The RIDING HANDBOOK

The Riding Handbook

Edited by Anne Wood
Editorial Assistant: Joanne Wood B.H.S.A.I.
Photography: Steve Evans and Ian Southall

Fifth Edition, April 1991

Published by:
Burlington Publishing Company Ltd
10 Sheet Street
Windsor
Berkshire
SL4 1BG

Produced by:
ABCo. Design Ltd
Unit 11 Stirling Industrial Centre
Stirling Way
Borehamwood
Herts WD6 2BT

Printed by:
Spottiswoode Ballantyne
Hawkins Road, The Hythe
Colchester, Essex CO2 8JT

Copyright © Burlington Publishing Company Limited, 1991

ISBN 1 873057 04 0

Acknowledgements: The Publishers would like to thank The Association of British Riding Schools for their help in preparing the "Where to Ride" Section, and to the many other companies and individuals who have given their invaluable advice and assistance in the production of this handbook.

The RIDING HANDBOOK

Edited by Anne Wood

From Burlington Publishing

Contents

SECTION 1:
WHERE TO RIDE

Chapter 1: And so to Ride   8

Chapter 2: The Worlds of Riding   14

Directory Section:

Riding Establishments   24

Riding Holidays   99

Estate Agents, Auctions and Auctioneers   124

Training   127

SECTION 2:
THE RESPONSIBLE RIDER

Chapter 3: Making the Decision   130

Chapter 4: Riding Wear   137

Chapter 5: Better Safe than Sorry   140

Chapter 6: Safety on the Road: Medical Emergencies   144

Chapter 7: Safety on the Road: Riding Out   148

Chapter 8: Public Rights of Way   151

Chapter 9: Some Human Faults and Problems   154

Chapter 10: Fencing   157

The Responsible Rider: Useful References & Listings   161

SECTION 3:
THE HEALTHY HORSE

Chapter 11: The Healthy Horse   179

Chapter 12: Feeding your Horse   189

Chapter 13: Tacking Up   190

Chapter 14: Bits   203

Chapter 15: No Foot No Horse 207

Chapter 16: Keeping a Horse at Grass 210

Chapter 17: Stabling your Horse 217

Chapter 18: At Livery 223

Chapter 19: Grooming 226

Chapter 20: Clipping 231

Chapter 21: Boots and Bandages 234

Chapter 22: Best-dressed Horse:
All Rugged Up 237

Chapter 23: Equine Faults and Vices 241

Chapter 24: Transporting your Horse 247

Chapter 25: Insurance 251

The Healthy Horse: Useful References
& Listings 254

Manufacturers and Suppliers of Horse-care
Products 297

SECTION 4:
THE WORLD OF HORSEMANSHIP

Chapter 26: The Pony Club 310

Chapter 27: Equestrian Organisations 316

Chapter 28: The World Equestrian Games 331

Useful References & Listings 346

SECTION 5:
A CAREER WITH HORSES

Chapter 31: Choosing a Career with Horses 348

Chapter 32: The Fortune Centre 353

SECTION 6:
TABLES OF SUPPLIERS

Table entries 357

INDEX

Foreword

Riding as a hobby is expanding in popularity and attracting not only the pony-mad youngster but also a growing number of adults who are making their first forays into riding/horse ownership, or are re-kindling an old enthusiasm.

This book is designed to provide a compendium of information about the subject in general, as well as detailed sources of supply for the various wants and needs that both the beginner and more experienced owner/rider have. However, no one book about riding and horses could hope to give all the answers! There simply could not be one definitive document - the diversity of the subject precludes this.

Fortunately, the sport enjoys a wealth of literature catering for the needs of the specialist. The role of The Riding Handbook is to provide a background of knowledge from which to begin the explorations which take you to an understanding of your own particular interests.

The task of distilling the vital elements from the absolute wealth of information available has been tackled in my own particular way. I trust that you will not find this to be too schizophrenic and feel that the logic of the various sections facilitates the mapping of a route to the information that you seek.

It is important to encourage the development of good practice in this sport and the editorial is geared towards the development of a responsible attitude with a strong emphasis on the safety aspects both for the horse and rider.

Whatever it is that motivates you to take part in riding what matters is that you enjoy it.

Anne Wood
April 1991

Section 1: Where to Ride

Chapter 1: And so to Ride   8
Chapter 2: The Worlds of Riding   14

Directory Section:

Riding Establishments:

England   24
Scotland   87
Wales   94
Northern Ireland   98

Riding Holidays:

England   99
Scotland   126
Wales   129
Northern Ireland   131
Estate Agents   124
Auctions/Sales Outlets 125

Training:

Dressage   127
Driving   127
Endurance   128
Eventing   128
Polo   128
Show Jumping   128
Side-saddle   128
Vaulting   128
Western   128

And so to Ride

Choosing the right place to learn to ride is vitally important. Here are some pointers to help with that choice.

Riding school provision throughout the country is vast. Schools range from the small, local stables where a few ancient, well-worn ponies provide endless hours of fun for local children, to the lavish, immaculate stables with a wide range of facilities that would be the envy of the majority of the horse owning population. Equally wide are the range of needs for those who wish to take up riding as a sport. Whether you are a newcomer or someone returning to the sport, it is important to choose a good school where you can ride safely and make progress.

At whatever age you decide to take up riding you will find friends to share the experience with.

All schools have to be licensed by the Local Authority. For someone to take payment for giving lessons on their horse is illegal unless they have the appropriate licence from the Local Authority. Before issuing a licence an officer from the authority and a veterinary surgeon carry out an inspection of the school. They ensure that the school's buildings and animals are in good condition, and that the school is insured and in the charge of a responsible person.

This licence, however, does not guarantee anything other than that the school is a safe place to be - it does not give a guide to the standards of tuition. The British Horse Society and the Association of British Riding Schools both run approval schemes for riding schools. Any school approved by either of these bodies must conform to their standards relating to stable management and instruction. these schemes are entirely voluntary: the school has to apply to the 'body' and present themselves for inspection and approval. The B.H.S. and A.B.R.S. are intent upon raising the standards of riding schools, and strongly recommend that anyone seeking riding tuition at any level should go to an approved riding school. There are, of course, many good riding schools that are well established and have not seen the need to apply for approval - these should not be overlooked.

You will probably have discussed your intention to ride with friends, some of whom may have the same interest. Listen to them, ask how they are improving, what the horses are like and what the tuition is like. If you get the right answers then make arrangements to go along and have a look. Alternatively you could consult the directory pages in this publication or the various publications available which provide this type of information. Your local Yellow Pages will list riding schools in the area, although this will not give you any idea of the standards that exist, merely the address and telephone number. You may also find advertisements for local riding schools displayed in your local tack shop.

Having researched the location of these establishments, the best way to find out what they are like is to go and have a look for yourself.

As a basic guide, we would suggest you pay particular attention to the following points:

First Impressions

Is it a friendly, clean, well-run centre? Or is it one where chaos reigns supreme and the staff are gruff and off-hand, and treat the customers as if they are nothing but a nuisance.

The Stable Yard

Sloppiness around the stable yard can often reflect a 'couldn't-care-less' attitude. This doesn't mean that the buildings have to be freshly painted and spotless but that it is tidy with a sense of order. Stable tools should be stored away neatly, not creating added hazards for horses and riders alike. The stabling area and yard should be swept clean of any remnants of stable debris. The muck heap should be squared up

The early Days

so that it is not sprawling all over the place. Hay and straw should be stacked neatly away in the barn or storage area, etc., etc.

The Tack Room

Is it organised in such a way that tack can be stored safely? Is the tack clean and supple and in a good state of repair, or is it hard, dirty and slung in a corner? If the latter is true then don't even bother to ride there. It's not safe for the rider and not comfortable for the horse, and probably reflects an irresponsible and un-professional attitude on the part of the school.

The Horses

Are they kept in clean stabling with plenty of room and clean bedding? Or are they kept in tatty, unclean conditions? They may be kept in the field, but wherever they are kept all should be healthy looking, clean and well turned-out when presented to someone to ride.

Stabling should be clean with plenty of room for the horse

The horses should be well covered with no ribs or haunches sticking out. Horses that are either too thin or too fat are not in top condition and it would be unfair to ask them to do any amount of work. Watch closely how the horses respond to handling by the staff. There should be no need for roughness when handling an animal.

The Instruction

Are lessons given by the instructor, or the teenage helper who gives a hand at week-ends and during school holidays? You are paying for instruction, so it would be appropriate to expect a suitably qualified person to take the lesson.

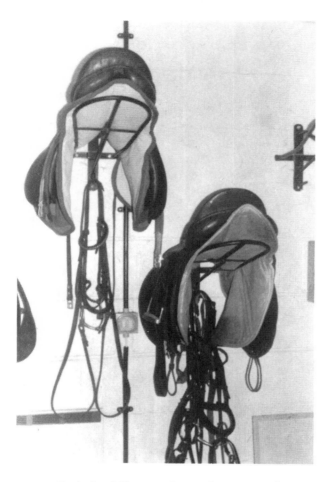

Tack should be stored away in a neat and orderly manner

The Instructor

Find out if the instructors are qualified. If they have the following letters after their names they will be qualified:

B.H.S.A.I. - British Horse Society Assistant Instructor

B.H.S.I.I. - British Horse Society Intermediate Instructor

B.H.S.I. - British Horse Society Instructor

F.B.H.S. - Fellow of the British Horse Society

The A.I. is the first step in the B.H.S. ladder of qualifications, and you may well find you are taught by someone at that level. It may be that they are working towards their A.I., in which case you will probably find a qualified person keeping an eye on them

Look at those taking part in the lesson. Are they all equipped to conform with basic riding safety standards - or are they allowed to ride in high heels and without hats?

Are the group under instruction making progress and taking part in a lesson that has variety and is stimulating and fun?

To be taught by someone with higher qualifications usually means paying more. As a newcomer, this is not really necessary, but as you progress and wish to gain a higher degree of skills, or participate in a different discipline, you may then wish to engage their services.

Facilities Available

Does the school have an indoor and/or outdoor riding arena, or are you expected to ride in a suitably fenced paddock?

Will your first lessons be on the lunge, in a beginners class, or on the leading rein? There are obvious advantages to being taught initially on the lunge: You have the undivided attention of your instructor, you can concentrate upon getting the feel of the horse's movements and getting the right position in the saddle, you can gain confidence and learn more rapidly when not overwhelmed with the dual problems of controlling the horse and maintaining your balance.

You may find that instruction is given whilst riding out under the direct guidance of the instructor. The obvious disadvantage in this is that the instructor is unlikely to be able to give you their sole attention as they will also be responsible for the others in the ride.

Whatever the school you eventually choose to be instructed at, make sure that it matches the standards that you have decided upon and is within a price range that you can afford.

Going out with a group can be an enjoyable experience

The Worlds of Riding

Riding as a sport is extremely diverse. Different aspects are explored by way of introduction to the sport.

Having mastered the basics of riding, you may well feel that it is time you branched out from the safe enclaves of your managed and well-ridden routes and looked at what particular aspect of the sport would suit you. For many, the sheer pleasure of ownership and communion with the horse will be sufficient, others will look for a different challenge. In the horse field there is such a diversity of activities that you may need to dip your toe into the water several times before coming up with the one for you.

Dressage riding is an aspect of equestrian sport that is growing in popularity

Dressage

All horses receive some degree of basic schooling so that they are obedient to the wishes of their riders. This is basic dressage. The development of this schooling and the refining of it into harmonious partnership between horse and rider is what we see in dressage at a higher level.

Dressage originated in the 4th or 5th century BC with the Greeks. It was developed as a series of disciplined schooling exercises for the cavalry by a general called Xenophon so that horses could be more easily controlled in combat. Dressage training, as we know it today, was developed in the late 17th century, early 17th century in Italy. By the 20th century it was established as a competitive sport. It was first included as an Olympic discipline in the 1912 Stockholm Olympics.

The growth of Dressage as a competition was slower to get started here in England than on the Continent but it is now fast growing in popularity both at national and local levels. Tests in England are split into five levels - Preliminary, Novice, Elementary, Medium and Advanced. An indication of the sport's growing popularity is that it now gets television coverage, however limited.

Show Jumping

An aspect of the sport that has grown tremendously in popularity in the past decade aided by television and the growth of show jumping personalities!

In show jumping, the style of the rider and the conformation of the horse are not judged at all, merely their ability to clear the fences - sometimes within a given time. The rules that govern jumping competitions are laid down by the British Show Jumping Association, that is in the case of those that are affiliated - although many unaffiliated shows will use the BSJA rules as a basic. In order to jump in an affiliated show jumping competition both horse and rider must be registered with the Association. The horses are graded according to their cash winnings: thus the horse starting out will be graded C, then when he has gained sufficient prize money to grade B, and finally to grade A; ponies are classified initially as JC, then JA. Once a horse or pony has been upgraded it can never be downgraded.

There are several types of fences and jumps in the show jumping ring, most of which have 'wings' or supports on either side to help the horse size up the obstacle. These jumps are usually brightly coloured, something that can be most off-putting for the inexperienced horse. If you are keen to 'have a go' at show jumping then consider arranging to have lessons from someone who is qualified and experienced; this will benefit both you and your horse.

Hunting

Hunting is not in itself competitive, although it has 'fathered' several other sports and equestrian activities, such as Point to Point Racing, Hunter Trials, Eventing etc.

Riding presents a great variety of challenges

Horses are trained for hunting by first going to the meet and being introduced to hounds. If they can cope with hounds without kicking and panicking and can be in a large group of equally excited horses without becoming a danger to themselves and those around them then you probably have the ingredients for a good hunter. A good horse that has good manners and goes well in the hunting field is a most valuable asset.

There is a great deal of protocol in the hunting field, and you would be well advised to have taken time to absorb some of it before venturing out.

Do

- remember that courtesy, good manners and consideration for others is essential.

- Be polite, hold gates, say thank you to others who extend a courtesy to you.

- Always obey the orders of the hunt staff without questioning.

- Make sure that if your horse is a kicker it sports a red ribbon on the tail, and if a youngster a green one.

- Shut gates behind you so that farm stock cannot escape, unless someone is directly behind you, assume that you are the last through.

- Ride within the limits of your horse's capabilities and fitness - a tired unfit horse can be hazardous for others in the hunting field.

- Be alert for anyone of the field who is experiencing difficulties and if you cannot help then make sure someone who can does.

- Familiarise your horse with the sound of the hunting whip being cracked - the sound could initially upset him.

Don't

- overtake hounds or get in front of the Master or field staff.

- Let your horse kick hounds, always keep his head turned towards hounds.

- Ride over crops.

- Jump when hounds are not running.

- Gallop through farm stock.

- Ride too close to the other horses, particularly when jumping.

- Barge at fences, gateways etc.

- Ignore the fact that your horse is tiring - go home, there's always another day.

- Hunt an unfit horse.

Horses ought not to be hunted until they are at least four years old; even then they ought not to be kept out all day. You will need to work out a fitness programme for your horse well in advance of the time you intend to attend your first meet.

By being careful when riding on the day of the hunt you can help conserve some of your horse's strength and energy. Don't gallop flat out on soft going, keep the horse in hand and slow up. If possible, ride around the soft places. Keep a watchful eye on the ground ahead and avoid any holes and rough patches. Never be tempted to gallop on metalled roads: not only is it dangerous to other road users as well as your horse and yourself, but it can be extremely injurious to the horse's legs. Learn to read the run of the hounds. If you can see that they are changing direction then see if you can safely take a short cut. It would be wise to get to know the country over which you are going to hunt. In this way you will be able to get some idea of the type of terrain you will be crossing and the obstacles you are likely to meet.

At the end of the day, you should be prepared to put in as much work caring for your horse as you did preparing him. A tired horse will not want to be unduly fussed over. He will need to be watered, groomed lightly (particularly removing wet mud from under the belly and on the legs), checked for injuries, rugged appropriately (an anti-sweat rug under the night rug if he is likely to break out) and given a light meal such as a bran and linseed mash before you go and clean your tack and eat. It is important to return to the horse later in the evening. At this point you should brush him off and make sure that he is comfortably rugged up. You may wish to give him another small feed at this time. Finally, check his hay and water and thank him for the day's sport!

For many the thrill of hunting is in the gallop in company across huge tracts of land that would probably otherwise be inaccessible to you as an individual.

Eventing

Events can be one, two or three days in duration. The horse and rider are required to complete three phases -

dressage, cross-country and show jumping. In three day events, a gruelling steeplechase course with rules of roads and tracks is also included.

It was during the days of the horse cavalry that the concept of events was first introduced. A 'series' be completed in one day. Obviously these are nowhere near as rigorous as the three-day event, but they are good training grounds for the trials riders of the future.

Hunter Trials

These are tests of the horse's speed and jumping ability over a course of natural fences such as would be encountered in the hunting field. A timed section is usually included to determine the winner. Heights of fences vary according to the class, but there is generally a novice class that will give those with very young or inexperienced horses a chance to school around a full set of cross country jumps.

Hunter trials are held at the start and end of the hunting season. Many riding clubs, pony clubs and hunt supporters' groups run these events, both for the pleasure and profit of those in their organisations.

Polo

Originating in Persia some 2000 years ago, this sport was introduced to this country in the 19th Century. The game is split up into four sections known as chukkas, each lasting seven minutes. Teams of four try to score as many goals as possible against the opposite side.

The cross-country event can be fast and furious

The teams are arranged with two players playing forward, one playing centre, one in defence. A handicap system operates for the ponies (they are in fact horses that average around 15HH) since they can only play for two chukkas in a match. Thus the player will have to have spare animals available in case of lameness and to use in the other two chukkas.

Understandably, the game is expensive and earns its name 'the sport of princes'. In recent years an interest has developed within the pony club for this particular sport and inter-branch competitions have developed.

Long Distance Riding

This aspect of equestrianism calls for extremely fit horses as well as riders who can cope with all the hardships that riding on all types of terrain and in any type of weather demands.

Two organisations undertake the organisation of long distance rides, the British Horse Society and the Endurance Horse and Pony Society, although local riding clubs may organise pleasure rides.

Anyone can enjoy the sport, starting with distances of 15 and 25 miles, working through 40 to 50 miles and maybe onto the ultimate test - 100 miles in 24 hours. You could, without too much extra training on top of your normal exercise, get your horse to the 25 mile stage. Beyond that demands a far more rigorous training schedule. The test is not only of your horse but also of your dedication.

When developing a training programme, the rider will not only have to consider the stamina of their horse, but also their ability to maintain speed in order to come within the time limits set. Pleasure rides are usually undertaken at speeds of around four to six miles an hour, whilst longer rides need to be ridden at an average of seven to eight mph. Obviously, since this is an average there will be times when the horse needs to travel faster.

Before, during and after rides the horses are vetted and the horse checked for any signs of injury. Penalties are incurred if the horse has been over-stressed, injured himself or sustains an injury through ill-fitting tack. A vet can withdraw a horse from a competition if he feels too much is being asked of it.

The winner is the fastest horse over the distance. Although this is a tough sport it does give the chance to experience riding through some of the most beautiful countryside in Britain. The most famous of these long distance rides is the Golden Horseshoe.

Driving

This is a sport which is growing in popularity and is open for people to enjoy at many different levels.

Driving clubs have developed throughout the country and do much to encourage the newcomer to the sport and to help develop his expertise. For many, it is a fun way to utilise the semi-retired and outgrown family pony by breaking it to harness and adding a new dimension to the family's participation in all things equestrian. However, for those who develop a growing interest it can prove to be as demanding and expensive as any horse sport. For those who find the rigours of mounted horse sports a little too demanding it is an ideal way to maintain a participating interest.

Should you really become an enthusiast for driving then you will find that competition is serious, physically demanding and requires a high degree of expertise. These are show driving classes and the more demanding 'combined driving' where presentation, dressage, marathon and obstacle driving are all elements in the competition.

Gymkhana

In years past at most local shows there would be a gymkhana class which was mainly for children to test their pony's skill in mounted games. Unfortunately, this type of event seems to be dying out with only the Pony Club maintaining it when their teams work towards the Prince Philip Cup - the finals of which are held every year at Wembley.

The gymkhana classes give children a chance to pit their horsemanship skills in such things as bending, musical sacks and potato races against others of the

The ultimate achievement in Gymkhana is to represent your club at Wembley

same age and ability in an atmosphere of friendly rivalry. The races are fast, furious and very intense - and they give children on the ordinary pony a chance to have a go.

Showing

Showing is an art in itself. You may have acquired a first class show horse, but without that partnership that is so essential you will not end up winning.

Your horse does not need to be trained to the high standard of the dressage horse but he must move evenly and his trot should be free yet balanced with only the lightest contact with your hands. His walk must be free and

appear unhurried, as should his canter. He must lead in hand and stand alertly in front of the judges with his ears pricked.

Your tack must be right too. Some classes require you to ride in a double bridle - do make sure that both you and your horse practice well in advance of your first class. Quiet hands are a must for a showing class, a horse that throws its head about will be marked down by the judges. A straight cut saddle will show off your horse's shoulders and should be worn without a breastplate or martingale.

In all but Mountain Moorland and Family Pony classes, your horse will need a plaited mane and a pulled or plaited tail. Small neat plaits are preferable to large loopy ones - although it may be hard to get the recommended seven plaits (it would , in fact, be better to go over that number). The tail should reach just below the hocks when carried.

The rider too must look neat and tidy and correctly attired as this can contribute towards the judges' decision. Make sure that your hair is tidy under your hat, that your gloves are holeless, that your whip is the accepted length, your boots polished and your clothes and tie neat, tidy and appropriate - then you will be ready to go.

Once in the ring keep your horse moving in a bold and well-balanced manner making sure that you are not in a bunch (you may not be picked out so easily if you are just part of a crowd). Remember to obey the instructions called out to you by the steward. If you are called in with the first six or seven horses you will be asked to give a show. You should have prepared for this beforehand. Dependent upon the type of class, the judges will want to see that your horse is obedient and well balanced. The most usual show is to walk and trot, then canter on either leg, followed by a halt and a rein back. Sometimes the judges may want to ride your horse. If this is the case then do make sure that your saddle is secure!

Pairs jumping takes both timing and judgement

After the ridden show you may be asked to unsaddle your horse. At this point it is helpful to have someone standing by with a brush or stable nibber so you can give your horse a quick once over. When your turn comes to lead your horse out make sure you stand your horse square, at the instruction from the judge trot your horse the required distance so that he demonstrates his good even paces. After you have been given the go-ahead by the judge return to your place in the line, tack up again and mount - ready for the final phase in this class.

Don't be too disappointed if you do not succeed straight away. If you get into the final line-up you have done well and it is worth persevering.

Working Pony

This is specifically a pony class and there are usually two sizes, 13.2 and under and 14.2 and under.

The rules and procedures are very similar to those in a showing class with the addition of jumping a small fence.

Working Hunter

This is usually a horse class which is divided by size.

The horse should be capable of jumping a course of rustic fences similar to those you would meet out hunting. It is usual for the jumping section to come first and those not eliminated will progress to the second section, which will be a test of conformation, manners and obedience suitable for hunting.

Handy Hunter/Handy Pony

There is a set course which must be completed correctly in the fastest possible time to win. The course may include backing between two bales, opening a gate, carrying an object between two points, leading over a fence, bending between poles or giving a show. Each show will develop their own specialities and if this is the first time you have competed then do wait and watch some other competitors have a go.

For this event you need a handy, bold obedient horse - you won't necessarily have paid a fortune for him since the competition is judged entirely on performance.

Riding Establishments

Several abbreviations have been used in this section - not just to confuse but to squeeze in more information. A list of these abbreviations is given below.

I/S	Indoor school	**J. Pd**	jumping Paddock	**B**	Breaking
G	Gallery	**X/C**	Cross country course	**H**	Hunting
E. Lt	Electric light	**X/J**	Cross country jumps	**Hkg**	Hacking
M	Menage	**L**	Livery	**C S**	Career students
Fl. Lt	Flood lit	**S**	Schooling		taken

England

Avon

Clevedon Riding Centre
Clevedon Lane, Clevedon, Avon, BS21 7AG.
Proprietor: Mrs J A Sims

Hunstrete Riding School
Hunstrete, Nr. Bristol, Avon.
Proprietor: Mr & Mrs T Warren

Leyland Court Riding School
Northwoods, Winterbourne, Bristol, Avon, BS17 1RY.
Proprietor: Mr & Mrs H M Irish

Montpellier Riding Centre
Weston Farm Lane, Weston, Bath, Avon.
Tel: 0225 23665
Proprietor: Mr & Mrs E Mills
Horses: 7 **Ponies:** 14

The Avon Riding Centre for the Disabled Ltd
Kings Weston Road, Henbury, Nr. Bristol, Avon, BS10 7QT.
Proprietor: Miss S Saywell

The Mendip Equestrian Centre
Lyncombe Lodge, Sandford, Avon, BS19 5PG.
Proprietor: Mr J Lee & Mrs S Lee

The Worlebury Riding School
Acres, 114 Worlebury Hill Road, Weston-Super-Mare, Avon, BS22 9TG.
Proprietor: Miss H Tonkin & Miss S Tonkin

Urchinwood Manor Equitation Centre
Congresbury, Nr. Bristol, Avon, BS19 5AP.
Tel: 0934 833248

Proprietor: Capt Peter Hall & Mrs S Hall
Horses: 25 **Ponies:** 15
Facilities available: Ind. Sch/Men(F.Lt)/J.Pd(in summer) /X-C/Dis.R - Limited /Hkg - Roads and woods, 5 miles from the Mendip Hills
Level: Teaching standards to: ABRS Test no. 10. P.C. tests to A. Ass. Grooms Diploma. NPS Examinations. BHS stages to 4 and Intermediate Teaching.
Specialisation: Client comps. Summer comps. - all disciplines.
Other details: F/P Livery. Breaking. Schooling. Hunting. Tuition in Dressage, eventing, side-saddle (beginner/advanced), polo. Stud standing with American Thoroughbreds and Hanoverian Stallions.
Member of Association of British Riding Schools

Villa Farm Riding School
Hewish, Weston-Super-Mare, Avon, BS24 6RQ.
Proprietor: Mrs P M A Moss

Wellow Trekking Centre
Little Horse Croft Farm, Wellow, Bath, Avon, BA2 8QE.
Proprietor: Mr & Mrs Shellard

White Cat Stables
Lyde View, Howsmoor Lane, Mangotsfield, Bristol, Avon, BS17 3AQ.
Tel: 0272 564370
Proprietor: Mrs P E Gough & Miss P E Gough
Horses: 13 Ponies: 5
Facilities available:
Ind.Sch/J.Pd/X-C/Hkg - to adult club members.
Level: Teaching standards to: ABRS Test no. 10. BHS Examinations. ABRS Grooms Diploma level 1 & 2 and Ass. Grooms Certificate.
Specialisation: Clients own riding club. Special 1, 2 & 3 day courses.
Other details: Livery. Evening classes. All Standards. YTS Together and Divided classes. Examination/Assessment centre. Brochure available.
Member of Association of British Riding Schools

Bedfordshire

Backnoe End Equestrian Centre
Keysoe Road, Thurleigh, Bedford, Bedfordshire, MK44 2OZ.
Proprietor: Sharon Dodson
Member of Association of British Riding Schools

Gransden Hall Riding School
Great Gransden, Bedfordshire
Tel: 076 77 366
Proprietor: Mrs Craze
Facilities available:
Liveries/ Ind Sch./Dress/X-C on own horse.

Highlands Riding Centre
Northill, Nr. Biggleswade, Bedfordshire, SG18 9AW.
Tel: 076727 528
Proprietor: Miss R Manning
Horses: 10 Ponies: 15
Facilities available: Men (F.Lt) /J.Pd/X-C Jumps/Hkg
Level: Teaching standards to: BHSAI.
Specialisation: Driving and side-saddle. Saddlery shop.
Other details: F/P Livery. Career students taken. YTS. Evening classes - Tues-Fri 8.00-10.00. Brochure available for school.
Member of Association of British Riding Schools

Millbrook Equitation Centre
Brook House Stables, Millbrook, Bedfordshire, MK45 2JB.
Proprietor: Mrs E H Shrive

Rocklane Riding Centre
Soulbury Road, Wing, Leighton Buzzard, Bedfordshire, LU7 0JL.
Tel: 0296 68867 3
Proprietor: Mrs J Joyce & Mr J Tossell
Horses: 8 Ponies: 9
Facilities available:
Ind.Sch/J.Pd/Dis.R/Hkg - Escorted rides only..
Level: Teaching standards to: ABRS Test no. 10. BHS HK & R to stage 3. BHSAI.
Specialisation: Own clients competitions in dressage, jumping and gymkhana.

Other details: Evening classes Mon-Fri. Instructional day courses. All standards. Divided classes. Brochure available. F/P Livery. Lecture room. Schooling. Breaking.
Member of Association of British Riding Schools

Rowan Lodge School of Equitation
Fildyke Close, Fildyke Road, Meppershall, Bedfordshire, SGI7 5LF.
Proprietor: Mrs J V Hirsh

Swallowfield Stables and Training Centre
Townside, Edlesborough, Nr. Dunstable, Bedfordshire.
Tel: 0525 220398
Proprietor: Mrs. C. Planton
Horses: 8 Ponies: 8
Facilities available:
Men(F.Lt)/J.Pd/Hkg
Level: Teaching Standards: Students to BHS Stages 1-3. ABRS Grooms Diploma. GCSE Horsemastership. Road Safety.
Specialisation: Courses run with Dunstable College.
Other details: Livery. Schooling. Breaking. Hunting. Evening classes. Brochure available. Tuition in Side-saddle and dressage.
Member of Association of British Riding Schools

Tinsleys Riding School
Green Lane, Clapham, Bedford, Bedfordshire.
Tel: 0254 68556
Proprietor: Mr & Mrs Thody
Horses: 2 Ponies: 6
Facilities available: Livery. Parkland. Unaffiliated riding club. No children under 6 Yrs.
Specialisation: Jumping

Wootton Riding School

25 Church Road, Wootton, Bedfordshire.
Tel: 0254 768241
Horses: 14 **Ponies:** 13
Facilities available: Gymkhanas/Riding Club activities
Specialisation: Hunter liveries

Berkshire

Bearwood Riding Centre

Bear Wood, Sindlesham, Wokingham, Berkshire, RG11 5GB.
Tel: 0734 760010
Horses: 12 **Ponies:** 8

Bradfield Riding Centre

The Maltings, Bradfield, Berkshire.
Tel: 0734 744048
Proprietor: Mrs J White
Horses: 8 **Ponies:** 10
Facilities available: Ind.Sch/Men/J.Pd/X-C Jumps/Hkg
Level: Teaching Standards: Students to BHS Stages 1-4.
Specialisation: Competitions - Pony Club and others.
Other details: Evening classes. All standards. Schooling. Breaking. Career students taken. YTS.
Member of Association of British Riding Schools

Cane End Stables Limited

Cane End, Nr. Reading, Berkshire, RG4 9HH.
Tel: 0734 724195
Proprietor: Mr & Mrs L E Hordern

Cloud Stables (School of Equitation)

Church Lane, Arborfield, Reading, Berkshire, RG2 9JA.
Tel: 0734 760238
Proprietor: Mr & Mrs W A Patrick
Facilities available: Evening Classes/Resid for working students.

Hall Place Riding Stables

Little Heath Road, Tilehurst, Reading, Berkshire, RG3 5TX.
Tel: 0734 426938
Proprietor: Mr & Mrs P Vincent
Horses: 15 **Ponies:** 15
Facilities available: Ind.Sch/Men/J.Pd/X-C/Dis.R/Hkg - Fields and woodland.
Level: Teaching Standards: BHS Stage 1-3.
Specialisation: Novice to advanced tuition. RDA.
Other details: Evening classes (Wed-Fri inclusive). All standards. Career students taken.
Member of Association of British Riding Schools

Pinnocks Wood Stables

Burchetts Green, Maidenhead, Berkshire.
Tel: 062 882 2031
Proprietor: Mrs Gilbert
Horses: 2 **Ponies:** 1

The Spanish Bit Riding School and Livery

Elm Farm, Boveney Road, Dorney Common, Nr. Windsor, Berkshire, SL4 6QD.
Tel: 06286 61275
Proprietor: Mrs K Hamilton
Horses: 9 **Ponies:** 14
Facilities available: Ind.Sch/Men(F.Lt)/J.Pd/Hkg - Common- land and bridleways

Level: Teaching standards to: ABRS Test no. 9. BHS Stages 1-4. BHSAI. BHS Intermediate. Riding and Road Safety.
Specialisation: Pub/Picnic rides. Competitions for clients.
Other details: F/P Livery. Schooling. Beginners to advanced on the flat and over jumps. Evening classes.
Member of Association of British Riding Schools

Wokingham Equestrian Centre

Chapel Green House, Chapel Green, Wokingham, Berkshire, RG11 3ER.
Proprietor: Mrs A C Adams

Buckinghamshire

Ashley Green Riding Centre

Flamstead Farm, Ashley Green, Nr. Chesham, Buckinghamshire, HP5 3PH.
Tel: 0494 772088
Proprietor: C F Robbins-Brown Esq
Number Horses/Ponies: 40
Facilities available: Ind.Sch/Men/Hkg
Level: Teaching Standards: All levels.
Specialisation: BHS approved.
Other details: Various types of riding activities available.

Brawlings Farm Livery Yard Limited

Horn Hill, Chalfont St Peter, Buckinghamshire, SL9 0RE.
Tel: 02407 2132
Proprietor: Mrs S M Fairbairns
Horses: 15 **Ponies:** 15

Facilities available: Ind.Sch /Men/J.Pd/X-C/Dis.R/Hkg - Rural country.
Level: Teaching standards to: ABRS test no. 5. Students to BHSAI.
Specialisation: Dressage.
Other details: Liveries. Schooling. Breaking. Career students taken. All standards taken. Evening classes - max. no.10.
Member of Association of British Riding Schools

Finmere Equestrian Centre

Town Farm, Finmere, Hoggeston, Buckingham, Buckinghamshire, MK18 4AS.
Proprietor: Mr D R Boyd

Hartwell Riding Stables

Oxford Road, Aylesbury, Buckinghamshire, HP17 8QR.
Proprietor: Miss M L Herring

Loughton Manor Equestrian Centre

Redland Drive, Childs Way, Loughton, Milton Keynes, Buckinghamshire, MK5 8AZ.
Tel: 0908 666434
Proprietor: Mr D R Benson
Horses: 14 **Ponies:** 15
Facilities available: Ind.Sch/Men(F.Lt)/J.Pd/X-C/Dis.R/Hkg
Level: Teaching standards to: ABRS Test no. 10. GCSE Horsemastership. BHS Stages 1-4. BHS Preliminary and Intermediate Instructor. ABRS Ass. Grooms Certificate.
Specialisation: Training riders to competition standard.
Other details: Tuition in Dressage, Show-jumping and X-country. Evening classes. Lecture room.

Schooling. Breaking. F/P Livery. Special residential courses.
Member of Association of British Riding Schools

Radnage House Riding School

Radnage House, Green End Road, Radnage, Buckinghamshire, HP14 4BZ.
Tel: 024026 3268
Proprietor: Mr & Mrs RH Pitt
Horses: 10 **Ponies:** 0
Facilities available: Ind. Sch/Men(F.Lt)/J.Pd/X-C/Hkg
Level: Teaching Standards: All ABRS Tests. BHSAI. BHS Intermediate Teaching. BHS Stage 4.
Specialisation: Only teach riders able to ride 15.2hh - 16.2hh.
Other details: Livery (12). Schooling. Breaking. Hunting. Evening classes Mon.-Thurs. All Standards taken - Beginners to advanced.
Member of Association of British Riding Schools

Ring Croft Farm Riding School

Cranfield Road, North Crawley, Newport Pagnell, Buckinghamshire.
Tel: 0234 751200
Proprietor: Mrs B Warner

Shana School of Riding

Walters Ash, Nr. High Wycombe, Buckinghamshire, HP14 4UZ.
Tel: 024024 2200
Proprietor: Mr R Huggard
Horses: 16 **Ponies:** 18

Facilities available: Ind.Sch /Men(F.Lt)/J.Pd/X-C/Hkg - National Trust woodlands and farmland.
Level: Teaching standards to: ABRS Test no. 10. BHSAI. BHSII.
Specialisation: Video camcorder and large screen. Lessons recorded for analysis.
Other details: Lecture room. F/P Livery. Schooling. Breaking. Evening classes. All standards. Brochure available. Divided classes.
Member of Association of British Riding Schools

Snowball Farm Riding and Livery Yard Limited

Dorney Wood Road, Burnham, Buckinghamshire.
Tel: 0628 666222
Proprietor: Mrs S Western-Kaye
Horses: 20 **Ponies:** 20
Facilities available: 2 Ind.Sch/Men(F.Lt)/J.Pd/3 X-C/Dis.R/Hkg
Level: Teaching Standards: BHS Stages 1-3. BHS Preliminary teaching and Intermediate teaching.
Specialisation: Dressage and jumping shows. Horse Trials. "Own a Pony" day.
Other details: F/Grass Livery. Schooling. Breaking. Hunting on request.
Member of Association of British Riding Schools

West End Farm

Worlds End Lane, Weston Turville, Aylesbury, Buckinghamshire.
Tel: 029 661 3205
Proprietor: Mr P Oldham
Facilities available: Client's own horse & pony.

Cambridgeshire

Cambridgeshire College of Agriculture & Horticulture

Landbeach Road, Milton, Cambridgeshire, CB4 4DB.
Tel: 0223 860701 **Fax:** 0223 860262
Proprietor: R Lancaster
Horses: 30 **Ponies:** 6
Facilities available: Ind.Sch /2 Men/J.Pd/X-C/Dis.R/Hkg
Level: Teaching Standards: All ABRS Tests. BHSAI. BHSII. BTEC. ANCEBM. HHSS. NCMH.
Specialisation: Examination /Assessment Centre.
Other details: Schooling. Breaking. YTS. Courses for both adults and children. Brochure available. Evening classes. Liveries.
Member of Association of British Riding Schools

Drift End Stables

The Drift, Bourn, Cambridgeshire, CB3 7JP.
Tel: 09544 565
Proprietor: Mrs Sandra Moore
Facilities available: Full Livery. Breaking/Schooling

Haggis Farm Stables

Cambridge Road, Barton, Cambridgeshire, CB3 7AT.
Tel: 0223 460353
Proprietor: Mrs B J Morris-Lowe
Member of Association of British Riding Schools

Hayacre Farm Ltd.

Ely Road, Waterbeach, Cambridge, Cambridgeshire, CB5 9PG.
Tel: 0223861108 **Fax:** 0223 440378
Proprietor: Miss R L Dickerson

Horses: 1 **Ponies:** 4
Facilities available: Ind.Sch /J.Pd/Hkg
Level: Teaching standards to: ABRS Test no. 9. Students to BHSAI.
Specialisation: Small yard with friendly atmosphere.
Other details: Livery. Schooling. Breaking. Hunting. Career students taken. YTS. Mainly private lessons.
Member of Association of British Riding Schools

Knights End Riding Centre

55, Elwyn Road, March, Cambridgeshire.
Tel: 0354 50334
Member of Association of British Riding Schools

Lodge Riding Stables

High Street, Great Abington, Cambridgeshire.
Tel: 0223 891101
Proprietor: Ms M H Parr

Lynch Farm Riding Centre

Wistow Way, Orton Wistow, Peterborough, Cambridgeshire, PE2 0XA.
Tel: 0773 234445
Proprietor: Mr & Mrs D M Brown
Horses: 12 **Ponies:** 9
Facilities available: Ind.Sch /J.Pd/Hkg - Open country
Level: Teaching standards to: ABRS test no.10. ABRS Ass. Groom Certificate. BHSAI. BHSII.
Specialisation: Day courses for examination candidates.
Other details: Career students taken. F/P Livery. Schooling. Breaking. Tuition in dressage,

advanced position analysis, understanding equine locomotion. Evening classes. Special residential courses.
Member of Association of British Riding Schools

Mill Cottage Riding & Livery Stables

Mill Cottage, Gidding Road, Sawtry, Cambridge, Cambridgeshire, PE17 5UJ.
Tel: 0487 831497
Proprietor: Mr & Mrs T Scott
Horses: 2 **Ponies:** 6
Facilities available: Men(F.Lt)
Level: Teaching Standards: Novice to ABRS Test no. 6.
Specialisation: Pony days for children.
Other details: Livery. Basic to novice standards taken.
Member of Association of British Riding Schools

Miss E A Pickard

New Farm, Fox Road, Bourn, Cambridgeshire, CB3 7TY.
Proprietor: Miss E A Pickard

New Farm

Fox Road, Bourn, Cambridge, Cambridgeshire, CB3 7TY.
Tel: 095 44 501
Proprietor: Miss E A Pickard
Horses: 4 **Ponies:** 12
Facilities available: Men(F.Lt)/X-C/Dis.R/Hkg
Level: Teaching Standards: Students to YTS Horse management. National Diploma. BHS stage 3. BHSAI.
Specialisation: Teaching children
Other details: Livery. Schooling. Breaking. Residential courses.
Member of Association of British Riding Schools

Ryecroft Riding Centre

Station Road, Longstanton, Cambridgeshire.
Tel: 0954 60251
Proprietor: Sharon Mott

Shade Stables

Ely Road, Soham, Cambridgeshire.
Tel: 0353 721922
Proprietor: Mrs Fox
Horses: 5 **Ponies:** 7
Facilities available: Men /J.Pd/Hkg - Flat open fenland
Level: Teaching standards to: ABRS Test no. 8. Students to Ass. Groom Cerificate
Specialisation: Day hacks. Pub rides.
Other details: F/P Livery. Schooling. Breaking. Hunting. Beginners to advanced. Evening classes - 5pm - 9pm.
Member of Association of British Riding Schools

Staughton Riding School

Hawthorn Lodge, The Town, Great Staughton, Huntingdon, Cambridgeshire.
Tel: 0480 860409
Proprietor: Sue Usher
Member of Association of British Riding Schools

Sue Usher

Staughton Riding School, Hawthorn Lodge, The Town, Great Staughton, Huntingdon, Cambridgeshire.
Tel: 0480 860409
Proprietor: Sue Usher
Facilities available: Jumping /X-C/accompanied hacking.

The Coach House Stables

Chippenham, Ely, Cambridgeshire CB7 5EV
Tel: 0638 720415
Member of Association of British Riding Schools

The Windmill Stables

Shepreth Road, Barrington, Cambridgeshire, CB2 5SB.
Tel: 0223 871487
Proprietor: Mrs Susan Tydeman
Horses: 5 **Ponies:** 8
Facilities available: 2 Men(1 F.Lt)/J.Pd/X-C
Level: Teaching standards to: ABRS Test no. 7. BHS HK & R 1-3. Prelim. teaching. ABRS Ass. Grooms Diploma.
Specialisation: Childrens Riding Holiday Courses, August.
Other details: Livery. Schooling. Evening classes. Training students for BHS exams. Special residential courses by arrangement.
Member of Association of British Riding Schools

White Hart Stables, Childrens Sch. of Riding

47 Main Street, Great Gidding, Huntingdon, Cambridge, Cambridgeshire, PE17 5NU.
Tel: 08323 277
Proprietor: Miss Racheal Giddens
Horses: 1 **Ponies:** 8
Facilities available: Lunging Sch./J.Pd/1 acre All Weather Track/Hkg/X-C
Level: Teaching Standards: Basic instruction.
Specialisation: Tiny tots. Super absolute first and family ponies.
Other details: Private tuition. Prptr. takes all lessons. Classes in pony care and management for Mums. Occasionally ponies available for sale. Courses and day sessions during holidays.
Member of Association of British Riding Schools

Woodhurst Riding & Livery Stables

Penny Farthing, Woodhurst, Huntingdon, Cambridgeshire, PE17 3BW.
Tel: 0487 822331
Proprietor: Margaret Benson
Member of Association of British Riding Schools

Oakington Riding School

High Street, Oakington, Cambrigeshire, CB45 AG.
Tel: 022023 3929
Proprietor: Miss Charlotte Jordan
Horses: 1 **Ponies:** 8
Facilities available: Men/Dis.R/J.Pd/Hkg - Country lanes and bridleways.
Level: Teaching standards to: ABRS Test no. 6. BHS Road Safety Test. ABRS Stable Management and Equitation Tests. Stable Helpers and Girl Guide Badge.
Specialisation: Annual Charity Horse Show. Written & drawing comps.
Other details: Specialise in Children, disabled and nervous riders. Junior dressage and jumping competitions for pupils. Evening classes. Regular 1 and 5 days in riding and stable management.
Member of Association of British Riding Schools

Channel Islands

La Corbiere Riding & Livery Stables

La Corbiere Forest, Guernsey, Channel Islands.
Proprietor: Miss G Brock

La Haie Fleurie Livery & Riding Centre

La Haie Fleurie, St Martin, Jersey, Channel Islands.
Proprietor: Miss C F Binet

Lovanne Riding Centre

St Peter, Jersey, Channel Islands.
Tel: 0534 43344
Proprietor: Mrs A M Honeycombe
Horses: 4 **Ponies:** 12

Multina Ridinch

Ville Au Neveu, St Ouen, Jersey, Channel Islands.
Proprietor: Mr & Mrs J Phillips

Cheshire

B 1st Riding School of Equitation Centre

1 Higherfold Farm, Windlehurst Road, High Lane, Stockport, Cheshire, SK6 8AQ
Tel: 061 427 3737
Proprietor: P M Booth Esq
Number Horses/Ponies: 15
Facilities available: Ind.Sch
Level: Teaching Standards: All level of instruction.
Other details: F/Livery.

Bold Heath Equestrian Centre

Heath House Farm, Bold Heath, Nr Widnes, Cheshire, WA8 0XT.
Tel: 051 424 5151
Proprietor: Mrs J E Baker
Horses: 11 **Ponies:** 18
Facilities available: Ind.Sch /J.Pd/Dis.R/Hkg - Arable and grassland 127 acres.
Level: Teaching standards to: ABRS test no.10. Students to ABRS Groom Diploma. BHS stages 1-4. BHSII standards. Pony Club D-A.

Specialisation: Up to Advanced Dressage. Grade C show-jumping.
Other details: YTS training scheme. Special residential courses. Evening classes. Schooling. Divided classes.
Member of Association of British Riding Schools

Broomhall Riding School

Heatley Lane, Broomhall, Nr Nantwich, Cheshire, CW5 8BA.
Proprietor: Mr C D Garside

Croft Riding Centre

Spring Lane, Croft, Nr Warrington, Cheshire.
Tel: 092576 3715
Proprietor: Mr P Graham
Number Horses/Ponies: 20
Facilities available: Hacking /Groups accompanied. Country roads.
Specialisation: 2-hour eventing lessons.

Foxes Farm and Riding Centre

Badgersrake Lane, Ledsham, South Wirral, Cheshire, L66 8PF.
Tel: 051 339 6797
Proprietor: Mrs J Davey
Horses: 23 **Ponies:** 15
Facilities available: 2 Ind.Sch/Men(F.Lt)/J.Pd/Dis.R/ Hkg
Level: Teaching standards to: BHS stages.
Specialisation: RDA.
Other details: Examination/Assesment centre. YTS. Evening classes. BHS stages and teaching. Career students taken - ET and WP. Novice to advanced. Brochure available.
Member of Association of British Riding Schools

Hope Farm Riding School

Halegate Road, Halebank, Widnes, Cheshire, WA8 8LZ.
Tel: 051 425 3878
Proprietor: P T & D R Brindle
Horses: 7 **Ponies:** 8
Facilities available: Ind.Sch /Men/J.Pd/X-C/Dis.R/Hkg - Rural country.
Level: Teaching standards to: ABRS Test no. 5.
Specialisation: Tuition in dressage and jumping.
Other details: Lecture room. Evening classes.
Member of Association of British Riding Schools

Mobberley Riding School

Oak House, Newton Hall Lane, Mobberley, Cheshire, WA16 7LQ.
Tel: 0565 873123
Proprietor: Miss P Rigby
Horses: 10 **Ponies:** 12
Facilities available: Ind.Sch /Men/X-C/Hkg - Country lanes
Level: Teaching standards to: ABRS Test no. 10.
Other details: Lecture room. Basic progressive instruction. Evening classes. Divided classes.
Member of Association of British Riding Schools

Tarden Farm Stables

100 Gibb Lane, Mellor, Cheshire, SK6 5LZ.
Tel: 061 427 3322
Proprietor: Miss Jean Goddard
Horses: 12 **Ponies:** 9
Facilities available: Men /J.Pd/Hkg - Country, moorland.
Level: Teaching Standards: Various standards.
Specialisation: Beginners.
Other details: P/Livery (4)
Member of Association of British Riding Schools

The Wirral Riding Centre
HaddenLane, Ness, South
Wirral, Cheshire, L64 8TA.
Proprietor: Mrs M Ward

Waverton Riding Centre
Whitchurch Road, Chester,
Cheshire, CH3 6AF.
Proprietor: Mrs M Banks

Cleveland

Cleveland Riding Centre
Skelton, Saltburn-by-Sea,
Cleveland, TS12 2AB.
Tel: 0287 50303
Proprietor: Mr & Mrs A G
Bonas
Horses: 10 **Ponies:** 10
Facilities available: Ind.Sch
/Men/J.Pd/Dis.R/X-C/Hkg -
Beach, moors and woodland.
Level: Teaching standards
to: ABRS Test no. 8. Students
to BHSAI. BHSII. Riding
Club Tests.
Specialisation: Hacking.
Other details: Lecture room.
Schooling. Breaking. Evening
classes.
*Member of Association of
British Riding Schools*

**Crimdon Park Rig
School**
Crimdon Park, Hartlepool,
Cleveland.
Proprietor: Mrs C F Ayre

Eston Equitation Centre
Occupation Road, Eston,
Cleveland.
Proprietor: J & E Thomson

**Ford Close Riding
Centre**
Brass Castle Lane, Marton,
Middlesborough, Cleveland,
TS8 9EE.
Tel: 0642 313772

Proprietor: Miss S Ritchie
Horses: 6 **Ponies:** 6

**Stainsby Grange Riding
Centre**
Stainsby Grange Farm,
Thornaby, Cleveland, TS17
9AB.
Proprietor: Mrs P Allen

**Whispers Equestrian
Centre**
Whispers, Whinney Hill,
Stockton, Cleveland, TS21
1BQ.
Proprietor: Miss M K
Jackson

**Wolviston Livery and
Riding School**
Bradley House Farm,
Durham Road, Wolviston,
Billingham, Cleveland, TS22
5LP.
Tel: 0740 644692
Proprietor: Mr I F Cross &
Mrs M E Cross
Horses: 5 **Ponies:** 4
Facilities available:
Men/J.Pd/Hkg
Level: Teaching standards
to: ABRS Test no. 8.
Specialisation: 1/2hr
lessons for 3-5 yr olds.
Other details: Evening
classes. Stable management
classes. Private lessons on
school and own ponies.
*Member of Association of
British Riding Schools*

Co Durham

**Durham Equestrian
Skills Limited**
New Moors, Training & Livery
Centre, Bishop Auckland, Co
Durham, DL14 9NN.
Proprietor: Messrs A & MA
& Miss G Lewis

**Hamsterley Riding
School**
Hamsterly, Bishop Auckland,
Co Durham, DL13 3NH.
Tel: 038888 328
Proprietor: Judy Dennis
Horses: 10 **Ponies:** 10
Facilities available: Men (F.Lt)
/J.Pd/3 X-C/Hkg - Moorland,
forest and farmland.
Level: Teaching standards
to: students to BHSAI.
Specialisation: High quality
holidays for adults.
Other details: F/P Livery.
Schooling. Confidence giving
safe horses. Unaccompanied
holidays for children.
Extensive hacking over
moorland.
*Member of Association of
British Riding Schools*

**Lowfold Farm Riding
Centre**
Sunnybrow, Crook, Co
Durham.
Tel: 0388 747313
Proprietor: Miss M J Hedley
Horses: 15 **Ponies:** 6

Cornwall

Calloose Riding Stables
Calloose Lane East,
Leedstown, Hayle, Cornwall,
TR27 5ET.
Proprietor: Mr & Mrs C J
Bonnick

Chiverton Riding Centre
Silverwell, Nr. Blackwater,
Truro, Cornwall.
Tel: 0872 560471
Proprietor: Mrs S Fawdry &
Miss V Jane
Horses: 10 **Ponies:** 10
Facilities available: Ind.Sch
/J.Pd/Dis.R/Hkg - Lanes and
tracks.

Level: Teaching standards to: ABRS Test no. 10. Students to BHSAI. BHSII. BHS HK & R Stages 1-4.
Specialisation: Managing agents for YTS. Students trained for career exams.
Other details: Evening classes. All ages and abilities. BHS Examination centre. Students trained for exams. Liveries. Schooling. Breaking.
Member of Association of British Riding Schools

Duchy College of Agriculture & Horticulture

Stoke Climsland, Callington, Cornwall, PL17 8PB.
Tel: 0579 70204
Proprietor: M Wharton Esq
Horses: 20 **Ponies:** 4/5
Facilities available:
Ind.Sch/Men(F.Lt)/J.Pd/X-C/H kg - Rural countryside.
Level: Teaching standards to: ABRS Test no. 10. NCMHB Tech. Dip. ABRS Exams. Diplomas and examinations up to and including BHSI. Courses normally up to BHSII level.
Specialisation: Training career students.
Other details: Max.no.in a ride 8. Special residential courses. All standards welcome. Livery. Schooling and breaking by arrangement.
Member of Association of British Riding Schools

Gooseham Barton Stables

Gooseham, Morwenstow, Nr. Bude, Cornwall, EX23 9PG.
Tel: 028883 204
Proprietor: Mr R Hamilton
Number Horses/Ponies: 20
Facilities available: Hkg - Peaceful scenic countryside.
Level: Teaching Standards: Basic

Specialisation: BHS approved.
Other details: Ponies approved by Ponies UK Ltd. Small children and beginners welcome.

Moss Farm Riding

Bradford, Blisland, Bodmin, Cornwall, PL30 4LF.
Proprietor: Mr & Mrs P J Dibb

Nine Tor Riding Centre

North Hill, Launceston, Cornwall, PL15 7PE
Tel: 056 682 232
Proprietor: Mr & Mrs Bloomfield
Number Horses/Ponies: 35
Facilities available: Hacking /Accompanied groups

Old Mill Stables

Lelant Downs, Hayle, Cornwall, TR27 6LN.
Tel: 0736 753045
Proprietor: Miss Renowden & Miss Scottings
Horses: 10 **Ponies:** 8
Facilities available:
Men(F.Lt)/J.Pd/X-C Jumps/Dis.R/Hkg
Level: Teaching standards to: ABRS Test no. 10+. Students trained for NVQ level 1. ABRS Ass. Grooms Certificate.
Specialisation: Competitions for own clients - mainly Dressage.
Other details: Livery. YTS. Assessment centre. Evening classes by arrangement. All riders taught on Classical Foundation - Confidence giving courses.
Member of Association of British Riding Schools

Polpever Riding Stables

Duloe, Liskeard, Cornwall.
Proprietor: Mrs S Kinver

Porth Hall Riding Centre

Porth Hall, Sticker, St. Austell, Cornwall.
Proprietor: Mrs J Philp

St Leonard's Equitation Centre

Polson, Launceston, Cornwall, PL15 9QR.
Tel: 0566 5543
Proprietor: Mr A Reeve
Number Horses/Ponies: 11
Facilities available:
Accompanied hacks

Sunrising Farm & Riding Centre

Henwood, Liskeard, Cornwall.
Tel: 0589 62895
Proprietor: Mrs Higgs
Horses: 5 **Ponies:** 17

T M International School of Horsemanship

Henwood, Nr. Liskeard, Cornwall, PL14 5BP.
Tel: 0579 48475
Fax: 0579 48475
Proprietor: Capt E Moore & Miss K Tyrrell
Horses: 10 **Ponies:** 15
Facilities available: Men /J.Pd/X-C/Dis.R/Hkg - Bodmin moor
Level: Teaching standards to: ABRS Gold award. BHSAI. ABRS Grooms Diploma.
Specialisation: Lessons analysed on video. Language tuition.
Other details: Livery. Schooling. Breaking. Career students taken. Common room with pool table.
Member of Association of British Riding Schools

Tall Trees Riding Centre

Davidstow, Camelford,
Cornwall, PL32 9XR.
Tel: 08406 249
Proprietor: Mrs M Harrison
Horses: 12 **Ponies:** 12
Facilities available: 2 Ind.
Sch /J.Pd/X-C Jumps/Dis.
R/Hkg - Moorland
Level: Teaching standards
to: ABRS Test no.10.
Students to ABRS Grooms
Diploma. BHSAI and BHSII.
Specialisation:
Show-jumping and dressage
competitions. RDA. BHS
approved.
Other details:
Examination/Assessment
centre. YTS. Evening classes.
Novices to advanced riders.
Video lessons.
*Member of Association of
British Riding Schools*

The Haven Equestrian Centre

Crackington Haven, Bude,
Cornwall, EX23 30LF.
Proprietor: Mrs C J Chalmers

Tracey's Riding Centre

Atlantic View, High Lanes,
St. Mary's Isles of Scilly,
Cornwall.
Proprietor: Mrs. Guy
*Member of Association of
British Riding Schools*

Trenance Riding Stables

Trenance Lane, Newquay,
Cornwall, TR7 2HS.
Tel: 0637 872699
Proprietor: Mrs J Burt
Horses: 20 **Ponies:** 10
Facilities available:
Men/J.Pd/X-C/Hkg - Seaside,
cliffland and sand dunes.
Level: Teaching standards
to: ABRS Tests as required.
Students to BHS Stages 1 & 2
Specialisation: Superb
riding area. No roads.

Other details: F/P Livery.
Novice and upwards. YTS.
Career students taken.
*Member of Association of
British Riding Schools*

Trenissick Riding Stables

Trenissick, Cubert,
Newquay, Cornwall, TR8
5PJ.
Tel: 0637 830413
Proprietor: Mrs S Yeo
Horses: 5 **Ponies:** 5
Facilities available:
Men/X-C/Hkg - Country
lanes, beach and
commonland.
Level: Teaching standards
to: ABRS Test no. 8.
Students to BHS
Horsemasters. Riding and
Road Safety.
Other details: F/P Livery.
Schooling. Hunting. Lecture
room.
*Member of Association of
British Riding Schools*

Wheal Buller Riding School

Buller Hill, Redruth, Cornwall
Tel: 0209 221182
*Member of Association of
British Riding Schools*

Woodlands Riding Stables

St Blazey, Par, Cornwall,
PL24 2SR.
Tel: 072 681 2963
Proprietor: Col T G
Alexander
Horses: 6 **Ponies:** 6
Facilities available:
Hacking/accompanied
groups. Very young children
accepted if accompanied on
foot.

Cumbria

Armathwaite Hall Equestrian Centre

Coalbeck Farm,
Bassenthwaite, Keswick,
Cumbria, CA12 4RE.
Proprietor: Mr C Graves

Bigland Hall Riding Centre

Backbarrow, Nr Ulverston,
Cumbria, LA12 8PB.
Tel: 05395 31728
Proprietor: R Bigland
Horses: 10 **Ponies:** 15
Facilities available: Ind.Sch
/Men/J.Pd/X-C/Dis.R/Hkg -
Lakeland. Hills. Fens. Tarns
Woods. Over 1 100 acres of
private country estate.
Level: Teaching Standards:
Novice to experienced
Specialisation: Trout fishing.
Clay pigeon shooting. Archery.
Wind-surfing.
Other details: Lecture room.
Mounting block with ramp for
RDA. F/P Livery. Schooling.
Breaking. Brochure available.
Private/class tuition.
*Member of Association of
British Riding Schools*

Blackdyke Farm & Riding School

Blackdyke Farm, Blackford,
Carlisle, Cumbria, CA6 4EY.
Tel: 0228 74633
Proprietor: Mr & Mrs J Collier
Horses: 6 **Ponies:** 12
Facilities available: Liveries
/Ind School/Menage /X-C/
S-Jumps

Holmescales Riding Centre

Holmescale, Old Hutton, Nr
Kendal, Cumbria, LA8 0NB.
Tel: 0539 729388
Proprietor: Mr & Mrs P
Jones

Number Horses/Ponies: 25
Facilities available: Ind.Sch
/Hkg - Open countryside.
Level: Teaching Standards:
All levels.
Specialisation: Quality
horses for BHS exams.
Other details: F/Livery. Tuition
in jumping and dressage.
Trekking. Examination centre.

Side Farm Trekking Centre
Side Farm, Patterdale,
Penrith, Cumbria, CA11 0NP.
Proprietor: Mr & Mrs
Taylforth

Stonerigg Riding Centre
Great Orton, Carlisle,
Cumbria, CA5 6NA.
Tel: 0288 576232
Proprietor: Mrs M Kendall
Number Horses/Ponies: 10
Facilities available: Dis.R
/Ind.Sch/J.Pd/Hkg
Level: Teaching Standards:
Beginners to Competitive
level.
Specialisation: BHS
approved. Tuition in jumping.
Other details: Qualified
staff. F/Working livery.
Schooling. Competitions.

The Claife & Grizedale Riding Centre
Sawrey Knotts, Far Sawrey,
Nr Ambleside, Cumbria,
LA22 0LG.
Proprietor: Mr & Mrs D Dand

Wynlass Beck Stables
Lakeland Equestrian
Enterprises, Wynlass Beck,
Windermere, Cumbria,
LA23 1EU.
Tel: 09662 3811
Proprietor: Mrs W M Oakden
Horses: 9 **Ponies:** 6
Facilities available: Men/X-C
Jumps/Hkg

Level: Teaching standards to:
ABRS Test no. 10. Students to
BHS Stages 1-3. NVQ level 1.
ABRS Grooms and Ass.
Grooms Certificate.
Other details: Livery. Breaking.
Schooling. BHS Examination
/Assessment centre
*Member of Association of
British Riding Schools*

Derbyshire

Alton Riding School
Alton, Chesterfield, Derbyshire,
S42 6AW.
Tel: 0246 590267
Proprietor: Mrs J D Fisher
Horses: 7 **Ponies:** 14
Facilities available: Ind.Sch
/Men(F.Lt)/Hkg - Open
countryside
Level: Teaching Standards:
Students to BHS Stages 1 &
2. BHSAI. BHSII.
Other details: Special
residential courses. Breaking.
Schooling. Hunting
*Member of Association of
British Riding Schools*

Belper Riding Centre
Whitehouse Farm, Belper
Lane, Belper, Derbyshire,
DE5 2UJ.
Tel: 0773 824080
Proprietor: Mrs Cooke &
Miss Morris
Horses: 10 **Ponies:** 4
Facilities available: Men
(F.Lt)/J.Pd/Hkg
Level: Teaching Standards:
BHS Stages 1, 2 & 3.
Specialisation: Instruction
for children and adults.
Beginners to BHS exams.
Other details: Liveries.
Schooling. Breaking. Very
good pass rate in exams.
*Member of Association of
British Riding Schools*

Birchwood Riding Centre
140 Birchwood Lane,
Somercotes, Derbyshire,
DE55 4NE.
Tel: 0773 604305
Proprietor: Mrs L Coyle
*Member of Association of
British Riding Schools*

Brimington Equestrian Centre
130 Manor Road,
Brimington, Chesterfield,
Derbyshire, SH3 1NN.
Tel: 0246 235465
Proprietor: Tracey E Priest
(BHSAI)
Horses: 7 **Ponies:** 6
Facilities available:
Men/J.Pd/X-C/Hkg -
Woodland and bridleways.
Level: Teaching Standards:
Training towards to BHSAI
Specialisation: "Own a
Pony" Week.
Other details: Lecture room.
P/Livery(5). Schooling.
Breaking. Beginner to novice
competition rider. Evening
classes. Residential courses
can be arranged over short
term.
*Member of Association of
British Riding Schools*

Buxton Riding School
Fern Farm, Fern Road,
Buxton, Derbyshire, SK17
9NG.
Proprietor: Mrs C
Andrew-Smith

Causeway Farm
Plaistow Green, Crich, Nr
Matlock, Derbyshire.
Tel: 0629 534248
Proprietor: Mr Bell & Mrs
Bell-Heather
Horses: 14 **Ponies:** 5
Facilities available:
Ind.Sch/Men(F.Lt)/J.Pd/X-C/H
kg

Level: Teaching standards to: ABRS Test no.10. Students to BHSAI and BHSII.
Specialisation: Side-saddle. Preparation for competitions /examinations
Other details: BHS Examination/Assessment Centre. BSJA Affiliated Jumping Centre - regular winter and summer indoor shows. YTS. Livery. Schooling. Breaking.
Member of Association of British Riding Schools

East Midlands Riding Ass for the Handicapped

Leathersley Lane, Scropton, Derbyshire, DE6 5PN.
Tel: 0283 812753
Proprietor: Miss Y Deakin
Horses: 11 **Ponies:** 12
Member of Association of British Riding Schools

Elvaston Castle Riding Centre

Thulston, Derby, Derbyshire, DE7 3EP.
Tel: 0332 751927
Proprietor: Mr & Mrs Coe, Mr & Mrs Anderson
Facilities available: 3 Men (F.Lt)/J.Pd/X-C/Dis. R/Hkg - 250 acres country park estate.
Level: Teaching standards to: BHSAI/BHSHM. BHS Stages 1-4. BHSII
Specialisation: Full competition schedule.
Other details: Full competition schedule includes: unaffiliated /affiliated dressage, Hunter trials and local level show-jumping. P/livery. Schooling. Breaking.
Member of Association of British Riding Schools

Field Farm Stables

The Field, Shipley, Nr Heanor, Derbyshire, DE7 7JH.
Proprietor: Mr & Mrs D G Barker

Hargate Hill Riding School

Hargate Hill, Glossop, Derbyshire, SK13 9JL.
Proprietor: Mr & Mrs Tyldesley

Hazelwood Equestrian Centre

Nether Lane, Hazelwood, Derbyshire DE6 4AP
Tel:077389 543
Member of Association of British Riding Schools

Markeaton Riding Centre and Stud

Markeaton Lane, Markeaton, Derbyshire, DE3 4NH.
Tel: 0332 40126
Proprietor: Mrs V Pollard
Horses: 9 **Ponies:** 6

Moorbridge Riding Stables

Sinfin Moor Lane, Chellaston, Derbyshire, DE7 1SP.
Tel: 0332 702508
Proprietor: Miss M A Rice
Member of Association of British Riding Schools

Northfield Farm Riding & Trekking Centre

Northfield Farm, Flash, Buxton, Derbyshire, SK17 0SW.
Tel: 0298 22543
Proprietor: Mr & Mrs D C Andrews
Horses: 20 **Ponies:** 10
Facilities available: Hkg
Level: Teaching Standards: Novice to experienced.
Specialisation: Self catering holidays.

Other details: Liveries. Breaking. Schooling. Open all year. 2 day trail rides by arrangement.

Quarnhill School of Equitation

Addcrofts Farm, Kirk Ireton, Derbyshire.
Tel: 0335 70335
Proprietor: Mrs J Yeomans

Red House Stables Carriage Museum

Old Road, Darley Dale, Matlock, Derbyshire, DE4 2ER.
Tel: 0629 733583
Proprietor: Mrs Caroline Dale-Leech
Number Horses/Ponies: 20
Facilities available: Men /Paddock/Hkg - Excellent riding country.
Level: Teaching Standards: For driving, the instructors are BDS Proficiency test 3 level.
Specialisation: All aspects of Driving.
Other details: Scenic tours by coach and/or carriage. Two day Victorian Tour by stage coach and Four in hand. Side-saddle. Tuition in dressage. Overnight liveries can be catered for.

Yew Tree Farm Stables

Hazelwood, Derbyshire, DE6 4AE.
Tel: 0332 841364
Proprietor: M & H Lester
Horses: 10 **Ponies:** 10
Facilities available: Ind.Sch /J.Pd/X-C/Hkg - Open countryside
Level: Teaching standards to: ABRS Test no. 10
Specialisation: Hunters for hire. Own pony days. Horses and ponies for sale.

Other details: Dressage lesssons. Private lessons. Schooling. Breaking. Livery. *Member of Association of British Riding Schools*

Devon

Bableigh Riding School
Bableigh House, Landkey, Barnstable, Devon.
Proprietor: Mrs V A Coles

Belle Vue Valley Equestrian Centre
Argyll Road, Pennsylvania, Exeter, Devon.
Proprietor: Mr & Mrs A Deams

Bicton College of Agriculture
East Budleigh, Budleigh, Salterton, Devon, EX9 7BY.
Proprietor: M Florey Esq

Blackslade Riding and Trekking Centre
Widecombe-in-the-Moor, Nr Newton Abbot, Devon, PQ13 7TF.
Tel: 036 42 304
Proprietor: M E Hares
Horses: 8 **Ponies:** 20

Budleigh Salterton Riding School
Heatherways Stables, Hatherways, Budleigh, Salterton, Devon, EX9 7AS.
Proprietor: Mrs B J & Miss M Howick

Capton Equestrian Centre
Capton Equestrian Centre, Capton, Dartmouth, Devon, TQ6 0JE.
Tel: 080421 341
Proprietor: Mrs Shirley Davis

Horses: 4 **Ponies:** 6
Facilities available:
Ind.Sch/Men/Hkg - Country lanes, bridleways, woodland.
Level: Teaching standards to: Students to BHSAI. BHS Stages 1-4. All Pony Club Tests up to and including A test. ABRS Ass. Grooms Certificate.
Specialisation: Tuition in dressage.
Other details: Livery. Schooling. Breaking. Hunting. Evening classes. *Member of Association of British Riding Schools*

Chagford Riding Centre
Waye barton, Chagford, Devon, TQ13 8DT.
Proprietor: Miss S J Davies

Cheston Farm Equestrian Centre
Cheston Farm, Wrangaton, South Brent, Devon, TQ10 9HL
Tel: 0364 73266
Proprietor: Mrs R A Cornish & Mrs M C Berry
Horses: 10 **Ponies:** 10
Facilities available:
Ind.Sch/Men/J.Pd/Dis.R/Hkg
Level: Teaching standards to: BHSAI.
Specialisation: Childrens Day Club. Adult Saddle Club.
Other details: Liveries. Schooling. Breaking. Career students taken.
Member of Association of British Riding Schools

Coombe Park Equestrian Centre
Little Hempston, Nr. Totnes, Devon, TQ9 6LW.
Tel: 0803 863473
Proprietor: Mr/Mrs Norris / Mr/Mrs Loffet

Number Horses/Ponies: 20+
Facilities available: Ind.Sch /Men/X-C/Hkg
Level: Teaching standards to: BHSII.
Other details: DIY/F Livery. Tuition in show-jumping, X-country, and dressage. Suppliers of bedding. Horse dealers.

Crossways Riding School
Axtown Lane, Yelverton, Devon, PL20 7EB.
Proprietor: Mr & Mrs Howard

Culm Vale Riding School
Willand, Cullompton, Devon EX15 3BZ
Tel: 0884 40674
Member of Association of British Riding Schools

Devenish Pitt Riding Centre
Farway, Nr. Colyton, Devon, EX13 6EG.
Proprietor: Mrs M & Miss A Banks

Doone Valley Riding Stables
Parsonage Farm, Oare Brendon, Lynton, Devon, EX35 6NU.
Tel: 059 87 234
Proprietor: Mr W Burge & Miss N Stafford
Horses: 20 **Ponies:** 5

Drywell Farm Riding Centre
Widecombe-in-the-Moor, Newton Abbot, Devon, TQ13 7PN.
Proprietor: Mr & Mrs D Parnell

Exeter & District Riding School

The Shieling, Ebford, Nr. Topsham, Exeter, Devon, EX3 0QT.
Proprietor: Mrs J Hewitt & Miss C Hewitt

Frogwell Riding Centre

Frogwell Farm, Tiverton, Devon.
Tel: 0884 252794
Proprietor: Mrs P Allanson-Bailey
Horses: 5 **Ponies:** 4

Heazle Riding Centre

Clayhidon, Cullompton, Devon, RX15 3TH.
Proprietor: Mr C Brake & Miss R Passy
Member of Association of British Riding Schools

Hilltop Riding School

Pennsylvania Road, Exeter, Devon.
Tel: 0392 51370
Proprietor: Miss J Portbury
Horses: 5 **Ponies:** 9
Facilities available: Men (F.Lt)/J.Pd/X-C/Dis.R/Hkg - Bridlepaths and woodland.
Level: Teaching standards to: BHSAI.
Specialisation: Competitions and courses regularly held for clients.
Other details: Livery. Schooling. Breaking. Career students taken. Beginners and riders to local competition standard. Evening classes.
Member of Association of British Riding Schools

Honeysuckle Farm Equestrian Centre

Haccombe With Combe, Newton Abbot, Devon.
Proprietor: Mr & Mrs I G Mackay

Horwood Riding Centre

West Barton, Horwood, Bideford, Devon.
Proprietor: Mrs J Congdon

Huxton Farm Riding Centre

Shaugh Prior, Plymouth, Devon, PL7 5EQ.
Tel: 075 539 484
Proprietor: Mr M Norman
Number Horses/Ponies: 11
Facilities available: Hacking/Accompanied groups

Lower Burston Riding School

Bow, Nr. Crediton, Devon.
Proprietor: Mrs A L Phillips

Lower Downstow Stables

South Brent, Devon, TQ10 9ED.
Tel: 036 47 3340
Proprietor: Mrs F Hayter & Mr R Hayter
Horses: 2 **Ponies:** 10

Lydford House Riding Stables

Lydford House, Lydford, Okehampton, Devon, EX20 4AU.
Tel: 082 282 347
Proprietor: Miss C Boulter
Number Horses/Ponies: 10
Facilities available: Hacking/Accompanied hacks

Manor House Riding School

Springfield House, Honiton, Devon, EX14 8TL.
Tel: 0297 42026
Proprietor: Mrs Jill Susan Hookings BHSAI **Ponies:** 6
Facilities available: Men /J.Pd/X-C/Hkg
Level: Teaching Standards: Basic

Other details: Livery. Schooling. Breaking. Special reidential courses.
Member of Association of British Riding Schools

North Haye Riding Centre

North Haye, North Bovey, Moreton Hampstead, Devon.
Tel: 064 722 304
Proprietor: Miss Gilbert

Northgate Riding Centre

Bye Field, 43 Gloucester Road, Barnstaple, Devon.
Proprietor: Miss T Benson

Northgate Riding School

Harepie Lane, Tawstock, Barnstaple, Devon.
Tel: 027185 330
Proprietor: Miss R B Jones
Horses: 6 **Ponies:** 4
Facilities available: Hacking /Accompanied groups

Otterdene Riding Stables

Venn Ottery, Ottery St Mary, Devon, EX11 1SG.
Proprietor: Mrs G Adamson

Rosehill Riding Centre

Station Road, North Tawton, Devon, EX20 2BA.
Tel: 0837 82375
Proprietor: Miss C Hedges
Horses: 2 **Ponies:** 7
Facilities available: Men/J.Pd
Level: Teaching standards to: ABRS Test no. 7.
Specialisation: Side-saddle. Stable management.
Other details: Livery. Nervous riders and beginners.
Member of Association of British Riding Schools

Shilstone Rocks Stud & Trekking Centre

Widecombe-in-the-Moor, Newton Abbot, Devon, TQ13 7TF.
Proprietor: Mr & Mrs R Newbolt-Young

Steele Hill Riding Club

Week St Marys, Holsworthy, Devon EX22
Tel: 0288 84553
Member of Association of British Riding Schools

The Beacons Riding School & Holiday Centre

Ivybridge, Devon.
Tel: 07554 2260
Proprietor: Mr & Mrs Greenhouse
Horses: 10 **Ponies:** 15

Wembury Bay Riding School

Hilltop, 83 Church Road, Wembury, Nr. Plymouth, Devon, PL9 0JW.
Tel: 0752 862676
Proprietor: Anne & Tony Bearne
Horses: 10 **Ponies:** 9
Facilities available: Men/ J.Pd/Dis.R/X-C/Hkg - Beach, woodlands and fields.
Level: Teaching standards to: ABRS Test no. 10. Students to BHS stages 1 & 2.
Other details: F/P Livery. Schooling. Breaking. Evening classes by arrangement.
Member of Association of British Riding Schools

Dorset

Ashtree Riding School

Purewell, Christchurch, Dorset.
Tel: 0202 482642
Proprietor: Mrs M Cook
Horses: 12 **Ponies:** 10

Claire's Riding School

Moorfields, Furselands Road, Three Legged Cross, Wimbourne, Devon, BH 21 6RZ.
Tel: 0202 822975
Proprietor: Miss C Speer
Ponies: 8
Facilities available: Men/ J.pd/ X-C Jumps/ Hkg - forest and heathland
Level: Teaching standards to: Students to BHSAI. Pony club tests. ABRS Ass. Grooms Certificate and Grooms Diploma.
Specialisation: Training to competition standard in dressage and jumping.
Other details: Livery. Breaking. Schooling. Hunting. Tuition on own horses is a speciality. Evening classes - only in the summer
Member of Association of British Riding Schools

Croft House School Limited

Shillingstone, Dorset, DT11 0QS.
Proprietor: Mrs E A Rawllinson

Forest Lodge Equestrian Centre

Motcombe, Nr. Shaftesbury, Dorset, SP7 9PL.
Proprietor: Mr & Mrs R I Roberts

Lanehouse Equitation Centre

Overbury Close, Weymouth, Dorset.
Proprietor: Mr R G Addison & Mrs Y Kennard

Leigh Equestrian Centre Limited

Three Gates, Leigh, Sherborne, Dorset, DT9 6JQ.
Tel: 096321 469
Proprietor: Mr & Mrs H Shuaib
Horses: 20 **Ponies:** 10
Facilities available: Ind.Sch /Men/J.Pd/X-C/Dis.R/Hkg - Dorset downs, fairly hilly country lanes.
Level: Teaching standards to: BHS Exams.
Specialisation: Hard tennis court.
Other details: F/P Livery. Schooling. Breaking. Hunting. Special residential courses. Evening classes. Brochure available.
Member of Association of British Riding Schools

Longham House

Longham, Hampreston, Nr. Wimbourne, Dorset, BH22 9AB.
Proprietor: Miss S R Bush

Lulworth Equestrian Centre

Kennel Farm, Coombe Keynes, Wareham, Dorset, BH20 5QR.
Tel: 0929 41396
Proprietor: Mr & Mrs W J Weld
Number Horses/Ponies: 44
Facilities available: Men(All weather surface)/Hkg - No road work.
Level: Teaching Standards: From novice to experienced.
Specialisation: Approved by BHS and Ponies (UK).
Other details: Qualified instructors up to BHSII. Livery - basic cost 50.

Pound Cottage Childrens Riding School

Pound Cottage, 13 Water Lane, Durweston, Nr. Blandford Forum, Dorset, DT11 0QB.
Proprietor: Mrs J Hardy

Pound Farm

Pound Farm, Madjeston, Gillingham, Dorset, SP8 5JH.
Tel: 07476 3189
Proprietor: Mr & Mrs G G Burden
Horses: 4 **Ponies:** 6
Facilities available:
Men/J.Pd/X-C Jumps/Hkg - Country lanes and bridleways
Level: Teaching Standards: Basic
Specialisation: Gymkhanas, Jumping, Handy Pony competitions for clients only.
Other details: F/P Livery. Special tuition for nervous riders. Evening classes in the summer.
Member of Association of British Riding Schools

Stocks Farm Equestrian Centre

Christchurch Road, West Parley, Dorset.
Tel: 0202 570288
Proprietor: Mr & Mrs P G Oliver
Horses: 12 **Ponies:** 8
Facilities available:
Ind.Sch/Men/J.Pd/Dis.R/Hkg - Open heathland and forest.
Level: Teaching standards to: up to BHSII level.
Specialisation: Courses for BHS stages 1-4. Riding and Road Safety Tests.
Other details: F/P Livery. Schooling. Breaking. Hunting by arrangement. Special courses. Evening classes. Lectures.
Member of Association of British Riding Schools

The Fortune Centre

Avon Tyrell, Bransgore, Christchurch, Dorset, BH23 8EE.
Tel: 0425 73297
Proprietor: Mrs Y Nelson
Facilities available:
Ind.Sch/Men/Hkg/Dis.R
Level: Teaching Standards: Instructors trained to BHSAI
Specialisation: Riding for the Disabled. BHS approved
Other details: Voltige. Lunging. Excellent facilities for the disabled.

East Sussex

Ashdown Forest Riding Centre

Whitehouse Farm, Duddleswell, Nr Uckfield, East Sussex.
Tel: 082 571 2738
Proprietor: M C Inglis
Horses: 9 **Ponies:** 10

Beauport Park Riding School

The Ridge West, St Leonards-on-Sea, East Sussex.
Tel: 0424 51424
Proprietor: Mr K Jackson
Horses: 28 **Ponies:** 12

Brendon Riding School

Pyecombe, East Sussex.
Tel: 079 18 2158
Proprietor: Mr & Mrs C J Light
Number Horses/Ponies: 15
Facilities available:
Hacking/Accompanied Groups. 2-3 Hour rides on South Downs

Canters End Riding School

Canters End Main Road, Hadlow Down, nr Uckfield, East Sussex, TN22 4HP.
Tel: 082 585 213

Proprietor: Miss M R Thompson
Horses: 3 **Ponies:** 10

Cophall Farm Stables

Eastbourne Roaed, Polegate, East Sussex, BN26 6QL.
Tel: 03212 3975
Proprietor: Mrs D & Miss L Baker-Beall
Horses: 5 **Ponies:** 10
Member of Association of British Riding Schools

Crockstead Equestrian Centre

Crockstead Farm, Halland, Nr Lewes, East Sussex, BN8 6PT.

Gatewood Stables

The Barn House, Robin Post Lane, Wilmington, East Sussex, BN26 6RP.
Tel: 032 12 3709
Proprietor: Mr & Mrs K Quicke
Horses: 10
Facilities available: Ind.Sch /Men/X-C Jumps/J.Pd/Hkg - Woods and downland
Level: Teaching standards to: BHS Stage 2.
Specialisation: Gymkhanas. Dressage to music. Downland picnics in summer.
Other details: Evening classes. Riders taking BHS stage 1 & 2. Together and divided classes.
Member of Association of British Riding Schools

Higham Farm

Chapel Lane, Guestling Green, Nr. Hastings, East Sussex, TN35 4HP.
Proprietor: Miss M Stokes

Horam Manor Riding Stables

Horam, Heathfield, East Sussex, TN21 0JD.
Tel: 043 53 2363
Proprietor: Sheila Elizabeth Guildford
Horses: 7 **Ponies:** 10
Facilities available: Ind.Sch /X-C/Hkg - Woodland and field.
Level: Teaching standards to: ABRS Test no. 8. Students to BHSAI.
Specialisation: Block bookings for Girl Guides, schools, etc.
Other details: Livery. Schooling. Breaking. Special residential course - accomodation available locally. Evening classes.
Member of Association of British Riding Schools

Magnum Equestrian Centre & Tutorial Academy

Cote Lodge, Cote Street, Worthing, East Sussex, BN13 3EX.
Tel: 0903 692745

Plumpton Agricultural College

Plumpton, Lewes , East Sussex, BN7 3AE.
Proprietor: J J Wilson Esq

Sky Farm Riding School

Cade Street, Chapel Cross, Old Heathfield, East Sussex.
Proprietor: C & D Sansom

Southdown Riding School

Bear Road, Brighton, East Sussex.
Tel: 0273 680953
Proprietor: R H Goodridge
Number Horses/Ponies: 10

The English Language and Equestrian Centre

Friars Gate Farm, Crowborough, East Sussex, TN7 1XH.
Proprietor: Mr D R C Forsyth

Whydown Riding School

Whydown Place, Bexhill-on-Sea, East Sussex, TN39 4RA.
Tel: 04243 6279
Proprietor: Mr Preston & Miss Price
Horses: 4 **Ponies:** 4
Facilities available: Ind.Sch /Dis.R/Hkg
Level: Teaching Standards: Various abilities.
Specialisation: Specialist classes for dressage and show-jumping.
Other details: Livery. Schooling. Indoor Shows. Examination/Assessment Centre.
Member of Association of British Riding Schools

Wilton House Riding Centre

Chisfield, Nr Battle, East Sussex, TW33 9DL.
Tel: 0424 892096
Proprietor: Mr M A Aver
Horses: 9 **Ponies:** 9
Facilities available: Ind Sch/Gallery/Men/J Pad/X-C Jumps Hkg. FL/Schooling /Hkg/Breaking/Hunting
Specialisation: Residential courses for French students only (max 40)
Member of Association of British Riding Schools

Winton Street Farm Stables

Winton Street, Alfriston, East Sussex.
Proprietor: Mrs H J Clark

Essex

Aldborough Hall Equestrian Centre Ltd

Aldborough Hall, Aldborough Hatch, Newbury Park, Ilford, Essex, IG2 7TE.
Tel: 081 590 1433
Proprietor: A R S Garrett
Horses: 20 **Ponies:** 4

Brentwood Riding Centre

Days Lanes, Pilgrims Hatch, Brentwood, Essex.
Tel: 0277 373647
Proprietor: Mrs Julie Stewart BHSII
Horses: 7 **Ponies:** 8
Facilities available: 2 Men (F.Lt)/J.Pd/Dis.R/Hkg
Level: Teaching standards to: BHSAI. Students trained to BHSAI and looking to do ABRS courses.
Specialisation: Driving. Wedding carriage hire.
Other details: Tuition in eventing, dressage and show-jumping. Evening classes. Beginners to experienced taken.
Member of Association of British Riding Schools

Brook Farm Equestrian Centre

Stock Road, Stock, Nr Ingatestone, Essex, CM4 9PH.
Tel: 0277 840425
Proprietor: Mr & Mrs C Golding
Horses: 20 **Ponies:** 20
Member of Association of British Riding Schools

Brook Farm Equestrian Centre

Radwinter, Safron Walden, Essex, CB10 2TH.
Proprietor: Mr & Mrs M Gay

Burches Riding School

Great Burchess Road,
Thundersly, Essex.
Tel: 0268 776654
Proprietor: Mr & Mrs J Bush
Horses: 4 **Ponies:** 6
Facilities available: Men
(F.Lt)/J.Pd/X-C/Dis.R/Hkg
Level: Teaching standards
to: ABRS test no. 6. Students
to BHSAI and ABRS exams.
Specialisation: Beginners.
Other details: Schooling.
Breaking. Liveries. Stable
management lessons.
Evening classes.
*Member of Association of
British Riding Schools*

Churchgate Farm

Churchgate Street, Old
Harlow, Essex, CM17 0NJ.
Proprietor: B Langemar Esq

Colne Valley Riding Stables

Brickhouse Farm, Coln
Engaine, Nr Colchester,
Essex.
Tel: 07875 2542
Proprietor: Mr J M Roberts
Horses: 6 **Ponies:** 6
Facilities available: Groups
accompanied on hacks.

De Beauvoir Farm Livery Yard

Church Road, Ramsden
Heath, Nr. Billericay, Essex,
CM11 1PW.
Proprietor: Mr B Greenan

East Anglian Farm Rides

Highfields Farm, Kelvedon,
Essex.
Tel: 0206 251790
Proprietor: N Dyson & R
Bunting
Facilities available: Hkg -
over 100 miles of Toll
Bridleways.
Other details: Livery available.

Eastern Equitation

Brickhouse Farm, Colne
Engaine, Nr. Colchester,
Essex, CO6 2HJ.
Tel: 0787 222542
Proprietor: Mr J M Roberts
Horses: 14
Facilities available: Ind.Sch
/J.Pd/X-C/Hkg - Farmland
and quiet lanes.
Level: Teaching standards
to: BHSII: BHS Stages 1-4.
ABRS Grooms Diploma..
Specialisation: Career
training - students WP's and
YTS to BHSII level .
Other details: Schooling.
Breaking. All standards
catered for. Free use of
indoor school and tuition for
liveries. BHS Exam centre.
Livery - Full from 38 to 55 +
VAT per week.
*Member of Association of
British Riding Schools*

Eastminster School of Riding Limited

Hooks Hall Farm, The Chase,
Rush Green, Romford, Essex,
RM7 055.
Proprietor: Mrs A Ackland

Folkes Farm Riding & Livery Stables

Folkes Lane, Upminster,
Essex, RM14 1TH.
Proprietor: Mr RA Nightingale

Foxhound Riding School Ltd

Baker Street, Orsett, Essex.
Tel: 0375 891367
Proprietor: Mrs M Cox
Horses: 10 **Ponies:** 8
Facilities available:
Ind.Sch/Men(F.Lt)/
Dis.R/X-C/J.Pd/Hkg -
Fenland and bridleways.
Level: Teaching standards
to: BHSAI Stage 4.
Specialisation: Hacking.

Other details: Evening
classes. All standards.
Liveries (20). P/ Livery (20).
Schooling. Breaking.
*Member of Association of
British Riding Schools*

Glebe Equestrian Centre

Mope Lane, Wickham
Bishops, Witham, Essex.
Proprietor: Miss R Osborne
& Miss J Osborne

Havering Park Riding School and Club,

Havering-Atte-Bower,
Romford, Essex.
Tel: 0708 46246
Proprietor: Joyce and David
Symth
Facilities available: Ind.Sch
/Men/X-C/Dis.R/Hkg -
Country park and farmland.
Level: Teaching standards
to: Students to ABRS
Grooms Diploma. BHSAI.
Specialisation: Riding for
the Disabled work with
MENCAP.
Other details: Daily or
weekly non-residential
courses on various
equestrian subjects. Livery.
Breaking. Schooling. Hunting.
*Member of Association of
British Riding Schools*

Heron Stream Stud

Burrells Farm, Curch Road,
Rawreth, Wickford, Essex,
SS11 8SH.
Tel: 0268 733008
Proprietor: Miss J R Van
Lennep
Horses: 7 **Ponies:** 3
Facilities available:
Ind.Sch/Men/J.Pd/X-C/Dis.R/H
kg - Limited and only when
escorted
Level: Teaching standards to:
BHS Intermediate Instructor.
NPS Diploma. Planned ABRS
and NVQ's exams.

Specialisation: Breeding. Show production. Tuition on clients own horses.
Other details: Highly disabled to expert riders taken. "Off the job" training for YTS. Lectures. Career students taken. Liveries. Schooling. Breaking. Dressage tuition.
Member of Association of British Riding Schools

High Beech Riding School

Pynest Green Lane, Waltham Abbey, Essex, EN9 3QL.
Tel: 01 508 8866
Proprietor: A J & G J Taylor
Horses: 12 **Ponies:** 9
Facilities available: Ind.Sch/Men/X-C Jumps/J.Pd/Hkg - In Epping forest and open countryside.
Level: Teaching standards to: ABRS Test no. 5.
Specialisation: Riding Clubs. HQ for 1st Essex Troop Rangers Association.
Other details: F/P Livery. Schooling. Lunge lessons. Brochure available. Evening classes. Tuition for dressage, show-jumping and nervous riders.
Member of Association of British Riding Schools

Hill Farm Riding Centre

Pan Lane, East Hanningfield, Chelmsford, Essex, CM3 8BJ.
Proprietor: Mr R Lawrence
Member of Association of British Riding Schools

Lillyputts Equestrian Centre

272 Wingletye Lane, Hornchurch, Essex, RM11 3BL.
Tel: 04024 53908
Proprietor: Mrs S J Ellis

Facilities available: Ind.Sch/Men(F.Lt)/X-C/Hkg - Farm-land, 127 acres grassland.
Specialisation: Specialised teaching. to BHSAI
Other details: P/Livery. Schooling. Breaking. Private lessons only.
Member of Association of British Riding Schools

Little Montrose Riding Establishment

Little Montrose, Birchwood Road, Purleigh, Chelmsford, Essex, CM3 6PR.
Tel: 0621 828231
Proprietor: Miss C Mercer & Mrs C S Mercer
Horses: 6 **Ponies:** 6
Facilities available: Men (F.Lt)/J.Pd/Hkg - Flat country.
Level: Teaching standards to: ABRS test no. 7. Students to BHSAI.
Other details: Career students taken. Together and divided classes.
Member of Association of British Riding Schools

Little Paddocks

Frating Road, Great Bromley, Colchester, Essex, CO7 7JL.
Tel: 0206 250921
Proprietor: Mr & Mrs J A Grant
Horses: 8 **Ponies:** 12
Facilities available: 2 Men (F.Lt)/J.Pd/X-C/Dis.R/Hk
Level: Teaching standards to: ABRS Test no. 6.
Specialisation: Canteen and cold drink facilities. Picnic benches.
Other details: Mounting blocks and ramps for the RDA. Internal and BHS Riding and Road Safety Examination Centre. Evening Classes. Schooling. Livery.
Member of Association of British Riding Schools

Longmead Riding School

Ardleigh Rad, Great Bromley, Colchester, Essex, CO7 7TL.
Proprietor: Miss K A Sheppard

Longwood Equestrian Centre

Dry Street, Basildon, Essex.
Tel: 0268 412184
Proprietor: Mr & Mrs Warren
Horses: 8 **Ponies:** 10

Medway Riding Centre

Medway Farm, Southminster Road, Althorne, Chelmsford, Essex, CM3 6EN.
Proprietor: Mr J S Castle

Mistley Riding School

Mistley, Manningtree, Essex, CO11 2NL.
Tel: 0206 392236
Proprietor: Y. Champness & A Barnard
Horses: 6 **Ponies:** 10
Facilities available: Men/J.Pd/Hkg - Rural lanes, some farmland
Level: Teaching standards to: ABRS test no. 7.
Specialisation: Young children. Novice adults.
Other details: Lecture room. Livery. Gymkhanas. Picnic rides in the summer.
Member of Association of British Riding Schools

Moor End Stables

Moor End, Great Sampford, Saffron Walden, Essex, CB10 2RQ.
Proprietor: Miss S J Green

New Hall School Riding Centre

Chelmsford, Essex.
Tel: 0245 467588
Proprietor: Sister Mary Francis
Horses: 24 **Ponies:** 28

Paglesham School of Equitation

Ingulfs, Paglesham,
Rochford, Essex, SS4 2DG.
Proprietor: Mr A K Judge

Park Lane Riding & Livery Stables

Park Lane, Ramsden Heath,
Billericay, Essex, CM11 1NN.
Tel: 0268 710145
Proprietor: Mr W White &
Mrs P Needham
Horses: 12 **Ponies:** 22

Pine Lodge Riding Centre

Springfield Farm, Lippitts
Hill, High Beech, Loughton,
Essex, IG10 4AL.
Tel: 081 508 7070
Proprietor: Mrs S A Stavrou
Horses: 12 **Ponies:** 6
Facilities available:
Ind.Sch/Men(F.Lt)/J.Pd/Dis.R
- Dependant on disability/Hkg
Level: Teaching standards
to: ABRS Test no. 10.
Specialisation: Training to
advanced medium dressage.
Other details: Evening
classes. Schooling.
Breaking. Career students
taken. Beginners to
advanced riders taken.
*Member of Association of
British Riding Schools*

Ragwood Riding Centre

Daws Heath Road,
Thundersly, Benfleet, Essex,
SS7 2TB.
Tel: 0702 556520
Proprietor: Mrs S Meggison
& Mrs C Lazell
Horses: 3 **Ponies:** 6
Facilities available: Ind.Sch
/Men/J.Pd/Hkg - Woodland.
Level: Teaching standards to:
ABRS Test no. 10. Students
to BHSAI and BHSHM. ABRS
Grooms Diploma.

Specialisation: Tuition in
dressage.
Other details: Schooling.
Breaking. Hunting. Livery.
Evening classes.
*Member of Association of
British Riding Schools*

Rayne Riding Centre

Fairy Hall Lane, Rayne,
Braintree, Essex, CM7 8SZ.
Proprietor: Mr & Mrs B R
Pewter

Red House Farm Riding & Livery Stables

Warren Lane, Doddinghurst,
Brentwood, Essex,
CM15 0JD.
Tel: 0277 72336
Proprietor: Ms C B Porter
Horses: 4 **Ponies:** 6
Facilities available:
Men(F.Lt)/J.Pd/Hkg - Lanes,
country park, farmland and
bridleways.
Level: Teaching Standards:
Various standards.
Specialisation: Childrens
holiday pony week.
Other details: F/P Livery.
Schooling. Breaking.
Hunting. Evening classes.
*Member of Association of
British Riding Schools*

The Grange Riding Club & Livery Yard

Murrels Lane, Hockley,
Essex SS5 6AX
Tel:0702 205727/203474
*Member of Association of
British Riding Schools*

Wethersfield Riding Stables

Hedingham Road,
Wethersfield, Nr. Braintree,
Essex.
Proprietor: Mr/Mrs Parker &
Mr/MrsMacKenzie

White's Place Riding Club

White's Place, Main Road,
Margaretting, Ingatestone,
Essex, CM4 0ES.
Tel: 0277 353243
Proprietor: Mrs C L Magness
Horses: 7 **Ponies:** 15
Facilities available: Ind
Sch/Gallery/J Pad/Leisure
Rm
Specialisation: Evening
Classes. Divided Classes.
*Member of Association of
British Riding Schools*

Woodredon Riding School

Woodredon Farm, Upshire,
Nr Waltham Abbey, Essex,
EN9 3QT.
Tel: 0992 714312
Proprietor: Mr & Mrs D L Gill
Horses: 14 **Ponies:** 16
Facilities available: Ind.Sch
/J.Pd/X-C/Hkg - forest
Level: Teaching standards
to: Students to BHSAI.
BHSHM.
Specialisation: Horses
qualified and trained for P to
P & Hunter-chasing.
Other details: Tuition in
dressage on own horse.
Evening classes. Divided
classes. Career students
taken. Livery. Schooling.
Breaking. Hunting.
*Member of Association of
British Riding Schools*

Gloucestershire

Horseshoe Farm Riding School

Horseshoe Farm, Brinkmarsh
Lane, Falfield, Gloucestershire,
GL12 8PT.
Tel: 0454 260318
Proprietor: Mrs Gladsby &
Mrs Paull

Horses: 4 **Ponies:** 9
Facilities available: Men
(F.Lt)/Hkg
Level: Teaching standards
to: ABRS Test no. 5. Novice
to intermediate riders taken.
Specialisation: Stable
management courses and
half day rides during holidays.
Other details: Schooling.
Evening classes.
*Member of Association of
British Riding Schools*

Huntley School of Equitation

Wood End, Huntley,
Gloucestershire, GL19 3EY.
Proprietor: Mrs M T Freeman

Littledean Trekking Centre

Wellington Farm, Sutton
Road, Littledean,
Gloucestershire, GL14 2TU.
Tel: 0594 23955
Proprietor: Mr & Mrs T
Chamberlain
Horses: 12 **Ponies:** 15

Long Distance Riding Centre

Fosseway, Bourton-on-the-
Water, Gloucestershire,
GL54 2DX.
Tel: 0451 21101
Proprietor: Miss J Davies
Horses: 5 **Ponies:** 4
Facilities available: Men
(F.Lt)/J.Pd/Hkg
Level: Teaching standard to:
ABRS Test no. 5. Students
trained towards ABRS Ass.
Grooms Diploma.
Specialisation: Long Distance
Courses - clients own horse.
L.D.R. day lectures.
Other details: Career
students taken. Horses
include 2 Cobs.
*Member of Association of
British Riding Schools*

Summerhouse Equitation Centre

Old Bath Road, Hardwicke,
Gloucestershire, GL2 6RG.
Tel: 0666 860249
Proprietor: Mrs S R Weston
Number Horses/Ponies: 35
Facilities available: Ind.Sch
/Men/X-C/Hkg
Level: Teaching Standards:
Beginners to advanced. BHS
stage 4.
Specialisation: Side-saddle.
Other details: Cater for
nervous riders and small
children. F/P/Working livery.
Schooling. Competitions.

The Playmate Riding School

Hardwicke House, Elmstone
Harwicke, Cheltenham,
Gloucestershire, GL51 9TD.
Proprietor: Mrs J Swambo

The Talland School of Equitation

Church Farm, Siddington,
Cirencester, Gloucstershire,
GL7 6EZ.
Tel: 0285 652318
Fax: 0285 658859
Proprietor: Colonel & Mrs R
C T Sivewright
Horses: 50 **Ponies:** 10
Facilities available: Ind.Sch
/Men/J.Pd/X-C/Dis.R-limited/H
kg - limited no casual hiring
Level: Teaching standards
to: ABRS Test no. 10+.
Students to any and all
ABRS, BHS and Pony Club
tests.
Specialisation: Comp.
Training. Junior and senior
eventers. PC Team prep.
Other details: Livery.
Schooling. Breaking. Hunting
(own horse). Career students
taken. Holiday courses.
Competition training in
Eventing and Dressage.
*Member of Association of
British Riding Schools*

Greater Manchester

Carrington Riding Centre

Nursery Farm, Isherwood
Road, Carrington, Urmston,
Greater Manchester,
M31 4BH.
Tel: 061 969 5853
Proprietor: Mr B Groos
Facilities available: Ind.Sch
/Men(F.Lt)/J.Pd/X-C/Dis.R/kg
- Cheshire, wooded, moss.
Level: Teaching standards
to: BHSAI - 2 year course in
conjunction with South
Trafford College of Further
Education.
Specialisation: BHS
Examination Centre.
Other details: Evening
classes. Special Residential
Courses. Tuition in
show-jumping and dressage.
*Member of Association of
British Riding Schools*

Deandane Riding Stables

397 Gathurst Road,
Shevington, Wigan, Greater
Manchester.
Proprietor: Mr M Whalley

Hampshire

Arniss Riding & Livery Stables

Godshill, Fordingbridge,
Hampshire.
Tel: 0425 54114
Proprietor: Miss A Finn
Horses: 20 **Ponies:** 25

Broadlands Riding Centre

Broadlands, Nr. Alton, Hampshire, GU34 5PX.
Proprietor: Mrs S M Stratford

Brocks Farm Equitation Livery & Training Ctre

Brocks Farm, Longstock, Stockbridge, Hampshire, SO20 6EE.
Proprietor: Mrs J & Misses P & L Buttenshaw

Burley Villa School of Riding

Bashley Common Road, New Milton, Hampshire.
Tel: 0425 610278
Proprietor: Miss Carter-Pennington
Horses: 10 **Ponies:** 10

Catherston Stud & Equestrian Centre

Black Knoll House, Brockenhurst, Hampshire, SO42 7QE.
Tel: 0590 22027
Proprietor: A G Lonston-Clarke Esq
Horses: 10 **Ponies:** 5

Causeway House Stables

Causeway House, The Causeway, Petersfield, Hampshire.
Proprietor: Mr J N Day

Chattis Hill Riding Centre

Chattis Hill Stables, Stockbridge, Hampshire.
Tel: 0264 810628
Proprietor: Mr & Mrs A G Lambert
Horses: 15 **Ponies:** 20

Decoy Pond Riding & Livery Stables

Decoy Pond Farm, Beaulieu Road, Beaulieu, Brockenhurst, Hampshire, SO4 7YQ.
Proprietor: D N Horton

Fir Tree Equestrian Centre

Fir Tree Farm, Ogdens, Fordingbridge, Hampshire, SP6 2PY.
Proprietor: Mrs Gail Mosley

Flanders Farm Riding Centre

Silver Street, Hordle, Hampshire SO41 6DF
Tel: 0590 682207
Proprietor: Mrs M Rogers

Fowlers Farm

Vernham Street, Nr Andover, Hampshire, SP11 0EL.
Proprietor: Mr & Mrs G Humphrey

Gleneagles Riding Centre

Allington Lane, West End, Southampton, Hampshire, SO3 3HQ.
Tel: 0703 473164
Proprietor: Mrs E H Walsh & Miss D K Walsh
Horses: 25 **Ponies:** 25
Facilities available: 2 Men (1 Olympic arena.F.Lt)/ J.Pd/X-C/Dis.R/Hkg - 300 acres of field and woodlands.
Level: Teaching standards to: ABRS Test No. 10. BHSAI. BHS Stages 1-3.
Specialisation: Pub and picnic rides. Shows and gymkhanas. Summer barbacues.
Other details: Lecture room. F/P Liveries. Schooling. Breaking. Hunting. Special

residential courses. Evening classes. Swimming pool on premises. Instruction from 3 BHSAI and 3 BHSII.
Member of Association of British Riding Schools

Harroway House

Penton Mewsey, Andover, Hampshire, SP11 0RA.
Tel: 0264 772295
Proprietor: Mrs E C Skelton
Horses: 10 **Ponies:** 19
Facilities available: Covered Sch/J.Pd/X-C Jumps/Hkg - Woods and downlands.
Level: Teaching Standards: General to elementary dressage, Intermediate Horse Trials, Grade B Show-jumping.
Specialisation: Side saddle tuition and hunting for known clients.
Other details: F/Livery. Schooling. Breaking. Hunting. Evening classes.
Member of Association of British Riding Schools

Headley Equestrian Centre

Frensham Lane, Headley, Nr Borden, Hampshire, GU35 8TB.
Tel: 0428 713858
Proprietor: Mr & Mrs C W Turner

Knight Bridge Riding, Training & Holiday Centre,

Knight Bridge, Sway, Lymington, Hampshire.
Tel: 0590 682271
Proprietor: Mrs J M Harris
Number Horses/Ponies: 35
Facilities available: Hacking /Accompanied groups

Meon Valley Equestrian Centre

Swanmore Park Farm,
Upper Swanmore,
Southampton, Hampshire.
Tel: 04893 2209
Proprietor: Mrs Richley

Merrie Stud Riding School

Merrie Stud, Corhampton,
Southampton, Hampshire,
SO3 1NB.
Proprietor: Mrs J D N Shaw

Mopley Farm Countryside Activity Centre

Blackfield, Southampton,
Hampshire, SO4 1YH.
Tel: 0703 891616
Proprietor: Brian Tillman
Horses: 8 **Ponies:** 8

Naval Riding Centre

HMS Dryad, Southwick, Nr.
Fareham, Hampshire, PO7
6EJ.
Tel: 0705 210522
Proprietor: Cdr. B W
Holden-Crawford
Horses: 35 **Ponies:** 15
Facilities available: 2 Ind.Sch
/Men(F.Lt)/J.Pd/X-C/Dis.R/Hkg
Level: Teaching standards
to: ABRS test no. 10.
Students trained to BHSAI
and BHSII.
Specialisation: Tuition in
dressage, driving and
show-jumping. Competitions.
Other details: Livery.
Schooling. Breaking. Career
students taken. Examination
/Assesment centre. Evening
classes. YTS.
*Member of Association of
British Riding Schools*

New Forest Equestrian Centre

Shirley Holms Farm, Shirley
Holms, Lymington,
Hampshire, SO41 8NH.
Proprietor: Mrs Y Tasker

New Forest Riding, Driving & Watersports

'The Old Barn', Dale Farm,
Manor Road, Nr.
Southampton, Hampshire,
SO4 5TJ.
Tel: 0703 843180
Proprietor: Ms Berridge
Horses: 15 **Ponies:** 15
Facilities available:
Men/J.Pd/Hkg - Excellent
New Forest
Level: Teaching standards
to; ABRS test no. 10+.
Grooms Diploma. Students
to Bhs stages 1-4 and up to
ITT
Specialisation: Activity
holidays. Riding and
watersports.
Other details: Livery.
Schooling. Breaking.
Hunting. Lecture room.
Tuition in dessage, eventing,
side-saddle and help with
problem horses. Pony trap
driving. Weddings.
*Member of Association of
British Riding Schools*

New Park Manor Equestrian Centre and Hotel

Lyndhurst Road,
Brokenhurst, Hampshire.
Tel: 0590 23467
Fax: 0590 22268
Proprietor: Mr P Lewis &
L.Lewis (StbleMan)
Horses: 6 **Ponies:** 2
Facilities available: Men
(F.Lt)/J.Pd/X-C/Dis.R/Hkg
Level: Teaching standards
to: ABRS Tests, BHSAI,
FBHS. Students trained to
BHSAI.

Specialisation: Competition
and Hunting Liveries.
Other details: F/P Livery.
Schooling. Breaking.
Hunting. Students welcome
to further training inc.
accomodation, food and
wages. Foreign students
welcome as 50% of Hotel
staff are French.
*Member of Association of
British Riding Schools*

Russell Equitation Centre

Black Farm, Gaters Hill,
West End, Southampton,
Hampshire, SO3 3HT.
Tel: 0703 473693
Proprietor: Mrs C Boulton
Horses: 10 **Ponies:** 12
Facilities available:
Men(F.Lt)/J.Pd/X-C/Hkg -
Bridleways, farmland and
downs/Dis.R
Level: Teaching standards
to: ABRS Test no.10. All
ABRS to Grooms Diploma.
BHS to stage 3,and stage 4
stable management.
Specialisation: Special
courses for adults/children.
Other details: F/P Livery.
Schooling. Breaking.
Evening classes. Special
loan system. Confidence
building for horse and riding.
*Member of Association of
British Riding Schools*

Rycroft School of Equitation

New Mill Lane, Eversley,
Hampshire, RG27 0RA.
Tel: 0734 732761
Proprietor: Mr & Mrs
Hundley
Facilities available: Ind.Sch
/2 Men(F.Lt)/J.Pd/X-C/Hkg -
Parkland
Level: Teaching standards to:
ABRS Test no. 10.
Examination level to BHSAI.
ABRS Ass. Grooms Cerificate.

Specialisation: Special daily or weekly courses.
Other details: F/P Livery. Schooling. Breaking. Hunting. Tuition in dressage, show-jumping and X-country. Evening classes. Career students taken.
Member of Association of British Riding Schools

School Farm Training Centre

School Farm, Canefield Cottage, Romsey Road, Lockerley, Nr. Romsey, Hampshire, SO5 0JA.
Proprietor: Mr & Mrs A Noordijk

Silver Horseshoe Riding Centre

Hale, Nr Fordingbridge, Hampshire.
Tel: 0725 20678
Proprietor: Mrs M Bryant
Horses: 8 **Ponies:** 4
Facilities available: Men(F.Lt)/J.Pd/X-C/Hkg - New Forest.
Level: Teaching standards to: Students to BHSAI. ABRS Grooms Certificate.
Specialisation: Stud. 6 Stallions. Young stock showing.
Other details: Evening classes. Special residential courses. Livery. Schooling. Breaking. Hunting. Brochure available.
Member of Association of British Riding Schools

Stockbridge Riding School

Stockbridge Downs, Winton Hill, Stockbridge, Hampshire.
Tel: 0264 810727
Proprietor: Mr & Mrs John Wrayton

Wellington Riding Limited

Basingstoke Road, Heckfield, Basingstoke, Hampshire, RG27 0LJ.
Tel: 0734 326308
Proprietor: Mr & Mrs John Goodman
Horses: 40 **Ponies:** 40
Facilities available: Ind.Sch /2 Men(F.Lt) /J.Pd /X-C/Dis.R /Hkg - Grassland and woodland
Level: Teaching standards to: ABRS Test no. 10. All BHS exams to BHSI.
Specialisation: Affiliated dressage and horse trials.
Other details: F/P Livery. Schooling. Breaking. Hunting. Tuition in X-country, side-saddle. Special residential courses. Junior unaccompanied holidays. Hunter trials and indoor jumping.
Member of Association of British Riding Schools

Westcroft Stables

147 Havant Road Hayling Island, Hampshire, PO11 0LF.
Tel: 465512
Proprietor: Mrs Dale Norman
Horses: 6 **Ponies:** 8
Facilities available: Men(F.Lt)/J.Pd/X-C Jumps /Hkg - Seaside
Level: Teaching standards to: Students to BHSAI.
Specialisation: Tuition in dressage and show-jumping.
Other details: F/P/DIY/ Working Liveries. Schooling. Breaking. Evening Classes.
Member of Association of British Riding Schools

Wickham Riding School & Stud

The White House, Wickham Common, Wickham, Fareham, Hampshire, PO17 6JQ.
Tel: 0329 832035

Proprietor: Mr & Mrs Schofield
Horses: 27 **Ponies:** 10
Facilities available: Ind.Sch /Men(F.Lt)/J.Pd/Dis.R/X-C/Hkg - countryside
Level: Teaching standards to: BHS stage 3. Students to BHSAI.
Specialisation: Pony trekking on the South Downs Way. Irish Draught Stud.
Other details: Evening classes Mon-Fri. Livery. Schooling. Breaking. Brochure available.
Member of Association of British Riding Schools

Willow Farm Livery

123 Frogmoor Lane, Lovedene, Portsmouth, Hampshire.
Tel: 0705 599817
Proprietor: Mrs J Auckland-Jones
Number Horses/Ponies: 20
Facilities available: Men/Hkg
Level: Teaching Standards: Novice to advanced.
Other details: Tuition in dressage. Suppliers for horse care products.

Woodcroft Riding Centre

Woodcroft Lane, Lovedean, Portsmouth, Hampshire
Tel: 0705 595069/592204

Hereford & Worcestershire

Castle Farm Livery Yard

Castle Farm Stables, Lea Castle Farm, Cookley, Kidderminster, Hereford & Worcester, DY10 3AD.
Proprietor: Mr G Knight & Miss W Wedgbury

Farm Forest Equestrian Centre

Far Forest Stables, James Place, Far Forest, Nr. Kidderminster, Hereford & Worcester, DY14 9DG.
Proprietor: Mr & Mrs A Fitzpatrick

Hallow Mill Equestrian Centre

Hallow, Nr. Worcester, Hereford & Worcester, WR2 6PR.
Proprietor: Mrs I Auty & Mrs R Johnson

Hanburies Riding Centre

Bishops Frome, Hereford & Worcester.
Tel: 053 186 312
Proprietor: Mrs C Hyett
Number Horses/Ponies: 40

Hartlebury Stables Ltd.

Warsely Manor Stables, Manor Lane, Hartlebury, Kidderminster, Hereford & Worcester, B60 1BJ.
Tel: 0299 250710
Proprietor: Miss Jenner & Mrs Clarke
Horses: 6 **Ponies:** 10
Facilities available: Ind.Sch /Men/J.Pd/X-C/Dis.R/Hkg - Quiet lanes and bridleways.
Level: Teaching standards to: ABRS Test no.10.
Specialisation: Tuition in dressage and side-saddle.
Other details: Lecture room. Livery. Schooling. Breaking. Evening classes. Divided classes.
Member of Association of British Riding Schools

High Crundalls Stables

Crundalls Lane, Bewdley, Hereford & Worcester DY12 1NB
Tel: 0299 404045
Member of Association of British Riding Schools

Honeybourne Stables Ltd.

28 Greenhill, Blackwell, Bromsgrove, Hereford & Worcester, B60 1BJ.
Tel: 021 445 4435
Proprietor: W A & E M Rogers
Horses: 5 **Ponies:** 5
Facilities available: Men/J.Pd/Dis.R/X-C/Hkg, Pleasant lanes and bridleways.
Level: Teaching Standards: Various standards.
Specialisation: Teaching, breaking and schooling. Lungeing.
Other details: Tuiton in dressage, show-jumping, X-country and stable management. Evening classes Career students taken.
Member of Association of British Riding Schools

Kyre Combined Training Club

Lower House Farm, Sutton, Tenbury Wells, Hereford & Worcester.
Tel: 088 54 10233
Proprietor: Mrs Durston-Smith
Horses: 5 **Ponies:** 7
Facilities available: Ind.Sch /Men/X-C/J.Pd/Hkg - Beautiful countryside.
Level: Teaching Standards: All levels catered for.
Specialisation: Private lessons on own or school horses.
Other details: Hacking - no casual hire. F/P/Grass Livery. Schooling.

Lea Bailey Riding School

Lea Bailey, Ross-on-Wye, Hereford & Worcester.
Tel: 098981 360
Proprietor: Mrs J Price
Horses: 10 **Ponies:** 20
Facilities available: Men/J.Pd/X-C/Hkg - Royal Forest of Dean.

Level: Teaching standards to: ABRS Test no. 10. YTS level 1 & 2. ABRS Side-saddle instructor 1-10. Road Safety Tests.
Specialisation: Holidays with/without own horse. Comps. Picnic rides/drives.
Other details: F/P Livery. Schooling. Breaking. Hunting. Stable management courses. Special residential courses. Tuition in side-saddle, dressage, driving and stable management.
Member of Association of British Riding Schools

Marches Equestrian College

Harewood End, Hereford & Worcester, HR2 8NG.
Member of Association of British Riding Schools

Moyfield Riding School

South Littleton, Evesham, Hereford & Worcester, WR11 5TR.
Tel: 0386 830207
Proprietor: Ms J Bomford
Horses: 50 **Ponies:** 50
Facilities available: 2 Ind.Sch/J.Pd/X-C/Dis.R/Hkg
Level: Teaching standards to: ABRS Test no. 10. All BHS Exams.
Specialisation: You name it, we do it!
Other details: Livery. Schooling. Breaking. Hunting. Career students taken. YTS. Examination/Assessment centre.
Member of Association of British Riding Schools

Portmans Farm

Newbridge Green, Upton-on-Severn, Hereford & Worcester, WR8 0QP.
Proprietor: Mrs J Challens

Rockmoor Stables

Rock, Nr. Kidderminster, Hereford & Worcester DY14 9RY.
Tel: 029 922 556
Proprietor: H D Maidment
Horses: 6 **Ponies:** 12
Facilities available: Men/X-C/J.Pd/Hkg - Farmland, country lanes, Wyre Forest.
Level: Teaching Standards: Novice.
Other details: F/Grass Livery.

Seechem Equestrian Centre

Rowney Green Lane, Alvechurch, Nr. Birmingham, Hereford & Worcester.
Tel: 021 445 2333
Proprietor: Mrs J Willetts
Horses: 10 **Ponies:** 10
Facilities available: Ind.Sch/Men(F.Lt)/J.Pd/X-C/Dis.R/Hkg
Level: Teaching standards to: ABRS Test no. 10. Students trained to BHSAI. ABRS Grooms Diploma.
Specialisation: Specialists in production of quality competition horses.
Other details: Livery. Schooling. Breaking. YTS. Examination/Assessment centre. Career students taken. Brochure available. Novice to advanced taken.
Member of Association of British Riding Schools

Severn Valley Riding Centre

Bewdley Road North, Stourport-on-Severn, Hereford & Worcester, DY13 8PX
Tel: 02993 2421
Proprietor: Susan Ketley
Horses: 10 **Ponies:** 3
Facilities available: Men (F.Lt)/J.Pd/X-C/Hkg - Undulating countryside.

Level: Teaching standards to: ABRS test no. 5. Students to ABRS Grooms Diploma.
Specialisation: Hunter liveries.
Other details: Livery. Schooling. Breaking. Hunting. Evening classes.
Member of Association of British Riding Schools

Springfield Stables Limited

The Durrance, Upton Warren, Bromsgrove, Hereford & Worcester, B61 9EL.
Proprietor: Mr R P Ingram

The Avenue Riding Centre

Hanley Road, Malvern, Hereford & Worcester.
Tel: 0684 310731
Proprietor: R P & Mrs Mayhew
Horses: 14 **Ponies:** 5
Facilities available: Men (F.Lt)/J.Pd/X-C/Hkg - Mixed countryside.
Level: Teaching standards to: ABRS exams.
Specialisation: Breaking and schooling horses to Western paces.
Other details: Pleasure, trail riding. Reining and Cutting. Tuition in Western Riding. Livery. Schooling. Breaking. Special residential courses.
Member of Association of British Riding Schools

The Marches Equestrian College

Harewood End, Hereford, Hereford & Worcester, HR2 8NG.
Tel: 0989 87234
Proprietor: Mrs Pippa Bacon
Horses: 22/50
Facilities available: Men /J.Pd/X-C/Hkg - Rural farmland, bridleways, woodland.

Level: Teaching standards to: ABRS Test no. 10. Students to ABRS vocational exams. BHS vocational exams. Side-saddle exams. Riding and road safety. First Aid exam.
Specialisation: YTS students. Competitions. Swimming pool.

Other details: Tuition in dressage, side-saddle and X-country. F/P Livery. Schooling. Breaking. Hunting. Special Residential courses.
Member of Association of British Riding Schools

The Mounts Equitation Centre

Crumpsbrook, Nr Cleobury Mortimer, Nr Kidderminster, Hereford & Worcester, DY14 0HX.
Tel: 0746 632 677
Proprietor: Mr & Mrs B Linington-Payne
Horses: 13 **Ponies:** 5
Facilities available: Ind Schl/Gallery/menage/X-C/X-C Jumps/Leis Rm/Hkg. Open countryside.
Level: Teaching standards to: ABRS Test no. 10, BHS Stages, Pony Club exams
Specialisation: Evening classes, special residential courses. Regular Compns
Other details: F/P Livery. Breaking

Top Holidays

Tops Limited, Hoe under Dinmore, Leominster, Hereford & Worcester, HR6 0PW.
Proprietor: Mr G Stansbridge

Hertfordshire

Ashridge Equestrian Centre

Ashridge Farm (Berkhamsted) Ld, Ringshall, Berkhamsted, Hertfordshire, HP4 1ND.
Proprietor: Mrs E Craib and Miss M Craib

Bambers Green Riding Centre

Takeley, Bishop's Stortford, Hertfordshire, CM22 6PE.
Tel: 0279 870320
Proprietor: Mr & Mrs I Dobson
Horses: 6 **Ponies:** 6

Batchworth Heath Farm Stud

London Road, Rickmansworth, Hertfordshire, WD3 1QB.
Proprietor: Mrs D Price

Birch Farm School of Equitation

White Stubbs Lane, Broxbourne, Hertfordshire, EN10 7QA.
Tel: 0992 467738
Proprietor: Mr A P Mead
Horses: 7 **Ponies:** 7

Chorleywood Equestrian Centre Ltd

Chenies Road, Chorleywood, Rickmansworth, Hertfordshire, WD3 5LY.
Tel: 0923 282713
Proprietor: Mr & Mrs Franklin
Number Horses/Ponies: 20
Facilities available: Men /Grass arenas/J.Pd/Hkg - 60 acres of grassland.
Level: Teaching Standards: Beginners to advanced.
Specialisation: BHS approved.

Other details: F/P/Working /Grass/ Livery. Tuition in driving, show-jumping, and dressage. Lessons from 6 to 20. Lead-rein lessons available.

Coltspring School of Riding Ltd

Sarratt Road, Chandlers Cross, Nr Rickmansworth, Hertfordshire.
Tel: 0923 774964
Proprietor: Mr C J Trigg
Horses: 15 **Ponies:** 11
Facilities available: Ind.Sch /X-C/J.Pd/Dis.R/Hkg - Local forest and woodland.
Level: Teaching Standards: Horsemasters to BHS stage 4.
Specialisation: Riding Club and club bar.
Other details: F/P Livery. Schooling. Breaking. Hunting. Evening classes. Special residential courses.
Member of Association of British Riding Schools

Contessa Arabian and Riding Centre

Willow Tree Farm, Colliers End, Nr. Ware, Hertfordshire, SG11 1EN.
Tel: 0920 821792
Proprietor: Miss T Layton & Mr & Mrs Layton
Horses: 20 **Ponies:** 5
Facilities available: Ind.Sch /Men(F.Lt)/J.Pd/X-C/Hkg - Over farmland
Level: Teaching standards: BHS Stages 1 to 4. Preliminary and Intermediate Instructors Teaching Exams. Students to BHSAI.BHSII. BHSI.
Specialisation: Examination orientated centre. Dressage.
Other details: Special residential courses for novice to advanced. GCSE Exam centre. Video filming.

YTS students taken. Livery (schooling only). Schooling. Breaking.
Member of Association of British Riding Schools

Courtlands Riding Stables

Todds Green, Stevenage, Hertfordshire, SG1 2JE.
Tel: 0438 313331
Proprietor: Mrs Halling & Miss Halling
Horses: 10 **Ponies:** 12
Facilities available: Ind.Sch /Men(F.Lt)/J.Pd/X-C/Dis. R/Hkg - Bridleways.
Level: Teaching standards to: BHSAI and similar.
Specialisation: Training young horses. Re-schooling.
Other details: F/P livery. Tuition in dressage and show-jumping. Career students taken. Weekly rallies for young riders.
Member of Association of British Riding Schools

Deanswood Equestrian Centre

Goose Lane, Little Hallingbury, Bishop's Stortford, Hertfordshire, CM22 7RG.
Tel: 0279 600660
Proprietor: Mr & Mrs J W Dean
Horses: 14 **Ponies:** 12
Facilities available: Ind.Sch / Men (F.Lt)/ J.Pd/ Hkg - excellent parkland
Level: Teaching standards to: BHSAI. Assistant Groom .
Specialisation: Dressage. Show-jumping.
Other details: Livery. Schooling. Breaking. Hunting. Evening classes.
Member of Association of British Riding Schools

Hadham Mill Riding Centre

Widford Road, Much Hadham, Hertfordshire, SG10 6EY.
Proprietor: Mr C & Ms L Wymer

Hallingbury Hall Equestrian Centre

Little Hallingbury, Bishop's Stortford, Hertfordshire, CM22 2RP.
Proprietor: Mrs Hardwick

Hastoe Hill Riding School

Tring , Hertfordshire, HP23 6LU.
Proprietor: Mr L R N Lewis

High Herts Farm Riding School

High Herts Farm, Pimlico, Hemel Hempstead, Hertfordshire, HP3 8ST.
Tel: 092 77 69265
Proprietor: Mr Peter Waterhouse
Horses: 8 **Ponies:** 14

Highfield Riding School

White Stubbs Lane, Broxbourne, Hertfordshire.
Tel: 0992 460206
Proprietor: Mr & Mrs Flanagan
Horses: 7 **Ponies:** 6

Mill Green Riding School

Millgreen , Hatfield, Hertfordshire.
Proprietor: Mrs Reeve & Mrs Reeve-Smith

North Herts Equitation Centre

Norton Road,, Baldock, Hertfordshire.
Tel: 0462892626
Proprietor: Mrs Deerness & Miss L Deerness
Horses: 15 **Ponies:** 15

Facilities available: Ind.Sch /Men/J.Pd/X-C/Hkg - Lanes and bridleways
Level: Teaching standards to: ABRS Test no. 10. BHS Stages. Horsemasters. BHS Preliminary Teaching. BHS Intermediate.
Specialisation: Quality show-jumpers and eventers produced and sold.
Other details: F/P Livery. Schooling. Breaking. Hunting. Evening classes. Special residential courses.
Member of Association of British Riding Schools

Patchetts Equestrian Centre

Hilfield Lane, Aldenham, Watford, Hertfordshire, WD2 8DP.
Tel: 092385 2255
Proprietor: Mrs. Wendy Hawkes
Horses: 21 **Ponies:** 18
Facilities available: 2 Ind.Sch /Men(F.Lt)/J.Pd/X-C/Hkg - Bridleways, woods and rivers.
Level: Teaching standards to: ABRS Test no. 10. ABRS Ass. Grooms Certificate. BHS exams up to 'Instructor' level.
Specialisation: Training for career students.
Other details: F/P Livery. Schooling. Breaking. Residential Career courses. Evening classes. Career exams. Tuition in Dressage, Show-jumping, X-country. Side-saddle.
Member of Association of British Riding Schools

Ponsbourne Riding Centre

Newgate Street Village, Nr Hertford, Hertfordshire.
Tel: 0707 874777
Proprietor: Mrs Godwin & Mrs Fitzgerald

Horses: 12 **Ponies:** 10
Facilities available: Ind.Sch /Men/J.Pd/Hkg
Level: Teaching standards to: ABRS Test no. 10. BHSAI. BHSII. BHSI.
Specialisation: Special residential courses.
Other details: Livery. Schooling. Breaking. Evening classes.
Member of Association of British Riding Schools

Pottersheath Riding Centre

Arnold's Farm, Potters Heath Road, Welwyn, Hertfordshire, AL6 9SZ.
Proprietor: Mr & Mrs Gudgin

Rose Hall Farm Riding and Livery Stables

Sarratt, Rickmansworth, Hertfordshire, WD3 4PA.
Tel: 0442 833267
Proprietor: Mr R Higgs
Horses: 5 **Ponies:** 6
Facilities available: Outdoor Men/J Pad/X-C fences /Livery/Breaking/ Schooling

Sunnydale Cottage

Upton End Road, Shillington, Hitchin, Hertfordshire.
Tel: 0462 711283
Proprietor: Mrs Armitage

The Ivory Equestrian Centre

Arnolds Farm, Potters Heath Road, Welwyn, Hertfordshire.
Tel: 0438 813070
Proprietor: Mr & Mrs P J Ivory
Horses: 12 **Ponies:** 8

Thorley Riding Centre

Brook Farm, Thorley, Bishop's Stortford, Hertfordshire.
Proprietor: Mrs D A James

Warrenwood Stables
Kentish Lane, Nr. Hatfield,
Hertfordshire, AL9 6JQ.
Proprietor: Mr S Robinson

Oxhey Grange School of Riding
Oxhey Lane, Watford, Herts.
Tel: 0923 31142
Proprietor: Mrs H Panton
Number Horses/Ponies: 6
Facilities available: Groups accompanied on hacks

Humberside

Bishop Burton College of Agriculture
Bishop Burton, Beverley,
Humberside, HU17 8QG.
Proprietor: Mr H W Petch

Bleach Yard Stables
New Walk, Beverley,
Humberside.
Tel: 0482 882557
Proprietor: Mrs Joyce Fearn
Horses: 8 **Ponies:** 4
Facilities available: Men/J.Pd/Hkg - Commonland.
Level: Teaching standards to: Riding Club Grade 3. Students to R.C.Grade tests. P.C.tests. BHSAI.
Specialisation: Tuition in dressage and eventing.
Other details: Livery. Schooling. Breaking. Evening classes.
Member of Association of British Riding Schools

Bramhill Riding School
Burton Pidsea, Nr Hull,
Humberside HU12 9AN
Tel: 0964 670999
Member of Association of British Riding Schools

Carrier House Riding School
Main Street,
Newton-on-Derwent,
Humberside, DN37 0QN.
Proprietor: Mrs I Pettigrew

Chestnut Farm Riding School
Brigsley Road, Ashby-cum-Fenby, Grimsby, Humberside, DN37 0QN.
Tel: 0472 825777
Proprietor: Mrs I Pettigrew
Horses: 3 **Ponies:** 10
Facilities available: Ind.Sch/J.Pd/Hkg
Level: Teaching standards to: ABRS Test no. 5. BHS Stages 1-3 and up to BHSAI.
Specialisation: Competitions for clients. Pony days in holidays.
Other details: Career students taken. Evening classes. Liveries. Schooling.
Member of Association of British Riding Schools

North Humberside Riding Centre
Easington, Nr Hull,
Humberside, HU12 0UA.
Tel: 0964 650250
Proprietor: Mrs Toni Biglin
Horses: 10 **Ponies:** 12
Facilities available: Ind.Sch/X-C/J.Pd/Hkg - River estuary, beach and country lanes
Level: Teaching standards to: ABRS Test no. 10. BHS Stable Manager. BHSAI. BHSII. ABRS Grooms Diploma. Novice to International
Specialisation: Specialised holiday courses and visiting instructors.
Other details: F/P Livery. Schooling. Breaking. Evening classes. Tuition in dressage.
Member of Association of British Riding Schools

Riverdale Riding Centre
East Butterwick,
Humberside, DN17 3AG.
Tel: 0724 783396
Proprietor: Miss Saunders
Number Horses/Ponies: 23
Facilities available: Hacking, accompanied & unaccompanied

Isle of Man

GGH Equitation Centre
Ballacallin Mooar, Crosby,
Isle of Man.
Tel: 0624 851450
Proprietor: Mrs Matthews and Mr & Mrs Gilbey
Horses: 3 **Ponies:** 12
Facilities available: Ind.Sch/Men(F.Lt)/X-C/Dis.R/Hkg - Unspoilt countryside.
Level: Teaching standards to: BHSAI.
Specialisation: Side-saddle.
Other details: Examination/Assessment centre. Lecture room. Evening classes. All standards.
Member of Association of British Riding Schools

Manx Equestrian Centre
Highton Stables, Ballanard
Douglas, Isle of Man.
Tel: 0624 21852
Proprietor: Mrs J C Britwistle.
Horses: 15 **Ponies:** 10
Facilities available: Men/J.Pd/X-C/Hkg - Mountains and beach rides.
Level: Teaching Standards: Various standards.
Specialisation: Show-jumping.
Other details: F/P Livery. Schooling. Breaking. Evening classes in the summer.
Member of Association of British Riding Schools

Isle of Wight

Allendale Stables
'Allendale', Godshill Ventnor, Isle of Wight.
Tel: 0983 840258
Proprietor: Mr & Mrs G S Allen
Horses: 10 **Ponies:** 8
Facilities available:
Men/J.Pd/Hkg - Downland
Level: Teaching standards to: Students to Horse Ranger Exams. BHSAI. Pony Club Exams.
Specialisation: Teaching students with little English (French speaking)
Other details: F/P Livery. Schooling. Breaking. Hunting. Evening classes. Special residential courses.
Member of Association of British Riding Schools

Brickfields Equestrian Centre
Brickfields, Newtham Road, Binstead, Rye, Isle of Wight.

Rosemary Riding School
Rosemary Lane, Ashey Road, Ryde, Isle of Wight.
Proprietor: L G W Moul

Kent

Appletree Stables
Starvenden Lane, Cranbrook Common, Cranbrook, Kent, TN17 2AN.
Tel: 0580 713833
Proprietor: Mrs V Nuthall
Number Horses/Ponies: 10
Facilities available: Groups accompanied on hacks. Children catered for

Bedgebury Park Riding Centre
Bedgebury School, Goudhurst, Nr Cranbrook, Kent, TN17 2SH.
Tel: 0580 211602
Proprietor: Mr S J Robbins
Horses: 9 **Ponies:** 4

Bitchet Farm Riding School
Bitchet Green, Sevenoaks, Kent.
Tel: 0732 62196
Proprietor: Mrs J A Thomson
Horses: 5 **Ponies:** 16
Facilities available: Paddock /J.Pd/Hkg - Excellent riding country.
Level: Teaching standards to: ABRS Ass.Grooms Diploma and Grooms Diploma. ABRS Test no. 5.
Specialisation: Four day courses and beginners courses.
Other details: F/P Livery. Career students taken. Speciality - children and weekly riders.
Member of Association of British Riding Schools

Blue Barn Riding Stables
Blue Barn Farm, Great Chart, Ashford, Kent, TN26 1JS.
Tel: 0233 6211863
Proprietor: Mrs S Draper
Horses: 15 **Ponies:** 15
Facilities available: 2 Ind. Sch/Men(F.Lt)/3 J.Pd/Dis.R/ X-C/ Hkg - Undulating countryside.
Level: Teaching standards to: ABRS and BHS exams
Specialisation: Affiliated and Unaffiliated Show-jumping and Dressage.
Other details: Liveries. Schooling. Residential courses. Hunting. Breaking.

Tuition in Show-jumping and Dressage. BHS approved. 24 hour attention.
Member of Association of British Riding Schools

Bradbourne Riding & Training Centre Ltd
Bradbourne Vale Road, Sevenoaks, Kent, TN13 3DH.
Proprietor: Mr P G Felgate

Chaucer Riding and Livery Stables
Waltham, Nr Canterbury, Kent, CT4 5SB.
Proprietor: Mrs M D Mervin

Chavic Park Farm
Jail Lane, Biggin Hill, Kent, TN16 3AU.
Proprietor: Mr & Mrs Palmer

Chelsfield Riding School
Church Road, Chelsfield, Orpington, Kent, BR6 7SY.
Tel: 0689 55603
Proprietor: Miss J M Golding
Horses: 10 **Ponies:** 10
Facilities available: Ind.Sch /Men(F.Lt)/J.Pd/X-C/Dis. R/Hkg - Bridleways and country lanes.
Level: Teaching standards to: ABRS test no. 5.
Specialisation: Nervous riders. Lunge lessons. Riding to music.
Other details: Livery. Evening classes.
Member of Association of British Riding Schools

Cobham Manor Riding Centre
Water Lane, Thurnham, Kent.
Tel: 0622 38497
Proprietor: Mr & Mrs J Brumer
Horses: 18 **Ponies:** 20
Facilities available: Ind.Sch /2 Men(F.Lt)/X-C/Dis.R/Hkg - Country set in Pilgrims Way

Level: Teaching standards to: Students to BHSAI. ABRS Grooms Diploma.
Specialisation: Managing agent for YTS scheme.
Other details: Pub rides. Camping weekends. X-C hire. Tack Shop. Taking pupils that are not eligible for the YTS scheme. Liveries. Schooling. Breaking.
Member of Association of British Riding Schools

Coombe Wood Stables

Woodside, Coombe Wood Lane, Hawkinge, Kent, CT18 7BZ.
Proprietor: Mr & Mrs M Fuller

Deepdene Riding School

Badlesmere, Nr Faversham, Kent, ME13 0NZ.
Tel: 023374 228
Proprietor: C J Harvey BHSII
Horses: 12 **Ponies:** 6
Facilities available: Ind.Sch /Men(F.Lt)/X-C/Hkg - Forest, farmland and bridleways.
Level: Teaching Standards: All ABRS exams. BHSII. Riding and Road safety exam. ABRS Equitation and Stable Management Exams.
Other details: F/P Livery. Schooling. Career students taken.
Member of Association of British Riding Schools

Eaglesfield Equestrian Centre

West Yoke, Ash, Nr. Sevenoaks, Kent, TN15 7HT.
Tel: 0474 872242
Proprietor: Mr Rowlands & Mrs Clark
Horses: 45 **Ponies:** 20
Facilities available: Ind.Sch /X-C/Hkg

Level: Teaching Standards: High level.
Specialisation: Evening classes.
Other details: Livery. Only open Mon-Fri. All standards. Brochure available.
Member of Association of British Riding Schools

Greenacres Riding School Limited

Greenacres, Ashmore Lane, Leaves Green, Keston, Kent, BR2 6DQ.
Proprietor: Mrs ME Warren & Miss SM Cutts

Hayne Barn Riding School

Hayne Barm, Saltwood, Hythe, Kent.
Tel: 0303 265512
Proprietor: Mr I Record
Horses: 6 **Ponies:** 8
Facilities available: Ind.Sch /Men/X-C/Hkg - Semi rural hilly area.
Level: Teaching Standards: Up to and including the BHSAI and the ABRS equivalent.
Specialisation: Tailor made courses. Family atmosphere encouraged.
Other details: F/P Livery. Schooling. Breaking. Hunting. Dressage and Stable Management courses. Nervous riders welcome. Indoor tennis courts on site. Evening classes - seasonal variations.
Member of Association of British Riding Schools

Heighstead Riding Centre

Heighstead, Chislet, Nr Canterbury, Kent.
Tel: 022 786 491
Proprietor: Mrs Lockhart

Hopes Grove Farm

Smallhythe Lane, Tenterden, Kent, TN30 7LT.
Tel: 05806 2482
Proprietor: Mrs M A Hankinson
Horses: 4 **Ponies:** 6
Facilities available: Ind.Sch /X-C/J.Pd/Hkg - Woodland.
Level: Teaching standards to: ABRS Test No. 6.
Specialisation: Welsh Cob Stud and Working Farm. ABRS exams.
Other details: Tuition for ladies, children and nervous riders. F/P Livery. Schooling. Breaking. Hunting. Annual Pony Week (August)
Member of Association of British Riding Schools

Horseshoes Riding School

Dean Street, East Farleigh, Maidstone, Kent, M15 0PH.
Tel: 0622 46161
Proprietor: Mr & Mrs R Hargreaves
Horses: 12 **Ponies:** 12
Facilities available: 2 Men(F.Lt)/Hkg - Orchard woodland, bridleway and weald.
Level: Teaching standards to: ABRS Test no.10. BHSAI/II. Grooms Diploma.
Other details: Schooling. Breaking. Livery. Career students taken. Evening classes.
Member of Association of British Riding Schools

Ilex Riding Centre

Hollybush Farm, Ruckinge, Ashford, Kent.
Tel: 023 373 3159
Proprietor: Mrs A C Maylam

Kersey Stables

Hawkenbury, Nr Staplehurst, Kent, TN12 0ED.
Tel: 0580 893205
Proprietor: Mrs Celia Wiggins.
Horses: 7
Facilities available: Men (F.Lt)/J.Pd/X-C Jumps
Level: Teaching standards to: ABRS test no. 10. All BHS stages. Pony Club tests.
Specialisation: Exam training. Individual needs.
Other details: Livery. Schooling. Breaking. Career students taken. Brochure available. Tuition in stable management. Evening classes.
Member of Association of British Riding Schools

Kingshill Riding School

Crouch Lane, Borough Green, Sevenoaks, Kent
Tel: 0732 882909
Member of Association of British Riding Schools

Limes Farm Equestrian Centre

Limes Farm, Pay Street, Hawkinge, Kent, CT18 7DZ.
Tel: 030389 2335
Proprietor: Miss A Berry
Horses: 20 **Ponies:** 6
Facilities available: Ind.Sch /Men/J.Pd/X-C/Hkg - Bridle-paths, openfields and quiet lanes
Level: Teaching standards to: BHSAI. BHSII. Ass. Grooms and Grooms Diploma.
Specialisation: Unaffiliated and Affiliated shows held throughout the year.
Other details: F/P Livery. Schooling. Breaking. Tuition in eventing, show-jumping and dressage. Evening classes. Special residential courses.
Member of Association of British Riding Schools

Lower Bell Riding School

BackLane, Boughton, Monchelsea, Maidstone, Kent.
Proprietor: Mr & Mrs A Harris

Lynx Park

Colliers Green, Goudhurst, Cranbrook, Kent, TN17 2LR.
Tel: 0580 211020
Proprietor: Ms S K Kindersley
Horses: 5 **Ponies:** 2
Facilities available: Ind.Sch
Level: Teaching standards to: ABRS Test no. 10. BHS Stages 1-3 including BHSAI.
Specialisation: Riding courses for horse enthusiasts.
Other details: Schooling. Breaking. F/P Livery. Lecture room. Evening classes.
Member of Association of British Riding Schools

Moat House

Benenden, Kent, TN17 4EU.

Mount Mascal Stables

Mascal Street, Vicarage Road, Bexley, Kent DA5 2AW
Tel: 081 300 3942

Nelson Park Riding Centre

St Margaret's Road, Woodchurch, Birchington, Kent, CT7 0HJ.
Tel: 0843 822251
Proprietor: Mrs S J Mathews
Horses: 5 **Ponies:** 7
Facilities available: 2 Men(F.Lt)All weather surfaces/J.Pd/X-C/Hkg
Level: Teaching standards to: ABRS Test no. 10. Students trained to ABRS, PHC & RC levels 1 & 2 and Ass. Grooms Certificate.

Specialisation: General instruction on the flat, jumping and X-country.
Other details: Childrens courses. Summer Camps. Clinics. Livery. Schooling. Breaking. Evening classes. Hacking and a Riding Club. Career students taken. YTS.
Member of Association of British Riding Schools

Oathill Farm Riding Centre

Pound Lane, Molash, Nr. Canterbury, Kent, CT4 8HQ.
Tel: 0233 74573
Proprietor: Mr A J Doree
Number Horses/Ponies: 35
Facilities available: Men/ Hkg - Forest and orchards.
Level: Teaching standards to: BHSAI.
Other details: F/P/Grass Livery. Tuition in dressage, show-jumping. Accomadation available.

Polhill Riding Centre

Otford Lane, Halstead, Nr Sevenoaks, Kent TN14 7EA
Tel: 0959 32530
Member of Association of British Riding Schools

Riding Farm

Riding Lane, Hildenborough, Kent, TN11 9LN.
Proprietor: Mr R Howe
Member of Association of British Riding Schools

St. Stephen's College Riding School

North Foreland, Broadstairs, Kent, CT10 3NP.

Taylor's Riding Establishment

Casita, Waverley Avenue, Minster, Sheerness, Kent, ME12 2JL.
Proprietor: Mr A J Taylor

The Royal Engineers Saddle Club

Royal School of Military Eng., Brompton Barracks, Chatham, Kent.
Proprietor: Capt P J Scanlan

Tollgate Riding Stables

Monks Buildings, Northumberland Bottom, Wrotham Road, Gravesend, Kent.
Tel: 0474 64681
Proprietor: Miss C Curtiss & Mr W Prielepp
Horses: 10 **Ponies:** 7
Facilities available: Ind.Sch/Men(F.Lt)/J.Pd/Hkg - Varied countryside.
Level: Teaching standards to: Students up to BHSAI.
Specialisation: Beginner children and adults.
Other details: Evening classes. F/P Livery. Schooling. Breaking.
Member of Association of British Riding Schools

Walmer Riding Centre

115 Station Road, Walmer, Deal, Kent, CT14 9JN.
Tel: 0304 362878
Proprietor: M Herriot
Horses: 4 **Ponies:** 7
Facilities available: Men(F.Lt)/Hkg - Bridlepaths and quiet country lanes.
Level: Teaching standards to: ABRS Test no. 6.
Specialisation: Pub hacks. Open days. Nervous and child riders.
Other details: Hacks - max. 4 . Lessons max. 8. Novice to intermediate standards taken. Evening classes.
Member of Association of British Riding Schools

Westerham Riding Centre

Hawley Corner, Westerham Hill, Kent, TN16 2HX.

Tel: 0959 73341
Proprietor: Gp Cpt H Tudor
Horses: 30 **Ponies:** 7

Willow Farm Horse Centre

Hansletts Lane, Ospringe, Nr. Faversham, Kent, ME13 0RS.
Proprietor: Mrs M J Openshaw

Lancashire

Becconsall Farm Stables.

Moss Hey Lane, Mere Brow, Tarleton, Nr. Preston, Lancashire, PR4 6LB.
Tel: 0772 813774
Proprietor: Mr & Mrs Walsh
Horses: 10 **Ponies:** 5
Facilities available: Ind.Sch/Men(F.Lt)/J.Pd/Hkg - Farmland.
Level: Teaching standards to: ABRS Test no.10.
Specialisation: Tuition in Showing.
Other details: F/P Livery. Schooling. Breaking.
Member of Association of British Riding Schools

Beech Tree Farm Riding Centre

Off Longheys Lane, Dalton, Nr Parbold, Lancashire, WN8 7RS.
Tel: 0695 622432
Proprietor: Mr A Watson
Horses: 4 **Ponies:** 6
Facilities available: Ind.Sch /Men(F.Lt)/J.Pd/Dis.R/X-C/Hkg - Rural country.
Level: Teaching standards to: Students to BHSAI.

Other details: F/P Livery. Schooling. Breaking. Hunting. "Own Pony" Club. Three day courses for children. Evening classes.
Member of Association of British Riding Schools

Beechmount Equitation Centre.

67 Fleetwood Road, Norbeck, Blackpool, Lancashire, FY5 1SB.
Tel: 0253 868310
Proprietor: Mr & Mrs Metcalf
Horses: 12 **Ponies:** 7
Facilities available: Men/J.Pd/Hkg - Beach.
Level: Teaching standards to: Students up to BHSAI. All BHS stages.
Specialisation: Horse-drawn carriages for Weddings. Driving instruction.
Other details: F/P Livery. Schooling. Breaking. YTS. Career students taken. Superb beach riding.
Member of Association of British Riding Schools

Crooklands Riding Establishment

Longley Lane, Goosnargh, Nr Preston, Lancashire PR3 2JU.
Proprietor: Mrs J & Mrs S Ward &Miss Turner

Douglas Farm Riding School

Bradshaw Lane, Parbold, Nr Wigan, Lancashire WN8 7NQ.
Tel: 025 76 2057
Proprietor: Miss S Barton
Horses: 2 **Ponies:** 8
Facilities available: Ind.Sch /Men(F.Lt)/J.Pd/Dis.R
Level: Teaching Standards: Varied standards.

Specialisation: Facilities for RDA riding and driving.
Other details: Tuition in dressage, show-jumping, side-saddle and vaulting. Lecture room. Schooling. Holidays can include painting and sketching days.
Member of Association of British Riding Schools

Earnsdale Farm Riding School

Earnsdale Farm, Off Lynwood Avenue, Darwen, Lancashire, BB3 0LB.
Tel: 0254702647
Proprietor: Mrs J Crook & Mrs M Comer
Horses: 6 **Ponies:** 14
Facilities available: Ind.Sch /Men/X-C
Level: Teaching Standards: Lessons by 2 BHSAI's 1 BHSII.
Other details: F/Livery - waiting list!. Tuition available in show-jumping, X-country, and dressage. Career students taken. Suppliers of riding clothing.

Eccleston Equestrian Centre

1 Lydiate Lane, Eccleston, Chorley, Lancashire, PR7 6LX.
Proprietor: Miss K A Green

Fenn's Equestrian Centre

Fenn's Farm, Moorbank Lane, Milnrow, Lancashire.
Tel: 0706 55611
Proprietor: Mrs S Temme

Fulwood Riding Centre

Sandyforth Lane, Off Lightfoot Lane, Fulwood, Preston, Lancashire, PR4 0AL.
Tel: 0772 864836
Proprietor: Nina Valerie Fawcett

Facilities available: Ind.Sch /Men/Hkg
Level: Teaching Standards: Various standards.
Other details: Liveries taken. Brochure available.
Member of Association of British Riding Schools

Halsall Riding & Livery Centre

Terra Nova, Gregory Lane, Halsall, Nr Ormskirk, Lancashire, L39 8SP.
Tel: 0704 840001
Proprietor: Mr & Mrs B Beilensohn
Horses: 14 **Ponies:** 3
Facilities available: Ind.Sch /Men(F.Lt)/Hkg - always escorted, farmland and beach tracks
Level: Teaching standards to: BHSAI.
Specialisation: Lectures/ Demonstrations. Winter dressage comps. Monthly shows.
Other details: Evening classes. F/P Livery. Schooling. Showing and Working Hunter tuition. Career students taken.
Member of Association of British Riding Schools

Hedley Riding School

Higher Elbut Farm, Elbut Lane, Birtle, Bury, Lancashire, BL9 7TU.
Proprietor: Mrs B D Hedley
Member of Association of British Riding Schools

Hollins Farm Riding School

Clerk Hill, Whally, Blackburn, Lancashire, BB6 9DR.
Tel: 025482 3135
Proprietor: Mrs M Taylor & Miss S Taylor
Horses: 5 **Ponies:** 5
Facilities available: Paddock (Fl Lt)/X-C/ Schlg /Hkg - Farmland, Moorland & Bridlepaths Show for own clients.
Level: Teaching standards to: ABRS Test no. 10. Highest test taken no. 2. Career Students taken. YTS. ABRS, Levels I, II & III. Grooms Dipl. BHS Stages & A1 Prelim.
Specialisation: Small grps. Begins, Childn/Adults. Tailor made.Evening classes.
Member of Association of British Riding Schools

Lassell House Riding Centre & Livery Stables

Mossy Lea Road, Wrightington, Nr Wigan, Lancashire, WN6 9RE.
Tel: 0257 427319
Proprietor: Mrs P S Brightcliffe
Horses: 10 **Ponies:** 10
Facilities available: Ind.Sch/Men(F.Lt)/J.Pd/X-C Jumps/Dis.R/Hkg
Level: Teaching Standards: BHS 1-3. BHS Preliminary teaching.
Specialisation: Riding and Road Safety Preparation Exam. Childrens courses.
Other details: Stable management courses. Livery. Schooling. Breaking. YTS. Career students taken. 6 ponies used in RDA lessons. Evening classes. All standards taken.
Member of Association of British Riding Schools

Longfield Stables
Middle Longfield Farm,
Todmorden, Lancashire,
OL14 6JN.
Tel: 070 681 2736
Proprietor: Miss C Farnaby
Horses: 7 **Ponies:** 10
Facilities available: Ind.Sch
/Men/J.Pd/Dis.R/X-C/Hkg -
Moorland.
Level: Teaching standards
to: ABRS test no. 10.
Students to ABRS Grooms
Diploma. BHSAI.
Specialisation: Show-livery.
Horses and ponies produced
for the show-ring.
Other details: F/P Livery.
Schooling. Breaking.
Evening classes. Tuition
available form a BHSI.
Unaccompanied childrens
riding holidays.Special
residential courses.
*Member of Association of
British Riding Schools*

Longton Riding Centre and Tack Shop
195 Chapel Lane, Longton,
Nr Preston, Lancashire
PR4 5NA.
Tel: 0772 613355
Proprietor: M L & J D
Murray
Horses: 8 **Ponies:** 14
Facilities available: Ind.Sch
/Men(F.Lt)/J.Pd/X-C
Level: Teaching standards
to: ABRS test no.10. BHSAI.
BHSII.
Specialisation: Toddler
rides. Driving. Over 30's
jumping.
Other details: Livery
boxes(42). Career students
taken. 3 One-day events per
yr. Annual Show Aug. Bank
Hol. Novice to advanced
riders taken.
*Member of Association of
British Riding Schools*

Midgeland Indoor Ridng School
Midgeland Road , Marton,
Blackpool, Lancashire,
FY4 5EE.
Tel: 0253 693312
Proprietor: Mr & Mrs Ellis
Horses: 8 **Ponies:** 7
Facilities available: Ind.Sch
/Men/J.Pd/Dis.R/Hkg - Local
countryside
Level: Teaching standards
to: Students to BHS stage 2.
Other details: Livery. YTS.
Career students taken.
*Member of Association of
British Riding Schools*

Northern Equitation Centre
Brookfield Lane, Aughton, Nr
Ormskirk, Lancashire.
Tel: 0695 423153
Proprietor: Mrs Mackert

Old Hall Mill Riding School
Old Hall Mill Lane, Atherton,
Lancashire.
Tel: 0942 677052
Proprietor: Mrs Monk
*Member of Association of
British Riding Schools*

Osbaldeston Hall Farm Riding Centre
Osbaldeston, Nr Blackburn,
Lancashire, BB2 7LZ.
Tel: 0254878452
Proprietor: Mr & Mrs N
Bargh
Specialisation: Riding/
competition yard.
Other details: Restaurant.
Lisenced bar. DIY/F livery.

Swordhill Equestrian Training Centre
The Grange, Stalmine, Black-
pool, Lancashire FY6 0JR
Tel: 0253 700216
*Member of Association of
British Riding Schools*

Whitemoor Stables
Whitemoor Bottom Farm,
Foulridge, Colne, Lancashire,
BB8 7LX.
Proprietor: Mrs R M Stanworth

Wrea Green Equitation Centre
Bryning Lane, Wrea Green,
Nr Kirkham, Lancashire,
PR4 1TN.
Tel: 0772 686576
Proprietor: Miss C A Pollitt
(BHSITT)
Horses: 12 **Ponies:** 8
Facilities available: Ind.Sch
/Men/J.Pd/X-C/Dis.R
Level: Teaching standards
to: BHSAI level
Specialisation: Mrs. Susan
Pimbley, BHSI by appoint-
ment. Side-saddle.
Other details: Lecture room.
Livery. Occasional schooling.
Breaking. Career students
taken. YTS. Side-saddle. All
standards taken. Brochure
available. Individual courses.
*Member of Association of
British Riding Schools*

Leicestershire

Brooklands Farm Riding School
Kirkby Lane, Barwell,
Leicestershire, LE9 8FT.
Proprietor: Mr T J Golding
& Miss D L Yates

Canaan Farm Riding School
Loughborough Road,
Costock, Loughborough,
Leicestershire, LE12 6XB.
Proprietor: Mrs J Chiasserini

Centaur School of Equitation

Cold Newton, Billesdon, Leicestershire.
Tel: 053 755 443
Proprietor: Mr J E Dobson
Horses: 14 **Ponies:** 7

Fleckney School of Equitation

Kilby Road, Fleckney, Leicestershire.
Tel: 0533 402336
Proprietor: Mr N Staines
Facilities available: Livery /Schooling
Specialisation: Evening tuition

Markfield Equestrian Centre

Stanton Lane Farm, Stanton Lane, Under Bardon, Markfield, Leicestershire, LE6 0TT.
Proprietor: J & P Duffield

Marsden School of Riding

Marsden House, Huncote Road, Stoney Stanton, Leicestershire.
Proprietor: Mrs M D Fray

Meadows School of Riding

The Stables, Stanford Court, Stanford-on-Soar, Loughborough, Leicestershire, LE12 5PY.
Proprietor: Mr D Allonby

Park View Leicester Equestrian Centre

Anstey Lane, Thurcaston, Leicestershire, LE7 7JA.
Proprietor: Mr & Mrs J L MacDonald

School of National Equitation

Bunny Hill Top, Costock, Loughborough, Leicestershire.
Tel: 0509 852366 **Fax:** 0602 848381
Proprietor: Mr R J Humphrey
Horses: 10 **Ponies:** 10
Facilities available: Ind.Sch/Men(F.Lt)/J.Pd/X-C/ Dis.R/Hkg - Roads and bridlepaths.
Level: Teaching Standards: All levels all ages.
Specialisation: Jousting. Side-saddle. Horses provided for film work. Other details: Livery (15). Schooling. Breaking. Hunting. Career students taken. Tuition in dressage, show-jumping, X-country, Point-to-Point. Evening classes. YTS.
Member of Association of British Riding Schools

South Leicestershire Riding Establishment

Kimberley House, Frolesworth Road, Leire, Nr Lutterworth, Leicestershire, LE17 5HP.
Tel: 0455 209407
Proprietor: Mr K W Clawson

Stone Lodge Equestrian Centre

Stone Lodge, Mere Lane, Oadby, Leicestershire.
Tel: 0533 712314
Proprietor: Miss L Jones-Fenleigh
Horses: 15 **Ponies:** 5
Facilities available: Dressage/X-C/Ind Schl/S-J arena/All-weather arena
Level: Students & working pupils to BHSAI, YTS welcome

Stretton Riding Centre

Manor Bungalow Farm, Stretton, Oakham, Leicestershire.
Tel: 078 081 323
Proprietor: Mrs J L Ward
Facilities available: Hacking. Woodlands & Bridleways

The Limes Equestrian Centre

Hinkley Road, Sapcote, Leicestershire, LE9 6LG.
Tel: 0455 272271
Proprietor: Mrs P Brown
Horses: 12 **Ponies:** 16

The Wharf

Market Overton, Oakham, Leicestershire, LE15 7PW.
Proprietor: Mrs J M Sturrock FBHS
Facilities available: Covered Sch/J.Pd/X-C/Men.
Level: Teaching standards to: FBHS
Specialisation: Training for working students.
Other details: Lessons per hour. Tuition in Jumping.

Witham Villa Riding School

Cosby Road, Broughton Ashley, Leicestershire.
Tel: 0455 282694
Proprietor: P A Cross
Number Horses/Ponies: 15
Facilities available: Ind.Sch/Hkg/X-C
Level: Teaching Standards: Beginners to advanced.

Lincolnshire

Auster Lodge Riding Stables

Edenham, Bourne,
Lincolnshire, PE10 0LH.
Tel: 077 832 287
Proprietor: Mr R W Haddow
Horses: 6 **Ponies:** 12

Becks Lane Riding Centre

C/O 12 Pinetree Avenue,
Scotter, Gainsborough,
Lincolnshire, DN21 3TY.
Tel: 0724 849900
Proprietor: Mrs R D Harbour
Member of Association of British Riding Schools

Better Tack Riding Centre

Middledene, Surfleet Road,,
Surfleet, Spalding, Lincs
PE11 4AG.
Proprietor: Mr & Mrs JP
Bettinson

Buckminster Lodge Equestrian Centre

Sewstern, Grantham,
Lincolnshire, NG33 5RW.
Tel: 057284 544
Proprietor: Mr & Mrs V
Gillingham

Four Acres Equestrian Centre

Station Road, Fulstow, Nr
Louth, Lincolnshire, LN11 0XQ.
Proprietor: Mr & Mrs N
Harrison

Four Winds Equitation Centre

Leaveslake Drove, West
Pinchbeck, Spalding,
Lincolnshire.
Tel: 0775 87533
Proprietor: Miss PV & Mrs
ED Matthews

Horses: 10 **Ponies:** 10
Facilities available: Ind.Sch/
Men(F.Lt)/J.Pd/Hkg
Level: Teaching standards
to: ABRS Test no. 10. BHS
Exams up to AI. ABRS Exams.
Specialisation: Evening
classes towards stage exams.
Other details: Career
students taken. Examination
/Assessment centre to Stage
3. YTS. All standards taken.
Breaking. Schooling. Liveries
Member of Association of British Riding Schools

Hill House Riding School

Sand Lane, Osgodby,
Market Rasen, Lincolnshire,
LN8 3TE.
Tel: 0673 843407
Proprietor: A D Pennell Esq

Ivy Lane Riding School & Livery Stables

Ivy Lane, Coningsby,
Lincolnshire, LN4 4RY.
Tel: 0526 42461
Proprietor: Jan Phillips
Horses: 5 **Ponies:** 10
Facilities available: Men
(F.Lt)/J.Pd/Dis.R/Hkg - Bridle-
ways.
Level: Teaching standards
to: ABRS test no. 10.
Students to YTS level 1 & 2.
BHS HK & R stages 1-3.
Specialisation: Ivy Lane
Saddle Club. RAF
Coningsby Saddle Club.
Other details: F/P livery.
Schooling. Breaking. Private
lessons on own horse.
Special residential courses.
Evening classes.
Member of Association of British Riding Schools

Lineside Riding Stables

Lineside Farm, Amberhill,
Boston, Lincolnshire.
Tel: 0205 820744
Proprietor: Miss J Key
Member of Association of British Riding Schools

Mill Farm Riding School

Main Road, Fotherby, Louth,
Lincolnshire, LN11 0UN.
Tel: 0507 602042
Proprietor: Mrs Ann
Campion
Horses: 6 **Ponies:** 6
Facilities available:
Men(F.Lt)/J.Pd/X-C Jumps
Level: Teaching standards
to: ABRS Test no. 10.
Specialisation: Side-saddle
instruction.
Other details: Lecture room.
P/Livery. Evening classes.
Divided classes.
Member of Association of British Riding Schools

Park Riding School & Livery Stables

Newland Street West,
Lincoln, Lincolnshire, LN1
1QE.
Tel: 0522 26168
Proprietor: Mr Arthur Baker
Horses: 12 **Ponies:** 8
Facilities available:
Men/J.Pd/X-C
Jumps/Dis.R/Hkg - Own
fields, bridleways and
riversides.
Level: Teaching Standards:
Various standards.
Specialisation: Affilated
Riding Club. Horse/ponies
and tack for sale
Other details: Hunting.
Career students taken.
Beach and country riding.
Self catering holidays at
Golden Sands Holiday
Estates.
Member of Association of British Riding Schools

Rednil Farm Equestrian Centre

Lincoln Road, Welton, Nr Lincoln, Lincolnshire, LN2 3JE.
Tel: 0673 60548
Proprietor: Mr & Mrs P J Linder
Horses: 12 **Ponies:** 12
Facilities available: Ind.Sch /Men(F.Lt)/J.Pd/X-C/Hkg
Level: Teaching standards to: ABRS Test no. 8. ABRS Ass. Groom. ABRS Preliminary levels 1 & 2. BHS Preliminary Teaching. BHS HK & R 1-3.
Specialisation: Driving.
Other details: Livery. Schooling. Breaking. Evening classes. Career students taken. YTS. All standards taken. Brochure available.
Member of Association of British Riding Schools

Saxilby Riding Club

High Street, Saxilby, Lincoln, Lincolnshire, LN1 2HA.
Tel: 0522 702240
Proprietor: Mr & Mrs M J Scott
Horses: 10 **Ponies:** 16
Facilities available: Ind.Sch/ Men(F.Lt)/J.Pd/Dis.R/X-C/ Hkg - Flatland.
Level: Teaching standards to: ABRS Test no. 8. BHSAI. Specialisation: Special residential courses.
Other details: F/Livery. Schooling. Breaking. Hunting. Evening classes. Tuition in show-jumping.
Member of Association of British Riding Schools

Thorpe Grange Equestrian Centre

Newark Road, Aubourn, Lincoln, Lincolnshire, LN5 9EJ.
Proprietor: Mrs E Poskitt

London

Aldersbrook Riding School Limited

Empress Avenue, Manor Park, London, E12 5HW.
Tel: 081 530 4648
Proprietor: Mrs I P Thorne
Number Horses/Ponies: 10
Facilities available: 2 Men (F.Lt)/J.Pd/Hkg - Forest.
Level: Teaching Standards: Lessons by BHSAI's.
Specialisation: No one over 14 stone.
Other details: F/livery. Private lessons. Schooling. Breaking. Lunge lessons.

Belmont Riding Centre

The Ridgeway, Mill Hill, London, NW7.
Proprietor: Mr G Parsons

Civil Service Riding Club

C/O The Royal Mews, Buckingham Palace Road, London, SW1W 0QH.
Tel: 071 9307232
Proprietor: C E Lister
Horses: 11
Facilities available: Ind.Sch /J.Pd/X-C Jumps/Hkg - Urban parks and some country riding
Level: Teaching standards to: ABRS Test no. 7. Students to BHSAI. Grooms Diploma. Horsemastership Certificate.
Specialisation: Adult beginners. Open to members only.
Other details: Evening classes. Divided classes.
Member of Association of British Riding Schools

Dulwich Riding School

Dulwich Common, London, SE21 7EX.
Tel: 081 693 2944
Proprietor: J T Bellman

Horses: 15 **Ponies:** 5
Facilities available: Ind.Sch /Men(F.Lt)/Dis.R/J.Pd
Level: Teaching standards to: BHSI Exams.
Specialisation: Free lecture on all subjects of the horse.
Other details: Schooling. Breaking. Evening classes. Only children over 10.
Member of Association of British Riding Schools

Equi Study Centre

44 Fleet Street, London, EC47 1BS.
Tel: 06972 383

Kentish Town City Farm

1 Cressfield Close, Off Grafton Road, London, NW5.
Proprietor: N Tuckett Esq

Lea Bridge Riding School

Lea Bridge Road,, Leyton, London, E10 7QL.
Tel: 081 556 2629
Horses: 14 **Ponies:** 5

Mottingham Farm Riding Centre

Mottingham Lane, London, SE9.
Proprietor: W L Collins Esq

Mudchute Park & Farm Riding School

Pier Street, Isle of Dogs, London, E14.

Newham Riding School & Association

Man.Comm. of Newham Riding Club, 96 Camel Road, London, E16 2DD.
Proprietor: Miss L Greaves

Richard Briggs Riding Stables

63 Bathurst Mews, London, W2 2SB.
Proprietor: Mr Richard Briggs

Roehampton Gate Stables Ltd

Priory Lane, London, SW15.
Tel: 081 876 7089
Proprietor: N. White
Horses: 7 **Ponies:** 3
Facilities available: Men/Hkg - in Richmond park and Wimbledon Common.
Level: Teaching Standards: Various standards.
Specialisation: Tuition for beginners.
Other details: F/P Livery.
Member of Association of British Riding Schools

Ross Nye's Riding Establishment

8 Bathurst Mews, Hyde Park, London, W2 2SB.
Tel: 071 262 3791
Proprietor: R A Nye & K Nye
Horses: 9 **Ponies:** 6
Facilities available: Men/J.Pd /Hkg - Tracks in Hyde Park.
Level: Teaching Standards: Novice to advanced.
Specialisation: BHS approved.
Other details: Tuition in Jumping to advanced levels. Hacking - 1hr - 20

Snaresbrook Riding School Limited

67/69 Hollybush Hill, Snaresbrook, London, E11 1QG.
Tel: 081 989 3256
Proprietor: Miss D Parfitt
Horses: 18 **Ponies:** 5

Totteridge Riding School

32 Totteridge Common, London, N20.
Tel: 081 959 7290
Proprietor: Jean West
Number Horses/Ponies: 12
Facilities available: Ind Sch /Outdoor Men./Livery/Hacking

Trent Park Equestrian Centre

Bramley Road,, Southgate, London, N14 4XS.
Proprietor: Mr K Beavan & Mrs A Short

Willow Tree Riding Establishment

Ronver Road,, London, SE12.
Tel: 081 857 6438
Proprietor: E A & R I Massey
Horses: 15 **Ponies:** 15
Facilities available: Ind.Sch /Men(F.Lt)/Dis.R
Level: Teaching Standards: All Pony Club tests. BHSAI.
Specialisation: Handicapped and sub-normal children
Other details: Evening classes. All standards. Special care taken with nervous children and adults. Suburban country.
Member of Association of British Riding Schools

Wimbledon Village Stables

24 A/B High Street, Wimbledon, London, SW19 5DX.
Tel: 081 946 8579
Proprietor: Mrs C A Andrews
Number Horses/Ponies: 20
Facilities available: Men/Hkg - Wimbledon Common and Richmond Park.

Level: Teaching Standards: All ages and abilities.
Specialisation: BHS approved. 13 stone limit.
Other details: F/Schooling liveries. Tuition in dressage and jumping. Qualified instructors.

Merseyside

Longacres Riding School

290 Southport Road, Lydiate, Nr Liverpool, Merseyside, L31 4EQ.
Tel: 051 526 0327
Proprietor: Mr & Mrs J Kirkham
Horses: 12 **Ponies:** 15
Facilities available: Ind.Sch /J.Pd/X-C/Dis.R/Hkg
Level: Teaching standards to: ABRS Test no. 10. BHS Stages 1-3. BHSAI. ABRS Ass. Grooms Certificate.
Specialisation: Dressage training. RDA. Very young children.
Other details: Beginners to advanced taken. Evening classes. Non-residential courses. Livery. School. Examination/Assessment Centre. YTS. Career students taken.
Member of Association of British Riding Schools

Northfield Riding Centre

Northfield Farm, Gorsey Lane, Bold, Nr St Helens, Merseyside, WA9 4SW.
Tel: 0744 816075
Fax: 0774 816018
Proprietor: Mr & Mrs Cotterill
Horses: 25 **Ponies:** 10
Facilities available: Ind.Sch /Men/J.Pd/Dis.R

Level: Teaching standards to: BHSII.
Specialisation: Event and Dressage training.
Other details: Livery. Schooling. Breaking. Career students taken. YTS.
Member of Association of British Riding Schools

Woodville Riding School
Raby Road, Thornton Hough, Wirral, Merseyside.
Proprietor: Mrs M P Walton

Bowlers Riding School
35 Brewery Lane, Formby, Mersyside, L37 7DY.
Tel: 0704 72915
Proprietor: Miss Mary Bowler
Horses: 5 **Ponies:** 20
Facilities available: Ind.Sch/Men/J.Pd/X-C/Dis.R/Hkg - Pinewoods and grass tracks.
Level: Teaching standards to: ABRS test no.10. All ABRS exams. BHS stage exams. BHS Preliminary Teaching exam.
Specialisation: Holiday course of 2-4 days. Picnic rides.
Other details: F/P Livery. Evening classes. Monthly competition for weekly riders.
Member of Association of British Riding Schools

Middlesex

Gillian's Riding School.
Brayside Farm, Beggars Hollow, Clay Mill, Enfield, Middlesex, EN2 9JL.
Tel: 081-366 5445
Proprietor: Mrs Gillian Head
Horses: 8 **Ponies:** 8

Facilities available: Men (F.Lt)/J.Pd/Dis.R/Hkg - Woodland and bridleways.
Level: Teaching standards to: ABRS test no.6. Students to BHSAI. BHS Road Safety.
Specialisation: Stable management courses.
Other details: F/P Livery. Schooling. Evening classes. Novice and beginners welcome.
Member of Association of British Riding Schools

Goulds Green Riding School
Goulds Green, Hillingdon, Middlesex.
Proprietor: Mr M W Jupp

Kings Oak Equestrian Centre Limited
Theobalds Park Road, Crews Hill, Enfield, Middlesex, EN2 9BL.
Tel: 081 363 7868
Proprietor: Mrs J Gill & Misses S & G Gill
Horses: 30 **Ponies:** 12

Park Farm School of Riding
Ducks Hill Road, Northwood, Middlesex.
Tel: 09274 25746
Proprietor: Mr R J Old
Horses: 13 **Ponies:** 5

Suzanne's Riding School
Brookshill Farm, Brookshill Drive, Harrow Weald, Middlesex.
Tel: 081-954 3618
Proprietor: Mrs S Marczak
Horses: 45 **Ponies:** 28
Facilities available: Ind.Sch /2 Men(F.Lt)/J.Pd /X-C/ Dis.R /Hkg - Farmlands and woods

Level: Teaching standards to: ABRS. Students to BHS Stage 2.
Specialisation: Pony Club and Riding Club activities.
Other details: F/P Livery. Schooling. Breaking. Lecture room. Special residential courses. Tuition in dressage and eventing. Evening classes. Career students taken.
Member of Association of British Riding Schools

Westway Riding School
Green Lane, Hounslow, Middlesex.
Tel: 081-570 1653
Proprietor: J E Radford Howes
Horses: 10 **Ponies:** 10
Facilities available: Men (F.Lt)/J.Pd/Dis.R/X-C Jumps/Hkg - Parks and own fields.
Level: Teaching standards to: Pony Club B test.
Other details: DIY livery.
Member of Association of British Riding Schools

Norfolk

Belton Riding Centre
Station Road, Belton, Gt Yarmouth, Norfolk, NR31 9AA.
Proprietor: Mrs H Jermy

Cringleford Riding School
The Loke, Cringleford, Norwich, Norfolk, NR4 6XA.
Tel: 0603 51719
Proprietor: Miss P Sykes
Horses: 4 **Ponies:** 22
Facilities available: Ind.Sch /J.Pd/X-C/Hkg - Fair countryside.

Level: Teaching standards to: ABRS test no. 10. Students - only YTS - To BHS stages 1-3. Pony Club tests. Side-saddle tests (ABRS). BHSAI.
Specialisation: Tuition in Side-saddle.
Other details: Non- residential courses. Livery. Schooling. Evening classes. Novice to intermediate riders taken.
Member of Association of British Riding Schools

Hillcrest Riding School Limited

Hillcrest Farm, Yarmouth Road, Filby Heath, Nr. Great Yarmouth, Norfolk, NR29 3JS.
Tel: 0493 730394
Fax: 0603 716567
Proprietor: Mrs N Wilkes
Horses: 8 **Ponies:** 8
Facilities available: 2 Men(F.Lt)/J.Pd/Hkg
Level: Teaching Standards: BHS Stages 1 & 2 and up to Elementary Dressage.
Specialisation: Show-jumping competitions throughout the summer.
Other details: Livery. Career students taken. YTS. Schooling.
Member of Association of British Riding Schools

Hockwold Lodge Riding School

Davey Lodge, Cowles Drove, Hockwold, Thetford, Norfolk, IP26 4JQ.
Tel: 0842 828376
Fax: 0842 828376
Proprietor: K M Ladell Esq
Horses: 14 **Ponies:** 21
Facilities available: Ind.Sch /Men(F.Lt)/J.Pd/X-C/Hkg
Level: Teaching standards to: ABRS Test no. 10. BHSAI. ABRS Grooms Diploma. NVQ level 1.

Specialisation: Side-saddle.
Other details: Career students taken. Liveries. Schooling. Breaking. Hunting. YTS. Examination/Assessment Centre.
Member of Association of British Riding Schools

Home Farm Riding Stables

Holme-next-the-Sea, Hunstanton, Norfolk, PF36 6LF.
Tel: 048 525 233
Proprietor: Miss N R Wheeler
Horses: 23 **Ponies:** 22

Newin Equestrian Centre

Woodrow Lane, Great Moulton, Norwick, Norfolk, NR15 2HZ.
Proprietor: Mrs M S Harvey

Rectory Road Riding School

Old Rectory, Suffield, Norwich, Norfolk, NR11 7ER.
Tel: 0263 761367
Proprietor: Mrs W Garrett
Horses: 3 **Ponies:** 15
Facilities available: Ind.Sch /J.Pd/Dis.R - by arrangement /Hkg - Country lanes, tracks and bridleways.
Level: Teaching standards to: ABRS Test no. 8. BHS Stages 1 & 2. BHS Riding and Road Safety.
Specialisation: Pupils taken to local competitions and Pony Club to participate.
Other details: F/P Livery. Schooling. Breaking. Beginners to Affiliated show-jumping. Flatwork for owners wishing to improve their performance.
Member of Association of British Riding Schools

Reeves Hall

Hepworth, Diss, Norfolk, IP22 2PP.
Proprietor: Mrs Richards & Mr & Mrs Allen

Rose-Acre Riding Stables

Back Mundesley Road, Gimingham, Nr. Mundesley, Norfolk, NR11 8HN.
Proprietor: Mrs J Self

Rosebrook Farm Equestrian Centre

South Lopham, Diss, Norfolk, IP22 2JP.
Tel: 037 988 278
Proprietor: Mr & Mrs J S Attenborough
Horses: 10 **Ponies:** 10

Runton Hall Stud

Church Farm, North Runton, Kings Lynn, Norfolk.
Proprietor: Mr & Mrs P Kemp

Salhouse Equestrian Centre

Farrer Farms Limited, Vicarage Farm, Salhouse, Norwick, Norfolk, NR13 6RW.

Stanbrook Riding Centre

Paddock Farm, Lower Road, Thetford, Norfolk, IP25 7EB.
Proprietor: Mrs BA Bates & Miss BT Bates

Stiffkey Valley Stables

Old Wells Road, Little Walsingham, Norfolk, NR22 6BZ.
Proprietor: Mr R Le-Bon Olive

Strumpshaw Riding Centre

Buckenham Road, Strumpshaw, Norwich, Norfolk, NR13 4NP.
Proprietor: Mrs F Beard

Swiss Cottage Stables & Saddlery

Swiss Cottage, West Winch, King's Lynn, Norfolk, PT33 0LZ.
Tel: 0553 760408
Proprietor: Carol Francis
Horses: 5 **Ponies:** 5
Facilities available: Men (F.Lt)/J.Pd/Dis.R/Hkg
Level: Teaching Standards: ABRS and BHS exams.
Specialisation: Picnic and pub rides. Tack and saddlery shop.
Other details: Livery. Schooling. Career students taken. YTS. Friendly riding school promotional instructional days.
Member of Association of British Riding Schools

West Runton Riding Stables

West Runton, Cromer, Norfolk, NR27 9QH.
Tel: 026375 339
Proprietor: Mrs J Bakewell
Horses: 10 **Ponies:** 15
Facilities available: Ind.Sch /Dis.R/Hkg - Costal and woodland
Level: Teaching Standards: All ages groups for basic instruction.
Specialisation: Home of the Norfolk Shire horse. Cart horse Demos. daily.
Member of Association of British Riding Schools

Willow Farm Riding School

Ormesby St Margaret, Gt Yarmouth, Norfolk.
Proprietor: Mrs J Russell

North Yorkshire

Barrowby Riding Centre

Kirkby Overblow, Nr Harrogate, North Yorkshire, NG3 1HU.
Proprietor: Mrs S Caley & Miss J Caley

Beck Isle Ponies

Wells Walk, The Rookers, Pickering, North Yorkshire, YO18 7JJ.
Tel: 0751 72982
Proprietor: Mrs M Cook
Horses: 1 **Ponies:** 10

Belmont Riding School & Livery

193 Forest Lane, Harrowgate, North Yorkshire, H62 7EF.
Tel: 0423 886997
Proprietor: Miss D M Atkinson

Bewerley School of Horsemanship

Bewerley Old Hall, Pateley Bridge, Harrogate, North Yorkshire, HG3 5JA.
Tel: 0423 711344
Proprietor: Mrs M Clark
Facilities available: Lessons, Livery, Breaking, Hacking

Breckonborough Riding Holiday Centre

Breckonborough Farm, Brough Park, Richmond, North Yorkshire, DI10 7PL.
Tel: 0748 811629
Proprietor: Messrs KA,M & Mrs PC Acaster
Number Horses/Ponies: 30
Facilities available: J.Pd/Hkg

Level: Teaching Standards: Beginners to competition riders.
Specialisation: BHS approved centre.
Other details: Ponies UK Purple star.

Brigg View Farm Stables

Hunmanby Gap, Sands Lane, Filey, North Yorkshire, YO14 9QW.
Tel: 0723 890205
Proprietor: Mr & Mrs Clemmit
Horses: 8 **Ponies:** 6
Facilities available: Men (F.Lt)/J.Pd/X-C/Dis.R/Hkg - Beaches and woods.
Level: Teaching standards to: Students to BHSAI. P.C 'B' test.
Other details: Livery. Schooling. Breaking. Hunting. Tuition in jumping and eventing.
Member of Association of British Riding Schools

Carlton Grange Riding Centre

Sexhon Lane , Carlton-in-Cleveland, North Yorkshire, TS9 7DX.
Tel: 0642 701027
Proprietor: Christine Hutchinson
Horses: 3 **Ponies:** 17
Facilities available: Ind.Sch /Men(F.Lt)/J.Pd/Hkg - Flat and open country.
Level: Teaching Standards: Various levels.
Other details: Working liveries. Schooling. All standards.
Member of Association of British Riding Schools

Catterick Army Saddle Club

Headquarters Catterick Garrison, Scotton Road, Catterick, North Yorkshire, DL9 3JE.
Proprietor: Mrs B Riley

Farsyde Stud and Riding Stables

Farsyde House, Robin Hood's Bay, Whitby, North Yorkshire, YO22 4UG.
Tel: 0947 880249
Proprietor: Mr & Mrs R V Green
Horses: 4 **Ponies:** 6

Friar's Hill Riding Stables

Friar's Hill, Sinnington, Nr Pickering, North Yorkshire, YO6 6NF.
Proprietor: Mrs C Gamble

Harrogate Equestrian Centre

Brackenthwaite Lane, Burn Bridge, Harrogate, North Yorkshire, HG3 1PW.
Tel: 0423 87 1894
Proprietor: Major J N D Birtwistle
Horses: 20 **Ponies:** 12
Facilities available: Ind.Sch/Men(F.Lt)/J.Pd/3 X-C/Dis.R - limited/Hkg
Level: Teaching standards to: Up to the Fellowship of the BHS.
Specialisation: Shop. Lisenced bar.
Other details: Tuition for competitors and horses for dressage, show-jumping and horse trials. Liveries (30). Career students taken. Schooling. Breaking. YTS. Evening classes.
Member of Association of British Riding Schools

Lacys Cottage Riding School

Scrayingham, York, North Yorkshire, YO4 1JD.
Proprietor: Mrs N Pimlott

Moor House Riding School

Sutton Road, Wagginton, York, North Yorkshire, YO3 8RB.
Proprietor: Mrs S Kemp-Welch

Naburn Grange Riding Centre

Naburn Grange, Naburn, North Yorkshire, YO1 4RU.
Tel: 090487 283
Proprietor: Mrs Della Horn
Horses: 8 **Ponies:** 18
Facilities available: Ind.Sch/Men/J.Pd/X-C/Hkg - Quiet country lanes. Farmland. Woodland.
Level: Teaching standards: From Novice to advanced.
Specialisation: Tailor made courses - all include stable management.
Other details: Tuition in dressage, Show-jumping, X-country and gymkhana. BHS qualified instructors. Livery. Schooling. Breaking. Class or Private tuition. Learn to drive a pony and trap.

Queen Margaret's Riding School

Escrick Park, York, North Yorkshire, YO4 6EA.
Proprietor: Miss G M Sanders

Rillington Manor Riding School

Rillington Manor, Rillington, Malton, North Yorkshire, YO17 8LL.
Tel: 09442 246
Proprietor: Mrs G T Russell

Number Horses/Ponies: 14
Facilities available: Men/X-C/J.Pd/Hkg - Bridlepaths.
Level: Teaching standards: Novice to Intermediate.
Specialisation: BHS approved.
Other details: P/Grass livery. Tuition in dressage, show-jumping and X-country.

Snainton Riding Centre

Snainton, Nr Scarsborough, North Yorkshire.
Tel: 0723 85218
Proprietor: Mr A Lyall & Mrs Lyall
Horses: 14 **Ponies:** 11
Facilities available: Ind.Sch/Men(F.Lt)/J.Pd/X-C/Dis.R/Hkg - Agricultural and forestry views.
Level: Teaching standards to: ABRS Test no. 10. Students to BHSAI. BHSII. BHSI. ABRS Ass. and Grooms Diplomas.
Specialisation: Training horses and riders for competition.
Other details: Lecture room. F/P Livery. Schooling. Breaking. Hunting. Career students taken. Comprehensive tuition in all disciplines.
Member of Association of British Riding Schools

The York Riding School

Wiggington Road, York, North Yorkshire, YO3 8RH.
Tel: 0904 763686
Proprietor: Mrs Holstead BHSI
Horses: 11 **Ponies:** 10
Facilities available: Ind.Sch/Men(F.Lt)/J.Pd/X-C/Dis.R
Level: Teaching Standards: All ABRS and BHS exams. ABRS test no.10+.

Specialisation: Warmblood Stud. Training for horses and ponies.
Other details: Livery. Schooling. Breaking. Hunting. Career students taken. Evening classes. Assessment centre - hopefully within the next 12 months.
Member of Association of British Riding Schools

Yafforth Equestrian Centre

Broomfield Farm, Yafforth, Northallerton, North Yorkshire.
Tel: 0609 71671
Proprietor: Mrs S Chapman
Horses: 2 **Ponies:** 9

Yorkshire Riding Centre

Markington, Harrogate, North Yorkshire, HG3 3PE.
Tel: 0765 87207
Proprietor: Jane & Chris Bartle
Number Horses/Ponies: 65
Facilities available: 2 Ind.Sch /Men/X-C/J.Pd
Level: Teaching standards: Novice to Advanced levels.
Specialisation: Dressage.
Other details: Training in Eventing, Dressage and Show-jumping.

Northamptonshire

Brampton Stables

Church Brampton, Northamptonshire, NN6 8AU.
Tel: 0604 842051
Proprietor: Mr & Mrs D A Ward
Horses: 12 **Ponies:** 20
Facilities available: Ind.Sch /2 Men(F.Lt)/X-C/J.Pd/Hkg - Pytchley Hunt Country.

Level: Teaching standards to: Students to BHS Stages 1-4. BHSAI and BHSII exams. Pony Club Tests Specialisation: Managing agents for YTS. Exam/ competition preparation.
Other details: Evening classes. Residential students. Breaking. Schooling. Lecture room. All standards. Exam training. Side-saddle. F/P Livery.
Member of Association of British Riding Schools

Chapman's Close Riding Establishment

Weedon Road, Nether Heyford, Northamptonshire.
Tel: 0327 41859
Proprietor: Mrs M E Cochran
Facilities available: Show Jumping/Show visits

Church Farm Stables

Church Brampton, Northamptonshire.
Tel: 0604 842313
Proprietor: J & E N Lamont
Facilities available: Hacking/Lessons. Open countryside

East Lodge Farm Riding Establishment

East Lodge Farm, Ecton, Northamptonshire, NN6 0QU.
Tel: 0604 810244
Proprietor: Mr & Mrs R D White
Horses: 5 **Ponies:** 5
Facilities available: Ind.Sch/Men(F.Lt)/J.Pd/X-C/H kg
Level: Teaching standards to: BHSAI.

Specialisation: Beginners specially catered for.
Other details: YTS. Children/Adult Stable and Horse Management Courses. Evening classes. Livery. Hunting.
Member of Association of British Riding Schools

Foxhill Farm Equestrian Centre

Sywell Road, Holcot, Northamptonshire, NN6 9SN.
Proprietor: Miss L J Stephenson

Greenacres Riding Centre

Puxley, Potterspury, Towcester, Northamptonshire, NN12 7QS.
Proprietor: Mrs S Smith
Member of Association of British Riding Schools

Holdenby Riding School

Holdenby, Northamptonshire, NN6 8DJ.
Tel: 0604 770003
Proprietor: Mr M Watkins & Miss T Watkins
Horses: 10 **Ponies:** 18
Facilities available: Ind.Sch/Men/Dis.R/Hkg - Open countryside and good bridleways.
Level: Teaching standards to: BHSAI.
Specialisation: Approved by the BHS.
Other details: Career students taken. Schooling. Evening classes - Tues.,Wed., and Thur.6pm-7.15pm. Special residential courses - accommodation available locally. Lecture room.
Member of Association of British Riding Schools

Manor Farm Equestrian Centre

Manor Farm, Maidwell, Northamptonshire, NN6 9JB.
Tel: 060 128 221
Proprietor: Miss S Stanier
Horses: 4 **Ponies:** 1

Moulton Riding School

Pound Lane, Moulton, Northamptonshire.
Tel: 0604 42006
Proprietor: Mr Woolman
Horses: 10 **Ponies:** 7
Facilities available: Hacking/Jumping. Weight limit 13 stone

Phoenix Stables

Brockhall Road, Flore, Northamptonshire.
Tel: 0327 42437
Proprietor: Mrs J A Quennell
Facilities available: Hacking/. Open countryside.

Shukburgh Riding Centre

Shuckburgh House, Naseby, Northamptonshire, NN6 7DA.
Proprietor: Mrs S Muirhead

Uplands Equestrian Centre Ltd

Loddington, Nr. Kettering, Northamptonshire, HU12 0UA.
Tel: 0964 650250
Proprietor: Toni Biglinn
Member of Association of British Riding Schools

Village Farm Riding & Livery Stables

Village Farm, Preston Capes, Nr Daventry, Northamptonshire.
Tel: 032736 392
Proprietor: Mrs Rathmill
Facilities available: Hacking, Cross country. Open countryside

Yelvertoft Equestrian Centre

Brookside Farm, Ashwells Lane, Yelvertoft, Northamptonshire, NN6 7LW.
Proprietor: Mr & Mrs B R Faulkner

Northumberland

Bay Horse Inn

West Woodburn, Hexham, Northumberland.
Tel: 0660 60218
Proprietor: H & J Wright
Facilities available: Hacking. Group hacking.

Benridge Riding School

Benridge Hagg, Hagg, Morpeth, Northumberland, NE61 3SB.
Tel: 0670 518507
Proprietor: D M Mancey Esq
Horses: 6 **Ponies:** 5
Facilities available: Men/J.Pd/Hkg - Undulating countryside.
Level: Teaching Standards: Various standards.
Specialisation: Hacking
Other details: Brochure available. Schooling. Livery. Lecture room.
Member of Association of British Riding Schools

Equi Study Centre

Hole House, Haltwhistle, Northumberland, NE49 0LQ.
Tel: 06977 47577
Proprietor: Mrs A L Midgley
Number Horses/Ponies: 3
Facilities available: Men
Level: Teaching standards to: BHSAI - 7 per 1/2hr lesson.
Specialisation: BHS approved.
Other details: Lecture room. Private tuition.

Kielder Adventure Centre

Kielder Water, Hexham, Northumberland, NE48 IBS.
Proprietor: P J V Cockerill

Kimmerston Riding Centre

Kimmerston, Wooler, Northumberland, NE71 6JH.
Proprietor: Mr & Mrs R Jeffreys

Whitton Farmhouse Hotel

Whitton Farm, Rothbury, Northumberland, NE65 7RL.
Proprietor: Mr T Clubley

Windy Edge Stables

Alnmouth Road, Alnwick, Northumberland, NE66 2QB.
Tel: 0665 602284
Proprietor: Miss White & Miss Sisterson
Horses: 6 **Ponies:** 6

Nottinghamshire

Bloomsgorse Trekking Centre

Bloomsgorse Farm, Bilsthorpe, Nr Newark, Nottinghamshire, ND22 8TA.
Proprietor: Mr & Mrs Z Grant

Brackenhurst College

Brackenhurst, Southwell, Nottinghamshire, NG25 0QF.
Tel: 0636 815404
Proprietor: J P Benson Esq
Horses: 40 **Ponies:** 0
Facilities available: Ind.Sch /Men/J.Pd/X-C/Hkg - Students only.
Level: Teaching standards to: BHS and NCMH Exams.
Specialisation: Students trained to BHSAI..

Other details: BHS Examination/Assessment Centre. Liveries(12). No beginners.YTS.
Member of Association of British Riding Schools

Carlton Forest Equestrian Centre

Glebe House, Blyth Road, Carlton Forest, Worksop, Nottinghamshire S81 0TP
Tel: 0909 731221
Member of Association of British Riding Schools

Cherry Tree Riding Centre

28 Plainspot Road, New Brinsley, Nottinghamshire.
Tel: 0773 721438
Proprietor: Mrs J Griffiths.
Member of Association of British Riding Schools

College Farm Equestrian Centre

West Markham, Tuxford, Nr Newark, Nottinghamshire, NG22 0PN.
Tel: 0777 870886
Proprietor: Victoria Hayton
Horses: 10 **Ponies:** 6
Facilities available: Men (F.Lt)/J.Pd/X-C/Dis.R/Hkg - Excellent riding country.
Level: Teaching standards to: Students to ABRS Grooms Diploma. BHSAI.
Specialisation: Side-saddle and Western riding.
Other details: Livery. Schooling. Breaking.
Member of Association of British Riding Schools

Hayside Stables

Moulton Crescent, Balderton, Newark, Nottinghamshire, NG24 3DY.
Tel: 0636 705384
Proprietor: Ms K S Murrell
Horses: 4 **Ponies:** 4

Facilities available: Men (F.Lt)/J.Pd/Hkg
Level: Teaching standards to: ABRS test no. 4. BHS stage 2.
Specialisation: Visiting instructors. Pony days. Competitions.
Other details: Possible exchanges with Portugal available for grooms. Evening classes. Livery. Schooling. Breaking.
Member of Association of British Riding Schools

Newark Equestrian Centre

Beaconfield Farm, Coddington, Newark, Nottinghamshire, NG24 2QG.
Proprietor: Mr & Mrs J Woodland

Nottingham Equestrian Centre

Leys Farm, Asher Lane, Ruddington, Nottinghamshire, NG11 6U.
Tel: 0602 842854
Proprietor: Mrs M J Worthington
Number Horses/Ponies: 30
Facilities available: Men /Ind.Sch/X-C/J.Pd/Dis.R/Hkg
Level: Teaching Standards: Novice up to BHS stage 3.
Specialisation: Eventing tuition.
Other details: F/Livery. Class or private tuition.

Selston Equestrian Centre

Hillbank Farm, Common Side, Selston, Nottinghamshire, NG16 6FJ.
Proprietor: Mrs Wild & Mrs Burr

St Clements Lodge Riding School

Woods Lane, Claverton, Nottinghamshire, NG14 6FF.
Tel: 0602 652524
Proprietor: Mr G Burrows & Mr N Burrows
Horses: 10 **Ponies:** 10
Facilities available: Ind.Sch/J.Pd/X-C Jumps/Hkg - hilly woods.
Level: Teaching standards to: ABRS Test no. 10. Students to BHSAI.
Specialisation: Clients take on own horse - special days for children in hols.
Other details: Tuition in dressage. Evening classes. Any standard. Divided classes. Brochure available. Video service. 100 seater lecture room.
Member of Association of British Riding Schools

Sutton Manor Farm Riding School

Sutton-cum-Lound, Retford, Nottinghamshire, DN22 8PJ.
Tel: 0777 705995
Proprietor: Mrs M Dunn
Ponies: 7
Facilities available: Men /X-C Jumps/Hkg
Level: Teaching standards to: ABRS test no. 10.
Specialisation: Dressage appreciated. Gymkhanas and Shows.
Other details: Beginners to advanced taken. Livery. Hunting.
Member of Association of British Riding Schools

Wellow Park Stables & Saddlery

Rufford Lane, Wellor, Nr Newark, Nottinghamshire, NG22 0EQ.
Tel: 0623 861040
Proprietor: Mrs M Willett
Horses: 20 **Ponies:** 10

Facilities available: Men (F.Lt)/J.Pd/X-C/Dis.R/Hkg
Level: Teaching Standards: BHS Stages to 4.
Specialisation: Driving ponies. BHS exam and horse trial centre.
Other details: Livery. Schooling. Breaking. Hunting. C.T competitions. Evening classes.
Member of Association of British Riding Schools

Oxfordshire

Barrington Stables
Home Farm, Little Barrington, Nr Burford, Oxfordshire, OX8 4TE.
Proprietor: Mrs J E Mills

Blenheim Riding Centre
Benson, Nr Wallingford, Oxfordshire, OX9 6PR.
Tel: 0491 36057
Proprietor: Mr & Mrs M W Jones
Number Horses/Ponies: 15
Facilities available: Hkg/ Accompanied group hacks/

Blewbury Riding & Training Centre Limited
Besselsway, Blewbury, Didcot, Oxfordshire, OX11 9NH.
Proprietor: Miss J Dexter & Mr B Knight

Cotswold Equitation Centre
93 Shilton Road, Carterton, Oxfordshire, OX8 3EN.
Proprietor: Mrs C A Hogg

Heathcote House
Little Tew, Oxfordshire, OX7 4JE.
Tel: 060883 617
Proprietor: Mrs F Johnson

Oakfield Riding School
Oakfield, Great Coxwell, Faringdon, Oxfordshire, RG9 6QU.
Proprietor: Mr D C Farrow

Oxford Riding School
Garsington, Oxfordshire, OX9 9DP.
Tel: 086736 383
Proprietor: Mr & Mrs C Akerman
Horses: 10 **Ponies:** 6
Facilities available: Ind.Sch /Men(F.Lt)/J.Pd/X-C Jumps /Dis.R/Hkg - Roads and bridleways.
Level: Teaching standards to: Students to BHS stages 1-3 and Preliminary teaching exam.
Specialisation: Jumping lessons on own horses.
Other details: Career students taken. P/ Livery. Schooling. Nervous adults taught.
Member of Association of British Riding Schools

Silverdown Riding School & Equitation Centre
Harwell, Didcot, Oxfordshire, OX11 0LU.
Tel: 023586 377
Proprietor: Mr & Mrs Skinner
Horses: 5 **Ponies:** 6
Facilities available: Ind.Sch /Hkg
Level: Teaching standards to: ABRS Test no. 10.
Specialisation: Novice and Experienced riders taken.
Other details: Evening classes. Career students YTS Livery. Schooling. Breaking.
Member of Association of British Riding Schools

The Malt House Stud Training Centre
Hanney Road, Steventon, Oxfordshire.
Proprietor: Mr P Tuckwell

Turville Valley Stud Riding
Turville, Henley On Thames, Oxfordshire, RG9 6QU.
Tel: 049163 338
Proprietor: Mrs N Thurman
Horses: 20 **Ponies:** 20
Facilities available: 2 Men (F.Lt)/J.Pd/X-C/Dis.R/Hkg
Level: Teaching standards to: ABRS Test no. 10. BHSAI. BHSII. Pony Club A Test. ABRS Tests.
Specialisation: Classical equitation. Lustiano Stud. P.C Mounted Games.
Other details: Schooling. Breaking. Career students taken. YTS.
Member of Association of British Riding Schools

Valley Farm Equestrian Centre
Shotteswell, Nr Banbury, Oxfordshire
Tel: 0295 730576
Member of Association of British Riding Schools

Waterstock House Training Centre
Waterstock, Nr Oxford, Oxfordshire.
Tel: 08447 616
Proprietor: Lars Sederholm
Horses: 8

Westfield Farm Riding Centre
Fenway, Steeple Aston, Oxfordshire, OX5 3SS.
Tel: 0869 47421
Proprietor: Mrs A Hillier
Horses: 15 **Ponies:** 10
Facilities available: Ind.Sch /Men/J.Pd/X-C/Dis.R/Hkg - Bridleways in open country-side.
Level: Teaching to: ABRS Test no. 6. Students to ABRS Grooms Diploma. BHS Prelim. teaching and Horsemasters.

Specialisation: Schooling problem horses with the rider. **Other details:** P/ Livery. Schooling. Breaking. Specialised tuition for nervous riders and absolute beginners. *Member of Association of British Riding Schools*

White Horse Stables

Goosey Glebe Smallholding, Goosey, Wantage, Oxfordshire. **Tel:** 03677 8806 **Proprietor:** Mrs Dianne Godfery **Horses:** 6 **Ponies:** 6 **Facilities available:** Men (F.Lt)/J.Pd/X-C Jumps /Hkg **Level:** Teaching Standards: Basic **Other details:** Livery. Schooling. Breaking. Evening classes. Riding and road safety exams. *Member of Association of British Riding Schools*

Shropshire

Berriewood Stud Farm

Condover, Shrewsbury, Shropshire, SY5 7NN. **Tel:** 074373 252 **Proprietor:** Mrs W Lock & Mrs P Cowdy **Horses:** 15 **Ponies:** 20 **Facilities available:** Ind.Sch /2 Men(F.Lt)/J.Pd/X-C/Dis.R/ Hkg - Farmland with surrounding hills. **Level:** Teaching standards to: Students to BHSAI and BHS Intermediate teaching. **Specialisation:** Affiliated Horse Trials and Dressage. **Other details:** Adult Saddle Club. Beginners to competition riders taken. F/P Livery. Schooling. *Member of Association of British Riding Schools*

Black Birches

Hadnell, Shrewsbury, Shropshire. **Tel:** 09397 380 **Proprietor:** J & M Jinks **Horses:** 9 **Ponies:** 1

Hope Equestrian Centre

The Tankerville, Hope, Minsterley, Shrewsbury, Shropshire SY5 0JB **Tel:** 0743 791418 *Member of Association of British Riding Schools*

Lilleshall Riding & Livery Stables

Child Pit Lane, Nr Newport, Shropshire, TF10 9AR. **Proprietor:** Mr & Mrs Francis

North Farm Riding Establishment

North Farm, Whitcliffe, Ludlow, Shropshire, SY8 2HD. **Proprietor:** Mr P Dickin **Horses:** 2 **Ponies:** 14

P G L Young Adventure Ltd

Boreatton Park, Baschurch, Nr Shrewsbury, Shropshire, SY4 2EZ. **Proprietor:** Mr B F Knell

Prescott Equestrian Centre

Prescott Farm, Baschurch, Nr Shrewsbury, Shropshire. **Tel:** 0939 260712 **Proprietor:** Mrs J Haydon & Mr R W Stone **Horses:** 6 **Ponies:** 16

The Inett Farm & Equestrian Centre

Pound Lane, Broseley, Shropshire, TF12 5AU. **Proprietor:** Mr & Mrs M S Gilmore

The Wyke Equestrian Centre

Shifnal, Shropshire, TF11 9PP. **Tel:** 0952 460560 **Proprietor:** L Phillips & R J Phillips **Horses:** 17 **Ponies:** 8 **Facilities available:** Ind.Sch /2 Men (F.Lt)/J.Pd/X-C/Hkg - Varied countryside **Level:** Teaching standards to: ABRS Test no. 10. Students to BHS Stages 1-4. BHSAI. BHSII. ABRS levels 1-2. ABRS Ass. Grooms Certificate and Diploma. **Specialisation:** Associated with Wyke Saddlery Comp and Wyke Equestrian Services **Other details:** F/P Livery. Schooling. Breaking. Hunting. Varied evening classes. Special residential courses. Brochure available. *Member of Association of British Riding Schools*

Tong Riding Centre Ltd

Church Farm, Tong, Shifnal, Shropshire, TF11 8PW. **Tel:** 090 722 2352 **Proprietor:** Mrs M J Garside-Bates **Horses:** 17 **Ponies:** 12

Tony Riding Centre

Shifnal, Shropshire, TF11 8PW. *Member of Association of British Riding Schools*

Somerset

Bayford Stud Farm and Training Centre

Riding Gate, Wincanton, Somerset. **Tel:** 0963 32827 **Proprietor:** Mrs Burt **Horses:** 10 **Ponies:** 10

Facilities available: Men /J.Pd/X-C Jumps/Hkg
Level: Teaching standards to: BHSAI. BHS stages 1-3. ABRS level 1-2
Specialisation: Training young horses, Re-schooling.
Other details: Career students taken. Livery. Schooling. Breaking. Hunting. Evening classes. Tuition in dressage, show-jumping and eventing.
Member of Association of British Riding Schools

Burcott Riding School
Lower Burcott, Wells, Somerset, BA5 1NQ.
Tel: 0749 73145
Proprietor: Mr N Payne
Number Horses/Ponies: 40
Facilities available: X-C/J.Pd /Men(All weather surface) /Hkg - No casual hiring.
Level: Teaching Standards: General instruction to BHSII level.
Other details: Working/F Livery. Private and group lessons seven days per week.

Camel Hill Farm Stables
Camel Hill Farm, Queen Camel, Yeovil, Somerset, BA22 7PL.
Proprietor: Mrs F Turner

Curland Equestrian Enterprises
Crosses Farm Stud, Curland, Taunton, Somerset, TA3 5SD.
Tel: 046 034 234
Proprietor: Mrs A L Brown
Horses: 14 **Ponies:** 6

Deepleigh Farm Riding Centre
Langley Marsh, Wiveliscombe, Somerset, TA4 2UU.
Proprietor: Mrs G Richardson

Ebborlands Farm & Riding Centre
Ebborlands Farm, Wookey Hole, Nr. Wells, Somerset, BA5 1AY.
Tel: 0749 72550
Proprietor: Mrs E A Gibbs
Horses: 10 **Ponies:** 7
Facilities available: Hacking /All-weather men/S.Jumps /X-C course. Accompanied groups in fields, lanes, Mendip Hills, Somerset Levels.

Greggs Riding School
Placket Lane, Off Weston Coker Road, Yeovil, Somerset, BA22 2HH.
Proprietor: Mr & Mrs G Bennett

Hill View Riding Centre
Sunnyside Farm, Portway, Crewkerne, Somerset, TA18 8PA.
Tel: 0460 72731
Proprietor: Mr & Mrs Congdon
Member of Association of British Riding Schools

Knowle Riding Centre
Timberscombe, Minehead, Somerset, TA24 6TZ.
Tel: 064384 342
Proprietor: J & K Lamacraft
Horses: 35 **Ponies:** 15
Facilities available: Ind.Sch /J.Pd/X-C/Hkg - Moorland, hilly countryside, parkland (National Trust)
Level: Teaching standards to: ABRS Test no. 6.
Specialisation: Riding and hunting holidays.
Other details: F/P Livery. Schooling. Hunting. Breaking. Tuition in jumping and X-country. Special residential courses. Ideal family holiday centre.
Member of Association of British Riding Schools

Millfield School
Street, Somerset, BA16 0AA.
Proprietor: Mr C R Atkinson

Old Stowey Farm
Wheddon Cross, Minehead, Somerset.
Tel: 064 384 268
Proprietor: Mr R Watson

Pevlings Farm Riding & Livery Stables
Cabbage Lane, Horsington, Templecombe, Somerset, BA8 0ER.
Tel: 0963 70990
Proprietor: Mr & Mrs Tytheridge
Horses: 3 **Ponies:** 8
Facilities available: Men (F.Lt)/J.Pd/Hkg - Quiet country lanes and bridle paths.
Level: Teaching Standards: Basic
Other details: F/P Livery. Special tuition for small groups of adults and children.
Member of Association of British Riding Schools

Porlock Vale Equitation Centre
Porlock Ford, Nr. Minehead, Somerset, TA24 8NY.
Tel: 0643 862 338
Proprietor: Mr & Mrs P Coxhead
Facilities available: 2 Ind.Sch /Men/J.Pd/X-C/Hkg - Woodland and open moorland
Level: Teaching Standards: Basic.
Other details: Lecture room. Livery. Schooling. Breaking.
Member of Association of British Riding Schools

The Quantock Riding Centre
Pardlestone Farm, Kilve, Nr. Bridgwater, Somerset, TA5 1SQ.
Tel: 027 874 374

Proprietor: Mr D Houghton & Ms R Moore
Horses: 20 **Ponies:** 25
Facilities available: Gen purp Livery/all weather Men./Hunt/Hack/Trek/X-C
Specialisation: S-J/X-C

The West Somerset Riding Centre
Moor Road, North Hill, Minehead, Somerset, TA24 5RT.
Proprietor: Miss L A Fisher

South Yorkshire

Barnes Green Riding School
Woodseats Farm, Barnes Green, Grenoside, Nr Sheffield, South Yorkshire.
Tel: 0742 460078
Proprietor: Miss C Walker
Horses: 10 **Ponies:** 10
Facilities available: Men (F.Lt)/J.Pd/X-C/Hkg.- Country woodland and forestry
Level: Teaching standards to: ABRS Test no.10. PC Tests. BHS Stages and ABRS Exams
Specialisation: Adult and children courses. Full BSJA jumping course
Other details: Career students taken. Lecture room.
Member of Association of British Riding Schools

Brockholes Farm Riding Centre
Branton , Doncaster, South Yorkshire, DN3 3QS.
Proprietor: Miss J H Turner

Cowley Riding School
Four Acres, Cowley Lane, Holmesfield, Sheffield, South Yorkshire, S18 5SD.
Proprietor: Mrs V E Oglesby

Horses: 11 **Ponies:** 6
Facilities available: Men (F.Lt)/X-C/Dis.R/Hkg - Hilly and moorland.
Level: Teaching standards to: Students to BHS stages 1-4. All ABRS.
Specialisation: ATO approved.
Other details: Schooling. Breaking. Hunting. Career students taken. Tuition in dressage and ODE. Evening classes. All standards. YTS managing agents.
Member of Association of British Riding Schools

Doe House Riding School
Bradfield Dale, Sheffield, South Yorkshire, S6 6LE.
Tel: 0742 81271
Proprietor: Mrs Grace Windle
Horses: 3 **Ponies:** 4
Facilities available: Men (F.Lt)/J.Pd/X-C/Dis.R - limited /Hkg - Hilly and bridlepaths.
Level: Teaching standards to: ABRS test no. 10. Students up to BHS stage 4.
Other details: P/ Livery. Schooling. Breaking. Career students taken. Special residential courses. Evening classes.
Member of Association of British Riding Schools

Finningley School of Equitation
Finningley, Doncaster, South Yorkshire, DN9 3BU.
Tel: 0302 770259
Proprietor: Mrs Baddiley & Mrs Cartwright
Horses: 20 **Ponies:** 28
Facilities available: Ind.Sch/J.Pd/X-C/Dis.R/Hkg - Flat, gravel and sand land.
Level: Teaching standards to: BHSAI. BHS Intermediate. BHS Stages 1-3. Pony Club Tests.

Specialisation: Managing agents for YTS (ATO status).
Other details: Special residential courses. F/P Livery. Schooling. Breaking. Career students taken - residential student accomodation available.
Member of Association of British Riding Schools

Massarella School of Riding
Thurcroft Hall, Brookhouse, Laughton, Sheffield, South Yorkshire, S31 9YO.
Tel: 0909 566429
Proprietor: Mr Massarella & Miss Liggins
Horses: 10 **Ponies:** 15

Millview Equestrian Centre
Mark Lane, Fulwood, Sheffield, South Yorkshire, S10 4PY.
Tel: 0742 305093
Proprietor: Mrs H M Greenwood
Horses: 6 **Ponies:** 9
Facilities available: Men /X-C Jumps/Dis.R/Hkg - Edge of Peak District.
Level: Teaching Standards: BHS Stage Exams.
Specialisation: RDA Long Distance Riding.
Other details: P/Livery. Schooling. Saddlery shop. Tuition in Riding and Road Safety and Stable management
Member of Association of British Riding Schools

Parklands Riding School Limited
Worksop Road, Aston, Sheffield, South Yorkshire, S31 0AD.
Proprietor: Mrs R Sampson

Rockingham House Farm Riding Centre

Upper Haugh, Rawmarsh, Rotherham, South Yorkshire, S62 7DP.
Tel: 0709 524045
Proprietor: Mrs J E Lindsey
Horses: 4 **Ponies:** 8
Facilities available: Ind.Sch /Dis.R/Hkg - Edge of a green belt.
Level: Teaching Standards: Various standards.
Specialisation: Improving young horses RDA (winner NAT Dressage Champs).
Other details: F/Livery. Schooling. Divided classes. Evening classes.
Member of Association of British Riding Schools

Stubley Hollow Riding Centre

Stubley Hollow, Dronfield, Woodhouse, Nr. Sheffield, South Yorkshire.
Tel: 0246 4192076
Proprietor: Mr & Mrs E H Mosley
Horses: 11 **Ponies:** 17
Facilities available: Ind.Sch /Men(F.Lt)/X-C/Hkg - Moorland
Level: Teaching standards to: ABRS test no.9. Students to BHS Stage 1-3 and BHS Preliminary Teaching.
Specialisation: Picnic rides in the summer months.
Other details: Lecture room. DIY/F Livery. Schooling. Breaking. Hunting. Tuition in driving. Evening classes. Special residential courses.
Member of Association of British Riding Schools

Staffordshire

Action Youth

P O Box 221, Stoke-on-Trent, Staffordshire.
Tel: 0782 262032
Member of Association of British Riding Schools

Dale School of Equitation

White House Farm, Bradley, Stafford, Staffordshire, ST18 9EA.
Proprietor: Miss H Kesson

Endon Riding School

Coltslow Farm, Stanley Moss Lane, Stockton Brook, Stoke-on- Trent, Staffordshire, ST9 9LR.
Tel: 0782 502114
Proprietor: Mr A Asplin & Mr D Machin
Horses: 15 **Ponies:** 10
Facilities available: Ind.Sch /Men/J.Pd/X-C/Dis.R/Hkg
Level: Teaching standards to: BHSAI.
Specialisation: Weekend Holidays.
Other details: Career students taken. Evening classes. Examination/Assessment centre. Career students taken.
Member of Association of British Riding Schools

Field House Equestrian Centre

Marchington, Uttoxeter, Staffordshire, ST14 8NX.
Tel: 0283 820310
Proprietor: Mrs M Snow & Miss S Snow
Horses: 24 **Ponies:** 12

Gartmore Riding School

Hall Lane, Hammerwich, Burntwood, Nr Walsall, Staffs
Tel: 054 36 6117
Proprietor: Miss T & Miss M Evans
Horses: 9 **Ponies:** 9
Facilities available: Ind.Sch /Men/J.Pd/X-C/Dis.R
Level: Teaching standards to: BHS Stages 1-3.
Specialisation: During holidays (school). Day courses. Lectures and demos.
Other details: Career students taken. Schooling. Jumping. Tuition in Eventing and Dressage. Evening classes. Brochure available. All standards. YTS.
Member of Association of British Riding Schools

Gunstone Hall Riding Centre

Whitehouse Lane, Codsall, Nr. Wolverhampton, Staffordshire, WV1 8QQ.
Tel: 09074 6693
Proprietor: Mr & Mrs Fish
Horses: 10 **Ponies:** 5
Facilities available: Ind.Sch/J.Pd/Hkg
Level: Teaching standards to: NVQ level 1. ABRS and BHS exams.
Specialisation: Regular shows on premises.
Other details: Career students taken. Liveries. Schooling. Breaking. Hunting. YTS. Novice to competitive standard.
Member of Association of British Riding Schools

Hurst Vale Riding School

Grange Road, Biddulph, Stoke-on-Trent, Staffordshire ST8 7RZ
Tel: 0782 522281
Member of Association of British Riding Schools

Ingestre Riding and Livery Stables

Ingestre, Staffordshire, ST18 0RE.
Tel: 0889 271165
Proprietor: Mr T Downes & Mr R Lovatt
Horses: 8 **Ponies:** 6
Facilities available: Ind.Sch /Men/J.Pd/X-C Jumps/Hkg
Level: Teaching standards to: BHSII/Stage 4. ABRS Grooms Diploma.
Specialisation: Dressage to advanced and Horse Trials.
Other details: Schooling. Breaking. Career students taken. YTS. Examination /Assessment Centre. Preparation of competition horses and riders.
Member of Association of British Riding Schools

Moddershall Riding School

Manor House Farm, Moddershall, Stone, Staffordshire, ST15 8TG.
Tel: 090 73 2359
Proprietor: Mr & Mrs Griffiths
Member of Association of British Riding Schools

Offley Brook Riding School

Heath House, Offley Brook, Eccleshall, Staffordshire, ST21 6HA.
Proprietor: Mrs N J Eyre-Walker

Westlands Riding Centre

Park Farm, Seabridge, Newcastle-under-Lyme, Staffordshire.
Tel: 0782 613996
Proprietor: Mr J Birch
Horses: 15 **Ponies:** 15

Westwood Riding Centre

Westwood Hall Farm, Leek, Staffordshire, ST13 8NW.
Proprietor: Mr & Mrs R Plant

Wood Farm Riding School

Wood Farm House, Gospel End, Sedgley, Staffordshire, ST15 8TG.
Tel: 0785 813919
Proprietor: Mrs S Carr
Member of Association of British Riding Schools

Suffolk

Barnby Training Centre

Church Farm, Beccles Road, Barnby, Beccles, Suffolk, NR34 7QN.
Proprietor: Mrs R Lambert

Brandon Riding Academy

Churh Farm, Church Farm Road, Brandon, Suffolk, IP27 0JB.
Tel: 0842 810089
Proprietor: Mrs Challis & Miss Challis
Horses: 1 **Ponies:** 8
Facilities available: Ind.Sch /Men(F.Lt)/J.Pd/Hkg
Level: Teaching Standards: Various standards taken.
Other details: Liveries. YTS.
Member of Association of British Riding Schools

Chimney Mill Riding School

Chimney Mill, West Stow, Bury St. Edmunds, Suffolk, IP27 0JB.
Tel: 028484 234
Proprietor: Mrs Gammell & Miss Wenn

Horses: 5 **Ponies:** 8
Facilities available: Men /J.Pd/X-C Jumps/Hkg - Woodlands.
Level: Teaching Standards: Basic.
Other details: Lecture room.
Member of Association of British Riding Schools

Kembroke Hall Riding School

Newbourn Road, Bucklesham, Nr Ipswick, Suffolk.
Tel: 03948 201
Proprietor: Mr R McAuley
Horses: 6 **Ponies:** 9
Facilities available: Ind.Sch /2 Men(F.Lt)/J.Pd/X-C Jumps /Hkg
Level: Teaching Standards: All ABRS Tests. BHS Stages 1, 2 & 3 and to BHSAI
Specialisation: Schools catered for. Instructional day courses.
Other details: P/Livery. Kiddies 1/2 hour lessons. Private lessons, group and jumping lessons. Quality horses and ponies for sale.
Member of Association of British Riding Schools

Laurels Stables

Horringer, Nr Bury St Edmunds, Suffolk.
Tel: 0284 735 281
Proprietor: Mrs A James
Facilities available: Hkg - Parkland.
Level: Teaching Standards: Dressage training available.
Specialisation: B & B. Boarding Kennels.
Other details: Season - April/December. B & B - 14 per night. Horse 6 per night. Dog - 2 per night.

Levington Equestrian Centre

Whitehouse Farm,
Levington, Ipswich, Suffolk.
Tel: 047388 342
Proprietor: Mrs S R Smith
Horses: 8 **Ponies:** 8

Millfields Riding Establishment

& Connemara Pony Stud,
Millfields, Stretchworth,
Newmarket, Suffolk,
CB8 9TR.
Tel: 063 876 210

Newton Hall Equitation Centre

Swilland, Nr. Ipswich,
Suffolk, IP6 9LP.
Tel: 0473 85 616
Proprietor: Mrs R Theobald
BHSI
Horses: 18 **Ponies:** 12
Facilities available: Ind.Sch
/Men(F.Lt)/J.Pd/X-C/Dis.R/
Hkg - Picturesque Suffolk
Countryside
Level: Teaching standards to:
BHSI. BHS stages 1-4.
Preliminary and Intermediate
Teaching. Progressive Riding
tests 1-12. Ass. Groom and
Grooms Diplomas.
Specialisation: Side-saddle.
Video and lectures.
Other details: Lecture room.
F/P Livery. Schooling.
Breaking. Hunting. Career
students taken. Lunge
lessons. Exam training.
*Member of Association of
British Riding Schools*

Pakefield Riding School

Carlton Road, Lowestoft,
Suffolk, NR32 4AA.
Tel: 0502 572257
Proprietor: Mrs Tessa Hardy
Horses: 17 **Ponies:** 14
Facilities available: Ind.Sch
/Men(F.Lt)/J.Pd/Dis.R/Hkg -
Beaches and countryside

Level: Teaching Standards:
All ages and stages. Students
to BHS stages 1-3. BHSAI.
Specialisation: Visiting
instructors. Driving for RDA
and able-bodied.
Other details: F/P Livery.
Schooling. Evening classes.
Own your own pony days.
*Member of Association of
British Riding Schools*

Poplar Park Equitation Centre

Hollesley, Woodbridge,
Suffolk, IP12 3NA.
Tel: 0394 411023
Proprietor: Mr & Mrs R
Leggett
Horses: 8 **Ponies:** 12
Facilities available: 2 X-C
/Ind.Sch/Men/J.Pd/Dis.R/Hkg
Level: Teaching standards
to: ABRS Test no. 10. BHSAI.
Specialisation: Western
riding.
Other details: Livery.
Schooling. Breaking. Hunting
- limited hire. Career
students taken. YTS.
Evening classes.
*Member of Association of
British Riding Schools*

Popples Equestrian Centre

Barrels Road, Thurston, Bury
St Edmunds, Suffolk, IP31
3SF.
Tel: 0359 31189
Proprietor: Mrs Mears & Mr
Le Bar
Horses: 10 **Ponies:** 10
Facilities available: Men
/J.Pd/Dis.R/Hkg
Level: Teaching standards
to: ABRS test no. 10. BHSAI.
Other details:
Examination/Assessment
centre. Evening classes.
Livery. Schooling. Breaking.
Hunting.
*Member of Association of
British Riding Schools*

Stoke-By-Clare Equestrian Centre

Stoke-by-Clare, Suffolk.
Tel: 0787 277266
Proprietor: Mr Reeve-Young

Tollgate Livery Centre

397 High Road, Walton,
Felixstowe, Suffolk, IP11
9QR.
Tel: 0474 564681
Proprietor: Mrs Thatcher
Number Horses/Ponies: 18
Facilities available: Ind.Sch
/Men/Hkg.
Level: Teaching Standards:
Beginners to advanced.
Other details: Tuition in
jumping and dressage.
Charges vary. F/Working
Livery. BHS exams.

Twinstead Riding School

Twinstead, Sudbury, Suffolk.
Tel: 078 729 283
Proprietor: Miss V Stebbing

Valley Farm Riding & Driving Centre

Wickham Market,
Woodridge, Suffolk, IP13
0ND.
Tel: 0728 746916
Proprietor: Mrs Ling
Horses: 5 **Ponies:** 8
Facilities available: 2
Men(F.Lt)/J.Pd/Dis.R/X-C/2
Enclosed lunging areas.
Level: Teaching standards
to: ABRS test no. 10. BHSAI.
Specialisation:
Driving-singles, pairs &
tandem. Vaulting. Horseball.
Other details: Livery.
Schooling. Breaking.
Weddings. Western riding.
Training for International
competitions in Voltige.
*Member of Association of
British Riding Schools*

Woodlands Stables (International) Ltd.

Holywell Row, Bury St Edmunds, Suffolk, IP28 8NB.
Tel: 0638 713825 **Fax:** 0638 510079
Proprietor: Mrs D B Johnstone
Horses: 5 **Ponies:** 11
Facilities available: 2 Men (F.Lt)/J.Pd/X-C/Dis.R/Hkg
Level: Teaching standards to: NVQ exams. BHS & ABRS exams. BHSII.
Specialisation: ½ yr courses in Equitation /Competition Riding
Other details: Livery. Schooling. Breaking. Hunting. Preparation for working in the Racing Industry. Specialise in Forgein students and provide English language lessons.
Member of Association of British Riding Schools

Surrey

Barnfield Riding School

Parkfields Road, Off Park Rd, Kingston, Surrey, KT2 5LL.
Tel: 01 546 3616
Proprietor: Mrs J Grayson
Horses: 6 **Ponies:** 3
Facilities available: Men(F.Lt)/Dis.R/J.Pd/Hkg.- Excellent all weather tracks.
Level: Teaching standards to: BHSAI and BHSII. BHS satges 1 & 2.
Specialisation: Group lessons - max. 4. All instructors have BHSAI or BHSII.
Other details: Pony weeks for children. Clear round jumping and dressage for clients. Stable management courses. All F/T Instructors hold First Aid Certificates. Brochure available.

Beechwood Riding School

Hillboxes Farm, Marden Park, Woldingham, Surrey, CR3 7JD.
Tel: 0883 342266
Proprietor: Miss J Garnham
Horses: 12 **Ponies:** 13
Facilities available: Ind.Sch /2 Men/J.Pd/X-C/Hkg - No casual hirings.

Oldencraig Equestrian Centre

Tandridge Lane, Lingfield, Surrey RH7 6LL
Tel: 0342 833317
Fax: 0342 835119
Proprietor: Mr B G Carlen
Number Horses/ Ponies: 15
Facilities available: Indoor/outdoor schools. Full livery. Beginners to advanced, BHS approved.

Wildwoods Riding Centre

Ebbisham Lane, Walton-on-the-Hill, Tadworth, Surrey KT20 5BH
Tel: 0737 812146
Proprietor: Mrs A C Chambers
Number Horses/Ponies: 28
Facilities available: Hacking/Riding Club/S Jumps/ X-C course/2 menages. Riding on National Trust heathlands and bridleways. All types and levels from nervous beginners to advanced dressage and show jumping.

Burstow Park Riding & Livery Centre

Antlands Lane, Horley, Surrey, CR3 7JD.
Tel: 0293 820766
Proprietor: Mr & Mrs J Skinner
Horses: 12 **Ponies:** 15
Facilities available: Ind.Sch/Men(F.Lt)/J.Pd/X-C Jumps/Dis.R
Level: Teaching standards to: BHS Stage 2.
Specialisation: Tuition in Showing, Driving and Dressage.
Other details: Livery. Schooling. Career students taken. Evening classes. YTS.
Member of Association of British Riding Schools

Bushy Park Riding School Limited

The Green, Hampton Court Road, Hampton Court, Surrey, KT8 9VW.
Proprietor: Mr & Mrs G M French

Dorking Riding School

Downs Meadow, Ranmore Road, Dorking, Surrey, RH4 1HW.
Tel: 0306 881718
Proprietor: Miss R B Fardon
Horses: 14 **Ponies:** 2
Facilities available: Ind.Sch/Hkg
Level: Teaching Standards: Students to beginners to post BHSAI. BHS Stages 1 & 2
Specialisation: All beginners taken solo until independant seat attained.
Other details: No-one under 9yrs. Groups limited to 6.
Member of Association of British Riding Schools

Ebbisham Farm Livery Stables
Ebbisham lane, Walton on the Hill, Tadworth, Surrey, KT20 7SA.
Proprietor: Mrs O J Rivett

Equus Equestrian Centre
Horton Country Park, Horton Lane , Epsom, Surrey, KT19 8PL.
Tel: 0372 743084
Fax: 0372 372543
Proprietor: D. Anderson & A Hackett-Jones
Horses: 16 **Ponies:** 6
Facilities available: Ind.Sch /Men(F.Lt)/J.Pd/X-C/Dis. R/Hkg - 36 square miles.
Level: Teaching standards to: ABRS test no. 10. All ABRS exams. BHS stages 1-4. BHSAI. BHSII. BHSI.
Specialisation: Polo for youngsters to grown-ups.
Other details: Liveries. Evening classes.
Member of Association of British Riding Schools

Farthing Down Stables
Drive Road, Coulsdon, Surrey, CR3 1HJ.
Proprietor: Mr & Mrs J Kennedy

Greenways Farm And Stables
Lower Eashing, Godalming, Surrey, GU7 2QF.
Proprietor: Mr & Mrs M Sprake

Headley Grove Riding & Livery Stables Ltd
Headley Common Road, Headley, Epsom, Surrey.
Proprietor: Mrs J Brown & Mr C Lewin

Huntersfield Farm Riding Centre
Fairlawn Road, (Off Croydon Lane), Banstead, Surrey, SM7 3AU.
Tel: 081 643 1333
Proprietor: Mr & Mrs D Horley
Horses: 17 **Ponies:** 13
Facilities available: Ind.Sch /Covered Sch/Men(F.Lt)/Hkg
Level: Teaching standards to: BHS Stage 4.
Specialisation: Children and beginners.
Other details: Livery. Schooling. Career students taken. Evening classes. All standards taken.
Member of Association of British Riding Schools

Kingston Riding Centre
38a Crescent Road, Kingston Upon Thames, Surrey.
Tel: 081 546 6361
Proprietor: J Mastroianni
Horses: 34 **Ponies:** 4

Langshot Equestrian Centre
Gracious Pond Road, Cobham, Surrey, GU24 8HJ.
Tel: 09905 6949
Proprietor: Mrs Kingsnorth & Mrs Stevenson
Member of Association of British Riding Schools

Little Brook Equestrian
East Park Lane, Newchapel, Lingfield, Surrey.
Proprietor: Mrs Rotberg & Mr & Mrs Marshall

Lower Farm Riding and Livery Stables
Stoke Road, D'Abernon, Cobham, Surrey.
Proprietor: Mr C Lewin & Mrs J Brown

Old Park Stables
Old Park Lane, Farnham, Surrey, GU9 0AN.
Proprietor: Mr J Ricketts

Oldencraig Equestrian Centre
Oldencraig Farm, Tandridge Lane, Blindley Heath, Surrey, RH7 6LL.
Proprietor: Mr & Mrs B G & Miss L Carlen

Orchard Cottage Riding Stables
Babylon Lane, Lower Kingswood, Surrey, KT20 6XA.
Tel: 0737 241311
Proprietor: Mr & Mrs P Howell & C.Brugger
Number Horses/Ponies: 20
Facilities available: Ind.Sch/J.Pd/Hkg - North downs and heathland.
Level: Teaching Standards: BHS stages 1-3.
Other details: Day courses.

Parkhurst Horse Training Facilities
Lodgelands, Bognor Road(A29), Beare Green, Dorking, Surrey.
Proprietor: Mr & Mrs P Larrigan

Partridge Stables
Partridge Lane, Newdigate, Dorking, Surrey, RH5 5EA.
Tel: 030 677 307
Proprietor: Miss Baldwin
Horses: 7 **Ponies:** 7

Priory School of Equitation
Millbridge, Frensham, Farnham, Surrey, GU10 3DP.
Tel: 025 125 4161
Proprietor: Mr & Mrs H Pays
Horses: 20 **Ponies:** 25

Facilities available: Hacking /Groups accompanied on hacks. Bridlepaths, forest & tracks

South Weylands Equestrian Centre
Esher Road, Hersham, Walton-on-Thames, Surrey, KT12 4LJ.
Tel: 0372 63010
Proprietor: Mr & Mrs P Bushnell
Horses: 12 **Ponies:** 20
Facilities available: 2 Ind.Sch /Men/J.Pd/X-C/Dis.R
Level: Teaching standards to: BHS Stage 2. Students to BHSII.
Specialisation: X-country driving course with obstacles (built to FEI standards)
Other details: Lecture room. Schooling. Breaking. All beginners on lunge. Horses/ponies broken to harness. Driving taught to good basic standard. Regular day courses for all ages. Video camera.
Member of Association of British Riding Schools

Southern Equitation Livery Centre
Frensham Lane, Wishanger Estate, Churt, Surrey, GU10 2QG.
Tel: 025 125 3461
Proprietor: T C Colgate

Stangrave Hall Stables
Bletchingley Road Godstone, Surrey, RH9 8NB.
Tel: 0883 842263
Proprietor: Mrs M G Tingley & L Reeves
Horses: 4 **Ponies:** 6
Facilities available: Ind.Sch /J.Pd/Hkg

Level: Teaching standards to: ABRS Test no. 10.
Other details: Livery. Evening classes.
Member of Association of British Riding Schools

Sylvandene Stud
Hare Lane, Blindley Heath, Surrey.
Tel: 0342 832234
Proprietor: D & M Mould
Facilities available: Show Jumping & Cross Country. Schooling

The Blindley Heath School of Equitation
Oldencraig Farm, Tandridge Lane, Blindley Heath, Surrey.
Tel: 0342 833317
Proprietor: Mrs J Tower
Horses: 6 **Ponies:** 9

The Clock Tower Riding School
Brighton Road, Kingswood, Tadworth, Surrey, KT20 6SY.
Proprietor: G B & J A Ayling-Rouse

The Diamond Centre for Handicapped Riders
Woodmansterne Road, Carshalton, Surrey.
Proprietor: Mr K Webb

The Kingston Riding Centre
38a Crescent Road, Kingston-Upon-Thames, Surrey
Proprietor: Joe Mastroianni & Ramon Osner

Triple Bar Riding Centre
Home Farm Cottage, Broadmoor, Abinger Common, Nr Dorking, Surrey.
Tel: 0306 730959

Vale Lodge Stables
Downs Lane, Off Dorking Road, Leatherhead, Surrey, KT22 8JG.
Tel: 0372 373184
Proprietor: Miss J Cooper
Number Horses/Ponies: 9
Facilities available: Men/X-C/J.Pd/Hkg - Excellent riding country.
Level: Teaching Standards: Beginners to advanced.
Other details: No one over 12 stone. F/Half livery. Tuition in jumping.

Wildwoods Riding Centre
Ebbisham Lane, Walton on the Hill, Tadworth, Surrey, KT20 5BH.
Tel: 073 781 2146
Proprietor: Mrs A Chambers
Horses: 18 **Ponies:** 5

Woldingham Equestrian Centre
Southfields Road, Woldingham, Surrey.
Proprietor: P Rodger Esq

Wyvenhoe Riding Centre Limited
Guilford Road, Little Bookham, Surrey, KT23 4HB.
Proprietor: RA Childs & JL Childs & LL Legg

Tyne & Wear

Barton Stud & School of Equitation
Middle Brunton, Newcastle-Upon-Tyne, Tyne & Wear NE3 5NA.
Proprietor: Mr L Barrass & Mrs L Barrass
Member of Association of British Riding Schools

Whittington Mill Riding Stables

Whittington Mill, Great Whittington, Newcastle-Upon-Tyne, NE19 2HU.
Proprietor: Mrs J Findeisen
Level: Teaching standards to: ABRS Test no.9. Ass. Grooms Diploma. NPS Stud Assistant. BHS Stages 1,2 & 3.
Specialisation: Children and adult day courses.
Other details: Career students taken. Examination /Assessment centre. Children and adult day courses. Brochure available. Evening classes. Novice to experienced taken.
Member of Association of British Riding Schools

Braymont Riding School

Stubbs Lane, Lower Kings-wood, Surrey, KT20 7AJ.
Tel: 07372 42935
Proprietor: T Gazzaniga
Horses: 6 **Ponies:** 6
Facilities available:
Hacking/Groups accompanied

Murton House Riding School

Murton Village, Shiremoor, Tyne & Wear, NE27 0LR.
Proprietor: Mr & Mrs S Sharp

Derwentoak Riding Centre

Hagg Farm, Rowlands Gill, Tyne and Wear, NE39 1ND.
Tel: 0207 542140
Proprietor: Mrs J Allison
Horses: 4 **Ponies:** 4
Facilities available: 2 Men(1 F.Lt)/J.Pd/X-C Jumps/Hkg - Woodland and farmland.
Level: Teaching standards to: ABRS test no. 5. Pony Management Institute Exams, theory and practical.

Other details: Working/F/P Livery. Schooling. Beginner and novice adults taken. Brochure available.
Member of Association of British Riding Schools

Warwickshire

Kimberley Riding & Livery Stables

Oakey Hill, Nr Baginton, Warkwickshire.
Tel: 0203 3020584
Proprietor: Mr T Habbits
Horses: 7 **Ponies:** 8

Pebworth Vale Equestrian Centre

Nr Dorsington, Stratford upon Avon, Warwickshire.
Tel: 0789 720505
Proprietor: R S Martindale
Number Horses/Ponies: 40

Warwick School of Riding

Guys Cliffe, Coventry Road, Warwick, Warkwickshire.
Tel: 0926 494313
Proprietor: Mrs Martinez
Horses: 23 **Ponies:** 23
Facilities available:
Men(F.Lt)/J.Pd/X-C/Dis.R/Hkg - Woodlands, bridleways and fields.
Level: Teaching Standards: Basic
Specialisation: Gymkhanas and jumping with rosettes and trophys.
Other details: F/P Livery. Schooling. Breaking. Hunting. Holidays for children throughout school leave - bring own pony or use ours.
Member of Association of British Riding Schools

British Equestrian Centre

Stoneleigh, Kenilworth, Warwickshire, CV8 2LR.
Proprietor: Mr J G Bramley

Caldecote Riding School

Anker Cottage Farm, Caldecote, Nuneaton, Warwickshire, CV10 0TN.
Tel: 0203 383103
Proprietor: Mrs Sandy Sandon
Horses: 5 **Ponies:** 7
Facilities available:
Men/J.Pd/Dis.R/Hkg
Level: Teaching standards to: ABRS test no. 8. Students to ABRS Ass. & Grooms Diploma.
Specialisation: Tuition for nervous riders and tiny tots.
Other details: Livery. Schooling. Breaking. Lunge lessons. Evening classes.
Member of Association of British Riding Schools

Carry on Stables

Rosebank, 407 Birmingham Road, Hertford Hill, Nr Warwick, Warwickshire.
Proprietor: Miss J A Cook

Castle Hill Riding School

Castle Lodge, Main Street, Brandon, Coventry, Warwickshire, CV8 3HQ.
Proprietor: Mrs P Potter

Coton Equitana

Newton Lane, Newton, Rugby, Warwickshire.
Proprietor: Mr & Mrs A Windsor

Highfield Stables Riding School

Deppers Bridge, Leaminton Spa, Warwickshire.
Proprietor: Mr & Mrs Jordan & Miss Starley

Holly Riding School

Hurley Common, Nr Altherstone, Warwickshire, CV9 2LR.
Tel: 0827 872205
Proprietor: Mr R A Brown
Horses: 7 **Ponies:** 8
Facilities available: Ind.Sch /Men/J.Pd/X-C/Hkg
Level: Teaching standards to: BHSAI.
Specialisation: Driving and harness tuition. Day courses for children.
Other details: Picnic rides in cart and on horseback pony camps. F/Livery. Schooling. Breaking. Career students taken. YTS. Evening classes
Member of Association of British Riding Schools

Kingswood School of Riding

Dalehouse Lane, Kenilworth, Warwickshire, CV8 2JZ.
Proprietor: Mrs Pauling

Moat House Farm

Ullenhall, Henley in Arden, Warwickshire.
Proprietor: Mrs P G Westwood

Pittern Hill Stables Limited

Pittern Hill, Kineton, Warwickshire, CV35 0JF.
Tel: 0926 640370
Proprietor: Mr R Philpot & Mrs P Spencer
Horses: 16 **Ponies:** 9
Facilities available: Ind.Sch /Men(F.Lt)/X-C/Dis.R/Hkg - Excellent bridleways

Level: Teaching standards to: ABRS Test no. 10. BHS Stages 1-4. BHSAI. BHSII. BHSI.
Specialisation: Leading side-saddle school in the Midlands. Tack shop.
Other details: Lecture room. P/F Livery. Schooling. Breaking. 6 side-saddle horses and saddles. Indoor show-jumping in winter. Riding Club.
Member of Association of British Riding Schools

Three Gates Equestrian Centre

Three Gates House, Fosse Way, Moreton Morrell, Warwickshire, CV35 9DE.
Tel: 0926 651946
Proprietor: Mrs L Lewis
Horses: 4 **Ponies:** 3
Facilities available: Men (F.Lt)/J.Pd/Dis.R - blind riders instructed/Hkg
Level: Teaching Standards: All ABRS standards.
Specialisation: No more than four in a group. Excellent for nervous riders.
Other details: Livery. Schooling. Breaking. Evening classes. All standards welcome.
Member of Association of British Riding Schools

Umberslade Riding School

Blunts Green Farm, Blunts Green, Nr Henley in Arden, Warwickshire.
Proprietor: P W Pettitt Esq

Warwickshire College of Agriculture

Moreton Hall, Moreton Morrell, Warwick, Warwickshire, CV35 9BL.
Tel: 0926 651 367
Proprietor: Mr R H G Suggett

Horses: 20
Facilities available: Ind.Sch/2 Men/J.Pd/X-C/Dis.R
Level: Teaching Standards: All ABRS Tests. National certificates and Diplomas. Higher National Diploma and BA degree in Horse studies.
Specialisation: Stud. Grant aided Full-time courses.
Other details: Livery. Schooling. Breaking. Career students taken. YTS. Proficient riders taken.
Member of Association of British Riding Schools

Waverley Riding School

Coventry Road, Cubbington, Leaminton Spa, Warwickshire.
Tel: 0926 22876
Proprietor: Mr & Mrs Ruyssevelt
Horses: 14 **Ponies:** 10
Facilities available: Ind.Sch /Men/X-C/Dis.R
Level: Teaching standards to: ABRS Tests to 10. BHSAI. BHS Stage 4. ABRS Ass. Grooms and Grooms Diploma.
Specialisation: Tuition in eventing and dressage.
Other details: F/P Livery. Schooling. Breaking. Hunting. Career students taken. Lecture room. Evening classes.
Member of Association of British Riding Schools

West Midlands

Bourne Vale Stables

Bourne Vale, Aldridge, Nr Walsall, West Midlands.
Tel: 021 353 7174
Proprietor: Mrs P Cooper
Horses: 9 **Ponies:** 14

Cottage Farm Stables

Illshaw Heath Road, Warings Green, Earlswood, Solihull, West Midlands, B94 6DL.
Proprietor: Mr V Perry

Four Oaks Livery & Training Stables

Hillwood Road, Four Oaks, Sutton Coldfield, West Midlands.
Tel: 021 308 7600
Proprietor: Mrs E M Coulthard
Facilities available: Ind.Sch /Men/Dis.R/Hkg
Level: Teaching standards to: ABRS Test no. 7. BHS Exams for students
Specialisation: Evening classes.
Other details: ABRS and BHS exams for students. Career students taken. Liveries. Schooling. Hunting.
Member of Association of British Riding Schools

Hole Farm, Watery Lane

Woodgate, West Midlands, B32.
Tel: 021 422 2400
Proprietor: Mr & Mrs B Adams.
Horses: 5 **Ponies:** 5
Facilities available: Men. (Olympic size)/Dis.R/Hkg - On green belt.
Level: Teaching Standards: Novice.
Specialisation: Trekking.
Other details: 1/2 Treks for beginners. Basic instruction for beginners.

Kingswood Equestrian Club

Kingswood Lodge, Country Lane, Abrighton, Nr Wolverhampton, West Midlands, WV7 3AH.
Proprietor: R Lickley Esq

Sandwell Valley Riding Centre

Wigmore Farm, Wigmore Lane, West Bromwich, West Midlands, B71 3SU.
Tel: 021 588 2103
Proprietor: Mrs M E Jones
Horses: 3 **Ponies:** 25
Facilities available: Men (F.Lt)/J.Pd/X-C/Hkg - Roads and tracks.
Level: Teaching Standards: ABRS tests. P.C Tests. BHS Riding and Road Safety test.
Specialisation: Horses/ ponies/ tack for sale. Club shows.
Other details: Lecture room. Livery. Schooling. Breaking. Evening classes.
Member of Association of British Riding Schools

Stourton Hill Stables

Bridgnorth Road, Stourton, Stourbridge, West Midlands, DY7 5BQ.
Tel: 0384 872865
Proprietor: Mrs P A Knight
Horses: 1 **Ponies:** 10
Facilities available: Men (F.Lt)/J.Pd/X-C Jumps/Hkg - Country lanes and bridleways
Level: Teaching standards to: ABRS Test no. 7. Students up to and including ABRS Ass. Grooms Certificate and BHSAI.
Specialisation: Summer camps. Day courses. Picnic rides.
Other details: Riding school for children. Brochure available. YTS places. Children 6 and over.
Member of Association of British Riding Schools

Silvretta Haflinger Stud & LDR Centre

Woodfield Lane, Romsley, Halesowen, West Midlands., B62 0LR.
Tel: 0562 710 245
Proprietor: Miss H Blair
Horses: 2 **Ponies:** 6
Facilities available: Ind.Sch /J.Pd/Hkg - National trust land.
Level: Teaching Standards: Students to BHSAI.
Specialisation: Haflinger ponies. Stallions at stud. Display team.
Other details: Livery. Schooling. Breaking. Hunting. Long distance riding - competitive trail rides and endurance.
Member of Association of British Riding Schools

West Sussex

Arundel Riding Centre

Park Place, Arundel, West Sussex.
Tel: 0903 882061
Proprietor: Mrs Joy Leggett
Horses: 16 **Ponies:** 13
Member of Association of British Riding Schools

Belmoredean Stub & Livery Stables

Little Champions Farm, Maplehurst Road, West Grinstead, West Sussex,
Proprietor: Miss L M Harnett

Bridge House Riding School

Five Oaks Road, Slinfold, Nr Horsham, West Sussex, RH20 1DL.
Tel: 0403 790163
Proprietor: Mr E Wheeler & Miss Fly
Horses: 8 **Ponies:** 11
Facilities available: Ind.Sch /Men/J.Pd/X-C/Hkg
Level: Teaching standards to: ABRS test no.8. BHSAI.
Other details: Livery. Schooling. Evening classes. Beginners to BHSAI taken.
Member of Association of British Riding Schools

Brinsbury College

North Heath, Pulborough, West Sussex, RH20 1DL.
Tel: 07982 5222
Proprietor: Mrs Anne Galloway
Horses: 30
Facilities available: Ind.Sch /Men(F.Lt)/J.Pd/X-C/Hkg
Level: Teaching Standards: Students to ABRS Ass. Grooms Diploma and Grooms Diploma.
Specialisation: No beginners. Only students taken.
Other details: YTS. Examination/Assessment centre. Livery.
Member of Association of British Riding Schools

Coldwaltham House

Nr. Pulborough, West Sussex, RH20 1LY.
Proprietor: Mrs E Esme Jack

Crabbet Park Equitation Centre

Worth, Crawley, West Sussex.
Tel: 0293 882601
Proprietor: Mr T Greenwood
Horses: 14 **Ponies:** 18

Ditchling Common Stud Riding School

Burgess Hill, West Sussex, RH15 0SE.
Tel: 04444 236678
Proprietor: P J M Dudeney
Horses: 25 **Ponies:** 15
Facilities available: 2 Ind.Sch /Men(F.Lt)/J.Pd/X-C/Dis.R/Hkg
Level: Teaching standards to: Students to BHSII.
Specialisation: Examination /Assessment Centre.

Other details: Preparation for eventing. Lecture room. Career students taken. Riding and Road Safety tests. Non-residential courses.
Member of Association of British Riding Schools

Grangefield Children's Riding School

Grangefield, Bepton, Midhurst, West Sussex, GU29 0JB.
Proprietor: Miss W Z Sugden

Naldretts Farm

Bucks Green, Nr. Horsham, West Sussex, RH12 3BU.
Proprietor: Miss V D Millwood

Pooh Corner Stables,

Goffs Park Road, Southgate, Crawley, West Sussex, RH11 8AY.
Tel: 0293 21805
Proprietor: Mrs Ann Sawyer
Horses: 5 **Ponies:** 12
Facilities available: Men (F.Lt)/J.Pd/X-C/Hkg - Forest.
Level: Teaching standards to: BHSAI.
Specialisation: Gymkhanas. Hunter trials. Picnic Rides.
Other details: Cater for all age groups. Livery. Schooling. Nervous beginners to advanced competitive riders.
Member of Association of British Riding Schools

Sands Farm Equitation Centre

Sands Farm, Warnham, Nr Horsham, West Sussex, RH12 3SQ.
Tel: 0403 52238
Proprietor: Linda Wayman
Horses: 4 **Ponies:** 2

Facilities available: Ind.Sch /Men/X-C/Hkg - Woodland and bridleways.
Level: Teaching Standards: Students to BHS stage exams from 1 to BHSII.
Specialisation: Jumping and dressage shows. Stable management courses.
Other details: F/P Livery. Schooling. Breaking. Competitions for clients
Member of Association of British Riding Schools

West Sussex College of Agriculture

Brinsbury, Pulborough, West Sussex, RH20 1DL.
Tel: 07982 3832
Proprietor: Anne Galloway
Member of Association of British Riding Schools

West Wolves Riding Centre

Ashington, West Sussex, RH20 3AY.
Proprietor: Mrs V Burton

Zara Stud and Training Centre

Highleigh Road, Sidlesham, Chichester, West Sussex, PO20 7NR.
Tel: 0243 641662
Proprietor: Mr & Mrs P Brown
Number Horses/Ponies: 6
Facilities available: Ind.Sch/Hkg
Level: Teaching Standards: All Levels.
Specialisation: Western riding.
Other details: Open all year. Excellent rates. Stud. Breaking. Re-schooling. Converting the average horse to Western riding.

West Yorkshire

Acre Cliffe Riding School

Ellar Ghyll , Bradford Road, Otley, West Yorkshire LS21 3DN.
Tel: 0943 73912
Proprietor: Mrs A Everall
Horses: 9 **Ponies:** 9
Facilities available: Ind.Sch /2 Men(F.Lt)/X-C/J.Pd/Hkg. - Semi Rural country
Level: Teaching standards to: ABRS test 10. Stable and Riding Management. BHS Stage Exams.
Specialisation: Side- saddle instruction. RDA. Stable management lectures
Other details: Monthly shows. Career students taken. Liveries. Schooling
Member of Association of British Riding Schools

Dean Hall Riding Livery Stables

Dean Hall Farm, Asquith, Morley, Leeds, West Yorkshire, LS27 9QZ.
Proprietor: Mr & Mrs D Miller

Field Bottom Riding Stables

Field Bottom Farm, Lower Shelf, Halifax, West Yorkshire.
Tel: 0422 201659
Proprietor: Mr B M Culpan
Horses: 3 **Ponies:** 5

Fly Laithe Stables

Pepper Hill, Shelf, Halifax, West Yorkshire.
Tel: 0274 886299
Proprietor: Mrs Hargreaves
Horses: 7 **Ponies:** 8
Facilities available: Men /J.Pd/X-C/Dis.R/Hkg - Hilly moorland.

Level: Teaching standards to: ABRS Diploma.
Specialisation: 'Whatever the rider wants to learn we will try to teach'.
Other details: F/P Livery. Schooling. Breaking. Lecture room. All standards.
Member of Association of British Riding Schools

Howarth Lodge Riding Centre

33 Bawtry Road, Brinsworth, Rotherham, West Yorkshire, S60 5NA.
Proprietor: Jill Davies
Member of Association of British Riding Schools

Moorside Equestrian Centre

Moorside Farm, Baildon, Shipley, West Yorkshire, BD17 6BJ.
Tel: 0274 587849
Proprietor: Mrs K Metcalfe
Horses: 11 **Ponies:** 10
Facilities available: Men (F.Lt)/J.Pd/X-C/Hkg
Level: Teaching standards to: ABRS Test no. 10. NVQ level 1. BHS Stages 1-3. BHS Preliminary Teaching.
Specialisation: BHS approved.
Other details: Examination /Assessment Centre for NVQ's. Liveries. Schooling. Breaking. Evening classes. Training on own horse or ours in show-jumping, dressage, or X-country. Lecture room.
Member of Association of British Riding Schools

Northowram Childrens Riding School

Royd Farm Hall Lane, Northowram, Halifax, HX3 7SN.
Tel: 0422 202180
Proprietor: Miss Lynn Jagger

Horses: 3 **Ponies:** 5
Facilities available: Men (F.Lt)/J.Pd/X-C/Dis.R/Hkg
Level: Teaching Standards: Basic.
Specialisation: Day courses. Picnic Rides. Birthday parties arranged.
Other details: Livery. Evening classes. B & B available on the premises.
Member of Association of British Riding Schools

Park Stables

Ewood Lane, Todmorden, West Yorkshire.
Proprietor: Mr R Miller

Raikes Hall Riding School

Raikes Lane, Tong, Bradford, West Yorkshire, BD4 0RN.
Tel: 0274 684722
Proprietor: Mrs Hanson
Horses: 25 **Ponies:** 10
Facilities available: Men(F.Lt)/J.Pd/X-C Jumps/Hkg - Rural country.
Level: Teaching standards to: Students to BHSAI.
Other details: F/Livery. Schooling. Breaking. Career students taken. Lecture room.
Member of Association of British Riding Schools

Shay Lane Stables & Saddlery

Ovenden, Halifax, West Yorkshire.
Tel: 0422 44247
Proprietor: Mr & Mrs S Yates
Horses: 6 **Ponies:** 9
Member of Association of British Riding Schools
Throstle Nest Riding School Fagley Lane, Eccleshill, Bradford, West Yorkshire, BD2 3NU.
Proprietor: Mrs B Howorth

Throstle Nest Riding School
Fagley Lane, Eccleshill,
Bradford, W Yorks BD2 3NU
Proprietor: Mrs B Howarth

Westways Riding School
The Homestead, Carr Lane,
Thorner, Leeds, West
Yorkshire, LS14 3HD.
Tel: 0532 892598
Proprietor: Miss Yolande
Catherine Beaumont
Horses: 10 **Ponies:** 20
Facilities available: 3
Men(2 F.Lt)/J.Pd/X-C/Hkg -
Rural area adjacent to Leeds
Level: Teaching standards
to: ABRS Test no. 10. ABRS
Prelim. Hores care and
Riding levels 1 & 2. BHS
Stages 1-3. ABRS Ass.
Grooms Certificate. ABRS
Grooms Diploma.
Specialisation: Traditional
Fare Shows. Christmas and
Hogmanay rides.
Other details: F/Livery.
Gymkhanas. Combined
events and Annual
Championships. Dog Fun
nights and Championships.
Summer evening classes.
Special non-residential
courses.
*Member of Association of
British Riding Schools*

Willow Royd Stables
Luddesden Foot, Halifax ,
West Yorkshire, HX2 6LG.
Tel: 0422 884095
Proprietor: Mrs J Ambler
Horses: 7 **Ponies:** 7
Facilities available: Ind.Sch
/Hkg - moorland
Level: Teaching Standards:
Basic
Other details: Livery.
Schooling. Breaking.
Evening classes
*Member of Association of
British Riding Schools*

Wiltshire

Applefield Riding School
Bourton, Nr. Swindon,
Wiltshire, SN6 8JN.
Tel: 0793 783016
Proprietor: Mr & Mrs Burton
Horses: 2 **Ponies:** 5
Facilities available:
Men(F.Lt)/J.Pd/X-C
Jumps/Hkg
Level: Teaching standards
to: ABRS test no. 10. ABRS
Weekly rider and stable
management tests.
Specialisation: Side-saddle
for all ages .
Other details:
Working/Liveries. Evening
classes during summer and
spring.
*Member of Association of
British Riding Schools*

Beech Equestrian Centre
Cortington Manor Stables,
Corton, Warminster,
Wiltshire.
Proprietor: Mr & Mrs R H
Caldecott

Brympton Riding School
Common Road , White-
parish, Nr. Salisbury,
Wiltshire.
Tel: 0794 884386
Proprietor: Mrs S A Near
Horses: 6/8 **Ponies:** 10/12
Facilities available: Men
/J.Pd/X-C Jumps/Hkg -
National Trust and Parkland.
Level: Teaching standards
to: BHS stage 3.
Specialisation: Small
children and novices. BHS
approved.

Other details: Liveries.
Schooling. Breaking.
Hunting. Evening Classes.
Divided classes.
*Member of Association of
British Riding Schools*

Equestrian Products International (UK) Ltd
Mere, Wiltshire, BA12 6LA.
Tel: 0747 860098

Hampsley Hollow Riding Centre
Heddington, Calne, Wiltshire,
SN11 0PQ.
Tel: 0380 850333
Proprietor: A Franks
Horses: 20 **Ponies:** 20
Facilities available: Ind.Sch
/Men/J.Pd/X-C/Dis.R/Hkg
Level: Teaching standards
to: ABRS test no. 10. BHSAI.
ABRS Ass. & Grooms
Diploma.
Other details: Beginners
and career students taken.
Livery.Schooling.Breaking.
Hunting.
*Member of Association of
British Riding Schools*

Heddington Wick Children's Riding School
3 Hillside, Heddington,
Caine, Wiltshire, SN11 0PH.
Tel: 0380 850796
Proprietor: Mrs I Gage
Horses: 2 **Ponies:** 12
Facilities available:
Men/Mini X-C/Dis.R/Hkg -
Downs, bridleways and
farmland.
Level: Teaching standards
to: ABRS Test no. 5.
Specialisation: Lunge
lessons. Riding and Road
safety tests taken.
*Member of Association of
British Riding Schools*

Hurdcott Livery Stables

Winterbourne Earls,
Salisbury, Wiltshire, SP4
7HR.
Tel: 0980 611276
Proprietor: Mrs C Bright
Other details: Livery only
establishment. Tack Shop.

Lacock Riding Centre

23 Bewley Lane, Lacock, Nr
Chippenham, Wiltshire,
SN15 2PM.
Proprietor: Miss L K George
*Member of Association of
British Riding Schools*

Malthouse Equestrian Centre

Bushton, Swindon, Wiltshire,
SN4 7PX.
Tel: 079373 342
Proprietor: Mr & Mrs Williams
Number Horses/Ponies: 14
Facilities available: Groups
accompanied on hacks

Pewsey Vale Riding Centre

Church Farm, Stanton St
Bernard, Malborough,
Wiltshire, SN8 4LJ.
Tel: 0672 851 400
Proprietor: Bryan Read Esq
Number Horses/Ponies: 30
Facilities available: Men
/Hkg/X-C/J.Pd
Level: Teaching standards
to: BHSII level.
Other details: Tuition in
X-country, show-jumping and
dressage. Video lessons.
Varied hacking.
F/Grass/Hunter/School
Livery.
*Member of Association of
British Riding Schools*

Stonar School

Atworth, Melksham,
Wiltshire, SN12 6LR.
Proprietor: Mrs A M C
Davies

White Horse Trekking Centre

Cleeve House, Codford,
War- minster, Wiltshire,
BA12 0JZ.
Proprietor: Mr W D Puddy

Widbrook Arabian Stud and Riding Centre

Trowbridge Road, Bradford
on Avon, Wiltshire.
Tel: 02216 2608
Proprietor: Mrs D Griggs
Horses: 14 **Ponies:** 10
Facilities available:
Ind.Sch/Men(F.Lt)/J.Pd/Dis.R/
X-C/Hkg
Level: Teaching standards
to: ABRS Ass. Grooms
Diploma. BHS Stage exams
to BHSAI.
Specialisation: Dressage
and show-jumping club,
holding comps. &
lecture/demos.
Other details: F/P Livery.
Schooling. Breaking.
Hunting. Lecture room.
Special non-residential
courses. All standards.
Career students taken.
Divided classes.
*Member of Association of
British Riding Schools*

Riding Establishments Scotland

Borders

Ferniehirst Mill Lodge
Jedburgh, Borders, TD8 6PQ.
Tel: 0835 63279
Proprietor: John & Beryl Tough
Number Horses/Ponies: 17
Facilities available: Hacking /Accompanied Groups/ Children not catered for.

Hazeldean Riding Centre
Hassendeanburn, Hawick, Borders.
Tel: 041 639 3011
Proprietor: Mr & Mrs Leslie
Horses: 6 **Ponies** 10
Facilities available: Ind.Sch /Men/X-C/J.Pd/Hkg - Good hacking country with many rights of way.
Level Teaching standards to: BHSAI. BHSII. BHSI.
Specialisation: Beginners to advanced.
Other details: Evening classes. Schooling. Breaking. Hunting. Lecture room.
Member of Association of British Riding Schools

Lumsdaine Farm Equestrian Centre
Lumsdaine Farm, Coldingham, Eyemouth, Berwickshire, Borders, TD14 5UA.
Proprietor: Mrs B Barbour

Nenthorn Stables
Nenthorn, Kelso, Borders, TD5 7RY.
Tel: 0573 2073
Proprietor: Alison Allan
Member of Association of British Riding Schools

Westertoun Farm Riding & Holiday Centre
Westruther, By Gordon, Berwickshire, Borders, TD3 6NE.
Tel: 057 84 275
Proprietor: Mr & Mrs A Isles
Number Horses/Ponies: 20
Facilities available: Men /Ind.Sch/Hkg - moorland
Level Teaching Standards: Beginners to intermediate riders.
Other details: Tuition in jumping and dressage. F/P/Hunter livery.

Central

Devon River Riding Centre
Howe Town, By Fishcross, Alloa, Central, FK10 3AN.
Proprietor: Miss J Holley

Drumbrae Riding Centre
Drumbrae Farm, Bridge of Allan, Stirlingshire, Central.
Proprietor: D McNicol

Ledard Riding Centre
Ledard Farm, Kinlochard, By Stirling, Central, FK8 3TL.
Tel: 08777 219

Myothyill Farm Riding Centre
Denny, Stirlingshire, Central, FK6 5HH.
Proprietor: Mr & Mrs Farquhar & Mrs Mowatt

Dumfries & Galloway

Barend Riding Centre
Sandyhills, By Dalbeattie, Kirkcudbrightshire, Dumfries & Galloway.
Proprietor: Mrs S Gourlay
Horses: 6 **Ponies** 10

Brighouse Bay Outdoor Activity Cntre
Brighouse Bay Holiday Park, Kirkcudbright, Dumfries & Galloway, DG6 4TS.
Tel: 05577 267
Proprietor: Mr & Mrs T C Gillespie
Horses: 3 **Ponies** 12

Rosebank Horse and Pony Centre
Bankend Road , Dumfries & Galloway, DG1 4TN.
Tel: 0387 55088
Proprietor: Mrs J Dempster
Horses: 7 **Ponies** 9

Facilities available: Men
/J.Pd/Dis.R/Hkg
Level Teaching Standards:
BHS stages 1-3. BHS
Preliminary teaching. Pony
Club Tests up to and
including 'H'.
Specialisation: Riding and
Stable management courses
and mini courses.
Other details: Career students
taken. RDA approved centre.
Examination/Assessment
Centre. Livery. Schooling.
Breaking.
*Member of Association of
British Riding Schools*

Deepwater Equitation Centre

Dalskairth, Dumfries and
Galloway, DG2 8ND.
Tel: 0387 68311
Proprietor: Mr & Mrs Slade
Horses: 8 **Ponies** 8
Facilities available: Ind.Sch
/J.Pd/Dis.R/Hkg
Level Teaching Standards:
Any standard of rider taken.
Other details: Livery.
Schooling. Breaking. Evening
classes.
*Member of Association of
British Riding Schools*

Fife

Glenrothes Riding Centre

Balgeddie Farm, Glenrothes,
Fife.
Tel: 0592 742428
Proprietor: Mr & Mrs Gilbert
Number Horses/Ponies: 20
Facilities available: Ind.Sch
/Hkg
Level Teaching Standards:
Beginners to BHSAI.
Other details: Livery.
Schooling. Breaking. One
hour hack - 7.

Lochore Meadows Riding Stables

Chapel Farm Road, Crosshill,
By Lochgelly, Fife, KY5 8LY.
Tel: 0592 861596
Proprietor: Dr Faith Anstey
BHS Int.T.
Horses: 7 **Ponies** 13
Facilities available: Ind.Sch
/J.Pd/X-C Jumps/Dis.R/Hkg -
Little or no roadwork.
Level Teaching standards
to: ABRS Test no. 7. BHS
Stage 3. Preliminary
Teaching Exam.
Specialisation: Hourly
trekking.
Other details: Livery -
working only. Career
students taken. YTS -
managing agent (ATO). BHS
Examination/Assessment
centre. Evening classes.
Brochure available. All
standards. Resident farrier.
*Member of Association of
British Riding Schools*

Shieldbank Stud Riding Centre

North Road, Saline, Fife,
KY12 9LN.
Proprietor: Mr & Mrs V F
Beasley

Grampian

Aberdeen Equestrian Training Centre

Hayfield, Hazlehead Park,
Aberdeen, Grampian AB1 8BB
Proprietor: Raymond
Strachen
Tel: 0860 409502
Fax: 0224 313834

Cathay Equestrian Centre

St Leonards Road, Forres,
Moray, Grampian.
Proprietor: Mrs M T Woolley

Grove Riding Centre

Whiterashes, Aberdeen,
Grampian, AB5 0RB.
Proprietor: Mrs E Taylor

Hayfield Equestrian Centre

Hazlehead Park, Aberdeen,
Grampian, AB1 8BB.
Tel: 0224 315703
Fax: 0224 313834
Proprietor: Mr J A Crawford
Horses: 20 **Ponies** 15
Facilities available: 2 Ind.Sch
/Men(F.Lt)/J.Pd/X-C/Dis.
R/Hkg - Varied town parkland
to forest and beaches.
Level Teaching standards
to: BHSI.
Specialisation: Side saddle.
Other details: F/P Livery.
Schooling. Breaking. Can
cater for foreign students
wishing to learn English and
ride. Evening classes.
*Member of Association of
British Riding Schools*

Hobby Holidays

Glencommon, Inchmarlo,
Banchory, Grampian.
Tel: 033 02 2628
Proprietor: Mrs Wardle

North Gellan Stables

Coull, Tarland, Grampian,
AB3 4YR.
Tel: 03398 81245
Proprietor: Mr & Mrs
Morrison
Horses: 8 **Ponies** 7
Facilities available:
Men(F.Lt)/J.Pd/X-C
Jumps/Hkg
Level Teaching standards
to: ABRS test no.10. BHS
stages 1-3. BHSAI.
Specialisation: Retailers of
Spillers & Dobson & Horrell
Feed.

Other details: Livery. Schooling. Breaking. Private and small groups. Lunge lessons. Evening classes.
Member of Association of British Riding Schools

The Grove Riding Centre
Whiterashes, Aberdeen, Grampian, AB5 0RB.
Tel: 0651 82263
Proprietor: R & E Taylor
Horses: 7 **Ponies** 13
Facilities available: Ind.Sch /J.Pd/2 X-C/Dis.R/Hkg - Little or no roadwork.
Level Teaching Standards: Novice to advanced riders.
Specialisation: Competitive dressage yard.
Other details: HQ for Gordon Dressage Group. Training centre for the British Baverian Warmblood Association. Livery. Schooling. Novice to Grand Prix Dressage.
Member of Association of British riding Schools

Tomintoul Pony Trekking Centre
Richmond Arms Hotel, Tomintoul, Ballindalloch, Bannffshire, Grampian, AB3 9ET.
Proprietor: Mr C McNiven

Highland

Attadale Trekking Centre
Attadale, Strathcarron, Highland.
Tel: 05202 385
Proprietor: Mrs A Smith
Ponies 10

Ballintean Riding Centre
Ballintean, Kincraig, Kingussie, Highland, PH21 1NX.
Tel: 05404 352
Proprietor: Miss G Henschel

Number Horses/Ponies: 10
Facilities available: Men/Hkg - Woodlands and meadows.
Level Teaching Standards: Novice to top level.
Other details: DIY/Grass/F Livery. Class lesson - £8 per hr. Private lesson - £15 per hr. Children under 12 £1 less per session.

Dores Riding Centre
Drummond Farm, Dores, Highland.
Tel: 046 375 251
Proprietor: Mrs C Cameron
Horses: 6 **Ponies** 10

Highland Riding Centre
Borlum Farm, Drumnadrochit, Inverness, Highland, IV3 6XN.
Tel: 04562 220
Proprietor: Capt & Mrs MacDonald-Haig
Horses: 12 **Ponies** 8
Facilities available: Ind.Sch/Men/J.Pd/X-C/Dis.R/H kg - Wood, parkland and hills over Loch Ness
Level Teaching Standards: Basic.
Specialisation: Riding and swimming horses in Loch Ness.
Other details: Special residential courses. Video camera. Centre is a working hill farm.
Member of Association of British Riding Schools

Killiemor Riding Centre
Aros, Isle of Mull, Highland.
Tel: 06803 302

Loch Ness Equi Centre
Drummond Farm, Dores, Inverness-shire, Highland, IV1 2TX.
Tel: 046 375251
Proprietor: Mrs Candy Cameron

Number Horses/Ponies: 15
Facilities available: Ind.Sch /Men/J.Pd/X-C/Hkg - Overlooking Loch Ness. Little road work.
Level Teaching Standards: Beginners to BHS stage 4.
Specialisation: BHS and STRA approved.
Other details: Short term full livery - 50 per week. Class and private lessons. No children under 8 yrs old. Training in eventing, show-jumping and endurance riding.

Logie Farm Riding Centre
Glenferness, Nairn, Highland, IV12 5XA.
Tel: 03095 226
Proprietor: Mrs S Hilleary
Horses: 7 **Ponies** 10
Facilities available: Men /X-C Jumps/J.Pd/Hkg - No unaccompanied rides.
Level Teaching Standards: Complete beginners to BHSII.
Other details: F/Grass Livery - from 16 per week. Schooling. Breaking.

Nethybridge Riding Centre
Nethybridge, Inverness-shire, Highland, PH25 3EB.
Tel: 047 982 693
Proprietor: Mr D N Taylor
Horses: 7 **Ponies** 3

Owenmore Stables
Altonburn Road, Nairn, Highland.
Proprietor: Miss B J Perceval

Torlundy Farm Riding Centre
By Fort William, Highland.
Tel: 0397 3015
Proprietor: Mrs Carver

Lothian

Appin Equestrian Centre
Drem, Nr North Berwick,
Lothian, EH39 5BL.
Proprietor: Mr & Mrs
Montgomery

Edinburgh & Lasswade Riding Centre
Kevock Road, Lasswade,
Lothian, EH18 1HX.
Proprietor: Mrs Beck/Mr J
Beck/Mr P Beck
Horses: 50 **Ponies** 50
Facilities available: Ind.Sch
/2 Men(F.Lt)/J.Pd/Mini X-C/
Dis.R/Hkg - Farmland and
tracks.
Level Teaching standards
to: Students to all ABRS
exams.
Specialisation: Catering for
large groups - free mini bus.
Other details: F/P Livery.
Schooling. Breaking. Hunting.
Forgeiners at reduced rates.
Tuition in dressage, show-
jumping and X-country.
Brochure available.
*Member of Association of
British Riding Schools*

Grange Riding Centre
West Calder, Lothian.
Tel: 0506 871219
Proprietor: Mrs E Knight
Horses: 5 **Ponies** 12

Houston Farm Riding School
1 Houston Mains, Broxburn,
Lothian, EH52 5HY.
Tel: 050681 351
Proprietor: Mr & Mrs Comrie
Horses: 15 **Ponies** 18
Facilities available: Ind.Sch
/Men(F.Lt)/J.Pd/X-C/Dis.
R/Hkg - Fringe of Beecraigs
country park.

Level Teaching standards
to: ABRS test no.10. BHSAI.
BHS stages. ABRS Ass. and
Grooms Diploma.
Specialisation: Working
hunter pony training. Driving
and side-saddle.
Other details: F/P Livery.
Schooling. Breaking.
Side-saddle and all aspects
of competition and driving.
*Member of Association of
British Riding Schools*

Kininmouth School of Horsemanship
Ecclesmachan, Broxburn,
Lothian, EH52 6NH.
Tel: 031 331 2545
Proprietor: C W Nixon Esq
Horses: 5 **Ponies** 9

Oatridge Agricultural College
Eccles Machan, Broxburn,
Lothian, EH52 6NH.
Tel: 0506 854387
*Member of Association of
British Riding Schools*

Silver Knowes Riding Centre
Muir House, Parkway,
Edinburgh 4, Lothian.
Tel: 031 332 7777
Horses: 15 **Ponies** 9
Facilities available: Ind.Sch
/Men/J.Pd/Dis.R/X-C Jumps
/Hkg
Level Teaching standards
to: ABRS Test no. 8.
Specialisation: Horse lease
system. Riding on Cramond
Lake. Tiny Tots lessons.
Other details: Livery. School-
ing. Breaking. Hunting.
Courses. YTS.
*Member of Association of
British Riding Schools*

Tower Farm Riding Stables
85 Liberton Drive, Edinburgh,
Lothian, EH16 6NS.
Tel: 031 664 3375
Proprietor: Mrs Judy
Forrest(BHSII (T))
Horses: 12 **Ponies** 14
Facilities available: Ind.Sch
/Men(F.Lt)/J.Pd/X-C/Dis.R/
Hkg - Excellent riding without
roadworks including views
over Edinburgh.
Level Teaching standards
to: ABRS Test No.10.
Students to BHS stages 1-3.
Riding and Road Safety.
ABRS Ass. Grooms
Diploma. BHS Progressive
tests. ABRS Weekly riders
tests.
Specialisation: Side-saddle.
Other details: Tuition in
side-saddle, dressage and
jumping. Evening classes.
Occasional special
residential courses. F/P
Livery. Schooling. Breaking.
Hunting. Lecture room.
*Member of Association of
British Riding Schools*

Veterinary Field Station
Easter Bush, Roslin, Lothian,
EH25 9RG.
Proprietor: Dr P Imlah

Weftmuir Riding Centre
Totley Wells Grange, 'Weft-
muir', Nr Winchburgh, Queens-
ferry, Lothian, EH52 7QJ.
Tel: 031 331 2990
Proprietor: Mr W J Stein
Horses: 11 **Ponies** 9

Strathclyde

Ardfern Riding Centre
Via Craobh Haven, Ardfern,
Argyll, Strathclyde, PA31 8QR.
Tel: 08525 632

Proprietor: Nigel & Lucia Boase
Number Horses/Ponies: 18
Facilities available: Men(All weather arena)
Level Teaching Standards: Western riding and British style riding. BHSII instructor available for tuition.
Specialisation: Western riding.
Other details: Hacks - 1-4 hr. Grass Livery. Schooling. Appaloosa and part-bred American Quarter horses. Stud. Lunge lessons. Wind-surfing. Canoeing. Skin-diving.

Ayrshire Equitation Centre

Castle Hill Stables, Hillfoot Road, Ayr, Strathclyde KA7 3LF.
Tel: 0292 266267
Proprietor: Mr K Galbraith
Horses: 10 **Ponies** 8
Facilities available: Men (F.Lt)/J.Pd/X-C/Hkg - Sandy beaches and country tracks.
Level Teaching standards to: BHS Stage 3. ABRS exams available.
Specialisation: Jumping. Evening classes. Carriage driving
Other details: Lecture room. Career students taken. F/P Livery. Evening classes. Tuition in jumping
Member of Association of British Riding Schools

Bowfield Riding Centre

Bowfield Riding & Country Club, Lands of Bowfield, Howwood, Renfrewshire, Strathclyde, PA9 1DB.
Tel: 050 57 5225
Proprietor: A S Campbell
Horses: 9 **Ponies** 6

Busby Equitation Centre Ltd

Wester Farm, Busby, Glasgow, Strathclyde G76 8JU.
Tel: 041 6441347
Proprietor: Mr R S Christie

Cairnhouse Trekking Centre

Cairnhouse, Blackwaterfoot, Isle of Arran, Strathclyde, K27 8EU.
Proprietor: Miss D MacAlister

Castle Riding Centre & Argyll Trail Riding

Brenfield, Loch Fyne, Ardnishaig, Argyll, Strathclyde, PA30 0ER.
Tel: 0546 3274
Proprietor: Mrs Stephens & Miss Thornburn

Corrow Trekking Centre

Failte, Lochgoilhead, Argylshire, Strathclyde.
Tel: 030 13 312
Proprietor: Mr D Campbell
Ponies 14

Dalchenna Riding Centre

Inverary, Strathclyde.
Tel: 0499 2194

Dean Castle Country Park Riding Centre

Assloss Road, Dean Castle, Country Park, Kilmarnock, Strathclyde, KA3 6BL.
Proprietor: D Hadley

Gleddoch Riding School

Gleddoch Farm, Langbank, Renfrewshire, Strathclyde.

Hazelden School of Equitation

Mearnskirk, Newton Mearns, Glasgow, Strathclyde, G77 6RR.
Proprietor: W Young Esq
Member of Association of British Riding Schools

Isle of Arran Riding Holidays

Shedock Farm, Shiskine, Isle of Arran, Strathclyde KA27 8EW.
Tel: 0770 86 472
Proprietor: Mrs G & Mrs J MacAlister
Horses: 6 **Ponies** 6
Facilities available: Men/Hkg - Beaches. Moorland. Hill. Farmland.
Level Teaching Standards: Basic instruction.
Specialisation: Hacking.
Other details: Hacks - 6.50 per hour. Trekking. All abilities catered for.

Kilmardinny Farm & Riding Establishment Ltd

Milngavie Road, Bearsdon, Glasgow, Strathclyde.
Tel: 041 942 4404
Proprietor: Mr W N Somerville

Ladyland Stables

The Stables, Ladyland, Kilbirnie, Strathclyde.
Tel: 0505 843478
Proprietor: Mrs Angela Warnock
Horses: 3 **Ponies** 4
Facilities available: Men (F.Lt)/J.Pd/Hkg
Level Teaching standards to: Students to BHSAI.
Other details: Livery. Schooling. Breaking. Career students taken. Evening classes.
Member of Association of British Riding Schools

Lanarkshire Riding Centre

Race Course Stables, Lanark, Strathclyde.
Tel: 0555 65652
Proprietor: Mrs E Taylor
Horses: 52
Facilities available: Men/J.Pd/X-C
Level Teaching Standards: Basic.
Specialisation: Licensed Resaurant.
Other details: YTS. Lunge area.
Member of Association of British Riding Schools

Lettershuna Riding Centre

Lettershuna House, Appin, Argyll, Strathclyde.
Tel: 063 173 227
Proprietor: Mr & Mrs D R Craig
Horses: 4 **Ponies** 10
Facilities available: Men/Hkg - accompanied only.
Specialisation: Approved by STRA and Ponies Association (UK).
Other details: Hacking on shoreline and hills.

Lomondside Stud & Equestrian Centre

Buchanan Home Farm, Drymen, By Glasgow, Strathclyde, G63 0HU.
Tel: 0360 60481
Proprietor: Misses E & P Rennie
Facilities available: Covered Sch.
Level Teaching Standards: All levels to BHSI.
Specialisation: Stud breeding services.
Other details: Experienced riders only. Basic/F Livery. Breaking. Schooling.

Shandon School of Equitation

Stuckenduff Farm, Shandon, Dumbartonshire, Strathclyde, G84 8NW.
Tel: 0436 820838
Proprietor: Mr B Black
Horses: 6 **Ponies** 12
Facilities available: Ind.Sch/Men/J.Pd/X-C/Dis.R/Hkg - Picturesque hill land and moors.
Level Teaching standards to: ABRS Test no. 10. BHSAI. Certificate of Horsemanship and Preliminary Teaching Grooms Diploma.
Specialisation: Instructional day rides and jumping competitions.
Other details: F/Livery. General improvement weekly riders. Evening classes. Brochure available. Riding Club base.
Member of Association of British Riding Schools

Shanter Riding Centre, Maidens

By Girvan, Strathclyde.
Tel: 0655 31636
Proprietor: Mr & Mrs Lord & Miss Young
Member of Association of British Riding Schools

The Melfort Riding Centre

Melford House, Kilmelford, By Oban, Argyll, Strathclyde, PA34 4XD.
Proprietor: C E Stott Esq

Woodfoot Riding School

Millheugh, Larkhall, Strathclyde, ML9 1QX.
Tel: 0698 881608
Proprietor: Mrs K McTear
Horses: 15 **Ponies** 10
Facilities available: Ind.Sch/Men(F.Lt)/Dis.R/Hkg

Level Teaching standards to: ABRS test no. 10.
Specialisation: Riding Club every Friday evening.
Other details: Livery. Schooling. Breaking. Tuition to Affiliated Show-jumping and Dressage. Career students taken.
Member of Association of British Riding Schools

Wrights Riding Academy

Sandhill Estate, Southwoods Road, Monkton, Strathclyde, KA9 1UP.
Tel: 0292 77979
Proprietor: Mrs M Wilson
Horses: 9 **Ponies** 10
Facilities available: Men (F.Lt)/J.Pd/X-C/Dis.R/Hkg - Wooded areas & beach riding
Level Teaching standards to: Students to BHSAI. ABRS Grooms Diploma.
Other details: F/P Livery. Hunting. Evening classes. Special residential courses.
Member of Association of British Riding Schools

Tayside

Balnakilly Riding Centre

Balnakilly Estate, Kirkmichael, Nr Pitlochry, Tayside, PH10 7NB.
Tel: 025 081 281
Proprietor: Mrs H Reid & Mrs D Main
Horses: 5 **Ponies** 3

Boreland Riding Centre

Fearnan, Lochtayside, By Aberfeldy, Perthshire, Tayside, PH15 2PG.
Tel: 08873 212
Proprietor: Mrs E M Menzies
Number Horses/Ponies: 20
Facilities available: Hkg

Level Teaching Standards: Basic instruction.
Specialisation: BHS & STRA approved.
Other details: Tuition in various riding disciplines. Trekking.

Caledonian Equestrian Centre

Pitskelly, Balbbeggie, Tayside, PH2 6AR.
Tel: 08214 426
Proprietor: Mr & Mrs J T Stuart Bruce
Horses: 8 **Ponies** 4
Facilities available: Men (F.Lt)/J.Pd/X-C/Dis.R/Hkg - Arable farmland and forest.
Level Teaching standards to: Students to ABRS Grooms. BHSAI
Specialisation: Private lessons for competition work.
Other details: F/P Livery. Schooling. Breaking. Hunting. Special residential course. Tuition in eventing, show-jumping and X-country. Young horses trained.
Member of Association of British Riding Schools

Glenfarg Riding School

Smiddyhill Farm, Glenfarg, Perth, Tayside, PH2 9NL.
Tel: 05773 262
Proprietor: Miss A M Stocks
Number Horses/Ponies: 8
Facilities available: Ind.Sch /J.Pd/Dis.R/X-C/Hkg
Level Teaching Standards: Basic instruction.

Specialisation: BHS approved.
Other details: No YTS.

Rowanlea Riding School Ltd

Westcotside, Barry, Carnoustie, Tayside, DD7 7SA.
Tel: 0382 532536
Proprietor: Mr & Mrs D Conchie
Horses: 3 **Ponies** 12

Scottish Equitation Centre

Sheriffmuir Road, Green-loaning, Dunblane, Perthshire, Tayside, FKI5 0ND.
Tel: 078 688 278
Proprietor: Mr & Mrs J A D MacFarlane

Strathearn Stables

Strathearn Hydro Ltd, Crieff, Perthshire, Tayside, PH7 3LQ.
Proprietor: Mr B Jamieson

The Gleneagles Mark Phillips Equestrian Ctre

Gleneagles Hotel, Auchterarder, Tayside, PH3 1NE.
Tel: 0764 63507
Proprietor: Capt Mark Phillips
Horses: 12 **Ponies** 8
Facilities available: 2 Ind.Sch /Men(F.Lt)/Dis.R/Hkg - Moorland
Level Teaching standards to: ABRS Test no.10. Students all BHS, RC and ABRS exams up to the FBHS.

Specialisation: Carriage driving. Vaulting. Side-saddle. Competition venue.
Other details: F/ Livery. Schooling. Breaking. Evening classes. From novice to advanced riders.
Member of Association of British Riding Schools

Tullochville Trekking Centre

Coshieville, By Aberfeldy, Tayside, PH15 2LG.
Tel: 08873 559
Proprietor: Mairi McCulloch
Horses: 2 **Ponies** 13
Facilities available: Men (F.Lt)/J.Pd/Hkg
Level Teaching standards to: ABRS test no.9.
Specialisation: Breeding and showing of Highland Ponies. Heavy horse centre.
Other details: Max. no. 6 per ride. Schooling. Breaking. Trekking and hacking all year around.
Member of Association of British Riding Schools

Whitewalls Farm Stables

Emmock Road, Dundee, Tayside.
Proprietor: Miss K Ashton

Woodlands Stables

Woodlands Road, Blairgowrie, Tayside, PH10 6LD.
Tel: 3475/4889
Proprietor: Anne Tedder
Member of Association of British riding Schools

Riding Establishments Wales

Clwyd

Haford Equestrian Centre
Hafod-y-Green, Trefnant, Denbigh, Clwyd, LL16 4UN.
Proprietor: Mrs S Cooper

Hwylfa Ddafydd Country Farm Holidays
Llysfean, Colwyn Bay, Clwyd, LL29 8TW.
Proprietor: Mrs E Jones

Peacehaven Riding Centre
Terrace Lane, Penyffordd, Nr Chester, Clwyd, CH4 0HB.
Tel: 0244 546819
Proprietor: Mr & Mrs G Williams
Number Horses/Ponies: 16
Facilities available: Men/ J.Pd/Hkg
Level: Teaching Standards: All ages and stages.
Other details: Tuition by BHSAI and BHSI. Exam training.

Ruthin Riding Centre
Cae Coch Farm, Ruthin, Clwyd, LL15 2YE.
Tel: 08242 2470
Proprietor: Mr & Mrs B Dewhurst
Member of Association of British Riding Schools

The Equestrian Centre
Caeau Farm, Gresford Road, Hope, Wrexham, Clwyd, LL12 9SD.
Tel: 0978 761349
Proprietor: Mr & Mrs Tytherleigh
Member of Association of British Riding Schools

The Golden Pheasant Riding Centre
Tay-Y-Garth, Glyn Cririog, Nr Llangollen, Clwyd.
Tel: 069172 408
Proprietor: Mrs J Rushworth
Number Horses/Ponies: 22
Facilities available: Men/ Hkg - Open moorland, forest.
Level: Teaching Standards: Novce to BHSAI.
Other details: Riding wear available. Coffee shop.

Dyfed

4 K's Riding Centre
Rhydyfallen Ganol, Rhycymeron, Llandeilo, Dyfed, SA19 7RS.
Tel: 05585 479
Proprietor: G J & D E Kemsley
Number Horses/Ponies: 14
Facilities available: Hacking on accompanied groups. Children not catered for.
Member of Association of British Riding Schools

Blue Well Riding Centre
Ffynnonlas, Llanllwni, Nr Pencader, Dyfed, SA39 9AY.
Tel: 026 789 274
Proprietor: Major & Mrs J B Gibbins
Horses: 1 **Ponies:** 13
Member of Association of British Riding Schools

Bowling Riding School
Meadow Farm, Bowling House, Rudbaxton, Haverfordwest, Pembrokeshire, Dyfed.
Tel: 043787 407
Proprietor: Mrs J Gibson & Mrs S Noott
Horses: 12 **Ponies:** 13
Member of Association of British Riding Schools

Caeiago Trekking Centre
Farmers, Llanwrda, Dyfed, SA19 8LZ.
Proprietor: Mr C Pollak & Mrs Pollak

Clyn-Du Riding Centre
Clyn-du Farm, Burry Port, Llanelli, Dyfed.
Tel: 055 46 2546
Proprietor: Mrs R Vaughan-Jones
Horses: 6 **Ponies:** 9

Derwen Stud
Ynshir, Pennant, Llanon, Dyfed , SY23 5JN.
Proprietor: Mr I J Roscoe-Lloyd

Glynhir Lodge Stables

Glynhir Road, Llandybie,
Ammanford, Dyfed.
Tel: 0269 850664
Proprietor: G. Rule
Horses: 7 **Ponies:** 12
Facilities available: Ind.Sch
/Men(F.Lt)/J.Pd/Hkg - Quiet
roads and farmland, hacking
on the Black Mountains.
Level: Teaching Standards:
BHS Stage 1 & 2
Specialisation: Training
clients on their own horses.
Other details: F/P Livery.
Schooling. Breaking.
Hunting. YTS students.
Basic dressage and jumping
tuition.
*Member of Association of
British Riding Schools*

Hendre Eynon Stables

Hendre Eynon, St David's,
Pembrokeshire, Dyfed,
SA62 6DB.
Tel: 0437 720 474
Proprietor: Mr & Mrs I A
Jamieson
Horses: 5 **Ponies:** 12

Mayeston

Cosheston, Pembroke,
Dyfed, SA72 4UQ.
Proprietor: Mrs M M
Hancock

Moelfryn Riding Centre

Bethania, Aberystwyth,
Dyfed, ST23 5NP.
Proprietor: Mr & Mrs R L
Davies

Moor Farm Riding Stables

Troopers Inn, Haverfordwest,
Dyfed.
Proprietor: Mr & Mrs D
Roscoe

Norchard Farm Riding School

Norchard Farm, Manorbier,
Tenby, Dyfed, SA70 8LD.
Tel: 083482 242
Proprietor: Mrs D H Mathias
Horses: 12 **Ponies:** 12
Facilities available: Ind.Sch
/J.Pd/X-C/Hkg - Undulating
farmland, beaches, tracks.
Level: Teaching Standards
to: ABRS test no. 1. BHSAI.
Specialisation: Trekking.
Evening Beach rides.
Other details: Livery.
*Member of Association of
British Riding Schools*

Pembrokeshire Riding Centre

Pennybridge Farm,
Hundleton, Pembroke, Dyfed.
Proprietor: Mrs S P
Scourfield
*Member of Association of
British Riding Schools*

The Dyfed Riding Centre

Maes-y-Felin, Bridell,
Cardigan, Dyfed, SA43 3DG.
Tel: 0239 612594
Proprietor: Mr Terence
Humfrey
Horses: 8 **Ponies:** 10

Towy Valley Riding Centre

Dan-y-Garn Farm,
Bethlehem, Dyfed.
Tel: 055 03 634
Proprietor: Mrs A Hooper
Horses: 10 **Ponies:** 12
Facilities available: Hacking
/Accompanied groups

Tregaron Pony Trekking Association

Tan-y-Bryn, Tregaron, Dyfed.
Tel: 097 44 364

Gwent

Earswood Riding Centre

Upper Tump Farm,
Earlswood, Chepstow,
Gwent, NP6 6AW.
Proprietor: Mr & Mrs R J
Raikes-May

Grange Pony Trekking

Capel-y-Ffin, Abergavenny,
Gwent.
Tel: 0873 82215
Proprietor: David & Mary
Griffiths
Number Horses/Ponies: 10

Trewysgoed Riding Centre

Fforest, Nr Abergavenny,
Gwent, NP7 7LW.
Tel: 0873 890296
Fax: 060072487
Proprietor: Mrs M S
Featherstonhaugh
Horses: 10 **Ponies:** 10
Facilities available: Ind.Sch
/Men/J.Pd/X-C/Dis.R/Hkg
Level: Teaching standards
to: BHSAI. ABRS Grooms
Diploma. Trek Leaders.
Specialisation: Trail rides.
Unaccompanied Childrens
Courses. Small classes.
Other details: Livery.
Schooling. Breaking. Career
students taken.
Examination/Assessment
centre. Residential courses.
Tuition in Dressage and
eventing. Mountain and
forest trekking.
*Member of Association of
British Riding Schools*

Gwynedd

Anglesey Equitation Centre Limited

Tanrallt Newydd, Bodedern, Anglesey, Gwynedd, LL64 3UE.
Proprietor: Mrs E M Manson

Cromloch Riding Centre

Tyn Y Gongl, Benllech Bay, Anglesey, Gwynedd.
Tel: 0248 853489
Proprietor: Mrs C Lomas
Number Horses/Ponies: 10

Llanddona Riding School

Llanddona, Nr Beaumaris, Anglesey, Gwynedd, LL58 8UB.
Tel: 0248 810813
Proprietor: Mrs K M Margeret
Horses: 5 **Ponies:** 11
Facilities available: Men /X-C/Hkg - Beaches and open countryside.
Level: Teaching standards to: Pony Club tests.
Other details: F/P Livery. YTS.
Member of Association of British Riding Schools

Pantiau Farm Trekking Holidays

Pantiau Farm, Rhosgadfen, Caernarfon, Gwynedd.
Tel: 0286 830002

Plas-y-Celyn Riding Centre

Ceunant, Nr Waunfawr, Caernarrfon, Gwynedd, LL55 4SA.
Proprietor: Mr & Mrs Wesemael

Rhiwiau Riding Centre

Llanfairfechan, Gwynedd,
Tel: 0248 680094
Proprietor: Miss R M & Miss S Hill
Number Horses/Ponies: 15
Facilities available: X-C/ Men/J.Pd/Hkg - Excellent countryside.
Level: Teaching Standards: Novice to experienced.
Specialisation: Western and side-saddle riding.
Other details: Picnic rides. Tuition in dressage & jumping. Stud. Video lessons. Gymkhanas arranged for clients.

Snowdonia Riding Stables

Weirglodd Fawr, Waunfawr, Caernarfon, Gwynedd, LL55 4PQ.
Tel: 028685 342
Proprietor: Mrs R Z Thomas

Ty 'N Lon Riding Centre

Llangybi, Pwllheli, Gwynedd.
Tel: 0766 618

Mid Glamorgan

Craig Fawr Livery Stables

Caerphilly, Mid Glamorgan.
Tel: 0222 883659
Proprietor: Mr & Mrs Jones & Mr Parry-Jones
Horses: 9 **Ponies:** 20

Green Meadow Riding Centre

Country Park, Aberdare, Mid Glamorgan, CF44 7PT
Tel: 0685 874961
Member of Association of British Riding Schools

Pencoed College

Pencoed, Bridgend, Mid Glamorgan, CF35 5LG
Tel: 0656 860202
Member of Association of British Riding Schools

Pengelli Fach Riding School

Pengelli Fach Farm, Pontsticil Vanor, Nr Merthyr Tydfil, Mid Glamorgan, CF48 2TU.
Tel: 0685 2169
Proprietor: Mr & Mrs C P Thomas

South Wales Equitation Centre

Heol-y-Cyw, Bridgend, Mid Glamorgan.
Proprietor: R & L Roberts

Powys

Black Mountain Riding Holidays

Peny-Bryn, Llangorse, Brecon, Powys.
Tel: 087 484 272

Camnant Centre

Camnant, Dolfor, Newtown, Powys, SY16 4BS.
Proprietor: Miss E Brooke & Miss M Coyne

Craen Riding Centre

Llanerfyl, Welshpool, Powys, SY21 0JB.
Tel: 093888 349
Proprietor: Mrs A V Wallace
Horses: 3 **Ponies::** 12

Cwmfforest Riding Centre

Pengenfford, Talgarth, Brecon, Powys, LD3 0EU.
Tel: 0874 711398
Proprietor: Michael W Turner
Horses: 1 **Ponies:** 30

Golden Castle Riding and Livery Stables

Golden Castle, Llangattock, Crickhowell, Powys
Tel: 0873 810469
Member of Association of British Riding Schools

Heart of Wales Riding School

Tyddu, Dolau, Llandrindod Wells, Powys LD1 5TD
Tel: 0597 87647
Member of Association of British Riding Schools

Llangorse Riding Centre

Gilfach Farm, Llangorse, Brecon, Powys.
Proprietor: J V M Thomas

Overland Pony Trek

Ddole Farm, Rhayader, Powys.
Tel: 0597 810 402
Proprietor: Mr H V Davies
Number Horses/Ponies: 42

Range Rides

Blaecwm, Llanwrthwl, Llandrindod Wells, Powys.
Tel: 0597 810627
Proprietor: Mr C Powell

The Lion Royal Hotel & Pony Trekking Centre

The Lion Royal Hotel, Rhayader, Powys, LD6 5AB.
Proprietor: E J & M E Collard

Tregoyd and Cadarn Riding and Trekking Centre

Tregoyd, Three Cocks, Brecon, Powys.
Proprietor: E L & D G Jones

Wern Riding Centre (Crickhowell) Limited

Llangattock Hillside, Crickhowell, Powys, NP8 1LG.
Tel: 0873 810899
Proprietor: Mr & Mrs Holland

Number Horses/Ponies: 30
Facilities available: Hkg - Excellent riding country.
Level: Teaching Standards: Basic instruction
Other details: Open April to October. Trail riding mountain and moorland. BS 4472 riding hats.

South Glamorgan

City of Cardiff Riding School

Pontcanna , Cardiff, South Glamorgan.
Tel: 0222 383908
Horses: 18 **Ponies::** 10

Down's-side Riding Centre

Sully Road, Penarth, South Glamorgan, CF6 2TY.
Tel: 0222 709719
Proprietor: M W Wilcox
Horses: 14 **Ponies::** 11
Facilities available: Ind.Sch /Dis.R/Hkg
Level: Teaching standards to: ABRS test no.10. Students trained for exams 1 & 2.
Other details: Livery. Schooling. Breaking. Evening classes (Tues. Wed. Thur.).
Member of Association of British Riding Schools

St Quentin's Stables

Llanblethian, Nr Cowbridge, South Glamorgan.
Tel: 04463 2682
Proprietor: Miss M E Northway
Member of Association of British Riding Schools

West Glamorgan

Copley Stables

Newpark Cottages, Copley, Bishopston, Swansea, W Glam
Tel: 044 128 4428
Proprietor: Mrs W P Hemns -Tucker
Horses: 3 **Ponies::** 7
Facilities available: Men (F.Lt)/J.Pd/Dis.R/X-C Jumps /Hkg - Open moor- land, wooded valleys, cliff- top bridleways, beaches
Level: Teaching standards to: ABRS Test no. 10. Students to BHSAI.
Specialisation: Tuition for beginners, side-saddle, show-jumping and dressage.
Other details: Livery. Schooling. Breaking. Brochure available. No hunting.
Member of Association of British Riding Schools

L & A Holiday & Riding Centre

Goytre, Port Talbot, W Glam
Proprietor: Mr & Mrs Holden

Pant-y-Sais Riding and Trekking Stables

Jersey Marine, Nr Swansea, West Glamorgan, SA10 6JF.
Tel: 0792 813213
Proprietor: D S Gorvett & R E Gorvett
Horses: 4 **Ponies:** 30

Par-le-Breos Trekking Centre

Parkmill, Gower, Nr Swansea, West Glamorgan, SA3 2EA.
Proprietor: Mr J Edwards

Woodlands Riding School

Vennaway Lane, Parkmill, Gower, W GlamSA3 2EA.
Proprietor: Miss T D Watts

Riding Establishments
Northern Ireland

Co Antrim

Ashfield Riding Centre
Middle Road, Islandmagee,
Larne, Co Antrim, BT40 3SL.
Tel: 096 03 73413
Proprietor: Mrs S Laird
Horses: 5 **Ponies:** 10

Galgorm Parks Riding School
112 Sand Road, Ballymena,
Co Antrim.
Tel: 0266 880269
Proprietor: Ms S R Kyle
Horses: 8 **Ponies:** 8

Co Down

Ballyknock Riding School
38 Ballyknock Road,
Hillsborough, Co Down,
BT26 6EF.
Proprietor: Miss J J Howes

East Hope Equestrian Centre
71 Killynure Road West,
Carryduff, Co Down, BT8 8EA.
Proprietor: Miss L J Adams
*Member of Association of
British Riding Schools*

Lessans Riding Stables
126 Monlough Road,
Saintfield, Co Down.
Proprietor: Miss Phillipa
Auret

Mill Bridge Riding Centre Limited
Ballystockart, Comber, Co
Down, BT23 5HZ.
Tel: 0247 872508
Proprietor: Mrs Denise Neill

Newcastle Riding Centre
35 Carnacaville Road,
Castlewellan, Co Down.
Tel: 039 67 22694
Proprietor: Mrs R & Miss E
Martin
Horses: 20 **Ponies:** 7

Co Fermanagh

Ashbrooke Riding Centre
Asbrooke, Brookeborough,
Co Fermanagh.
Tel: 036553 242
Proprietor: The Viscountess
Brookeborough
Horses: 1 **Ponies:** 2

Co Tyrone

Edergole Riding Centre
70 Moneynore Road,
Cookstown, Co Tyrone,
BT80 8PY.
Proprietor: Mr D W H Short

Moy Riding Centre
21 Killyman Street, Moy,
Dungannon, Co Tyrone,
BT71 7SJ.
Tel: 086 87 84309
Proprietor: Mrs M Corr
Horses: 7 **Ponies:** 7

Riding Holidays England

Avon

Urchinwood Manor Equitation Centre

Congresbury, Nr. Bristol, Avon, BS19 5AP.
Tel: 0934 833248
Proprietor: Capt Peter Hall & Mrs S Hall
Holiday details: Adults, children and family groups. Max. no. taken 20. All standards. Divided classes. Brochure available. See also entry under 'Riding Schools'
Member of Association of British Riding Schools

Bedfordshire

Gransden Hall Riding School

Great Gransden, Bedfordshire.
Tel: 076 77 366
Proprietor: Mrs Craze
Holiday details: Accommodation available.

Berkshire

Cane End Stables Limited

Cane End, Nr. Reading, Berkshire, RG4 9HH.
Tel: 0734 724195
Proprietor: Mr & Mrs L E Hordern
Holiday details: Holiday guests may bring own horse

Buckinghamshire

Brawlings Farm Livery Yard Ltd

Horn Hill, Chalfont St Peter, Buckinghamshire, SL9 0RE.
Tel: 02407 2132
Proprietor: Mrs S M Fairbairns
See also entry under 'Riding Schools'
Member of Association of British Riding Schools

Loughton Manor Equestrian Centre

Redland Drive, Childs Way, Loughton, Milton Keynes, Buckinghamshire, MK5 8AZ.
Tel: 0908 666434
Proprietor: Mr D R Benson
Holiday details: Children. Max.no.10. All standards.

Divided classes. Brochure available. See also entry under 'Riding Schools'
Member of Association of British Riding Schools

Snowball Farm Riding and Livery Yard Ltd

Dorney Wood Road, Burnham, Buckinghamshire.
Tel: 0628 666222
Proprietor: Mrs S Western-Kaye
Holiday details: Camp. Children. Brochure available. See also entry under 'Riding Schools'
Member of Association of British Riding Schools

Cambridgeshire

New Farm

Fox Road, Bourn, Cambridge, Cambridgeshire, CB3 7TY.
Tel: 095 44 501
Proprietor: Miss E A Pickard
Holiday details: Children. Max. no. 8-10. Divided classes. See also entry under 'Riding Schools'
Member of Association of British Riding Schools

The Windmill Stables

Shepreth Road, Barrington, Cambridgeshire, CB2 5SB.
Tel: 0223 871487
Proprietor: Mrs Susan Tydeman
Holiday details: Childrens Holiday courses in August.
See also entry under 'Riding Schools'
Member of Association of British Riding Schools

Woodhurst Riding & Livery Stables

Penny Farthing, Woodhurst, Huntingdon, Cambridgeshire, PE17 3BW.
Tel: 0487 822331
Proprietor: Margaret Benson

Oakington Riding School

High Street, Oakington, Cambridgeshire, CB45 AG.
Tel: 022023 3929
Proprietor: Miss Charlotte Jordan
Holiday details: Children. Max.no.6. Divided classes.
See also entry under 'Riding Schools'
Member of Association of British Riding Schools

Cleveland

Eston Equitation Centre

Occupation Road, Eston, Cleveland.
Proprietor: J & E Thomson
Holiday details: Children's instructional holiday courses.

Wolviston Livery and Riding School

Bradley House Farm, Durham Road, Wolviston, Billingham, Cleveland, TS22 5LP.
Tel: 0740 644692

Proprietor: Mr I F Cross & Mrs M E Cross
Holiday details: Children. All standards. Divided classes.
See also entry under 'Riding Schools'
Member of Association of British Riding Schools

Co Durham

Hamsterly Riding School

Hamsterly, Bishop Auckland, Co Durham, DL13 3NH.
Tel: 038888 328
Proprietor: Judy Dennis
Holiday details: Adult, children and family groups. Max. no.8. Brochure available. Excellent riding country. Quiet surroundings.
See also entry under 'Riding Schools'
Member of Association of British Riding Schools

Cornwall

Duchy College of Agriculture & Horticulture

Stoke Climsland, Callington, Cornwall, PL17 8PB.
Tel: 0579 70204
Proprietor: M Wharton Esq
Holiday details: Special residential courses.
See also entry under 'Riding Schools'
Member of Association of British Riding Schools

Gooseham Barton Stables

Gooseham, Morwenstow, Nr. Bude, Cornwall, EX23 9PG.
Tel: 028883 204
Proprietor: Mr R Hamilton

Holiday details: Adults, children and family groups. Excellent self-catering accommodation to sleep 4-5. Well equipped.
See also entry under 'Riding Schools'

Killiworgie Mill Riding Centre

Black Cross, Newquay, Cornwall.
Tel: 0637 880570
Proprietor: Mrs C Carne
Holiday details: Unaccompanied children 9-15 years old welcome. Holiday guests may bring own horse.

Nine Tor Riding Centre

North Hill, Launceston, Cornwall, PL15 7PE.
Tel: 056 682 232
Proprietor: Mr & Mrs Bloomfield

Old Mill Stables

Lelant Downs, Hayle, Cornwall, TR27 6LN.
Tel: 0736 753045
Proprietor: Miss Renowden & Miss Scotting
Holiday details: Adults and family groups. Brochure available. All standards.
See also entry under 'Riding Schools'
Member of Association of British Riding Schools

St Leonard's Equitation Centre

Polson, Launceston, Cornwall, PL15 9QR.
Tel: 0566 5543
Proprietor: Mr A Reeve

Sunrising Farm & Riding Centre

Henwood, Liskeard, Cornwall.
Tel: 0589 62895
Proprietor: Mrs Higgs

T M International School of Horsemanship

Henwood, Nr. Liskeard,
Cornwall, PL14 5BP.
Tel: 0579 48475
Fax: 0579 48475
Proprietor: Capt E Moore &
Miss K Tyrrell
Holiday details: Adults,
children and family groups.
Brochure available. Novice to
advanced taken. Dorm. sleeps
14. Double rooms for adults.
See also entry under 'Riding
Schools'
*Member of Association of
British Riding Schools*

Tall Trees Riding Centre

Davidstow, Camelford,
Cornwall, PL32 9XR.
Tel: 08406 249
Proprietor: Mrs M Harrison
Holiday details: Holiday
guests may bring own horse.
See also entry under 'Riding
Schools'
*Member of Association of
British Riding Schools*

Trenissick Riding Stables

Trenissick, Cubert,
Newquay, Cornwall, TR8
5PJ.
Tel: 0637 830413
Proprietor: Mrs S Yeo
Holiday details: Children.
8-16yrs. Max. no. 6. All
standards. Divided classes.
Brochure available.
See also entry under 'Riding
Schools'
*Member of Association of
British Riding Schools*

Trevillet Parc Farm Riding Centre

Tintagel, Cornwall, PL34 0HL.
Tel: 0840 770662

Trewalla Equestrian Centre

Liskeard, Cornwall.
Tel: 0579 42385
Proprietor: Mrs Phillips &
Mrs Priest

Woodlands Riding Stables

St Blazey, Par, Cornwall,
PL24 2SR.
Tel: 072 681 2963
Proprietor: Col T G Alexander
Holiday details: Holiday
guests may bring own horse.

Cumbria

Blackdyke Farm & Riding School

Blackdyke Farm, Blackford,
Carlisle, Cumbria, CA6 4EY.
Tel: 0228 74633
Proprietor: Mr & Mrs J
Collier

Grey Horse Riding Stables

Brough, Kirkbystephen,
Cumbria.
Tel: 093 04 651
Proprietor: Mr Atkinson
Holiday details: Riding hols
for all ages, unaccompanied
children from 12 years. Hotel
accomodation & camping

Holmescales Riding Centre

Holmescale, Old Hutton, Nr
Kendal, Cumbria, LA8 0NB.
Tel: 0539 729388
Proprietor: Mr & Mrs P
Jones

Holiday details: Children
only. Includes competitions,
outings and instruction.
See also entry under 'Riding
Schools'

Robin Hood Riding Centre

Robin Hood House,
Bassenthwaite, Keswick,
Cumbria.
Tel: 059681 296

Side Farm Trekking Centre

Side Farm, Patterdale,
Penrith, Cumbria, CA11 0NP.
Proprietor: Mr & Mrs
Taylforth

Wynlass Beck Stables

Lakeland Equestrian Enter-
prises, Wynlass Beck, Winder-
mere, Cumbria, LA23 1EU.
Tel: 09662 3811
Proprietor: Mrs W M Oakden
Holiday details: Adult,
children and family groups.
Brochure available. All
standards taken. Unaccom-
panied children welcome.
See also entry under 'Riding
Schools'
*Member of Association of
British Riding Schools*

Derbyshire

Alton Riding School

Alton, Chesterfield,
Derbyshire, S42 6AW.
Tel: 0246 590267
Proprietor: Mrs J D Fisher
Holiday details: Adults,
children and family groups.
Max. no. 8. Any standard.
Divided classes See also
entry under 'Riding Schools'
*Member of Association of
British Riding Schools*

Belper Riding Centre

Whitehouse Farm, Belper Lane, Belper, Derbyshire, DE5 2UJ.
Tel: 0773 824080
Proprietor: Mrs Cooke & Miss Morris
Holiday details: Adult and children. Brochure available. See also entry under 'Riding Schools'
Member of Association of British Riding Schools

Brimington Equestrian Centre

130 Manor Road, Brimington, Chesterfield, Derbyshire, SH3 1NN.
Tel: 0246 235465
Proprietor: Tracey E Priest (BHSAI)
Holiday details: Children. Max.no.8 - these are special weeks only and are camping weeks. See also entry under 'Riding Schools'
Member of Association of British Riding Schools

Causeway Farm

Plaistow Green, Crich, Nr Matlock, Derbyshire.
Tel: 0629 534248
Proprietor: Mr Bell & Mrs Bell-Heather
Holiday details: Adults, children and family groups. Any standard.
See also entry under 'Riding Schools'
Member of Association of British Riding Schools

Elvaston Castle Riding Centre

Thulston, Derby, Derbyshire, DE7 3EP.
Tel: 0332 751927
Proprietor: Mr & Mrs Coe, Mr & Mrs Anderson

Holiday details: Adults, children and family groups. Max. no. 6.(more if have own accomodation). Any standard. See also entry under 'Riding Schools'
Member of Association of British Riding Schools

Markeaton Riding Centre and Stud

Markeaton Lane, Markeaton, Derbyshire, DE3 4NH.
Tel: 0332 40126
Proprietor: Mrs V Pollard
Holiday details: Holiday guests may bring own horse.

Northfield Farm Riding & Trekking Centre

Northfield Farm, Flash, Nr. Buxton, Derbyshire, SK17 0SW.
Tel: 0298 22543
Proprietor: Mr D C & Mrs M E Andrews
Holiday details: Self catering hols. with or without riding. Excellent accom.. Any standard or age. Own horse welcome. Easy access. See also entry under 'Riding Schools'

Quarnhill School of Equitation

Addcrofts Farm, Kirk Ireton, Derbyshire.
Tel: 0335 70335
Proprietor: Mrs J Yeomans

Red House Stables Carriage Museum

Old Road, Darley Dale, Matlock, Derbyshire, DE4 2ER.
Tel: 0629 733583
Proprietor: Mrs Caroline Dale-Leech
Holiday details: Tailor made courses to suit the individual - do not include accom. and food. See also entry under 'Riding Schools'

Devon

Capton Equestrian Centre

Capton Equestrian Centre, Capton, Dartmouth, Devon, TQ6 0JE.
Tel: 080421 341
Proprietor: Mrs Shirley Davis
Holiday details: Adults, children and family groups. Max. no. 8. All standards. Divided classes. See also entry under 'Riding Schools'
Member of Association of British Riding Schools

Cheston Farm Equestrian Centre

Cheston Farm, Wrangaton, South Brent, Devon, TQ10 9HL.
Tel: 0364 73266
Proprietor: Mrs R A Cornish & Mrs M C Berry
Holiday details: Adults, children and family groups. Beginners to advanced taken. See also entry under 'Riding Schools'
Member of Association of British Riding Schools

Coombe Park Equestrian Centre

Little Hempston, Nr. Totnes, Devon, TQ9 6LW.
Tel: 0803 863473
Proprietor: Mr/Mrs Norris & Mr/Mrs Loffet
Holiday details: Adults, children and family groups. Unaccompanied children taken. Farmhouse accomodation. See also entry under 'Riding Schools'

Hillside Riding Centre

Merrivale, Princetown,
Yelverton, Devon.
Tel: 082 289 458
Proprietor: Mr & Mrs M Peck
Holiday details: Riding hols
with full board. Unaccompanied children welcome.
Holiday guests may bring
own horse.

Huxton Farm Riding Centre

Shaugh Prior, Plymouth,
Devon, PL7 5EQ.
Tel: 075 539 484
Proprietor: Mr M Norman
Holiday details: Holiday
guests may bring own horse.

Lydford House Riding Stables

Lydford, Okehampton,
Devon EX20 4AU
Tel: 082282 321
Fax: 082282 442
Proprietor: Mrs Claire Knight
Holiday details: En-suite
rooms with all facilities, avail
all year. Escorted riding on
Dartmoor. Private and class
tuition at all levels.

Lower Downstow Stables

South Brent, Devon
TQ10 9ED.
Tel: 036 47 3340
Proprietor: Mrs F Hayter &
Mr R Hayter

Manor House Riding School

Springfield House, Honiton,
Devon, EX14 8TL.
Tel: 0297 42026
Proprietor: Mrs Jill Susan
Hookings BHSAI

Holiday details: Children.
Max.no.8. All standards.
Divided classes.
See also entry under 'Riding
Schools'
*Member of Association of
British Riding Schools*

North Haye Riding Centre

North Haye, North Bovey,
Moreton Hampstead, Devon.
Tel: 064 722 304
Proprietor: Miss Gilbert

Northgate Riding School

Harepie Lane, Tawstock,
Barnstaple, Devon.
Tel: 027185 330
Proprietor: Miss R B Jones

Shilstone Rocks Stud & Trekking Centre

Widecombe-in-the-Moor,
Newton Abbot, Devon
TQ13 7TF.
Proprietor: Mr & Mrs R
Newbolt-Young

Wembury Bay Riding School

Hilltop, 83 Church Road,
Wembury, Nr. Plymouth,
Devon, PL9 0JW.
Tel: 0752 862676
Proprietor: Anne & Tony
Bearne
Holiday details: Adults,
children and family groups.
Max. no. 15. All standards.
Divided classes. Brochure
available.
See also entry under 'Riding
Schools'
*Member of Association of
British Riding Schools*

Dorset

Leigh Equestrian Centre Limited

Three Gates, Leigh,
Sherborne, Dorset, DT9 6JQ.
Tel: 096321 469
Proprietor: Mr & Mrs H
Shuaib
Holiday details: Adults and
children. Max. no. 10. All
standards. Divided classes.
See also entry under 'Riding
Schools'
*Member of Association of
British Riding Schools*

Milton Lodge Hotel

Milton-on-Stour, Gillingham,
Dorset.
Tel: 074 76 2262
Proprietor: Mr & Mrs
Roberts

Pound Farm

Pound Farm, Madjeston,
Gillingham, Dorset, SP8 5JH.
Tel: 07476 3189
Proprietor: Mr & Mrs G G
Burden
Holiday details: Children.
Max.no.6. Any level.
Brochure available. Divided
classes. See also entry
under 'Riding Schools'

Stocks Farm Equestrian Centre

Christchurch Road, West
Parley, Dorset.
Tel: 0202 570288
Proprietor: Mr & Mrs P G
Oliver
Holiday details: Adults,
children and family groups.
Must live out. See also entry
under 'Riding Schools'
*Member of Association of
British Riding Schools*

West Dorset Equestrian Centre
New Road Farm, Uploders, Bridport, Dorset.
Tel: 0308 24384
Proprietor: Mrs M Leigh

East Sussex

Ashdown Forest Riding Centre
Whitehouse Farm, Duddleswell, Nr Uckfield, East Sussex.
Tel: 082 571 2738
Proprietor: M C Inglis
Holiday details: Holiday guests may bring own horse

Brendon Riding School
Pyecombe, East Sussex.
Tel: 079 18 2158
Proprietor: Mr & Mrs C J Light
Holiday details: Holiday guests may bring own horse.

Horam Manor Riding Stables
Horam, Heathfield, East Sussex, TN21 0JD.
Tel: 043 53 2363
Proprietor: Sheila Elizabeth Guildford
Holiday details: Adults, children and family groups. Max.no.10. All standards taken. Brochure available. See also entry under 'Riding Schools'
Member of Association of British Riding Schools

Whydown Riding School
Whydown Place, Bexhill-on-Sea, East Sussex, TN39 4RA.
Tel: 04243 6279
Proprietor: Mr Preston & Miss Price

Holiday details: From next Spring when brochures will be available. See also entry under 'Riding Schools'
Member of Association of British Riding Schools

Essex

High Beech Riding School
Pynest Green Lane, Waltham Abbey, Essex, EN9 3QL.
Tel: 01 508 8866
Proprietor: A J & G J Taylor
Holiday details: Adults and children. Max.no.8. All standards. All lessons graded. Adults and children seperate. See also entry under 'Riding Schools'
Member of Association of British Riding Schools

Little Paddocks
Frating Road, Great Bromley, Colchester, Essex, CO7 7JL.
Tel: 0206 250921
Proprietor: Mr & Mrs Grant
Holiday details: Adults, children and family groups. Beginners from lead-rein upwards.
See also entry under 'Riding Schools'
Member of Association of British Riding Schools

Gloucestershire

Littledean Trekking Centre
Wellington Farm, Sutton Road, Littledean, Gloucestershire, GL14 2TU.
Tel: 0594 23955
Proprietor: Mr & Mrs T Chamberlain

Long Distance Riding Centre
Fosseway, Bourton-on-the-Water, Glos GL54 2DX.
Tel: 0451 21101
Proprietor: Miss J Davies
Holiday details: Guests may bring own horse by prior arrangement. See also entry under 'Riding Schools'
Member of Association of British Riding Schools

The Talland School of Equitation
Church Farm, Siddington, Cirencester, Glos GL7 6EZ.
Tel: 0285 652318
Fax: 0285 658859
Proprietor: Colonel & Mrs R C T Sivewright
Holiday details: Adults, children and family groups. Brochure available. Novice to advanced taken. Divided classes. See also entry under 'Riding Schools'
Member of Association of British Riding Schools

Greater Manchester

Carrington Riding Centre
Nursery Farm, Isherwood Rd, Carrington, Urmston, Greater Manchester, M31 4BH.
Tel: 061 969 5853
Proprietor: Mr B Groos
Holiday details: Adult, children and family groups. Max. no. 12. Beginners to advanced. See also entry under 'Riding Schools'
Member of Association of British Riding Schools

Hampshire

Burley Villa School of Riding
Bashley Common Road,
New Milton, Hampshire.
Tel: 0425 610278
Proprietor: Miss
Carter-Pennington

Chattis Hill Riding Centre
Chattis Hill Stables, Stock-
bridge, Hampshire.
Tel: 0264 810628
Proprietor: Mr & Mrs A G
Lambert
Holiday details: Holiday
guests may bring own horse.

Flanders Farm Riding Centre
Silver St, Hordle, Lymington,
Hampshire, SO41 6DF.
Tel: 0590 682207
Proprietor: Mrs M Rogers

Fleetwater Stud
Park Farm, Minstead,
Lyndhurst, Hampshire
SO4 7FY.
Tel: 0703 812534
Proprietor: Mrs King

Gleneagles Riding Centre
Allington Lane, West End,
Southampton, Hampshire,
SO3 3HQ.
Tel: 0703 473164
Proprietor: Mrs E H Walsh
& Miss D K Walsh
Holiday details: Adult,
children and family groups.
Max.no.10. Beginners to
BHSAI riders taken. Divided
classes. See also entry
under 'Riding Schools'
*Member of Association of
British Riding Schools*

Harroway House
Penton Mewsey, Andover,
Hampshire, SP11 0RA.
Tel: 0264 772295
Proprietor: Mrs E C Skelton
Holiday details: Chidrens
instructional holidays. Guest
may bring own horse. See also
entry under 'Riding Schools'
*Member of Association of
British Riding Schools*

Knight Bridge Riding, Training & Holiday Centre
Holiday Centre, Knight
Bridge, Sway, Lymington,
Hampshire.
Tel: 0590 682271
Proprietor: Mrs J M Harris
Holiday details: Holiday
guests may bring own horse.

Meon Valley Equestrian Centre
Swanmore Park Farm,
Upper Swanmore,
Southampton, Hampshire.
Tel: 04893 2209
Proprietor: Mrs Richley

Mopley Farm Countryside Activity Centre
Blackfield, Southampton,
Hampshire, SO4 1YH.
Tel: 0703 891616
Proprietor: Brian Tillman

Naval Riding Centre
HMS Dryad, Southwick, Nr.
Fareham, Hampshire
PO7 6EJ.
Tel: 0705 210522
Proprietor: Cdr. B W
Holden-Crawford
Holiday details: Children.
Brochure available.
Beginners to international
standard taken..
See also entry under 'Riding
Schools'
*Member of Association of
British Riding Schools*

New Forest Riding, Driving & Watersports
'The Old Barn', Dale Farm,
Manor Road, Nr.
Southampton, Hampshire,
SO4 5TJ.
Tel: 0703 843180
Proprietor: Ms Berridge
Holiday details: Adults,
children and family groups.
Max.no.8. All standards.
Brochure available.
See also entry under 'Riding
Schools'

New Park Manor Equestrian Centre and Hotel
Lyndhurst Road, Brokenhurst,
Hampshire.
Tel: 0590 23467
Fax: 0590 22268
Proprietor: Mr P Lewis &
L.Lewis (StbleMan)
Holiday details: Adult,
children and family groups.
Brochure available. Novice
to experienced taken.
See also entry under 'Riding
Schools'
*Member of Association of
British Riding Schools*

Russell Equitation Centre
Black Farm, Gaters Hill,
West End, Southampton,
Hampshire, SO3 3HT.
Tel: 0703 473693
Proprietor: Mrs C Boulton
Holiday details: Adults,
children and family groups.
Max. no. 20. Experienced
riders only. Divided classes.
See also entry under 'Riding
Schools'
*Member of Association of
British Riding Schools*

Wellington Riding Limited

Basingstoke Road, Heckfield, Basingstoke, Hampshire, RG27 0LJ.
Tel: 0734 326308
Proprietor: Mr & Mrs John Goodman
Holiday details: Holiday courses - Adults and children. Max. no. 50 residential. All standards. Divided classes. Brochure available.
See also entry under 'Riding Schools'
Member of Association of British Riding Schools

Hereford & Worcestershire

Hanburies Riding Centre

Bishops Frome, Hereford & Worcester.
Tel: 053 186 312
Proprietor: Mrs C Hyett
Holiday details: Holiday guests may bring own horse.

Lea Bailey Riding School

Lea Bailey, Ross-on-Wye, Hereford & Worcester.
Tel: 098981 360
Proprietor: Mrs J Price
Holiday details: Adults, children and family groups. Max.no.6. All Standards. Brochure available. See also entry under 'Riding Schools'
Member of Association of British Riding Schools

Moyfield Riding School

South Littleton, Evesham, Hereford & Worcester, WR11 5TR.
Tel: 0386 830207
Proprietor: Ms J Bomford

Holiday details: Adults, children and family groups. All standards taken. Brochure available. See also entry under 'Riding Schools'
Member of Association of British Riding Schools

Seechem Equestrian Centre

Rowney Green Lane, Alvechurch, Nr. Birmingham, Hereford & Worcester.
Tel: 021 445 2333
Proprietor: Mrs J Willetts
See also entry under 'Riding Schools'
Member of Association of British Riding Schools

The Avenue Riding Centre

Hanley Road, Malvern, Hereford & Worcester.
Tel: 0684 310731
Proprietor: R P & Mrs Mayhew
Holiday details: Adults. Max. no. 6. Average ability to experienced. Divided classes. Brochure available. See also entry under 'Riding Schools'
Member of Association of British Riding Schools

The Marches Equestrian College

Harewood End, Hereford, Hereford & Worcester HR2 8NG.
Tel: 0989 87234
Proprietor: Mrs Pippa Bacon
Holiday details: Adults, children and family groups. Max. No. 45 (children). All standards. Divided classes. See also entry under 'Riding Schools'
Member of Association of British Riding Schools

The Mounts Equitation Centre

Crumpsbrook, Nr Cleobury Mortimer, Nr Kidderminster, Hereford & Worcester, DY14 0HX.
Tel: 0746 632 677
Proprietor: Mr & Mrs B Linington-Payne
Holiday details: Special residential courses arranged. See also entry under 'Riding Schools'
Member of Association of British Riding Schools

Longtown Outdoor Education Centre

The Court House, Longtown, Hereford & Worcestershire.
Tel: 087 387225
Proprietor: Mr Van Laun
Holiday details: Courses in equitation, pony trekking and all outdoor activities.

Hertfordshire

Contessa Arabian and Riding Centre

Willow Tree Farm, Colliers End, Nr. Ware, Hertfordshire, SG11 1EN.
Tel: 0920 821792
Proprietor: Miss T Layton & Mr & Mrs Layton
Holiday details: Adults, children over 14 and family groups. Max. no. 6. Any standard. Dressage holiday courses. Self-catering bungalows.
See also entry under 'Riding Schools'
Member of Association of British Riding Schools

Courtlands Riding Stables
Todds Green, Stevenage,
Hertfordshire, SG1 2JE‹
Tel: 0438 313331
Proprietor: Mrs Halling &
Miss Halling
Holiday details: Children.
Max. no. 10. All standards.
Classes together and divided.
See also entry under 'Riding
Schools'
*Member of Association of
British Riding Schools*

Deanswood Equestrian Centre
Goose Lane, Little Hallingbury,
Bishop's Stortford,
Hertfordshire, CM22 7RG.
Tel: 0279 600660
Proprietor: Mr & Mrs J W
Dean
Holiday details: Children.
Max. no. 10. Summer
holiday residential courses
for children. Any standard.
Brochure available. See also
entry under 'Riding Schools'
*Member of Association of
British Riding Schools*

North Herts Equitation Centre
Norton Road,, Baldock,
Hertfordshire.
Tel: 0462892626
Proprietor: Mrs Deerness &
Miss L Deerness
Holiday details: Adults. Any
standard. Brochure
available.. See also entry
under 'Riding Schools'
*Member of Association of
British Riding Schools*

Patchetts Equestrian Centre
Hilfield Lane, Aldenham,
Watford, Hertfordshire
WD2 8DP.
Tel: 092385 2255
Proprietor: Mrs. W Hawkes

Holiday details: Adults and
children. Any standard
accepted. Divided classes.
Brochure available. See also
entry under 'Riding Schools'
*Member of Association of
British Riding Schools*

Ponsbourne Riding Centre
Newgate Street Village, Nr
Hertford, Hertfordshire.
Tel: 0707 874777
Proprietor: Mrs Godwin &
Mrs Fitzgerald
Holiday details: Adults,
children and family groups.
Max. no. 10. Divided classes.
Brochure available. See also
entry under 'Riding Schools'
*Member of Association of
British Riding Schools*

Sunnydale Cottage
Upton End Road, Shillington,
Hitchin, Hertfordshire.
Tel: 0462 711283
Proprietor: Mrs Armitage

Humberside

Bleach Yard Stables
New Walk, Beverley,
Humberside.
Tel: 0482 882557
Proprietor: Mrs Joyce Fearn
Holiday details: Children.
Max.no.25. All standards.
See also entry under 'Riding
Schools'
*Member of Association of
British Riding Schools*

North Humberside Riding Centre
Easington, Nr Hull,
Humberside, HU12 0UA.
Tel: 0964 650250
Proprietor: Mrs Toni Biglin

Holiday details: Adults and
children. Max.no. adults - 20,
children - 16. Preliminary to
advanced riders taken. See
also entry under 'Riding
Schools'
*Member of Association of
British Riding Schools*

Isle of Man

Manx Equestrian Centre
Highton Stables, Ballanard
Douglas, Isle of Man.
Tel: 0624 21852
Proprietor: Mrs J C
Britwistle.
Holiday details: Children.
All standards. See also entry
under 'Riding Schools'
*Member of Association of
British Riding Schools*

Isle of Wight

Allendale Stables
'Allendale', Godshill Ventnor,
Isle of Wight.
Tel: 0983 840258
Proprietor: Mr & Mrs G S
Allen
Holiday details: Adults,
children and family groups.
Max. no. 12. All standards.
Brochure available. See also
entry under 'Riding Schools'
*Member of Association of
British Riding Schools*

Kent

Bladbean Stud
Ekham, Nr Canterbury, Kent.
Tel: 030 384 245
Proprietor: Mrs Sewell

Blue Barn Riding Stables

Blue Barn Farm, Great Chart, Ashford, Kent, TN26 1JS.
Tel: 0233 6211863
Proprietor: Mrs S Draper
Holiday details: Adult, children and family groups. No limit on numbers. Non-residential. Any standard. See also entry under 'Riding Schools'
Member of Association of British Riding Schools

Cobham Manor Riding Centre

Water Lane, Thurnham, Kent.
Tel: 0622 38497
Proprietor: Mr & Mrs Brumer
Holiday details: Children. All standards. See also entry under 'Riding Schools'
Member of Association of British Riding Schools

Hayne Barn Riding School

Hayne Barm, Saltwood, Hythe, Kent.
Tel: 0303 265512
Proprietor: Mr I Record
Holiday details: Courses for children from the ages of 8 to 15. See also entry under 'Riding Schools'
Member of Association of British Riding Schools

Horseshoes Riding School

Dean Street, East Farleigh, Maidstone, Kent, M15 0PH.
Tel: 0622 46161
Proprietor: Mr & Mrs R Hargreaves
Holiday details: Adults, children and family groups. Max.no.12. All standards. Divided classes. See also entry under 'Riding Schools'
Member of Association of British Riding Schools

Limes Farm Equestrian Centre

Limes Farm, Pay Street, Hawkinge, Kent, CT18 7DZ.
Tel: 030389 2335
Proprietor: Miss A Berry
Holiday details: Adult, children and family groups. Max.no.12. All standards. Divided classes. Brochure available See also entry under 'Riding Schools'
Member of Association of British Riding Schools

Lynx Park

Colliers Green, Goudhurst, Cranbrook, Kent, TN17 2LR.
Tel: 0580 211020
Proprietor: Ms S K Kindersley
Holiday details: Adults. Max.no.4. Standard of riding, novice - elementary. Divided classes. Brochure available. See also entry under 'Riding Schools'
Member of Association of British Riding Schools

Oathill Farm Riding Centre

Pound Lane, Molash, Nr. Canterbury, Kent, CT4 8HQ.
Tel: 0233 74573
Proprietor: Mr A J Doree
See also entry under 'Riding Schools'

Tollgate Riding Stables

Monks Buildings, North-umberland Bottom, Wrotham Road, Gravesend, Kent.
Tel: 0474 64681
Proprietor: Miss C Curtiss & Mr W Prielepp
Holiday details: Children. Max no. 7. Any standard. Divided Classes.
See also entry under 'Riding Schools'
Member of Association of British Riding Schools

Westerham Riding Centre

Hawley Corner, Westerham Hill, Kent, TN16 2HX.
Tel: 0959 73341
Proprietor: Gp Cpt H Tudor

Lancashire

Becconsall Farm Stables.

Moss Hey Lane, Mere Brow, Tarleton, Nr. Preston, Lancashire, PR4 6LB.
Tel: 0772 813774
Proprietor: Mr & Mrs Walsh
Holiday details: Adults, childrn and family groups. Max. no. 14. All standards taken. See also entry under 'Riding Schools'
Member of Association of British Riding Schools

Douglas Farm Riding School

Bradshaw Lane, Parbold, Nr Wigan, Lancashire WN8 7NQ.
Tel: 025 76 2057
Proprietor: Miss S Barton
Holiday details: Adults and family groups. Max. no. 6. All standards. Divided classes. Brochure available. See also entry under 'Riding Schools'
Member of Association of British Riding Schools

Hollins Farm Riding School

Clerk Hill, Whally, Blackburn, Lancashire, BB6 9DR.
Tel: 025482 3135
Proprietor: Mrs M Taylor & Miss S Taylor
Holiday details: Children. Family Grps, max 8. All Standards. Divided classes
Member of Association of British Riding Schools

Longfield Stables
Middle Longfield Farm,
Todmorden, Lancashire,
OL14 6JN.
Tel: 070 681 2736
Proprietor: Miss C Farnaby
Holiday details: Children.
Max.no.5. Not suitable for
beginners.
See also entry under 'Riding
Schools'
*Member of Association of
British Riding Schools*

Northern Equitation Centre
Brookfield Lane, Aughton, Nr
Ormskirk, Lancashire.
Tel: 0695 423153
Proprietor: Mrs Mackert
Holiday details: Holiday
guests may bring own horse.
*Member of Association of
British Riding Schools*

Wrea Green Equitation Centre
Bryning Lane, Wrea Green,
Nr Kirkham, Lancs
Tel: 0772 686576
Proprietor: Miss Christine
Pollitt
Holiday details: Various
courses available. See entry
under 'Riding Schools'.

Leicestershire

Stone Lodge Equestrian Centre
Stone Lodge, Mere Lane,
Oadby, Leicestershire.
Tel: 0533 712314
Proprietor: Miss L Jones-
Fenleigh
Holiday details: Residential
courses, tailored to suit
needs.

The Wharf
Market Overton, Oakham,
Leicestershire, LE15 7PW.
Proprietor: Mrs Sturrock FBHS
See also entry under 'Riding
Schools'

Witham Villa Riding School
Cosby Road, Broughton
Ashley, Leicestershire.
Tel: 0455 282694
Proprietor: P A Cross
Holiday details: Adults.
Courses in jumping and
dressage.

Lincolnshire

Ivy Lane Riding School & Livery Stables
Ivy Lane, Coningsby,
Lincolnshire, LN4 4RY.
Tel: 0526 42461
Proprietor: Jan Phillips
Holiday details: Children.
Max. no. 6. Standards taken
- novice to test 10. See also
entry under 'Riding Schools'
*Member of Association of
British Riding Schools*

Orchard Farm
Hogsthorpe, Nr Skegness,
Lincolnshire.
Tel: 0754 72319
Proprietor: Mrs J M
Blanchard

Park Riding School & Livery Stables
Newland Street West
Lincoln, Lincolnshire, LN1 1QE.
Tel: 0522 26168
Proprietor: Mr Arthur Baker
Holiday details: Adults,
children and family groups.
All standards. See also entry
under 'Riding Schools'
*Member of Association of
British Riding Schools*

Saxilby Riding Club
High Street, Saxilby, Lincoln,
Lincolnshire, LN1 2HA.
Tel: 0522 702240
Proprietor: Mr & Mrs M J
Scott
Holiday details: Children.
Max.no.16. Only riders taken
that are of the lead-rein.
Divided classes. Brochure
available.
See also entry under 'Riding
Schools'
*Member of Association of
British Riding Schools*

London

Belmont Riding Centre
The Ridgeway, Mill Hill,
London, NW7.
Proprietor: Mr G Parsons

Civil Service Riding Club
C/O The Royal Mews,
Buckingham Palace Road,
London, SW1W 0QH.
Tel: 071 9307232
Proprietor: C E Lister
See also entry under 'Riding
Schools'
*Member of Association of
British Riding Schools*

Ross Nye's Riding Establishment
8 Bathurst Mews, Hyde Park,
London, W2 2SB.
Tel: 071 262 3791
Proprietor: R A Nye & K Nye
Holiday details: Adults and
children. Shared
accomodation. Excellent
hacking. Tuition in dressage,
show-jumping and X-country.
See also entry under 'Riding
Schools'

Merseyside

Bowlers Riding School
35 Brewery Lane, Formby, Mersyside, L37 7DY.
Tel: 0704 72915
Proprietor: Miss Mary Bowler
Holiday details: Holiday courses of 2-4 days.
See also entry under 'Riding Schools'
Member of Association of British Riding Schools

Northfield Riding Centre
Northfield Farm, Gorsey Lane, Bold, Nr St Helens, Merseyside, WA9 4SW.
Tel: 0744 816075
Fax: 0774 816018
Proprietor: Mr & Mrs Cotterill
Holiday details: Adults, children and family groups. Brochure available. Beginners to advanced taken. See also entry under 'Riding Schools'

Middlesex

Suzanne's Riding School
Brookshill Farm, Brookshill Drive, Harrow Weald, Middlesex.
Tel: 081-954 3618
Proprietor: Mrs S Marczak
Holiday details: Adults, children and family groups. Max.no.10. All standards. Brochure available. See also entry under 'Riding Schools'
Member of Association of British Riding Schools

Westway Riding School
Green Lane, Hounslow, Middlesex.
Tel: 081-570 1653
Proprietor: J E Radford Howes
Holiday details: Children and family groups. Max. no. 10. Brochure available. See also entry under 'Riding Schools'
Member of Association of British Riding Schools

Norfolk

Barnham Broom Hotel Golf & Country Club
Barnham Broom, Nr Norwich, Norfolk.
Tel: 060545 393
Holiday details: Riding & instruction arranged with Mr & Mrs Guest of Dereham Riding School.

Hockwold Lodge Riding School
Davey Lodge, Cowles Drove, Hockwold, Thetford, Norfolk, IP26 4JQ.
Tel: 0842 828376
Fax: 0842 828376
Proprietor: K M Ladell Esq
Holiday details: Adults, chidren and family groups. Brochure available. All standards welcome..
See also entry under 'Riding Schools'
Member of Association of British Riding Schools

Rectory Road Riding School
Old Rectory, Suffield, Norwich, Norfolk, NR11 7ER.
Tel: 0263 761367
Proprietor: Mrs W Garrett
Holiday details: Children. Max.no.6. All standards. Divided classes. Brochure available. See also entry under 'Riding Schools'
Member of Association of British Riding Schools

Swiss Cottage Stables & Saddlery
Swiss Cottage, West Winch, King's Lynn, Norfolk, PT33 0LZ.
Tel: 0553 760408
Proprietor: Carol Francis
Holiday details: Adult, children and family groups. Brochure available. Beginners to advanced taken. See also entry under 'Riding Schools'
Member of Association of British Riding Schools

West Runton Riding Stables
West Runton, Cromer, Norfolk, NR27 9QH.
Tel: 026375 339
Proprietor: Mrs J Bakewell
Holiday details: Holiday guests may bring own horse.
Member of Association of British Riding Schools

North Yorkshire

Beck Isle Ponies
Wells Walk, The Rookers, Pickering, North Yorkshire, YO18 7JJ.
Tel: 0751 72982
Proprietor: Mrs M Cook
Holiday details: Holiday guests may bring own horse.

Breckonborough Riding Holiday Centre

Breckonborough Farm,
Brough Park, Richmond,
North Yorkshire, Dl10 7PL.
Tel: 0748 811629
Proprietor: Messrs KA,M &
Mrs PC Acaster
Holiday details: Children and
adults and unaccompanied
children. 4hrs daily. See also
entry under 'Riding Schools'

Brownside Trekking Centre

Ravenscar, Scarborough,
North Yorkshire.
Tel: 0947 880295
Proprietor: Mrs Brechon
Holiday details: Riding
holidays for adults, families
and unaccompanied
children. Experienced and
novice riders welcome.

Farsyde Stud and Riding Stables

Farsyde House, Robin
Hood's Bay, Whitby, North
Yorkshire, YO22 4UG.
Tel: 0947 880249
Proprietor: Mr & Mrs Green
Holiday details: Holiday
guests may bring own horse.

Harrogate Equestrian Centre

Brackenthwaite Lane, Burn
Bridge, Harrogate, North
Yorkshire, HG3 1PW.
Tel: 0423 87 1894
Proprietor: Major J N D
Birtwistle
Holiday details: Adults,
children and family groups.
Brochure available. See also
entry under 'Riding Schools'
*Member of Association of
British Riding Schools*

Naburn Grange Riding Centre

Naburn Grange, Naburn,
North Yorkshire, YO1 4RU.
Tel: 090487 283
Proprietor: Mrs Della Horn
Holiday details: Adults,
children and family groups.
Full board Farmhouse
accomodation. Excellent
facilities. See also entry
under 'Riding Schools'

Snainton Riding Centre

Snainton, Nr Scarsborough,
North Yorkshire.
Tel: 0723 85218
Proprietor: Mr A Lyall & Mrs
Lyall
Holiday details: Adults and
children (accompanied only)
- B & B in village. All
standards. Divided classes.
See also entry under 'Riding
Schools'
*Member of Association of
British Riding Schools*

The York Riding School

Wiggington Road, York,
North Yorkshire, YO3 8RH.
Tel: 0904 763686
Proprietor: Mrs Holstead
BHSI
Holiday details: Adults,
children and family groups.
Brochure available. All
standards taken.
See also entry under 'Riding
Schools'
*Member of Association of
British Riding Schools*

Trew Well Hall

Gooseye, Keighley, North
Yorkshire.
Tel: 0535 603292
Proprietor: Mrs Pickles

Yafforth Equestrian Centre

Broomfield Farm, Yafforth,
Northallerton, North Yorkshire.
Tel: 0609 71671
Proprietor: Mrs S Chapman

Yorkshire Riding Centre

Markington, Harrogate, North
Yorkshire, HG3 3PE.
Tel: 0765 87207
Proprietor: Jane & Chris
Bartle
See also entry under 'Riding
Schools'

Northamptonshire

Chapman's Close Riding Establishment

Weedon Road, Nether
Heyford, Northamptonshire.
Tel: 0327 41859
Proprietor: Mrs M E Cochran
Holiday details: Holiday flat
available on farm. Pool/Trout
lake.

Holdenby Riding School

Holdenby, Northamptonshire,
NN6 8DJ.
Tel: 0604 770003
Proprietor: Mr M Watkins &
Miss T Watkins
Holiday details: Adults,
children and family groups.
Max.no.6. From beginners.
See also entry under 'Riding
Schools'
*Member of Association of
British Riding Schools*

Phoenix Stables

Brockhall Road, Flore,
Northamptonshire.
Tel: 0327 42437
Proprietor: Mrs J A Quennell
Holiday details: Holiday
tuition.

Village Farm Riding & Livery Stables
Village Farm, Preston Capes, Nr Daventry, Northamptonshire.
Tel: 032736 392
Proprietor: Mrs Rathmill
Holiday details: B & B accommodation, children welcome.

Northumberland

Border Trails
Bellingham, Hexham, Northumberland, NE48 2JE.
Tel: 0660 40335
Holiday details: Open all year, non riders welcome, golf, sailing & shooting available.

Nottinghamshire

College Farm Equestrian Centre
West Markham, Tuxford, Nr Newark, Nottinghamshire, NG22 0PN.
Tel: 0777 870886
Proprietor: Victoria Hayton
Holiday details: Adults and children(4). Novice to experienced taken. See also entry under 'Riding Schools'
Member of Association of British Riding Schools

Wellow Park Stables & Saddlery
Rufford Lane, Wellor, Newark, Nottinghamshire, NG22 0EQ.
Tel: 0623 861040
Proprietor: Mrs M Willett
Holiday details: Adults and children. All standards. Brochure available. See also entry under 'Riding Schools'
Member of Association of British Riding Schools

Oxfordshire

Heathcote House
Little Tew, Oxfordshire, OX7 4JE.
Tel: 060883 617
Proprietor: Mrs F Johnson

Turville Valley Stud Riding
Turville, Henley On Thames, Oxfordshire, RG9 6QU.
Tel: 049163 338
Proprietor: Mrs N Thurman
Holiday details: Adults and children. Beginner to advanced dressage taken. See also entry under 'Riding Schools'
Member of Association of British Riding Schools

Westfield Farm Riding Centre
Fenway, Steeple Aston, Oxfordshire, OX5 3SS.
Tel: 0869 47421
Proprietor: Mrs A Hillier
Holiday details: Adults, children and family groups. All standards. Divided clases. Brochure available. See also entry under 'Riding Schools'
Member of Association of British Riding Schools

White Horse Stables
Goosey Glebe Smallholding, Goosey, Wantage, Oxfordshire.
Tel: 03677 8806
Proprietor: Mrs Dianne Godfery
Holiday details: Children and Beginners taken. See also entry under 'Riding Schools'
Member of Association of British Riding Schools

Shropshire

Berriewood Stud Farm
Condover, Shrewsbury, Shropshire, SY5 7NN.
Tel: 074373 252
Proprietor: Mrs W Lock & Mrs P Cowdy
Holiday details: Children only. Max.no.12. Any standard. Divided classes. Brochure available. See also entry under 'Riding Schools'
Member of Association of British Riding Schools

Llanrhaedr Y M Pony Trekking Centre
Tanyffordd, Llanrhaedr Y M, Nr Oswestry, Shropshire.
Tel: 069 189 349
Proprietor: Mrs D Williams & Sons
Holiday details: Unaccompanied children welcome over 8 years. Holiday guests may bring own horse.

Somerset

Bayford Stud Farm and Training Centre
Riding Gate, Wincanton, Somerset.
Tel: 0963 32827
Proprietor: Mrs Burt
Holiday details: Adults and children. See also entry under 'Riding Schools'
Member of Association of British Riding Schools

Curland Equestrian Enterprises
Crosses Farm Stud, Curland, Taunton, Somerset, TA3 5SD.
Tel: 046 034 234
Proprietor: Mrs A L Brown
Holiday details: Holiday guests may bring own horse.

Ebborlands Farm & Riding Centre
Ebborlands Farm, Wookey Hole, Nr. Wells, Somerset, BA5 1AY.
Tel: 0749 72550
Proprietor: Mrs E A Gibbs
Holiday details: Holiday guests may bring own horse.

Gallon House
Simonsbath, Minehead, Somerset.
Proprietor: Mr & Mrs P E Hawkins

Knowle Riding Centre
Timberscombe, Minehead, Somerset, TA24 6TZ.
Tel: 064384 342
Proprietor: J & K Lamacraft
Holiday details: Adults, children and family groups. Max.no.35. All standards. Divided classes. See also entry under 'Riding Schools'
Member of Association of British Riding Schools

North Wheddon Farm
Wheddon Cross, Nr Minehead, Somerset, TA24 7EX.
Tel: 064 384 224
Proprietor: Mr Trouton

Old Stowey Farm
Wheddon Cross, Minehead, Somerset.
Tel: 064 384 268
Proprietor: Mr R Watson

Pevlings Farm Riding & Livery Stables
Cabbage Lane, Horsington, Templecombe, Somerset, BA8 0ER.
Tel: 0963 70990
Proprietor: Mr & Mrs Tytheridge
Holiday details: Children Max. No. 4. All standards. Divided classes. See also entry under 'Riding Schools'
Member of Association of British Riding Schools

Porlock Vale Equitation Centre
Porlock Ford, Nr. Minehead, Somerset, TA24 8NY.
Tel: 0643 862 338
Proprietor: Mr & Mrs P Coxhead
Holiday details: Holiday courses available, full board and B & B. See also entry under 'Riding Schools'
Member of Association of British Riding Schools

The Quantock Riding Centre
Pardlestone Farm, Kilve, Nr. Bridgwater, Somerset, TA5 1SQ.
Tel: 027 874 374
Proprietor: Mr D Houghton & Ms R Moore
Holiday details: 28 Houses, 12 Cottages all self-catering

South Yorkshire

Doe House Riding School
Bradfield Dale, Sheffield, South Yorkshire, S6 6LE.
Tel: 0742 81271
Proprietor: Mrs Grace Windle

Holiday details: Children. Max.no. 6. All standards. See also entry under 'Riding Schools'
Member of Association of British Riding Schools

Finningley School of Equitation
Finningley, Doncaster, South Yorkshire, DN9 3BU.
Tel: 0302 770259
Proprietor: Mrs Baddiley & Mrs Cartwright
Holiday details: Adult, children and family groups. Max. no. 15. Any standard. Brochure available. See also entry under 'Riding Schools'
Member of Association of British Riding Schools

Stubley Hollow Riding Centre
Stubley Hollow, Dronfield, Woodhouse, Nr. Sheffield, South Yorkshire.
Tel: 0246 4192076
Proprietor: Mr & Mrs E H Mosley
Holiday details: Children. Max.no.6. All standards. Divided classes. See also entry under 'Riding Schools'
Member of Association of British Riding Schools

Staffordshire

Endon Riding School
Coltslow Farm, Stanley Moss Lane, Stockton Brook, Stoke-on-Trent, Staffordshire, ST9 9LR.
Tel: 0782 502114
Proprietor: Mr A Asplin & Mr D Machin

Holiday details: Children and family groups during winter. Weekend holidays. Brochure available. See also entry under 'Riding Schools' *Member of Association of British Riding Schools*

Ingestre Riding and Livery Stables

Ingestre, Staffordshire, ST18 0RE.
Tel: 0889 271165
Proprietor: Mr T Downes & Mr R Lovatt
Holiday details: Children only. Novice to advanced taken. See also entry under 'Riding Schools'
Member of Association of British Riding Schools

Moorlands Trail Riding

Glenwood House Farm, Ipstones, Staffordshire.
Tel: 0583 71762
Proprietor: Miss K Rielev

Westlands Riding Centre

Park Farm, Seabridge, Newcastle-under-Lyme, Staffordshire.
Tel: 0782 613996
Proprietor: Mr J Birch

Wood Farm Riding School

Wood Farm House, Gospel End, Sedgley, Staffordshire, ST15 8TG.
Tel: 0785 813919
Proprietor: Mrs S Carr
Member of Association of British Riding Schools

Suffolk

Kembroke Hall Riding School

Newbourn Road, Bucklesham, Nr Ipswick, Suffolk.
Tel: 03948 201
Proprietor: Mr R McAuley
See also entry under 'Riding Schools'
Member of Association of British Riding Schools

Laurels Stables

Horringer, Nr Bury St Edmunds, Suffolk.
Tel: 0284 735 281
Proprietor: Mrs A James
Holiday details: DIY holiday. Bring your own horse. Hunting available. Egon Ronay Public house adjacent. Near to local Town centre.
See also entry under 'Riding Schools'

Levington Equestrian Centre

Whitehouse Farm, Levington, Ipswich, Suffolk.
Tel: 047388 342
Proprietor: Mrs S R Smith
Holiday details: Holiday guests may bring own horse.

Newton Hall Equitation Centre

Swilland, Nr. Ipswich, Suffolk, IP6 9LP.
Tel: 0473 85 616
Proprietor: Mrs R Theobald BHSI
Holiday details: Adults and children. Numbers negotiable.
See also entry under 'Riding Schools'
Member of Association of British Riding Schools

Pakefield Riding School

Carlton Road, Lowestoft, Suffolk, NR32 4AA.
Tel: 0502 572257
Proprietor: Mrs Tessa Hardy
Holiday details: Adults, children and family groups. Max.no.15. All standards. See also entry under 'Riding Schools'
Member of Association of British Riding Schools

Poplar Park Equitation Centre

Hollesley, Woodbridge, Suffolk, IP12 3NA.
Tel: 0394 411023
Proprietor: Mr & Mrs R Leggett
Holiday details: Adults and children. All standards taken. Brochure available. See also entry under 'Riding Schools'
Member of Association of British Riding Schools

Popples Equestrian Centre

Barrels Road, Thurston, Bury St Edmunds, Suffolk, IP31 3SF.
Tel: 0359 31189
Proprietor: Mrs Mears & Mr Le Bar
Holiday details: Adults, children and family groups. Brochure available. Beginners to advanced taken. See also entry under 'Riding Schools'
Member of Association of British Riding Schools

Twinstead Riding School

Twinstead, Sudbury, Suffolk.
Tel: 078 729 283
Proprietor: Miss V Stebbing

Valley Farm Riding & Driving Centre

Wickham Market, Wood-ridge, Suffolk, IP13 0ND.
Tel: 0728 746916
Proprietor: Mrs Ling
Holiday details: Adults, children and family groups. Brochure available. All standards.
See also entry under 'Riding Schools'
Member of Association of British Riding Schools

Woodlands Stables (International) Ltd

Holywell Row, Bury St Edmunds, Suffolk, IP28 8NB.
Tel: 0638 713825
Fax: 0638 510079
Proprietor: Mrs D B Johnstone
Holiday details: Adults and children. Brochure available. From novice to BSJA Grade 'A' and BHS Intermediate Eventing See also entry under 'Riding Schools'
Member of Association of British Riding Schools

Surrey

Burstow Park Riding & Livery Centre

Antlands Lane, Horley, Surrey, CR3 7JD.
Tel: 0293 820766
Proprietor: Mr & Mrs J Skinner
Holiday details: Childrens holidays. See also entry under 'Riding Schools'
Member of Association of British Riding Schools

Dorking Riding School

Downs Meadow, Ranmore Rd, Dorking, Surrey, RH4 1HW.

Tel: 0306 881718
Proprietor: Miss R B Fardon
See also entry under 'Riding Schools'
Member of Association of British Riding Schools

Equus Equestrian Centre

Horton Country Park, Horton Lane , Epsom, Surrey,
Tel: 0372 743084
Fax: 0372 372543
Proprietor: D. Anderson & a Hackett-Jones
Holiday details: Adults, children and family groups. Beginners to experienced
See also entry under 'Riding Schools'
Member of Association of British Riding Schools

Priory School of Equitation

Millbridge, Frensham, Farnham, Surrey, GU10 3DP.
Tel: 025 125 4161
Proprietor: Mr & Mrs H Pays
Holiday details: Specialist residential courses.

Southern Equitation Livery Centre

Frensham Lane, Wishanger Estate, Churt, Surrey, GU10 2QG.
Tel: 025 125 3461
Proprietor: T C Colgate

Stangrave Hall Stables, Bletchingley Road

Godstone, Surrey, RH9 8NB.
Tel: 0883 842263
Proprietor: Mrs M G Tingley & L Reeves
Holiday details: Children. Summer camp. Brochure available. Novice plus taken. See also entry under 'Riding Schools'
Member of Association of British Riding Schools

Triple Bar Riding Centre

Home Farm Cottage, Broad-moor, Abinger Common, Nr Dorking, Surrey.
Tel: 0306 730959

Wildwoods Riding Centre

Ebbisham Lane, Walton on the Hill, Surrey, KT20 5BH.
Tel: 073 781 2146
Proprietor: Mrs A Chambers

Warwickshire

Caldecote Riding School

Anker Cottage Farm, Caldecote, Nuneaton, Warcs CV10 0TN.
Tel: 0203 383103
Proprietor: Mrs S Sandon
Holiday details: Adults, children and family groups. All standards taken. See also entry under 'Riding Schools'
Member of Association of British Riding Schools

Holly Riding School

Hurley Common, Nr Alther-stone, Warks, CV9 2LR.
Tel: 0827 872205
Proprietor: Mr R A Brown
Holiday details: Children. Max.no.15. All standards. Divided classes. See also entry under 'Riding Schools'
Member of Association of British Riding Schools

Pebworth Vale Equestrian Centre

Nr Dorsington, Stratford upon Avon, Warwickshire.
Tel: 0789 720505
Proprietor: R S Martindale
Holiday details: Holiday guests may bring own horse.

Warwick School of Riding

Guys Cliffe, Coventry Road, Warwick, Warwickshire.
Tel: 0926 494313
Proprietor: Mrs Martinez
Holiday details: Adults, children and family groups. Max. no. 40. All standards. Divided classes. Brochure available. See also entry under 'Riding Schools'
Member of Association of British Riding Schools

West Midlands

Bourne Vale Stables

Bourne Vale, Aldridge, Nr Walsall, West Midlands.
Tel: 021 353 7174
Proprietor: Mrs P Cooper

Sandwell Valley Riding Centre

Wigmore Farm, Wigmore Lane, West Bromwich, West Midlands, B71 3SU.
Tel: 021 588 2103
Proprietor: Mrs M E Jones
Holiday details: Children. All standards.
See also entry under 'Riding Schools'
Member of Association of British Riding Schools

West Sussex

Crabbet Park Equitation Centre

Worth, Crawley, West Sussex.
Tel: 0293 882601
Proprietor: Mr T Greenwood
Holiday details: Holiday guests may bring own horse.

Pooh Corner Stables

Goffs Park Road, Southgate, Crawley, West Sussex, RH11 8AY.
Tel: 0293 21805
Proprietor: Mrs Ann Sawyer
Holiday details: Children. Max.no.12. Beginner to BHSAI level. See also entry under 'Riding Schools'
Member of Association of British Riding Schools

Zara Stud and Training Centre

Highleigh Road, Sidlesham, Chichester, West Sussex, PO20 7NR.
Tel: 0243 641662
Proprietor: Mr & Mrs P Brown
Holiday details: Instructional holidays. Facilities for own horse. See also entry under 'Riding Schools'

West Yorkshire

Fly Laithe Stables

Pepper Hill, Shelf, Halifax, West Yorkshire.
Tel: 0274 886299
Proprietor: Mrs Hargreaves
Holiday details: Adults, children and family groups. Max.no.15. Any standard. Brochure available. See also entry under 'Riding Schools'
Member of Association of British Riding Schools

Moorside Equestrian Centre

Moorside Farm, Baildon, Shipley, West Yorkshire, BD17 6BJ.
Tel: 0274 587849
Proprietor: Mrs K Metcalfe

Holiday details: Adults, children and family groups. Beginners to advanced. See also entry under 'Riding Schools'
Member of Association of British Riding Schools

Northowram Childrens Riding School

Royd Farm Hall Lane, Northowram, Halifax, West Yorkshire, HX3 7SN.
Tel: 0422 202180
Proprietor: Miss Lynn Jagger
Holiday details: Adults, children and family groups. All ages from 2yrs. to advanced work. See also entry under 'Riding Schools'
Member of Association of British Riding Schools

Raikes Hall Riding School

Raikes Lane, Tong, Bradford, West Yorkshire, BD4 0RN.
Tel: 0274 684722
Proprietor: Mrs Hanson
Holiday details: Adults and children. Max.no.30. All standards. See also entry under 'Riding Schools'
Member of Association of British Riding Schools

Westways Riding School

The Homestead, Carr Lane, Thorner, Leeds, West Yorkshire, LS14 3HD.
Tel: 0532 892598
Proprietor: Miss Yolande Catherine Beaumont
Holiday details: Adult, children and family groups. All non-residential. Max. no. 6-8. All standards. Divided classes. Brochure available. See also entry under 'Riding Schools'
Member of Association of British Riding Schools

Willow Royd Stables
Luddesden Foot, Halifax ,
West Yorkshire, HX2 6LG.
Tel: 0422 884095
Proprietor: Mrs J Ambler
Holiday details: Children.
Max. no. 10. - non- residential.
Divided classses. Brochure
available. See also entry
under 'Riding Schools'
*Member of Association of
British Riding Schools*

Wiltshire

**Hampsley Hollow
Riding Centre**
Heddington, Calne, Wiltshire,
SN11 0PQ.
Tel: 0380 850333
Proprietor: A Franks
Holiday details: Children.
Brochure available. See also
entry under 'Riding Schools'
*Member of Association of
British Riding Schools*

**Heddington Wick
Children's Riding School**
3 Hillside, Heddington,

Caine, Wiltshire, SN11 0PH.
Tel: 0380 850796
Proprietor: Mrs I Gage
Holiday details: Children
only. All standards. Classes
together.
*Member of Association of
British Riding Schools*

**Malthouse Equestrian
Centre**
Bushton, Swindon, Wiltshire,
SN4 7PX.
Tel: 079373 342
Proprietor: Mr & Mrs
Williams
Holiday details: Holiday
guests may bring own horse.

*Riding Holidays
Scotland*

Borders

**Bowmont Trekking
Centre**
Belford on Bowmont,
Yetholm Kelso, Borders.
Tel: 057 382 362
Proprietor: Mrs Johnson
Holiday details: Full board,
farm house accommodation.
Non-residents welcome.

Ferniehurst Mill Lodge
Jedburgh, Borders, TD8 6PQ.
Tel: 0835 63279
Proprietor: John & Beryl
Tough

Hazeldean Riding Centre
Hassendeanburn, Hawick,
Borders.
Tel: 041 639 3011

Proprietor: Mr & Mrs Leslie
See also entry under 'Riding
Schools'
*Member of Association of
British Riding Schools*

**Westertoun Farm
Riding & Holiday Centre**
Westruther, By Gordon,
Berwickshire, Borders,
TD3 6NE.
Tel: 057 84 275
Proprietor: Mr & Mrs A Isles
Holiday details:
Unaccompanied children live
in with family in Farmhouse.
7-16yrs taken. Beginners to
experienced riders. See also
entry under 'Riding Schools'

Dumfries &
Galloway

**Brighouse Bay Outdoor
Activity Cntre**
Brighouse Bay Holiday Park,
Kirkcudbright, Dumfries &
Galloway, DG6 4TS.
Tel: 05577 267
Proprietor: Mr & Mrs Gillespie

Grampian

**Hayfield Riding School
(Aberdeen) Limited**
Hazelhead Park, Aberdeen,
Grampian, AB1 8BB.
Tel: 0224 315703
Proprietor: Mr & Mrs J A
Crawford

Holiday details: Adults, chidren and family groups. All standards. Max.no.8. Divided classes. Brochure available. See also entry under 'Riding Schools'
Member of Association of British Riding Schools

Highland Horseback
Auchinandoch, Glass, By Huntley, Aberdeenshire, Grampian.
Tel: 046 685 277
Proprietor: T Montgomery

Hobby Holidays
Glencommon, Inchmarlo, Banchory, Grampian.
Tel: 033 02 2628
Proprietor: Mrs Wardle

North Gellan Stables
Coull, Tarland, Grampian, AB3 4YR.
Tel: 03398 81245
Proprietor: Mr & Mrs Morrison
Holiday details: Adults. Brochures available. All standards. See also entry under 'Riding Schools'
Member of Association of British Riding Schools

Tanarside Riding Centre
Glen Tanar, Aboyne, Aberdeenshire, Grampian.
Tel: 0339 2030
Proprietor: Miss F Chittleborough

Tomintoul Pony Trekking Centre
Richmond Arms Hotel, Tomintoul, Ballindalloch, Bannffshire, Grampian, AB3 9ET.
Proprietor: Mr C McNiven

Highland

Dores Riding Centre
Drummond Farm, Dores, Highland.
Tel: 046 375 251
Proprietor: Mrs C Cameron

Garry Gualach
Invergarry, Invernesshire, Highland.
Tel: 08092 230
Proprietor: Captain Teddy Grey
Holiday details: Instruction for unaccommpanied children from 14 years.

Highland Riding Centre
Borlum Farm, Drumnadrochit, Inverness, Highland, IV3 6XN.
Tel: 04562 220
Proprietor: Capt & Mrs MacDonald-Haig
Holiday details: Adult, children and family groups. Max.no.25. Inclusive holidays in farmhouse or self-catering cottages. See also entry under 'Riding Schools'
Member of Association of British Riding Schools

Killiemor Riding Centre
Aros, Isle of Mull, Highland.
Tel: 06803 302

Logie Farm Riding Centre
Glenferness, Nairn, Highland, IV12 5XA.
Tel: 03095 226
Proprietor: Mrs S Hilleary
Holiday details: Self- catering Farmhouse. Full board cottage. Facilities for own horse incl stables and grass. See also entry under 'Riding Schools'

Torlundy Farm Riding Centre
By Fort William, Highland.
Tel: 0397 3015
Proprietor: Mrs Carver

Lothian

Edinburgh & Lasswade Riding Centre
Kevock Road, Lasswade, Lothian, EH18 1HX.
Proprietor: Mrs Beck/Mr J Beck/Mr P Beck
Holiday details: Special residential courses by arrangement with local hotels. Any number taken with prior arrangement. All standards. See also entry under 'Riding Schools'
Member of Association of British Riding Schools

Houston Farm Riding School
1 Houston Mains, Broxburn, Lothian, EH52 5HY.
Tel: 050681 351
Proprietor: Mr & Mrs Comrie
Holiday details: Adults and children. Brochure available. See also entry under 'Riding Schools'
Member of Association of British Riding Schools

Kininmouth School of Horsemanship
Ecclesmachan, Broxburn, Lothian, EH52 6NH.
Tel: 031 331 2545
Proprietor: C W Nixon Esq

Silver Knowes Riding Centre
Muir House, Parkway, Edinburgh 4, Lothian.
Tel: 031 332 7777

Holiday details: Adults, children and family groups. Any standard taken. See also entry under 'Riding Schools'
Member of Association of British Riding Schools

Tower Farm Riding Stables

85 Liberton Drive, Edinburgh, Lothian, EH16 6NS.
Tel: 031 664 3375
Proprietor: Mrs J ForrestBHSI
Holiday details: Children. Any standard. Divided classes. Brochure available. See also entry under 'Riding Schools'
Member of Association of British Riding Schools

Strathclyde

Ardfern Riding Centre

Via Craobh Haven, Ardfern, Argyll, Strathclyde, PA31 8QR.
Tel: 08525 632
Proprietor: Nigel & Lucia Boase
Holiday details: Riding packages. Self-catering available in Mansion house. Inns and hotels locally. See also entry under 'Riding Schools'

Ayrshire Equitation Centre

Castle Hill Stables, Hillfoot Rd, Ayr, Strathclyde, KA7 3LF.
Tel: 0292 266267
Proprietor: Mr K Galbraith
Holiday details: Adults, children and family groups. Max. no 15. Any standard. All ages and experiences. One week holiday - 150 + VAT. See also entry under 'Riding Schools'
Member of Association of British Riding Schools

Bowfield Riding Centre

Bowfield Riding & Country Club, Lands of Bowfield, Howwood, Renfrewshire, Strathclyde, PA9 1DB.
Tel: 050 57 5225
Proprietor: A S Campbell
Holiday details: Holiday guests may bring own horse.

Castle Riding Centre & Argyll Trail Riding

Brenfield, Loch Fyne, Ardrishaig, Argyll, Strathclyde, PA30 8ER.
Tel: 0546 3274
Proprietor: Mrs Stephens & Miss Thornburn

Connel Trekking Centre

Ardoran, Connel, Argyll, Strathclyde.
Tel: 063171 237
Proprietor: K & A Mackinson

Corrow Trekking Centre

Failte, Lochgoilhead, Argyleshire, Strathclyde.
Tel: 030 13 312
Proprietor: Mr D Campbell

Dalchenna Riding Centre

Inverary, Strathclyde.
Tel: 0499 2194

Isle of Arran Riding Holidays

Shedock Farm, Shiskine, Isle of Arran, Strathclyde, KA27 8EW.
Tel: 0770 86 472
Proprietor: Mrs G & Mrs J MacAlister
Holiday details: Trekking and other holidays available. See also entry under 'Riding Schools'

Ladyland Stables

The Stables, Ladyland, Kilbirnie, Strathclyde.
Tel: 0505 843478
Proprietor: Mrs Angela Warnock
Holiday details: Children. Brochure available. Beginners to advanced taken. See also entry under 'Riding Schools'
Member of Association of British Riding Schools

Wrights Riding Academy

Sandhill Estate, Southwoods Road, Monkton, Strathclyde, KA9 1UP.
Tel: 0292 77979
Proprietor: Mrs M Wilson
Holiday details: Children. Max. no. 10. All standards. Divided classes. Brochure available. See also entry under 'Riding Schools'
Member of Association of British Riding Schools

Tayside

Caledonian Equestrian Centre

Pitskelly, Balbbeggie, Tayside, PH2 6AR.
Tel: 08214 426
Proprietor: Mr & Mrs J T Stuart Bruce
Holiday details: Adults, children and family groups. Max. no. 10. All standards See also entry under 'Riding Schools'
Member of Association of British Riding Schools

Scottish Equitation Centre

Sheriffmuir Road, Greenloaning, Dunblane, Perthshire, Tayside, FKl5 0ND.
Tel: 078 688 278
Proprietor: Mr & Mrs J A D MacFarlane

The Gleneagles Mark Phillips Equestrian Ctre

Gleneagles Hotel, Auchterarder, Perthshire, Tayside, PH3 1NE.
Tel: 0764 63507
Proprietor: Capt Mark Phillips

Holiday details: Adults, children and family groups. Normally 6 in a group. All standards. Together if required. Brochures available. See also entry under 'Riding Schools'
Member of Association of British Riding Schools

Riding Holidays Wales

Clwyd

Peacehaven Riding Centre

Terrace Lane, Penyffordd, Nr Chester, Clwyd, CH4 0HB.
Tel: 0244 546819
Proprietor: Mr & Mrs G Williams
Holiday details: Courses for children. Beginners welcome. See also entry under 'Riding Schools'

The Golden Pheasant Riding Centre

Tay-Y-Garth, Glyn Cririog, Nr Llangollen, Clwyd.
Tel: 069172 408
Proprietor: Jane Turner
Holiday details: Adults and children. Farmhouse accomodation. Restaurant. Lisensed bar.
See also entry under 'Riding Schools'

Dyfed

Blaenau Farm

Landdeusant, Llamgadog, Dyfed, SA19 9UN.
Tel: 05504 277
Proprietor: Patrick Dobbs
Holiday details: Pony trekking & riding tours. Holiday guests may bring own horse.

Blue Well Riding Centre

Ffynnonlas, Llanllwni, Nr Pencader, Dyfed, SA39 9AY.
Tel: 026 789 274
Proprietor: Maj & Mrs Gibbins

Clyn-Du Riding Centre

Clyn-du Farm, Burry Port, Llanelli, Dyfed.
Tel: 055 46 2546
Proprietor: Mrs R Vaughan-Jones

Hendre Eynon Stables

Hendre Eynon, St David's, Pembrokeshire, Dyfed, SA62 6DB.
Tel: 0437 720 474
Proprietor: Mr & Mrs Jamieson

Loveston Mill Stables

Loveston, Kilgetty, Nr Tenby, Dyfed.
Tel: 0834 856 78
Proprietor: Mr P M Goldsworthy
Holiday details: Residential riding holidays for unaccompanied children. Novice and experienced welcome.

Norchard Farm Riding School

Norchard Farm, Manorbier, Tenby, Dyfed, SA70 8LD.
Tel: 083482 242
Proprietor: Mrs D H Mathias

Holiday details: Spring and autumn weekend rides with Farmhouse or self catering accomadation.See also entry under 'Riding Schools'
Member of Association of British Riding Schools

Towy Valley Riding Centre
Dan-y-Garn Farm, Bethlehem, Dyfed.
Tel: 055 03 634
Proprietor: Mrs A Hooper

Tregaron Pony Trekking Association
Tan-y-Bryn, Tregaron, Dyfed.
Tel: 097 44 364

Gwent

Cwmyoy Pony Trekking Centre
Daren Farm, Cwmyoy, Abergavenny, Gwent.
Tel: 087 382 565
Proprietor: Mr A R Smith

Grange Pony Trekking
Capel-y-Ffin, Abergavenny,
Tel: 0873 82215
Proprietor: David & Mary Griffiths

Trewysgoed Riding Centre
Fforest, Nr Abergavenny, Gwent, NP7 7LW.
Tel: 0873 890296
Proprietor: Mrs M S Featherstonhaugh
Holiday details: Adults, children and family groups. Brochure available. All standards taken. See also entry under 'Riding Schools'
Member of Association of British Riding Schools

Gwynedd

Bodysgallen Hall Farm
Llandudno, Gwynedd, LL30 IRS.
Tel: 04928 3537
Proprietor: Mr & Mrs Faulks

Cromlech Riding Centre
Tyn Y Gongl, Benllech Bay, Anglesey, Gwynedd.
Tel: 0248 853489
Proprietor: Mrs C Lomas

Llanddona Riding School
Llanddona, Nr Beaumaris, Anglesey, Gwynedd LL58 8UB.
Tel: 0248 810813
Proprietor: Mrs K M Margeret
Holiday details: Adults, children and family groups with own horses/ponies. Any standard. Divided classes. See also entry under 'Riding Schools'
Member of Association of British Riding Schools

Pantiau Farm Trekking Holidays
Pantiau Farm, Rhosgadfen, Caernarfon, Gwynedd.
Tel: 0286 830002

Pen-Llyn Stud & Trekking Centre
Tyddyn Corn, Mynydd Rhiw, Pwllheli, Gwynedd.
Tel: 075 883 360
Proprietor: Mr Pendelbury

Rhiwiau Riding Centre
Llanfairfechan, Gwynedd, LL33 0EH.
Tel: 0248 680094
Proprietor: Miss R M & Miss S Hill

Holiday details: Adults and children. See also entry under 'Riding Schools'

Snowdonia Riding Stables
Weirglodd Fawr, Waunfawr, Caernarfon, LL55 4PQ.
Tel: 028685 342
Proprietor: Mrs R Z Thomas

Ty 'N Lon Riding Centre
Llangybi, Pwllheli, Gwynedd.
Tel: 0766 618

Mid Glamorgan

Pengelli Fach Riding School
Pengelli Fach Farm, Pont-sticil Vanor, Nr Merthyr Tydfil, Mid Glamorgan, CF48 2TU.
Tel: 0685 2169
Proprietor: Mr & Mrs C P Thomas

Powys

Black Mountain Riding Holidays
Peny-Bryn, Llangorse, Brecon, Powys.
Tel: 087 484 272

Cefn Coch Pony Trekking Centre
Cefn Coch Inn, Cefn Coch, Nr Welshpool, Powys.
Tel: 0938 810 247
Proprietor: Mr R M Oliver

Craen Riding Centre
Llanerfyl, Welshpool, Powys, SY21 0JB.
Tel: 093888 349
Proprietor: Mrs A V Wallace

Cwmfforest Riding Centre

Pengenfford, Talgarth, Brecon, Powys, LD3 0EU.
Tel: 0874 711398
Proprietor: Michael Turner

Overland Pony Trek

Ddole Farm, Rhayader, Powys.
Tel: 0597 810 402
Proprietor: Mr H V Davies

South Glamorgan

Down's-side Riding Centre

Sully Road, Penarth, South Glamorgan, CF6 2TY.
Tel: 0222 709719
Proprietor: M W Wilcox
Holiday details: Children . All standards taken. See also entry under 'Riding Schools'
Member of Association of British Riding Schools

West Glamorgan

Copley Stables

Newpark Cottages, Copley, Bishopston, Swansea, West Glamorgan.
Tel: 044 128 4428
Proprietor: Mrs W P Hemns-Tucker
Holiday details: Adult, children and family groups. Max.no.6. Any standard..
See also entry under 'Riding Schools'
Member of Association of British Riding Schools

Northern Ireland

Newcastle Riding Centre

35 Carnacaville Road, Castlewellan, Co Down.
Tel: 039 67 22694
Proprietor: Mrs R & Miss E Martin

Useful References and Listings

Riding Establishments:

England	24
Scotland	87
Wales	94
Northern Ireland	98

Riding Holidays:

England	99
Scotland	126
Wales	129
Northern Ireland	131
Estate Agents	124
Auctions/Sales Outlets	125

Training:

Dressage	127
Driving	127
Endurance	128
Eventing	128
Polo	128
Show Jumping	128
Side-saddle	128
Vaulting	128
Western	128

Where to Ride: Useful References and Listings

Estate Agents

Abbotts
3A Butter Market, Ipswich,
Suffolk, IP1 1BB
Tel: 0473 212666

Abott (Chartered Surveyors)
69 Duke Street, Chelmsford,
Essex, CM1 1HL
Tel: 0245 83266

Abotts
14/16 Queen Street,
Norwich, Norfolk, NR2 4SQ
Tel: 0603 630083

Agriservices
Bitton, Bristol, Avon
Tel: 0272 322448

Bairstow Eves
London & County Homes,
Tindal House, Tindal Square,
Chelmsford, Essex
Tel: 02425 358232

Bairstow Eves
1 Holly Hill, Hampstead,
London, NW3
Tel: 071 431 2328

Buckinghams Property Consultants
543 Green Lanes, London,
N13 4DR
Tel: 081 882 8282

Carter Jonas
42 High Street, Marlborough,
Wilts, SN8 1HT
Tel: 0672 54545

Churchill Equestrian Est Agnts
Cobwebs House, Copsale
Lane, Copsale, Horsham,
Sussex
Tel: 0403 732222

David Bedford
15 Guildhall Street, Bury St
Edmunds, Suffolk
Tel: 0284 2822

Dickinson Dary & Markham
7 Cornmarket, Louth, Lincs
Tel: 0507 604712

Fox & Sons
5-7 Salisbury Street,
Fordingbridge, Hants
Tel: 0425 52121

Frank Hill & Son
18 Market Place, Patrngton,
Hull, Humberside, HU12 0RB
Tel: 0964 630531 Fax: 0964
631206

GA Property Services
Hartley House, High Street,
Chipping Sodbury, Bristol,
Avon, BS17 6BG
Tel: 0454 313395

Hampton & Sons
18 Imperial Square,
Cheltenham, Gloucs, GL50
1QZ
Tel: 0242 514849

Harrods Estate Offices
12 Brompton Place,
Knightsbridge, London, SW3
Tel: 071 589 1490

Henry Smith & Son
50 Carfax, Horsham, West
Sussex, RH12 1BP
Tel: 0403 53271

Hobbs & Chambers
Market Place, Faringdon,
Oxon
Tel: 0367 20356

Hobbs Parker
Romney House, Ashford
Market, Elwick Road,
Ashford, Kent, TN23 1PG
Tel: 0233 622222 Fax: 0233
646642

Humberts
25 Grosvenor Street,
London, W1X 9FE
Tel: 071 629 6700

Hunters
3 Market Place, Sturminster
Newton
Dorset, DT10 1AF
Tel: 0258 72362

Husseys
Chartered Surveyors, Alphin
Brook Road, Exeter
Devon, EX2 8TH
Tel: 0392 50441 Fax: 0392
50610

Januarys
7 King Street, Saffron Walden
Essex, CB10 1HE
Tel: 0799 21176

John H James & Co
16 Whitehouse Street,
Baldock, Herts
Tel: 0462 894221

Kays
225-229 Church Street,
Blackpool, Lancs
Tel: 0253 23486

King & Chasemore
Station Road, Pulborough
W Sussex
Tel: 07982 2081

Kivell & Sons
Stanhope Chambers, 12 The
Square, Holsworthy
Devon
Tel: 0409 253 275

Knight Frank & Rutley
20 Hanover Square
London, W1R OAH
Tel: 071 629 8171

Knight Frank & Rutley
14 Broad Street, Hereford,
Hereford & Worcs HR4 9AL
Tel: 0449 711783

Mawer Mason & Bell
Horncastle
Lincs
Tel: 06582 2222

Merry Pierce Thorpe
14 Bridge Street,
Northampton
Northants
Tel: 0604 32266

**Messenger May
Baverstock**
4 Castle Street, Farnham,
Hants
Tel: 0252 714164

**Messenger May
Baverstock**
31 High Street, Alton, Hants
Tel: 0420 86868

Pearson Cole
279 High Street, Dorking,
Surrey
Tel: 0306 880800

**Phillips, Sanders &
Stubbs**
4 Cross Street, Barnstaple,
Devon
Tel: 0271 75784

Rendells
13 Market Square, Newton
Abbot, Devon, TQ12 2RL
Tel: 0626 3881

Richard Mayers
58 Crown Street,
Stowmarket, Suffolk, IP14
1HY
Tel: 0449 71183

**Russell Baldwin &
Bright**
16, Castle Street,
Hay-on-Wye, Herefordshire,
HR3 5DF
Tel: 0497 820622

Savills
21 Horse Fair, Banbury,
Oxon, OX16 0AW
Tel: 0295 3535

Savills (Colchester)
8 West Stockwell Street,
Colchester, Essex

Senior & Godwin
Salisbury Street, Blandford
Forum, Hereford
Tel: 0285 52327

Senior & Godwin
High Street, Gillingham,
Dorset
Tel: 07476 3133

Senior & Godwin
92 Cheap Street, Sherborne,
Dorset, DT9 3LR
Tel: 0935 812115

Senior & Godwin
The Market Place,
Sturminster, Newton, Dorset
Tel: 0258 72244

Senior & Godwin
High Street, Wincanton,
Somerset
Tel: 0963 33251

Stags
19 Brampton Street,
Tiverton, Devon
Tel: 0884 356331

Tufnell & Partners
40 Chobham Road,
Sunningdale, Ascot, Berks
Tel: 0990 23411

Wallhead Gray & Coates
Central Chambers, Hexham,
Northumberland
Tel: 0434 603802

Woosham & Tyler
Dolarreg, North Road, Builth
Wells, Powys, LD2 3DD
Tel: 0982 553248

Auctions,
Auctioneers &
Sales Outlets

**Aberdeen & Northern
Marts Ltd**
Central Mart, 51 Powis
Terrace, Aberdeen,
Grampian AB9 2UQ
Tel: 0224 41331

Andrew Oliver & Son Limited
Auction Mart Offices, Hawick, Borders TD9 9NN
Tel: 0450 3261

Avon Livestock Centre
Crew Road, Winford, Nr Bristol
Avon BS18 8HB
Tel: 0275 87 2171

Biggar Auction Market Co Ltd
Biggar, Lanark, Scotland

Blackburn Auction Mart Co. Ltd
The Cattle Market, Sumner Street, Blackburn, Lancashire
Tel: 0254 53626

Botterills Ascot Bloodstck Sals
The Lodge, Flaxton, Yorkshire YO6 7PZ
Tel: 0904 56240 Fax: 0904 56626

C M Stanford & Son
Stanford House, 12 Culver Street, Colchester, Essex
Tel: 0206 573165

Cambs Horse & Pony Agency
42 Abington Grove, Elm, Wisbech, Cambs
Tel: 0945 860076

Cheffin Grain & Chalk Messrs
49-53 Regent Street, Cambridge, Cambridgeshire CB2 1AR
Tel: 0223 358721

Coles Knapp & Kennedy, Ross-on-Wye, Herefordshire
Tel: 0989 762225 Fax: 0989 66082

Doncaster Bloodstock Sales Ltd
Auction Mart Offices, Hawick, Roxburghshire TD9 9NN
Tel: 0450 72222 Fax: 0450 78017

Frank Hill & Son
18 Market Place, Patrngton, Hull, Humberside HU12 0RB
Tel: 0964 630531 Fax: 0964 631206

Hobbs Parker
Romney House, Ashford Market, Elwick Road, Ashford, Kent TN23 1PG
Tel: 0233 622222 Fax: 0233 646642

Hopes Auction Co
93 High Street, Wigton, Cumbria CA7 9PG
Tel: 0965 42202

Husseys
Chartered Surveyors, Alphin Brook Road, Exeter, Devon EX2 8TH
Tel: 0392 50441 Fax: 0392 50610

J J Morris
Broyan House, Priory Street, Cardigan, Dyfed SA43 1DA
Tel: 0239 612343

King Thomas Lloyd-Jones & Co
36 High Street, Lampeter, Dyfed SA48 7BB

Kivell & Sons
Stanhope Chambers, 12 The Square, Holsworthy, Devon
Tel: 0409 253 275

Lawrie & Symington Limited
Auction Market, Hawick, Roxburghshire TD9 9NN
Tel: 0450 73261
Fax: 0450 74022

Lodge & Thomas
77 Lemon Street, Truro, Cornwall TR21 2PY
Tel: 0872 72722

Mawer Mason & Bell, Horncastle, Lincs
Tel: 06582 2222

Messrs Sawdye & Harris
13 West Street, Ashburton, Devon TQ13 7DT
Tel: 0364 52304

Messrs Taylor & Fletcher
The Square, Stow on-the-Wold, Gloucestershire GL54 1BL
Tel: 0451 30383

Midland Marts Limited
P O. Box 10, Banbury Stockyard, Banbury, Oxon OX16 8EP
Tel: 0295 50501

Montague Harris & Co
30 Lion Street, Abergavenny, Gwent
Tel: 0873 3041

Norris & Duvall
106 Fore Street, Hertford, Hertfordshire SG14 1AH
Tel: 0992 52249

Pattullo & Partners
Castle Market, 154 London Road, Sevenoaks, Kent TN13 1DJ
Tel: 0732 52329

Penrith Farmers & Kidds plc
Agricultural Hall, Skirsgill, Penrith, Cumbria CA11 0DN
Tel: 0768 62323

Rennies
Newmarket Chambers, Lion Street, Avergavenny, Gwent
Tel: 0873 2327

Rugby Livestock Sales Ltd
Cattle Market, Craven Road,
Rugby, Warwickshire

Russell Baldwin & Bright
16, Castle Street,
Hay-on-Wye, Herefordshire
HR3 5DF
Tel: 0497 820622

Stephenson & Son
Wetherby Horse Sales,
Market Place, Easingwold
N Yorkshire YO6 3AA
Tel: 0347 21145

Thimbleby & Shorland
31 Great Knollys Street,
Reading, Berks RG1 7HU
Tel: 0734 508611

Thomdon Roffick & Laurie Ltd
24 Lowther Street
Carlisle, Cumbria
Tel: 0228 289939

W S Johnson & Co
40 High Street
Leighton Buzzard, Beds
Tel: 0525 372414

Walker Walton Hanson
Wilton Lodge
1, Wilton Road
Melton Mowbray LE13 0UJ
Tel: 0664 67555

Wallets Mart Ltd
Castle Douglas
Dumfries DC7 1HY
Tel: 0556 2381

Warner Sheppard & Wade Ltd
The Racecourse, Leicester Road, Oadby
Leicestershire , LE2 4AL
Tel: 0533 736438

Wright-Manley Auctioneers
Gresty Road,
Crewe
Cheshire

Training

Training, Dressage

Brampton Stables
Church Brampton, North-
ampton, Northamptonshire
NN6 8AU
Tel: 0604 842051

Holmescales Riding Centre
Holmescales, Old Hutton
Nr Kendal, Cumbria LA8 0NB
Tel: 0539 729388

Kyre Combined Training Club
Lower House Farm, Sutton,
Tenbury Wells, Hereford &
Worcester WR15 8RL
Tel: 0885410233

Laurels Stables
Horringer, Bury St Edmunds,
Suffolk IP29 5SN
Tel: 0284 735 281

North Humberside Riding Centre
Easington, Nr Hull, North
Humberside HU12 0UA
Tel: 0964 650250

Nottingham Equestrian Centre
Asher Lane, Ruddington
Nottinghamshire NG11 6JX
Tel: 0602 842854

Peacehaven Riding Centre
Terrace Lane, Penyffordd
Nr Chester, CH4 0HB
Tel: 0244 546819

Tall Trees Riding Centre
Davidstow, Camelford,
Cornwall PL32 9XR
Tel: 0840 6249

Yorkshire Riding centre
Markington
Harrogate
North Yorkshire HG3 3PE
Tel: 0765 87207 Fax: 0765 667065

Training, Driving

Chorleywood Equestrian Ctre Ltd
Chenies Road,
Chorleywood,
Rickmansworth,
Hertfordshire WD3 5LY
Tel: 0923 282713

Poplar Park Equestrian Centre
Heath Road, Hollesley,
Woodbridge, Suffolk
IP12 3NA
Tel: 0394 411023 Fax: 0394
411553

Red House Stables Carriage Mus
Old Road, Darley Dale,
Matlock, Derbyshire
DE4 2ER
Tel: 0629 733583

Endurance

Loch Ness Equicentre
Drummond, Dores,
Invernesshire IV1 2TX
Tel: 046 375251

Eventing

Kyre Combined Training Club
Lower House Farm, Sutton,
Tenbury Wells, Hereford &
Worcester WR15 8RL
Tel: 0885410233

Loch Ness Equicentre
Drummond, Dores,
Invernesshire IV1 2TX
Tel: 046 375251

Nottingham Equestrian Centre
Asher Lane, Ruddington
Nottinghamshire NG11 6JX
Tel: 0602 842854

Yorkshire Riding centre
Markington, Harrogate
North Yorkshire HG3 3PE
Tel: 0765 87207 Fax: 0765
667065

Training, Polo

Equitus Ltd
Stoney Hill Farm, Brimpsfield,
Gloucester, Gloucestershire
GL4 8LF
Tel: 0452 864412

Show Jumping

Holmescales Riding Centre
Holmescales, Old Hutton, Nr
Kendal, Cumbria LA8 0NB
Tel: 0539 729388

Kyre Combined Training Club
Lower House Farm, Sutton,
Tenbury Wells, Hereford &
Worcs WR15 8RL
Tel: 0885410233

Loch Ness Equicentre
Drummond, Dores,
Invernesshire IV1 2TX
Tel: 046 375251

Peacehaven Riding Centre
Terrace Lane, Penyffordd,
Nr Chester, CH4 0HB
Tel: 0244 546819

Tall Trees Riding Centre
Davidstow, Camelford,
Cornwall PL32 9XR
Tel: 0840 6249

Yorkshire Riding centre
Markington, Harrogate
North Yorkshire HG3 3PE
Tel: 0765 87207
Fax: 0765 667065

Side Saddle

Lea Bailey Riding School
Nr Ross-on-Wye, Hereford &
Worcester HR9 5TY
Tel: 0989 81360

Wrea Green Equitation Centre
Bryning Lane, Wrea Green,
Nr Kirkham, Lancs
Tel: 0772 686576

Training, Vaulting

Poplar Park Equestrian Centre
Heath Road, Hollesley,,
Woodbridge, Suffolk
IP12 3NA
Tel: 0394 411023
Fax: 0394 411553

Training, Western

Ardfern Riding Centre
Craobh Haven, Ardfurn,
Lochgilphead, Dumfries &
Galloway PA31 8QR
Tel: 08525 270

Poplar Park Equestrian Centre
Heath Road, Hollesley,
Woodbridge, Suffolk
IP12 3NA
Tel: 0394 411023 Fax: 0394
411553

Zara Stud & Training Centre
Highleigh Road, Sidlesham,
Chichester, Sussex PO20
7NR
Tel: 0243 641662

Section 2: The Responsible Rider

Chapter 3: Making the Decision   130
Chapter 4: Riding Wear   137
Chapter 5: Better Safe than Sorry 140
Chapter 6: Safety on the Road:
Medical Emergencies   144
Chapter 7: Safety on the Road:
Riding Out   148
Chapter 8: Public Rights of Way   151
Chapter 9: Some Human Faults
and Problems   154
Chapter 10: Fencing   155

Useful References & Listings

Aqua Sprays   162
Clothing Manufacturers:
Boots   162
Breeches & Jodphurs   163
Chaps   164
General   164
Hats   165
Jackets   166
Waterproofs   168
Clothing Retailers   169
Equestrian Fine Art   169
Galleries   169
Hat Covers   170
Insurance Brokers/Valuers   170
Magazines & Books   171
Mail Order Supplies   172
Name Plates   173
Portraits & Momentos   173
Riding Equipment, Chaps   173
Riding Equipment, Clothing   173
Show Jumps/Sundries   174
Side-Saddle Habits   174
Spurs   175
Tack Shops   175
Ties & Stocks   175
Video Services   175
Whips   176

Making the Decision

Buying your first horse or pony can be a nerve-racking experience. However, a knowledge of what's involved can make the decision easier.

Having decided that riding is the sport for you, the next decision to make is 'shall I continue riding at a school and gaining experience that way, or shall I embark upon horse ownership?'. The most vital consideration to make initially is can you afford it? There are two factors to take into consideration - the initial cash outlay for buying the horse and all the essential tack and, perhaps most importantly, the weekly up-keep. You should be able to get a rough idea of the average cost of horses/ponies by making enquiries at your local riding school and checking the adverts in horse journals such as the *Horse and Hound*. This will help give you a rough guide to your initial outlay. To this figure you should add the incidental costs of travelling to view, telephone calls, veterinary fees and collection costs. This could be a one-off, but not everyone is lucky enough to find the right horse straight away so costs could mount.

The weekly costs are, to some extent, determined by where you are going to keep your horse. If you have access to a field and possibly some sort of shelter then you may decide to keep the horse there. However, you do need to know how to look after a horse or at least have someone who can give you expert, informed advice. Alternatively, you may decide to keep it at a local livery yard where you will be paying for their expertise and facilities. Add to this the incidental costs for things like tack, worming, shoeing and veterinary care - then you are beginning to get an idea of the financial dimensions of the task in hand!

So you have made up your mind and got over the dent it is going to make in your bank balance! The next step in the planning stage is to consider what purposes will the horse/pony be used for. Do you intend to use it just for hacking and gaining further experience, or do you intend to try show-jumping, cross-country, showing, hunting etc. If you are a novice and are embarking upon your first purchasing venture then you may well be advised to start with an animal that is an 'all-rounder' - an animal that can perform a variety of tasks. When you have gained in experience and confidence as a horse owner and know which particular discipline you wish to concentrate on, then you will know what type of horse you want to look for as your second purchase.

Making the right decision when choosing a child's pony is vital

Size is the next consideration, the horse must suit the rider and the purpose for which the horse is going to be used. It is important not to be either under-horsed or over-horsed. Size is particularly important when choosing a children's pony since the qualifying size of the pony in children's competition classes is usually linked to the age of the child who is competing. If in doubt about the correct size of horse/pony to choose then consult someone experienced who knows both your basic requirements and your level of expertise.

When considering the age of animal to purchase, there are probably as many schools of thought as people offering you advice, and in the end the choice is yours. However, we offer you a few thoughts to take into consideration when making your choice:

1. Age has a direct bearing upon the price and the resale value of the animal

2. Age has a bearing upon the working years, suitability and life expectancy.

3. Horses are regarded as mature at five years.

4. Horses/ponies reach their prime at around six or seven years.

5. Up to seven years of age they are appreciating in value.

6. After twelve years of age they are depreciating in value.

7. Horses/ponies are termed 'aged' over eight years.

Since there are no hard and fast rules for you to apply when deciding whether an animal's age is acceptable, you should perhaps look at the age as just one of the factors to be taken into consideration. Often for the younger, less experienced or nervous rider an older 'school-master' is ideal, and is often of inestimable value when considering purchase price.

Unless you are experienced both as a rider and in training, then it is inadvisable to buy a young horse, i.e. three or four years old. It is a mistake to think that purchasing so young a horse will give the horse and rider a chance to grow together since, in this particular sport, two such novices could be a devastating combination.

Good temperament is essential and for most people, particularly the young, inexperienced or nervous rider, the most important factor. The phrase 'good temperament' implies obedience, willingness, docility and gentleness. When being ridden, handled or out in traffic, animals that have any vices such as biting, napping, kicking, rearing, bolting, etc. should in general be avoided by the young or less experienced, as should animals that are difficult to catch.

Conformation is a vast area to cover and not something that one can expect to learn just from a book but basically describes the horses basic structure. There are, however, some points to keep in mind:

1. Serious conformation faults can lead towards a horse becoming unsound.

2. The head should be well proportioned and well defined. Pricked ears and a kind prominent eye set on the side are generally regarded as signs of a generous horse. Small, piggy eyes and laid back ears are considered to be a sign of bad temper. Excess white in the eye suggests the possibility of an excitable and ill tempered animal.

   Ensure that the incisor teeth meet; a horse with an overshot jaw (parrot mouth) or an undershot jaw (sow mouthed) will have increasing problems with grazing.

3. The neck should have a good unbroken line fitting into a good sloping shoulder and well-developed withers. Too thick a neck denotes strength that could be used against the rider, and will tire the arms. A concave neck, known as an 'ewe neck' results in difficulty for the horse to achieve the desirable head carriage.

   Shoulders should have a good slope. Too straight a shoulder will limit the forward movement of the front legs and front legs will show wear faster.

4. The chest should be broad enough to allow plenty of room for the heart and lungs. If the chest is too narrow the front legs will be closer together thus increasing the likelihood of the horse 'brushing' (knocking one leg against the other).

    Conversely, if the chest is too wide the horse will have a rolling gait and produce an uncomfortable ride. There should be great depth from the withers to the elbow. Horses that are flat sided often lack stamina.

5. The back should not be disproportionately long to the overall height of the horse. The loins should be muscular, the round with well developed muscles and strong thighs. The lower part of the belly should curve up slightly, not run up between the legs like a greyhound, referred to as 'run up light' which denotes the overall condition which may go with hard training, hard work or lack of food.

    The tail should be set high not low on drooping quarters.

6. Since the legs have to carry the whole of the horse's weight they are the part that is most susceptible to unsoundness. The forelegs are the principal weight bearers, the hind legs are used more as a means of propulsion. Thus, good legs are of prime importance.

Legs should be free of any unwarranted lumps or bumps. There are, however, some lumps that do come with time and work and are acceptable, but of course the advice of a veterinary surgeon should always be sought before buying. The joints should be large and flat, the tendons and ligaments clearly defined.

The feet of the forelegs should point straight ahead. Feet that point inwards (pigeon-toed) and outwards (splay- footed) will increase disjointed action and put more stress on the joints.

Viewed from the side, the knees should be convex. Concave knees, known as 'calf-knees' or turned 'back at the knee', should be avoided as this is a serious weakness.

If a horse appears to be standing over his legs when standing this is termed as 'over at the knee'. This should, however, not be looked on as a weakness as it does actually help alleviate any undue pressure on the tendons increase the shock absorbing properties of the leg. In reverse 'back at the knee' should be avoided, as it puts too great a strain on the tendons.

The hind legs should not be overbent (sickle-hocked) as horses with this condition will have the tendency to throw 'curbs' - a thickening of the tendon or ligament at the back of the hock.

Ensure that the horse you are buying will perform the tasks you require it for

If the toes turn outwards and the hocks turn inwards, horses are said to be 'cow-hocked' and will not therefore be able to move straight. The opposite condition, toes in-hocks out, is known as 'bowed-hocks'. This results in a twisting action when the foot hits the floor and could be detrimental.

7. The hoof should not be too narrow and broad at the heel. Feet should always look as though they are a pair and if not then should be regarded with suspicion. A concave foot with a number of ridges could indicate that the horse/pony has had laminitus (inflammation of the sensitive wall of the foot). Care should be taken that this is not confused with grass ridges which are an indication that the horse has been out at grass for some time and then stabled affecting the growth in the hoof. The foot is susceptible to a number of diseases and unsoundness. The maxim 'No foot-no horse' is most wise, and one that any experienced horse owner will whole-heartedly agree with.

Details of the structure of the hoof and the diseases that it is prone to are too vast to deal with in this book, and could indeed fill volumes. It is not the intention of this book to provide the definitive answer to choosing a horse but merely to give pointers, and present sufficient information to enable intelligent questions to be asked.

Equipped with this knowledge, the search begins in earnest! Initial contact with the seller may well be via the telephone. If this is the case, then it is a good idea to make a list of the questions that you would like answered. Equally important are a pen and paper to make a note of the answers that you receive.

The first question should be "why is the horse for sale". Make sure you tell the vendor what you require the horse for, although you cannot rely upon the verdict of the vendor for the suitability of his horse for your purpose. Always ask if the horse suffers from any vices such as: biting, weaving, crib-biting, wind-sucking, shying, kicking, rearing, box walking, bolting, striking out with forelegs, bad to shoe, difficult to catch, bad to travel/box, bad in traffic.

Should the vendor discuss the horses performance at an event where information is recorded and logged e.g. B.S.J.A or B.H.S., it is possible to confirm these by contacting the organisation who, possibly for a small fee, will search their records.

When you go to view the horse, make certain that your first view of it is in the stable. Try to confirm whether this is the stable that the horse is usually kept in. Be aware of telltale signs of vices such as crib-biting which will be indicated by teeth marks on fixed, projecting objects. Indentations in the floor by the door that are approximately 16 - 25" apart could be wear marks from a weaver, it may be a previous occupant or it may be this horse. Hoof marks on the wall could indicate a box kicker. Keep your eyes open and you could well pick up information that will guide you when making your decision.

Take careful note of how the horse reacts when it is approached and tacked up - does it accept the bit easily, does it hollow when the saddle is placed on, does it stand calmly when the girth is tightened. Maybe not things that would encourage or prevent you buying a horse, but things that you add to your overall picture.

One of your queries of the owner will have been about lameness or leg problems. You will need to see the horse trotted out, ensure that this is done on a hard, level surface. Should the horse trot up lame and the owner insists that this is only a temporary lameness and the horse in all other respects suits your needs, do proceed with extreme caution. When the animal is examined, careful scrutiny of the legs should be made and a history of the lameness taken.

Initially, it is wise to ask to see the horse ridden before you attempt. Take careful note how the horse moves, the way in which he leaves the stable yard or companions - a nappy horse can prove troublesome. Is it placid or excitable? Ask for the horse to be ridden at all paces and, if required, to tackle a few obstacles. Be aware of how the horse performs. When it is your turn, spend time in walk to get the feel of the horse and its responsiveness. Try it through all paces and both left and right to ascertain how stiff it is. If you are going to be asking the horse to jump either immediately or in the future, ask the owner if you can try him over a few jumps. If there is a course already set up then ask for it to be varied as he may be familiar with the layout. Try a number of fences away from home to see if he is willing to tackle these.

Having reached this point and you feel that the horse will meet your requirements in every respect, the horse should undergo a thorough vetinary examination. The vet should be told for what purpose the horse/pony is required so as to allow an informed diagnosis which takes into account the general level of activity the horse will be required to attain, as well as the particular nature of this activity i.i. if just for hacking or for 3-Day Eventing.

When arranging for a veterinary examination, ensure that all details you have been given about any vices or problems the horse may have had are passed on. Make sure that the veterinary is aware of the purpose for which the horse is required - this will influence his assessment in as much as minor problems in conformation could be overlooked if the horse were only required for hacking, but not for a showing animal.

A few words of caution for parents buying ponies for their children. Buying a horse that is plainly unsuited to the needs and experience of the child is both unwise and potentially dangerous. It is a complete fallacy for example, to buy a young horse for a novice child under the illusion that they will grow and learn together - two novices together could be courting disaster. Aim to find a horse that is suitable for the child at that point in time - 'under horsing' and 'over-horsing' can create problems and, in the end, turn out to be a false economy. It is far better to let the child enjoy a pony that it feels confident and comfortable with, and is thus not always dependent upon an adult for help. The choice of the first pony is critical since it could make or mar any future interest in horses.

Riding Wear

Nowadays, it is not necessary to forsake smart fashionable wear for the sake of safety and practicability - safety and style can be combined!

The range of colourful and stylish riding wear available nowadays may leave the rider spoilt for choice and this has created a much more competitive market. Although it must be said that, even if the choice is greater, the buyer should not be swayed into buying merely for economy but take into consideration the quality of the goods since durability, practicality and safety are pre-requisites in riding wear.

If you are new to the sport it would be foolish to rush out and buy the whole outfit without first knowing you are going to carry on.

What is essential to buy is a good riding hat. Even the most competent of competitive riders will attest to this, and could probably regale you with a whole host of examples of how serious injuries had been avoided because of appropriate headgear. The riding hat is not decorative or something reserved for wearing when competing, it should be worn whenever you ride.

There are many different types and makes of riding hat - the ones most highly recommended are the ones with the British Standards Institute 'kitemark' and numbers BS 4472 AND BS 6473. Most important, is the fit of the hat, after all the last thing you want is a hat that lands on the floor before you do! There are a greater number of hats on the market now that are fitted with a safety harness/chin strap. When trying on a hat make sure that it is a comfortable fit when worn correctly, i.e. the hat is parallel with the ground and not tipped back on the head. The laces inside the hat are designed for adjustment in order to obtain a snug fit and to act as a shock absorbing 'cushion'.

The modern type of helmet hunting cap has a flexible peak rather than the old rigid type. This will bend as it hits any hard surface, thereby avoiding any jarring or whiplash effect. The jockey skull is equally popular at the moment, particularly in cross-country events and for exercise.

It is advisable to keep hair off the face and under your riding cap either by tying it back or putting it in a net. Hair blowing in the face can be annoying and dangerously distractive.

Equally important is safe footwear. The best types of footwear are the specially designed jodhpur boot or long leather/rubber riding boots. Both these types of footwear have small heels and relatively smooth soles. The heel will prevent the foot slipping too far through the stirrup and getting stuck. Equally, the smooth sole is a safety precaution since a ridged sole could get stuck and prevent the rider quitting the stirrups quickly in the event of an emergency. If you are in the early stages of learning to ride and do not as yet, possess boots, then a strong pair of walking shoes with smooth soles and a small heel will serve the purpose. Do not attempt to ride wearing the following:

a.   Heel-less or wedge heeled shoes - your feet could slip through the stirrups.

b.   High-heeled shoes with a high in-step - your feet could get stuck on the in-step.

c.   Shoes/boots with a ridged sole - you will not be able to slip your feet from the stirrups in case of an emergency.

The rest of your outfit is largely up to you. Initially you may ride in any trousers you happen to own - although jeans would probably be most suitable since they are a tough, thick material. The disadvantage of loose fitting trousers is that you could end up with rubbing or nipping from the stirrup leathers. Obviously the best riding wear are jodhpurs or riding breaches since they are designed to fit closely and are reinforced in the places where the leg makes maximum contact with the saddle.

Whatever you choose to ride in should be practical and comfortable. It is unwise to wear loose fitting, flapping clothes since they can hinder movements and could frighten the horse - as can clothes that are too tight. Take account of the weather you are riding in - there is a variety of quilted waistcoats and anoraks on the market that are shower and wind proof and designed not to restrict movements. Wax jackets are equally useful since they are wind-proof and waterproof, and, unlike many waterproofs, have air holes to prevent undue sweating. However, do be aware of the cheap imitations that the popularity of the wax jacket to the non-riding public has encouraged. Although they will be adequate for wear around the stable yard, they are not entirely suitable for riding unless the skirt is vented and the zip opens both top and bottom.

Whatever you choose to wear make sure that it is neat, well-fitted, and falls within the safety rules that common sense dictates.

For competitive riding there is a far more clearly defined dress code. In competitions, it is usual for the rider to wear a hat, jacket, jodhpurs, boots, shirt and tie, gloves and to carry a stick. For some events, such as gymkhana, the coat may be replaced by a sweater. At cross-country events, a sweater with distinctive colours would be the order of the day whereas, at a hunter trial, a jacket would be prescribed wear. The schedule of events for a competition is likely to tell you what is acceptable wear.

Better Safe than Sorry

The rider who takes every possible care to protect their horse from theft is taking a responsible attitude to horse ownership

The rider who takes every possible care to protect their horse from theft is taking a responsible attitude to horse ownership.

As a responsible owner you will of course take every precaution to safeguard the health and safety of your horse. Insurance helps in the event of loss or injury, but there is a method that will help you apply the adage 'prevention is better than cure' - freeze marking.

Every year the number of horses and ponies lost by theft increases. There are no nationwide statistics available at present since horse thefts are recorded along with cattle thefts on one list. The police make every effort to trace stolen animals, but are greatly hindered by the lack of positive identification. A description of the horse and it's markings is not enough in most cases.

The marking is noticeable at a glance

If a rustler takes a horse or pony they can change the appearance by altering the coloration, i.e. if an animal has a white sock, this can be 'blacked out'. Similarly, a white star could be added where previously there was none. The only characteristic which cannot be altered, and is the equivalent to the human fingerprint, is the whorl. A whorl is a radial arrangement of horse hair and is totally unique to each individual animal. It is wise to keep an illustration of the whorls of your animal on a diagram indicating where they are situated and with a photograph, if possible, to show the shape of the whorls.

Freeze marking is a way of marking your horse positively and this has become increasingly popular in recent years. There are a number of firms who have developed this method of marking, but by far the largest is MMB Farmkey. Established in 1978, the MMB Farmkey system of identification and nationwide registration was introduced with the full support of the B.H.S. and crime prevention officers. This humane method gives positive, unique and permanent identification that will act as a deterrent to would-be horse rustlers. MMB Farmkey has the sole authorisation for the maintenance of a National Security Register. A four figure number is allocated to each animal, and the details of the animal are recorded, together with any subsequent change of ownership. All the information contained in the Register is available to the police seven days a week, twenty-four hours a day, in order to assist in tracing lost or stolen horses.

How is the mark applied? It is quite unlike the other methods of marking such as hot branding, hoof marking or lip tattooing. A super-chilled marker which operates at -70°C is applied to a clipped area on the left hand side of the saddle patch. This kills the pigment cells in the hair which then re-grows white within a few weeks. The distinctive, permanent mark that is left can be recognised at a glance by owners, traders and police. Light coloured animals can also be marked by the same method, but in these cases a bald marking is produced which is usually placed on the horses shoulder.

Since the organisation operates a nationwide service, arrangements can be made quite easily for one of their operatives to call at your stables and do the job. The success and popularity of the whole operation is attested to by the growing number of people who have taken advantage of this method of identification; there are now some 75,000 horses on their register. Further confirmation of the success of this preventative method is that, out of the 48 freeze-marked horses which were stolen, 38 were recovered. MMB Farmkey pride themselves upon their after-care service and will happily deal with any queries either by police, telephone or, if necessary, a personal visit.

1990 was one of MMB's busiest years so far as there has been a dramatic increase in the incidence of thefts. Many people wait until they are altered by a theft in the area before deciding to take preventative measures. The recent theft of 5 horses/ponies in the

Halesowen, West Midlands area has bought about a rush to get horses in this area marked.

How, you may ask, will freeze marking help prevent thefts when your horse is rugged up? There are badges that can be attached to the rugs and signs to display that will confirm that those animals are freeze-marked.

One area that is giving rising cause for concern is the change which is due to take place in 1992 regarding the law relating to the transporting of live horses to the continent. Fears that there will be an increase in the number of horses stolen are very real for the horse owning population and is shared by the authorities. MMB Farmkey have begun to discuss the problem with various Port Authorities, and are in the process of developing a Port Watch scheme. With this sort of responsible attitude you must have increased confidence.

There are, of course, many questions the prospective client may wish to ask. Following are some of the questions that could arise, with answers supplied by Mary Awre, Manager of MMB Farmkey.

Q. Is freeze marking painful?

A. It is a humane way of marking a horse permanently.

Q. How soon can a horse be ridden after being freeze marked?

A. For a horse marked on the saddle area, it is recommended that you do not ride for four days to a week. There can, of course, be variable reactions, and for particularly sensitive horses, it is best to leave it a little longer. The recommended lay off for horses that are marked on the shoulder is only two days. Discretion should be used.

Q. How do you mark a light coloured horse?

A. Instead of killing the pigmentation in the hair cells to produce white hair, a small amount of hair is killed so that the skin shows through. This process is usually carried out on the shoulder area.

Q. Should I use a numnah after the horse has been marked?

A. It is essential to use a thick numnah or saddle cloth until such time as the hair has grown through, possibly with a hole cut out over the brand so as to reduce pressure on that particular area.

Q. What is the youngest age a horse can be marked?

A. Preferably not under the age of 12 months.

Q. Will freeze marking affect the results of horses being shown in hand?

A. The B.H.S. has recommended freeze marking to the various breed societies. There have been no reports that marking has had an adverse effect upon marking in these events.

Q. Does freeze marking have an effect on insurance companies?

A. It certainly does. The majority of companies give a reduction on the annual premium, some up to 10%.

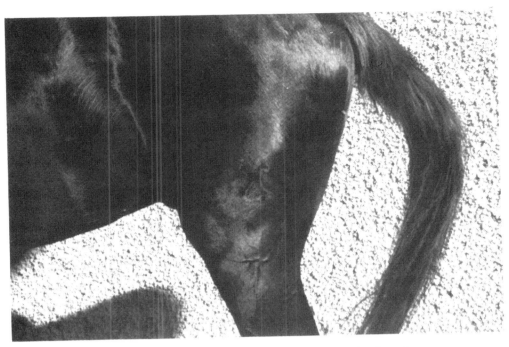

Hanovarian horses are marked with a distinctive brand

Q. Can I arrange for my horse to be marked singly, or do I have to be part of a group?

A. Some firms operate on a local basis, but with MMB Farmkey, which is a nationwide operation, operatives are based throughout the regions.

Q. What happens when the horses coat grows in winter?

A. It may be necessary to clip the marked area with those that are bald marked in order to give better visibility.

Q. What should you do in the event of a marked horse going missing?

A. Contact the local police immediately, and the firm responsible for the freeze marking. MMB Farmkey will notify ports, horse sales and slaughterhouses, and liaise with the police. They also offer a reward of £5,000 for anyone who gives information that leads to the conviction of a freeze marked horse thief.

Costs, of course, will vary according to the firm you employ. If you arrange for a group of horses to be marked at the same time then it is likely that you will get a reduction of the costs. At a cost of under £40, you will find it money well spent! Further reductions may be available for those who belong to B.H.S. riding and pony clubs.

Safety on the Roads - Medical Emergencies

> Riding is a high-risk sport. The rider needs to be aware of the dangers and prepared to act swiftly when problems arise.

Riding is a high-risk sport. The rider needs to be aware of the dangers and prepared to act swiftly when problems arise.

Whilst not wishing to dwell too much upon all the things that can go wrong, we would be failing if we did not point out the precautions that any wise and considerate rider would undertake.

We talked briefly in the 'Riding Out' section about taking a First Aid course in order to deal with any emergencies. This is a wise and sensible precaution and knowing what to do in the event of an accident or injury could mean the difference between aggravating an injury or helping the casualty to recover more quickly.

Accidents often happen when you least expect them and, with riding, can happen where you would least want them to but with a little knowledge and improvisation you could deal with the matter until you are able to obtain expert help.

The St. John's Ambulance Brigade and the British Red Cross both run basic First Aid classes which will give you the necessary knowledge to handle emergencies and inform you of what to do and what not to do! To find out where your local branch is situated check in the directory or your local Yellow Pages under Charitable and Benevolent Organisations. You may find that if there is a group of you who want to take lessons the branch will organise instruction exclusively for you. You will find that the type of group activity will not only be instructional but fun!

It would be sensible to keep a First Aid box handy in the stable area. As a guide we would suggest that your First Aid box includes the following:

- Bandages: Various types, lengths and widths.
- Sterile Gauzes
- Antiseptic wipes.
- Adhesive tape.
- Plasters: A variety.
- Safety pins.

- Antiseptic: Cream or liquid.
- Triangular bandage.
- Pair of scissors.

Always keep your First Aid box topped-up. Make sure that the box is returned to the same place each time it is used, and that everyone who uses the stable area is aware of where it is kept.

If an accident occurs where someone is seriously injured or unconscious, try not to panic! By drilling into yourself the following procedure, your help could be invaluable.

Emergency Drill:

1. Do not move the injured person unless leaving them where they are will place them in further danger.

2. Call the emergency services or a doctor.

3. Check that the casualty is in a position where his breathing is unimpeded.

4. Arrest bleeding.

5. Immobilise broken bones.

6. Treat for shock.

Let us look in greater detail at the last four items where a little knowledge of emergency procedures coupled with common sense could help alleviate unnecessary suffering.

Breathing:

If the person has stopped breathing then you have no alternative but to give them artificial respiration since a delay could prove fatal.

Clear the mouth of any debris that could cause an obstruction to the air passages. Loosen clothing around the neck. Move to the side of the casualty and gently lever them onto their back. Tilt the head backwards and the jaw upwards - this will straighten the wind pipe and give a straight access to the lungs. Pinch the nostrils tight, make a seal over the mouth with yours and breathe deeply into the lungs of the casualty. Watch for the chest to rise. If it does not check that the tongue hasn't fallen back and blocked the air passage. If this has happened hold the lower jaw - pull forwards - then tilt the head further back. Your first few breaths should be given rapidly, and thereafter at a rate of ten breaths per minute.

Bleeding

If the cut is a minor one then cleanse with an antiseptic wipe, cover with a clean, dry dressing and bandage. If the bleeding is more severe then you must treat straight away. Bright red blood that is spurting out will be from an artery. the bleeding must. be stopped immediately by applying pressure. If you do not have any gauze available any clean piece of material will suffice. Place the pad over the area and bandage firmly. If the bleeding seeps through do not remove the bandage, just add another layer.

Treating for shock

Place the casualty in the recovery position - unless there are broken bones that would be immobilised - keep the head low and turn to the side and raise the legs. Wrap the casualty in rugs, coats or blankets and loosen clothing. Do not give the casualty anything to drink as they may need anaesthetic and will need to have an empty stomach - your actions could delay treatment.

Broken Bones:

You may suspect broken bones if any of the following factors are present: The limb lying in an unnatural position; the injured area cannot be moved naturally; there is swelling or discolouration. Do not attempt to move the patient or the limb, this could cause further complications. Keep the patient warm and await professional help.

It is advisable for anyone spending time around horses to keep up-to-date with tetanus shots as tetanus germs are particularly prevalent where there are horses.

There are two magazines serving the Airgun market.

One is the leading publication, with an officially audited circulation

The other does not submit its circulation for scrutiny.

One is universally regarded as the voice of authority in the sport.

One is not.

One carries colour editorial in every issue.

One does not.

One is called **Airgun World.**

The other isn't.

There is only one

Safety on the Roads - Riding Out

> Horses can be extremely unpredictable, especially when frightened. Riders should owe it to themselves to develop strategies to deal with emergenceies on the road

Horses can be extremely unpredictable, especially when frightened. Riders owe it to themselves to develop strategies to deal with emergencies on the roads.

The time will come for the rider to leave the safe confines of the menage or school fields. When venturing outside the menage onto paths or roads that are used by the general public, on foot or on wheels, then you must be more aware of your surroundings. You must be alert at all times and able to react according to the situation.

It is your job to take all the precautions you can and adopt the Boy-Scouts' motto 'Be prepared'! There is no such thing as a 'car-proof' horse or pony. You cannot possibly anticipate all the situations that could happen on the road, but what you should have is a sound knowledge of the Highway Code. Today's roads are overcrowded and you cannot assume that all drivers have an understanding of the needs of the horse and rider.

Apart from reading the Highway Code, how can you prepare yourself?

Arrange to take the 'Riding and Road Safety Test' which is organised and operated by the British Horse Society and Pony Club. The aim of the test is to promote safety on the roads. It does this by recognising riders who conduct themselves responsibly, with courtesy and who obey the law, the Highway Code and comply with the rules as laid down in the British Horse Society Riding and Road Safety Manual.

This test can be taken either through your Pony Club or through your local Riding Club. If you are unable to locate a place to take it, then contact the Riding and Road Safety Officer at the B.H.S.

The test is conducted in three sections:

Prior to the ridden section there is a Tack and Turnout Inspection. This is as the title implies, an inspection of both horse and rider to ensure that their equipment is both suitable and safe for riding out on the roads.

Theoretical Test - This is to test the rider's knowledge of the Highway Code and the generally accepted rule of riding on the highway. This test can be given either orally or in the form of a test paper.

Simulated Road Test - Prior to going out on the roads, the examiners assure themselves that the rider is capable of dealing with a series of simulated hazards and situations. This test contains road junctions where riders must correctly demonstrate their ability to use arm signals. Hazards are included and placed in such a position that the candidates have to trot between them.

Road Test on the Public Highway - A practical test of the riders' knowledge of roadcraft. A piece of road suitable for testing the range of knowledge is chosen for this part.

In order to gain the Certificate, riders must pass all parts of the test - theory, simulated, and actual road test. In order to progress to the last part of the test the candidates must have passed the theory and simulated sections. Any manoeuvre that is judged by the examiners to be dangerous to other road users results in instant failure.

Pony Club members who are working for tests have to pass the Riding and Road Safety Test before they can progress to the higher tests.

It may take you some time to arrange to take the Riding and Road Safety Test, and in the meantime I am sure that you will want to use the road. The following are a few suggested do's and dont's.

Do

a. Check your tack before riding out. Make sure that it is comfortably fitted and in good repair.

b. Make sure that you are properly equipped, particularly your head and feet!

c. Check your horse's shoes - ensure that they are not loose or badly worn.

d. Keep away from busy main roads if at all possible.

e. Ride on the left of the road.

f. Give clear and accurate road signals that can be seen and understood by other road users.

g. Be courteous to other road users and acknowledge a courtesy.

h. Plan your rides so that you are returning before dusk, or alternatively, make sure that both you and your horse are equipped with appropriate reflective or fluorescent clothing.

i. Tell someone where you are going to ride, and roughly how long you are going to be.

j. Carry a pocket first aid kit and money for a phone call - BE PREPARED!

k. Make sure that you have labels inside your clothes and hat, and a disc marked with your 'phone number attached to your tack.

l. Stay alert to what is happening on the road.

m. Be considerate to pedestrians.

n. Enrol in some basic first aid classes - it may help you and your friends.

Don't

a. Take an over-fresh horse on the roads if it can possibly be avoided.

b. Ride along in a bunch - remember, two abreast is the maximum.

c. Take a young, inexperienced horse out on the roads without a steadier, more experienced horse.

d. Trot on road surfaces known to be slippery.

e. Trickle across a main road - cross in a group.

f. Ride in the fog or after dark, unless completely unavoidable.

g. Ride out on roads known to be dangerous from snow and ice.

h. Panic if your horse slips and falls. Keep calm, let the animal find it's feet, move to a safe area and check for injuries before re-mounting.

i. Tense in anticipation of something happening as this will transmit to the horse.

j. Have a battle royal in the middle of a busy road if your horse is spooking; either wait for the traffic to clear or, if this doesn't happen, dismount and lead the horse around the obstacle.

k. Ride on pavements or ornamental verges.

l. Canter on the roads or trot downhill on slippery roads.

m. Lead a horse on a busy road in a head collar only, you won't have enough control if anything goes wrong.

n. Be put off riding out by the number of Do's and Dont's listed here!!

We must stress the need for courtesy towards other road users. Don't forget that you are ambassadors for other riders - the motorist is likely to remember a courteous acknowledgment and smile, and respond to other riders with the same degree of courtesy afforded to you.

Public Rights of Way

by Ian Southall BHSII

Bridleways are falling into missuse due to the publics ignorance of their right. Vigilance is needed from the riding public if the current network of bridleways is to be maintained

To the horse rider, the single most important way of gaining access to the countryside is by the network of public rights of way. The term 'public right of way' means a path, track, bridleway or unmetalled road, over which the general public have the right to walk and, in some cases, ride horses and bicycles, and possibly drive motor vehicles.

Imagine being able to set out on your horse for a morning's hack and being able to use fields, bridleways and quiet country lanes for the duration of the ride. The bridleways would be wide enough for two horses to pass and would have a dry, springy surface such as wood-chips or sand. The gates would be hung correctly on secure posts and fastened with easy to use catches. There would be signposts at every junction to keep riders well informed, especially when the bridleway crosses a field. Where fields have been seeded or ploughed the surface would be restored around the edge or across the field. Unfortunately, for the majority of riders, this scenario is just a dream.

A quiet hack in the countryside can be more of a nightmare than a way to relax. In a recent survey undertaken by the Countryside Commission it was stated that we have about 140,000 miles of public right of way. Of this amount there are 106,000 miles (76%) of footpath and 28,000 miles (20%) of bridleway. The remaining 6,000 miles (4%) are by-ways open to all traffic, or roads used as public paths. It was also stated that 75% of the bridleways were shown to be satisfactory, 17% are poor, and 8% are unusable. The main problems associated with the unusable bridleways are:

Ploughed surfaces, or growing crops.

Overgrown vegetation.

Fences, hedges or walls across a path without a gate.

Boggy or flooded areas.

Due to these problems England and Wales have about 22,000 miles of unusable rights of way.

Important changes to the law on ploughing and cropping of public footpaths and bridleways came into effect on 13th August 1990. The Rights of Way Act 1990 gives councils the power to take farmers to court, or to go in and put matters to rights after giving notice to the farmer.

Every year the number of people riding horses increases. Every year more of the countryside is developed, and what land remains is farmed with increasing intensity. Farmers, or other landowners, cannot legally prevent riders from using bridleways which cross their land.

If riders are to have adequate riding places in the future, then existing bridleways must be retained and many new ones created. Bridleways are kept open by establishing their legal existence, and by clearing them and maintaining their surfaces. Riders should get to know the route and condition of all bridleways in their area. Public rights of way are shown in the 1:25000 outdoor leisure maps and the definitive maps held by local authorities. The definitive map is accompanied by a statement which describes each right of way in detail. If the statement defines the position or width of a right of way shown on the definitive map, then that is conclusive evidence of the position of the right of way at the relevant date. Any amendments to the definitive map should be available for public inspection.

If an obstruction occurs then the landowner can be approached directly. If the landowner is not known, or if there are other reasons why a personal approach would not be productive, the local highway authority should be asked to begin procedures for the removal of obstructions.

1991 has been designated as the year of the ARROW (Access and Riding Rights of Way) by the British Horse Society. The aim of ARROW is to ensure that, within the next ten years, there should be an established basic network of public bridleways and by-ways in all counties, with cross-country and regional links. Hopefully individual riders will come forward to help identify one circular county route with links across the borders to other county routes. The routes will eventually be mapped and shown on leaflets, along with points of interest and appropriate information.

Now we come to what most of us have to do on a regular basis - riding on the road. With the weight of today's traffic, everyone who uses any road is at risk. We can, however, take precautions before using the road. Firstly, a thorough knowledge of the Highway Code is essential. A current edition of the Highway Code is on sale in most bookshops, and some motoring shops. Riders must show consideration for other road users and be courteous to those who show consideration in return. Thanking a driver for slowing down when near to your horse goes a long way. Exercising common sense by avoiding peak traffic times and major roads is very important.

Without safe and well fitting tack, all of our efforts will be a waste of time. How can a horse be expected to behave if his saddle is pinching, or his bit is jangling against his teeth? The riders clothe's are another major consideration. Firstly, the headgear must conform to BSI standards BS6473 or BS4472 (for the jockey skull cap). the hat must fit correctly with the harness securely fastened. Boots should be worn and should have hard soles and heels. Plimsole or training shoes should not be worn - they can be dangerous. It is also dangerous to wear an unfastened coat. A gust of wind can make the coat flap with dire consequences as your horse, or a following horse, takes flight.

If you ride on the roads after lighting-up time you must wear reflective clothing and a safety stirrup lamp fitted in accordance with the Highway Code. Obviously, the riders experience should be considered. An inexperienced rider should not be tempted to go on the road.

Finally, the horse. All necessary precautions can be taken, but if the horse has not been prepared for what it may have to face, then the rider, the horse and other road users could be placed in a very dangerous situation.

To help prepare for riding on the road, the British Horse Society and the Pony Club run the Riding and Road Safety Test which covers all areas necessary to ensure safety in the future.

If anyone would like to volunteer their services to help improve the bridleways network, or would like further information about bridleways or the Riding and Road Safety Test, they should contact the British Horse Society. They are based at Stoneleigh, Warwickshire, and the telephone number is (0203) 696697.

Some Human Faults and Problems

> *Bad habits, once developed, can be extremely difficult to correct. Attention to avoiding developing these must surely pay off.*

Bad habits, once developed, can be extremely difficult to correct. Attention to avoiding developing these must surely pay off.

Not all faults can be attributed to the horse of course. Even the mildest well-mannered experienced horse cannot be expected to perform to its full potential if the rider has developed or perpetuated some bad habits. Let us look at some of the common problems that are encountered.

A Bad Seat

This is undoubtedly a serious fault. You may be sitting too far back in the saddle, thus pushing your legs into a forward position. This position will make it harder for the horse to carry your weight and the only way you will achieve any movement with the horse is by waving your legs backwards and forwards in an unsightly manner.

You should sit in the centre of the saddle and be able to fit a hand between yourself and the centre - a deep-seated saddle will help you to achieve this position. Your legs should be as near to the horse as possible, but leaving the lower part to draw an imaginary line from your knee to the ground with it passing through the tip of your toe (through your ankle and your legs are too far forwards, through space and your legs are too far back).

A Weak Seat

This could be as a result of the way you sit, or just your general unfitness. If the latter is the case then you need to make sure your diet and exercise routine improve your level of fitness.

The rider who leans too far forward, who is 'in front' of the horse has a weak seat. If riding a horse that is prone to stumbling or sudden stops he could soon find himself over the horse's head! Until the rider is able to sit deep in the saddle and use his legs properly, he will achieve less than adequate control over his horse.

If you feel that this is a fault you may have then to work hard on correcting it - ask your riding companions to correct you, or even invest in some professional help at your local riding school or riding club.

Bad Hands

If you are the sort of person who's always in a hurry and tends to pull the horse where you want it to go rather than push it then bad hands could be your problem. The reins are not there for you to balance yourself with and, if you find that your horse is snatching at the bit - developing a sore mouth or pulling till your arms ache then inconsiderate hands may be your problem. Your hands may be wrong because of your seat, its's hard to separate the two.

Good hands are those that go with the horse and know when to give and when to take. Your hands should not be fixed, nor should they be moving all the time - a rider with good quiet hands can stop a well-schooled horse by merely closing his fingers. A rider with good hands will be able to move them independently of each other.

If you feel that your hands are bad, then try to begin by making them independent of your seat. Ask someone to lunge you while you ride either with your arms outstretched or folded. When you feel you are achieving some degree of mastery then try the same movement, but this time without your stirrups. Progress with these movements through walk to trot and canter, making sure you work both

ways round the circle. Once you become confident and feel there is some improvement try riding in a reasonably enclosed space with your reins knotted using both your legs and seat to control the horse. With a reasonably well-schooled horse try bringing your weight forward and using your legs correctly to get the horse to move forwards, bring your weight back and he should stop. Never rush at this procedure, a little time spent in the early stages could save a lot of anguish later on. Remember - never use your hands alone - your seat and legs should work in combination with your legs.

Calf Cuddling

This is when the calves of your legs are almost permanently pressed against the sides of the horse. For the well-schooled horse this can be most frustrating since you will so often come to the point where your legs are saying 'go faster' and your hands are saying 'stop'.

The fault here lies in your seat. Try riding for a time without stirrups, but maintaining a correct position and making sure that when you look down you can see the tip of your toe. Also check the length of your stirrups.

Nervousness

Although you may never cure this completely you must try to gain confidence.

If you can, try to find a kind, calm and experienced horse to ride. There is nothing worse than trying to ride something that you are afraid of and is beyond your capabilities.

Don't try to run before you can walk. You should not be pushed into jumping before you have achieved a good independent seat. Try riding out with a group who are sympathetic to your problems and who can be of assistance to you if something goes wrong. Once you know you can ride out with confidence and relax you are more than half way towards conquering your problems.

Horses can be extremely sensitive towards the moods and feelings of the rider so do try hard to conquer your fears as a nervous horse and rider can be a pretty lethal combination out on the highways.

Fencing

Fencing has always been a traditional art but increased concern over safety has led to the use of new materials and techniques in order to provide this vital function

Fencing Problems Taped

An accident to a horse in 1984 led to the conception of the most revolutionary safe fencing it is possible to obtain for the containment of horses and quite changed people's attitude to what constitutes a 'safe' fence.

A French horse breeder bought a finely bred horse from the United Kingdom and just before shipment the horse became tangled in a barbed wire fence for many hours. As is usual with barbed wire, the damage was bad and ruined the horse for any future competitive work. Both the horse's breeder and her new owner decided to try to invent a form of fencing that was totally safe for the containment of horses.

First the various options currently available were studied. Post and rail is expensive, needs to be professionally installed and then is subject to constant maintenance as horses rub, chew and break it. The breaking strain of a normal wood rail is roughly 150 lbs (75 kilos) and a horse can very easily smash

through a three rail fence as if it did not exist. The added terror of wood fencing being that it is brittle and breaks leaving a jagged edge that can lance into a horse's chest or slice into legs with ease. Many expensive, highly bred horses have been put down with a wood 'lance' bedded deep inside the chest from a split rail and many more have broken legs by forceful contact with wood or concrete rails. Normal wire is inexpensive but is virtually invisible to horses, particularly when in flight. It slices animals up like salami and, if broken or badly installed can wind round a leg with ease applying a sharp edged touriquet that kills the flesh below within forty minutes. Barbed wire has all the disadvantages of ordinary wire but with the added problem of the jagged edges that can slice a horse open in seconds. It conducts arbitrary, unselective surgery in seconds.

The various equine fences were also studied. Stock fencing does hold equines very effectively but needs to be installed under tension and with precision. As horses lean over to attempt to get at rich grass on the other side they will tend to pore the ground. Should a hoof go through the stock fencing they will attempt to withdraw and the speed determines how much damage is inflicted. It is not unusual for the entire hoof to be removed. Electric string was too fragile whilst electric wire had the same preventative characteristics as drawn wire.

Fencing of wide plastic bands usually need to be professionally installed and can quickly become slack and unsightly. Some become brittle after a few years' weathering and once this happens they crack and splinter. Any horse rubbing alongside can be sliced by these splinters. The general conclusion was that most forms of accepted equine fencing had been designed mainly by non horse owners and utilising existing technology.

One year later the French owner, who by profession was a marketing ideas man, came up with the solution. A unique concept that appeared to have none of the disadvantages of any existing form of conventional fencing and many inbuilt advantages. The result no doubt, of a horse breeder and owner who held no pre-conceived ideas about fencing but seeking a simple goal - totally safe equine fencing.

Serge Lecachuer had sat down with an open mind. He learned that an effective barrier for a bolting horse need to no more than 2 inches (40 mm) wide. The most flexible item 2 inches wide was a medical bandage and he found that it did hold animals back. Being flexible

and soft even if they did become entangled it did no harm. He worked on a more robust bandage that would stand weathering and then found that a woven band of nylon not only accomplished his objective but also retained a very high breaking strain about seven times greater than a wood rail. It also proved to be rot proof and durable. When horses became entangled, once they stopped struggling it fell away with no harm being inflicted on the animal due to the width of the tape and no sharp edges.

The problem of safely containing bolting horses was solved. However, the problem of grazing horses sliding gently under this flexible band as they grazed was not solved. The fence needed to 'bite', The answer was already in existences in the form of electric string so a number of filaments were incorporated into the band of nylon tape and current passed through. It worked beyond his wildest dreams and the revolution in fencing was born.

The fence was totally 'bolt' proof, stronger than any conventional fencing except barbed wire, incapable of harming a horse, eye appealing, simple to install and about one fifth the price of post and rail fencing. Today, with the price increases in drawn wire, it is about the same price as barbed wire. Additionally it only needed two strands. One to stop bolting horses and a second, lower strand to discourage grazing animals going underneath where their manes provide natural insulation.

He then set out to exhaustively test the system and it was subject to intense heat and sunlight in Saudi Arabia, 60+ below temperatures in Northern Canada. Each brought forward some weakness in the system most particularly the problems of degradation under ultra violet light but as each problem emerged so it was overcome. Subsequently with wide use it has been constantly refined until it became a safe, complete fencing system that far outstrips anything else in cost effectiveness, simplicity to install and durability. It also happens to be incapable of harming animals in any way. The fence is light and easy to handle. It also has the advantage that if badly installed it will only look untidy but can do no damage of any sort to a horse. All horses respect it and it has proved ideal for 'hot' or very young animals. The fencing is now finding many outlets in other animal containment spheres.

In 1986, whilst still being estensively tested around the world, the fencing was presented at the Salon du Cheval de Paris where it won three of the twelve awards given - best product, best original idea, best technical achievement. The first time in the 100 years' history of the Salon that one product had gained more than two awards.

As well as its enormous advantages over every other form of animal fencing the one of cost is significant. It aggregates a total installed price well below most other systems. Post and rail averages £6-£8 per metre. A combination wire and stock fence £4 with plain wire at £2. Most wide plastic band systems tend to run at around £5 per metre whilst the tape comes in at approximately £1.50 per metre. It utilises the thinnest stakes possible placed five metres apart.

Once it became widely known and used many other advantages soon became apparent when horses are familiar with its properties. Horses respect its ability to 'bite' and this can be used to great advantage. Tape can be used to encourage reluctant horses into confined spaces. Fields can be temporarily sub divided in minutes. Stallions can be allowed to graze free close to other horses because horses will communicate over or through the fence but NEVER attempt to cross or break through it. Tape gates are far simpler and easier to handle than oconventional 'solid' gates and can be used to cut out one horse from a a herd. All horses respect the tape and none will attempt to jump over it. The making of menages and round pens is a matter of hours and at about a quarter the cost of any other material. One trainer has dispensed with horse walkers and has a series of tape corridors side by side. Each is around 100 yards long and 10 yards wide. A horse put into each corridor will run up and down competing with its neighbour and so self-exercise at a natural pace to suit its development.

It has proved a boon to stud farms for, apart from keeping visiting mares and foals safe it also allows stallions to lead a more natural and contented life as they also respect its properties and can be safely left grazing in their own paddocks. Because it is so easily mobile people who rent grazing can install and ultimately remove their own safe fencing when they move on. Studs and training facilities with grass management machinery geared to large acrages tend to install permanent runs around the perifery and use the temporary system for internal field division. When paddocks that are too small for this type of equipment need to be worked it is a matter of minutes to dismantle the temporary fencing to allow the large machines access to the increased acrage. Similarly the use of tape gates rather than solid gates enables field entrances to be up to 6 metres wide - sufficient width for the very largest equipment.

Once the original testing had been completed a number of other horse owners and breeders then undertook to market the product in their own countries rather than having the system marketed through fencing companies or Agricultural wholesalers. Where the marketing cover may not be so good the strength of this approach is long term for each has their own equine installation so that they can advise customers from personal experience.

Since its introduction a considerable number of plagiarist tapes have appeared throughout the world but, regrettably, the manufacturers, through lack of experience of this new medium have applied electric string or wire techniques to their products so that although the tapes are all fairly similar the attendant parts that make up the complete system are derivatives of what amounts to an alien technique that renders the total installation not very durable nor reliable.

More than 600,000 systems have been sold throughout the world and in countries such as France and Sweden it is now the accepted horse fencing. It is also finding outlets in other fields and successfully translates to containing pigs, elephants, deer, cattle, sheep, goats and Llamas. The tape system is marketed in the United Kingdom by Fieldguard Limited.

Tape really is the fencing of the future.

Useful References
& Listings

Aqua Sprays   162

Clothing Manufacturers:

Boots   162
Breeches & Jodphurs   163
Chaps   164
General   164
Hats   165
Jackets   166
Waterproofs   168

Clothing Retailers   169
Equestrian Fine Art   169
Galleries   169
Hat Covers   170
Insurance Brokers/Valuers   170
Magazines & Books   171
Mail Order Supplies   172
Name Plates   173
Portraits & Momentos   173
Riding Equipment, Chaps   173
Riding Equipment, Clothing   173
Show Jumps/Sundries   174
Side-Saddle Habits   174
Spurs   175
Tack Shops   175
Ties & Stocks   175
Video Services   175
Whips   176

The Responsible Rider:
Useful References and
Listings

Aqua Sprays

The Wyke Equestrian Services
Shifnal, Shropshire TF11 9PP
Tel: 0952 462982
Fax: 0952 462981

H J Fagg & Son
Driberg Way, Braintree,
Essex CM7 7NB
Tel: 0376 22026

Clothing Manufacturers: Boots

Allen & Caswell
Regent Works, Cornwall
Road, Kettering, Northants
NN16 8PR
Tel: 0536 512804
Fax: 0536 411085

Bridgedale
Samuel Street, Leicester,
LE1 1RU

British Bata Shoe Co Ltd
East Tilbury, Essex RM18
8RL
Tel: 03752 3400

Burton McCall
Samuel Street, Leicester,
Leicestershire
Tel: 0533 538781

Carbex-Munroe (Handles)
11a St Nicholas Lane,
Lewes, East Sussex BN7 2JZ
Tel: 0273 478111

Casual Riding Manufacturing Ltd
533 Twickenham Road,
Isleworth, Middlesex
Tel: 081 8927710

Champion & Wilton Limited
112/122 Tabernacle Street,
London, EC2M 4LE
Tel: 071 251 2701

Coleman Croft Saddlery
Sutton's Farm, Cooper's
Green, Nr St Albans,
Hertfordshire AL4 9HJ
Tel: 07072 74239

Cottage Ind. (Equestrian) Ltd
Crown Lane, Wychbold,
Droitwich, Worcestershire
Tel: 052786 582

Crockett & Jones
Perry Street, Northampton,
Northamptonshire
Tel: 0604 31515

Derriboots
C Mills Derriboots, Princess
Margaret Road, East Tilbury,
Essex RM18 8RL
Tel: 03752 3400

Equestrian Manufacturing & Supply
52 Mount Street, Walsall,
West Midlands WS1 3PL

G T Hawkins Ltd

Overstone Road,
Northampton, NN1 3JJ
Tel: 0604 32293
Fax: 0604 231413

Hebden Cord Co Limited
Hebden Bridge, West
Yorkshire HX7 6SW
Tel: 0422 843152

Higham Ferrers Boot Co
Moor Road, Rushden,
Northants
Tel: 0933 50808

Horse Requisites Newmarket Ltd
Black Bear Lane,
Newmarket, Suffolk CB8 0JT
Tel: 0638 664619
Fax: 0638 661562

Hydrophane Laboratories Limited
Ickleford Manor, Hitchin, Hertfordshire
Tel: 0462 32596

J Barbour & Sons Limited
Simonside, South Shields, Tyne & Wear NE34 9PD
Tel: 091 455 4444
Fax: 091 454 2944

J C Footwear
137/141 Regent Street, Kettering, Northants
Tel: 0536 84797

L W Faulkner & Son
5 Station Road, Woodford Halse, Daventry, Northants NN11 6RB
Tel: 0327 60306

Lady Northampton Boot Co Ltd, The
Regent Street, Northampton, Northants
Tel: 0604 38122/3/4

Leyland & Birmingham Rubber Co
Golden Hill Lane, Leyland, Lancs PR5 1VB

M J Ainge & Co. Ltd
Porthouse Farm Industrial Est., Bromyard, Herefordshire HR7 4NP
Tel: 0885 83601

R E Tricker Ltd
St Michaels Road, Northampton, Northants NN13JX
Tel: 0604 30595/6/7

RPM Western Trading
The Avenue Riding Centre, Hanley Road, Malvern, Worcs
Tel: 0684 310783

Schnieder Riding Boot Company
16, Clifford Street, New Bond Street, London WIX 1RG
Tel: 071 734 0433
Fax: 071 287 2536

Trickers (London)
67 Jermyn street, St James's, London SW1
Tel: 071 930 6395

Tuc Plastics Ltd
104 Blackdown Rural Industries, Haste Hill, Hazelmere, Surrey
Tel: 0426 52026

Turners Footwear & Country Clo.
241 Drayton High Road, Hellesdon, Norwich, Norfolk

Vale Bros Ltd
Defiance Brush Works, Long Street, Walsall, W Mids
Tel: 0922 24363

W & H Gidden Ltd
15d Clifford Street, New Bond Street, London W1X 1RF
Tel: 071 734 2788
Fax: 071 494 2388

Walkers Outdoor Leisure Ltd
6 Bell Court Precinct, Stratford-upon-Avon, Warwickshire
Tel: 0789 68937

Breeches & Jodhpurs

Birrs Sportswear Ltd
9 Erskine Street, Leicester, Leics LE1 2AT
Tel: 0533 25780

Bob Church & Co. Limited
16 Lorne Road, Northampton, NN1 3RN
Tel: 0604 713674
Fax: 0604 250051

Brian Lindsay
19 Ledra Closem, Cagwith Ruan Minor, Helston, Cornwall TR12 7LD
Tel: 0326 290595

Bryan Lawrence & Co
Rowney Priory, Dane End, Ware Hertfordshire SG12 0JY
Tel: 0920 438684

Caldene Clothing Co Ltd
Burnley Road, Mytholmroyd, Hebden Bridge, West Yorkshire
Tel: 0422 883393

Castle Sportswear Ltd
Unit 39/44, Barkston House, Domestic Street Ind Estate, Leeds LS11 9RT
Tel: 05322 452858

Casual Riding Manufacturing Ltd
533 Twickenham Road, Isleworth, Middlesex
Tel: 081 8927710

Champion & Wilton Limited
112/122 Tabernacle Street, London, EC2M 4LE
Tel: 071 251 2701

Chevalier Ltd
P O Box 8, Pethworth, Sussex EU28 OPE
Tel: 079 86418

Coleman Croft Saddlery
Sutton's Farm, Cooper's Green, Nr St Albans, Hertfordshire AL4 9HJ
Tel: 07072 74239

Dressage of London
Beadman Place, London,
London SE27 ODN
Tel: 081 670 1115

Gorringe Sportswear Limited
Arclive House, 2 Short
Street, Walsall, West
Midlands WS2 9EB
Tel: 0922 28131

Hac Tac
P O Box 164, Oxford, Oxon
OX1 5JN
Tel: 08677 2796

Harris Meyer (E.P.) Limited
Burnley Road, Mytholmroyd,
Hebden Bridge, West
Yorkshire
Tel: 0422 884938

Harry Hall Limited
P.O. Box 3, Thirsk, North
Yorkshire

Hebden Cord Co Limited
Hebden Bridge, West
Yorkshire HX7 6SW
Tel: 0422 843152

Horse Requisites Newmarket Ltd
Black Bear Lane,
Newmarket, Suffolk CB8 0JT
Tel: 0638 664619
Fax: 0638 661562

Hydrophane Laboratories Limited
Ickleford Manor, Hitchin,
Hertfordshire
Tel: 0462 32596

M J Ainge & Co. Ltd
Porthouse Farm Industrial
Est, Bromyard, Herefordshire
HR7 4NP
Tel: 0885 83601

McHardy's of Carlisle
South Henry Street, Carlisle,
Cumbria
Tel: 0228 23988

Merage Clothing Co (Ipswich)Ltd
St Clements, Church Lane,
Fore Street, Ipswich, Suffolk
IP4 1JH
Tel: 0473 215265

Outdoor Life
533 Twickenham Road,
Isleworth, Middlesex
Tel: 081 892 7710

Stylo Manufacturing International Ltd
Matchmakers House,
Clayton Wood Bank, Leeds
Tel: 0532 783501

Chaps

J & C Gibbins
Lodge Road, Hollesley,
Woodbridge, Suffolk
IP12 3RR
Tel: 0394 411 195
Fax: 0394 410 015

Clothing, General

Aerborn Equestian
Pegasus House, 198
Sneinton Dale, Nottingham,
Notts NG2 4HJ
Tel: 0602 505631
Fax: 0602 483273

Allen & Caswell
Regent Works, Cornwall
Road, Kettering, Northants
NN16 8PR
Tel: 0536 512804
Fax: 0536 411085

Beaver of Bolton Limited
Gilnow Mill, Spa Road,
Bolton, Lancashire BL1 4LF
Tel: 0204 386824
Fax: 0204 365522

Belstaff Int. Limited
Caroline Street, Longton,
Stoke on Trent, Staffs
ST3 1DD
Tel: 0782 317261

Bob Church & Co. Limited
16 Lorne Road,
Northampton, NN1 3RN
Tel: 0604 713674
Fax: 0604 250051

Bramham Sweaters
Roseberry Cottage, Bishop
Thornton, Harrogate,
Yorkshire

Buckingham Harness
Ardington, Wantage, Oxon
OX12 8PN
Tel: 0235 833719

Burton McCall
Samuel Street, Leicester,
Leicestershire
Tel: 0533 538781

Castle Sportswear Ltd
Unit 39/44, Barkston House,
Domestic Street Ind Estate,
Leeds, LS11 9RT
Tel: 05322 452858

Casual Riding Manufacturing Ltd
533 Twickenham Road,
Isleworth, Middlesex
Tel: 081 8927710

Charles Owen & Co (Bow) Ltd
61/65 Cae Gwilym Lane,
Cefn Mwr, Wrexham,
Clwydn LL14 3LS
Tel: 0978 810671
Fax: 0978 810670

Cottage Ind. (Equestrian) Ltd
Crown Lane, Wychbold, Droitwich, Worcestershire
Tel: 052786 582

Cross Country (Equestrian) Ltd
Luttwytche Road, Church Stretton, Shropshire SY6 6AT
Tel: 0694 722919

David Marsh (Manchester) Ltd
Riverside Works, Edward Street, Lower Broughton, Manchester M7 9SJ

Denewear
In Park Barn, Capistock, Nr Dorchester, Dorset
Tel: 093583 638

Donalds McLellan (Saddler), Saddle & Harness
Maker
146, Busby Road, Clarkston, Glasgow G76 8BH
Tel: 041 644 4880

Emsby Field Sportswear Limited
Granville Chambers, Midland Road, Wellingborough, Northants
Tel: 0933 224482

Epic, Equestrian Product Innovation Co Ltd
Sales & Marketing House, Beacon Street, Lichfield, Staffs WS13 7AA
Tel: 0543 414040
Fax: 0543 256024

Fancy Free Race & Event Wear
The Heath, Stoke Prior, Leominster, Herefordshire
Tel: 056 882 662

George Jeffries Gloves
Fairfield Road, Warminster, Wilts BA12 9DL
Tel: 0985 212716

Hebden Cord Co Limited
Hebden Bridge, West Yorkshire HX7 6SW
Tel: 0422 843152

Hydrophane Laboratories Limited
Ickleford Manor, Hitchin, Hertfordshire
Tel: 0462 32596

Irene Wilson
The Smithy, Waddington, Clitheroe, Lancs BB7 3HW
Tel: 0200 22976

Lavenham Rug Company Ltd
Long Melford, Suffolk CO10 9LL
Tel: 0787 79535

M J Ainge & Co. Ltd
Porthouse Farm Industrial Est., Bromyard, Herefordshire HR7 4NP
Tel: 0885 83601

Mark Saddler Limited
Gayton House, Well Lane, Gayton, Wirral, Cheshire
Tel: 051 342 7722

P I Associates
The Red House, Tuddenham, Bury St Edmunds, Suffolk IP28 6TB
Tel: 0638 717521

Ridry Waterproof Clothing
Cobbacombe Farm, Huntsham, Nr Tiverton, Devon EX16 7QJ
Tel: 03983 711

RPM Western Trading
The Avenue Riding Centre, Hanley Road, Malvern, Worcs
Tel: 0684 310783

Turners Footwear & Country Clo.
241 Drayton High Road, Hellesdon, Norwich, Norfolk

Vale of Belvoir Leathers
26 Park Road, Melton Mowbray, Leics
Tel: 0664 65199

Wrangler, Bluebell Apparell
Park Road East, Nottingham, Nottinghamshire

Yorkshire Horse Rug Co
1256 Manchester Road, Linthwaite, Huddersfield, Yorkshire
Tel: 0484 844897

Hats

Beaver of Bolton Limited
Gilnow Mill, Spa Road, Bolton, Lancashire BL1 4LF
Tel: 0204 386824
Fax: 0204 365522

Black Horse International Trading Ltd
Church Lane, Pitsford, Northampton, Northants NN6 9AJ
Tel: 0604 880230

Caldene Clothing Co Ltd
Burnley Road, Mytholmroyd, Hebden Bridge, West Yorkshire
Tel: 0422 883393

Casual Riding Manufacturing Ltd
533 Twickenham Road, Isleworth, Middlesex
Tel: 081 8927710

Charles Owen & Co (Bow) Ltd

61/65 Cae Gwilym Lane, Cefn Mwr, Wrexham, Clwyd LL14 3LS
Tel: 0978 810671
Fax: 0978 810670

Christy & Co Limited
Stockport, Cheshire

Denewear
In Park Barn, Capistock, Nr Dorchester, Dorset
Tel: 093583 638

Emsby Field Sportswear Limited
Granville Chambers, Midland Road, Wellingborough, Northants
Tel: 0933 224482

F B Davis Saddlery Limited
Tolsons Mill, Mitchfield Street, Fazeley, Tamworth, Staffordshire B78 3QB
Tel: 0827 280550

Gecko Leisure Products Ltd
Sutton Industrial Park, Reading, Berks RG6 1AZ
Tel: 0734 669333

Hebden Cord Co Limited
Hebden Bridge, West Yorkshire HX7 6SW
Tel: 0422 843152

Herbert Johnson, Wholesale/Export
4 New Burlington Street, London W1 1LA
Tel: 071 434 4330

James Lock & Co Limited
6 St James Street, London SW1A 1EF
Tel: 071 930 5849

Jofa UK
P O Box 8, Petworth, Sussex
Tel: 07986 418

John Partridge Sales Ltd
Trent Meadows, Rugeley, Staffs WS15 2HS
Tel: 0889 584438
Fax: 0889 576746

Lee Bennett
3 Bailiffs' Close, Axbridge, Somerset
Tel: 0934 732545

M J Ainge & Co. Ltd
Porthouse Farm Industrial Est., Bromyard, Herefordshire HR7 4NP
Tel: 0885 83601

Merage Clothing Co (Ipswich)Ltd
St Clements, Church Lane, Fore Street, Ipswich, Suffolk IP4 1JH
Tel: 0473 215265

S Patey (London) Ltd
1 Amelia Street, Walworth Road, London SE17 3PY
Tel: 071 703 6528

The Gatehouse Range
The GatehouseEwood Lane, Newdigate, Surrey
Tel: 0306 77374

Thomas Townend & Co Ltd
31-35 East Dulwich Road, London SE22 9AW
Tel: 081 693 8182

Jackets

Aerborn Equestrian
Pegasus House, 198 Sneinton Dale, Nottingham NG2 4HJ
Tel: 0602 505631
Fax: 0602 483273

Beaver of Bolton Limited
Gilnow Mill, Spa Road, Bolton, Lancashire BL1 4LF
Tel: 0204 386824
Fax: 0204 365522

Belstaff Int. Limited
Caroline Street, Longton, Stoke on Trent Staffs ST3 1DD
Tel: 0782 317261

Bob Church & Co. Limited
16 Lorne Road, Northampton, Northamptonshire NN1 3RN
Tel: 0604 713674
Fax: 0604 250051

Bob Lillie Leisurewear
Gold Street, Clipson Market Harborough Leics LE16 9RZ

Caldene Clothing Co Ltd
Burnley Road, Mytholmroyd, Hebden Bridge, West Yorkshire
Tel: 0422 883393

Castle Sportswear Ltd
Unit 39/44, Barkston House, Domestic Street Ind Estate, Leeds, LS11 9RT
Tel: 05322 452858

Casual Riding Manufacturing Ltd
533 Twickenham Road, Isleworth, Middlesex
Tel: 081 8927710

Catworth Manufacturing Co. Ltd
34 Market Road, Thrapston, Kettering, Northants NN14 4JU
Tel: 08012 3280

Denewear
In Park Barn, Capistock, Nr Dorchester, Dorset
Tel: 093583 638

Earnsdale Farm Riding School
Off Lynwood Avenue, Darwen, Lancs BB3 0LB
Tel: 0254 702647

Gorringe Sportswear Limited
Arclive House, 2 Short Street, Walsall, West Midlands WS2 9EB
Tel: 0922 28131

Hadleigh Equestn & Sportswr Ltd
Keynsham Road, Keynsham, Avon BS18 2DE
Tel: 02756 4356

Harris Meyer (E.P.) Limited
Burnley Road, Mytholmroyd, Hebden Bridge, West Yorkshire
Tel: 0422 884938

Harry Hall Limited
P.O. Box 3, Thirsk, North Yorkshire

Hebden Cord Co Limited
Hebden Bridge, West Yorkshire HX7 6SW
Tel: 0422 843152

Horse Requisites Newmarket Ltd
Black Bear Lane, Newmarket, Suffolk CB8 0JT
Tel: 0638 664619
Fax: 0638 661562

Husky of Tostock Limited
115 Bury Street, Stowmarket, Suffolk IP14 1HE
Tel: 0449 674471
Fax: 0449 674853

Irene Wilson
The Smithy, Waddington, Clitheroe, Lancs BB7 3HW
Tel: 0200 22976

J Barbour & Sons Limited
Simonside, South Shields, Tyne & Wear NE34 9PD
Tel: 091 455 4444
Fax: 091 454 2944

Jaytone Riding Wear
Yew Tree Cottage, Potters Hill, Felton, Avon

John Partridge Sales Ltd
Trent Meadows, Rugeley, Staffs WS15 2HS
Tel: 0889 584438
Fax: 0889 576746

Kampkit Limited
237 Royal College Street, 257 West Green, London NW1
Tel: 071 485 9989

Kingfisher Ltd
Lichfield Street, Rugely, Staffs
Tel: 08894 5032

Lavenham Rug Company Ltd
Long Melford, Suffolk CO10 9LL
Tel: 0787 79535

M J Ainge & Co. Ltd
Porthouse Farm Industrial Est., Bromyard Herefordshire HR7 4NP
Tel: 0885 83601

Matlock Brown Ltd
Bath Road, Kettering, Northants NN16 8NH
Tel: 0536 512435
Fax: 0536 513146

McHardy's of Carlisle
South Henry Street, Carlisle, Cumbria
Tel: 0228 23988

Merage Clothing Co (Ipswich)Ltd
St Clements, Church Lane, Fore Street, Ipswich, Suffolk IP4 1JH
Tel: 0473 215265

P I Associates
The Red House, Tuddenham, Bury St Edmunds, Suffolk IP28 6TB
Tel: 0638 717521

Puffa Ltd
Parka House, Little Waldingfield, Suffolk CO10 OSY
Tel: 0787 248474
Fax: 0787 248133

RCR Sales
4 The Approach Aldsworth Cheltenham Gloucestershire

Sporting Developments Int Ltd
210 Hermitage Road, Whitchurch Road, Whitchurch, Leicester, Leics
Tel: 0530 37236

Stylo Manufacturing Int. Ltd
Matchmakers House, Clayton Wood Bank Leeds
Tel: 0532 783501

The Gatehouse Range
The Gatehouse, Ewood Lane, Newdigate, Surrey
Tel: 0306 77374

Thornproof Riding Wear, Carr Day & Martin Limited
Newton Works, Great Dunmow, Essex

Wychwood Sportswear
Wellesbourne House, Wellesbourne, Warwick, CV35 9JB
Tel: 0789 842330

Yorkshire Horse Rug Co
1256 Manchester Road, Linthwaite, Huddersfield, Yorkshire
Tel: 0484 844897

Waterproofs

Allen & Caswell
Regent Works, Cornwall Road, Kettering Northants NN16 8PR
Tel: 0536 512804
Fax: 0536 411085

Beaver of Bolton Limited
Gilnow Mill, Spa Road, Bolton, Lancashire BL1 4LF
Tel: 0204 386824
Fax: 0204 365522

Belstaff Int. Limited
Caroline Street, Longton, Stoke on Trent, Staffs ST3 1DD
Tel: 0782 317261

Bob Church & Co. Limited
16 Lorne Road, Northampton, Northamptonshire NN1 3RN
Tel: 0604 713674
Fax: 0604 250051

Fawcett's Tarpaulins Ltd
Longton, Lancs PR4 5JA
Tel: 0772 612125
Hebden Cord Co Limited
Hebden Bridge, West Yorkshire HX7 6SW
Tel: 0422 843152

Husky of Tostock Limited
115 Bury Street Stowmarket Suffolk IP14 1HE
Tel: 0449 674471
Fax: 0449 674853

J Barbour & Sons Limited
Simonside, South Shields, Tyne & Wear NE34 9PD
Tel: 091 455 4444
Fax: 091 454 2944

James Calder
Caroline Street, Longton, Stoke On Trent, Staffordshire ST3 1DD
Tel: 0782 317261

John Partridge Sales Ltd
Trent Meadows, Rugeley Staffs WS15 2HS
Tel: 0889 584438
Fax: 0889 576746

P I Associates
The Red House, Tuddenham Bury St Edmunds Suffolk IP28 6TB
Tel: 0638 717521

Rainbow Horse Suppliers
Plasman Industrial Centre, Peter Moss Way, Levenshulme, Manchester M19 3JH
Tel: 061 224 0333

Ridry Waterproof Clothing
Cobbacombe Farm, Huntsham, Nr Tiverton, Devon EX16 7QJ
Tel: 03983 711

Talat International Leather Co
Talat House, Upper Northam Drive, Hedge End, Southampton, Hants SO3 4BG
Tel: 0703 462908

Vita Salford, (Division of British Vita PLC)
Seaford Road, Salford,
Manchester, G Man M6 6NA
Tel: 061 736 5343

Wychwood Sportswear
Wellesbourne House,
Wellesbourne, Warwick,
CV35 9JB
Tel: 0789 842330

Clothing Retailers

Ride-Away
Stillington Road, Sutton-on-Forest York YO6 1EH
Tel: 0347 810443
Fax: 0347 8107464

School of National Equitation
Bunny Hill Top, Costock,
Leicestershire LE12 6XE
Tel: 0509 852366
Fax: 0602 848381

W & H Gidden Ltd
15d Clifford Street, New Bond
Street, London W1X 1RF
Tel: 071 734 2788
Fax: 071 494 2388

Equestrian Fine Art

Michael Stewart Fine Art Ltd
The Georgian House, Broad
Street, Wrington Bristol,
Tel: 0934 862458
Fax: 0483 575109

Galleries

Andrew Thomas
The Old Vicarage, West
Pennard, Glastonbury,
Somerset BA6 8NT
Tel: 0458 32818

Animal Portraiture
Spinney Cottage, The
Ashlands, Illston on the Hill,
Leicestershire

Berrisford Hill
Down Cottage, The Dell,
Kingsclere, Nr Newbury,
Berks
Tel: 0635 298568

David Cemmick
Smithy House Farm, Great
Smeaton, Northallerton
N Yorks
Tel: 0325 483271

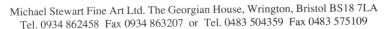

Henry-Brett Galleries
Halford House, Burton-on-the-Water, Gloucester, Glos
Tel: 0451 20443

Jane Neville Gallery
Elm House, Abbey Lane, Aslockton, Notts NG13 9AE
Tel: 0949 50220

John & Judith Nead
The Barn Book Supply, 88 Crane Street, Salisbury Wilts
Tel: 0722 27767

Michael Stewart Fine Art Ltd
The Georgian House, Broad Street, Wrington, Bristol, Avon BS18 7LA
Tel: 0934 862458
Fax: 0934 863207

Hat Covers

Charles Owen & Co (Bow) Ltd
61/65 Cae Gwilym Lane, Cefn Mwr Wrexham, Clwyd LL14 3LS
Tel: 0978 810671
Fax: 0978 810670

S Patey (London) Ltd
1 Amelia Street, Walworth Road, London SE17 3PY
Tel: 071 703 6528

The Gatehouse Range
The Gatehouse Ewood Lane, Newdigate, Surrey
Tel: 0306 77374

Insurance Brokers and Valuers

Avon Insurance PLC
Church Street, Stratford-upon-Avon, Warwickshire
Tel: 0789 204211

Baker Reeve & Co
63/66 Cannon House, West India Dock London E14 9ST
Tel: 071 987 3522

Bloodstock & General Insurance
Brokers Limited, 162 High Street, Newmarket Suffolk CB8 9AQ
Tel: 0638 661411
Fax: 0638 665013

British Equestrian Insurance
Hildenbrook House The Slade Tonbridge Kent TN9 1HY
Tel: 0732 771719
Fax: 0732 359982

Charles Wilkinson Ins Brokers
27 Walmgate, York, N Yorks
Tel: 0904 31839

Devitt Midland Limited
Tricorn House, Five Ways, Hagley Road, Edgbaston, Birmingham B16 8TP
Tel: 021 454 7881

E J Wood & Associates
50, Caynham Road, Bartley Green, Birmingham B32 4EY
Tel: 021 477 2001
Fax: 021 477 2865

Entertainment & Leisure
Box 100, Great Ouseburn, York, YO5 9SZ
Tel: 0901 30711

Equine & Livestock Ins. Co Ltd
Grove House 551 London Road, Isleworth, Middx TW7 4EP
Tel: 081 568 3431

Farmkey Limited
Universal House, Riverside, Banbury, Oxon OX16 8TF
Tel: 0295 52544

Frank Hill & Son
18 Market Place, Patrington, Hull, Humberside HU12 0RB
Tel: 0964 630531
Fax: 0964 631206

General Accident Fire & Life, Insurance Co. Ltd
General Buildings, Perth, Tayside PH2 0NH
Tel: 0738 21202
Fax: 0738 21843

George S Forbes
(Bloodstock Agents Ltd)
Burley Lodge, Hyde End road, Shinfield, nr Reading, Berkshire

Hobbs Parker
Romney House, Ashford Market, Elwick Road Ashford, Kent TN23 1PG
Tel: 0233 622222
Fax: 0233 646642

Horse & Rider Insurance Service
4 Augusta Place, Leamington Spa Warks CV31 5EL
Tel: 0203 452626
Fax: 0203 888999

Langbury Assoc Services Ltd
Langbury House, 19 High Street, Lambourn, Berks
Tel: 0488 71990

Matthews Comfort & Co Ltd

PO Box 37, Tuns Lane,
Henley-on-Thames Oxon
RG9 1BR
Tel: 0491 572083
Fax: 0491 410143

Norwich Union Insurance Group

P O Box 48, Norwich,
Norfolk NR1 3NG
Tel: 0603 622200
Fax: 0603 683007

P G Flower & Co

Insurance Brokers, 83
Station Road, Chingford,
London E4 7BU
Tel: 081 524 631515

Prudential Assurance Co Limited

142 Holborn Bars, London
EC1N 2NH
Tel: 071 405 9222

Richard Field Insurance Brokers

280/282 High Street,
Orpington, Kent

Rondo Horse Insurance

29 High Street, Newhaven,
East Sussex BN9 9PD
Tel: 0273 611555
Fax: 0273 611666
*'We represent policies by
eight leading underwriters
and are thus in a position
to offer a wide selection
and unbiased advice'*

South Essex Ins Brokers Ltd

South Essex House, North
Road, South Ockendon,
Essex RM15 6NU
Tel: 0708 853456
Fax: 0708 851520

Magazines and Books

B T Batsford Ltd

4 Fitzhardinge Street,
London W1H OAH
Tel: 071 486 8484

British Equestrian Directory

E.M.C., Wothersome Grange,
Bramham Nr Wetherby, West
Yorkshire
Tel: 0532 892267

Chiltern Connemara Stud

Combe Cottage, Presteigne,
Powys LD8 2LH
Tel: 0544 267026

Coleman Croft Saddlery

Sutton's Farm, Cooper's
Green, Nr St Albans,
Hertfordshire AL4 9HJ
Tel: 07072 74239

Dartmoor Pony Society

Weston Manor, Corscombe,
Dorchester Dorset DT2 OPB
Tel: 093 589 466

Elliot Right Way Books

7-31 Kingswood Buildings,
Kingswood Tadworth, Surrey
KT20 6TD
Tel: 0737 832202

Equestrian Book Society, Readers Union,

P.O.Box 6, Brunel House
Newton Abbott Devon
TQ12 2DW
Tel: 0626 69881
Fax: 0626 64463

Equi-Study

Hole House, Haltwistle,
Northumberland NE49 0LQ
Tel: 06977 47577
Fax: 06977 47661

Irish Draught Horse Society

4th Street, N A C, Stoneleigh,
Kenilworth, Warwickshire
CV8 2LG
Tel: 0203 696549
Fax: 0203 696729

Horse & Hound

King's Reach Tower, Stamford
Street, London SE1 9LS
Tel: 071 261 6315

Horse & Jockey Limited

High Street, Peterchurch,
Herefordshire HR2 0RP
Tel: 0981 550467

Horse & Pony Magazine

EMAP National Publications,
Bretton Court, Bretton,
Peterborough Lincs PE3 8DZ
Tel: 0733 264666

Horse & Rider

D J Murphy (Pulishers) Ltd,
104 Ash Road, Sutton,
Surrey
Tel: 081 641 4911

J A Allen & Co, The Horseman's Bookshop Ltd

1, Lower Grosvenor Place,
Buckingham Palace Road,
London SW1W 0EL
Tel: 071 834 5606 Fax: 071
233 8001

Mail Order Supplies

Acorn Rugs
Gair Shield Farm, Steel, Hexham, Northumberland NE47 OHS
Tel: 043 473 562

Alison Hammett (Equest Servces)
98 Robert Street, Ynysybwl, Pontypridd, Mid Glam CF3 3EA
Tel: 0443 790833

B F P Rosettes
39 Manor Road, Pawlett Nr Bridgewater, Somerset TA6 4SN
Tel: 0278 683455
Fax: 0278 684425

Brian Lindsay
19 Ledra Closem, Cagwith Ruan Minor,Helston, Cornwall TR12 7LD
Tel: 0326 290595

CAM Equestrian Joinery & Equip
Eardisley, Hereford, Hereford & Worcs HR3 6NS
Tel: 05446 611

CAM Stables & Farmbldgs Ltd
Eardisley, Hereford Hereford & Worcs HR3 6NS
Tel: 054 46611
Fax: 054 46210

Equi-Study
Hole House, Haltwistle, Northumberland NE49 0LQ
Tel: 06977 47577
Fax: 06977 47661

J P Rug Co
Downs House, Childrey, Oxon OX12 9UF
Tel: 023 559 400

John & Judith Nead
The Barn Book Supply, 88 Crane Street, Salisbury, Wilts
Tel: 0722 27767

Methuen London Ltd
11 New Fetter Lane, London, London EC4P 4EE
Tel: 071 583 9855

Pelham Books
44 Bedford Square, London WC1B 3DP
Tel: 071 323 3200

Pony
D J Murphy (Publishing) Limited, 104 Ash Road, Sutton, Surrey
Tel: 081 641 4911

Pony Press
Ellis Horwood Limited, Market Cross House, Copper Street, Chichester Sussex PO19 1EB
Tel: 0243 789942

Purnell Books
Poulton, Nr Bristol Avon

Riding
King's Reach Tower, Stamford Street, London SE1 9LS
Tel: 071 261 5487

The Barn Book Supply
88 Crane Street, Salisbury Wilts
Tel: 0722 27767

The Bloodstock Breeders Review
Sagittarius Bloodstock Ass. Ltd, Suite 53, 26 Charing Cross Road, London WC2H 0DJ

The National Stallion Assocn
96 High Street, Edenbridge Kent TN8 5AR
Tel: 0732 866277

Your Horse
National Publications Ltd Bretton Court, Bretton, Peterborough, Cambs PE3 8DZ
Tel: 0733 264666
Fax: 0733 265515

Zenophon Publication
44 Fleet Street London EC4Y 1BS

Zenophon Publication
Hole House, Haltwistle, Northumberland NE49 OLQ
Tel: 069 72383

K G Products
247/251 City Road, Fenton,
Stoke-on-Trent Staffs
ST4 2PY
Tel: 0782 44866

M J Ainge & Co. Ltd
Porthouse Farm Ind. Est.,
Bromyard, Hereford & Worcs
HR7 4NP
Tel: 0885 83601

M S Racegear
High Nentesberry Farm,
Alston, Cumbria CA9 3LZ
Tel: 0498 81998

Newton Horse Ltd
Hotham Hall, Hotham, E
Yorkshire YO4 3UN
Tel: 0430 423636

Rainbow Rosettes
FREEPOST, PO Box 110,
Norwich, Norfolk NR3 4BR
Tel: 0800 378364

Ride-Away
Stillington Road,
Sutton-on-Forest, York,
N Yorks YO6 1EH
Tel: 0347 810443
Fax: 0347 810746

V E Byrom (Mail Order)
Dept H & P,22 Regent Road,
Altringham, Cheshire
WA14 1RP
Tel: 061 928 6793

Name Plates

**CAM Equestrian
Joinery & Equip**
Eardisley, Hereford, Hereford
& Worcs HR3 6NS
Tel: 05446 611

Engraved Signs
Offenham, Evesham, Worcs
Tel: 0386 2712

Forecourt Signs Limited
73 Woodham Park Road,
Woodham, Weybridge,
Surrey
Tel: 093 2346639

Instant Signs
Fordes, Ropley, Alresford,
Hants
Tel: 096277 3373

K D Hampson
221 Hodges Street
Wigan, Lancs WN6 7JG
Tel: 0942 45102

**Loddon Livestock
Equipment Ltd**
Beccles Road, Loddon,
Norwich, Norfolk NR14 6JJ
Tel: 0508 20744
Fax: 0508 28055

Parry's Signs
Church Street, Malverton
Worcestershire
Tel: 06845 4077

Signs Familiar
Howdale, Downham Market,
Norfolk PE38 9AL
Tel: 0366 382511

Portraits and Momentos

Andrew Thomas
The Old Vicarage, West
Pennard, Glastonbury,
Somerset BA6 8NT
Tel: 0458 32818

Animal Portraiture
Spinney Cottage, The
Ashlands, Illston on the Hill,
Leicestershire

Animals Unlimited
Herb House, Draycott,
Moreton-in-Marsh, Gloucs
Tel: 0386 700453

Eclipse Jewellery
5 Lymouth Grove, Prestwich
Manchester M25 8TL

Foto Focus
7 The Parade, Trumpsgreen
Road, Virginia Water, Surrey
Tel: 09904 3900

**Michael Stewart Fine
Art Ltd**
The Georgian House, Broad
Street, Wrington, Bristol, Avon
BS18 7LA
Tel: 0934 862458
Fax: 0934 863207

Riding Equipment: Chaps

J & C Gibbins
Lodge Road, Hollesley,
Woodbridge, Suffolk
IP12 3RR
Tel: 0394 411 195
Fax: 0394 410 015

Riding Equipment: Clothing

Brian Lindsay
19 Ledra Close, Cagwith
Ruan Minor, Helston, Cornwall
TR12 7LD
Tel: 0326 290595

**Lavenham Rug
Company Ltd**
Long Melford, Suffolk
CO10 9LL
Tel: 0787 79535

Leyland & Birmingham Rubber Co
Golden Hill Lane, Leyland,
Lancs PR5 1VB

Matlock Brown Ltd
Bath Road, Kettering,
Northants NN16 8NH
Tel: 0536 512435
Fax: 0536 513146

Puffa Ltd
Parka House, Little
Waldingfield, Suffolk
CO10 0SY
Tel: 0787 248474
Fax: 0787 248133

Show Jumps and Sundries

Asthall Show Jumps
Hill Building, Blenheim hill,
Shipton-under-Wychwood,
Oxon
Tel: 0993 831454

B F P Rosettes
39 Manor Road, Pawlett, Nr
Bridgewater, Somerset
TA6 4SN
Tel: 0278 683455
Fax: 0278 684425

B G S Plastics Ltd
Unit 4, Crossways Ind
Estate, Church Stretton,
Shropshire
Tel: 0694723478

CMS Trim
34 Spon End, Coventry,
West Midlands CV1 3GY
Tel: 0203 20363

D & J Watson
T/A Watson's Quality
Products, Red House Farm,
Stoke Mandeville, Aylesbury,
Bucks HP22 5XD
Tel: 029661 2392

E Williams & Co
23 Glebe Street, Walsall,
West Midlands WS1 3PA
Tel: 0922 23333

Horse Advancement Co. Ltd
44 Ferry Road, London
SW13 9PW
Tel: 081 748 6843

Instant Signs
Fordes, Ropley, Alresford,
Hants
Tel: 096277 3373

James H Wood Printers Ltd
Don Press Penistone,
Sheffield, S Yorks S30 6AR
Tel: 0226 762207

Newson Show Jumps
Whitefriars, Vicarage Lane,
North Weald, Epping, Essex

Quality Showjumps
Mick Chips, Bowyers,
Steepmarsh, Petersfield,
Hampshire

R W Stephen Equestrian Products Ltd
Honeycombe Leaze,
Cirencester, Gloucestershire
Tel: 0285 712438

Rainbow Rosettes
FREEPOST, PO Box 110,
Norwich, Norfolk NR3 4BR
Tel: 0800 378364

Salcey Forest Timber Products
Hartwell, Northants
Tel: 0604 406373

Silver Fox Showjumps
Snape Hill, Darfield, Barnsley,
South Yorkshire
Tel: 0226 758215

Sportsline Plastics Ltd
370 Melton Road, Leicester,
Leics
Tel: 0533 681212

Surewood Products
3 Moss Cottage, New Cut
Lane, Merseyside L33 3AH
Tel: 051 548 9052

Sustan Showjumps
5 Rose Cottage, Mill Street,
Hastingwood, near Marlow
Common, Essex
Tel: 0279 415802

Taunton Show Jumps
Curland Equestrian Enterprises
Crosses Farm, Curland,
Taunton, Somerset TA3 5SD
Tel: 0460 34234

Thanet Show Jumps
Chestnuts, Woolpack
Corner, Biddenden, nr
Ashford, Kent TN27 8BN

Watson's Quality Products
Red House Farm, Stoke
Mandeville, Aylesbury,
Bucks HP21 9DR
Tel: 029 661392

Side-saddle Habits

Hippomatic Ltd
Sandon, Buntingford, Herts
SG9 0QW
Tel: 076 387 453

Judith Cochran
Stoneyhills Alnwick,
Northumberland NE66 2AB
Tel: 0665 602930

Keith Luxford (Saddlery) Ltd
H Q 57 High Street,
Teddington, Middlesex
Tel: 081 977 4964

Spurs

Carbex-Munroe (Handles)
11a St Nicholas Lane, Lewes
East Sussex BN7 2JZ
Tel: 0273 478111

Equiquip Ltd
7 Pepper Alley, Banbury,
Oxon OX16 OTF
Tel: 0295 3913

Impala Sales and Marketing
The Cottage, Creation Road
Hollowell, Northampton,
Northants NN6 8RP
Tel: 0604 740687

Newton Horse Ltd
Hotham Hall, Hotham
E Yorkshire YO4 3UN
Tel: 0430 423636

Tack Shops

Derby House Saddlery
Newburgh, Parbold,
Lancashire WN8 7NG
Tel: 0257 462228
Fax: 0257 464421

Hurdcott Livery Stables & Saddlery
Hurdcott Lane, Winterbourne
Earls, Salisbury, Wilts SP4 6HR
Tel: 0980 611276

Kiln Saddlery
The Folley, Layer de la
Haye, Colchester, Essex
CO2 OHZ
Tel: 0206 34695

Ride-Away
Stillington Road, Sutton-
on-Forest, York N Yorks
YO6 1EH
Tel: 0347 810443
Fax: 0347 810746

Rondo Horse Insurance
29 High Street, Newhaven,
East Sussex BN9 9PD
Tel: 0273 611555
Fax: 0273 611666

School of National Equitation
Bunny Hill Top, Costock
Leics LE12 6XE
Tel: 0509 852366
Fax: 0602 848381

Tall Trees Riding Centre
Davidstow, Camelford,
Cornwall PL32 9XR
Tel: 0840 6249

Tower Farm Riding Stables
85 Liberton Drive, Edinburgh
EH16 6NS
Tel: 031 664 3375

West Essex & Kernow Saddlery
113 Station Road, Chingford,
London E4 7BU

Ties and Stocks

Casual Riding Manufacturing Ltd
533 Twickenham Road,
Isleworth, Middlesex
Tel: 081 8927710

Emsby Field Sportswear Limited
Granville Chambers, Midland
Road, Wellingborough,
Northants
Tel: 0933 224482

Fancy Free Race & Event Wear
The Heath, Stoke Prior,
Leominster, Hereford &
Worcs
Tel: 056 882 662

Faulks & Jaques
27 Innage Park, Holly Lane,
Atherstone, Warwickshire
CV9 2HA
Tel: 08277 67003

Irene Wilson
The Smithy, Waddington,
Clitheroe, Lancs BB7 3HW
Tel: 0200 22976

J W E Banks & Sons Ltd
Crowland, Peterborough,
Cambs PE6 OJP
Tel: 0733 210318

Video Services

Champion Services Ltd
P.O. Box 20, Ryton on
Dunsmore, Coventry
CV8 3LQ
Tel: 0203 542112

IPC Video
Surrey House, Throwley
Way, Sutton, Surrey

Lloyds Bank PLC
Public Relations Department
Head Office, 71 Lombard
Street, London EC3P 3BS
Tel: 071 626 1500

Notts Equestrian Video Library
Thorlea, Askham, Newark,
Notts NG22 ORN
Tel: 0777 83234

Quadrant Video
37a High Street, Carshalton,
Surrey SM5 3BB
Tel: 081 669 1114

Smith, Kline Animal Health Ltd
Cavendish Road,
Stevenage, Hertfordshire
Tel: 0438 67881

Sterivet Supplements
C/o Epsom Veterinery
Remeds Ltd
The Old Manor, Upper
Lambourn, Newbury, Berks
Tel: 0488 71657

Town and Country Prodns Ltd
Parry's Lodge, Threapwood,
Malpas, Cheshire SY14 7AW
Tel: 0948 81309

Vet Health
The Animal Care Centre,
Colne Road, Coggeshall,
Colchester, Essex
Tel: 0376 61548

Video Replay
Equestrian Video Agents,
Southwater Ind Estate,
Southwater, West Sussex
RH13 7UD
Tel: 0403 731515

Whips

Allen & Caswell
Regent Works, Cornwall
Road, Kettering, Northants
NN16 8PR
Tel: 0536 512804
Fax: 0536 411085

Cross Country (Equestrian) Ltd
Luttwytche Road, Church
Stretton, Shropshire SY6 6AT
Tel: 0694 722919

Equequip Ltd
7 Pepper Alley, Banbury
Oxon OX16 OTF
Tel: 0295 3913

Horse Requisites Newmarket Ltd
Black Bear Lane, Newmarket
Suffolk CB8 0JT
Tel: 0638 664619

Section 3: The Healthy Horse

Chapter 11: The Healthy Horse 179
Chapter 12: Feeding your Horse or Pony 185
Chapter 13: Tacking Up 190
Chapter 14: Bits 203
Chapter 15: No Foot No Horse 207
Chapter 16: Keeping a Horse at Grass 210
Chapter 17: Stabling your Horse 217
Chapter 19: Grooming 226
Chapter 20: Clipping 231
Chapter 21: Boots and Bandages 234
Chapter 22: Best-dressed Horse: All Rugged Up 237
Chapter 23: Equine Faults and Vices 241
Chapter 24: Transporting your Horse 247
Chapter 25: Insurance 251

Useful References & Listings

Allergy-Free Horse Hay 256
Allweather Riding Surfaces 256
Aqua Sprays 257
Bedding 257
Bits 258
Bridles 258
Cavaletti 259
Clippers 259
Compound Feeds 260
Disinfectants 261
Draw Reins 261
Dressage Supplies 262
Drinking Troughs 262
Driving Vehicles and Accessories 262
Equestrian Engineers 264
Farriery Supplies 264
Feed Additives & Supplements 265
Feed Manufacturers 266
Feed Storage Bins 267
Feed Suppliers, General 268
Fencing 268
Fencing Suppliers 268
Fencing Contractors 269
Fencing Gates and Shelters 269
Floor Covering 271
Freeze Marking 271
Girths 271
Harness Manufacturers 272
Hoof-care Products 272
Horse Boots 274
Horse Boxes 275
Horse-care Products 276
Horse Dealers 277
Horse Eye Protectors 277
Horse Feed Suppliers 277
Horse Holiday Homes 277
Horse Hoods 278
Horse Trailers & Accessories 278
Horse Transporters & Agents 280

Horse Treats	280	Stable Equipment	291
Horse Walkers	280	Surcingles & Rollers	294
Hydroponic Grass Machines	280	Tack Repairers	295
Indoor School Maintenance		Towing Vehicles and	
Equipment	280	Accessories	296
International Forwarding		Watering Devices	296
Agents	281	Manufacturers and Suppliers of	
Lead Ropes	281	Horse-care Products	
Leather-care Products and		Anti-inflammatory Treatments	297
Supplies	281	Antiseptics	297
Leg Guards	282	Bandages	297
Linseed and Barley Boilers	282	Blood Tonics	298
Lungeing Equipment	282	Cod Liver Oils	299
Measuring Sticks	282	Coat Glosses and Dressings	299
Numnahs	282	Cough and Cold Treatments	300
Nutritionists	284	Crib-biting Preventatives	300
Pasture Maintenance	284	Digestive Treatments	300
Plaits, Bands, Threads and		Fly and Insect Repellants	306
Needles	284	Healing Creams and Gels	306
Reins	284	Hoof-care Products	307
Riding Equipment, Tack	284	Liniments	307
Riding Surfaces	285	Louse Powder	307
Rosettes and Trophies	285	Milk Replacers	308
Rubber Stops and Pads	286	Poultices	308
Rugs & Blankets/Tail Guards	286	Shampoos and Conditioners	308
Saddle Manufacturers & Sole		Skin-care Products	309
Agents	288	Treatments and Tonics	309
Saddle Stands and Racks	290	Vaccines	310
Saddles, Retailers	290	Veterinary Equipment	310
Safety Equipment	290	Veterinary and Homeopathic	
Show Jumps/Sundries	290	Remedies	310
Small Tractors	291	Vitamin/Mineral Supplement	311
Stirrups and Leathers	291	Wormers	307
		Wound Dressings	313

The Healthy Horse

Maintaining the health of your horse can appear to be a relentless task but the resulting healthy animal can be a reward in itself

You should never take chances with a horse's health. If the horse is obviously unwell, lame or injured then, in the majority of cases, the recommended course of action is to call the vet. But, with a basic knowledge of First Aid, you can help to alleviate minor symptoms yourself.

It is strongly recommended that every stable yard should have a well equipped First Aid kit. This kit should be stored in a suitable medical cabinet and placed in an accessible location for all who may need to use it. Recommended contents are:

1. Veterinary clinical thermometer.

2. Surgical scissors (blunt).

3. Wool and crepe bandages.

4. Gamgee tissue (gauze covered cotton wool).

5. Cotton wool.

6. Packets of lint.

7. Cough electuary.

8. Colic drink - available from the Vet.

9. Epsom salts - sprinkled in food or water will act as a laxative.

10. Lanoline or glycerine for sore or cracked heels.

11. Iodine - for wounds and fungi.

12. Antibiotic powder - dusting powder for wounds.

13. Animalintex or kaolin for poulticing and reducing inflammation.

14. Lead lotion - for cooling.

15. Boracic lotion or ointment - for eyes.

16. Worming preparations.

17. Methylated or surgical spirits - for girth galls etc.

18. Ordinary salt.

As you can imagine, you will need a large medical cabinet! Keep the contents of the cabinet topped-up, and do make sure that any treatments that are out of date are disposed of safely.

Fitness and good health shine through

Some horse ailments will be pretty obvious to spot and treat. A horse cannot tell you what is wrong with it, but by careful observation - plus a little knowledge - you should be able to ascertain whether your horse is off colour. Observe:

The Coat

The coat mirrors the horses health. It should lie flat and have a sheen on it. If the coat is dull and staring you should begin looking for any signs of ill health.

The skin should move easily when pinched. there should not be too much scurf. A tight skin could be due to dehydration, malnutrition or lice.

Excessive sweating is not normal. Hot sweats usually indicate a fever, whilst cold sweats suggest that the animal is in pain.

Appetite

Always check that your horse is eating and drinking normally. A loss of appetite can be a sign of ill health.

Urine and Droppings

The healthy horse will pass urine and droppings regularly.

If the horse does not pass droppings then this could indicate that there could be a blockage. Colour of droppings vary with the diet. A stable fed horses will be golden brown, whilst those of a horse at grass will be greenish in colour. They should be passed in small balls, which break as they hit the floor.

Urine should be pale yellow in colour. If it is thick or cloudy it could indicate some disorder. A horse will pass 2-10 litres of urine per day - dependent upon the water intake, the amount of sweating and the water content of the droppings.

Temperature

The normal temperature of a horse is 100.5°F (38°C). The temperature should not vary by more than 1.5°F over 24 hours, any variation over 2° is abnormal. Temperature is taken in the rectum using a veterinary thermometer:

-Make sure the mercury level is down below the normal level.
-Coat thermometer with Vaseline.
-Gently lift tail and insert thermometer.
-Stand to the side when doing this.
-Hold the thermometer firmly throughout this operation

Limbs

If your horse begins to rest or point a foreleg, then be warned - something is amiss. Check the legs daily for signs of heat lumps or bumps.

Eyes

The healthy horse has bright eyes. Check the eyes by rolling the eyelid back and observing the colour of the membranes. Salmon pink is the normal colour for eye, nose and mouth membranes. Deep red indicates a fever.

Yellow indicates a liver disorder. Paleness indicates anaemia. Purple spotting usually indicates impurity of the blood.

Pulse and Respiration

The resting pulse rate should be between 35 and 40 beats per minute. The pulse is taken where the facial artery passes under the jaw, or at the median artery in the centre of the inside surface of the foreleg, level with the elbow.

Respiration should be even and regular at a resting rate of 8-12 breaths per minute. There should only be a slight movement of the nostrils and ribs - you cannot hear a healthy horse breathing.

Knowing what to look for is part of the battle - what to do is the next step. Treating:

Wounds

If the wound is severe, your first priority is to stop the bleeding. A severed artery will produce bright red blood that pumps out in spurts. Apply a sterile pad of gauze and bandage firmly, making sure that you keep the pressure evenly distributed both above and below the wound. If a bandage is not available, use a clean cloth, towel or even your shirt in the case of emergency. DO NOT apply a tourniquet - this can do more harm than good. If the wound is in a place that cannot be bandaged, e.g. belly, then apply direct pressure. In the case of a wound of any severity, it is always safest to call the vet.

For slight wounding, allow the bleeding to stop on its own. Cleanse with a mild antiseptic, a little salt and water, or allow a hose pipe to trickle over it for 10 minutes or so. Do not use anything to clean the wound (cloth or sponge) since it may contain germs. Dust with antibiotic powder. Allow the wound to remain free of bandages in order to aid the healing process - but do make sure that you keep it scrupulously clean.

Puncture Wounds

These are caused by sharp objects such as nails, thorns, glass etc. Just occasionally, a farrier may misdirect a nail when shoeing. This could result in a nail bind - where the nail rubs along the sensitive part too close to the white line, thus causing bruising. Since the foot has a hard outer casing it can't swell and the result is lameness. A nail prick will damage the wall of the foot. Since there is very often little blood the injury may initially go unnoticed, even though the penetration could be quite deep. One of the major hazards here, apart from the lameness incurred, is the risk of tetanus. As the surface of the wound heals rapidly the air is excluded, thereby creating ideal conditions in which the tetanus germ can thrive. With all puncture wounds, a further danger is that, as a result of the rapid healing of the wound's surface, puss can be enclosed in the wound. This will need poulticing. Once puss is clear then pack the wound with Stockholm tar and a plug of cotton wool.

Poulticing

Hot poulticing will soften the tissue in the areas where puss has accumulated and allow it to come to the surface.

There are several different ways to poultice:

Kaolin paste should be heated either by placing the tin in boiling water, or by spreading the paste between two pieces of gauze, putting it on a heatproof dish and heating in the oven. Test the temperature on the back of the hand first. Apply to the leg on the gauze - this allows you to remove it quickly if it is too hot. Cover the gauze with cotton wool or lint, then bandage fairly loosely to allow for swelling.

Poultices for the foot can be made with bran. Pour a little boiling water on the bran - enough to make it damp but not wet. Put the hot bran onto a piece of sacking, place the horses foot into the centre of the sacking then tie the sacking securely up around the fetlock. Bandage the ends of the sacking with a stable bandage.

To achieve maximum effect from a poultice, it ought to be changed every 12 hours at least. Epsom salts made into a paste with cold water will take the heat out of a horses leg. This should be applied around the cannon bones and tendons, covered with cotton wool, bandaged and left overnight.

Sprains and Bruises

You will notice injuries where the skin is not broken as they will be apparent from the presence of heat and/or swelling. These can be reduced by running cold water from the hose over the affected part. Allow the water to trickle over the affected area.

Sprained tendons are a serious matter. Occurring most frequently in the forelegs, they can be caused by many things such as landing heavily from a fence, too much galloping, faulty shoeing, etc. They can also be as a result of poor conformation. The symptoms are: pain, tenderness, heat and swelling in the tendons at the back of the cannon bone. Rest is an essential in the treatment of sprains and, although cold water hosing may be adequate in mild cases, it is probably wisest to consult a vet.

Saddle and Girth Galls

These are patches on the horses skin that are a result of bad management. Galls are usually a result of saddles that don't fit properly, inadequate cleaning of coat under saddle and girth area, or horses that are still 'soft' after coming up from grass.

Prevent these by:

-Making sure your tack is clean.
-Grooming has been done thoroughly under saddle and girth areas.
-The girth is not rubbing - if it is, look for an alternative or encase it in a sheepskin girth sleeve.
-If the horse is raw, apply a cooling lotion.
-If skin is becoming tender, rub with surgical spirits or a mild solution of salt and water.
-Keep the horse off the saddle until the sores have healed.

Colic

This pain can be compared with a pain in the stomach in humans.

The following symptoms will appear:

-Restlessness, pawing the ground and looking at flanks.

-May try to roll.
-Will break out in a sweat
-Breathing will be laboured.
-Pulse rate will increase.

At the first signs:
-Put a head collar on the horse and lead him so that he cannot lie down or roll.
-Do not give anything to eat or drink.
-Keep him warm with extra rugs or blankets.
-Walk him.
-If the symptoms persist after an hour, then call the vet.

DO NOT:
-Administer a colic drench unless you have expert help.
-Leave him on his own until you are sure he has recovered.

There are many causes of colic. It may be due to:
-A sudden change in feeding.
-Drinking large quantities after a big meal.
- Too much food.
- A stoppage.
- Worms.
- Fermenting food.
- Working after a heavy meal.
- Sand in the stomach.
- Stones in the bowels, kidneys or bladder.
- Twisted gut.

Worming

It is a salutary thought that many people either do not bother to worm their horses, or feel that once every six months is enough. If you are one of these people it could well be an eye-opener to have your horses droppings analysed by the vet - you would be shocked!

Most worming preparations are aimed at the straggle group of worms. This is because they cause most damage to the horses and are most numerous. These include:

-Small straggles (red worm). These can cause damage to the caecum and colon.

-Large straggles. These also occur in the caecum and colon and as adult worms are bloodsuckers and cause anaemia.

-Pin worms. Present in the caecum, colon and rectum, they cause skin irritation and tail rubbing.

-Stomach Bots. Here the adult bot flies attach eggs to horses hair in summer. Larvae migrate through tissue of mouth and tongue and attach themselves to the stomach wall. These worms can cause tissue damage, impaired digestion and perforation of the stomach wall.

A good wormer will kill off 100% adult worms in the horses intestines. The result will be that the horses droppings do not contain any worm eggs for the next six weeks. By the time 8-10 weeks have passed, the horse will again have adult worms in the intestines and be passing worm eggs. These worms will have developed from the worm eggs that were present at the time of worming, but were not killed off.

The recommended frequency for administering a wormer is every eight weeks - depending upon the drug used. Regular worming is an insurance for the future of your horse.

General Pointers

Try to treat a sick horse as you would like to be treated if you were sick! Handle wounds carefully, rough handling could cause more suffering. Make him comfortable with as little fuss as possible, ensuring a good, clean bed. If the horse has a leg injury, don't make the bed too thick as this could hinder his movements. Make sure that clean, fresh water is available at all times - the bucket should be scoured regularly to minimise risk of germs. Dispense with any grooming other than a light rub over until the horse is feeling better. Don't create too much dust in the stable by shaking up bedding unnecessarily. Keep the horse warm with an adequate number of rugs and, possibly, stable bandages. Ensure that the stable has plenty of fresh air, but avoid draughts. Adapt your horses diet to his needs. A horse that is not being exercised should not be given heating foods such as maize, barley or oats. Try to tempt his appetite with succulent foods such as carrots, turnips, etc. Clean all uneaten food from the manger.

All these points are to help with minor problems. If you are in any doubt at all, ring the vet and get him to visit.

Feeding your Horse or Pony

The development of a successful and balanced feeding regime should be the aim of all horse owners, but choosing from the vast array of options can be difficult

Feeding your horse or pony correctly is an art. The horse in its natural state satisfied all its food requirements from grass, wandering from place to place selecting the most succulent food and seldom expending any undue amount of energy unless pursued by enemies. Man has altered this. As a domesticated animal the horse is expected to work and is largely dependent upon man for the food he eats. The horse will, therefore, need a more concentrated diet in a balanced form both to maintain the body and to supply additional energy.

In order to understand what we need to feed we should also try to understand a little about the horse's digestive system. There are two main features peculiar to horses that need to be understood in order to manage their feeding regime successfully:-

1. The stomach is small in comparison to the size of the gut. Food is masticated by the teeth, passed to the stomach where it remains for an hour or so. Then the digestive juices start to act on it and prepare it for the final digestive process in the gut. Large feeds, especially if they are eaten quickly, could overload the stomach resulting in the food being passed into the gut without the digestive process having taken place properly.

The stomach and gut react adversely to sudden change due to their extreme sensitivity.

As a rule of thumb the following points should be noted:-

a) Don't make any sudden changes in your animal's feeding routine. Any adjustments should be gradual and over a number of days.

b) Attempt to imitate the horse's natural feeding methods - a little and often.

c) Feed plenty of roughage (hays and chaff). A successful digestive process in the horse is impossible without roughage.

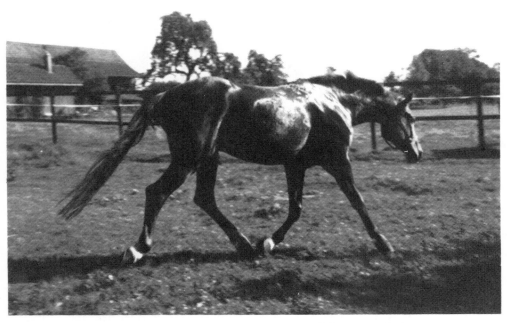

A happy healthy horse is one that has received the correct balance of feeding and exercise

d) Make sure that water is readily available. Water before feeding so that undigested food will not be washed prematurely out of the stomach.

e) Develop a regular feeding routine - stick to the same times.

f) Feed according to the amount of work the animal is doing and its size. If the work is demanding then increase the amounts of concentrates (oats etc.). If your horse is laid off, even for a short while then cut down to a mere maintenance level the amounts of concentrates but increase the bulk feed to compensate.

g) Feed only good quality forage - the horse is a very fussy feeder.

h) Include some succulent foods in his diet (e.g. carrots) to compensate for the lack of grass.

i) Do not work a horse immediately after he has eaten. The horse's stomach lies next to the his chest and this could press onto the horse's lungs and restrict his breathing.

Bulk Foods

Hay

Hay is one of the most useful forms of forage and the only one upon which the horse can live and perform some light work, apart from grass. Feeding bad hay is a false economy since the horse is unlikely to thrive on it. Older hay is less likely to cause digestive upsets and on no account should you feed hay under six months old, since it is still undergoing changes. There is a variety of hays to feed:

Meadow Hay

This comes from pasture that is permanently laid down to grass. This type of hay is generally greener than seed hay and also softer and sweeter. The nutritional value of the hay may vary tremendously, depending upon the types of grass it contains.

Seed Hay

Also known as 'mixture' hay this hay comes from land that has been re-seeded. It is an excellent food for horses and can contain such grasses as rye, clover, timothy and meadowrescue - all extremely attractive to horses. A good seed hay should be greenish brown, sweet to smell, hard and crisp. Yellow or dark brown hay usually indicates that deterioration has taken place and should be seen as a warning.

Chaff (Chopped Hay)

This is hay that has been through a chaff cutter and is then mixed with the corn feed to add bulk. Oat straw is sometimes mixed in with the hay. Chaff adds bulk to the corn feed, and aids digestion by encouraging mastication, preventing the horse from bolting its food.

Horsage, Haylage

This is a cross between silage and hay. It is particularly useful for feeding horses who are allergic to hay or straw. Some Horsage and Haylage has a high protein content and this must be taken into account in your overall feeding plan.

Oat Straw

Sometimes used in conjunction with hay, either on its own or in chaff. Should be given as only about one third of the total bulk feed.

Silage

Can be fed to horses, but is more usually used for cattle. This should only provide a maximum of one third of the horse's bulk feed.

Concentrated Foods

Oats

These are probably the best all-round concentrated feed for horses. They should be fed with care as they can cause the animal to 'hot-up'.

Oat grains should be large, hard and clean, but since whole grains may be more difficult to digest they are usually rolled, crushed or bruised.

Barley

Barley can be used as a substitute for oats, either rolled, crushed or flaked. Barley is a high energy food that is less heating than oats.

A more recently-popular method of treating barley is extrusion cooking. Extrusion cooking uses a combination of friction and steam to raise the temperature of the feed to over 180°C in eight seconds. This is then forced through the extruder as a boiling mass which then flash dries and is cut into pieces by a revolving knife. This method is most successfully used by Burgess Endeavour PLC who include with their barley mineral trace elements, vitamins, linseed oil and molasses. The product is sold under the trade-name 'Supa-Barley'.

Cubes (Nuts or Pellets)

Cubes are made from a carefully formulated mixture of ingredients - including added vitamins. There are several varieties - 'Horse and Pony', 'Stud', 'Racehorse', 'Grass', etc.

Cubes can be used as a substitute for a part or all of the oat ration. Three quarters to one and a half pounds dependent upon the type of cube you are feeding can replace one pound of oats.

There are many advantages to feeding cubes, not the least of which is the fact that you do not have to store a large variety of feeds. You must, however, make sure that you are not inadvertently feeding too much protein.

Flaked Maize

This is a fattening food, but should be used sparingly since it could cause over-heating of the blood.

Bran

Wheat bran can be used to encourage mastication and digestion and to provide bulk. Fed in moderation, this is a beneficial product for horses.

Served as a BRAN MASH this is most useful for horses after hard exercise or hunting. A bran mash is made by filling a bucket three quarter full of bran, pouring boiling water over it until thoroughly wet, adding salt and a handful of oats, covering with sacking and leaving until cool enough to feed. Bran has a laxative effect.

Linseed

This should be fed sparingly, and care should be taken as to its preparation. Linseed will help improve a horse's condition and give a gloss to the coat. The correct amount of feed-between one quarter and one half pound (dry weight) - may be fed twice a week.

Preparations are LINSEED JELLY: a handful of linseed is placed in the saucepan, covered with water and allowed to soak until the following day. The following day add more water and bring to the boil (un-boiled linseed is poisonous). Once the boiling process is completed, remove the pan and allow to cool. This should, if properly made, set as a jelly which can be mixed with the evening feed. LINSEED TEA or gruel is made in a similar way but with more water.

Dried Sugar-Beet Pulp

A source of both energy and roughage which helps to maintain weight and provide heat and bulk.

Dried sugar-beet pulp, whether shredded or cubes, should be soaked for at least 12 hours prior to feeding. It should be soaked in a ratio of 2 1/2 parts water to 1 part beet. No more than 3 1/2 lbs soaked weight should be fed per day. Once soaked, beet should be used immediately as the fermentation process begins as soon as the beet is mixed with water.

The sugar beet should be stored in a cool dry place and away from any other cubes you may have in store.

Succulent Foods

Succulent foods that are within the horse's natural food range and are green or juicy. They will make the food more appetizing, in addition to providing bulk and variety. They can help towards providing an acceptable substitute for grass.

Root vegetables, such as carrots, turnips, parsnips, swedes, mangels and beetroot are particularly acceptable to the horse in winter months. Do make sure that these vegetables are free from dirt when fed and sliced into 'fingers' - square or round pieces must not be fed as these can cause choking if they become lodged in the throat.

Storing your Feed

If at all possible, store forage away from the stables and in a closed storage unit. Feed should be stored in a vermin-proof bin in order to prevent it from becoming infected.

Hay and straw should be staked on wooden pallets in order to keep them away from dampness and to allow the air to circulate around.

Amounts to Feed

It is very difficult to give any strict mathematical formula as to what you should feed any given horse.

The following factors should be taken into consideration:-

- The work required of the horse.

- The type, age and temperament of the horse.

- Its condition and level of fitness.

- The weather and time of year.

- The feeding habits of the horse.

- Whether the horse is unclipped, clipped or part clipped.

- The amount of 'clothing' the horse requires.

- The amount of grass available if the horse is turned out during the day.

Good feeding is a great skill that demands experience and a great deal of skill. Horses and ponies should be continually observed so that any falling- off in condition or performance can be noted in the early stages and the feeding regime adjusted accordingly.

Tacking Up

Tack is the second-most expensive item after buying your horse. The choice of good-quality suitable tack is most important

In terms of initial expenditure when buying a horse the largest single cost after the purchasing of the animal is the tack (Tack is a term that is commonly used in the Horse World to refer to any item of saddlery that is used for the horse). Frequently when purchasing an animal the tack is passed on. Providing that the tack is in good repair and is suitable for your requirements, it is advisable to accept it as this will help in reducing the initial expenditure.

Tack should be both comfortable and suitable for the horse and the rider. It should be of good quality, for the sake of safety, durability and appearance it is advisable to have good quality leather and metalwork.

Tack should be comfortable and suitable for both horse and rider

The Saddle

The framework of the saddle is known as 'the tree'. It was originally made of beechwood, but now is usually made of laminated wood. The 'spring tree' saddle is most popularly used and has two pieces of tempered steel running length-ways along the tree from the front arch to the cantle. This gives the seat of the saddle more resilience and thus allows the rider to feel and follow the horses movements more closely. The parts of the saddle are:

1. The seat - built onto the tree and usually made of pig-skin.

2. The saddle flaps - attached to the seat.

3. The panels - stuffed with wool or shaped felt and act as a cushion between the tree and horse.

4. Waist

5. Seat

6. Pommel - front of the saddle.

7. Cantle - back of the saddle.

8. Skirt - flap of leather to cover stirup bars.

9. Girth straps or tabs to attach girth.

10. Gullet - Channel in the centre underneath of saddle.

11. Surcingle loop - to hold surcingle in place.

Varieties of saddles

All saddles are designed to distribute the riders weight evenly on either side of the backbone without causing undue pressure. In the various riding disciplines there is a need to adopt different riding positions, thus saddles are designed to create the most comfortable ride for both horse and rider. For example, in racing the horse, is extended and the rider's weight needs to be well forward over the horse's point of gravity.

Jumping Saddle

Designed to encourage the rider to assume a forward, jumping/galloping position.

Bars for stirrups are placed well forward.

Panels extended and cut forward with rolls to support knee and thigh.

Cut back head at the pommel.

Deep seat.

General Purpose Saddle

Similar to jumping saddle. Most commonly used all-round saddle for the non-specialist.

Panels not so forwardly cut, thus allowing longer stirrup length.

Dressage Saddle

Saddle designed to seat the rider in the deepest part of the saddle and allow maximum contact with the horse.

Allows for riding with longer stirrups than would be required for hacking.

Straight-cut saddle.

Roll for lower thigh positioned on forward edge of saddle.

Longer girth straps to allow closer leg contact by moving buckles lower down.

Show Saddle:

Designed more to show off the horse than for the comfort of the rider.

Straight cut to the extreme.

Fits closely to the horse. Half panel used with little padding and no knee rolls.

Racing Saddle

Seat is unimportant since the rider seldom uses it. Designed more for the riders balance than grip. Weight is a vital factor - usually 0.5 to 1 Kg.

Light materials used.

Panels cut to a minimum.

Usually no stirrup bars - leathers passed over side bars of the tree.

Endurance Saddle

Designed to give maximum comfort for both horse and rider over a long period of time.

Seat extra-well padded.

Knee block pads on flaps for extra support when riding downhill.

Extra D-rings front and rear for carrying equipment.

Extended panels on back to give greater weight distribution and added comfort for the horse.

Saddle fittings come in three basic sizes - narrow, medium and broad. It is important to get the correct width fitting for your horse, and often your search will be helped if you can find a saddler/tack shop prepared to bring a selection of saddles out to your stables and try them until you achieve the correct fit - you may be afraid that this could be a costly experience, but not nearly as costly as buying the wrong saddle and having to go through the process of returning it or buying yet another.

Fitting the Saddle

Saddles should be tested for correct fitting both with rider on board and without. Do not use a numnah or saddle cloth at this stage as this could affect the way the saddle sits.

All saddles must clear the withers and along the length of the backbone.

The rider must be able to fit a minimum of three fingers between the withers and the saddle arch.

Looking from the back of the saddle to the pommel there should be a clear channel along the horses spine.

The forward cut of the saddle should not intrude upon the horses shoulder, thus restricting movement.

Girths should be kept clean and supple

Panels need to be stuffed so that the rider sits in the correct position. Incorrect stuffing or wrong tilting can result in the rider not being in contact with the horse and/or sliding backwards.

It is possible to break the tree. DO NOT use the saddle in this case - it could damage the horses back.

If your saddle is coming to the stage where it needs stuffing then use a wither pad and 'phone the saddler.

You may not want to buy new tack immediately and decide upon looking for second hand. If you are doing this, check the items carefully for splits, cracks, loose stitching and broken tree.

To test the saddle for broken tree:

Press the cantle of the saddle against your thigh, hold the pommel with one hand and pull back. A spring tree will usually give about an inch, but some old spring trees may flex a little more if the stuffing in the panels is thin.

Gently twist the pommel in the opposite direction to the cantle - there should be no movement.

Using both hands, press both sides of the pommel in towards each other and then apart.

A creaking noise or a movement denotes a broken tree.

Keep on looking!

Saddle Accessories

In addition to the saddle you will need to buy stirrup irons and leathers, girth and a numnah/saddle cloth.

The Girth

This is a means of securing the saddle. There are various types, all of which have their virtues. They are:

Leather

These must be used with caution on soft, unfit horses as they can cause girth galls.

Leather girths can be shaped, straight, cross over or three fold. All leather girths need careful attention to cleaning otherwise they could become stiff and rub the animal.

Web

Web girths are single strips of webbing and it is best to use two at a time in case they snap. This girth needs brushing each time it is used or it will become stiff.

Padded

There are a great many of these on the market nowadays. They are made of soft, durable material which is padded and reinforced with nylon straps. The girth should be brushed after use to remove clinging mud and washed thoroughly at intervals.

String/Nylon

Made of thin, rounded pieces of string/nylon with woven strips at intervals to maintain the shape. These girths rarely rub because they allow the air to circulate. As with all material girths, they should be washed regularly as they absorb sweat.

Stirrup Leathers

These should never be regarded as an item to economise on! Always buy the best leather and, if buying second hand, pay careful attention to stitching, cracking or any other signs of wear.

Check your leathers at regular intervals for any sign of wear or stretching. The greatest strain will be on the nearside from when you are mounting; changing them around should even this out. The strongest are buffalo hide - not pretty but practical.

Stirrup Irons

Hand forged, stainless steel stirrups are the best type of stirrup. Rubber treads are a useful addition as they help to prevent the riders foot slipping. Safety irons are a useful item, particularly for children. These irons are open at the side with a thick rubber band, which will come loose in the event of a fall, securing the gap on the outside of the stirrup. The disadvantage of this type is that they do not hang level, and the rubber often breaks.

The rider should try the stirrup before purchasing and ensure that there is a gap of ½ inch on either side between the foot and the iron. Less gap than this means that the foot may get wedged in the event of a fall. More than ½ inch could result in the whole foot slipping through - both are equally dangerous.

The snaffle bridle

The bridle: There are two types of bridle - the Snaffle bridle and the Double bridle.

The Snaffle bridle consists of:

Headpiece and throat lash (or latch)

Brow band

Two cheek pieces - these attach at one end to the headpiece, the other end to the bit.

Noseband - fitted on its own headband. The various

types include:

The Canesson which fastens below the protruding cheek bones.

The Dropped Noseband which fastens under the bit and prevents the horse evading the bit by opening its mouth.

The Flash Noseband which is basically a Canesson with a loop attached to the centre front through which a narrower strap fastened to the bit is attached.

The Grackle Noseband which has crossed straps that fasten above and below the bit.

The Bit - attached to the cheek pieces and reins by stitches, studs or buckles.

The Rein - two leather straps joined by a central buckle and attached to the bridle at the bit.

The Double Bridle has all the same pieces as the Snaffle Bridle, plus:

The double bridle

Bridoon Headpiece with one cheek piece.

The Bits - bridoon, a thin snaffle curb bit, referred to as 'the bit'.

Additional pair of Reins - made of plain leather with the bridoon rein wider than the curb rein.

The Curb Chain - attached by two hooks on either side of the curb bit.

Hip Strap - attached to the 'D's on the curb bit and running through the fly link on the curb chain.

Fitting the bridle

The following pointers will help when fitting a bridle:

The throat lash should be loose enough to allow an adults fist to fit between it and the jaw bone. Too tight restricts the breathing and flexion, too loose and it will not prevent the bridle slipping over the horses head in the event of a fall.

The brow band should not be so high that it touches the ears or pulls on the headpiece. the purpose of the brow band is to prevent the bridle slipping back.

The noseband - a canesson should lie halfway between the projecting cheekbone and the corners of the mouth.

It should normally be loose enough to fit two fingers between it and the nose, although it can be tightened to help keep the mouth closed.

The dropped noseband can only be used with a snaffle bridle. It should be fitted with the front part of the strap well above the nostrils so that it does not restrict breathing, and goes behind the jaw under the bit, fitting into the horses chin groove. A dropped noseband should never be used with a standing martingale. Incorrect fitting can cause extreme distress to the horse.

The bit should not be so high or so narrow that it wrinkles or pinches the horses lips. Neither should it be so low that it falls on the horses teeth. The bridoon should fit above the curb in a double bridle.

The curb should be attached to the offside hooks on the bit, and twisted until flat, then attached to the near-side. The length should be such that when the bit is drawn back to an angle of 45 degrees it comes into play.

The Breastplate Martingle

The Martingale

Martingales are used to prevent the horses head from going beyond the point of control. There are various types:

The Standing Mart- ingale: This consists of a strap running from the girth to a canesson or flash nose band

with a neck strap. This martingale prevents the horse throwing its head in the air. A standing martingale which is fitted too short will force the horses head into an unnatural position and thereby impede the flow of its movements. When fitted correctly the standing martingale should be long enough to reach up to the junction of the horses head and neck.

The Running Martingale: Consists of a strap which runs from the girth and divides into two at the point of the neck strap, ending in two rings which run along the reins. Thus the effect of the martingale is felt upon the bit.

The martingale should not be too short, but fit so that the rings attached to the reins are in line with the withers when fully extended. The neck strap should not be too tight. Leather or rubber stops should be attached to the martingale at the point where it joins the neck strap to prevent it riding up, and on the reins to prevent the rings catching on the buckles or bit.

The Bib Martingale: Is an adaptation of the running martingale, and has the addition of a triangular piece of leather which fits between the branched straps. This martingale is particularly helpful when riding a young, excitable horse that is likely to get its teeth caught in one of the branches.

The Irish Martingale: Is a 6 inch leather strap with a metal ring at each end which fit onto the reins. These are used to prevent the reins going over the head in the event of a fall.

This type of martingale is used almost entirely in racing.

Other Devices

There are a wide range of devices which will help the rider to gain greater control, and eventually a greater union with the horse. Such devices as the Market Harborough, Chanbon, balancing reins and draw reins are devised to alter and control the position of the head.

Cleaning Tack

In terms of safety, tack cleaning could be regarded as one of the most important stable chores. It is at this time that you can carry out a thorough inspection of the tack and check that there is no loose stitching and that the leather is supple. Your basic tack cleaning equipment should include:

Towel/sponge for washing.

Sponge for saddle soap.

Chamois leather for drying.

Saddle soap.

Metal polish.

Soft cloths for applying metal polish and for buffing up afterwards.

Brush for cleaning girths and cloth linings.

Leather dressing and brush for application.

Vaseline/glycerine for covering tack to be stored.

A saddle horse is a useful piece of equipment to have when cleaning the saddle since it keeps it firm. Equally important is a hook or nail to hang the bridle on.

Tack should be wiped over after every ride with a sponge that is coated with one of the leather care products. This will make your task easier when you come to your weekly/monthly full-scale cleaning!

On the next right hand page following this one, you will find a list of the shooting magazines in Great Britain that have achieved any or all of the following in relation to **Shooting Times.**

1. Published in an unbroken, weekly sequence since 1882.

2. Carried, each year, more pages of features, news, advice and information to its readers on a weekly, monthly or yearly basis.

3. Carried more pages of classified advertising each year than the rest of the publications put together.

4. Remained Great Britain's largest selling shooting magazine since first being published more than 108 years ago.

5. Is the official magazine of the British Association for Shooting and Conservation.

New tack should be given particular attention BEFORE it is used. The bridle should be dismantled and given a coating of leather dressing. This, when applied with a brush, will reach into all those nooks and crannies and act as a water proofing agent. The same process applies to the saddle. However, dressings should not be applied to the upper part of the saddle unless you enjoy walking around with dark stains on your jodhpurs!

A few do's and don'ts:

DO: Undo all buckles and remove attachments (bit, stirrup leathers, irons etc.) before doing a full-scale clean.

Wash leather and metal with lukewarm water.

Dry with a chamois leather.

Apply saddle soap with a sponge using as little water as possible. If using a bar of soap, it is best to dampen the soap rather than the sponge.

Apply metal polish to metal, then clean off.

Put tack together when task is completed.

Use pure soap and not detergent on any parts of tack which need washing.

Coat leather in glycerine/vaseline if storing it away.

DON'T   Saturate your tack with water.

Use soda or hot water for cleaning tack.

Dry too close to strong heat.

Use leather dressing each time you clean - some products can cause the stitches to rot over a period of time.

Use metal polish on the bit.

Remove 'jockies' (round, black spots of accumulated dirt and grease) by scraping them off. Make a pad out of horse hair (mane or tail) and rub gently until they are gone.

Modern products have taken a lot of the hard work out of tack cleaning, but the final glow you get on your tack is best achieved by elbow grease!

Storing your Tack

Tack should be stored neatly in order to prevent it getting damaged, and so that air can circulate around it.

With the bridle, place the rein through the throat lash and noseband outside the cheek pieces. There is no need to buckle it up, just push the end of the strap through the keepers. Put the bridle on a hanging rack to maintain its correct shape - not on a nail or a hook. An empty saddle soap tin nailed to the wall makes a perfectly adequate hanger.

The saddle should be placed on an 18 inch bracket attached to the wall. This will keep it out of the way of accidental

Well, you didn't expect anything else, did you?

SHOOTING TIMES

& Country magazine

Britain's number one shooting magazine

damage and any vermin that may be around. It also allows the air to circulate around it. If you do have to place the saddle on the floor. then place it on the pommel with the girth underneath to prevent scratching. Saddles thrown down carelessly may end up with damaged trees.

If you are going to store your tack away for any length of time, cover all leather parts with a coat of glycerine or Vaseline. This will help prevent the leather from drying out or decomposing. Keep the dust off by either covering it with sheets or packing it away in a container.

You may find tack cleaning a chore, but it is a very important one. Well cared for tack will give you years of service.

Tack should be suitable for the horse and for the type of riding that you do

Bits

> *The choice of the correct bit to suit you, your horse and the type of riding that you do is of the greatest importance. It is a choice that affects not only the safety but also the health of the horse*

To get your horse working properly will take a combination of factors, not least of which is the use of the correct bit. There is no virtue in using a snaffle with your horse out of control and pulling you all over the place when, for the sake of using a slightly more severe bit, you can exert a little more control. Conversely there is no need to weight a horse down with more and more severe bits just because it has been known to blink in the wrong place. The rider who 'always' rides their horses in one type of severe bit is probably the type who relies upon the bit to exert control rather than themselves.

The bit is just one part of the system which controls the horse. Best control is achieved when the bit is used in conjunction with the riders seat and legs. The pressure of the bit in the mouth conveys a message to the horse. The horse receives this message and accordingly relaxes his jaw and responds. The different bits apply varying degrees of pressure to the mouth and chin. An appropriate bit in the hands of a rider with a firm seat and good hands is on the way towards being a winning combination.

Bits can be made from:

Nickel - This is the most economical. It is slightly yellowish in colour. It does not wear well and tends to develop rough edges, bend and break.

Plated Steel - Stronger and brighter, but does have a tendency to chip. Within the readily affordable range.

Hard-Forged Steel - Strongest of all but also the most expensive.

Rubber - Often too soft unless used in conjunction with another substance.

Vulcanite - A tough substance that lacks the coldness of the metal bit.

There are many varieties of bit but they can be put into three main categories - the snaffle, the curb and the pelham.

The Snaffle

This is generally accepted as the mildest form of bit. It can either be made of one piece or jointed. The action is three-fold.

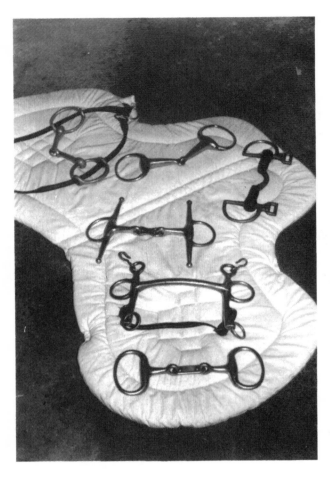

There is a wide variety of bits available

The straight bar snaffle, or half-moon, is a very mild bit, especially when made of rubber. These are particularly useful for young, sensitive horses, or those who have a sensitive mouth.

The single jointed snaffle has a 'nut-cracker' action and, therefore, applies more pressure than the straight bar. All of the bits have loose rings, except for the Egg-Butt, so that they can revolve in holes made in the side of the bit. This gives more play in the horses mouth so that, especially with young horses, the animal keeps a wet mouth.

Care must be taken with these bits as they wear both on the ring holes and on the joint. Check the bits carefully now and then to find wear, cracks or breaks in the bit before it is too late.

a)   Upwards against the corners of the lips particularly when the horses head is low.

b)   On the bars of the lower jaw - particularly when the horses head is high.

c)   On the tongue.

There are many varieties of the snaffle bit, all of which perform a variation on the function of the basic snaffle. Some are:

German Hollow Mouth Snaffle - This has a thicker mouthpiece. Often made lighter by being manufactured hollowed out rather than being solid metal.

Racing Snaffle - A thin snaffle - works on the principle the thinner the mouthpiece the more severe it is.

Egg-butt Snaffle - The rings are fixed to the mouthpiece. In order to prevent pinching of the lips, the rings are straight where attached to the mouthpiece.

Fulmer Snaffle - Snaffle bit with metal cheek pieces to prevent the bit from rubbing the mouth and to ensure that it is not pulled through. The rings are loose. Keepers are needed for this type of bit. These are small pieces of leather connected from the cheek pieces to the top bar, and they keep the bit from revolving in the mouth.

Twisted Snaffle - To prevent the horse leaning on the bit, this increases the pressure on the mouth. This should only be used on hard mouthed horses.

Gag Snaffle - Rounded leather cheek pieces pass through holes at the top and bottom of the bit rings. The headpiece fastens to the top strap, and the rein to the bottom. The action caused therefore, is like that of a lever with the pressure pulled down from the poll and the bit rising against the corners of the mouth. This is an extremely severe bit and should only be used as a last resort in the hands of someone who understands it.

Cheek Snaffle - This is very similar to a Fulmer snaffle. They are always an egg-butt snaffle, but have a bar going either up or down or, in some cases, both ways. These bars are fixed to the egg-butt part. This bit is useful in helping to turn a horse, and is

particularly good for use on a child's pony, where the child may pull the bit through the horses mouth.

A slight variation of the snaffle is the **Double Jointed Snaffle**. Such bits as the French Bridoon and the Doctor Bristol come within this category. The two joints have the effect of reducing the 'nut-cracker' action. The bit does not rest so low on the horses tongue and therefore gives it more room. Sensitive horses and horses which have a tendency to put their tongues over the bit are usually more relaxed with this type of bit.

The Curb Bit

The curb bit acts on the tongue, the pressure being greatest when the mouthpiece is straight. Some have parts which allow the tongue to move and concentrate upon pressure on the bars of the mouth. The metal cheek pieces can be fixed, which will make the action more direct, or moveable. Whichever way, it produces a lever action that places pressure on the bars of the mouth. As the metal cheek is pulled back, it causes the curb chain to apply pressure on the curb groove. The longer the cheek piece, the greater the severity of the action of the bit.

This is an extremely harsh bit, and should never be used by the beginner.

The Pelham

The pelham aims to combine the effects of both the snaffle and the curb in one mouthpiece. The cheeks have two rings and a curb chain attached. The top ring is for the snaffle rein - this has no leverage effect. The lower ring is for the curb rein - this acts as a lever.

The mouthpiece can be vulcanite or metal, straight or half-moon, with a part or even jointed.

Leather roundings, or 'D' straps, are curved couplings that can be used to attach the snaffle and curb rings, thus allowing for one rein to be used.

The effects of this bit are very much dependent upon the reins that are pulled - it can be mild or severe.

The Kimblewick bit has built-in roundings - there is a single metal 'D' running from above the mouthpiece to the bottom of the cheek. This bit is very severe.

The Double Bridle has two bits - The Bridoon, which is a thinner type of simple snaffle, and The Curb, which provides additional control and facilitates more refined aids.

The Bitless Bridle has no bit but places pressure on the nose and on the chin. **The Hackamore** is probably the best known of all the bitless bridles. The two metal cheeks are curved so that their leather attachments act across the nose and behind the chin when the reins are pulled.

Resistance

A horse that is not comfortable will, in some way, try to evade or resist the bit. There are various ways in which this happens:

Tongue Over the Bit - A bit with a port or that is double jointed could help this.

Behind the Bit - The horse tucks his head in an effort to evade the action of the bit. Consider using a less severe bit.

Above the Bit - The horse raises his head. This can be due to lack of training, fear of a severe bit, or simply a hard mouth.

Problems with the Teeth - Can be due to an injury, sharp teeth or maloclusion. Consult the Vet or a horse dentist for corrective treatment.

No Foot - No Horse

The choice of a good blacksmith is extremely important but the rider himself must be aware of the needs of his horse

A good farrier is worth his weight in gold, and has to be the horse owners greatest asset! Good feet are important to the health and fitness of the horse and it is up to the owner to make sure they are maintained. The good farrier can help correct faults in conformation, improve the condition of the feet and prevent weakness developing. Conversley, a bad one can lame the horse for life.

The main functions of the hooves are to support the body weight, absorb the jarring and keep a good grip on the ground.

The three crucial parts of the foot are:

The Wall
Made of horn and constantly growing downwards from the coronary band which encircles the foot between the hoof and the postern. On the underside where it meets the sole, there is a strip of softer horn called the white line.

The Sole
This protects the foot from injury and, as long as it remains concave, gives a better grip.

The Frog
Without doubt, the most vital part of the hoof. The frog is the 'V' shaped rubbery part on the underside of the hoof. It is the anti-concussion and anti-slipping device. It is the part of the foot which bears the brunt of the first contact with the ground.

How often should you have an animal shod? This depends upon the amount and type of work you are doing and upon the conditions that are prevalent when you are riding. Shoes will generally need attention every 4-6 weeks. If you are doing very little roadwork then your shoes will be less likely to need replacing and you will be able to get away with 'removes'. This is when the shoe is removed, the hoof trimmed and the same shoe re-fitted. It is essential that the hoof receives attention every 4-6 weeks and is trimmed in order to avoid problems caused by overgrown, chipped or cracked feet.

Take note of the indications that re-shoeing is necessary:

Loose shoe - you can not mistake the clanking!

Day to day hoof care is vital to the horse's health

'Cast' shoe - one that has been lost.

Shoe wearing thin.

Clenches rising and standing out from wall.

Long foot and/or one that has lost its shape.

Many people have little real choice about which blacksmith to use. The lifestyle and habits of 'smiths have changed, and blacksmiths who run a permanent forge are few and far between. The travelling blacksmith is more common these days. Recommendation is the best way to make your choice, together with a look at some of their work. If the blacksmith you choose is a popular choice in your district, you may have to find out when he is visiting local horses and make arrangements to have your horse shod there.

There are two methods of shoeing - hot and cold. With cold shoeing the farrier makes the shoes beforehand, and nails them on cold. He will be able to make only minor adjustments in this method. It is important that the farrier has seen your horse and taken careful measurements of the feet before making the shoes. If this is the case, then there are likely to be few problems with fitting. The real danger here must obviously be when an attempt is made to fit a wrong size/shape shoe, and the foot is altered to fit the shoe. The resultant problems could be quite far reaching and long term.

Hot shoeing can be done at a permanently sited forge, or by the farrier who travels with a portable forge. The shoe is heated, tried on and adjusted before it is cooled and nailed on. With this method the shoe should be a perfect fit.

When the shoe has been fitted the following checks should be made:

That the type of shoe fitted is suitable for the work you will require from your horse, and that the weight of iron is proportional to the size of the horse (horses 4-5lbs, ponies 12.2oz - 2.5lbs).

That the shoe is made to fit the horse, not the foot to fit the shoe (severe paring back of the hoof and too much rasping could well indicate this).

That the frog touches the ground.

That the length of the foot is reduced evenly at both toe and heel.

That the appropriate number of nails have been used (usually three on the inside, four on the outside).

That the clenches are neat, in line and the right distance up the wall.

That no daylight can be seen between the shoe and the foot.

That the clips fit well.

Having stressed the importance of a good farrier, it must also be stated what part you as the careful owner should be doing.

Daily inspection of the shoes could show you one of several things -

That the shoes are wearing evenly. Uneven wear could be attributed to bad conformation or ill-fitting shoes.

That there are no stones, mud or stable debris impacted in the hoof that could cause heat or lameness.

That the hoof is healthy and not a breeding ground for micro-organisms that could lead to such conditions as thrush.

Checking on feet should come as naturally to you as part of the stable routine as brushing your teeth - and is equally important!

In addition to regular shoeing and inspection, the application of hoof oils and various other hoof-care preparations is important. These reinforce the foot's natural moisture and prevent brittleness.

Keeping a Horse at Grass

---

*Living out is natural for horses but living in a field
does not always answer all the horses nutritional needs
and the owner must be aware of what is lacking in the diet*

Living out in the wild, wandering in herds over unlimited tracts of land, finding food, water and shelter, is the natural habitat of the horse. During their daily wanderings they would keep their muscles in trim, their feet in shape, and would enjoy a life of variety. Then along came man!

Now the horse living in its domestic state, relies entirely upon man for his well-being. Man, therefore, carries the responsibility for ensuring his safety. It is not sufficient to turf a horse or pony out onto a fenced patch of grass and think that is enough - he may survive, but is that enough?

If you are going to keep a horse at grass, whether it be part-time or full-time, ask yourself the following questions:

1. Is the field large enough for the animals needs?

As a general guide, ponies need about 1.5 acres, horses somewhat more.

If the field is used throughout the year, ideally it should be large enough to be used in rotation (one part is used, whilst the other part is rested). Land that is in constant use can become 'horse sick', and is a breeding ground for the multitude of worms to which horses are prone. Don't forget that droppings need to be picked up regularly or you may find that large portions become unusable since horses are very 'picky' grazers. If you are able to turn cattle out on the field, even for a short period, it would be advantageous since they will eat the rank grass and swallow the worm larvae which will not survive in the intestines of the cattle. If possible, set aside a period to fertilise the field, usually in the early spring. During this operation, you will need to remove the horse for at least three weeks, the rain has to wash all traces of fertiliser into the soil. If it is possible arrange for the field to be harrowed, this will aerate the soil and allow the fertiliser to sink in.

2. Is the quality of the grass sufficient to maintain the horse?

A horse at grass eats for about 16 out of 24 hours. You will often observe that horses graze to a pattern, always at the same part of the field at the same time each day. They will eat the sweetest grass available for the longest periods, often leaving this quite bare. They are extremely selective eaters, preferring shorter grass to crop. There is a variety of grasses that have their individual qualities, and varying appeal to the horses. First-grade pasture contains 30% or more of perennial rye grass, and a mixture of several of the following: cocks-foot, timothy, meadow fescue, fine leaved fescues and white clover. Long grass should be 'topped' when over a foot high. This, left on the pasture, helps act as a mulch, and protects the young grass from scorching by the sun.

Regard for quality as well as quantity is therefore extremely important.

3. Is the field fairly level and well drained?

Very hilly fields are unsuitable for horses, particularly younger ones, since they impose a strain on their limbs. The benefits of good drainage are obvious, not only will excessive surface water be reduced, but it will also allow adequate ventilation below the surface where aeration is essential.

Horses develop their own grazing patterns

Gates held together with old ironmongery are unsightly and also a potential danger

Large, boggy areas of your field will cut down the amount of grazing land available.

4. Is the fencing appropriate and adequate?

The horse owner has a responsibility, both to his horse and to others who could be affected by a straying horse. Many accidents are caused by horses escaping through poorly maintained and inadequate fences and becoming hazards on the highway. It is wise to make sure that your horse is covered (on your insurance policy) against damage caused by straying .

Safe, sound fencing is a must in any paddock. Make-shift railings, bedsteads, thorn bushes, etc. are not only unsightly but dangerous.

Of all forms of fencing the POST AND RAIL type is considered to be the safest, both for looks and durability. For preference these should be either three or four barred, and reaching to a height of about 4'6" - this should be high enough to discourage the horse from jumping out. More-recent developments have substituted tape for the rail and these are considered to be even safer.

A well kept cut and laid HEDGE is also a popular form of fencing but is more usually found in older, well-established pasture. One of the big drawbacks is that it is apt to develop weak spots and gaps. An inner rail may be necessary to prevent the horses pushing their way through.

STONE WALLS are equally effective. These are usually confined to areas where stone is plentiful. These need frequent checking for loose stones and mortar, and to ensure that a regular height is maintained.

Probably the most popular, and the most economical form of fencing is the heavy gauge type PLAIN WIRE fence. This should be erected with regularly-placed posts, the bottom wire stretched taught and at least 2' from then ground. This type of fence needs regular maintenance in order to ensure that the wire does not slacken, thus allowing the horse to get caught up in it. Ideally, some form of top rail should be fitted so the horse can see it easily. Alternatively, pieces of cloth could be tied at intervals along the top strand to make it easily visible.

ELECTRIC fencing can be dangerous. It's thin, single strand can be difficult for horses to see, especially if they are travelling at speed. It is probably best to keep this for use in emergencies only.

BARBED WIRE is an absolute no-no - even as a stop gap. The injuries that can result from a horse getting caught up in the barbed wire are horrific and the responsible horse owner will avoid them at any cost.

Strong fencing is an essential. Don't forget that horses are inquisitive creatures too, and often adhere to the view that 'the grass is greener on the other side'!

5. Are there any hazards in the field on which the horse may injure himself?

The field should be inspected for any debris that may be lying around before the horse is turned out. If your field is near a road, make sure that there is no litter thrown over into the field. Broken bottles, tin cans and plastic bags can be dangerous. If you have fed hay in the field make sure you remove the string from the bales.

6. Is there adequate shelter?

Horses, however hardy, will need some form of shelter in the more extreme weather.

A good thick hedge or a clump of trees will prove an adequate place for a horse to shelter, although the amount of shelter depends upon the direction of the prevailing wind.

Obviously, the best form of shelter is the purpose-built field shelter. There are many types and sizes available on the market. Make sure that the site on which you construct your field shelter is well drained, and that the entrance to the building faces away from the prevailing wind. It is best to lay some form of bedding inside the shelter, preferably straw, as the ground can get very churned up, particularly if there is more than one horse using it. it could well be a wise precaution to lay some form of covering down at the entrance to the shelter as this can get very boggy.

7. Have you taken precautions to prevent increased worm infestation?

All horses harbour a certain number of worms. With careful management of both horse and pasture, they can be kept down to a level that will not have any injurious effect upon the horse.

Since both adult worms and eggs live in the horses droppings, it is essential to tackle the worm problem both from a curative and preventative viewpoint. By developing an effective and regular worming programme, you can cure the immediate problem with the horse and prevent greater worm infestation developing. Droppings should be removed from the field very regularly. This will mean that the larvae have no chance to hatch and infect the grass.

If you have a new horse coming into the field, it will be wise to ensure that adequate worming has taken place, and that the owner (if it is someone other than yourself) agrees to follow a similar worming programme.

8. Is there water available at all times?

A horse will drink 8-10 gallons per day, a pony between 4 and 8.

A constant supply of water in the field is essential. A natural, free-running stream is best, preferably with a gravel bottom and gently sloping, firm approaches. If the stream is muddy, the banks steep and the stream bottom either sand or mud, then you should consider fencing it off.

Obviously, it is better to have a water supply laid on to the field. The alternative calls for an awful lot of fetching and carrying! A water trough is the best container, preferably one

that is galvanised and has a ball-cock mechanism that is protected by a cover. An old bath with cracked and broken edges is not suitable. Horses do not like stagnant water - make sure that whatever receptacle you use, you are able to empty it easily. It will need to be cleared at regular intervals.

9. Are there any poisonous weeds in the field?

The major causes of poisoning in horses are ragwort, yew, oak, laburnum and bracken. All fields should be inspected at the time you take them over, and regularly thereafter, for any signs of poisonous plants and weeds. If you are unsure whether a weed comes into then poisonous category, then take it to someone who recognises plants and have it checked out.

Some of the weeds/plants that cause problems are:

Ragwort: Yellow, multi-headed flower, with ragged edged leaves. This is most deadly and can be fatal within a few days. Horses in fields with sufficient grass will avoid this. It is most dangerous when dried in hay, or in silage. Ragwort should be removed from the field and burnt.

Yew: Most poisonous tree in Britain. All parts of the tree are poisonous - including the leaves, berries and twigs.

Oak: Both acorns and leaves are poisonous.

Bracken: the rhyzomes are much more poisonous than the fronds. Most commonly dangerous between August and October, when the fronds turn brown.

Buttercup: Dangerous only when eaten in excess. They are completely harmless when dry in hay.

Cowbane or Water Hemlock: Very poisonous - roots contain most poison, although stems and leaves can prove fatal. Grows in marshes and damp places. Cowbane has a white, umbrella shaped flower head.

Spotted Hemlock: Identifiable by the purple spots on the stem. All parts of the plant are poisonous.

Laburnum: All parts, particularly the seeds, are poisonous. Poisoning is fairly common, although large doses are needed before it is fatal.

Deadly Nightshade: A deadly poison.

Privet: Poisoning is rare and will usually only occur when horses have unlimited access.

10. Are you able to give daily attention?

Horses at grass need to be looked at every day. No matter how safe you think your field is, you would never be able to anticipate all the silly things the horse in the field can do!

The horse should be inspected each day for cuts, lumps or scratches. Check his feet to make sure the shoes are in place and not creating any further problems. Inspect the horses coat, although you may not necessarily be grooming every day.

Some foals are extremely inquisitive - they look for fun as much as for food

Horses can suffer from a skin condition known as 'rain scald' which thrives in wet conditions. Check on heels, especially with horses in muddy fields, for 'cracked heels'. This condition, if allowed to deteriorate, is often referred to as 'mud fever' and can end up with an extremely sore inflammation of the legs and heels. If this happens you will need to consult the vet, but prevention can be as simple as the application of a thick layer of Vaseline.

A horse that is wintering out will, naturally, need daily attention. If the horse is wearing a New Zealand Rug, it will need to be checked for wear-and-tear and fitting.

You will also need, at some point, supplementary feed. It is impossible to say how much the horse needs as there are so many factors to take into account. You will be able to judge from the horses general condition when additional feeding is needed. In the most extreme weather, the feed would need to be given at least twice a day, mornings and evenings. It should consist of both hay and dry feed in sufficient quantities dependent upon the size of the horse and the amount of work it is asked to do.

Safety First

Please do not forget this aspect of keeping a horse or pony at grass. In our section 'Better Safe Than Sorry' we stress the advantages of freeze marking. It is a process that could end up saving you an awful lot of heartache, not to mention money.

It is also advisable to have some form of locking device on the gate, not forgetting that gates can be lifted off their hinges. Do remember, though, that horse thieves are determined people who have already made up their minds. They are less likely to bother the owner who runs a tight, secure field.

Stabling Your Horse

Many factors must be taken into account when keeping your horse in the stable environment. Safety, convenience and cost must blend together

Your stable doesn't necessarily have to look smart, but it does have to be safe. It is only the very few, and the very fortunate, who are in the position to have their own stables built. The majority of people have to make do with what is already there, or convert an old one. Whichever type you have you should consider the safety aspects.

Are there any danger points or anything the horse could hurt himself on?

Is it big enough?

Is it sited where there is good natural drainage and facing away from the cold North wind?

Brick built stables are ideal, but do tend to be expensive

Is it in a place that is easily accessible for you from your home?

Let us look in more detail at some of the requirements:-

Size

The size of stable you require depends upon the size of horse you have. However, do look to your future needs in terms of the size of your horse.

Standard boxes are 14' x 12' for a horse 15.2hh and above, below this height 12' x 10' is quite adequate. The ceilings should be high enough to allow the horse head room, even if he rears and to allow room for the circulation of air.

Materials

If you are starting to build your stables from scratch then what you will choose will depend upon preference, cost and availability.

The brick-built stable is ideal, but unfortunately very expensive nowadays. A suitable substitute are concrete blocks which are cheaper and easier to lay - you will, however, have to put up with the starkness they present!

Probably the cheapest and easiest solution is to invest in one of the modern wooden portable stables that are now quite readily available. These come either in kit form with instructions on how to "do-it-yourself" or you can arrange for the manufacturer to erect them for you. A cautionary word - unless you or someone you know is competent in this type of constructing it would be wise to invest in 'professional' help.

Whichever stables you choose it is important to treat all new wood with a liberal coating of creosote or similar preparation in order to make it less attractive for chewing as well as preserving it.

When you have made the decision about the type of material with which you will construct your stables, do bear in mind that you will need storage space for tack and feed.

N.B. If you are considering a building in which to store hay and straw then do make sure that it is away from where the horses are stabled in case of fire.

Floors and Drainage

The most important things about floors are that they are

a)   non-slip

b)   long lasting

c)   Impervious to moisture.

Cement and concrete floors are long lasting, but you must ensure that the surface is roughened otherwise they become very slippery when wet. Ordinary bricks are very porous and prone to uneven wear. Clay or hard packed earth are also a possibility, although used more abroad than here. They are, however, very difficult to keep clean. Probably the best and, incidentally - the most expensive, is Staffordshire brick. These bricks are grooved on the upper surface, long lasting and non slip.

Although it is important to have good drainage in your stables it is not essential to invest in an expensive and complicated system. A gentle slope towards the door will be sufficient - although do make sure that it is gentle as a slope that is too steep could put a certain amount of strain on your horse's legs.

Water

Do consider the proximity of a water outlet to your stable - a horse drinks anything from 4 to 10 gallons of water a day - an awful lot to carry in containers.

The easiest way to ensure a constant and clean supply of water for your horse is to install self-filling water bowls. These have many advantages but you may wish to discount them because of the expense or because you will have no idea how much, or more specifically how little your horse is drinking each day.

The alternative is to have a fixed point where a filled water bucket can be sited. Make sure that you can easily place the filled bucket there (and just as easily remove it to clean it!) and that it does not have any sharp projections that might injure the horse.

Ventilation

Unlike many humans, horses do not necessarily thrive in an over-warm atmosphere. A stable needs to be well ventilated to allow the often noxious odours of decomposing manure to be carried away. Fresh air should be pure and plentiful, germs will breed in a muggy atmosphere and thereby increase the risk of coughs and colds.

As the weather gets colder, instead of closing up the stable doors, add more clothing. It really shouldn't be necessary to close both sections of the stable door, except in extreme weather conditions.

However, good ventilation does not imply draughts. As with humans draughts can be extremely detrimental, for example swollen legs are often the result of a continuous draught coming under the stable door.

To test if your horse is warm enough feel his ears. If they are cold he may well need an extra item of clothing.

Windows

Windows should be sited on the same side as the door in order to prevent a cross draught. Best for stables are those made of some type of shatter-proof material. All windows should be guarded by a metal grille or iron bars in order to prevent the horse poking his nose through them. You may wish to choose a louvred window, but these can, unless fitted properly, be draughty. Probably the best type of window opening is the hopper type which, opening inwards, directs the current of air towards the roof thus avoiding any draughts on the animal's back.

Doors

Ideally, stable doors should have two halves, not only to provide ventilation but also to allow the horse to look out and take an interest in what's going on around him.

Make sure the top bolt is fastened firmly

A Kick bolt will help foil the escape of even the most persistant horse

Ensure that the doors open outwards and that the top door has a catch or fixture that it can be fastened onto to prevent it swinging and banging.

The stable door should be high enough and wide enough for your horse to fit through easily without risk on banging either sides or head.

It is essential to have two bolts on the bottom door - one towards the top and one at the bottom. This may seem a nuisance but some horses devote days to working out how to undo bolts and then make a bolt for freedom!

Electric Fittings

All light fittings, bulbs, switches or sockets should be out of reach of the horse or fitted with a strong guard. Stables can be very dusty places so make sure that your light bulbs are behind a grille that is easily removed to accommodate easy cleaning. Wiring should be behind metal cases and firmly fixed in a place least accessible to the horse.

Mangers

There is a variety of types of manger and many varied opinions on the type that should be used. There are some people who argue that a horse eats naturally from the ground and those who argue that you shouldn't feed from the ground because the food is in danger of contamination from stable matter and vermin and too prone to being knocked over. Whatever method you choose, it should be done so with the safety, health and hygiene of the horse in mind.

A manger fixed to the wall is undoubtedly safer from being knocked over, and as long as the underneath is boxed in so that the horse cannot knock its knees or get cast when rolling, seems a practical method of dispensing feed. If you are at the planning stage with your stable then do consider placing the manger where it is easily accessible from the door, in this way you can exit safely without risking getting clipped by a fidgety horse.

Hay-Feeding

The most economical and clean way to feed hay is in a net tied to a ring in the wall. Do make sure that the net is high up in order to avoid the horse getting his foot caught if he paws. Don't forget, nets do get longer when they are empty! You can counteract this by pulling the drawstring through one of the lower meshes and pulling it up tightly before fastening.

The older types of hay rack fastened to the wall are not now recommended, they force the horse to hold his head in an unnatural position when he eats, and you also risk hay-seeds falling into the horse's eyes.

Fire Safety

Without doubt the most frightening experience that could happen in any stable block is fire. Most horses are terrified of fire and panic to the extent that they freeze.

With careful thoughtful management you can minimise the chances of a serious outbreak of fire.

1. Post 'No Smoking' notices in prominent positions and make sure this rule is adhered to.

2. Keep fire-fighting equipment handy and in an up-to-date state.

3. Have a regular fire drill.

4. Phone numbers of Emergency services, doctor, vet etc. should be prominently displayed.

5. Have a regular maintenance check by a qualified electrician of all the electrical appliances and wiring.

6. Store hay and straw away from your main stable block.

Bedding

There are many different types of bedding, but whatever you choose make sure that it is adequate. It would be foolish to skimp on the bed and end up with a horse that knocks his joints resulting in swellings known as 'capped hocks', 'capped elbows' or 'big knees'.

OAT STRAW is the most readily available straw, but since it is quite palatable horses are inclined to eat it.

WHEAT STRAW is generally accepted to be the best bedding straw. It makes a warm, comfortable bed, with good drainage and is sweet smelling.

BARLEY STRAW can be quite prickly and less acceptable to the more sensitive horses.

SHAVINGS make quite a good bed, but if you buy from the mill make sure there are no sharp chips of wood or nails. Shavings are available in bales and come neatly packaged in polythene.

SAWDUST and PEAT are also suitable for bedding, but need a lot of working to keep it dry and clean. If you use this type of bedding do make sure that you pick out your horse's feet at regular intervals as it does tend to ball up.

SAND may be cheap, but if it is sea-sand the horses may lick it for the salt it contains. Swallowed in any quantity, sand can cause colic.

PAPER is also an acceptable form of bedding when shredded. It is quite absorbant but tends to get soggy quickly and can be quite uneconomical if you are a meticulous 'mucker out'!

At Livery

Finding a suitable place to stable your horse
is a priority

You, as an owner, are in the fortunate position of being able to choose your livery yard. Your choice should be an informed one, not just the yard that is most convenient to you, but one that is going to give you and your horse the best possible service and value for money.

It is your responsibility to do your homework and find out what are the best places to suit your needs and are within your pocket. It would be foolish to commit yourself to a livery that you cannot afford to maintain and then have to go through the upheaval of moving.

It is important to assess what the yard has to offer and to be in no doubt as to what the service is that you are paying for.

Liveries fall into the following categories:-

Full Livery

This will normally cover the complete care of your horse. He will be stabled, fed, groomed, exercised and your tack cleaned.

Part Livery

This is similar to the full livery but does not include exercise.

Working Livery

This type of livery is generally offered only in riding schools that take in liveries in addition to giving lessons. Here the horse is cared for either as a full or part livery and charged at a reduced rate in return for the horse being used by the school for an agreed number of hours in return.

Livery plus Schooling

These can be either full or part livery but have the additional benefit that rather than receiving just exercise they receive schooling towards a particular discipline.

Do-it yourself Livery

Here you pay for the use of the stable and possibly grazing - but everything else you do yourself.

The cost of livery will vary according to the service you require. Generally the 'Livery plus Schooling' will be the most expensive followed by the 'Full Livery', with DIY the cheapest.

In addition to the livery charges there will be additional costs such as worming and shoeing. You may be asked to pay extra for any nursing care your horse has to receive as a result of illness or accident.

If you have paid for exercising as part of your livery then do check exactly what this means both in terms of frequency, amount and type of exercise to be received. Normally a yard will only exercise from Monday to Friday, working on the assumption that you will want to take advantage of riding your own horse at the weekend. In addition to riding at the weekends it is likely that you will want to ride some summer evenings because it is still light. If this is the case, do inform the yard of your intentions unless you want to arrive there and have to wait around while your horse digests its evening meal. Also, if you have announced your intention to ride in the evenings and can't make it then try and let them know so that your horse can be fed with all the others and isn't getting increasingly hungry and frustrated in his box.

One of the most common causes for complaint at a livery yard are the additional cost of extras that you may suddenly find added to your bill. In order to avoid this sort of frustration enquire if the following are included or charged for as extras:-

1. Damage to stables, yard or equipment.

2. Bedding that is different from that generally used on the yard.

3. Specialised feed stuffs or supplements.

4. Worming - both purchasing and administering.

5. Turning out or bringing in if you are a DIY Livery.

6. Clipping (although this would generally be seen as extra since it is your choice).

7. Plaiting/Trimming Up.

8. Administering medications or giving treatments.

If you are aware that any of the above are extras and you ask for them to be undertaken then you have made the choice and be expected to pay the cost. Making an assumption can lead you into many arguments and situations that will cause irritation on both sides.

Looking at Facilities

Some yards are better off for facilities than others, but in the end you will make the choice of yard for what you consider to be essentials. You may, for example, feel that a covered arena is an essential if you take into consideration the climate in this country, your leisure hours available on an all-year-round basis and the type of equestrian activity you intend to participate in. If this is your priority then you can bet on it that it will be others' too! You may end up out-bidding them, or just looking for an acceptable alternative. You may find that facilities are available, but at an extra cost. It would be wise to check on the folllowing points before taking up a livery:-

1. The facilities available, e.g. Covered arena, floodlit arena, show jumps, cross country jumps. Whether these are covered in the cost of the livery you choose or whether they are extra. Ask about the limits of use - all the time - certain days - a set number of times per week, etc.

2. The type of riding available in the area, including any bridleways and any restricted areas.

3. If grazing is available - to what extent (including limitations) and if your horse will be turned out and fetched in.

4. Does the yard have a resident blacksmith and, if it does, are there any limitations about the one you already use coming onto the yard to shoe your horses.

5. If you are a DIY livery ask if the yard supplies tools for mucking out.

6. Does the yard have any secure facilities where you can store your equipment?

7. Does the yard have any staff who can give you extra instruction if you want it, and do they mind if you bring your own instructor if that is what you prefer.

Remember that taking up a place at a livery yard can be as much a gamble for the proprietors as it can for you - except that you probably have more choice than them. Do try to keep your side of the bargain by being thoughtful and responsible. Try to make sure that you pay your bills on time - this may be a hobby for you, but it's a business for the owners.

Grooming

> *Grooming is an essential part of horse ownership, it helps to maintain the health of your horse, as well as making it look good*

Grooming is necessary for the well-being of any horse or pony. First and foremost it keeps the horse clean. It also massages, stimulates the circulation and improves the muscle tone. Attention to the coat, therefore, promotes the animals health.

A list of essentials for your Grooming Kit follows on the next page.

Make sure the foot is held securely when using a hoof pick

ITEM	PURPOSE	METHOD
Hoof Pick	To remove dirt and stones from feet.	Pick out each foot in turn and remove mud, stones, bedding etc. with the point of the pick. Work from the heel to the toe in order to avoid accidental piercing of the frog. Take care not to press down too hard on the side or on the cleft or the frog.
Dandy Stiff bristled Brush	removes mud and sweat	This is best used on horses or ponies with thick coats. Do not used on clipped horses or on the tender parts such as the head, around the eyes and between the hind legs. Use a vigorous motion, starting at the neck and working with the lay of the hair.
Rubber Curry	To remove hair and dirt from the coat.	Use in a way similar to the Dandy, beginning at the neck to remove mud and sweat stains. Do not use on bony areas.
Body Brush	To remove dust and dirt from coat. Also used on mane and tail.	Using long, sweeping, round strokes, follow the lie of the hair, thus removing dust and scurf. Apply strong pressure without thumping it down on the horse. Clean by drawing brush through curry comb. Brush mane and tail by separating a few locks at a time.
Metal Curry	To remove dirt from the body brush.	Working with the curry comb in one hand and the body brush in the other, draw the curry comb through the body brush every 5 or 6 strokes to remove dirt. Clean curry by banging one end on the floor. Do not use on horses body.
Wisp	To stimulate circulation and massage.	Bring down vigorously with a bang on the muscles of the neck, quarters and thighs in the direction of the lie of the coat. Do not use on tender or bony areas.
Sponges	To clean eyes, nostrils, lips and dock.	Using one dampened sponge, gently clean around the eyes, then nostrils and lips. With a separate sponge, lift the tail and clean the dock area. Colour code the sponges to prevent them getting mixed up.

ITEM	PURPOSE	METHOD
Mane Comb	To shorten or remove hair from mane and/or tail.	Thinning of the mane and tail should not be attempted by the inexperienced. Lay hair flat with spare hand to determine long pieces. Pulling a few at a time, wrap the comb around them and remove with a vigorous yank. Collect all loose hair.
Water Brush	To dampen mane and tail and wash feet.	Dampen brush to lay the mane. Work from the roots downwards. Wash feet if necessary.
Sweat Scraper	To remove water and/or sweat from the coat.	Run sweat scraper firmly over the wet or sweaty areas, following the lie of the hair. Not used during normal grooming but only to scrape off sweat or water if the horse has been vigorously exercised, out in the rain, or washed.
Stable Rubber	To give a final polish after grooming.	Dampen cloth, arrange in a bundle, and wipe over the coat following the lie of the hair.

When to Groom

The ideal time to groom is immediately after exercise, when the horse is still warm and the pores are still open, and the dirt and scurf will rise to the surface. However, you will want your horse looking clean and smart before exercising.

Quartering

This is a fine, ten-minute grooming routine that takes place before stabled horse is exercised.

1. Pick out hooves (hold hoof over a 'mucking out' skip to prevent debris falling into the bedding).

2. Remove stable marks with dandy or damp sponge.

3. Brush mane and tail with body brush and lay with water brush.

4. Sponge eyes, muzzle and dock.

The Grooming Kit

Cooling and Drying
On return to the stable

1. Wash and pick out the feet if muddy.

2. Remove dry sweat marks with a dandy brush.

3. Cover with anti-sweat sheet or straw under rug if horse is likely to 'break out' in the stable.

4. Do not rug until you are positive the horse has cooled down properly.

Strapping
The most thorough grooming routine where the most beneficial effects are felt through the application of 'elbow grease'!

1. Remove mud and sweat marks with dandy brush or rubber curry.

2. Using a body brush, with firm vigorous movements, start at the neck on the nearside and work along the body. Transfer to the offside one nearside is clean.

3. Clean areas between forelegs, belly and flank.

4. Using a body brush, gently but firmly clean head.

5. Using a wisp, give stimulating massage to muscles in neck, quarters and thighs.

6. Groom mane and tail using a body brush.

7. Lay mane with a dampened water brush.

8. Sponge eyes and nose, then dock, remembering to use separate sponges.

9. Oil hooves.

10 Finally, wipe over the surface of the coat with a dampened stable rubber.

Setting Fair

When setting a stabled horse down for the night and maybe putting on an additional blanket or thicker rug, this is a good opportunity to give a quick brush over, or wisping.

The Grass Kept Horse

Grass kept horses do not need nearly so much grooming. The grease in their coats acts as a waterproofing agent that protects them from the elements, and

The metal curry comb is used to remove dirt and hairs from the body brush.

because the horse in the field moves around freely, it doesn't need grooming to stimulate it's circulation.

There is, however a routine to follow:

Pick out hooves and check feet or heels for any injury or inflammations such as 'mud fever'.

Brush mud from coat using a dandy brush - checking at the same time for any unexplained lumps or bumps.

Clean out eyes and nose then dock with your colour coded sponges.

As always, when around horses, do not take any unnecessary risks:

-Never kneel by the horses legs.

-When grooming the hindquarters of the horse, try to stand to the side.

-Keep in contact with the horse by running your hand down it's leg and leaving it resting just above the hock, will help you to feel if the horse tenses up ready to kick.

-Hold the tail when grooming at the back or between the hind legs, this will stop the tail swishing in your face and, hopefully, make him feel less inclined to kick.

Always use extreme caution when standing behind even the most docile of horses - accidents do happen.

Clipping

> *The horse's natural coat needs to be removed for a variety of practical reasons, many associated with the amount of work it is expected to do*

For the horse which is in regular work during the winter months, the removal of part or all of the coat is essential.

During the winter months the horse grows a thicker coat and, round about October time, you will probably notice that the higher gloss of the summer coat has disappeared and the coat is taking on a woolly appearance. The best time to perform the first clip is when the winter coat is established.

Clipping is, essentially, not a cosmetic exercise, but is performed for practical reasons. The horses which are in heavy, fast work such as racehorses, hunters and eventers, will benefit from having a large proportion of their coat removed. The owner will be the judge of what type of clip their horse needs, and this will be gauged by the amount of work the horse is required to do and by the amount of time and attention the owner is able to lavish on the animal. The four basic types of clip are:

The Full Clip

All the hair is removed from the head (except for the muzzle and inside the ears), neck, body and legs. This clip makes it easier to dry off and groom neck, legs and back. It does not leave any protection. This type of clip is most popularly used on racehorses.

The Hunter Clip

The head, neck and body are clipped out, leaving a saddle shaped area of hair on the back. The hair is left on the legs as this helps give protection against knocks, bangs, twigs and thorns. The hair left on the saddle area will form an extra cushion against soreness and injury.

The Blanket Clip

The hair is removed from the head, neck, shoulders, belly, part of the thighs and a thin strip up the back of the quarters. The remaining hair resembles a blanket - hence the origin of the clips name. This type of clip will afford the horse maximum protection on the back and sides, whilst leaving clipped areas which are most likely to get wet, sweaty and muddy.

Just removing the hair from under the belly is sufficient for the pony only doing light work

It would be extremely unwise to even attempt to clip your horse if you have little experience. Horses can become very nervous and frightened of the clippers, and you could well find yourself in a dangerous situation. If you have a burning desire to participate in clipping you horse, then enlist the services of someone to clip your horse who will not be averse to allowing you to have a go on some of the easier, less sensitive areas. Don't forget though that the skilled person can make it look a lot easier than it is, and the last thing you want is to have great weal marks where the clippers have been.

The Trace High Clip

The coat is removed from the belly (to the height the traces would have come if the horse had been pulling a cart), chest, under the neck to the throat, part of the thighs, and up the back of the quarters. Theoretically you can turn the horse clipped in this manner out at night, as long as they have a New Zealand on.

Clipping is a job that takes both time and patience. before starting check that a) the clippers are in good working order - sharp, well-oiled, and that the tension is correct b) that you have taken the precaution to check that the plug is well earthed and that you are wearing rubber boots, and c) that the horses coat is dry and as well groomed as possible.

Keep talking to and patting your horse to give him reassurance. It is a good idea to let the clippers run for a short time before starting so that he becomes accustomed to the noise. Start clipping in the areas that are least sensitive and ticklish - not the head, belly or groin. You would be well advised to leave the head until last. It may be necessary at some point to use 'twitch' to keep the horse still. a 'twitch' is an implement with a handle, usually of wood, with a loop of rope on the end. This is looped around the upper lip and twisted until it is firm. Don't twist so hard that it causes him pain and he begins to fight, but just tight enough to make him keep his head still.

Do not clip into

a)   the sides of the mane or the root of the tail

b)   the insides of the ears or

c)   the backs of the tendons or fetlocks. These are best done with a pair of rounded, blunt ended scissors and a comb.

Having clipped your horse you will then have to make sure that he has sufficient clothing to compensate for his loss of hair.

The full clip is most practical if your horse is working throughout the winter

Boots and Bandages

> Legs need protection against bumps and bangs and undue strain

Boots and bandages are used as a protection against brushing, over-reaching, blows and as a means of support. However, both boots and bandages that are put on incorrectly can do more harm than good.

Brushing Boots

These can be made of various types of materials - felt. leather, rubber etc. They are worn around the cannon bone and the upper half of the fetlock joint, and have a shaped, reinforced area to protect the fetlock area.

Brushing boots are essential equipment when working a horse on the lunge, particularly youngsters. They protect the horse from knocking itself.

They are used in all aspects of the sport, both in competition and schooling at home. One should always consider the weather conditions when fitting. If the going is muddy and deep it is probably a good idea to leave them off as pieces of grit and mud can work up between the boot and the leg. This rubs the horse and causes soreness.

Yorkshire Boots:

This is another type of brushing boot. They are worn to protect the hind fetlocks and/or coronet.

Tendon Boots

These provide a good protection measure, and support for weak tendons. They can be used in many equestrian pursuits - lunging, schooling, exercising, show-jumping and travelling.

Hock Boots

Are made of heavy wool or felt material. They are worn over the hocks to protect the horse when travelling, or in the stable in the case of a kicker.

Over Reach Boots:

These are bell-shaped boots made of rubber. they fit over the hoof to protect the heels of the forelegs. They are made both with and without fastenings. the latter should be pulled over the hoof inside out and upside down, then turned the correct way once they are on.

Knee Boots:

Usually made of felt with shaped leather reinforcements. they fit with buckles above the knee, the bottom being left loose. these are an ideal item of equipment for young horses or those who have to use roads with slippery surfaces. Anyone who has seen the injuries sustained from 'broken knees' would not hesitate to make these an essential purchase.

These boots can be worn as an extra protection when jumping over fixed fences as well as exercising.

Travelling Knee Caps

These are similar in construction to the knee boot except that they have a loose fitting strap at the bottom. They provide an added protection when travelling but are also suitable for use when exercising. It is inadvisable to jump in them since they are quite restrictive.

Travelling Boots

Made from a durable foam-filled material, these boots are designed to give maximum

Boots should be fitted carefully and checked regularly whilst in use

protection to the legs when travelling. Although some may be fitted with straps and buckles, velcro fastenings are becoming more and more popular. This type of fastening has the advantage that the boots are quick and easy to both fit and remove. They have the disadvantage that they slip more easily than the conventional, well fitted travelling boot.

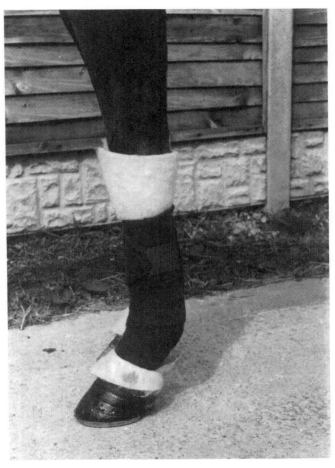

It is best to trim the Gamgee before bandaging

Bandages

The main functions of bandages are to provide protection for the legs when travelling and support when exercising - particularly to the back tendons and suspensory ligaments.

Stable or Travelling Bandages

These are made of flannel or wool and are usually about 4" wide by 7-8 feet long. They fasten with tape or velcro and should be applied over gamgee or cotton wool. They should cover as much of the leg as possible from the knee/hock to the coronet. They should be fitted firmly but not too tight. Start at the top and wind it around until the starting point is reached. If the bandages are secured with tapes, make sure you fasten them firmly on the outside of the cannon bones, never in the front or back of the legs as the pressure can cause lumps and bumps. Tuck any loose ends away under the bandage.

Exercise Bandages

These are made of stockinette or elasticated crepe. They are between 2 ½ and 3" wide. They should be applied over gamgee under the knee and above the fetlock joint. Too high or too low could interfere with the horses action. the tapes should be double knotted on either side of the leg, never at the front or back, and the loose ends tucked away. If used in a competition, the fastening tapes should be covered with adhesive tape to make them more secure.

A word of caution - once you start working a horse in bandages, you may have to continue doing so.

Best Dressed Horse - All Rugged up

The development of new types of rugs has led to a boom in the horse 'clothes' market

Most horses doing any kind of hard work during the winter months will be clipped and stabled - at least at night. Once you have removed the horse's natural coat, you must provide him with rugs for warmth.

There are a wide variety of rugs available, some being multi-purpose and can be used both day and night. But before rushing out and buying a rug, make sure you know what size the horse needs, and what functions it is

The rug should be a snug, comfortable fit

The New Zealand gives winter protection

going to serve. To measure him take a tape from the centre of the chest, around his shoulder and along the side to an imaginary vertical line drawn from the horses dock.

The Jute Rug

The traditional stable rug is the **Jute** rug. This can be used for day or night wear. The Jute rug is a heavy, close-woven material with a blanket lining. Although this is warm enough for mild nights, in the depths of winter or with horses particularly sensitive to the cold, you would need to put an appropriate number of blankets underneath. If you are putting blankets underneath then be careful and follow the correct procedure for fitting:

Fold the blanket to the appropriate size.

Place on the horses back with the extra blanket high on the horses neck and just fitting up to the dock.

Make sure that there are no wrinkles and the coat is lying smoothly - all one way.

Fold the front corners over the base of the neck to form a triangle with the apex pointing towards the horses neck.

Throw a rug over the horses back, making sure that the blanket remains in position.

Fold the triangular piece back over the rug, ensuring that it is unwrinkled over the shoulders.

The anti-cast roller is a 'must' for those horses that are in danger of being cast

Secure the blanket and rug with a surcingle.

Make sure you have some sort of buffer pad between the surcingle and rugs to prevent the covers creating undue pressure on the spine.

The Quilted Rug:

This is an extremely popular stable rug. It has the advantages of being light, easily washable and it comes in a wide range of colours. The quilted rug usually has an attached surcingle, either of the conventional style or the more recent cross-over type.

The Day Rug:

This is a woollen rug often decorated with braid. Although originally intended for use on stabled horses during the day, it is more generally seen at shows or when transporting horses.

Anti-Sweat Sheets:

These are used on horses that are hot, cold or wet. The sheet is made of an open cotton mesh, rather like a string vest, that allows good ventilation whilst trapping a layer of warm air. Used in conjunction with a rug, it provides a form of insulation against both heat and cold. This allows the horse to cool down slowly and dry out quickly, thus helping to prevent a horse from 'breaking out' (sweating) after heavy, strenuous work.

The Travelling Rug:

This serves a similar purpose to the anti-sweat rug, and also acts as an under blanket or travelling sheet.

Summer Sheets:

These can be used to protect the horse against dust and flies during the summer period. They are particularly useful for throwing over your horse when it is at a show waiting to enter the ring.

Nylon Sheets:

These are also useful if you are going to a show and need some sort of waterproof protection to keep your horse and tack dry whilst waiting for your turn in a competition.

The New Zealand Rug:

This is made of waterproof canvas that is partially lined with wool. It has special straps that pass between the horses legs to prevent it from slipping. It is used to keep horses warm and dry when they are turned out at grass. For a hardy horse out at grass, this type of protection is likely to prove unnecessary. But for thin-skinned horses, or horses who are turned out for a few hours in cold weather, it is an essential. Particular care must be taken in fitting this rug. The front of the rug must not rest on the withers but should follow the line of his own neck, otherwise it will rub. These rugs are usually shaped at the back and should fit neatly over the rump up to the top of the dock.

Rollers are used to keep rugs in place. They can be made of leather, webbing or jute, and are padded on either side to prevent pressure forming on the spine.

The Anti-Cast Roller:

This has a metal hoop joining the two pads. As the name suggests, this is used to ensure that the horse cannot roll over and become cast in the stable.

As a general rule, rugs should be removed for a period each day. This is done in order to allow the skin to breathe, to check for rubs and abrasions, and to make sure that the coat is laid flat. When not in use, rugs and blankets should be brushed and cleaned, then stored ready for the next time they are needed. It is good practice to get any rips, tears or broken stitching repaired before they are put away.

Equine Faults and Vices

Some equine faults and vices are irritating whilst others are extremely dangerous. Understanding these can be the first step along the road to a cure

---

Unless you are extremely lucky you will certainly come up against horses who present problems at some point during your riding career. Let us look at some of these problems, together with possible explanations and ways of dealing with them.

Bucking

Sheer high-spirits can be one of the reasons a horse bucks - when he literally wants to kick up his heels for the fun of it. One way round this particularly with the younger horse, is to lunge him for a time before riding. This may take a few of the kinks out Keep your horse's lead up, don't forget that if his leads are going to go up his head will go down. However, tensing in anticipation of bucking occuring can take a lot of the pleasure out of your ride both for yourself and the horse.

Another thing you should do is consider your horse's diet - is he having too many oats - if so cut them down.

The other type of bucking is the rodeo type and this is far more serious. It is most certainly possible that he is doing it just to get rid of YOU. There may be other reasons and these should be eliminated.

- Check your saddle - it may be pressing or pinching the back and making it sore.

- Check the girth, make sure no skin is pinched

- He may be cold backed, try putting a numnah under the saddle, or lungeing him in his track first.

You should always ride a potential bucker forward, keeping him on the bit. Try to anticipate his makes and drive him forwards using your legs and a whip if necessary.

If you have tried all these measures and the problem persists to the extent where you are finding little pleasure in riding - or becoming afraid - then consider replacing your horse for something without the problem. There are too many good horses around to have to put up with a bad one.

Rearing

This is a most serious fault. Anything higher than a half-rear is dangerous - and no-one other than an extremely competant rider should be put on a horse that is known to be a rearer.

If you should be unfortunate enough to be on a horse that rears then lean forwards to one side of the horse's neck - and wait for him to come down. When he does come down turn him round at once and keep on turning, using your whip at the same time. When you think he is ready then ride him forwards - as fast as you can and keep him going. If you feel there is a likelihood of the horse rearing again try to anticipate it and turn a circle.

You may find there is a reason for a horse starting to rear, such as an ill-fitting saddle, or a bit that is wrongly fitted. If this is the case then obviously you can do something about it. If the horse rears through exitement, or happiness then you can take steps to deal with it. However, the horse that is a persistent and incurable rearer is a danger to all.

Napping

A nappy horse doesn't like to leave his friends or his stable, often because he doesn't feel safe without them. Horses/ponies are natural herd animals and generally prefer to be with a group.

You must be firm with a nappy horse. It's no good simply flapping your legs ineffectually like a windmill. A well schooled horse who responds to the rider's aids is unlikely to be persistently nappy because he has been taught to go

forward. You may be well advised to go back to basics with a nappy horse - teaching him to move forwards when you squeeze with your legs. If he persists with being nappy then use the whip, not as an aid on its own but to reinforce the leg aids that the horse is ignoring.

Nappiness and going behind the bit can lead to rearing - yet another good reason for riding him forward. You must always win any argument with your horse, although if you are in the middle of traffic it can be a little difficult. Try to make all your battles at home, and if necessary enlist the help of a friend.

Bolting

Horses that are botling are taking charge of the situation. If you have lost control the horse will take you where it wants to go - some horses are just terrified and running for safety. A nappy horse may gallop you back to where he wants to go - these are not really bolters.

A rider who loses control is usually over-horsed, losing control is a terrifying experience which only the brave survive without permanent scarring!

If your horse runs away, try to find out why. Are you over-feeding? Have you changed your bit? The problem is that once a horse has run away it is likely to do it again, so be prepared. Keep contact with his mouth, ride him forwards between your hands and legs, be ready for a sudden swing round or buck. If he is making for home, turn him round in the other direction before he gets into his stride, or turn him round in a circle. When you do eventually halt make him rein back - not so roughly that you will jab him in the mouth, but firmly enough to show him that you are in control. Having got control again, steel yourself and take him back to the point he started to bolt from and make him walk back.

Basically, a well-schooled horse will not present this problem, unless it is frightened into it. You may want to try a different bit, or a martingale that will give you greater control. The problem may be with the horse, but it may be a combination of both yours and your horse's shortcomings.

Stumbling

This fault may be due to the fact that the horse is half asleep, or it may be that he needs his hoofs cut back, or he may have a problem with his forelegs. Obviously, the latter problem is the worst because it is often incurable. However, the majority of stumbles occur because the horse is bored and badly ridden.

Take control, sit up, bring your horse onto the bit and concentrate upon the task in hand. If the horse still persists in stumbling, check his feet, or better still explain the problem to your blacksmith and get him to check it out. If the problem is still there then call in the vet - get him to check it out.

Shying

This can be caused by the horse being truly afraid, or just by him being determined to do what he wants to do. Some horses will pass anything, others will find a piece of paper lying innocently in the road quite terrifying.

If your horse is a persistant shyer then you must do something to prevent you and your horse becoming a danger to yourselves and other road users. Try riding out in the company of an older horse, ride on the inside keeping him in contact with hands legs and seats. If you have to ride out on your own then try a shoulder-in position with your horse's head bent inwards as for a circle - this should stop him swinging his quarters into oncoming traffic.

Kicking

Kickers can be very difficult to cure. Mares will sometimes kick when they are in season, others kick because they are excited or afraid, or just because they see a potential enemy.

Kicking in a crowd can be extremely dangerous, and you must take precautions: don't get into the middle of a crowd of horses - keep to the edge and keep your horse's head turned towards the other horses; don't go into the collecting ring until the last minute; wear a red ribbon on the horse's tail if you are not hunting; keep him on the bit and you should be able to feel the kick winding up; punish when the horse is actually in the act of kicking.

If your horse kicks for fear of punishment, e.g. knocking down a fence - then rethink your strategy. Try an alternative method of dealing with the problem, go back to basics.

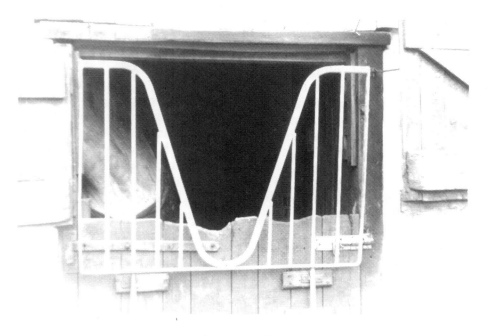

Aniti-weave bars

Headshaking

There can be several reasons why a horse will headshake:-

Ill fitting bridle
Unsuitable bit
Painful tooth
Appalling hands

You should begin a process of ellimination. Check your bridle, pay particular attention to the browband as this may be catching the ears and causing irritation; check that the bit is in the right position in the mouth and is not too severe. Appalling hands are a far more difficult problem to deal with. If you are hauling your horse around by the mouth and using the reins to balance yourself then you could be guilty of creating the problem. There is only one thing to do in this case: get yourself some lessons that will help you to develop an independent secure seat.

Plunging

This is leaping in the air and lungeing forwards. This usually occurs with a horse who is trying to get his own way. A horse that is a plunger should be kept moving with his head up, turning a circle before he can get his head down can help in this.

Stargazing

This is when the horse pulls with its head up in the air. Most stargazers have light necks, in fact, some may even be ewe-necked. Often these horses have developed this condition because they are afraid of their mouths. If this appears to be the case then a lighter bit should be considered. A standing martingale may act as a temporary solution, although it would be unsuitable for competition riding.

You should begin working on this fault by riding on a loose rein, practise halting using your legs and encouraging him to drop his nose and flex his jaw. The schooling you are doing should develop the muscles in the neck and encourage overall flexibility.

Overbending

It isn't natural for the horse to move with his head tucked tightly into his chest. When a horse tucks his head in to the extent where he would be termed 'overbent' then he is attempting to escape something. It may be your hands, or those of a rider he remembers from the past, a fierce bit, tight draw reins, whatever it is, the action he has taken is to evade the bit.

Overbending can lead to jibbing or to rearing and, once it decides to go forward, to bolting. The overbent horse is bending from the neck rather than the poll. When you are riding at the trot the horse's poll, not the crest of the neck, should be the highest point.

You need to work hard to try and get the horse to relax. Try to do this by changing the bit to the mildest one you feel you allow you to maintain control. Then, try to get him to stretch his neck, starting with a loose rein walk. This process does not work in five minutes, you will need a great deal of time and patience. Once you have achieved a relaxed walk, try for some relaxed halts, talk to your horse or sing to him if this helps him relax.

Behind the Bit

This can mean overbent, but more usually it is a term applied to a horse that lacks impulsion and never actually goes on the bit. You need to ride the horse foward using lots of leg and, more than likely, a lot of schooling. You need to ride using a combination of legs, seat and back to achieve the necessary impulsion to bring the horse onto the bit.

In Front of the Bit

A horse that hangs on the bit needs reschooling. A horse that is in front of the bit will be inclined to pull, this may be due to over-excitement, over-eating, or even over-pulling from previous riders. Whichever it is, you may find that your horse has developed a habit that is both irritating and hard work.

Try using a squeezing action with your hands, giving when the horse does. Attempt walking on a loose rein and circling if he starts to pull - it's much harder to pull when you're circling. Gradually pick up the pace through the trot to the slow canter - however, don't attempt to rush, this is a long, slow process that requires a great deal of patience.

If you find that your horse is opening his mouth and pulling then try using a dropped noseband.

Weaving

A horse is said to be a weaver when it sways its head and neck from side to side and at the same time lifting one leg after another.

Once this habit has developed it is very difficult to cure. Since other animals are prone to copy this sort of behaviour it would be unwise to put the horse in the middle of a stable yard where others are likely to copy. Weaving may cause loss of condition and action as if the action is constant the horse will get insufficient rest and uselessly fatigue its muscles.

This condition can be perpetuated by boredom. If possible turn the horse out, although the most confirmed weavers will still tend to weave when they have eaten their fill. You can close the stable door, since most weavers will weave over a door and this can be effective. The anti-weave device that can be fitted onto the top of the bottom door will allow the horse to put its head out of the stable but restrict the sideways movement.

Wind Sucking

The horse snatches the head - as though snapping at something in the air - purses the lips, arches the neck and swallows air.

Crib Biting

The horse grasps the edge of a solid object - manger door, railings etc. arches the neck and swallows air.

Both wind-sucking and crib-biting appear to be two forms of the same vice, and both may cause colic and chronic digestive trouble. Crib-biting also causes wear of the incisor teeth, which in excessive cases may mean that the horse's teeth are unable to meet properly, causing trouble with grazing.

The application of a broad leather strap which fits round the neck immediately behind the ears and has a metal 'tongue' fitting under the throat can help since it causes pain when the horse arches its neck prior to wind sucking and crib-biting. Another preventative is a hollow perforated bit which means that a horse cannot produce the vaccuum in its mouth necessary for wind-sucking.

There are various surgical procedures that can be performed but it is best to consult your vet before giving these any real consideration.

Transporting your Horse

Try to take the anxiety out of transporting your horse, both for your sake and his!

There will come a time in most horses' lives when they have to transported from one place to another. This will, in most cases, involve the use of some mechanical means, either a trailer or a horse box. One cannot assume that all horses will take to it naturally, although, thank goodness, the majority of them do. However, you cannot make that assumption if this is a new experience for you and your horse. Planning and groundwork play a large part in your preparations.

The Preparations

Have a trial run at loading your horse before you plan on going to that all important show or event. If the horse is young or nervous or if you are new to loading the horse, it will be a useful learning experience.

The first time you try loading a horse it is wise to choose a day that is calm, where there are not an undue number of distractions and things to frighten. Never try to load on your own, particularly into a trailer - you will need an assistant to fasten the tail bar once the horse has been loaded in order to prevent him reversing out. Make sure that your assistant, be he putting up the tail bar, breeching strap or ramp, stands on the side.

Load the horse in a headcollar with a longish lead rope attached - just in case the horse attempts to snatch his head up. If the horse becomes extremely difficult you may find it easier to control him by having the bridle on over the headcollar.

You may find it easier to load if you position the trailer up against a wall or a hedge. This will form a natural wing. Horses are often nervous about walking into dark places so try to position the trailer where natural light falls into the back. The hollow sound of feet on the ramp should be deadened by laying down a thick bed of straw. If your ramp has a thick covering of coconut matting this will be unnecessary.

Give the horse time to look around and familiarise himself with, what to him will be, this awesome object! It is often a good ploy to give the horse some feed

A vehicle with a low gently sloping ramp is more inviting to horses

as he is standing at the bottom of the ramp, then gradually tempt him up into the box. Once there you should allow the horse to finish his feed before unloading. Try this a few times and, if you are successful you will be able to rest easy with the knowledge that at least one anxiety of going to a show is taken away! However, if you are still experiencing difficulties - 'Nil Desperandum'! Patience is the keynote when loading a difficult horse - together with stubbornness - yours! Ask two assistants to stand on either side of the ramp with a rope or lunge line between them. Then, as you firmly lead the horse firmly onto the ramp, they should take up the slack and tighten the line across the horse's buttocks. Remind them before undertaking this procedure to stand to the side, just in case.

Patience and persistence - together with a strong arm and nerves of steel - can be needed with those horses who are difficult to box. It is, however, better to get this done at home rather than battling in public and being overwhelmed with the advice and help of the well meaning onlookers whose methods may vary drastically from yours.

Make sure your horsebox/trailer is roadworthy. I am fairly sure that the majority of people will check their horse box before setting off on a journey - as they would their car. How many will carry out such a rigorous check on the trailer? The trailer is like a car in all ways, except that it doesn't have an engine or gearbox.

Horses must be protected against knocks and bumps when travelling

A pamphlet entitled 'Trust your trailer - Maintenance hints' is available at a modest cost from the British Horse Society.

Alternatively, you may consult the maintenance booklet supplied with your trailer, or contact the manufacturer.

There are moves afoot to get the Ministry of Transport to make annual trailer testing compulsory. They have not as yet been successful, but the intention is to continue to pursue this in view of the savings such a small cash expenditure could make in terms of humans' and horses' lives.

One thing that you should do after each journey is clear out all droppings and wet straw from the body of the vehicle since this will surely have an adverse effect regardless of how the floor is constructed. Similarly, a regular inspection of the floor from inside and underneath is advisable, since rotting floors are not always obvious until they have gone far enough to prove a hazard to the horse.

Check that the car you intend to tow with is appropriate. Just because you have a towing hitch doesn't mean that you can tow any trailer regardless of its size. You will need to check what is the maximum towing weight of your car, either in the handbook or with your manufacturer. The towing weight is established through a number of factors that relate to the design details of the vehicle.

If you are new to transporting horses then do proceed with thought. You may want to try towing the trailer without an animal in it. This will give you an idea of how both your car and the trailer handle together. Once you have the animal aboard, then do :

a) Adjust your speed appropriately. Towing at speed can cause a whiplash effect with the trailer ending up weaving about at the back - and you could end up with it jack-knifed.

b) Anticipate when you are going to brake - your passengers may have some warning but the horse in the back doesn't, and could end up being severely jarred.

c) Take corners and roundabouts wide and slow, although they have a leg at each corner, horses can easily become unsettled.

d) If a horse is travelling for the first time, do not make the journey too long.

e) Plan your route so that you take the easiest way - even if it is slightly longer. That way you can all arrive calm and collected!

These may all seem minor points to you, but they could make all the difference between a horse being a willing or an unwilling traveller who is difficult to load.

Since the horse needs to be comfortable when travelling, make sure that he is dressed for the event - not only for comfort and warmth, but most importantly for safety.

To protect the legs, put on knee boots/hock boots, plus travelling bandages/boots. These will afford extra protection in case the horse bangs around in the box, either whilst travelling or loading and unloading.

In order to balance themselves, horses will often lean back against something solid, thereby rubbing their tails. A tail bandage or tail guard will help prevent this.

Should the weather be cold, or the box draughty, you may need to put a rug on your horse. However, do be aware that if your horse is nervous or excited, and sweats as a result, a thick rug may make matters worse.

If your horse is inclined to throw its head up, and is likely to bump it, then a poll guard would be advisable.

Although many people travel their horses to the hunt in full tack with a rug over them, it is not generally a practice that should be encouraged. The risk of some part of the tack getting caught is not one that you should choose to take if it can be avoided.

The final word of caution I would add is - make sure that your car, trailer and horse insurance are in order. Better to have them and not need them than to need them and not have them.

Insurance

Riding may be your favourite hobby but your horse could be one of your largest investments. Insurance can safeguard this investment

One of the costs that we would recommend you take into account when calculating the cost of keeping a horse is the annual insurance premium.

To adopt the attitude 'it will never happen to me' is an optimistic view and, in many instances, foolhardy. For example, what if your horse is injured in an accident? This could leave you with heavy vet's fees. What if your horse should die following an accident? What if your horse should injure a third party, or what if your horse should develop a problem which leaves it unable to perform the tasks for which you bought it? A lot of what-if's! but for the horse owner who has taken out insurance, all these questions are answered.

As with many things, the question of cost comes into discussion, although that will depend upon the type of cover which you require, and the horse you wish to insure. Whatever the cost, you will find it a relatively small price to pay for the broad cover you will receive. There are a number of companies who specialise in horse insurance, and if you are in doubt, the most sensible thing to do would be to consult an insurance broker, or a representative of an insurance company which specialises in horse insurance. They will help you to determine what is the best cover to suit your needs.

Let us look at some of the types of cover available, given that each company will vary slightly.

Death of the Horse

Here the company will pay the owner the market value of the horse, or the amount insured, whichever is the lesser, in the event of death or humane slaughter. This will be for a horse who suffers an accident or contracts an illness which causes death during the period of insurance.

Economic Slaughter and Permanent Loss of Use

If the horse becomes permanently incapable of fulfilling the purpose for which it was bought, then economic, humane slaughter may be the recommended course of action. However, the owner may decide that they would prefer to keep the animal. In this case, they can arrange to keep the horse whilst still claiming under the terms of the insurance policy. This usually involves accepting a percentage of the agreed insured sum, and accepting that the horse is no longer insurable.

Veterinary Fees

The amount covered again varies from company to company. What is covered in this section is the vet's fee paid for treatment following an accident or a disease contracted during the period of insurance. It is important to note what is NOT covered by your policy, although this is unlikely to change your decision about calling the vet in. There is usually a clause in the policy which commits you to paying a set sum per claim. This again varies with the company.

Theft or Straying

It is usual for the company to pay the market value, or the insured sum, whichever is the lesser, in the event of the loss of a horse through theft or straying. In addition to this, the company will make an allowance of a set sum to be paid to you in order to cover advertising or rewards which lead to the recovery of the horse. Many companies will give a 10% discount if the horse is freeze marked.

Saddlery and Tack

Both saddlery and tack are covered against accidental loss or damage and against theft. The company will pay up to an agreed amount stated in your policy, but excluding a set sum e.g. you may have to pay the first £25 of the claim. With most companies this usually includes both the policy holder and their immediate family who permanently reside in the same household. It will not cover equipment left in an unlocked place, or tack that is damaged through the owner's negligence.

Personal Injury

Although this is not included in all policies, it is important to consider whether you should ensure that yours has. The policy should include death by accident, loss of one or more limbs or eyes, permanent total disability from following any occupation. It will not cover you if you are engaged in professional racing of any kind or if you are under the influence of any intoxicating liquor or drugs.

Public Liability

It is vital to have third party liability cover. Should your horse cause damage to property or injure someone, you could end up facing a substantial claim. Although the claimant would have to prove negligence on your part before any claim was met, it could prove to be a time-consuming and costly business with you paying out substantial amounts in legal fees. The amount for which you are covered under the public liability clause varies with the company and type of plan you have taken out.

This is not a totally comprehensive list since there are other covers offered by different companies, e.g. horse-drawn vehicles, horse trailers, stable cover, hire or replacement. You will, of course, only get what you pay for.

Before filling in your proposal form, do give careful consideration to the class of cover you require. Some insurance companies operate two scales, whilst others have three. As a rule of thumb, the classes usually cover the following categories:

Class A - Hacking, gymkhana, showing, driving or pony club events, stallions, brood mares, young horses, heavy horses (breeding and showing), endurance and long distance riding.

Class B - As for Class A plus show-jumping under B.S.J.A., hunting, polo, hunter trials, combined training, one and three day events, trotting.

Class C - As for Classes A and B plus point-to-point racing, team/hunter chasing, drag hunting, intermediate or advanced horse trials.

Having decided the class of insurance, you need to determine the cover you require. Usually there are three types and, although the names vary with the companies, they are basic, standard and standard plus.

Make sure that you are realistic when declaring the value of your horse on the proposal form. Insurance companies do not go on agreed value, but on a market value basis. Whatever you choose to insure your horse at, if it comes to claiming for the loss of your horse, under whatever circumstances, the policy will pay at the current market value. The only thing you will have done if you over estimate the value is waste your premium! On the other hand, if your horse is competing in B.H.S. or B.S.J.A. events and is gaining points, then it is appreciating in value and this should be reflected on your proposal form.

Finally, before you sign the declaration at the end of the proposal form, do make sure that your answers are correct to the best of your knowledge. Ensure that any vices are declared. Don't be caught out - if your declaration is not wholly true, then the insurers would be within their right to void the contract.

One can think of many adages that point to the advantages of insuring your horse. Perhaps the most apt is - there's no point in closing the stable door after the horse has bolted!

Useful References and Listings

Allergy-Free Horse Hay	256	Harness Manufacturers	272
Allweather Riding Surfaces	256	Hoof-care Products	272
Aqua Sprays	257	Horse Boots	274
Bedding	257	Horse Boxes	275
Bits	258	Horse-care Products	276
Bridles	258	Horse Dealers	277
Cavaletti	259	Horse Eye Protectors	277
Clippers	259	Horse Feed Suppliers	277
Compound Feeds	260	Horse Holiday Homes	277
Disinfectants	261	Horse Hoods	278
Draw Reins	261	Horse Trailers & Accessories	278
Dressage Supplies	262	Horse Transporters & Agents	280
Drinking Troughs	262	Horse Treats	280
Driving Vehicles and		Horse Walkers	280
Accessories	262	Hydroponic Grass Machines	280
Equestrian Engineers	264	Indoor School Maintenance	
Farriery Supplies	264	Equipment	280
Feed Additives & Supplements	265	International Forwarding	
Feed Manufacturers	266	Agents	281
Feed Storage Bins	267	Lead Ropes	281
Feed Suppliers, General	268	Leather-care Products and	
Fencing	268	Supplies	281
Fencing Suppliers	268	Leg Guards	282
Fencing Contractors	269	Linseed and Barley Boilers	282
Fencing Gates and Shelters	269	Lungeing Equipment	282
Floor Covering	271	Measuring Sticks	282
Freeze Marking	271	Numnahs	282
Girths	271	Nutritionists	284

Pasture Maintenance	284	Antiseptics	297
Plaits, Bands, Threads and		Bandages	297
Needles	284	Blood Tonics	298
Reins	284	Cod Liver Oils	299
Riding Equipment, Tack	284	Coat Glosses and Dressings	299
Riding Surfaces	285	Cough and Cold Treatments	300
Rosettes and Trophies	285	Crib-biting Preventatives	300
Rubber Stops and Pads	286	Digestive Treatments	300
Rugs & Blankets/Tail Guards	286	Fly and Insect Repellants	306
Saddle Manufacturers & Sole		Healing Creams and Gels	306
Agents	288	Hoof-care Products	307
Saddle Stands and Racks	290	Liniments	307
Saddles, Retailers	290	Louse Powder	307
Safety Equipment	290	Milk Replacers	308
Show Jumps/Sundries	290	Poultices	308
Small Tractors	291	Shampoos and Conditioners	308
Stirrups and Leathers	291	Skin-care Products	309
Stable Equipment	291	Treatments and Tonics	309
Surcingles & Rollers	294	Vaccines	310
Tack Repairers	295	Veterinary Equipment	310
Towing Vehicles and		Veterinary and Homeopathic	
Accessories	296	Remedies	310
Watering Devices	296	Vitamin/Mineral Supplement	311
Manufacturers and Suppliers of		Wormers	307
Horse-care Products		Wound Dressings	313
Anti-inflammatory Treatments	297		

The Healthy Horse: Useful References and Listings

Allergy-free Horse Hay

Horse Requisites Newmarket Ltd
Black Bear Lane, Newmarket, Suffolk CB8 0JT
Tel: 0638 664619
Fax: 0638 661562

Hydrodan (Corby) Ltd
74 Earlstrees Road, Corby, Northamptonshire
Tel: 0536 361185

Mark Westaway & Son
Love Lane Farm, Marldon, Paignton, Devon TQ3 1SP
Tel: 0803 527257
Fax: 0803 528010

Natural Animal Feeds Ltd
Penrhos, Raglan, Gwent NP5 2DJ
Tel: 0600 85256

Propack
Coppice Farm, Akeley Wood, Buckingham, Bucks
Tel: 0280 812141

Somerset Zero Grass Ltd
37a Market Place, Cirencester, Gloucestershire
Tel: 0285 69228

All-weather Riding Surfaces

British Gates & Timber Ltd
Biddenden, Nr Ashford, Kent TN27 8DD
Tel: 0580 291 555
Fax: 0580 292011

Dormit Riding Surfaces
Lakeside Sawmills, South Cerney, Cirencester, Gloucestershire GL7 5UH
Tel: 0285 860781
Fax: 0285 861033

Equitred
'Luceme', Maury's Lane, West Wellow, Hampshire SO5 0DA
Tel: 0774 220303

H S Jackson & Son (Fencing) Ltd
140 Stowting Common, Nr Ashford, Kent
Tel: 023 375 393

H S Jackson & Son (Fencing) Ltd
Wrexhan Road, Belgrave, Chester, Cheshire
Tel: 0244 674804

H S Jackson & Son (Fencing) Ltd
Ramshawfield, Bardon Mill, Hexham, Northumberland
Tel: 04984 555

H S Jackson & Son Ltd (Bath)
New Rock, Chilcompton, Nr Bath, Somerset
Tel: 0761 232666

Irrigation & Slurry Services
Louvain, Quavey Road, Redlynch, Wiltshire SP5 2HH
Tel: 0725 20377

Monomet Ltd
3 Church Road, Croydon, Surrey CRO 1SG
Tel: 081 686 4311

Muir Landscape Services
112 Main Road, Ravenshead, Nottingham, Nottinghamshire
Tel: 0603 796469

Osborne Poultry Services Ltd
Crookford Hill, Elkesley, Retford, Nottingham, Nottinghamshire
Tel: 0777 83670/641

Parkway UK Ltd
Paines Corner, Swife Lane,
Broad Oak, Heathfield, East
Sussex TN21 8UT
Tel: 0435 883553

Singleton Flint
Newland Works, Deacon
Road, Lincoln, Lincolnshire
LN2 4LE
Tel: 0522 524542
Fax: 0522 514426

**The Wyke Equestrian
Services**
Shifnal, Shropshire TF11 9PP
Tel: 0952 462982
Fax: 0952 462981

Unitex Ltd
Knaresborough, North
Yorkshire HG5 OPP
Tel: 0423 862677

**Ushers Equestrian
Services**
46 Chandos Avenue, London
N20 9DX
Tel: 081 446 2311

**Woodland Riding
Surfaces**
Warren Camp,
Crowborough, Sussex
Tel: 034282 4612

Aqua Sprays

**The Wyke Equestrian
Services**
Shifnal, Shropshire TF11 9PP
Tel: 0952 462982
Fax: 0952 462981

W H J Fagg & Son
Driberg Way, Braintree,
Essex CM7 7NB
Tel: 0376 22026

Bedding

**Animal Bedding
Company**
Unit 10D, Trinity Trading
Estate, Mill Way,
Sittingbourne, Kent
Tel: 0795 26578

C P Backhurst & Co

Strawberry Farm, Glaziers
Lane, Normandy, Guildford,
Surrey GU3 2DF
Tel: 0483 811360
Weekly Deliveries (30-mile
radius). Cash and Carry
open 6 ½ days per week.

**Charnwood Milling Co
Ltd**
Framlingham, near
Woodbridge, Suffolk
1P13 9PT
Tel: 0728 723435
Fax: 0728 724359

**Coombe Park
Equestrian Centre**
Littlehempston, Totnes,
Devon TQ9 6LW
Tel: 0803 863473

Equi-Bed
6 Sandall Road, Wisbeach,
Cambridgeshire PB13 2ZZ
Tel: 0733 78928

**Mallon Brother
Transport Ltd**
Brades Road, Prees, Nr
Whitchurch, Shropshire
Tel: 0948 840420

**Newport Shredded
Paper Products**
Unit 6, Hogwood Lane
Industrial Estate,
Finchampstead,
Wokingtham, Berkshire

Proctors Woodflakes
Dunkeswell, Honiton, Devon
EX14 0QH
Tel: 040489 2451

R S Assemblies Ltd
Coppice Farm, Akeley
Wood, Buckingham,
Buckinghamshire
Tel: 0280 812141

Remploy
231/233 Alder Road,
Parkstone, Poole, Dorset
BH12 4AP
Tel: 0202 749108

Sawdust Marketing Co
Standon, Hertfordshire

Shreddabed
W Cawthorne & Sons Ltd,
Corporation Street, Nuneaton
Warcs CV11 5AG
Tel: 0203 641212
Fax: 0203 370766

SMC Ltd
Standon, Hertfordshire
SG11 1PH
Tel: 0920 821777

**Snowflakes Wood
Shavings Ltd**
Marsh Lane, Boston,
Lincolnshire
Tel: 0205 65457

**Willow Farm Livery
Stables & RS**
123A, Frogmore Lane,
Lovedean, School,
Waterlooville,
Hampshire PO8 9RD
Tel: 0705 599817

Woodpecker Products Ltd
Brades Road, Press, Nr Whitchurch, Shropshire
Tel: 0948 840 420
Fax: 0948 841 195

Bits

Carbex-Munroe (Handles)
11a St Nicholas Lane, Lewes, East Sussex BN7 2JZ
Tel: 0273 478111

Cottage Industries (Equestrian) Ltd
Crown Lane, Wychbold, Droitwich, Worcestershire
Tel: 052786 582

Horse Requisites Newmarket Ltd
Black Bear Lane, Newmarket, Suffolk CB8 0JT
Tel: 0638 664619
Fax: 0638 661562

Impala Sales and Marketing
The Cottage, Creation Road, Hollowell, Northampton, Northamptonshire NN6 8RP
Tel: 0604 740687

Thoroughbred Saddlery Company
Ickleford Manor, Hitchin, Hertfordshire
Tel: 0462 325596

Bridles

Acorn Bridle Manufacturers
18 Vicarage Place, Walsall, West Midlands

Acorn Rugs
Gair Shield Farm, Steel, Hexham, Northumberland NE47 OHS
Tel: 043 473 562

British Leathergoods' Association
10 Vyse Street, Birmingham, West Midlands B18 6LT
Tel: 021 236 2657
Fax: 021 236 3921

Champion & Wilton Ltd
112/122 Tabernacle Street, London, EC2M 4LE
Tel: 071 251 2701

Chris Adams
Park Farm House, Cornworthy, Totnes, Devon
Tel: 080 423 454

Clare Lawson
Vine Cottage, Winchester Rd, Waltham Chase, South-ampton, Hampshire SO3 2LX
Tel: 0329 832366

Coleman Croft Saddlery
Sutton's Farm, Cooper's Green, Nr St Albans, Hertfordshire AL4 9HJ
Tel: 07072 74239

Colin Whittaker (Saddler)
Fore Street, Castle Gray, Somerset
Tel: 0963 50929

Cross Country (Equestrian) Ltd
Luttwytche Road, Church Stretton, Shropshire SY6 6AT
Tel: 0694 722919

Diane Onions (Harness Maker)
Pilgrim Cottage, Milton-under-Wychwood, Oxfordshire OX7 6LE
Tel: 0993 830128

Donalds McLellan (Saddler)
Saddle & Harness Maker, 146, Busby Road, Clarkston, Glasgow, Strathclyde G76 8BH
Tel: 041 644 4880

Equestrian Manufacturing & Supply
52 Mount Street, Walsall, West Midlands WS1 3PL

F B Davis Saddlery Ltd
Tolsons Mill, Mitchfield Street, Fazeley, Tamworth, Staffordshire B78 3QB
Tel: 0827 280550

G Fieldhouse Saddlery
(Walsall) Ltd, 18-19 Green Lane, Walsall, West Midlands WS2 8HE
Tel: 0922 38094
Fax: 0922 22921

Ideal Saddle Co. Ltd
14/19 Green Lane, Walsall, West Midlands WS2 8HE
Tel: 0922 20233

Impala Sales and Marketing
The Cottage, Creation Road, Hollowell, Northampton, Northamptonshire NN6 8RP
Tel: 0604 740687

Kangol Equestrian
Norfolk Street, Carlisle, CA2 5HX
Tel: 0228 31711

Keith Bates
Harness Maker, 36 Stonedale, Sutton Hill, Telford, Shropshire
Tel: 0952 582551

Keith Luxford (Saddlery) Ltd
57 High Street, Teddington, Middlesex
Tel: 081 977 4964

Mitre Bridles
59/61 Wednesbury Road, Walsall, West Midlands

Peter Vastl Saddler
4/5 Taroveor Road, Penzance, Cornwall TR18 2DB
Tel: 0736 61280

Reed Saddlery & Co Ltd
Unit 2D, Fryers Works, Abercombe Avenue, High Wycombe, Buckinghamshire
Tel: 0494 452374

RPM Western Trading
The Avenue Riding Centre, Hanley Road, Malvern, Worcestershire
Tel: 0684 310783

Sabre Leather Co Ltd
19-21 Sandwell Street, Walsall, West Midlands WS1 3DR
Tel: 0922 29925
Fax: 0922 723463

Talat International Leather Co
Talat House, Upper Northam Drive, Hedge End, Southampton, Hampshire SO3 4BG
Tel: 0703 462908

Thoroughbred Saddlery Co
Ickleford Manor, Hitchin, Hertfordshire
Tel: 0462 325596

Turf & Travel Saddle & Harness Centre
Originality House, 93 High Street, Elton, Berkshire
Tel: 0753 840753

Turner Griffiths Ltd
Bridge Street Mill, Whitney, Oxfordshire
Tel: 0993 75899

W H Gidden Ltd
15d Clifford Street, New Bond Street, London W1X 1RF
Tel: 071 734 2788

Cavaletti

Newson Show Jumps
Whitefriars, Vicarage Lane, North Weald, Epping, Essex

Surewood Products
3 Moss Cottage, New Cut Lane, Merseyside L33 3AH
Tel: 051 548 9052

Sustan Showjumps
5 Rose Cottage, Mill Street, Hastingwood, near Marlow Common, Essex
Tel: 0279 415802

Clippers

A & E Woodward
Northbridge Works, Lime Street, Hull, Humberside HU8 7AB
Tel: 0482 29185

Alfred Cox (Surgical) Ltd
Edgware Road, Coulsdon, Surrey
Tel: 081 686 2131

Alfred Cox (Surgical) Ltd
Edward Road, Coulsdon, Surrey
Tel: 081 668 2131

Brookwick Ward & Co Ltd
88 Westlaw Place, Whitehall Estate, Glenrothes, Fife KY6 2QB
Tel: 0592 630052
Fax: 0592 630109

Coleman Croft Saddlery
Sutton's Farm, Cooper's Green, Nr St Albans, Hertfordshire AL4 9HJ
Tel: 07072 74239

D Thurgood
Rear 27a Bell Street, Reigate, Surrey
Tel: 07372 49101

Equequip Ltd
7 Pepper Alley, Banbury, Oxfordshire OX16 OTF
Tel: 0295 3913

Euroclip Ltd
P.O.Box 57, Banbury, Oxfordshire

H Cameron Gardner Ltd
Bath Road, Woodchester, Stroud, Gloucestershire GL5 5EX
Tel: 045 383 2526

Hydrophane Laboratories Ltd
Ickleford Manor, Hitchin, Hertfordshire
Tel: 0462 32596

K G Products
247/251 City Road, Fenton, Stoke-on-Trent, Staffs ST4 2PY
Tel: 0782 44866

Listers Clippers
Lister Shearing Equipment Ltd, Long Street, Dursley, Gloucestershire GL11 4HS
Tel: 0453 544832
Fax: 0453 545110

Compound Feeds

Badminton Horse Feeds
3A West Market Place,
Cirencester, Gloucestershire
GL7 2NJ
Tel: 0285 68884

Bailey's Horse Feeds
Four Elms Mills, Bardfield
Saling, Braintree, Essex
CM7 5EJ
Tel: 0371 850247
Fax: 0371 851269

British Horse Feeds Ltd
Victoria House, 50, Albert
Street, Rugby, Warcs
CV21 2RH
Tel: 0788 567475

Charnwood Milling Co Ltd
Framlingham, near
Woodbridge, Suffolk
1P13 9PT
Tel: 0728 723435
Fax: 0728 724359

D I & J G Young
Bracken Barn, Holmes
Chapel Road, Somerford,
Congleton, Cheshire
Tel: 026 02 2623

Dodson & Horrell Ltd
Ringstead, Northamptonshire
Tel: 0933 624221

Equimix Feeds Ltd
Sandy Lane Trading Estate,
Tilton, Stourport on Severn,
Worcestershire DY13 9QA
Tel: 0299 827744

Equine Products UK Ltd
Smithy Side, Ponteland,
Newcastle-upon-Tyne
NE15 8SJ
Tel: 091 264 5536

Equivite
(Milk Pellets) Beecham
Animal H Health, Beecham
House, Brentford, Middlesex

Four Seasons(British Sugar PLC)
P O Box 11, Oundle Rd, Peterborough, Cambs PE2 9QX
Tel: 0733 63171

Horse Requisites Newmarket Ltd
Black Bear Lane, Newmarket,
Suffolk CB8 0JT
Tel: 0638 664619
Fax: 0638 661562

Main Ring from Rumenco
Stretton House, Derby Road, Burton-on-Trent, Staffordshire DE13 ODW
Tel: 0283 511211
Fax: 0283 46152

Parkwood Feeds Ltd
Byers Lane, South Godstone, Surrey RH9 8JJ
Tel: 0342 893264

Pentac
Hammersley Lane, Penn, Buckinghamshire
Tel: 049481 2183

R & E Bamford
Bretherton, Preston, Lancs PR5 7BD
Tel: 0772 600671
Fax: 0772 600340

Spillers Horse Feeds
Dalgety Agricultural Ltd, Dalgety House, The Promenade, Clifton, Bristol, Avon BS8 3
Tel: 0272 738981

The Mill Feed Co Ltd
Navenby, Lincoln, Lincs LN6 OEX
Tel: 0522 810741

Wagg Foods Ltd
Dalton Airfield, Topcliffe, Thirsk, North Yorkshire YO7 3HE
Tel: 0845 578111
Fax: 0845 577990

Disinfectants

B G S Plastics Ltd
Unit 4, Crossways Ind Estate, Church Stretton, Shropshire
Tel: 0694723478

Equine Products UK Ltd
Smithy Side, Ponteland, Newcastle-upon-Tyne NE15 8SJ
Tel: 091 264 5536

Horse Advancement Co. Ltd
44 Ferry Road, London SW13 9PW
Tel: 081 748 6843

Horse Requisites Newmarket Ltd
Black Bear Lane, Newmarket, Suffolk CB8 0JT
Tel: 0638 664619
Fax: 0638 661562

Ollard Westcombe & Co Ltd
Cameo Works, Downpatrick, Down
Tel: 0396 2355

Steve Russell Sales
24 Maltings Wharf, Manningtree, Essex CO11 1XF
Tel: 0206 395171
Fax: 0206 395171

Talat International Leather Co
Talat House, Upper Northam Drive, Hedge End, Southampton, Hampshire SO3 4BG
Tel: 0703 462908

Vet Health
The Animal Care Centre, Colne Road, Coggeshall, Colchester, Essex
Tel: 0376 61548

Draw Reins

Clare Lawson
Vine Cottage, Winchester Road, Waltham Chase, Southampton, Hampshire SO3 2LX
Tel: 0329 832366

Coleman Croft Saddlery
Sutton's Farm, Cooper's Green, Nr St Albans, Hertfordshire AL4 9HJ
Tel: 07072 74239

Cottage Industries (Equestrian) Ltd
Crown Lane, Wychbold, Droitwich, Worcestershire
Tel: 052786 582

F B Davis Saddlery Ltd
Tolsons Mill, Mitchfield Street, Fazeley, Tamworth, Staffordshire B78 3QB
Tel: 0827 280550

Jabez Cliff & Co. Ltd
Globe Works, Lower Forster Street, Walsall, West Midlands WS1 1XG
Tel: 0922 21676

Kangol Equestrian
Norfolk Street, Carlisle, CA2 5HX
Tel: 0228 31711

Keith Luxford (Saddlery) Ltd
H Q 57 High Street, Teddington, Middlesex
Tel: 081 977 4964

Keith Luxford(Saddlery)Ltd
57 High Street, Teddington, Middlesex
Tel: 081 977 4964

M J Ainge & Co. Ltd
Porthouse Farm Industrial Est., Bromyard, Herefordshire HR7 4NP
Tel: 0885 83601

Ollard Westcombe & Co Ltd
Cameo Works, Downpatrick, Down
Tel: 0396 2355

Peter Vastl Saddler
4/5 Taroveor Road,
Penzance, Cornwall
TR18 2DB
Tel: 0736 61280

**Talat International
Leather Co**
Talat House, Upper Northam
Drive, Hedge End,
Southampton, Hampshire
SO3 4BG
Tel: 0703 462908

Dressage
Supplies

B G S Plastics Ltd
Unit 4, Crossways Ind
Estate, Church Stretton,
Shropshire
Tel: 0694723478

**CAM Equestrian
Joinery & Equip**
Eardisley, Hereford
Hereford & Worcester
HR3 6NS
Tel: 05446 611

**Horse Requisites
Newmarket Ltd**
Black Bear Lane Newmarket
Suffolk CB8 0JT
Tel: 0638 664619
Fax: 0638 661562

Instant Signs
Fordes, Ropley, Alresford,
Hampshire
Tel: 096277 3373

**Leyland & Birmingham
Rubber Co**
Golden Hill Lane, Leyland,
Lancs PR5 1VB

Newson Show Jumps
Whitefriars, Vicarage Lane,
North Weald, Epping, Essex

Parkway UK Ltd
Paines Corner, Swife Lane,
Broad Oak, Heathfield, East
Sussex TN21 8UT
Tel: 0435 883553

Sportsline Plastics Ltd
370 Melton Road, Leicester,
Leics
Tel: 0533 681212

Sustan Showjumps
5 Rose Cottage, Mill Street,
Hastingwood, near Marlow
Common, Essex
Tel: 0279 415802

W R Outhwaite & Son
Ropemakers, Town Foot,
Hawes, North Yorkshire
DL8 3NT
Tel: 09697 487

**Watson's Quality
Products**
Red House Farm, Stoke
Mandeville, Aylesbury,
Buckinghamshire HP21 9DR
Tel: 029 661392

Drinking
Troughs

**CAM Equestrian
Joinery & Equipment**
Eardisley, Hereford, Hereford
& Worcester HR3 6NS
Tel: 05446 611

Faulks & Jaques
27 Innage Park, Holly Lane,
Atherstone, Warwickshire
CV9 2HA
Tel: 08277 67003

Fisher Foundries Ltd
Albion road, Greet,
Birmingham B11 2PB
Tel: 021 772 0197
Fax: 021 771 1242

**Horse Requisites
Newmarket Ltd**
Black Bear Lane,
Newmarket, Suffolk CB8 0JT
Tel: 0638 664619
Fax: 0638 661562

**Loddon Livestock
Equipment Ltd**
Beccles Road, Loddon,
Norwich, Norfolk NR14 6JJ
Tel: 0508 20744
Fax: 0508 28055

Driving
Vehicles and
Accessories

**Bennington Artistic Iron
Products**
Sparrow Lane, Long
Bennington, Newark,
Nottinghamshire
NG23 5DL
Tel: 0400 81280

Buckingham Harness
Ardington, Wantage,
Oxfordshire OX12 8PN
Tel: 0235 833719

Clare Lawson
Vine Cottage, Winchester
Road, Waltham Chase,
Southampton Hampshire
SO3 2LX
Tel: 0329 832366

**Croford Coachbuilders
Ltd**
Dover Place, Ashford, Kent
Tel: 0233 23455

**Diane Onions
(Harness Maker)**
Pilgrim Cottage,
Milton-under-Wychwood,
Oxfordshire OX7 6LE
Tel: 0993 830128

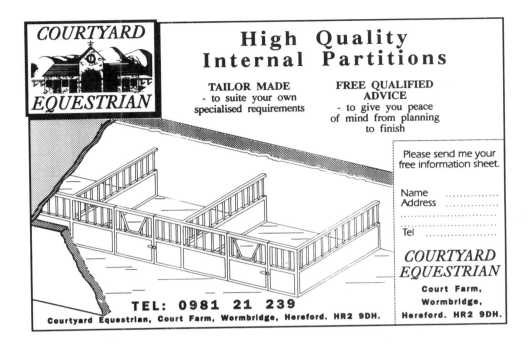
Fenix Enterprizes (Equestrian)
Saxley Hill Barn, Meath
Green Lane, Horley, Surrey
Tel: 0293 784903

G M Daly
The Laurels, Wood Ditton, Nr
Newmarket, Suffolk CB8 9SQ
Tel: 0638 730950

Gordon Ford Carriages
Adswood Road, Stockport,
Cheshire
Tel: 061 480 02811

H Belfield & Sons Ltd
Rocks Mill, Smallbridge,
Rochdale, Lancashire
Tel: 0706 47014

Horse & Rider Insurance Service
4 Augusta Place, Leamington
Spa, Warks CV31 5EL
Tel: 0203 452626
Fax: 0203 888999

Horse Requisites Newmarket Ltd
Black Bear Lane, Newmarket,
Suffolk CB8 0JT
Tel: 0638 664619
Fax: 0638 661562

Horsedrawn Ltd
Pinkey Park, Malmesbury,
Wiltshire
Tel: 0666 840920

J C Gapp
Point Farm, Litcham, Kings
Lynn, Norfolk
Tel: 0328 701204

J M H Harness Makers
1 Woodside Cottages, Gate
Hill, Dunkirk, Faversham,
Kent ME13 9LW
Tel: 0227 751553

Jabez Cliff & Co. Ltd
Globe Works, Lower Forster
Street, Walsall, West Midlands
WS1 1XG
Tel: 0922 21676

Keith Bates, Harness Maker
36 Stonedale, Sutton Hill,
Telford, Shropshire
Tel: 0952 582551

Keith Luxford (Saddlery) Ltd
H Q 57 High Street,
Teddington, Middlesex
Tel: 081 977 4964

M J Ainge & Co. Ltd
Porthouse Farm Industrial
Est., Bromyard, Herefordshire
HR7 4NP
Tel: 0885 83601

McRostie of Glasgow
The Harness Room,
Templeton Business Centre,
Templeton Street, Glasgow,
Strathclyde G40 1DA
Tel: 041 554 4338

Monfort
The Mount, 11 The Wych,
Kington, Herefordshire
HR5 3AQ
Tel: 0544 230629

Newton Horse Ltd
Hotham Hall, Hotham, E.
Yorkshire YO4 3UN
Tel: 0430 423636

Peter Vastl Saddler
4/5 Taroveor Road, Penzance,
Cornwall TR18 2DB
Tel: 0736 61280

Raud & Malet
Boxfarm, Stockwell Lane,
Woodmancote, Nr Chelten-
ham,Gloucestershire
Tel: 04515 477

Richard Gill & Son Ltd
Brame Lane, Norwood,
Harrogate, North Yorkshire
Tel: 0943 88622

S W Halford & Son
8 South Street, Crowland,
Peterborough, Cambs
PE6 0AJ
Tel: 0733 210605

**Talat International
Leather Co**
Talat House, Upper Northam
Drive, Hedge End, South-
ampton,Hampshire SO3 4BG
Tel: 0703 462908

Tedman Harness
58 Clifden Road, Worminghall,
Buckinghamshire HP18 9JP
Tel: 084 47 318

**The Wellington Carriage
Co**
Long Lane, Telford, Shropshire
TF6 6HD
Tel: 0952 42495

Tim Hawks
Lockanbreck, Mansegate,
Dunscore, Dumfries
Tel: 038782 468

**Turf & Travel Sadd &
Harnss Ctr**
Originality House, 93 High
Street, Elton, Berkshire
Tel: 0753 840753

Turner Griffiths Ltd
Bridge Street Mill, Whitney,
Oxfordshire
Tel: 0993 75899

Wm R Pangbourne
1-2 Queens Parade, Bounds
Green Road, London N11 2DN
Tel: 081 889 0422

Equestrian
Engineers

Courtyard Equestrian
Court Farm, Wormbridge, Here-
ford and Worcester HR2 9DH
Tel: 0981 21239

Farriery
Supplies

Acorn Rugs
Gair Shield Farm, Steel,
Hexham, Northumberland
NE47 OHS
Tel: 043 473 562

Alfred Cox (Surgical) Ltd
Edgware Road, Coulsdon,
Surrey
Tel: 081 686 2131

**Andell Equestrian
Services Ltd**
Winterbottom Farm, Mere,
Knutsford, Cheshire
WA16 0QQ
Tel: 0565 830464

**Brookwick Ward & Co
Ltd**
88 Westlaw Place, Whitehall
Estate, Glenrothes, Fife
KY6 2QB
Tel: 0592 630052
Fax: 0592 630109

Buckingham Harness
Ardington, Wantage,
Oxfordshire OX12 8PN
Tel: 0235 833719

Equicushion Ltd
Berricot Green, Warrengate,
Tewin, Welwyn, Hertfordshire
AL6 0JE
Tel: 043871 7708

G M Daly
The Laurels, Wood Ditton, Nr
Newmarket, Suffolk CB8 9SQ
Tel: 0638 730950

Harris Meyer (E.P.) Ltd
Burnley Road, Mytholmroyd,
Hebden Bridge, West Yorkshire
Tel: 0422 884938

**Horse Requisites
Newmarket Ltd**
Black Bear Lane,
Newmarket, Suffolk CB8 0JT
Tel: 0638 664619
Fax: 0638 661562

J & C Gibbins
Lodge Road, Hollesley,
Woodbridge, Suffolk
IP12 3RR
Tel: 0394 411 195
Fax: 0394 410 015

Judith Cochran
Stoneyhills Alnwick,
Northumberland NE66 2AB
Tel: 0665 602930

Ridry Waterproof Clothing
Cobbacombe Farm,
Huntsham, Nr Tiverton,
Devon EX16 7QJ
Tel: 03983 711

S R Jefferd (RRS)
The Forge, Burpham,
Arundel, Sussex
Tel: 0903 883176

Station House Farriery Supplies
The Forge, Coppice Lane,
Heapey, Nr Chorley, Lancs
Tel: 02572 76452

Stromsholm
B & D J Thompson, South
Cottage, Stockgrove Park,
Leighton Buzzard, Beds
Tel: 052 523 477

Feed Additives and Supplements

Badminton Horse Feeds
3A West Market Place,
Cirencester, Gloucestershire
GL7 2NJ
Tel: 0285 68884

Battle, Hayward Bower Ltd
Victoria Chemical Works,
Crofton Drive, Allenby Road
Industrial Estate, Lincoln,
Lincolnshire
Tel: 0522 29206

Bayer (UK) Ltd
Agrochem Div, Eastern Way,
Bury St Edmunds, Suffolk
IP32 7AH
Tel: 0284 63200

British Cod Liver Oils Ltd
Hedon Road, Marfleet, N
Humberside HU9 5NJ
Tel: 0482 75234

Carr Day & Martin Ltd
Lloyds House, Alderly Road,
Wilmslow, Cheshire SK9 1QT
Tel: 0625 539135
Fax: 0625 526962

Champerene Ltd
19 Meadow Close,
Lavenham, Suffolk CO10 9RU
Tel: 0787 217564

Charnwood Milling Co Ltd
Framlingham, Nr Woodbridge,
Suffolk 1P13 9PT
Tel: 0728 723435
Fax: 0728 724359

Chase Organics (GB) Ltd
Termina House, Shepperton,
Middlesex
Tel: 0932 221212

Day Son & Hewitt Ltd
10 Grant Street, Bradford, W
Yorkshire
Tel: 0774 722005

Dodson & Horrell Ltd
Ringstead, Northamptonshire
Tel: 0933 624221

Equestrian Agencies Ltd
The Post House, Filkins,
Lechlade, Gloucestershire
Tel: 036 786249

Equestricare
6 Bevans Lane,
Hinton-on-the-Green,
Eveshan, Warks WR11 6QT
Tel: 0386 48424

Equiform Nutrition Ltd
379 Victoria Street, Grimsby,
Sth Humberside DN31 1PX
Tel: 0472 44766

Equimix Feeds Ltd
Sandy Lane Trading Estate,
Tilton, Stourport on Severn,
Worcestershire DY13 9QA
Tel: 0299 827744

Equine Products UK Ltd
Smithy Side, Ponteland,
Newcastle-upon-Tyne
NE15 8SJ
Tel: 091 264 5536

Equivite (Milk Pellets) Beecham Animal H Health
Beecham House, Brentford,
Middlesex

F B Davis Saddlery Ltd
Tolsons Mill, Mitchfield
Street, Fazeley, Tamworth,
Staffordshire B78 3QB
Tel: 0827 280550

F J Alton & Partners Ltd
Lower Madeley Farm,
Belbroughton, Stourbridge,
Stourbridge, Worcestershire
Tel: 0562 710293

Faulks & Jaques
27 Innage Park, Holly Lane,
Atherstone, Warwickshire
CV9 2HA
Tel: 08277 67003

Feedmark Ltd
St Cross, Harleston, Norfolk
IP20 0NY
Tel: 098 682368

Goldswell Ltd
Manor Farm cottage, Ryme
Intrinseca, Nr Sherborne,
Dorset DT9 6JX
Tel: 0935 872 699

H-M Veterinary Ltd
1 Spencer Street, Ringstead,
Kettering, Northamptonshire
NN14 4BX
Tel: 0933 625544

**Horse Advancement
Co. Ltd**
44 Ferry Road, London
SW13 9PW
Tel: 081 748 6843

**Horse Requisites
Newmarket Ltd**
Black Bear Lane, Newmarket,
Suffolk CB8 0JT
Tel: 0638 664619
Fax: 0638 661562

Intervet Laboratories Ltd
Science Park, Milton,
Cambridge, Cambridgeshire
Tel: 0223 311221

**Main Ring from
Rumenco**
Stretton House, Derby Road,
Burton-on-Trent, Staffordshire
DE13 ODW
Tel: 0283 511211
Fax: 0283 46152

**Maxicrop International
Ltd**
21 London Road, Great
Shelford, Cambs CB2 5DF
Tel: 0223 844024

Medi Equus PLC
Gibbs House, Kennel Ride,
Ascot, Berkshire SL5 7NT
Tel: 0344 890662
Fax: 0344 886531

**Smith, Kline Animal
Health Ltd**
Cavendish Road, Stevenage,
Hertfordshire
Tel: 0438 67881

Sterivet Supplements
C/o Epsom Veterinery
Remeds Ltd, The Old Manor,
Upper Lambourn, Newbury,
Berkshire
Tel: 0488 71657

The Mill Feed Co Ltd
Navenby, Lincoln, Lincs
LN6 OEX
Tel: 0522 810741

**Thomas Pettifer and Co.
Ltd**
Animal Health & Nutrition
Products, Seabright Chemicals
Ltd, 72-76 River Road,
Barking, Essex
Tel: 081 594 4074

Vet Health
The Animal Care Centre,
Colne Road, Coggeshall,
Colchester, Essex
Tel: 0376 61548

Wagg Foods Ltd
Dalton Airfield, Topcliffe,
Thirsk, North Yorkshire
YO7 3HE
Tel: 0845 578111
Fax: 0845 577990

**Willow Farm Livery
Stables & RS**
123A, Frogmore Lane,
Lovedean, School, Waterloo-
ville, Hampshire PO8 9RD
Tel: 0705 599817

**Woodpecker Products
Ltd**
Brades Road, Press, Nr
Whitchurch, Shropshire
Tel: 0948 840 420
Fax: 0948 841 195

Feed
Manufacturers

**ACA Forage
(Buckingham) Ltd**
Coppice Farm, Akeley Wood,
Buckingham, Buckinghamshire
Tel: 0280 812141

**ACA Forage Ltd
(Warnford)**
Rooksgrove, Warnford, Nr
Southampton, Hampshire
Tel: 096 279385

Animart Ltd
Ashbrook, Shipley, Horsham,
West Sussex
Tel: 0403 87546

Bailey's Horse Feeds
Four Elms Mills, Bardfield
Saling, Braintree, Essex
CM7 5EJ
Tel: 0371 850247
Fax: 0371 851269

Belvoir Horse Feeds
Navenby, Lincoln, Lincs
LN5 OEX
Tel: 0522 810741

British Horse Feeds Ltd
Victoria House, 50, Albert St,
Rugby, Warcs CV21 2RH
Tel: 0788 567475

British Sugar Plc
Trident Feeds, P.O. Box 11,
Oundle Road, Peterborough,
Cambs PE2 9QX
Tel: 0733 63171
Fax: 0733 63068

Champerene Ltd
19 Meadow Close, Lavenham,
Suffolk CO10 9RU
Tel: 0787 217564

Charnwood Milling Co Ltd
Framlingham, near Wood-
bridge Suffolk 1P13 9PT
Tel: 0728 723435
Fax: 0728 724359

D I & J G Young
Bracken Barn, Holmes
Chapel Road, Somerford,
Congleton, Cheshire
Tel: 026 02 2623

Dodson & Horrell Ltd
Ringstead, Northamptonshire
Tel: 0933 624221

Equestricare
6 Bevans Lane, Hinton-on-
the-Green, Eveshan, Warks
WR11 6QT
Tel: 0386 48424

Equiform Nutrition Ltd
379 Victoria Street, Grimsby,
Sth Humberside DN31 1PX
Tel: 0472 44766

Equimix Feeds Ltd
Sandy Lane Trading Estate,
Tilton, Stourport on Severn,
Worcestershire DY13 9QA
Tel: 0299 827744

Equine Products UK Ltd
Smithy Side, Ponteland,
Newcastle-upon-Tyne
NE15 8SJ
Tel: 091 264 5536

Equivite (Milk Pellets)
Beecham Animal Health,
Beecham House, Brentford,
Middlesex

F J Alton & Partners Ltd
Lower Madeley Farm
Belbroughton, Stourbridge,
Stourbridge, Worcestershire
Tel: 0562 710293

Feedmark Ltd
St Cross, Harleston, Norfolk
IP20 0NY
Tel: 098 682368

Four Seasons(British Sugar PLC)
P O Box 11, Oundle Road,
Peterborough, Cambs
PE2 9QX
Tel: 0733 63171

Friendly Feeds
Friendship Estates Ltd,
Stubbs Walden, Doncaster,
South Yorkshire
Tel: 0302 700220

G R Bailey Ltd
Four Elms Mills, Bardfield
Saling, Braintree, Essex
CM7 5EJ
Tel: 0371 850247

Main Ring from Rumenco
Stretton House, Derby Road,
Burton-on-Trent, Staffordshire
DE13 ODW
Tel: 0283 511211
Fax: 0283 46152

Mark Westaway & Son
Love Lane Farm, Marldon,
Paignton, Devon TQ3 1SP
Tel: 0803 527257
Fax: 0803 528010

Mr & Mrs Wiegersma
Tregenbo, Relubbus, Nr
Penzance, Cornwall
Tel: 073676 2445

Parkwood Feeds Ltd
Byers Lane, South
Godstone, Surrey RH9 8JJ
Tel: 0342 893264

R & E Bamford
Bretherton, Preston, Lancs
PR5 7BD
Tel: 0772 600671
Fax: 0772 600340

RHM Pegasus Horse Feeds
Deans Grove House, Coleshill,
Wimborne, Dorset

Spillers Horse Feeds
Dalgety Agricultural Ltd,
Dalgety House, The
Promenade, Clifton, Bristol,
Avon BS8
Tel: 0272 738981

The Mill Feed Co Ltd
Navenby, Lincoln, Lincs
LN6 OEX
Tel: 0522 810741

Thomas Pettifer and Co. Ltd
Animal Health & Nutrition
Pro., Seabright Chemicals
Ltd, 72-76 River Road,
Barking, Essex
Tel: 081 594 4074

Feed Storage Bins

CAM Equestrian Joinery & Equipment
Eardisley, Hereford, Hereford
& Worcester HR3 6NS
Tel: 05446 611

Faulks & Jaques
27 Innage Park, Holly Lane,
Atherstone, Warwickshire
CV9 2HA
Tel: 08277 67003

Highlight Hardware
Unit 9, Bulwark Industrial
Estate, Cheptow, Gwent
NP6 5QZ
Tel: 0633 412243

Hopperstore Bins
Kilnside Farm, More Park
Lane, Farnham, Surrey
GU10 1NS
Tel: 0252 712062

Strong Fabrications
Hamble Road, Stourbridge,
Worcestershire DY8 3SZ
Tel: 0384 394396

Feed Suppliers, General

British Sugar Plc
Trident Feeds, P.O. Box 11,
Oundle Road, Peterborough,
Cambs PE2 9QX
Tel: 0733 63171
Fax: 0733 63068

C P Backhurst & Co

Strawberry Farm, Glaziers
Lane, Normandy, Guildford,
Surrey GU3 2DF
Tel: 0483 811360
Weekly Deliveries (30-mile
radius)
Cash and Carry open 6 1/2
days per week.

Tower Farm Riding Stables
85 Liberton Drive, Edinburgh
EH16 6NS
Tel: 031 664 3375

Willow Farm Livery Stables & RS
123A, Frogmore Lane,
Lovedean, School,
Waterlooville, Hampshire
PO8 9RD
Tel: 0705 599817

Fencing

Fieldguard Ltd
Equine Fencing Division,
Grove Heath Farm, Ripley,
Woking, Surrey, GU23 6ES

Fencing Suppliers

Animart Ltd
Ashbrook, Shipley, Horsham,
West Sussex
Tel: 0403 87546

Beta Fencing Ltd
Gloucester Close,
Petersfield, Hampshire

Calders & Grandidge Ltd
London Road, Boston,
Lincolnshire PE21 7HJ
Tel: 0205 66660
Fax: 0205 52592

D & J Watson
T/A Watson's Quality
Products, Red House Farm,
Stoke Mandeville, Aylesbury,
Buckinghamshire HP22 5XD
Tel: 029661 2392

David Wells Fencing
Fellnaw Cottage, Ringford,
Castle Douglas, Dumfries &
Galloway DG7 2AP
Tel: 055 722 291

Denefencing
In Park Barn, Cattistock,
Near Sherbourne, Dorset
Tel: 0935 83638

Dennis Coe Supplies
Ballysox, Curragh, Co Kildare,
Eire
Tel: 45 41663

Equifence
Allcot, Chester High Road,
Gayton, Wirral, Cheshire
Tel: 051 342 3020

Farmkey Ltd
Universal House, Riverside,
Banbury, Oxfordshire
OX16 8TF
Tel: 0295 52544

Fencing and Farm Services
4 Poultmoor Cottage,
Barnsley, Near Cirencester,
Gloucestershire GL7 5EQ
Tel: 028 574 428

Fieldguard Ltd
Grove Heath Farm, Ripley,
Woking, Surrey GU23 6ES
Tel: 0483 225224
Fax: 0483 222087

G K Parson & Sons
Millbay, Roehook, Horsham,
West Sussex
Tel: 0403 790675

G L C Williams
Rodmarton Forge, Nr
Cirencester, Gloucestershire
GL7 6PE
Tel: 028 584 272

H S Jackson & Son (Fencing) Ltd
140 Stowting Common, Nr
Ashford, Kent
Tel: 023 375 393

Livestock Fencing Ltd
P O Box 73, Gloucester,
Gloucestershire GL3 4AF
Tel: 0452 64573

Loddon Livestock Equipment Ltd
Beccles Road, Loddon,
Norwich, Norfolk NR14 6JJ
Tel: 0508 20744
Fax: 0508 28055

P J Godsmark
19 Smugglers Way, Barnes
Green, Horsham, West Sussex
Tel: 0403 731557

R Ellis
North Sydmonton Farm,
North Sydmonton, Near
Newbury, Berkshire
Tel: 0635 23623

South Lincs Fencing
Northfield Road, Market
Deeping, Lincs
Tel: 0778 342458

Sparkford Sawmills Ltd
Sparkford, Yeovil, Somerset
BA22 7LH
Tel: 0968 40505

Sparkford Sawmills Ltd
Sparkford, Yeovil, Somerset
BA22 7LH
Tel: 0963 40505

Fencing Contractors

British Gates & Timber Ltd
Biddenden, Nr Ashford, Kent
TN27 8DD
Tel: 0580 291 555
Fax: 0580 292011

Fencing Gates and Shelters

Broadfield Stables
Kings Barn Lane, Steyning,
Sussex
Tel: 0903 816404

Calders & Grandidge Ltd
London Road, Boston,
Lincolnshire PE21 7HJ
Tel: 0205 66660
Fax: 0205 52592

CAM Equestrian Joinery & Equip
Eardisley, Hereford, Hereford
& Worcester HR3 6NS
Tel: 05446 611

CAM Stables & Farmbldgs Ltd
Eardisley, Hereford,
Herefordshire HR3 6NS
Tel: 054 46611
Fax: 054 46210

D Mears ,
Old Mill, Buckingham Road,
Brackley, Northants
Tel: 0280 703804

Davis Mead & Partners
41 Gay Street, Queens
Square, Bath, Avon

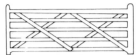

British Gates & Timber Ltd
Biddenden, Nr Ashford, Kent
TN27 8DD
Tel: 0580 291 555
Fax: 0580 292011

F J Lucas
West Dereham, Kings Lynn,
Norfolk
Tel: 0366 500502

G K Parson & Sons
Millbay, Roehook, Horsham,
West Sussex
Tel: 0403 790675

G L C Williams
Rodmarton Forge, Nr
Cirencester, Glos GL7 6PE
Tel: 028 584 272

H S Jackson & Son (Fencing) Ltd
140 Stowting Common, Nr
Ashford, Kent
Tel: 023 375 393

Harlow Bros. Limited
Long Whatton, Nr Lough-
borough, Leics 5DE
Tel: 050 9842561

J J Robinson & Son Ltd
Timber Buildings, Eden
Lane, Gainford, Near
Darlington, Co Durham
Tel: 0325 730241

Ken Johnson
Beechwood Cottage,
Southview Road, Headly
Down, Bordon, Hants
GU35 8NY
Tel: 0428 713885

Loddon Livestock Equipment Ltd
Beccles Road, Loddon,
Norwich, Norfolk NR14 6JJ
Tel: 0508 20744
Fax: 0508 28055

Passmores Portable Bldgs Ltd
High Street, Strood,
Rochester, Kent
Tel: 0634 722500

Ruari Construction
Warf Way, Glen Parva,
Leicester, Leics
Tel: 0533 771667

Sparkford Sawmills Ltd
Sparkford, Yeovil, Somerset
BA22 7LH
Tel: 0968 40505

Supreme Stables
Fenhurst Saw Mills, Henley
Common, Haslemere, Surrey
Tel: 0428 52362

Surewood Products
3 Moss Cottage, New Cut
Lane, Merseyside L33 3AH
Tel: 051 548 9052

W S Hodgson & Co Limited
Cotherstone, Nr Barnard
Castle, Co Durham
DL12 9PS
Tel: 0833 50274

Floor Covering

Avon Industrial Polymers
Melksham, Wilts
Tel: 0225 73101

CAM Equestrian Joinery & Equip
Eardisley, Hereford, Hereford & Worcester HR3 6NS
Tel: 05446 611

Faulks & Jaques
27 Innage Park, Holly Lane, Atherstone, Warwickshire CV9 2HA
Tel: 08277 67003

Format Ltd
Unit 27, Taunton Trading Estate, Norton Fitzwarren, Taunton, Somerset
Tel: 0823 53966

Granilastic Haltopex
PO Box 8, Petworth, W Sussex
Tel: 07986 418

Nuway Manufacturing Co Ltd
Telford, Shropshire TF8 7HX
Tel: 0952 581800

Springfield Horseboxes
Springfield House, Harrington Road, Desborough, Kettering, Northants
Tel: 0536 762038

Freeze Marking

MMB Farmkey
28 West Bar, Banbury, Oxfordshire OX16 9RR
Tel: 0295 252544

Girths

Acorn Rugs
Gair Shield Farm, Steel, Hexham, Northumberland NE47 OHS
Tel: 043 473 562

Ambassador Saddlery Limited
Embassy Buildings, Bath Street, Walsall, West Midlands
Tel: 0922 644826

Chris Adams
Park Farm House, Cornworthy, Totnes, Devon
Tel: 080 423 454

Clare Lawson
Vine Cottage, Winchester Road, Waltham Chase, Southampton, Hampshire SO3 2LX
Tel: 0329 832366

Coleman Croft Saddlery
Sutton's Farm, Cooper's Green, Nr St Albans, Hertfordshire AL4 9HJ
Tel: 07072 74239

Cottage Ind. (Equestrian) Ltd
Crown Lane, Wychbold, Droitwich, Worcestershire
Tel: 052786 582

Cross Country (Equestrian) Ltd
Luttwytche Road, Church Stretton, Shropshire SY6 6AT
Tel: 0694 722919

Donalds McLellan (Saddler)
Saddle & Harness Maker, 146, Busby Road, Clarkston, Glasgow G76 8BH
Tel: 041 644 4880

Equequip Ltd
7 Pepper Alley, Banbury, Oxon OX16 OTF
Tel: 0295 3913

Equinomic Products Limited
South Lodge, Newark Lane, Ripley, Surrey GU23 6BZ
Tel: 0483 224999
Fax: 0483 211673

Jabez Cliff & Co. Limited
Globe Works, Lower Forster Street, Walsall, West Midlands WS1 1XG
Tel: 0922 21676

John James Hawley, (Speciality Works) Ltd
Lichfield Road, Walsall, West Midlands WS4 2HX
Tel: 0922 25641
Fax: 0922 720163

Kangol Equestrian
Norfolk Street, Carlisle, CA2 5HX
Tel: 0228 31711

Keith Luxford (Saddlery) Ltd
57 High Street, Teddington, Middx
Tel: 081 977 4964

Ollard Westcombe & Co Ltd
Cameo Works, Downpatrick, Down
Tel: 0396 2355

Peter Vastl Saddler
4/5 Taroveor Road, Penzance, Cornwall TR18 2DB
Tel: 0736 61280

RPM Western Trading
The Avenue Riding Centre, Hanley Road, Malvern, Worcs
Tel: 0684 310783

Talat International Leather Co
Talat House, Upper Northam Drive, Hedge End, Southampton Hants SO3 4BG
Tel: 0703 462908

Thoroughbred Saddlery Co
Ickleford Manor, Hitchin, Herts
Tel: 0462 325596

Turner Griffiths Ltd
Bridge Street Mill, Whitney, Oxon
Tel: 0993 75899

Harness Manufacturers

British Leathergoods' Manufacturers Association
10 Vyse Street, Birmingham, West Midlands B18 6LT
Tel: 021 236 2657
Fax: 021 236 3921

Hoof-care Products

B G S Plastics Ltd
Unit 4, Crossways Ind Estate, Church Stretton, Shropshire
Tel: 0694723478

Bellet Ltd
Main Road, Arlesford, Colchester, Essex CO7 8OH
Tel: 0206 223360

Brookwick Ward & Co Ltd
88 Westlaw Place, Whitehall Estate, Glenrothes, Fife KY6 2QB
Tel: 0592 630052
Fax: 0592 630109

C Vet Ltd
Western Way, Bury St Edmunds, Suffolk IP33 3SU
Tel: 0284 61131

Charnwood Milling Co Ltd
Framlingham, near Wood-bridge, Suffolk 1P13 9PT
Tel: 0728 723435
Fax: 0728 724359

Conquest Remedies
Norwood House, Lockerbie, Dumfrieshire, Dumfries & Galloway DG11 2QU
Tel: 052 786582

Constant Laboratories
Gores Road, Knowsley Industrial Park, Liverpool, Merseyside
Tel: 051 547 3711

Cottage Ind. (Equestrian) Ltd
Crown Lane, Wychbold, Droitwich, Worcestershire
Tel: 052786 582

Equicushion Ltd
Berricot Green, Warrengate, Tewin, Welwyn, Herts AL6 0JE
Tel: 043871 7708

Equine Products UK Ltd
Smithy Side, Ponteland, Newcastle-upon-Tyne NE15 8SJ
Tel: 091 264 5536

Goldswell Ltd

Effol

Manor Farm Cottage, Ryme Intrinseca, Nr Sherborne, Dorset DT9 6JX
Tel: 0935 872 699

H-M Veterinary Ltd
1 Spencer Street, Ringstead, Kettering, Northants NN14 4BX
Tel: 0933 625544

Horse Advancement Co. Ltd
44 Ferry Road, London SW13 9PW
Tel: 081 748 6843

Hydrophane Laboratories Limited
Ickleford Manor, Hitchin, Hertfordshire
Tel: 0462 32596

J & C Gibbins
Lodge Road, Hollesley, Woodbridge, Suffolk IP12 3RR
Tel: 0394 411 195
Fax: 0394 410 015

Leyland & Birmingham Rubber Co
Golden Hill Lane, Leyland, Lancs PR5 1VB

M J Ainge & Co. Ltd
Porthouse Farm Industrial Est., Bromyard, Herefordshire HR7 4NP
Tel: 0885 83601

Manspence Developments
59 Edinburgh Drive, Spalding, Lincs
Tel: 0406 370809

Mars Oil Co.
Withycombe Farmhouse,
Drayton, Nr Banbury, Oxon
OX15 6EE
Tel: 0295 262844
Fax: 0295 273164

Radiol Chemicals
Stepfield, Witham, Essex
Tel: 0376 512538

**Stylo Manufacturing Int.
Ltd**
Matchmakers House, Clayton
Wood Bank, Leeds
Tel: 0532 783501

Unitex Limited
Knaresborough, North
Yorkshire HG5 OPP
Tel: 0423 862677

W H Cowie Limited
26a Dene Street, Dorking,
Surrey
Tel: 0306 887074

W H Tildesley Ltd
Clifford Works, Willenhall,
W Mids WV13 2AN
Tel: 0902 65441

Horse Boots

Acorn Rugs
Gair Shield Farm, Steel,
Hexham, Northumberland
NE47 OHS
Tel: 043 473 562

Aerborn Equestian
Pegasus House, 198
Sneinton Dale, Nottingham
Nottinghamshire NG2 4HJ
Tel: 0602 505631
Fax: 0602 483273

**CAM Equestrian
Joinery & Equip**
Eardisley, Hereford, Hereford
& Worcester HR3 6NS
Tel: 05446 611

**Casual Riding
Manufacturing Ltd**
533 Twickenham Road,
Isleworth, Middlesex
Tel: 081 8927710

Clare Lawson
Vine Cottage, Winchester
Road, Waltham Chase,
Southampton Hampshire
SO3 2LX
Tel: 0329 832366

**Cottage Ind.
(Equestrian) Ltd**
Crown Lane, Wychbold,
Droitwich, Worcestershire
Tel: 052786 582

**Cross Country
(Equestrian) Ltd**
Luttwytche Road, Church
Stretton, Shropshire SY6 6AT
Tel: 0694 722919

Eqinis Polymer Ltd
Willenhall, West Midlands

Equiquip Ltd
7 Pepper Alley, Banbury,
Oxon OX16 OTF
Tel: 0295 3913

**Horse Advancement
Co. Ltd**
44 Ferry Road, London
SW13 9PW
Tel: 081 748 6843

**Hydrophane
Laboratories Limited**
Ickleford Manor, Hitchin,
Hertfordshire
Tel: 0462 32596

J & C Gibbins
Lodge Road, Hollesley,
Woodbridge, Suffolk
IP12 3RR
Tel: 0394 411 195
Fax: 0394 410 015

Jabez Cliff & Co. Limited
Globe Works, Lower Forster
Street, Walsall, West
Midlands WS1 1XG
Tel: 0922 21676

JAI
P O Box 72, Northampton,
NN4 OLT
Tel: 0604 862236

Jane Bertram Products
Dognests, Grimston, Melton
Mowbray, Leics
Tel: 0664 812751

**Leyland & Birmingham
Rubber Co**
Golden Hill Lane, Leyland,
Lancs PR5 1VB

Limbuffs Limited
22 Wadsworth Road,
Perivale, Middlesex

M J Ainge & Co. Ltd
Porthouse Farm Industrial
Est., Bromyard, Herefordshire
HR7 4NP
Tel: 0885 83601

Newton Horse Ltd
Hotham Hall, Hotham, E
Yorkshire YO4 3UN
Tel: 0430 423636

Peter Vastl Saddler
4/5 Taroveor Road, Penzance,
Cornwall TR18 2DB
Tel: 0736 61280

Sabre Leather Co Ltd
19-21 Sandwell Street,
Walsall, West Midlands
WS1 3DR
Tel: 0922 29925
Fax: 0922 723463

**Shires Equestrian
Products**
158 Bromyard Road,
Worcester, Hereford &
Worcester
Tel: 0905 422421

Witney Horse Blanket Co
12 Corn Street, Witney, Oxon
Tel: 0993 3456

Yorkshire Horse Rug Co
1256 Manchester Road,
Linthwaite, Huddersfield,
Yorkshire
Tel: 0484 844897

Horse Boxes

Acreliff Stables
Bradford Road, Otley, West
Yorks
Tel: 0943 73912

**Arden Horsebox
Company**
Unit 6, Kew Trading Area,
Kew Works, Meols Cop Rd,
Southport, Merseyside
PR8 5JU
Tel: 0704 38282

ATG Horseboxes
Acton Turville Garage,
Badminton, Avon
Tel: 045 421 220

Autosteer Controls Ltd
Moorfield Ind Estate,
Yeadon, Leeds, W Yorks
LS19 7BN
Tel: 0532 506011

**Bedford Horsebox Co
Ltd**
Stanwell New Road, Staines,
Middx
Tel: 0784 53148

Bristol Horseboxes
Haberfield Hall,
Easton-in-Gordano, Bristol
Avon BS20 0QH
Tel: 0272 665141

CB Horseboxes
Park Lane, Cottingham,
North Humberside
Tel: 0482 847373

Enterprise Biddenden
Tenterden Road, Biddenden,
Kent TN27 8BH
Tel: 0580 291088

Flettner Ventilator Ltd
2 Basing Hill, London
NW11 8TH
Tel: 081 455 7469

G C Smith (Coachworks)
Long Whatton, Loughborough,
Leicestershire LE12 5BY
Tel: 0509 842451

Gordon Ford Carriages
Adswood Road, Stockport,
Cheshire
Tel: 061 480 02811

Harrops Horseboxes Ltd
Thornyfield Farm, Thornyfield
Lane, Stafford, Staffs
Tel: 0785 48890

Highbarn Horseboxes
Green Trees Farm, Tendring,
Nr Clacton-on-Sea, Essex
CO1 6DD
Tel: 025587 505

**Horse & Rider
Insurance Service**
4 Augusta Place, Leamington
Spa, Warks CV31 5EL
Tel: 0203 452626
Fax: 0203 888999

**Horsemaster
Coachbuilders Ltd**
15B Bennetts Field Trading
Est, Wincanton, Somerset
BA9 9DT
Tel: 0963 33689

Integral Cabs
18 Brookthorpe Drive,
Stonegate Estate, Willenhall,
West Midlands
Tel: 0902 636877

J Gordon Stirrat
Rockbank, Kilmacolm,
Renfrewshire
Tel: 050587 2371

**Jennings Coachwork
Ltd**
Second Avenue, Weston
Road, Crewe, Cheshire
CW1 1BD
Tel: 0270 583358

**Lambourn
Coachbuilders Ltd**
Station Road, Lambourn,
Newbury, Berkshire
RG16 7PH
Tel: 0488 72623

Oakley Coachbuilders
High Cross, Ware,
Hertfordshire SG11 1AD
Tel: 0920 66781
Fax: 0920 467895

Pearce Horseboxes
Unique Farm, Kenn Road,
Kenn, Avon BS21 6TT
Tel: 0934 838174

Red Rose Horseboxes
Shaw Road, Royton, Nr
Oldham, Leics.
Tel: 067 620 866666

Sinclairs Trailers
Wargate Bridge, Gosberton,
Spaldings, Lincolnshire
PE11 4HH
Tel: 0775 840442

Springfield Horseboxes
Springfield House,
Harrington Road,
Desborough, Kettering,
Northants
Tel: 0536 762038

Thorndon Horse Boxes
24 Horndon Industrial Park,
West Horndon, Brentwood,
Essex CM13 3XE
Tel: 0277 811668

Thoroughbred Horseboxes
Brunswichmill, Rye Street,
Preston, Lancashire
Tel: 0772 52873

Ward Trailers of Easingwold
Yorkshire
Tel: 0347 21359

Horse-care Products

Acorn Rugs
Gair Shield Farm, Steel,
Hexham, Northumberland
NE47 OHS
Tel: 043 473 562

Alfred Cox (Surgical) Ltd
Edgware Road, Coulsdon,
Surrey
Tel: 081 686 2131

Battle, Hayward Bower Limited
Victoria Chemical Works,
Crofton Drive, Allenby Road
Industrial Estate, Lincoln,
Lincolnshire
Tel: 0522 29206

Bellet Ltd
Main Road, Arlesford,
Colchester, Essex CO7 8OH
Tel: 0206 223360

Brookwick Ward & Co Ltd
88 Westlaw Place, Whitehall
Estate, Glenrothes, Fife
KY6 2QB
Tel: 0592 630052
Fax: 0592 630109

Caldene Clothing Co Ltd
Burnley Road, Mytholmroyd,
Hebden Bridge, West
Yorkshire
Tel: 0422 883393

CAM Equestrian Joinery & Equip
Eardisley, Hereford,
Hereford & Worcester
HR3 6NS
Tel: 05446 611

Carbex-Munroe (Handles)
11a St Nicholas Lane,
Lewes, East Sussex BN7 2JZ
Tel: 0273 478111

Carr Day & Martin Limited
Lloyds House, Alderly Road,
Wilmslow, Cheshire SK9 1QT
Tel: 0625 539135
Fax: 0625 526962

Coleman Croft Saddlery
Sutton's Farm, Cooper's
Green, Nr St Albans,
Hertfordshire AL4 9HJ
Tel: 07072 74239

Constant Laboratories
Gores Road, Knowsley
Industrial Park, Liverpool,
Merseyside
Tel: 051 547 3711

Cottage Ind. (Equestrian) Ltd
Crown Lane, Wychbold,
Droitwich, Worcestershire
Tel: 052786 582

Cross Country (Equestrian) Ltd
Luttwytche Road, Church
Stretton, Shropshire SY6 6AT
Tel: 0694 722919

Crown Chemical Co. Limited
Lamberhurst, Kent TN3 8DJ
Tel: 0892 890491

Faulks & Jaques
27 Innage Park, Holly Lane,
Atherstone, Warwickshire
CV9 2HA
Tel: 08277 67003

Fisons Animal Health

12 Derby Road, Lough-
borough, Leicestershire
LE11 0BB
Tel: 0509 611001
Fax: 0509 235285

Goldswell Ltd
Manor Farm Cottage, Ryme
Intrinseca, Nr Sherborne,
Dorset DT9 6JX
Tel: 0935 872 699

Hippomatic Ltd
Sandon, Buntingford, Herts
SG9 OQW
Tel: 076 387 453

Hydrophane Laboratories Limited
Ickleford Manor, Hitchin,
Hertfordshire
Tel: 0462 32596

Impala Sales and Marketing
The Cottage, Creation Road,
Hollowell, Northampton,
Northants NN6 8RP
Tel: 0604 740687

John Palmer Ltd
Victory Brushes, Victory
House, Cornwall Road,
Portsmouth, Hants PO1 5JT
Tel: 0705 826441

Kiln Saddlery
The Folley, Layer de la Haye,
Colchester, Essex CO2 OHZ
Tel: 0206 34695

Mars Oil Co.
Withycombe Farmhouse,
Drayton, Nr Banbury, Oxon
OX15 6EE
Tel: 0295 262844

Newton Horse Ltd
Hotham Hall, Hotham,
E Yorkshire YO4 3UN
Tel: 0430 423636

Robinson Healthcare
Hipper House, Chesterfield,
Derbyshire S40 1YF
Tel: 0246 3220022
Fax: 0246 208164

Sterivet Supplements
C/o Epsom Veterinery
Remedies Ltd. The Old
Manor, Upper Lambourn,
Newbury, Berks
Tel: 0488 71657

Steve Russell Sales
24, Maltings Wharf,
Manningtree, Essex
CO11 1XF
Tel: 0206 395171
See advertisement under
'Disinfectants'

Vale Bros ltd
Defiance Brush Works, Long
Street, Walsall, W Mids
Tel: 0922 24363

Vet Health
The Animal Care Centre,
Colne Road, Coggeshall,
Colchester, Essex
Tel: 0376 61548

W H Tildesley Ltd
Clifford Works, Willenhall, W
Mids WV13 2AN
Tel: 0902 65441

Wagg Foods Ltd
Dalton Airfield, Topcliffe,
Thirsk, North Yorkshire
YO7 3HE
Tel: 0845 578111
Fax: 0845 577990

Horse Dealers

**Coombe Park
Equestrian Centre**
Littlehempston, Totnes,
Devon TQ9 6LW
Tel: 0803 863473

Equitus Ltd
Stoney Hill Farm,
Brimpsfield, Gloucester,
Gloucestershire GL4 8LF
Tel: 0452 864412

**John Goodwin
(International) Ltd**
Wychnor Manor, Wychnor,
Nr Burton-on-Trent, Staffs
DE13 8BU
Tel: 0283 791056
Fax: 0283 790249

Laurels Stables
Horringer, Bury St Edmunds,
Suffolk IP29 5SN
Tel: 0284 735 281

Horse Eye Protectors

**Cottage Ind.
(Equestrian) Ltd**
Crown Lane, Wychbold,
Droitwich, Worcestershire
Tel: 052786 582

M J Ainge & Co. Ltd
Porthouse Farm Industrial
Est., Bromyard,
Herefordshire HR7 4NP
Tel: 0885 83601

**Ridry Waterproof
Clothing**
Cobbacombe Farm,
Huntsham, Nr Tiverton,
Devon EX16 7QJ
Tel: 03983 711

Horse Feed Suppliers

British Horse Feeds Ltd
Victoria House, 50, Albert
Street, Rugby, Warcs
CV21 2RH
Tel: 0788 567475

British Sugar Plc
Trident Feeds, P.O. Box 11,
Oundle Road, Peterborough,
Cambs PE2 9QX
Tel: 0733 63171
Fax: 0733 63068

C P Backhurst & Co

Strawberry Farm, Glaziers
Lane, Normandy, Guildford,
Surrey GU3 2DF
Tel: 0483 811360
Weekly Deliveries (30-mile
radius) Cash and Carry
open 6 ½ days per week.

R & E Bamford
Bretherton, Preston, Lancs
PR5 7BD
Tel: 0772 600671
Fax: 0772 600340

Horse Holiday Homes

Laurels Stables
Horringer, Bury St Edmunds,
Suffolk IP29 5SN
Tel: 0284 735 281

Horse Hoods

Horse Advancement Co. Ltd
44 Ferry Road, London
SW13 9PW
Tel: 081 748 6843

Hydrophane Laboratories Limited
Ickleford Manor, Hitchin,
Hertfordshire
Tel: 0462 32596

Jane Bertram Products
Dognests, Grimston, Melton
Mowbray, Leics
Tel: 0664 812751

Keith Luxford (Saddlery) Ltd
57 High Street, Teddington,
Middx
Tel: 081 977 4964

M J Ainge & Co. Ltd
Porthouse Farm Industrial
Est., Bromyard, Herefordshire
HR7 4NP
Tel: 0885 83601

Ridry Waterproof Clothing
Cobbacombe Farm, Hunts-
ham, Nr Tiverton Devon
EX16 7QJ
Tel: 03983 711

Horse Trailors and Accessories

Acreliff Stables
Bradford Road, Otley, West
Yorks
Tel: 0943 73912

Bahill Trailers
Melbourne Works, Buxton
Road, Bakewell, Derbyshire
Tel: 062 9813401

Bateson Trailers Ltd
Doodfield Works,
Windlehurst Road, Marple,
Stockport, Cheshire
Tel: 061 427 2663

Bryan Lawrence & Co
Rowney Priory, Dane End,
Ware, Hertfordshire
SG12 0JY
Tel: 0920 438684

C & T Trailors
Eastfield Mills, Horley Green,
Halifax, W Yorks
Tel: 0422 53930

E F Birchall
Moors Avenue Garage,
Hartlebury, Nr Kidderminster,
Worcestershire
Tel: 02996 320

E Ward & Sons
Easingwold, Yorks
Tel: 034721473

Enterprise Biddenden
Tenterden Road, Biddenden,
Kent TN27 8BH
Tel: 0580 291088

Feeney & Johnson Ltd
Alperton Lane, Wembley,
Middlesex HA0 1JJ
Tel: 081 998 4458

G C Smith (Coachworks)
Long Whatton, Loughborough,
Leicestershire LE12 5BY
Tel: 0509 842451

George Hobbs Trailers
Millbay, Roebook, Horsham,
W Sussex
Tel: 0403 790675

Haywood Design
11 Oldfield Crescent, Great
Haywood, Staffordshire
Tel: 0889 881764

Henry Bowers
Furnham Road, Chard,
Somerset
Tel: 046 06 2295

Ifor Williams Trailers Ltd
Cynwyd, Corwen, Clwyd
Tel: 0490 2626

Integral Cabs
18 Brookthorpe Drive,
Stonegate Estate, Willenhall,
West Midlands
Tel: 0902 636877

J & B Towing
The Trailer Centre,
Cottismore Farm, Kingsclere,
Newbury, Berks RG15 8SY
Tel: 0635 298928

J Gordon Stirrat
Rockbank, Kilmacolm,
Renfrewshire
Tel: 050587 2371

Mechanical Services (Trailer Engineers) Ltd
Belmont Road, Bolton, Lancs
Tel: 0204 58434

Newmaster Ltd
Pebworth Vale, Darsingtan,
Statford-upon-Avon, Warks
Tel: 0789 720118

Pearce Horseboxes
Unique Farm, Kenn Road,
Kenn, Avon BS21 6TT
Tel: 0934 838174

R B Biddescombe Ltd
13/15 Dene Road, Andover,
Hants SP10 2AA
Tel: 0264 3941

Rice Trailers Limited
Portland Works, Cosby,
Leicestershire LE9 5TG
Tel: 0533 866666
Fax: 0533 750439

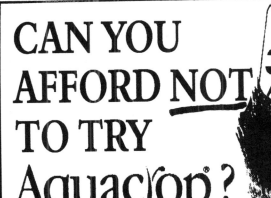

Richardson Trailers
Primrose Hill Works,
Shipton-by-Beningborough,
York, N Yorks YO6 1AB
Tel: 0904 470282

Sinclairs Trailers
Wargate Bridge, Gosberton,
Spaldings, Lincolnshire
PE11 4HH
Tel: 0775 840442

Springfield Universal
Springfield House, Harrington
Road, Desborough, Dettering,
Northants NN14 2NJ
Tel: 0536 762038

Horse Transporters and Agents

B & R International Horse Transport
Furze Hill Stud, Churt,
Farnham, Surrey
Tel: 0428 714313

Crook Brothers
Station Road Depot, Hoghton,
Nr Preston, Lancashire

Enterprise Biddenden
Tenterden Road, Biddenden,
Kent TN27 8BH
Tel: 0580 291088

George Hobbs Trailers
Millbay, Roebook, Horsham,
W Sussex
Tel: 0403 790675

LEP Bloodstock Limited
75/77 High Street, Tunbridge
Wells, Kent TN1 1XZ
Tel: 0892 39244

Peden International Transport Ltd
Orchard Garage, Oxford
Road, Chieveley, Newbury,
Berkshire RG16 8RU
Tel: 0635 248911

Horse Treats

Battle, Hayward Bower Limited
Victoria Chemical Works,
Crofton Drive, Allenby Road
Industrial Estate, Lincoln,
Lincolnshire
Tel: 0522 29206

Equimix Feeds Ltd
Sandy Lane Trading Estate,
Tilton, Stourport on Severn,
Worcestershire DY13 9QA
Tel: 0299 827744

Goldswell Ltd
Manor Farm cottage, Ryme
Intrinseca, Nr Sherborne,
Dorset DT9 6JX
Tel: 0935 872 699

Woodpecker Products Ltd
Brades Road, Press, Nr
Whitchurch, Shropshire
Tel: 0948 840 420
Fax: 0948 841 195

Horse Walkers

Equitus Ltd
Stoney Hill Farm,
Brimpsfield, Gloucester,
Gloucestershire GL4 8LF
Tel: 0452 864412

Horsegear Ltd
Gable House, Holcot Road,
Brixworth, Northants
Tel: 0604 880640

Hydroponic Grass Machines

Aquacrop
Hewing Bere, Crewkerne,
TA18 7TG
Tel: 0785 59670

Coombe Park Equestrian Centre
Littlehempston, Totnes,
Devon TQ9 6LW
Tel: 0803 863473

Hydrodan (Corby) Limited
74 Earlstrees Road, Corby,
Northants
Tel: 0536 361185

Somerset Zero Grass Ltd
37a Market Place,
Cirencenster, Gloucs
Tel: 0285 69228

Indoor School Maintenance Equipment

Irrigation & Slurry Services
Louvain, Quavey Road,
Redlynch, Wiltshire SP5 2HH
Tel: 0725 20377

Parkway UK Ltd
Paines Corner, Swife Lane,
Broad Oak, Heathfield, East
Sussex TN21 8UT
Tel: 0435 883553

International Forwarding Agents

International Air Cargo Services
Shirley Lodge, 470 London Road, Slough, Berkshire

LEP Bloodstock Inc (USA)
251 Hempstead Turnpike, Elmont, New York 11003
Tel: (516) 3286677

LEP Bloodstock Limited
75/77 High Street, Tunbridge Wells, Kent TN1 1XZ
Tel: 0892 39244

Peden International Transport Limited
Orchard Garage, Oxford Road, Chieveley, Newbury, Berkshire RG16 8RU
Tel: 0635 248911

Lead Ropes

Equequip Ltd
7 Pepper Alley, Banbury, Oxon OX16 OTF
Tel: 0295 3913

F B Davis Saddlery Limited
Tolsons Mill, Mitchfield Street, Fazeley, Tamworth, Staffordshire B78 3QB
Tel: 0827 280550

Impala Sales and Marketing
The Cottage, Creation Road, Hollowell, Northampton, Northants NN6 8RP
Tel: 0604 740687

Jabez Cliff & Co. Limited
Globe Works, Lower Forster Street, Walsall, West Midlands WS1 1XG
Tel: 0922 21676

John James Hawley, (Speciality Works) Ltd
Lichfield Road, Walsall, West Midlands WS4 2HX
Tel: 0922 25641
Fax: 0922 720163

S Robb & Son
18 East Street, St Ives, Huntingdon, Cambs PE17 4PB
Tel: 0480 62150

Leather-care Products and Supplies

Allen & Caswell
Regent Works, Cornwall Road, Kettering, Northants, NN16 8PR
Tel: 0536 512804
Fax: 0536 411085

Battle, Hayward Bower Limited
Victoria Chemical Works, Crofton Drive, Allenby Road Industrial Estate, Lincoln, Lincolnshire
Tel: 0522 29206

Bellet Ltd
Main Road, Arlesford, Colchester, Essex, CO7 8OH
Tel: 0206 223360

Carbex-Munroe (Handles)
11a St Nicholas Lane, Lewes, East Sussex, BN7 2JZ
Tel: 0273 478111

Carr Day & Martin Limited
Lloyds House, Alderly Road, Wilmslow, Cheshire, SK9 1QT
Tel: 0625 539135
Fax: 0625 526962

Caswell & Co Ltd
St Michaels Road, Kettering, Northants, NN15 6AY
Tel: 0536 518340

F B Davis Saddlery Limited
Tolsons Mill, Mitchfield Street, Fazeley, Tamworth, Staffordshire, B78 3QB
Tel: 0827 280550

Flexalan Products Limited
Hunters of Chester, 8 Canal Street, Chester, Cheshire

Goldswell Ltd
Manor Farm Cottage, Ryme Intrinseca, Nr Sherborne, Dorset, DT9 6JX
Tel: 0935 872 699
Fax: 0935 872592

Horse Advancement Co. Ltd
44 Ferry Road, London, SW13 9PW
Tel: 081 748 6843

Hydrophane Laboratories Limited
Ickleford Manor, Hitchin, Hertfordshire
Tel: 0462 32596

Impala Sales and Marketing
The Cottage, Creation Road, Hollowell, Northampton, Northants, NN6 8RP
Tel: 0604 740687

**Joseph Clayton & Sons
(Chesterfield) Ltd**
Clayton St Tannery,
Chesterfield, Derbyshire,
S41 ODU
Tel: 0246 32863

M J Ainge & Co. Ltd
Porthouse Farm Industrial
Est., Bromyard, Herefordshire
HR7 4NP
Tel: 0885 83601

Mars Oil Co.
Withycombe Farmhouse,
Drayton, Nr Banbury, Oxon,
OX15 6EE
Tel: 0295 262844
Fax: 0295 273164

Newton Horse Ltd
Hotham Hall, Hotham,
E. Yorkshire, YO4 3UN
Tel: 0430 423636

Leg Guards

Acorn Rugs
Gair Shield Farm, Steel,
Hexham, Northumberland,
NE47 OHS
Tel: 043 473 562

Aerborn Equestian
Pegasus House, 198
Sneinton Dale, Nottingham,
Notts, NG2 4HJ
Tel: 0602 505631
Fax: 0602 483273

**Casual Riding
Manufacturing Ltd**
533 Twickenham Road,
Isleworth, Middlesex
Tel: 081 8927710

Coleman Croft Saddlery
Sutton's Farm, Cooper's
Green, Nr St Albans,
Hertfordshire, AL4 9HJ
Tel: 07072 74239

**Cross Country
(Equestrian) Ltd**
Luttwytche Road, Church
Stretton, Shropshire,
SY6 6AT
Tel: 0694 722919

JAI
P O Box 72, Northampton,
NN4 OLT
Tel: 0604 862236

Newton Horse Ltd
Hotham Hall, Hotham,
E Yorkshire, YO4 3UN
Tel: 0430 423636

Peter Vastl Saddler
4/5 Taroveor Road, Penzance,
Cornwall, TR18 2DB
Tel: 0736 61280

**Talat International
Leather Co**
Talat House, Upper Northam
Drive, Hedge End,
Southampton, Hants,
SO3 4BG
Tel: 0703 462908

Yorkshire Horse Rug Co
1256 Manchester Road,
Linthwaite, Huddersfield,
Yorkshire
Tel: 0484 844897

Linseed and
Barley Boilers

W J Farvis & Sons Ltd
Temple Works, Morley Road,
Southville, Bristol, Avon,
BS3 1DT
Tel: 0272 666677
Fax: 0272 669893

Lungeing
Equipment

Clare Lawson
Vine Cottage, Winchester
Road, Waltham Chase,
Southampton, Hampshire
SO3 2LX
Tel: 0329 832366

**Cottage Ind.
(Equestrian) Ltd**
Crown Lane, Wychbold,
Droitwich, Worcestershire
Tel: 052786 582

**F B Davis Saddlery
Limited**
Tolsons Mill, Mitchfield
Street, Fazeley, Tamworth,
Staffordshire B78 3QB
Tel: 0827 280550

**Impala Sales and
Marketing**
The Cottage, Creation Road,
Hollowell, Northampton,
Northants NN6 8RP
Tel: 0604 740687

Jabez Cliff & Co. Limited
Globe Works, Lower Forster
Street, Walsall, West
Midlands WS1 1XG
Tel: 0922 21676

**John James Hawley
(Speciality Works) Ltd**
Lichfield Road, Walsall, West
Midlands WS4 2HX
Tel: 0922 25641
Fax: 0922 720163

**Loddon Livestock
Equipment Ltd**
Beccles Road, Loddon,
Norwich, Norfolk NR14 6JJ
Tel: 0508 20744
Fax: 0508 28055

Ollard Westcombe & Co Ltd
Cameo Works, Downpatrick, Down
Tel: 0396 2355

Peter Vastl Saddler
4/5 Taroveor Road, Penzance, Cornwall TR18 2DB
Tel: 0736 61280

S Robb & Son
18 East Street, St Ives, Huntingdon, Cambs PE17 4PB
Tel: 0480 62150

Talat International Leather Co
Talat House, Upper Northam Drive, Hedge End, Southampton, Hants SO3 4BG
Tel: 0703 462908

Turf & Travel Saddle & Harness Centre
Originality House, 93 High Street, Elton, Berks
Tel: 0753 840753

Yorkshire Horse Rug Co
1256 Manchester Road, Linthwaite, Huddersfield, Yorkshire
Tel: 0484 844897

Measuring Sticks

Talat International Leather Co
Talat House, Upper Northam Drive, Hedge End, Southampton, Hants SO3 4BG
Tel: 0703 462908

Numnahs

Acorn Rugs
Gair Shield Farm, Steel, Hexham, Northumberland NE47 OHS
Tel: 043 473 562

Aerborn Equestian
Pegasus House, 198 Sneinton Dale, Nottingham, Notts NG2 4HJ
Tel: 0602 505631
Fax: 0602 483273

Canac Horse Products
Becks Mill, Westbury Leigh, Westbury, Wiltshire
Tel: 0373 864775

Casual Riding Manufacturing Ltd
533 Twickenham Road, Isleworth, Middlesex
Tel: 081 8927710

Coleman Croft Saddlery
Sutton's Farm, Cooper's Green, Nr St Albans, Hertfordshire AL4 9HJ
Tel: 07072 74239

Cottage Ind. (Equestrian) Ltd
Crown Lane, Wychbold, Droitwich, Worcestershire
Tel: 052786 582

Cross Country (Equestrian) Ltd
Luttwytche Road, Church Stretton, Shropshire SY6 6AT
Tel: 0694 722919

Equequip Ltd
7 Pepper Alley, Banbury, Oxon OX16 OTF
Tel: 0295 3913

Equinomic Products Limited
South Lodge, Newark Lane, Ripley, Surrey GU23 6BZ
Tel: 0483 224999
Fax: 0483 211673

F B Davis Saddlery Limited
Tolsons Mill, Mitchfield Street, Fazeley, Tamworth, Staffordshire B78 3QB
Tel: 0827 280550

Greenmeadow Designs
'B' Cwmpen Graig, Velindre, Llandysul, Dyfed, Wales
Tel: 0559 370625

Horse Advancement Co. Ltd
44 Ferry Road, London SW13 9PW
Tel: 081 748 6843

Hydrophane Laboratories Limited
Ickleford Manor, Hitchin, Hertfordshire
Tel: 0462 32596

J P Rug Co
Downs House, Childrey, Oxon OX12 9UF
Tel: 023 559 400

Jabez Cliff & Co. Limited
Globe Works, Lower Forster Street, Walsall, West Midlands WS1 1XG
Tel: 0922 21676

John James Hawley (Speciality Works) Ltd,
Lichfield Road, Walsall, West Midlands WS4 2HX
Tel: 0922 25641
Fax: 0922 720163

Keith Luxford (Saddlery) Ltd
57 High Street, Teddington, Middx
Tel: 081 977 4964

Mark Saddler Limited
Gayton House, Well Lane,
Gayton, Wirral, Cheshire
Tel: 051 342 7722

Newton Horse Ltd
Hotham Hall, Hotham, E
Yorkshire YO4 3UN
Tel: 0430 423636

Nursey & Son Ltd
Upper Olland Street, Bungay,
Suffolk NR35 1B4
Tel: 0986 2821

P I Associates
The Red House, Tuddenham,
Bury St Edmunds, Suffolk
IP28 6TB
Tel: 0638 717521

Peter Vastl Saddler
4/5 Taroveor Road, Penzance,
Cornwall TR18 2DB
Tel: 0736 61280

Redport Equestrian
Asker Works, 94 East Street,
Bridport, Dorset
Tel: 0308 22592

**Shaw Mills Chrome
Leather Co**
Shaw Mills, Nr Harrogate, N
Yorks HG3 3HU
Tel: 0423 770294

Yorkshire Horse Rug Co
1256 Manchester Road,
Linthwaite, Huddersfield,
Yorkshire
Tel: 0484 844897

Nutritionists

Bailey's Horse Feeds
Four Elms Mills, Bardfield
Saling, Braintree, Essex,
CM7 5EJ
Tel: 0371 850247
Fax: 0371 851269

Pasture Maintenance

Fieldguard Ltd
Grove Heath Farm, Ripley,
Woking, Surrey GU23 6ES
Tel: 0483 225224
Fax: 0483 222087

**Murphy Chemicals
Limited**
Latchmore Court, Brand
Street, Hitchin, Hertfordshire

Plaits, Bands, Threads and Needles

**Casual Riding
Manufacturing Ltd**
533 Twickenham Road,
Isleworth, Middlesex
Tel: 081 8927710

**Hydrophane
Laboratories Limited**
Ickleford Manor, Hitchin,
Hertfordshire
Tel: 0462 32596

Sterivet Supplements
C/o Epsom Veterinery
Remeds Ltd, The Old Manor,
Upper Lambourn, Newbury,
Berks
Tel: 0488 71657

Reins

**Cross Country
(Equestrian) Ltd**
Luttwytche Road, Church
Stretton, Shropshire, SY6
6AT
Tel: 0694 722919

**Horse Advancement
Co. Ltd**
44 Ferry Road, London,
SW13 9PW
Tel: 081 748 6843

Kangol Equestrian
Norfolk Street, Carlisle, CA2
5HX
Tel: 0228 31711

**Keith Luxford
(Saddlery) Ltd**
57 High Street, Teddington,
Middx
Tel: 081 977 4964

Newton Horse Ltd
Hotham Hall, Hotham, E
Yorkshire, YO4 3UN
Tel: 0430 423636

S Robb & Son
18 East Street, St Ives,
Huntingdon, Cambs,
PE17 4PB
Tel: 0480 62150

**Thoroughbred Saddlery
Co**
Ickleford Manor, Hitchin,
Herts
Tel: 0462 325596

Riding Equipment, Tack

**Andell Equestrian
Services Ltd**
Winterbottom Farm, Mere,
Knutsford, Cheshire,
WA16 0QQ
Tel: 0565 830464

Chris Adams
Park Farm House,
Cornworthy, Totnes, Devon
Tel: 080 423 454

Coleman Croft Saddlery
Sutton's Farm, Cooper's
Green, Nr St Albans,
Hertfordshire, AL4 9HJ
Tel: 07072 74239

**Donalds McLellan
(Saddler)**
Saddle & Harness Maker,
146, Busby Road, Clarkston,
Glasgow, G76 8BH
Tel: 041 644 4880

G Fieldhouse Saddlery
(Walsall) Ltd, 18-19 Green
Lane, Walsall, West
Midlands, WS2 8HE
Tel: 0922 38094
Fax: 0922 22921

**Horse Advancement
Co. Ltd**
44 Ferry Road, London,
SW13 9PW
Tel: 081 748 6843

Jabez Cliff & Co. Limited
Globe Works, Lower Forster
Street, Walsall, West
Midlands, WS1 1XG
Tel: 0922 21676

Kangol Equestrian
Norfolk Street, Carlisle,
CA2 5HX
Tel: 0228 31711

**Keith Luxford
(Saddlery) Ltd**
57 High Street, Teddington,
Middx
Tel: 081 977 4964

L W Faulkner & Son
5 Station Road, Woodford
Halse, Daventry, Northants,
NN11 6RB
Tel: 0327 60306

Peter Vastl Saddler
4/5 Taroveor Road, Penzance,
Cornwall, TR18 2DB
Tel: 0736 61280

Turner Griffiths Ltd
Bridge Street Mill, Whitney,
Oxon
Tel: 0993 75899

Riding Surfaces

Parkway UK Ltd
Paines Corner, Swife Lane,
Broad Oak, Heathfield, East
Sussex, TN21 8UT
Tel: 0435 883553

Singleton Flint
Newland Works, Deacon
Road, Lincoln, Lincolnshire,
LN2 4LE
Tel: 0522 524542
Fax: 0522 514426

Rosettes and Trophies

B F P Rosettes
39 Manor Road, Pawlett, Nr
Bridgewater, Somerset,
TA6 4SN
Tel: 0278 683455
Fax: 0278 684425

Cone Rosettes
Woods, Penistone, Sheffield
South Yorkshire

Corby Rosettes
Moat Cottage, Great
Staughton, Cambridgeshire

Darby Rosettes
10 Cavalry Ride, Norwich,
Norfolk
Tel: 0603 24385

Fiesta Rosettes
4 Belmore Road, Thorpe,
Norwich, Norfolk, NR7 0PT
Tel: 0603 35924

**James H Wood Printers
Ltd**
Don Press Penistone,
Sheffield, S Yorks, S30 6AR
Tel: 0226 762207

Knight & Co
135 St Michaels Hill, Bristol,
Avon, BS2 8BT
Tel: 0272 265681
Fax: 0272 745365

Mogridge Rosettes Ltd
3 Greenbank Road, Easton,
Bristol, Avon, BS5 6EZ
Tel: 0272 354880
Fax: 0272 354773

Norfolk Rosettes
Norfolk House, Beaconsfield
Road, Norwich, Norfolk,
NR3 4PW
Tel: 0603 616238

**Presfield Fabrics
Limited**
Mant Street, Accrington,
Lancashire
Tel: 0254 393711

Rainbow Rosettes
FREEPOST, PO Box 110,
Norwich, Norfolk, NR3 4BR
Tel: 0800 378364

**Regent of Huddersfield
Limited**
Newsome Mills, Hart Street,
Newsome, Huddersfield,
Yorkshire, HD4 6JG
Tel: 0484 21233

Woods Rosettes
Penistone, Sheffield, South
Yorkshire

Rubber Stops and Pads

Carbex-Munroe (Handles)
11a St Nicholas Lane,
Lewes, East Sussex,
BN7 2JZ
Tel: 0273 478111

Casual Riding Manufacturing Ltd
533 Twickenham Road,
Isleworth, Middlesex
Tel: 081 8927710

Eqinis Polymer Ltd
Willenhall, West Midlands

F B Davis Saddlery Limited
Tolsons Mill, Mitchfield
Street, Fazeley, Tamworth,
Staffordshire, B78 3QB
Tel: 0827 280550

Jabez Cliff & Co. Limited
Globe Works, Lower Forster
Street, Walsall, West
Midlands, WS1 1XG
Tel: 0922 21676

Leyland & Birmingham Rubber Co
Golden Hill Lane, Leyland,
Lancs, PR5 1VB

Ridgeway Rug Co
Astra House, Childrey,
Wantage, Oxon, OX12 9UF
Tel: 023 559 495

Talat International Leather Co
Talat House, Upper Northam
Drive, Hedge End,
Southampton, Hants,
SO3 4BG
Tel: 0703 462908

Thoroughbred Saddlery Co
Ickleford Manor, Hitchin, Herts
Tel: 0462 325596

Rugs and Blankets/Tail Guards

Acorn Rugs
Gair Shield Farm, Steel,
Hexham, Northumberland,
NE47 OHS
Tel: 043 473 562

Aerborn Equestian
Pegasus House, 198 Sneinton
Dale, Nottingham, Notts,
NG2 4HJ
Tel: 0602 505631
Fax: 0602 483273

Bryan Lawrence & Co
Rowney Priory, Dane End,
Ware, Hertfordshire,
SG12 0JY
Tel: 0920 438684

Casual Riding Manufacturing Ltd
533 Twickenham Road,
Isleworth, Middlesex
Tel: 081 8927710

Coleman Croft Saddlery
Sutton's Farm, Cooper's
Green, Nr St Albans,
Hertfordshire, AL4 9HJ
Tel: 07072 74239

Cross Country (Equestrian) Ltd
Luttwytche Road, Church
Stretton, Shropshire,
SY6 6AT
Tel: 0694 722919

Eldonian Brookes Limited
Marsh Street, Walsall, West
Midlands
Tel: 0922 31121

Equinomic Products Limited
South Lodge, Newark Lane,
Ripley, Surrey, GU23 6BZ
Tel: 0483 224999
Fax: 0483 211673

Equiquip Ltd
7 Pepper Alley, Banbury,
Oxon, OX16 OTF
Tel: 0295 3913

Fancy Free Race & Event Wear
The Heath, Stoke Prior,
Leominster, Herefordshire
Tel: 056 882 662

Greenham Saddlery Co Ltd
Ridge House, Greenham,
Wellinton, Somerset,
TA21 OJS
Tel: 0823 672304

Hurdcott Livery Stbles & saddly
Hurdcott Lane, Winterbourne
Earls, Salisbury, Wilts,
SP4 6HR
Tel: 0980 611276

Hydrophane Laboratories Limited
Ickleford Manor, Hitchin,
Hertfordshire
Tel: 0462 32596

Impala Sales and Marketing
The Cottage, Creation Road,
Hollowell, Northampton,
Northants, NN6 8RP
Tel: 0604 740687

J P Rug Co
Downs House, Childrey,
Oxon, OX12 9UF
Tel: 023 559 400

J W Wilkinson & Co Ltd
Newin Works, Highgate,
Kendal, Cumbria, LA9 4HG
Tel: 0539 20013

James Walkers & Son Ltd
Holme Bank Mills, Mirfield,
Yorks, NF14 8NA
Tel: 0924 492277

Jane Bertram Products
Dognests, Grimston, Melton
Mowbray, Leics
Tel: 0664 812751

Jaytone Riding Wear
Yew Tree Cottage, Potters
Hill, Felton, Avon

Jean Goodman Riding
Watling Street, Hockliffe,
Beds, LU7 9NP
Tel: 0525 210138

John James Hawley (Speciality Works) Ltd
Lichfield Road, Walsall, West
Midlands, WS4 2HX
Tel: 0922 25641
Fax: 0922 720163

Keith Luxford (Saddlery) Ltd
57 High Street, Teddington,
Middx
Tel: 081 977 4964

Lavenham Rug Company Ltd
Long Melford, Suffolk,
CO10 9LL
Tel: 0787 79535

Linthwaite Textiles Ltd
Guardian Buildings, Bridge St,
Slaithwaite, Huddersfield, W
Yorks, HD7 5JN
Tel: 0484 845442

Mark Saddler Limited
Gayton House, Well Lane,
Gayton, Wirral, Cheshire
Tel: 051 342 7722

Newton Horse Ltd
Hotham Hall, Hotham, E
Yorkshire, YO4 3UN
Tel: 0430 423636

Ollard Westcombe & Co Ltd
Cameo Works, Downpatrick,
Down
Tel: 0396 2355

Ordell Enterprises
The Forest House, Hatchet
Lane, Winkfield, Berkshire,
SL4 2EG
Tel: 0344 885857

P I Associates
The Red House,
Tuddenham, Bury St
Edmunds, Suffolk, IP28 6TB
Tel: 0638 717521

Paramount Horse Clothing Co
Tolson Mill, Fazeley,
Tamworth, Staffs, B78 3QB
Tel: 0827 280450

Polywarm Products Ltd
Cambuslang Road, Farme
Cross, Rutherglen, Glasgow,
Strathclyde, G73 1RS
Tel: 041 647 2392
Fax: 041 613 1569

Rainbow Horse Suppliers
Plasman Industrial Centre,
Peter Moss Way,
Levenshulme, Manchester,
M19 3JH
Tel: 061 224 0333

Redport Net Co Ltd
Asker Works, 94 East Street,
Bridport, Dorset
Tel: 0308 22592

Ridgeway Rug Co
Astra House, Childrey,
Wantage, Oxon, OX12 9UF
Tel: 023 559 495

Scotrug Ltd
Park Head House,
Hareshaw, Cleland, By
Motherwell, Strathclyde
Tel: 0698 861706

Talat International Leather Co
Talat House, Upper Northam
Drive, Hedge End,
Southampton, Hants,
SO3 4BG
Tel: 0703 462908

Turf & Travel Saddle & Harness Centre
Originality House, 93 High
Street, Elton, Berks
Tel: 0753 840753

W & H Gidden Ltd
15d Clifford Street, New
Bond Street, London,
W1X 1RF
Tel: 071 734 2788
Fax: 071 494 2388

Wearite Clothing Co
Parkview Works, 275 West
Green Road, London,
W15 5EE
Tel: 081 802 3399

Witney Horse Blanket Co
12 Corn Street, Witney, Oxon
Tel: 0993 3456

Yorkshire Horse Rug Co
1256 Manchester Road,
Linthwaite, Huddersfield,
Yorkshire
Tel: 0484 844897

Saddle Manufacturers and Sole Agents

A D Mackenzie
Brodrick, Isle of Arran

Acorn Rugs
Gair Shield Farm, Steel,
Hexham, Northumberland,
NE47 OHS
Tel: 043 473 562

Ambassador Saddlery Limited
Embassy Buildings, Bath St,
Walsall, West Midlands
Tel: 0922 644826

Brian Scrivener
Rear of 168 High Street,
Newmarket, Suffolk
Tel: 0638 664856

British Leathergoods' Manufacturers Assoc
10, Vyse Street Birmingham,
West Midlands B18 6LT
Tel: 021 236 2657
Fax: 021 236 3921

Bryan Fradgley
Dordale House, Chaddesley
Corbett, Nr Kidderminster,
Worcs
Tel: 056283 452

CAM Equestrian Joinery & Equip
Eardisley, Hereford, Hereford
& Worcester, HR3 6NS
Tel: 05446 611

Champion & Wilton Limited
112/122 Tabernacle Street,
London, EC2M 4LE
Tel: 071 251 2701

Chris Adams
Park Farm House,
Cornworthy, Totnes, Devon
Tel: 080 423 454

Clare Lawson
Vine Cottage, Winchester
Road, Waltham Chase,
Southampton, Hampshire,
SO3 2LX
Tel: 0329 832366

Coleman Croft Saddlery
Sutton's Farm, Cooper's
Green, Nr St Albans,
Hertfordshire, AL4 9HJ
Tel: 07072 74239

Colin Whittaker (Saddler)
Fore Street, Castle Gray,
Somerset
Tel: 0963 50929

Cottage Ind. (Equestrian) Ltd
Crown Lane, Wychbold,
Droitwich, Worcestershire
Tel: 052786 582

Cross Country (Equestrian) Ltd
Luttwytche Road, Church
Stretton, Shropshire, SY6 6AT
Tel: 0694 722919

Diane Onions (Harness Maker)
Pilgrim Cottage, Milton-under-
Wychwood, Oxon, OX7 6LE
Tel: 0993 830128

Eldonian Brookes Limited
Marsh Street, Walsall, West
Midlands
Tel: 0922 31121

Equestrian Manufactng & Supply
52 Mount Street, Walsall,
West Midlands, WS1 3PL

F B Davis Saddlery Limited
Tolsons Mill, Mitchfield
Street, Fazeley, Tamworth,
Staffordshire, B78 3QB
Tel: 0827 280550

F J Chandler (Saddler) Ltd
Hilliers Yard, High Street,
Marlborough, Wiltshire,
SN8 1BE
Tel: 0672 52633

G Fieldhouse Saddlery
(Walsall) Ltd, 18-19 Green
Lane, Walsall, West Midlands,
WS2 8HE
Tel: 0922 38094
Fax: 0922 22921

G T Palmer & Son Ltd
59 - 61 Wednesbury Road,
Walsall, West Midlands
Tel: 0922 29408

George Parker & Sons Ltd
12 Upper Street, St Martins
Lane, London, WC2H 9DU
Tel: 071 836 1164

Hippomatic Ltd
Sandon, Buntingford, Herts,
SG9 OQW
Tel: 076 387 453

Horse Advancement Co. Ltd
44 Ferry Road, London,
SW13 9PW
Tel: 081 748 6843

Ian McNeill Saddlery
Redhill Farm, Medstead, Nr
Alton, Hampshire, GU34 5EE
Tel: 0420 62249
Fax: 0420 63897

Ideal Saddle Co. Ltd
14/19 Green Lane, Walsall,
West Midlands, WS2 8HE
Tel: 0922 20233

Impala Sales and Marketing
The Cottage, Creation Road, Hollowell, Northampton, Northants, NN6 8RP
Tel: 0604 740687

International Saddlery Ltd
James House, Northgate, Aldridge, West Midlands

Jabez Cliff & Co. Limited
Globe Works, Lower Forster Street, Walsall, West Midlands, WS1 1XG
Tel: 0922 21676

James Walkers & Son Ltd
Holme Bank Mills, Mirfield, Yorks, NF14 8NA
Tel: 0924 492277

John Goodwin (International)
Wynchnor Manor, Wynchnor, Burton on Trent, Staffordshire, DE13 8BU
Tel: 0283 791056
Fax: 0283 790249

John James Hawley (Speciality Works) Ltd
Lichfield Road, Walsall, West Midlands, WS4 2HX
Tel: 0922 25641
Fax: 0922 720163

Kangol Equestrian
Norfolk Street, Carlisle, CA2 5HX
Tel: 0228 31711

Keith Bates
Harness Maker, 36 Stonedale, Sutton Hill, Telford, Shropshire
Tel: 0952 582551

Keith Luxford (Saddlery) Ltd
57 High Street, Teddington, Middx
Tel: 081 977 4964

Larkin the Saddlers
40 South Street, Eastbourne, E Sussex

Leonard Coombe
13 Highweek Street, Newton Abbott, Devon
Tel: 0626 4099

New Forest Saddlers Limited
Lyndhurst Road, Brockenhurst, Hampshire, SO42 7RO
Tel: 0590 22313

Newton Horse Ltd
Hotham Hall, Hotham, E Yorkshire, YO4 3UN
Tel: 0430 423636

Ollard Westcombe & Co Ltd
Cameo Works, Downpatrick, Down
Tel: 0396 2355

Pennwood Saddlery
Pennwood Lane, Penn, Wolverhampton, West Midlands, WV4 4JQ
Tel: 0902 338 552

Pentac
Hammersley Lane, Penn, Bucks
Tel: 049481 2183

Peter Vastl Saddler
4/5 Taroveor Road, Penzance, Cornwall, TR18 2DB
Tel: 0736 61280

Reed Saddlery & Co Ltd
Unit 2D, Fryers Works, Abercombe Avenue, High Wycombe, Bucks
Tel: 0494 452374

Rimell Saddlers
1 West Street, Shipston on Stour, Warwickshire, CV36 4AL
Tel: 0608 62000

RPM Western Trading
The Avenue Riding Centre, Hanley Road, Malvern, Worcs
Tel: 0684 310783

S Robb & Son
18 East Street, St Ives, Huntingdon, Cambs, PE17 4PB
Tel: 0480 62150

S W Halford & Son
8 South Street, Crowland, Peterborough, Cambs, PE6 OAJ
Tel: 0733 210605

Sabre Leather Co Ltd
19-21 Sandwell Street, Walsall, West Midlands, WS1 3DR
Tel: 0922 29925
Fax: 0922 723463

Saddle Craft
3 Cropwell Road, Radcliffe on Trent, Nottinghamshire, NG12 2FJ
Tel: 0602 332800

Sandon Saddlery Co
Sandon, Buntingford, Hertfordshire, SG9 0QW
Tel: 076 387 247

Talat International Leather Co
Talat House, Upper Northam Drive, Hedge End, Southampton, Hants, SO3 4BG
Tel: 0703 462908

Taunton Saddlery
141 Staplegrove Road, Taunton, Somerset, TA2 6AF
Tel: 0823 251553

The Boston Saddlery Co.
118 Skirbeck Road, Boston, Lincolnshire

Thoroughbred Saddlery Co
Ickleford Manor, Hitchin, Herts
Tel: 0462 325596

Turf & Travel Saddle & Harness Centre
Originality House, 93 High Street, Elton, Berks
Tel: 0753 840753

Turner Griffiths Ltd
Bridge Street Mill, Whitney, Oxon
Tel: 0993 75899

W H Gidden Ltd
15d Clifford Street, New Bond Street, London, W1X 1RF
Tel: 071 734 2788

Yorkshire Horse Rug Co
1256 Manchester Road, Linthwaite, Huddersfield, Yorkshire
Tel: 0484 844897

Saddle Stands and Racks

Bryan Fradgley
Dordale House, Chaddesley Corbett, Nr Kidderminster, Worcs
Tel: 056283 452

CAM Equestrian Joinery & Equip
Eardisley, Hereford, Hereford & Worcester, HR3 6NS
Tel: 05446 611

D & J Watson
T/A Watson's Quality Products, Red House Farm, Stoke Mandeville, Aylesbury, Bucks, HP22 5XD
Tel: 029661 2392

F B Davis Saddlery Limited
Tolsons Mill, Mitchfield Street, Fazeley, Tamworth, Staffordshire, B78 3QB
Tel: 0827 280550

Faulks & Jaques
27 Innage Park, Holly Lane, Atherstone, Warwickshire, CV9 2HA
Tel: 08277 67003

Greenmeadow Designs
'B' Cwmpen Graig, Velindre, Llandysul, Dyfed, Wales
Tel: 0559 370625

J J Robinson & Son Ltd
Timber Buildings, Eden Lane, Gainford, Near Darlington, Co Durham
Tel: 0325 730241

W B Stubbs (Hawksworth) Ltd
Progress Works, Hawksworth, Nottingham, Nottinghamshire
Tel: 0949 50218

Walsall Riding Saddle Co. Ltd
Olympic Works, Garden Street, Walsall, West Midlands
Tel: 0922 24768

Saddle Retailers

L W Faulkner & Son
5 Station Road, Woodford Halse, Daventry, Northants, NN11 6RB
Tel: 0327 60306

Ride-Away
Stillington Road, Sutton-on-Forest, York, N Yorks, YO6 1EH
Tel: 0347 810443
Fax: 0347 810746

W & H Gidden Ltd
15d Clifford Street, New Bond Street, London, W1X 1RF
Tel: 071 734 2788
Fax: 071 494 2388

West Essex & Kernow Saddlery
113 Station Road, Chingford, London, E4 7BU

Safety Equipment

Charles Owen & Co (Bow) Ltd
61/65 Cae Gwilym Lane, Cefn Mwr, Wrexham, Clwyd, LL14 3LS
Tel: 0978 810671
Fax: 0978 810670

Personalite Ltd
Ridealite, PO Box 45, Barnet, Herts, EN5 4NA
Tel: 081 449 9117

Show Jumps and Sundries

Asthall Show Jumps
Hill Building, Blenheim hill, Shipton-under-Wychwood, Oxon
Tel: 0993 831454

B F P Rosettes
39 Manor Road, Pawlett, Nr Bridgewater, Somerset TA6 4SN
Tel: 0278 683455
Fax: 0278 684425

B G S Plastics Ltd
Unit 4 , Crossways Ind Estate, Church Stretton, Shropshire
Tel: 0694723478

CMS Trim
34 Spon End, Coventry,
West Midlands CV1 3GY
Tel: 0203 20363

D & J Watson
T/A Watson's Quality
Products, Red House Farm,
Stoke Mandeville, Aylesbury,
Bucks HP22 5XD
Tel: 029661 2392

E Williams & Co
23 Glebe Street, Walsall,
West Midlands WS1 3PA
Tel: 0922 23333

Horse Advancement Co. Ltd
44 Ferry Road, London
SW13 9PW
Tel: 081 748 6843

Instant Signs
Fordes, Ropley, Alresford,
Hants
Tel: 096277 3373

James H Wood Printers Ltd
Don Press Penistone,
Sheffield, S Yorks S30 6AR
Tel: 0226 762207

Newson Show Jumps
Whitefriars, Vicarage Lane,
North Weald, Epping, Essex

Quality Showjumps
Mick Chips, Bowyers,
Steepmarsh, Petersfield,
Hampshire

R W Stephen Equestn Prods Ltd
Honeycombe Leaze,
Cirencester, Gloucestershire
Tel: 0285 712438

Rainbow Rosettes
FREEPOST, PO Box 110,
Norwich, Norfolk NR3 4BR
Tel: 0800 378364

Salcey Forest Timber Products
Hartwell, Northants
Tel: 0604 406373

Silver Fox Showjumps
Snape Hill, Darfield,
Barnsley, South Yorkshire
Tel: 0226 758215

Sportsline Plastics Ltd
370 Melton Road, Leicester,
Leics
Tel: 0533 681212

Surewood Products
3 Moss Cottage, New Cut
Lane, Merseyside L33 3AH
Tel: 051 548 9052

Sustan Showjumps
5 Rose Cottage, Mill Street,
Hastingwood, near Marlow
Common, Essex
Tel: 0279 415802

Taunton Show Jumps
Curland Equestrian
Enterprises, Crosses Farm,
Curland, Taunton, Somerset
TA3 5SD
Tel: 0460 34234

Thanet Show Jumps
Chestnuts, Woolpack
Corner, Biddenden, nr
Ashford, Kent TN27 8BN

Watson's Quality Products
Red House Farm, Stoke
Mandeville, Aylesbury,
Bucks HP21 9DR
Tel: 029 661392

Small Tractors

Lely Iseki Tractors
Station Road, St. Neots,
Cambs PE16 1QH
Tel: 0480 76971

Wessex Farm Machinery Sales Ltd
Trading Estate, Oakhanger
Road, Bordon, Hampshire
GU35 9HH
Tel: 04203 8111

Stirrups and Leathers

Charles Walker & Co Ltd
Beta Works, John Espritt
Road, Bingley, West Yorks
BD16 2SU

Chris Adams
Park Farm House, Corn-
worthy, Totnes, Devon
Tel: 080 423 454

Clare Lawson
Vine Cottage, Winchester
Road, Waltham Chase,
Southampton, Hampshire
SO3 2LX
Tel: 0329 832366

Cross Country (Equestrian) Ltd
Luttwytche Road, Church
Stretton, Shropshire
SY6 6AT
Tel: 0694 722919

Donalds McLellan (Saddler)
Saddle & Harness Maker,
146, Busby Road, Clarkston,
Glasgow G76 8BH
Tel: 041 644 4880

F B Davis Saddlery Limited
Tolsons Mill, Mitchfield
Street, Fazeley, Tamworth,
Staffordshire B78 3QB
Tel: 0827 280550

Horse Advancement Co. Ltd
44 Ferry Road, London
SW13 9PW
Tel: 081 748 6843

Jabez Cliff & Co. Limited
Globe Works, Lower Forster
Street, Walsall, West
Midlands WS1 1XG
Tel: 0922 21676

Peter Vastl Saddler
4/5 Taroveor Road, Penzance,
Cornwall TR18 2DB
Tel: 0736 61280

Talat International Leather Co
Talat House, Upper Northam
Drive, Hedge End, South-
ampton, Hants SO3 4BG
Tel: 0703 462908

Wm R Pangbourne
1-2 Queens Parade, Bounds
Green Road, London,
London N11 2DN
Tel: 081 889 0422

Stable Equipment

Abbey Chase Stables
Bridge Road, Chertsey,
Surrey
Tel: 09328 66112

ACA Forage Ltd (Warnford)
Rooksgrove, Warnford, Nr
Southampton, Hants
Tel: 096 279385

Acorn Rugs
Gair Shield Farm, Steel,
Hexham, Northumberland
NE47 OHS
Tel: 043 473 562

Alfred Cox (Surgical) Ltd
Edgware Road, Coulsdon,
Surrey
Tel: 081 686 2131

Andell Equestrian Services Ltd
Winterbottom Farm, Mere,
Knutsford, Cheshire
WA16 0QQ
Tel: 0565 830464

Battle, Hayward Bower Limited
Victoria Chemical Works,
Crofton Drive, Allenby Road
Industrial Estate, Lincoln, Lincs
Tel: 0522 29206

Bellet Ltd
Main Road, Arlesford,
Colchester, Essex CO7 8OH
Tel: 0206 223360

Bowley & Coleman Trucks Ltd
Stanley Works, Kempston
Hardwick, Bedford, Beds
MK45 3JD
Tel: 0234 49591

British Gates & Timber Ltd
Biddenden, Nr Ashford, Kent
TN27 8DD
Tel: 0580 291 555
Fax: 0580 292011

Browns of WEM Ltd
Four Lane Ends, Wem, Salop
SY4 5UQ
Tel: 0939 32382

Caldene Clothing Co Ltd
Burnley Road, Mytholmroyd,
Hebden Bridge, West Yorks
Tel: 0422 883393

CAM Equestrian Joinery & Equip
Eardisley, Hereford,
Hereford & Worcester
HR3 6NS
Tel: 05446 611

CAM Stables & Farmbuildings Ltd
Eardisley, Hereford,
Herefordshire HR3 6NS
Tel: 054 46611
Fax: 054 46210

Carbex-Munroe (Handles)
11a St Nicholas Lane,
Lewes, East Sussex
BN7 2JZ
Tel: 0273 478111

Chaskit New Zealand Rugs
Chaskit House, Langton
Green, Nr Tunbridge Wells,
Kent TN3 OEG
Tel: 0892 863113
Fax: 082 581 2192

Cottage Ind. (Equestrian) Ltd
Crown Lane, Wychbold,
Droitwich, Worcestershire
Tel: 052786 582

Cross Country (Equestrian) Ltd
Luttwytche Road, Church
Stretton, Shropshire
SY6 6AT
Tel: 0694 722919

Crown Chemical Co. Limited
Lamberhurst, Kent TN3 8DJ
Tel: 0892 890491

D & J Watson
T/A Watson's Quality
Products, Red House Farm,
Stoke Mandeville, Aylesbury,
Bucks HP22 5XD
Tel: 029661 2392

D Mears
Old Mill, Buckingham Road,
Brackley, Northants
Tel: 0280 703804

Equimix Feeds Ltd
Sandy Lane Trading Estate,
Tilton, Stourport on Severn,
Worcestershire DY13 9QA
Tel: 0299 827744

Equine Products UK Limited
Smithy Side, Ponteland,
Newcastle-upon-Tyne
NE15 8SJ
Tel: 091 264 5536

Equivite (Milk Pellets)
Beecham Animal Health,
Beecham House, Brentford,
Middlesex

F B Davis Saddlery Limited
Tolsons Mill, Mitchfield
Street, Fazeley, Tamworth,
Staffordshire B78 3QB
Tel: 0827 280550

F J Lucas
West Dereham, Kings Lynn,
Norfolk
Tel: 0366 500502

Faulks & Jaques
27 Innage Park, Holly Lane,
Atherstone, Warwickshire
CV9 2HA
Tel: 08277 67003

Fisher Foundries Limited
Albion road, Greet,
Birmingham B11 2PB
Tel: 021 772 0197
Fax: 021 771 1242

Fredericks Stables
Ingleby House, Fernhurst,
Hazlemere, Surrey
GU27 3HF
Tel: 0428 3262

G K Parson & Sons
Millbay, Roehook, Horsham,
West Sussex
Tel: 0403 790675

G L C Williams
Rodmarton Forge, Nr
Cirencester, Glos GL7 6PE
Tel: 028 584 272

Goldswell Ltd
Manor Farm cottage, Ryme
Intrinseca, Nr Sherborne,
Dorset DT9 6JX
Tel: 0935 872 699

H-M Veterinary Ltd
1 Spencer Street, Ringstead,
Kettering, Northants
NN14 4BX
Tel: 0933 625544

Harlow Bros. Limited
Long Whatton, Nr Lough-
borough, Leicestershire
LE12 5DE
Tel: 050 9842561

Highlight Hardware
Unit 9, Bulwark Industrial
Estate, Cheptow, Gwent
NP6 5QZ
Tel: 0633 412243

Horse Advancement Co. Ltd
44 Ferry Road, London
SW13 9PW
Tel: 081 748 6843

Horsegear Limited
16 Beech Road, Purley,
Reading, Berkshire
Tel: 0604 880640

Impala Sales and Marketing
The Cottage, Creation Road,
Hollowell, Northampton,
Northants NN6 8RP
Tel: 0604 740687

Irrigation & Slurry Services
Louvain, Quavey Road,
Redlynch, Wiltshire
SP5 2HH
Tel: 0725 20377

J E Goodrick & Co Ltd
Derwent Valley Ind Est,
Dunnington, York, N Yorks
YO1 5LP
Tel: 0904 489948

J J Robinson & Son Ltd
Timber Buildings, Eden
Lane, Gainford, Near
Darlington, Co Durham
Tel: 0325 730241

Ken Johnson
Beechwood Cottage,
Southview Road, Headly
Down, Bordon, Hants GU35
8NY
Tel: 0428 713885

Levett Burchett
Squires Farm, Easons
Green, Nr Uckfield, E Sussex
Tel: 082 584641

Loddon Livestock Equipment Ltd
Beccles Road, Loddon,
Norwich, Norfolk NR14 6JJ
Tel: 0508 20744
Fax: 0508 28055

Passmores Portable Bldgs Ltd
High Street, Strood,
Rochester, Kent
Tel: 0634 722500

Peter Cliffe
Grove Road, Harrogate,
Yorkshire
Tel: 0423 57252

R S Assemblies Ltd
Coppice Farm, Akeley
Wood, Buckingham, Bucks
Tel: 0280 812141

R W Stephen Equestrian Prods Ltd
Honeycombe Leaze,
Cirencester, Gloucestershire
Tel: 0285 712438

Rednal Products Ltd
Long Itchington, Southam,
Nr Rugby, Warks
Tel: 0926 812666

Robsons of Wolsingham
Durham Road, Wolsing-
ham-in-Weardale, Co Durham
Tel: 0325 730241

Roddimore Stud
Winslow Road, Great
Horwood, Milton Keynes,
Bucks MK17 ONY
Tel: 029671 2147

Ron Barry & Co
Rosehead Cottage, Pooley
Bridge, Penrith, Cumbria
CA10 2LT
Tel: 07684 86436

Ruari Construction
Warf Way, Glen Parva,
Leicester, Leics
Tel: 0533 771667

Rycovet Ltd
127 Houldsworth Street,
Glasgow, Strathclyde
G3 8JT

S Robb & Son
18 East Street, St Ives,
Huntingdon, Cambs
PE17 4PB
Tel: 0480 62150

Scotts of Thrapston
Bridge Street, Thrapston,
Northants NN14 4LR
Tel: 08012 2366
Fax: 08012 3703

**Sparkford Sawmills Ltd
(Herriard)**
Basingstoke, Hants
RG25 2PH
Tel: 0256 83585

Sparkford Sawmills Ltd
Sparkford, Yeovil, Somerset
BA22 7LH
Tel: 0968 40505

Sterivet Supplements
C/o Epsom Veterinery
Remedies Ltd, The Old
Manor, Upper Lambourn,
Newbury, Berks
Tel: 0488 71657

Steve Russell Sales
24, Maltings Wharf,
Manningtree, Essex
CO11 1XF
Tel: 0206 395171

Supreme Stables
Fenhurst Saw Mills, Henley
Common, Haslemere, Surrey
Tel: 0428 52362

Surewood Products
3 Moss Cottage, New Cut
Lane, Merseyside L33 3AH
Tel: 051 548 9052

Tiverton Timberware
Hillcrest, Maundown,
Wiveliscombe, Taunton,
Somerset
Tel: 0984 23679

Tuka Limited
1-2 St Johns Place, Banbury,
Oxon
Tel: 0295 87419

**W B Stubbs
(Hawksworth) Ltd**
Progress Works,
Hawksworth, Nottingham,
Nottinghamshire
Tel: 0949 50218

**W S Hodgson & Co
Limited**
Cotherstone, Nr Barnard
Castle, Co Durham
DL12 9PS
Tel: 0833 50274

Windsor Stables
Fenhurst Sawmills, Henley
Common, Hazlemere, Surrey
Tel: 0428 52362

Withington Hill Stables
189 Windlehurst Road, High
Lane, Stockport, Cheshire
Tel: 061 427 1209

Woodward (UK)
105 Lulworth Avenue, Leeds,
W Yorks LS15 8LW
Tel: 0532 645130

Surcingles and Rollers

Acorn Rugs
Gair Shield Farm, Steel,
Hexham, Northumberland,
NE47 OHS
Tel: 043 473 562

Clare Lawson
Vine Cottage, Winchester
Road, Waltham Chase,
Southampton, Hampshire,
SO3 2LX
Tel: 0329 832366

Equiquip Ltd
7 Pepper Alley, Banbury,
Oxon, OX16 OTF
Tel: 0295 3913

**F B Davis Saddlery
Limited**
Tolsons Mill, Mitchfield
Street, Fazeley, Tamworth,
Staffordshire, B78 3QB
Tel: 0827 280550

**Fancy Free Race &
Event Wear**
The Heath, Stoke Prior,
Leominster, Herefordshire
Tel: 056 882 662

**Hydrophane
Laboratories Limited**
Ickleford Manor, Hitchin,
Hertfordshire
Tel: 0462 32596

John James Hawley
(Speciality Works) Ltd,
Lichfield Road, Walsall, West
Midlands, WS4 2HX
Tel: 0922 25641
Fax: 0922 720163

Keith Luxford
(Saddlery) Ltd
H Q 57 High Street,
Teddington, Middx
Tel: 081 977 4964

Newton Horse Ltd
Hotham Hall, Hotham, E
Yorkshire, YO4 3UN
Tel: 0430 423636

Ollard Westcombe & Co
Ltd
Cameo Works, Downpatrick,
Down
Tel: 0396 2355

Talat International
Leather Co
Talat House, Upper Northam
Drive, Hedge End,
Southampton, Hants,
SO3 4BG
Tel: 0703 462908

Yorkshire Horse Rug Co
1256 Manchester Road,
Linthwaite, Huddersfield,
Yorkshire
Tel: 0484 844897

Tack Repairers

Brian Scrivener
Rear of 168 High Street,
Newmarket, Suffolk
Tel: 0638 664856

Chaskit New Zealand
Rugs
Chaskit House, Langton
Green, Nr Tunbridge Wells,
Kent, TN3 OEG
Tel: 0892 863113
Fax: 082 581 2192

Donalds McLellan
(Saddler)
Saddle & Harness Maker,
146, Busby Road, Clarkston,
Glasgow, G76 8BH
Tel: 041 644 4880

Fred Sales (Jersey) Ltd
The Old Tack Room,
Grasford, Gorey, Jersey,
Channel Islands
Tel: 0534 54131

Jump Off
11 Bishopsmeade Parade,
East Horsley, Surrey,
KT24 6RT
Tel: 04865 2086

Keith Luxford
(Saddlery) Ltd
H Q 57 High Street,
Teddington, Middx
Tel: 081 977 4964

Kiln Saddlery
The Folley, Layer de la
Haye, Colchester, Essex,
CO2 OHZ
Tel: 0206 34695

L M Hickling
The Laurels Workshop,
Stane Street, Ockley,
Dorking, Surrey
Tel: 0306 79215

McRostie of Glasgow
The Harness Room,
Templeton Business Centre,
Templeton Street, Glasgow,
Strathclyde, G40 1DA
Tel: 041 554 4338

Sandon Saddlery Co
Sandon, Buntingford,
Hertfordshire, SG9 0QW
Tel: 076 387 247

Tim Hawks
Lockanbreck, Mansegate,
Dunscore, Dumfries
Tel: 038782 468

Tie Rings

Brian Scrivener
Rear of 168 High Street,
Newmarket, Suffolk
Tel: 0638 664856

Chaskit New Zealand
Rugs
Chaskit House, Langton
Green, Nr Tunbridge Wells,
Kent, TN3 OEG
Tel: 0892 863113
Fax: 082 581 2192

Donalds McLellan
(Saddler)
Saddle & Harness Maker,
146, Busby Road, Clarkston,
Glasgow, G76 8BH
Tel: 041 644 4880

Fred Sales (Jersey) Ltd
The Old Tack Room,
Grasford, Gorey, Jersey,
Channel Islands
Tel: 0534 54131

Jump Off
11 Bishopsmeade Parade,
East Horsley, Surrey,
KT24 6RT
Tel: 04865 2086

Keith Luxford
(Saddlery) Ltd
H Q 57 High Street,
Teddington, Middx
Tel: 081 977 4964

Kiln Saddlery
The Folley, Layer de la
Haye, Colchester, Essex,
CO2 OHZ
Tel: 0206 34695

L M Hickling
The Laurels Workshop,
Stane Street, Ockley,
Dorking, Surrey
Tel: 0306 79215

McRostie of Glasgow
The Harness Room,
Templeton Business Centre,
Templeton Street, Glasgow,
Strathclyde, G40 1DA
Tel: 041 554 4338

Sandon Saddlery Co
Sandon, Buntingford,
Hertfordshire, SG9 0QW
Tel: 076 387 247

Tim Hawks
Lockanbreck, Mansegate,
Dunscore, Dumfries
Tel: 038782 468

Towing Vehicles and Accessories

Birmingham Land-Rover Serv Ltd
480 College Road,
Erdington, Birmingham,
W Mids
Tel: 021 382 7111

Continental Car Centre
Church Road, Stanmore,
Middlesex
Tel: 081 954 0077

Crook Brothers
Station Road Depot,
Hoghton, Nr Preston,
Lancashire

Dunsford Land-Rovers (Bath) Ltd
Bath Road Garage, Colerne,
Bath, Avon
Tel: 0225 743337

H & W Auto's (Ewell) Ltd
138 Ruxley Lane, West
Ewell, Surrey
Tel: 081 397 2462

J W E Banks & Sons Ltd
Crowland, Peterborough,
Cambs, PE6 OJP
Tel: 0733 210318

James Windsor of Mansfield Ltd
59/67 Nottingham Road,
Mansfield, Notts, NG18 1BX
Tel: 0623 33171

Kingsthorpe Garage
50 Harborough Road,
Kingsthorpe, Northampton,
Northants
Tel: 0604 716716

Lex Mead Cheltenham
Princess Elizabeth Way,
Cheltenham,
Gloucestershire, GT1 6TQ
Tel: 0242 520441

Pinewood (Toyota)
Coulsden Road, Caterham,
Surrey
Tel: 0883 46499

Rice Trailers Limited
Portland Works, Cosby,
Leicestershire, LE9 5TG
Tel: 0533 866666
Fax: 0533 750439

Sachs Motor Services Ltd
The Maltings, Tamworth
Road, Ashby-de-la-Zouch,
Leics
Tel: 0530 414313

Townley Cross Country Vehicles
701 Sidcup Road, Eltham,
London, London, SE9
Tel: 081 851 4511

Watering Devices

ACA Forage Ltd (Warnford)
Rooksgrove, Warnford, Nr
Southampton, Hants
Tel: 096 279385

Irrigation & Slurry Services
Louvain, Quavey Road,
Redlynch, Wiltshire,
SP5 2HH
Tel: 0725 20377

Manufacturers and Suppliers of Horse Care Products

Anti-inflammatory Treatments

Alfred Cox (Surgical) Ltd
Edgware Road, Coulsdon,
Surrey
Tel: 081 686 2131

C P Backhurst & Co
Strawberry Farm, Glaziers
Lane, Normandy, Guildford,
Surrey GU3 2DF
Tel: 0483 811360

Horse Advancement Co. Ltd
44 Ferry Road, London
SW13 9PW
Tel: 081 748 6843

Pharmacia Ltd
Pharmacia House,
Midsummer Boulevard,
Milton Keynes, Bucks
MK9 3HP
Tel: 0908 66101

Robinson Healthcare
Hipper House, Chesterfield,
Derbyshire S40 1YF
Tel: 0246 3220022
Fax: 0246 208164

School of National Equitation
Bunny Hill Top, Costock,
Leics LE12 6XE
Tel: 0509 852366
Fax: 0602 848381

Antiseptics

Alfred Cox (Surgical) Ltd
Edgware Road, Coulsdon,
Surrey
Tel: 081 686 2131

C P Backhurst & Co
Strawberry Farm, Glaziers
Lane, Normandy, Guildford,
Surrey GU3 2DF
Tel: 0483 811360

Crown Chemical Co. Limited
Lamberhurst, Kent TN3 8DJ
Tel: 0892 890491

Epsom Veterinary Remedies Ltd
Kingswood Stud, Lambourn,
Newbury, Berkshire
RG16 7RS
Tel: 0488 71657

Horse Advancement Co. Ltd
44 Ferry Road, London
SW13 9PW
Tel: 081 748 6843

Horse Requisites Newmarket Ltd
Black Bear Lane,
Newmarket, Suffolk CB8 0JT
Tel: 0638 664619
Fax: 0638 661562

Robinson Healthcare
Hipper House, Chesterfield,
Derbyshire S40 1YF
Tel: 0246 3220022
Fax: 0246 208164

School of National Equitation
Bunny Hill Top, Costock,
Leics LE12 6XE
Tel: 0509 852366
Fax: 0602 848381

Bandages

Acorn Rugs
Gair Shield Farm, Steel,
Hexham, Northumberland
NE47 OHS
Tel: 043 473 562

Aerborn Equestian
Pegasus House, 198
Sneinton Dale, Nottingham,
Notts NG2 4HJ
Tel: 0602 505631
Fax: 0602 483273

Alfred Cox (Surgical) Ltd
Edgware Road, Coulsdon,
Surrey
Tel: 081 686 2131

C P Backhurst & Co
Strawberry Farm, Glaziers
Lane, Normandy, Guildford,
Surrey GU3 2DF
Tel: 0483 811360

Carbex-Munroe (Handles)
11a St Nicholas Lane,
Lewes, East Sussex
BN7 2JZ
Tel: 0273 478111

Coleman Croft Saddlery
Sutton's Farm, Cooper's
Green, Nr St Albans,
Hertfordshire AL4 9HJ
Tel: 07072 74239

Equequip Ltd
7 Pepper Alley, Banbury,
Oxon OX16 OTF
Tel: 0295 3913

F B Davis Saddlery Limited
Tolsons Mill, Mitchfield
Street, Fazeley, Tamworth,
Staffordshire B78 3QB
Tel: 0827 280550

Glentona Textiles (1977) Ltd
44 Ferry Road, London
SW13 3PW
Tel: 081 748 6843

Horse Requisites Newmarket Ltd
Black Bear Lane,
Newmarket, Suffolk CB8 0JT
Tel: 0638 664619
Fax: 0638 661562

Hydrophane Laboratories Limited
Ickleford Manor, Hitchin,
Hertfordshire
Tel: 0462 32596

James Walkers & Son Ltd
Holme Bank Mills, Mirfield,
Yorks NF14 8NA
Tel: 0924 492277

M J Ainge & Co. Ltd
Porthouse Farm Industrial
Est., Bromyard, Herefordshire
HR7 4NP
Tel: 0885 83601

Mike Doyle Marketing Ltd
2 Wordsworth Close,
Towcester, Northants
Tel: 0604 770601

Newton Horse Ltd
Hotham Hall, Hotham, E
Yorkshire YO4 3UN
Tel: 0430 423636

Ordell Enterprises
The Forest House, Hatchet
Lane, Winkfield, Berkshire
SL4 2EG
Tel: 0344 885857

Redport Equestrian
Asker Works, 94 East Street,
Bridport, Dorset
Tel: 0308 22592

Robinson Healthcare
Hipper House, Chesterfield,
Derbyshire S40 1YF
Tel: 0246 3220022
Fax: 0246 208164

School of National Equitation
Bunny Hill Top, Costock,
Leics LE12 6XE
Tel: 0509 852366
Fax: 0602 848381

Yorkshire Horse Rug Co
1256 Manchester Road,
Linthwaite, Huddersfield,
Yorkshire
Tel: 0484 844897

Blood Tonics

C P Backhurst & Co
Strawberry Farm, Glaziers
Lane, Normandy, Guildford,
Surrey GU3 2DF
Tel: 0483 811360

Equine Products UK Limited
Smithy Side, Ponteland,
Newcastle-upon-Tyne
NE15 8SJ
Tel: 091 264 5536

Goldswell Ltd
Manor Farm cottage, Ryme
Intrinseca, Nr Sherborne,
Dorset DT9 6JX
Tel: 0935 872 699

School of National Equitation
Bunny Hill Top, Costock,
Leics LE12 6XE
Tel: 0509 852366
Fax: 0602 848381

Smith, Kline Animal Health Ltd
Cavendish Road,
Stevenage, Hertfordshire
Tel: 0438 67881

Sterivet Supplements

C/o Epsom Veterinery
Remeds Ltd, The Old Manor,
Upper Lambourn, Newbury,
Berks
Tel: 0488 71657

Vet Health

The Animal Care Centre,
Colne Road, Coggeshall,
Colchester, Essex
Tel: 0376 61548

Wagg Foods Ltd

Dalton Airfield, Topcliffe,
Thirsk, North Yorkshire YO7
3HE
Tel: 0845 578111
Fax: 0845 577990

Breeding Supplements

C P Backhurst & Co

Strawberry Farm, Glaziers
Lane, Normandy, Guildford,
Surrey GU3 2DF
Tel: 0483 811360

Charnwood Milling Co Ltd

Framlingham, near
Woodbridge, Suffolk 1P13
9PT
Tel: 0728 723435
Fax: 0728 724359

Equine Products UK Limited

Smithy Side, Ponteland,
Newcastle-upon-Tyne
NE15 8SJ
Tel: 091 264 5536

Equivite

(Milk Pellets) Beecham
Animal H Health, Beecham
House, Brentford, Middlesex

Horse Advancement Co. Ltd

44 Ferry Road, London
SW13 9PW
Tel: 081 748 6843

Medi Equus PLC

Gibbs House, Kennel Ride,
Ascot, Berks SL5 7NT
Tel: 0344 890662
Fax: 0344 886531

School of National Equitation

Bunny Hill Top, Costock,
Leics LE12 6XE
Tel: 0509 852366
Fax: 0602 848381

Sterivet Supplements

C/o Epsom Veterinery
Remedies Ltd, The Old
Manor, Upper Lambourn,
Newbury, Berks
Tel: 0488 71657

The Wyke Equestrian Services

Shifnal, Shropshire
TF11 9PP
Tel: 0952 462982
Fax: 0952 462981

Wagg Foods Ltd

Dalton Airfield, Topcliffe,
Thirsk, North Yorkshire
YO7 3HE
Tel: 0845 578111
Fax: 0845 577990

Willow Farm Livery Stables & Riding School

123A, Frogmore Lane,
Lovedean, School,
Waterlooville, Hampshire
PO8 9RD
Tel: 0705 599817

Cod Liver Oils

British Cod Liver Oils Limited

Hedon Road, Marfleet,
N. Humberside HU9 5NJ
Tel: 0482 75234

C P Backhurst & Co

Strawberry Farm, Glaziers
Lane, Normandy, Guildford,
Surrey GU3 2DF
Tel: 0483 811360

Charnwood Milling Co Ltd

Framlingham, near Wood-
bridge, Suffolk 1P13 9PT
Tel: 0728 723435
Fax: 0728 724359

Mark Westaway & Son

Love Lane Farm, Marldon,
Paignton, Devon TQ3 1SP
Tel: 0803 527257
Fax: 0803 528010

School of National Equitation

Bunny Hill Top, Costock,
Leics LE12 6XE
Tel: 0509 852366
Fax: 0602 848381

Willow Farm Livery Stables & Riding School

123A, Frogmore Lane,
Lovedean, School,
Waterlooville, Hampshire
PO8 9RD
Tel: 0705 599817

Coat Glosses and Dressings

C P Backhurst & Co
Strawberry Farm, Glaziers Lane, Normandy, Guildford, Surrey GU3 2DF
Tel: 0483 811360

Carr Day & Martin Limited
Lloyds House, Alderly Road, Wilmslow, Cheshire
SK9 1QT
Tel: 0625 539135
Fax: 0625 526962

Mars Oil Co.
Withycombe Farmhouse, Drayton, Nr Banbury, Oxon
OX15 6EE
Tel: 0295 262844
Fax: 0295 273164

School of National Equitation
Bunny Hill Top, Costock, Leics LE12 6XE
Tel: 0509 852366
Fax: 0602 848381

Willow Farm Livery Stables & Riding School
123A, Frogmore Lane, Lovedean, School, Waterlooville, Hampshire
PO8 9RD
Tel: 0705 599817

Cough and Cold Treatments

C P Backhurst & Co
Strawberry Farm, Glaziers Lane, Normandy, Guildford, Surrey GU3 2DF
Tel: 0483 811360

Epsom Veterinary Remedies Ltd
Kingswood Stud, Lambourn, Newbury, Berkshire
RG16 7RS
Tel: 0488 71657

Equine Products UK Limited
Smithy Side, Ponteland, Newcastle-upon-Tyne
NE15 8SJ
Tel: 091 264 5536

Horse Advancement Co. Ltd
44 Ferry Road, London
SW13 9PW
Tel: 081 748 6843

Horse Requisites Newmarket Ltd
Black Bear Lane, Newmarket, Suffolk CB8 0JT
Tel: 0638 664619
Fax: 0638 661562

School of National Equitation
Bunny Hill Top, Costock, Leics LE12 6XE
Tel: 0509 852366
Fax: 0602 848381

Crib-biting Preventatives

C P Backhurst & Co
Strawberry Farm, Glaziers Lane, Normandy, Guildford, Surrey GU3 2DF
Tel: 0483 811360

Carr Day & Martin Limited
Lloyds House, Alderly Road, Wilmslow, Cheshire SK9 1QT
Tel: 0625 539135
Fax: 0625 526962

School of National Equitation
Bunny Hill Top, Costock, Leics LE12 6XE
Tel: 0509 852366
Fax: 0602 848381

Willow Farm Livery Stables & Riding School
123A, Frogmore Lane, Lovedean, School, Waterlooville, Hampshire PO8 9RD
Tel: 0705 599817

Digestive Treatments

C P Backhurst & Co
Strawberry Farm, Glaziers Lane, Normandy, Guildford, Surrey GU3 2DF
Tel: 0483 811360

Equine Products UK Limited
Smithy Side, Ponteland, Newcastle-upon-Tyne
NE15 8SJ
Tel: 091 264 5536

Radiol Chemicals
Stepfield, Witham, Essex
Tel: 0376 512538

School of National Equitation
Bunny Hill Top, Costock, Leics LE12 6XE
Tel: 0509 852366
Fax: 0602 848381

The Wyke Equestrian Services
Shifnal, Shropshire
TF11 9PP
Tel: 0952 462982
Fax: 0952 462981

Fly and Insect Repellants

Bellet Ltd
Main Road, Arlesford,
Colchester, Essex CO7 8OH
Tel: 0206 223360

C P Backhurst & Co
Strawberry Farm, Glaziers
Lane, Normandy, Guildford,
Surrey GU3 2DF
Tel: 0483 811360

Carr Day & Martin Limited
Lloyds House, Alderly Road,
Wilmslow, Cheshire
SK9 1QT
Tel: 0625 539135
Fax: 0625 526962

Epsom Veterinary Remedies Ltd
Kingswood Stud, Lambourn,
Newbury, Berkshire
RG16 7RS
Tel: 0488 71657

Fisons Animal Health
12, Derby Road,
Loughborough,
Leicestershire LE11 OBB
Tel: 0509 611001
Fax: 0509 235285

Glentona Textiles (1977) Ltd
44 Ferry Road, London,
London SW13 9PW
Tel: 081 748 6843

Goldswell Ltd

Effol

Manor Farm cottage, Ryme
Intrinseca, Nr Sherborne,
Dorset DT9 6JX
Tel: 0935 872 699

Horse Requisites Newmarket Ltd
Black Bear Lane,
Newmarket, Suffolk CB8 0JT
Tel: 0638 664619
Fax: 0638 661562

Radiol Chemicals
Stepfield, Witham, Essex
Tel: 0376 512538

School of National Equitation
Bunny Hill Top, Costock,
Leics LE12 6XE
Tel: 0509 852366
Fax: 0602 848381

Steve Russell Sales
24 Maltings Wharf,
Manningtree, Essex
CO11 1XF
Tel: 0206 395171
Fax: 0206 395171

Willow Farm Livery Stables & Riding School
123A, Frogmore Lane,
Lovedean, School,
Waterlooville, Hampshire
PO8 9RD
Tel: 0705 599817

Healing Creams and Gels

C P Backhurst & Co
Strawberry Farm, Glaziers
Lane, Normandy, Guildford,
Surrey GU3 2DF
Tel: 0483 811360

Carr Day & Martin Limited
Lloyds House, Alderly Road,
Wilmslow, Cheshire
SK9 1QT
Tel: 0625 539135
Fax: 0625 526962

F B Davis Saddlery Limited
Tolsons Mill, Mitchfield
Street, Fazeley, Tamworth,
Staffordshire B78 3QB
Tel: 0827 280550

Fisons Animal Health
12, Derby Road,
Loughborough,
Leicestershire LE11 OBB
Tel: 0509 611001
Fax: 0509 235285

Goldswell Ltd

Effol

Manor Farm cottage, Ryme
Intrinseca, Nr Sherborne,
Dorset DT9 6JX
Tel: 0935 872 699

Horse Advancement Co. Ltd
44 Ferry Road, London
SW13 9PW
Tel: 081 748 6843

Horse Requisites Newmarket Ltd

Black Bear Lane,
Newmarket, Suffolk CB8 0JT
Tel: 0638 664619
Fax: 0638 661562

Hydrophane Laboratories Limited

Ickleford Manor, Hitchin,
Hertfordshire
Tel: 0462 32596

Radiol Chemicals

Stepfield, Witham, Essex
Tel: 0376 512538

School of National Equitation

Bunny Hill Top, Costock,
Leics LE12 6XE
Tel: 0509 852366
Fax: 0602 848381

Sterivet Supplements

C/o Epsom Veterinery
Remeds Ltd, The Old Manor,
Upper Lambourn, Newbury,
Berks
Tel: 0488 71657

Tranby Equestrian Services

Tranby House, West End,
Long Whatton, Leics LE12
5DW
Tel: 0509 843079

Willow Farm Livery Stables & Riding School

123A, Frogmore Lane,
Lovedean, School, Waterloo-
ville, Hampshire PO8 9RD
Tel: 0705 599817

Hoof-care Products

Brookwick Ward & Co Ltd

88 Westlaw Place, Whitehall
Estate, Glenrothes, Fife
KY6 2QB
Tel: 0592 630052
Fax: 0592 630109

C P Backhurst & Co

Strawberry Farm, Glaziers
Lane, Normandy, Guildford,
Surrey GU3 2DF
Tel: 0483 811360

Carr Day & Martin Limited

Lloyds House, Alderly Road,
Wilmslow, Cheshire SK9 1QT
Tel: 0625 539135
Fax: 0625 526962

Fisons Animal Health

12, Derby Road, Lough-
borough, Leicestershire
LE11 OBB
Tel: 0509 611001
Fax: 0509 235285

Mars Oil Co.

Withycombe Farmhouse,
Drayton, Nr Banbury, Oxon
OX15 6EE
Tel: 0295 262844
Fax: 0295 273164

Robinson Healthcare

Hipper House, Chesterfield,
Derbyshire S40 1YF
Tel: 0246 3220022
Fax: 0246 208164

School of National Equitation

Bunny Hill Top, Costock,
Leics LE12 6XE
Tel: 0509 852366
Fax: 0602 848381

Wagg Foods Ltd

Dalton Airfield, Topcliffe,
Thirsk, North Yorkshire
YO7 3HE
Tel: 0845 578111
Fax: 0845 577990

Willow Farm Livery Stables & Riding School

123A, Frogmore Lane,
Lovedean, School, Waterloo-
ville, Hampshire PO8 9RD
Tel: 0705 599817

Liniments

Fisons Animal Health

12, Derby Road,
Loughborough,
Leicestershire LE11 OBB
Tel: 0509 611001
Fax: 0509 235285

School of National Equitation

Bunny Hill Top, Costock,
Leics LE12 6XE
Tel: 0509 852366
Fax: 0602 848381

Willow Farm Livery Stables & Riding School

123A, Frogmore Lane,
Lovedean, School, Waterloo-
ville, Hampshire PO8 9RD
Tel: 0705 599817

Louse Powders

C P Backhurst & Co

Strawberry Farm, Glaziers
Lane, Normandy, Guildford,
Surrey GU3 2DF
Tel: 0483 811360

F B Davis Saddlery Limited

Tolsons Mill, Mitchfield Street, Fazeley, Tamworth, Staffordshire B78 3QB
Tel: 0827 280550

Horse Requisites Newmarket Ltd

Black Bear Lane, Newmarket, Suffolk CB8 0JT
Tel: 0638 664619
Fax: 0638 661562

School of National Equitation

Bunny Hill Top, Costock, Leics LE12 6XE
Tel: 0509 852366
Fax: 0602 848381

Thoroughbred Saddlery Co

Ickleford Manor, Hitchin, Herts
Tel: 0462 325596

Willow Farm Livery Stables & RS

123A, Frogmore Lane, Lovedean, School, Waterlooville, Hampshire PO8 9RD
Tel: 0705 599817

Milk Replacers

C P Backhurst & Co

Strawberry Farm, Glaziers Lane, Normandy, Guildford, Surrey GU3 2DF
Tel: 0483 811360

Carr Day & Martin Limited

Lloyds House, Alderly Road, Wilmslow, Cheshire SK9 1QT
Tel: 0625 539135
Fax: 0625 526962

Charnwood Milling Co Ltd

Framlingham, near Woodbridge, Suffolk 1P13 9PT
Tel: 0728 723435
Fax: 0728 724359

Equimix Feeds Ltd

Sandy Lane Trading Estate, Tilton, Stourport on Severn, Worcestershire DY13 9QA
Tel: 0299 827744

Equivite

(Milk Pellets) Beecham Animal H Health, Beecham House, Brentford, Middlesex

Horse Requisites Newmarket Ltd

Black Bear Lane, Newmarket, Suffolk CB8 0JT
Tel: 0638 664619
Fax: 0638 661562

School of National Equitation

Bunny Hill Top, Costock, Leics LE12 6XE
Tel: 0509 852366
Fax: 0602 848381

The Wyke Equestrian Services

Shifnal, Shropshire TF11 9PP
Tel: 0952 462982
Fax: 0952 462981

Willow Farm Livery Stables & Riding School

123A, Frogmore Lane, Lovedean, School, Waterlooville, Hampshire PO8 9RD
Tel: 0705 599817

Poultices

C P Backhurst & Co

Strawberry Farm, Glaziers Lane, Normandy, Guildford, Surrey GU3 2DF
Tel: 0483 811360

Crown Chemical Co. Limited

Lamberhurst, Kent TN3 8DJ
Tel: 0892 890491

Horse Requisites Newmarket Ltd

Black Bear Lane, Newmarket, Suffolk CB8 0JT
Tel: 0638 664619
Fax: 0638 661562

K/L Pharmaceutical Ltd

25 Macadam Place, South Newmoor Industrial Estate, Irvine, Strathclyde KA11 4HP
Tel: 0294 215951

Robinson Healthcare

Hipper House, Chesterfield, Derbyshire S40 1YF
Tel: 0246 3220022
Fax: 0246 208164

School of National Equitation

Bunny Hill Top, Costock, Leics LE12 6XE
Tel: 0509 852366
Fax: 0602 848381

Shampoos and Conditioners

Battle, Hayward Bower Limited

Victoria Chemical Works, Crofton Drive, Allenby Road Industrial Estate, Lincoln, Lincs
Tel: 0522 29206

Bellet Ltd
Main Road, Arlesford,
Colchester, Essex CO7 8OH
Tel: 0206 223360

C P Backhurst & Co
Strawberry Farm, Glaziers
Lane, Normandy, Guildford,
Surrey GU3 2DF
Tel: 0483 811360

**Carr Day & Martin
Limited**
Lloyds House, Alderly Road,
Wilmslow, Cheshire
SK9 1QT
Tel: 0625 539135
Fax: 0625 526962

Constant Laboratories
Gores Road, Knowsley
Industrial Park, Liverpool,
Merseyside
Tel: 051 547 3711

**Crown Chemical Co.
Limited**
Lamberhurst, Kent TN3 8DJ
Tel: 0892 890491

**F B Davis Saddlery
Limited**
Tolsons Mill, Mitchfield
Street, Fazeley, Tamworth,
Staffordshire B78 3QB
Tel: 0827 280550

Fisons Animal Health
12, Derby Road,
Loughborough,
Leicestershire LE11 OBB
Tel: 0509 611001
Fax: 0509 235285

Goldswell Ltd
Manor Farm cottage, Ryme
Intrinseca, Nr Sherborne,
Dorset DT9 6JX
Tel: 0935 872 699

Hippomatic Ltd
Sandon, Buntingford, Herts
SG9 OQW
Tel: 076 387 453

**Horse Advancement
Co. Ltd**
44 Ferry Road, London
SW13 9PW
Tel: 081 748 6843

**Horse Requisites
Newmarket Ltd**
Black Bear Lane,
Newmarket, Suffolk CB8 0JT
Tel: 0638 664619
Fax: 0638 661562

**Hydrophane
Laboratories Limited**
Ickleford Manor, Hitchin,
Hertfordshire
Tel: 0462 32596

Mars Oil Co.
Withycombe Farmhouse,
Drayton, Nr Banbury, Oxon
OX15 6EE
Tel: 0295 262844 **Fax:** 0295
273164

**School of National
Equitation**
Bunny Hill Top, Costock,
Leics LE12 6XE
Tel: 0509 852366
Fax: 0602 848381

**Willow Farm Livery
Stables & Riding School**
123A, Frogmore Lane,
Lovedean, School, Waterloo-
ville, Hampshire PO8 9RD
Tel: 0705 599817

Skin-care Products

C P Backhurst & Co
Strawberry Farm, Glaziers
Lane, Normandy, Guildford,
Surrey GU3 2DF
Tel: 0483 811360

Constant Laboratories
Gores Road, Knowsley
Industrial Park, Liverpool,
Merseyside
Tel: 051 547 3711

**Horse Advancement
Co. Ltd**
44 Ferry Road, London
SW13 9PW
Tel: 081 748 6843

**Horse Requisites
Newmarket Ltd**
Black Bear Lane,
Newmarket, Suffolk CB8 0JT
Tel: 0638 664619
Fax: 0638 661562

**School of National
Equitation**
Bunny Hill Top, Costock,
Leics LE12 6XE
Tel: 0509 852366 **Fax:** 0602
848381

Treatments and Tonics

**Battle, Hayward Bower
Limited**
Victoria Chemical Works,
Crofton Drive, Allenby Road
Industrial Estate, Lincoln, Lincs
Tel: 0522 29206

C P Backhurst & Co
Strawberry Farm, Glaziers
Lane, Normandy, Guildford,
Surrey GU3 2DF
Tel: 0483 811360

**School of National
Equitation**
Bunny Hill Top, Costock,
Leics LE12 6XE
Tel: 0509 852366
Fax: 0602 848381

Vaccines

**Coopers Animal Health
Ltd**
Crewe Hall, Crewe, Cheshire
CW1 1UB
Tel: 0270 580131

Hoechst UK Limited
Walton Manor, Walton,
Milton Keynes,
Buckinghamshire MK7 1AJ

Holly Stud
Holly Farm, Alston,
Axminster, Devon

**School of National
Equitation**
Bunny Hill Top, Costock,
Leics LE12 6XE
Tel: 0509 852366
Fax: 0602 848381

**Smith, Kline Animal
Health Ltd**
Cavendish Road,
Stevenage, Hertfordshire
Tel: 0438 67881

Veterinary Equipment

**Brookwick Ward & Co
Ltd**
88 Westlaw Place, Whitehall
Estate, Glenrothes, Fife
KY6 2QB
Tel: 0592 630052
Fax: 0592 630109

K G Products
247/251 City Road, Fenton,
Stoke-on-Trent, Staffs
ST4 2PY
Tel: 0782 44866

**Loddon Livestock
Equipment Ltd**
Beccles Road, Loddon,
Norwich, Norfolk NR14 6JJ
Tel: 0508 20744
Fax: 0508 28055

M J Ainge & Co. Ltd
Porthouse Farm Industrial
Est., Bromyard,
Herefordshire HR7 4NP
Tel: 0885 83601

**School of National
Equitation**
Bunny Hill Top, Costock,
Leics LE12 6XE
Tel: 0509 852366
Fax: 0602 848381

**The Wyke Equestrian
Services**
Shifnal, Shropshire
TF11 9PP
Tel: 0952 462982
Fax: 0952 462981

Veterinary and Homeopathic Remedies

**Battle, Hayward Bower
Limited**
Victoria Chemical Works,
Crofton Drive, Allenby Road
Industrial Estate, Lincoln, Lincs
Tel: 0522 29206

C P Backhurst & Co
Strawberry Farm, Glaziers
Lane, Normandy, Guildford,
Surrey GU3 2DF
Tel: 0483 811360

Champerene Ltd
19 Meadow Close,
Lavenham, Suffolk
CO10 9RU
Tel: 0787 217564

Conquest Remedies
Norwood House, Lockerbie,
Dumfrieshire, Dumfries &
Galloway DG11 2QU

**Epsom Veterinary
Remedies Ltd**
Kingswood Stud, Lambourn,
Newbury, Berkshire
RG16 7RS
Tel: 0488 71657

Equicushion Ltd
Berricot Green, Warrengate,
Tewin, Welwyn, Herts
AL6 0JE
Tel: 043871 7708

Fisons Animal Health
12, Derby Road, Lough-
borough, Leicestershire
LE11 OBB
Tel: 0509 611001
Fax: 0509 235285

Horse Advancement Co. Ltd
44 Ferry Road, London
SW13 9PW
Tel: 081 748 6843

K/L Pharmaceutical Ltd
25 Macadam Place, South
Newmoor Industrial Estate,
Irvine, Strathclyde KA11 4HP
Tel: 0294 215951

Magnetopulse Ltd
16 Grafton Place,
Northampton, Northants
Tel: 0604 31764

Magnevet Therapies Ltd
Magnevet House, 29 Enfield
Road, London, London N1
5AZ

School of National Equitation
Bunny Hill Top, Costock,
Leics LE12 6XE
Tel: 0509 852366
Fax: 0602 848381

Vitamin/Mineral Supplements

Bailey's Horse Feeds
Four Elms Mills, Bardfield
Saling, Braintree, Essex
CM7 5EJ
Tel: 0371 850247
Fax: 0371 851269

Battle, Hayward Bower Limited
Victoria Chemical Works,
Crofton Drive, Allenby Road
Industrial Estate, Lincoln, Lincs
Tel: 0522 29206

Bayer (UK) Ltd
Agrochem Div, Eastern Way,
Bury St Edmunds, Suffolk
IP32 7AH
Tel: 0284 63200

British Cod Liver Oils Limited
Hedon Road, Marfleet, N
Humberside HU9 5NJ
Tel: 0482 75234

C P Backhurst & Co
Strawberry Farm, Glaziers
Lane, Normandy, Guildford,
Surrey GU3 2DF
Tel: 0483 811360

Carr Day & Martin Limited
Lloyds House, Alderly Road,
Wilmslow, Cheshire
SK9 1QT
Tel: 0625 539135
Fax: 0625 526962

Charnwood Milling Co Ltd
Framlingham, near
Woodbridge, Suffolk
1P13 9PT
Tel: 0728 723435
Fax: 0728 724359

Chase Organics (GB) Ltd
Termina House, Shepperton,
Middx
Tel: 0932 221212

Day Son & Hewitt Ltd
10 Grant Street, Bradford,
W Yorkshire
Tel: 0774 722005

Equestricare
6 Bevans Lane,
Hinton-on-the-Green,
Eveshan, Warks WR11 6QT
Tel: 0386 48424

Equiform Nutrition Ltd
379 Victoria Street, Grimsby,
Sth Humberside DN31 1PX
Tel: 0472 44766

Equimix Feeds Ltd
Sandy Lane Trading Estate,
Tilton, Stourport on Severn,
Worcestershire DY13 9QA
Tel: 0299 827744

Equine Products UK Limited
Smithy Side, Ponteland,
Newcastle-upon-Tyne
NE15 8SJ
Tel: 091 264 5536

Equivite
(Milk Pellets) Beecham
Animal H Health, Beecham
House, Brentford, Middlesex

F B Davis Saddlery Limited
Tolsons Mill, Mitchfield
Street, Fazeley, Tamworth,
Staffordshire B78 3QB
Tel: 0827 280550

F J Alton & Partners Ltd
Lower Madeley Farm,
Belbroughton, Stourbridge,
Stourbridge, Worcs
Tel: 0562 710293

Fisons Animal Health
12, Derby Road, Lough-
borough, Leicestershire
LE11 0BB
Tel: 0509 611001
Fax: 0509 235285

Goldswell Ltd
Manor Farm cottage, Ryme
Intrinseca, Nr Sherborne,
Dorset DT9 6JX
Tel: 0935 872 699

H-M Veterinary Ltd
1 Spencer Street, Ringstead, Kettering, Northants
NN14 4BX
Tel: 0933 625544

Horse Advancement Co. Ltd
44 Ferry Road, London
SW13 9PW
Tel: 081 748 6843

Horse Requisites Newmarket Ltd
Black Bear Lane, Newmarket, Suffolk CB8 0JT
Tel: 0638 664619
Fax: 0638 661562

Intervet Laboratories Ltd
Science Park, Milton, Cambridge, Cambridgeshire
Tel: 0223 311221

Main Ring from Rumenco
Stretton House, Derby Road, Burton-on-Trent, Staffordshire DE13 0DW
Tel: 0283 511211
Fax: 0283 46152

Medi Equus PLC
Gibbs House, Kennel Ride, Ascot, Berks SL5 7NT
Tel: 0344 890662
Fax: 0344 886531

School of National Equitation
Bunny Hill Top, Costock, Leics LE12 6XE
Tel: 0509 852366
Fax: 0602 848381

Smith, Kline Animal Health Ltd
Cavendish Road, Stevenage, Hertfordshire
Tel: 0438 67881

Sterivet Supplements
C/o Epsom Veterinery Remeds Ltd, The Old Manor, Upper Lambourn, Newbury, Berks
Tel: 0488 71657

The Wyke Equestrian Services
Shifnal, Shropshire
TF11 9PP
Tel: 0952 462982
Fax: 0952 462981

Vet Health
The Animal Care Centre, Colne Road, Coggeshall, Colchester, Essex
Tel: 0376 61548

Willow Farm Livery Stables & Riding School
123A, Frogmore Lane, Lovedean, School, Waterloo-ville, Hampshire PO8 9RD
Tel: 0705 599817

Wormers

Battle, Hayward Bower Limited
Victoria Chemical Works, Crofton Drive, Allenby Road Industrial Estate, Lincoln, Lincs
Tel: 0522 29206

Bayer (UK) Ltd
Agrochem Div, Eastern Way, Bury St Edmunds, Suffolk
IP32 7AH
Tel: 0284 63200

C P Backhurst & Co
Strawberry Farm, Glaziers Lane, Normandy, Guildford, Surrey GU3 2DF
Tel: 0483 811360

Coopers Animal Health Ltd
Crewe Hall, Crewe, Cheshire
CW1 1UB
Tel: 0270 580131

Crown Chemical Co. Limited
Lamberhurst, Kent TN3 8DJ
Tel: 0892 890491

Holly Stud
Holly Farm, Alston, Axminster, Devon

Horse Requisites Newmarket Ltd
Black Bear Lane, Newmarket, Suffolk CB8 0JT
Tel: 0638 664619
Fax: 0638 661562

Kiln Saddlery
The Folley, Layer de la Haye, Colchester, Essex
CO2 0HZ
Tel: 0206 34695

MSD Agvet
Merck, Sharp & Dohme Ltd, Hoddesdon, Herts
Tel: 0992 467272

Pfizer Limited
Sandwick, Kent
Tel: 0304 616161

R & E Bamford
Bretherton, Preston, Lancs
PR5 7BD
Tel: 0772 600671
Fax: 0772 600340

School of National Equitation
Bunny Hill Top, Costock, Leics LE12 6XE
Tel: 0509 852366
Fax: 0602 848381

Smith, Kline Animal Health Ltd

Cavendish Road,
Stevenage, Hertfordshire
Tel: 0438 67881

Willow Farm Livery Stables & Riding School

123A, Frogmore Lane,
Lovedean, School, Waterloo-
ville, Hampshire PO8 9RD
Tel: 0705 599817

Wound Dressings

Battle, Hayward Bower Limited

Victoria Chemical Works,
Crofton Drive, Allenby Road
Industrial Estate, Lincoln, Lincs
Tel: 0522 29206

Bayer (UK) Ltd

Agrochem Div, Eastern Way,
Bury St Edmunds, Suffolk
IP32 7AH
Tel: 0284 63200

Crown Chemical Co. Limited

Lamberhurst, Kent TN3 8DJ
Tel: 0892 890491

Horse Requisites Newmarket Ltd

Black Bear Lane,
Newmarket, Suffolk CB8 0JT
Tel: 0638 664619
Fax: 0638 661562

Hydrophane Laboratories Limited

Ickleford Manor, Hitchin,
Hertfordshire
Tel: 0462 32596

Mike Doyle Marketing Ltd

2 Wordsworth Close,
Towcester, Northants
Tel: 0604 770601

School of National Equitation

Bunny Hill Top, Costock,
Leics LE12 6XE
Tel: 0509 852366
Fax: 0602 848381

Section 4: The World of Horsemanship

Chapter 26: The Pony Club   310
Chapter 27: Equestrian
Organisations   316
Chapter 28: The World
Equestrian Games   331

Useful References & Listings

Stud Breeding Services   346
Stud Management Equipment   346
Western Saddles and Wear   346

The Pony Club

> *The Pony Club is a youth organisation which is dedicated to the development and encouragement of good skills and practice within the spheres of riding and horsemastership*

The Pony Club is a youth organisation which is dedicated to the development and encouragement of good skills and practice within the spheres of riding and horsemastership. Affiliated to the British Horse Society, it could rightly be known as their youth branch and has certainly been the training ground for many of our national and international riders. It has been granted constituent membership to the National Council of Voluntary Youth Services (N.C.V.Y.S.) and is therefore officially a National Youth Organisation.

The advantages of this are quite far reaching since, as a recognised member, it will come within the auspices of the Youth Service and can be represented at Local Authority level. It is hoped that this will allow for a more sympathetic attitude towards riding in general, and the Pony Club in particular, by local authorities and other influential bodies. It is, however, incumbent upon each branch to make representations to the N.C.V.Y.S. councils and gain a place on their committees, thus maximising the advantage already gained.

The overall aims of the Pony Club are threefold:

To encourage young people to ride and to learn to enjoy all kinds of sport connected with horses and riding.

To provide instruction in riding and horsemastership and to instil in members the proper care of their animals.

To promote the highest ideals of sportsmanship, citizenship and loyalty, thereby cultivating strength of character and self-discipline.

Membership of the Pony Club is available to all young people under the age of 21. Ordinary membership is held by those up to the age of 17 years, and Associate membership from 17-21 years.

At an annual cost per member of £13.50, plus a joining fee of £1, with maximum family contributions of £32, this has to be one of the best value for money clubs in the country! Throughout the year a series of rallies will be organised - these will be both mounted and unmounted - 1989 an

	1990	1989	1988	1987
Members - Ordinary		32,526	31,116	28,613
Associates		3,594	3,846	3,714
		36,120	34,962	33,327
Boy members		5,825	5,439	5,097
Branches		366	367	368
Working Rallies (average per branch)		18	17	16
Branches holding camps or 3/4 day rallies		330	329	332
Members attending camps		16,843	17,477	17,

average of 18 rallies were held per branch per annum. In addition, there are annual camps, additional training sessions, social events and mounted events - not bad for a mere £13.50!

There are, of course, the hidden extras - specialised clothing and equipment, entry fees, transport etc - all of which you would incur by attending commercially-organised events anyway. The greatest hidden cost is, in my opinion, on the time and energy of those parents who do not make a timely exit when volunteers are being asked for! Many parents who show a keen and lively interest in the horse/pony club world, often find themselves in the position where all their spare time and energies are taken up in 'The Cause'! It is good to be involved in the activities of your children and give them support and encouragement outside of the more competitive environment of the show ring - but beware the willing horse!

Looking back at the growth of the Pony Club, let us look at some of the vital statistics - this will enable you to judge its strengths for yourself. The following are statistics for the past 4 years.

Let us look at the origins of the Pony Club. As far back as 1928, thought was being given to encouraging the younger generation in the mastery of riding and horsemastership. The then 'Institute of the Horse' had formed a series of sub-branches in different parts of the country to encourage riding. In addition to running those functions for adults, many began to organise paper chases and gymkhanas for the children. On November 1st (still the start of the Pony Club subscription year) 1929, the 'Institute of the Horse' inaugurated a junior branch which was to be known at the Pony Club. The objectives were for the purpose of interesting young people in riding and sport and at the same time offering the opportunity of higher education in this direction that many of them cannot obtain individually?

The country was divided into a series of districts which correspond with the different Hunts, and each district was under the control of a District Commissioner aided by a Local Committee. The intention was to keep each district in close touch with hunting.

The member were enroled with an entrance fee of 2s 6d (a fee that remained unchanged until 1976 when inflation and decimalisation caught up!) and an annual fee of 5s. Each member was given a badge upon joining - the pattern of which is still in use today.

A 'Central Committee of the Pony Club' was formed by the 'Institute of the Horse and Pony Club' under the directions of the then chairman Major Faudel-Phillips and the secretary Brig. Gen. T.H.S. Marchant. These two together with other members of the committee were responsible for drawing up the constitution of the new club.

In January 1930 the Central Committee held its first meeting, and by May, District Commissioners had been appointed to the founding branches. The branches were Belvoir, Cottesmere, Craven, Essex, Essex Union, Fernie, Grafton, Ludlow, Shropshire (North and South), Old Surrey, Burstow, V.W.H. and Wynstey. These 14 branches formed the backbone of the Pony Club in Great Britain and commanded a membership

of 700. 1930 also saw the formation of the Royal Calpe Hunt Pony Club (Gibraltar), the first affiliated overseas branch.

By 1931 the concept of the Pony Club had really taken off and the 14 branches had grown to 59, with a membership of 4,442. During this year, the first Pony Club Camp was held. Growth continued and by 1934 the number of branches totalled 103 with a membership of 8,350.

The war years saw the temporary suspension of many Pony Club activities. By 1947 the Pony Club was in full swing again with 64 new branches having been formed, and the membership more than double to 17,082/ The number of branches overseas had now increased to 13. The Pony Club was well established and going from strength to strength - supply had created an even greater demand.

This year, 1947, was significant for the horse world since it saw the establishment of the world-acclaimed 'British Horse Society' which was formed from the amalgamation of the 'Institute of the Horse and Pony Club' and the 'National Horse Association of Great Britain'. The 'British Horse Society' took on the role of parent organisation for the Pony Club.

The Pony Club is organised into branches, each organised by a District Commissioner, Secretary and Local Committee - all working on a purely voluntary basis. Each of these branches is financially independent and raises capital from subscriptions, profits from events and interest upon investments.

The D.C. and the committee are responsible for organising a balanced programme of events and rallies that take account of the differing levels of ability and need.

Support is given to the branches by an area representative who acts as a vehicle between the branches and the Central Pony Club Council and works towards the smooth running of the branch. In addition to the help given to branches through the area representatives and through the Council itself, there are a number of specialised committees upon which the branch can call for assistance.

n order to help each member improve, there are a series of proficiency tests; these are D, C, C+, B, H, A, in that ascending order.

These tests will be taken in order, and preferably spaced throughout the member's Pony Club career, 'B' test for those who are 14 years or over - but preferably 15 years of age, and for 'H' test the minimum age is 17 years. Members will be given a list of requirements for the test, and also be given help in working towards them at both mounted and unmounted rallies. Each test is designed to help the member to progress both in riding and horsemastership, and to aid them by giving some measure of their improvement. Once they have attained the test standard, the member is given a felt or plastic disc to wear with their membership badge - the colour denotes the tests passed:-

D - Yellow

C - Green

C+- Pink

B - Red

H - Orange

A - Blue

(Honours) A - Purple

Yet another proficiency award that is now obligatory if the member wishes to take any tests of C standard or above is the B.H.S. Riding and Road Safety Test. This test includes a series of simulated and actual road tests as well as a written test on questions including basic highway code knowledge. The candidates will be examined by two people, one a riding examiner who is also an experienced driver, the other a road safety examiner (Police, Road Safety Officer, or Pony Club Examiner who has attended a Road Safety Course in basic road safety). Successful candidates are given a certificate and badge to show they have attained that standard.

The backbone of the Pony Club has to be the working rally. Here members benefit from teaching by well-qualified people within a group that is commensurate with their ability. The number of rallies may vary from branch to branch, but hopefully the standards will all be similarly high.

Members must attend at least 3 rallies in the year to qualify for entry to Pony Club organised competitions. The Chief Instructor for the branch will organise the instructional programme and ensure that the range of instruction available is suitable to the members who have expressed an intention to attend the rally. Usually rallies will take place at weekends, (although Sunday rallies are generally avoided), evenings during the summer period, and school holidays.

Dress must be suitable for the job that is being undertaken, and although it is neither necessary nor advisable that best riding gear should be worn, it is important that it is clean and neat. Suitable headgear is an absolute must - as is appropriate footwear. Hats bearing the BSI kitemark must be worn at all times when the member is mounted - preferably the BSI No. 4472 which is compulsory in all Pony Club competitions. Footwear should be in the form of jodhpur boots, rubber or leather riding boots or shoes that have smooth sole and a heel and with no further adornments that could catch on the side of a stirrup.

Equally important is that the horse/pony should be suitable and in good condition and that tack is in good repair and suitable to the needs of the rider. Each rally will begin with a tack inspection. Here it is important that the instructors handle what could be potentially tricky situations with tact and understanding. Many youngsters joining the Pony Club may find the first rallies a little daunting - particularly if their experience in the horse field is limited and neither themselves nor their parents have any knowledge of the standards and routines of the Pony Club. However, the object of the Pony

Club is not to reprimand or condemn but to encourage.

The basis of the Pony Club is not strictly speaking competitive although there are organised events at which Pony Club members can pit their skills against each other. It dwells rather in the development of team effort. Inter branch/area competitions are a feature of the Pony Club and a means whereby the development of a corporate spirit and loyalties are developed. The concept that the Pony Club is an elitist organisation is not one that is encouraged, rather that it is a group of people with common aims and similar aspirations to join together in order to increase their skills and awareness in the spheres of riding and horsemastership.

One subject I touched upon earlier was the role of parents in the Pony Club. Since the Pony Club is run by a group of people giving their time and effort on a voluntary basis, then the presumption must be that there may be an occasion or situation where parents can contribute towards the Pony Club. My own involvement began 14 years ago when my eldest daughter was attending her second rally and I was chatting to the branch secretary. I mentioned that I was involved with working with groups of children in both a formal and informal sphere and had some first aid knowledge. By the time I had transported my daughter home, got the pony bedded down and retired to the sitting room with a well-earned drink, the phone was ringing and the D.C. asking if I could possibly spare a week in the summer to take on the role of matron cum first aider at the annual residential camp. Since then I have had 14 years of almost uninterrupted involvement at various Pony Club events - sitting on bleak hillsides with the rain dripping on my score sheets at hunter trials and events; testing my maths to the full when working out scores at one-day events, and feeding 60 hungry youngsters and helpers 3 square meals a day for a week (most daunting since I am very aware of the limitations of my culinary skills!). Of course, not everyone will want to be involved, or, if so involved only on a limited basis. The thing that I have found as a Pony Club parent is the more the merrier is probably a good maxim.

Equestrian Organisations

British Horse Society

Formed in 1947 as a result of the amalgamation of the National Horse Association and Institute of the Horse and Pony Club. In its charter it was laid down that the Society existed to promote the interests of the horse and pony breeding, further the art of riding and encourage horsemastership and the welfare of the horse.

At the time of its foundation there were some 5000 members, but by the time the Society moved from its London headquarters to its present venue at the National Equestrian Centre in Stoneleigh in 1967 membership had risen to some 15000.

When the Society was first formed there was only an Executive Committee and sub committees representing the different interests in riding at that time such as combined training and dressage. In the early 50's there were around six different committees, but by 1978 this had expanded to eighteen. In addition to the General Purposes and Finance Committee these consisted of:-

1.   Dressage Committee

2.   Combined Training Committee

3.   Welfare Committee

4.   Training and Exam Committee

5.   Development and Liaison Committee

6.   Riding Clubs Committee

7.   Combined Driving Committee

8.   L D R Committee

9.   Riding Establishments Act Committee

10. Horse & Pony Breeds Committee

11. The English Committee

12. The Scottish Committee

13. The Welsh Committee

14. The Northern Ireland Committee

15. The International Horse Show Committee

16. Sponsorship Committee

17. The Pony Club Committee - which maintains autonomy.

In addition to representatives from these bodies there were also representatives from the British Show Jumping Association, the Hunters' Improvement Society, the Society of Master Saddlers, the National Master Farriers and Blacksmiths Association, the Thoroughbred Breeders Association and the British Driving Society.

Both the Council and General Purposes Committee had in fact become too large and unwieldy. A move was made in 1978 to redraft the Constitution so that there was a smaller and more stream-lined Council and an Executive Committee which consists of two sub-committees - Finance and Policy. The Society has organised itself into regions which coincide with the regions of the BSJA and Pony Club.

The work of the Society can be said to be divided into two sections the competitive side and the services side. The former deals with dressage, Combined Training and Combined Driving. The latter deals with everything from welfare, examinations, riding schools etc. The competitive side of the Society is obviously the largest money earner and to some extent subsidises the services.

The Society's work on the welfare side is often overlooked. Not only does it inspect Riding Schools and investigates any complaints made about them, it also looks to the general welfare of the horse and pony, looks at Road Safety, bridleways and administers the BHS examinations.

The BHS caters as much for the ordinary horseman as for the expert.

The British Show Jumping Association

The BSJA was formed in 1923 when it became obvious that there was a need to draw up a set of rules that would be understood by competitors, judges and spectators alone. There was an almost immediate improvement in the standards of competition, although it wasn't until after the 2nd World War when we adopted the International rules of the Federation Equestre Internationale that Britain began to make any real impact on the International competition scene. The objectives of the Association are:-

1. To improve the standard of jumping

2. To provide for representation of Great Britain in International Competitions.

3. To prescribe the general standard of height of obstacles for show jumping.

4. To promote and encourage the holding of shows where jumping competitions are held.

5. To make rules for judging of jumping competitions.

6. To arrange the registration of horses and ponies.

9. To record the results and winnings of horses and ponies in show jumping competitions.

Because the majority of the membership of the BSJA are actively involved in a competitive sport their interest is very lively and vital. The BSJA is acknowledged as one of the most effective ruling bodies of show jumping in the world.

The Hunter Improvement and Light Horse Society

Founded well over 100 years ago this Society provides a useful service by ensuring that good stallions are available to the owners of useful part-bred mares who would not ordinarily be able to afford the services of a top notch stallion. Because of a subsidy from the Levy Board the HIS is able to subsidise approved stallions so that only a small fee is payable by the mare's owner.

An annual show is held at Newmarket each March. Premiums are awarded to those stallions the judges feel worthy of them on a regional basis so that the HIS ensures that in each region there is an HIS stallion that can be bought for a reasonable fee.

The National Pony Association

This is the official organisation which controls all the pony world activities in the same way as the BHS controls its various disciplines and the BSJA controls show jumping.

The Society is organised into area branches, each of which organise their own shows and social events for the members in the different regions.

Federation Equestre Internationale

This international organisation, recognised by the abbreviatiion FEI, was founded in 1921 under the Presidency of Baron du Teil.

The purpose of the FEI is:-

1. To be the sole international authority for equestrian sports of dressage, jumping, three-day events, driving and any other forms of sport which the General Assembly may from time to time decide.

2. To promote the organisation of international equestrian competitions throughout the world.

3. To co-ordinate, standardise and publish the rules and to supervise the organisation of international equestrian events, while allowing the National Federations the widest possible freedom in the arrangement of their programmes.

4. To standardise and approve the rules and programmes for International Championship Regional and Olympic Games and to control their technical organisation.

5. To provide the means for discussion and understanding between National Federations and to give them support and encouragement and to strengthen their authority and prestige.

6. To encourage instruction in riding, driving and horsemastership for recreational purposes.

The Riding for the Disabled Association

The Riding for the Disabled Association was first registered in 1960 and developed from an idea in the 1950's to give the opportunity to ride to groups of handicapped people.

The Association is administered from its headquarters at the National Equestrian Centre in Stoneleigh, Warwickshire, but run by volunteer groups throughout the country. Disabled adults and children are encouraged to take an interest in horses and riding in order to widen their horizons and add to their interests in life by developing their interest and skills in horses.

Before a group can become a recognised member of the RDA they have to be recommended by the regional chairman to the headquarters at Stoneleigh. When the application is made the regional chairman has to check on the facilities available and the level of help to ensure they meet the criteria laid down by the RDA. These area:-

a)   A source of horses and ponies that are reliable.

b)   Tack which is safe and sound.

c)   A reasonably confined area in which to ride.

d)   A responsible person who is able to take charge of the ride.

e)   Physio/occupational therapists to deal with those who are physically handicapped.

f)   A group of voluntary helpers.

If the group is approved then it is given provisional membership which lasts for a year, during which time it is monitored. When the group has functioned for a year and been given the final approval it is made a full member. As a full member they will be given the right to vote at RDA general meetings and to apply to the main offices for grants and loans.

Long Distance Riding Association

This Association is responsible for the development and organisation of this particular sport and comes under the broad umbrella of the British Horse Society.

To participate in LDR association events you will need an animal that is 14HH or over and is registered with the British Horse Society. The general concept of the LDR is not to develop a sense of competition in the same way that say show jumping or eventing does, rather to reach the standards that you have realistically set for yourself.

The most famous long distance ride is the Golden Horseshoe over a distance of 75 miles in two days. In this event you can try for either a gold which requires a speed of approximately 8 mph, a silver at approx. 6 mph, or a bronze with the target of approx. 4 mph. This is an extremely gruelling ride over Exmoor with frequent veterinary inspections and marks allowed for conditions en route. In order to enter the Golden Horseshoe you must have successfully completed rides of 40 miles.

The Association of British Riding Schools

The Association of British Riding Schools is the professional body for riding school proprietors and represents the interests of those who use Riding Schools by approving Riding Establishments.

The objectives of the Association of British Riding Schools are:

a) To raise the standard of instruction, horsemastership, welfare of horses and ponies in riding establishments.

b) To deal with any problems of common concern to the proprietors of riding establishments.

c) To act generally as a professional association for proprietors and managers of riding establishments.

The objectives of the ABRS Approval Scheme are:-

a) To provide members of the public with information where, in the opinion of the Association, good riding instruction can be obtained and to provide an accurate description of the facilities offered by each approved school.

b) To assist in raising the standards of riding instruction, horsemastership and horsemanship by visiting and assisting riding schools.

c) To provide an advisory service to Riding School proprietors and to give publicity to their business in the Association Handbook.

The Association administers and runs a series of tests in equitation and stable management. These tests are available to people who have regularly ridden at a School or Schools of a member. The equestrian tests number 10 in all and aim to provide a series of tests for the rider in order to provide nationally recognised standards of competance in equitation. There are also 10 Stable Management tests. Their objective is:- to provide a series of tasks for those interested in the care, welfare and management of horses, in order to provide nationally recognised standards of competance in Stable Management.

The ABRS have also developed an examination structure for those interested in a career with horses. There are two courses of qualifications open - the traditional examination structure or the New Vocational Qualifications.

Traditional Examination Structure

The ABRS Preliminary Horse Care and Riding Certificate Levels 1 and 2

The first step in ABRS qualifications. Open to all persons 16 years and over in full-time training or work with horses. Successful candidates are considered employable but need to work under supervision.

The ABRS Assistant Grooms Certificate

Open to candidates with reasonable practical experience in the handling and care of a variety of horses throughout all seasons of the year. Holders of this certificate are considered capable of working on their own but still require some supervision.

The ABRS Grooms Diploma

Intended for those with a wide knowledge of and experience with a wide variety of horses. Candidates must hold the ABRS Grooms certificate, a current First Aid certificate, be in their 18th year and have a minimum of two years full-time occupation training with horses.

National Vocational Qualification

This method is by continual assessment during training.

There are 13 Units of Competance - 12 compulsory 'core' units and Unit 13 - Equitation which is optional.

The units may be gained collectively or individually, and there is no time limit within which the student has to work.

As the units are gained they may be added to the student's record of achievement. The NVQ level 1 Certificate in Horse Care and Management is awarded after all 13 units have been completed and is equivalent to the ABRS Preliminary Horse Care and Riding Certificate Level 2.

This course can be entered either through a Youth Training Package or as a 'working pupil'.

Clubs and Associations

Amateur Riders Association of Great Britain

Premier House, P O Box 27, Loushers Lane, Warrington, Cheshire WA4 6RQ

Tel: 0925 33500 **Fax:** 0925 230992

The aims of the Amateur Riders' Association are to represent the status of Amateur Jockeys within racing in the United Kingdom. The Association is the spokesman for Amateurs on all issues and it is recognised by all sectors of racing.

The Association has approximately 250 members and this is increasing on an annual basis. The members have a presiding President, Gay Kindersley; Secretary, John Greenall and an elected committee.

Animal Health Trust

PO BOX 5, Newmarket, Suffolk CB8 7DW

Tel: 0638 661111

Arab Horse Society

Windsor House, Lye Green, Ramsbury, Marlborough, Wiltshire SN8 2LP

Tel: 0672 20782 **Fax:** 0672 20880

The Arab Horse Society maintains Stud Books and Registers for Pure bred, Anglo and Part Bred Arab horses (nearly 2000 were registered in 1990), and encourages the use of Arab blood in light horse and pony breeding. he Society, and related organisations, hold hundreds of events annually for its 4000 members, including the Annual Summer Show, Malvern (25-27 July 1991), and twenty race meetings including Kempton Park Internationals on 10th August and 28th September 1991. The range of activities demonstrates the famous versatility of Arab blood. Membership includes free admission to two annua breed shows, free racemeeting ticket, two magazines and four Newsletters annually.

Arabian Horse Breeders Club

The Mount Hill Stud, The Fringes, Roixies Lane, Wendron, Helston, Cornwall TR13 0PS

Tel: 03265 61128

Association of Show and Agricultural Organisations

The Showgound, Winthorpe, Newark, Nottinghamshire NG24 2NY

Tel: 0636 702627 **Fax:** 0636 610642

Blue Cross Horse Protection Scheme

Blue Cross Field Centre, Shilton Road, Burford, Oxon OX8 4PF

Tel: 0993 822651

The purpose of the modern Horse Protection Scheme remains the same as in the Balkan War days: to alleviate the suffering of horses, ponies and donkeys in a practical way. Horses are accepted under the scheme as gifts from owners, who can no longer afford to care for their animals, but wish to ensure a secure and happy future for them. Such horses remain the Society's property for life, but may be loaned under agreement to knowledgeable horse lovers, who offer good homes which are regularly inspected. The Blue Cross prefers that horses should lead useful, working lives but some pensioned horses do stay at Blue Cross rest fields. Blue Cross horses attend shows and sporting events in many parts of this country.

British Appaloosa Society

c/o 2 Frederick Street, Rugby, Warwickshire CV21 2EN

Tel: 0788 860535

British Driving Society

27, Dugard Place, Barford, Warwickshire CV35 8DX

Tel: 0926 624420

Secretary: Mrs Jennifer Dillon

The British Driving Society aims to encourage and assist those interested in the Driving of horses and ponies.

British Equine Veterinary Associaton

Hartham Park, Corsham, Wiltshire SN13 0QB

Tel: 0249 715723

The British Equine Veterinary Association promotes the cultural, scientific and professional activities of veterinary surgeons and others interested in equine practice, teaching and research.

British Horse Society

The British Equestrian Centre, Stoneleigh, Kenilworth, Warwickshire CV8 2LR

Tel: 0203 696697 **Fax:** 0203 692351

The British Horse Society is the national governing body for riders, playing an active role in welfare, riding and road safety, access and rights of way, training and careers. It is also the governing body for five equestrian disciplines - dressage, horse driving trials, horse trials, endurance riding and vaulting,which are entirely self supporting. The more members, the more influence the Society (which is a registered charity), will have in working for the horse. Members' benefits include third party (legal) liability insurance up to £2,000,000 and personal accident insurance for your equestrian activities, a Members' Yearbook plus regular issues of the BHS Magazine "Horseshoe", special facilities at major functions, and money saving discounts.

British Leathergoods Manufacturers Association

10 Vyse Street, Birmingham B18 6LT

Tel: 021 236 2657 **Fax:** 021 236 3921

British Quarter Horse Association

4th St, NAC, Stoneleigh, Kenilworth, Warwickshire CV8 2LG

Tel: 0203 696549 **Fax:** 0203 696729

The British Quarter Horse Association runs a stud book to promote the breeding of pure partbred Quarter Horses in the British Isles.

A sub-committee organises race meetings. The association hods a Breed Show and several shows affiliate and hold classes for Quarter Horses. Clinics and demonstrations are also organised.

British Sporting Art Trust

BSAT Gallery, 99 High Street, Newmarket, Suffolk CB8 8JL

Tel: 0491 571294

The aim of the Trust is to promote interest in British Sporting Art and its permanent public exhibition.

British Spotted Pony Society

Weston Manor, Corscombe, Dorset DT2 0PB

Chairman/General Secretary: Mrs E C M Williamson

Tel: 0935 891466

The aims of the British Spotted Pony Society are to promote the breeding and use of the British Spotted Pony.

The socity publishes the stud book, keeps all breed records and holds a breed show each year. These ponies are NOY miniature Apaloosas, being of true pony type, limited to 14.2 and under and have been bred in Britain for many years. No stock has been imported from the USA.

The ponies have and adequate bone and substance, are hardy and active with real pony character of small riding or cob type, up to and including 14.2". These ponies should NOT be described as 'Miniature Horses'. The small type has been bred from pony stock.

British Veterinary Association

7, Mansfield Street, London W1M 0AT

Tel: 071 636 6541 **Fax:** 071 436 2970

Chief Executive: James Baird

The British Veterinary Association is the professional association representing veterinary surgeons. It aims to serve the interests of animal health, science, welfare and good veterinary practice and, of course, thos eof veterinary surgeons and their clients. The association has a number of specialist divisions covering pets, horses, farm animals and exotic species. The may be contacted through the BVA.

Coaching Club

8 Parthenia Road, London SW6 4BD

Tel: 071 384 1165

Country Landowners Association

16, Belgrave Square, London
SW1X 8PQ

Tel: 071 235 0511 **Fax:** 071 235 4969

Contact: Mrs Tamara Strapp

The CLA offers a free legal, tax and economics advisory service to its members. The policies it pursues promote a strong, thriving rural economy for the long-term benefit of the countryside and the community. The CLA lobbies in the Uk and Europe on a variety of issues from access to tenancy reform.

Dales Pony Society

196 Springvale Road, Walkley, Sheffield

S6 3NU

Tel: 0742 683992

The Dales Pony Society exists for the registration of Pure Bred Dales ponies, and the maintenance and publishing of the Dales Pony Stud book. The Society runs three breed shows annually, and is concerned with the sales and general welfare of the Dales pony.

The Donkey Sanctuary

Sidmouth, Devon EX10 0NU

Tel: 0395 578222 **Fax:** 0395 579266

The Donkey Sanctuary is a charity to protect donkeys and mules in the United Kingdom. Nearly 5,000 donkeys have been taken into care; many from a life of hardship and they are given care and protection for the rest of their lives. Welfare officers cover the whole country, following up any complaint of cruelty or neglect and protect the rights of donkeys. Visitors are welcome at the sanctuary.

Exmoor Pony Society

Glen Fern, Waddicombe, Dulverton, Somerset TA22 9RY

Tel: 03984 490

Exmoor Ponies are a "Rare Breed". The Society, formed in 1921, exists to encourage the breeding of pure bred Exmoor Ponies, to publish a stud book, institute an annual show, examine and approve all pony stallions and examine and approve all foals eligible for registrations.

English Connemara Pony Society

2, The Leys, Salford, Chipping Norton OX7 5FD

Tel: 0608 643309

Secretary: Mrs M V Newman

The English Connemara Pony Society was founded in 1947, starting its own stud book in 1978. The official magazine of the society is the Connemara Chronicle which is published annually.

The society holds two shows a year, the Breed In-Hand Show in July and the Ridden Show in August and operates a Performance Award scheme which runs throughout the year.

Highland Pony Society

Beechwood, Elie, Fife KY9 1DH

Tel: 0333 330 696

Horses and Ponies Protection Association

Happa House, 64 Station Road, Padiham, Nr Burnley, Lancashire BB12 8EF

Tel: 0282 79138

The association supervises the care of some 1000 animals. Its three rescue centres, Capel House, Enfield, Middlesex; Gregory Farm at Brockweir in Gwent; and Shores Hey, Burnley, Lancashire, strive to restore the health of formerly ill treated horses, ponies and donkeys.Throughout the year, many horses fall victim to neglect. Horses cost time, money and responsibility. Where they have been let down by ignorant and often callous owners, HAPPA exists to give them a warm stable, plenty of food and the chance to make a fresh start. Furthermore HAPPA educates the offenders and brings the guilty to justice. Our loan scheme has placed more than 600 animals in caring, monitored homes. HAPPA relies solely upon voluntary aid.

Lusitano Breed Society of Great Britain

Foxcroft, Bulstrode Lane, Felden, Hemel Hempstead, Hertfordshire HP3 0BP

Tel: 0442 250806

The Lusitano, also known as the Iberian or until the 17th Century as the Spanish horse, is the oldest saddle horse in Europe, and one of the founders of many of the modern breeds we know today, including the Thoroughbred. Lusitanos are hot blood horses, with a superb temperament, kind, willing and very intelligent, varying in height from 15.2 - 16.3 h.h. and are of any true colour, including bay, black, dun, chesnut and grey. With their temperament and natural athleticism they are ideal for High School work, hunting, hacking, long distance riding, show jumping and driving, or simply as a pleasure horse. In breeding they produce an ideal cross when put to suitable English mares, particularly those posessing Iberian genes.

National Stallion Association

96 High Street, Edenbridge, Kent TN8 5AR

Tel: 0732 866277

New Forest Pony Breeding and Cattle Society

Beacon Cottage, Burley, Ringwood, Hants BH24 4EW

Tel: 04253 2272

Hon Sec: Miss D Macnair

Point-to-Point Owners Association

Crispins, 91A Ellis Road, Crowthorne, Berkshire RG11 6PN

Tel: 0344 778438

The Fishing Handbook

Britain's most comprehensive guide to fishing, angling suppliers and fishing locations in the UK.

Packed with information and advice on how to fish, its listings of tackle shops and suppliers have been thoroughly researched to ensure up to date accuracy. This is an indispensable companion for all fishing enthusiasts as well as an invaluable reference book for everybody involved in the trade itself.
It covers all forms of fishing – game, course and sea – with advice on the background of the sport, plus information and listings which are of equal value to both the novice and the experienced angler.

THE FISHING HANDBOOK is edited by James Marchington, himself an experienced angler and journalist who has written for both The Field and Shooting Times as well as having contributed valuable guides to shotgun and airgun shooting.

Published by Burlington Publishing, THE FISHING HANDBOOK forms a companion to the Riding and Shooting Handbooks which together provide a complete guide to the world of country sports in the UK.

Available from Booksellers and Newsagents or direct from Burlington Publishing Co. Ltd.
10 Sheet Street, Windsor, Berkshire SL4 1BG

The Open Spaces Society

25A Bell Street, Henley-on-Thames, Oxfordshire RG9 2BA

Tel: 0491 573535

The Open Spaces Society, (formerly the Commons, Open Spaces and Footpaths Preservation Society) campaigns to create and conserve common land, village greens, open spaces and rights of public access, in town and country, in England and Wales. Founded in 1865, it is Britain's oldest National conservation body.

Permit Trainers Association

Tel: 028 5720 304 **Fax:** 028 5720 614

The Permit Trainers Association is the representative body for permit holders. It has a seat on both the General and Executive Councils of H.A.C and liaises closely with the National Trainers Federation over matters concerning all Trainers and Permit holders.

Pony Club

The British Equestrian Centre, Stoneleigh, Kenilworth, Warwickshire CV8 2LR

Tel: 0203 696697 **Fax:** 0203 692351

The objects of the BEC are to encourage young people to ride and to learn to enjoy all kinds of sport connected with horses and riding, to provide instruction in riding and horse mastership and to instil in members the proper care of their animals, and to promote the highest ideals of sportsmanship, citizenship and loyalty, thereby cultivating strength of character and self-discipline.

Pony Trekking & Riding Society of Wales

Pencelli-fach, Pontsticill, Merthyr Tydfil, Mid Glamorgan CF48 2TY

Tel: 0685 722 169

Racecourse Association Ltd

Winkfield Road, Ascot, Berkshire SL5 7HX

Tel: 0344 25912 **Fax:** 0344 27233

Racehorse Transporters Association

21 Lisburn Road, Newmarket, Suffolk CB8 8HS

Tel: 0638 663155

Riding for the Disabled Association

Avenue R, National Agricultural Centre, Stoneleigh, Kenilworth, Warwickshire CV8 2LY

Tel: 0203 696510 **Fax:** 0203 696532

We currently provide the opportunity for riding to over 25,000 children and adults of all disabilities at our 700 Member Groups throughout the United Kingdom. Funds are always needed to meet the growing demands of this very active charity in providing facilities, horses and saddlery. Supported by over 13,500 volunteers without whom the charity could not work, we have grown to our present size in 22 years. Many more disabled people would like the opportunity to ride with us. Help us to help them do so.

Shire Horse Society

East of England Showground, Peterborough, Cambridgeshire
PE2 0XE

Tel: 0733 390696 **Fax:** 0733 390720

The Shire Horse Society has been concerned with the welfare of heavy horses since its inception in 1878. Its reason for existence is to improve the breed; to eliminate as far as possible hereditary defects which are not only distressing for the animal but render it unfit for work; and to encourage good horsemanship. The Society's National Shire Horse Show takes place on the third Saturday in March each year at the East of England Showground, Peterborough. New members and supporters are always welcome and further information may be obtained by writing to the Sectretary.

Side Saddle Association

Highbury House, 19 High Street, Welford, Northampton NN6 7HT

Tel: 0858 575300 **Fax:** 0858 575051

Hon Sec: Mrs R N James

The side saddle association was formed in 1974 with the aim of reviving the art of riding side saddle and encouraging more riders to take it up.

England, Scotland and Wales are organised into 14 areas, each with its own Committee which organises shows, instructional courses, Grade Tests and social events. Each area committee is represented on the Association's Council by its elected Chairman.

Reciprocal links are also established with overseas side saddle groups in Australia, Canada, Eire, Japan, New Zealand and the USA.

Society for the Welfare of Horses and Ponies

Folly Cottage, Whitebrook, Monmouth, Gwent NP5 4TU

Tel: 0600 860482

Society of Equestrian Artists

4 Woolgars Farm, Blakes Lane, West Horsley, Leatherhead, Surrey KT24 6EA

Tel: 0483 222992

The Society is a registered charity and aims to present a wide cross- section of the gest in contemporary equine art. A major part of its activities is to hold an annual London Exhibition which includes Members' work. No style or medium is excluded, the sole criterion for exhibition being artistic and technical merit. Three dimensional work plays a notable part alongside drawings and paintings, the whole aimed to interest and stimulate the public into a greater appreciation of equine art. Commissions can be arranged from a vast selection of the top equestrian artists.

St John Ambulance

1 Grosvenor Crescent, London SW1X

Tel: 071 235 5231 **Fax:** 071 235 0796

For over 100 years St John Ambulance Brigade have been administering and teaching first aid.

Today, St John Ambulance is completely staffed by over 60,000 voluntary members who give over 4 million hours each year to provide first aid cover at every event from garden fetes, point-to-points, equestrian events to the London Marathon.

St John Ambulance has long been known for the excellent first aid and ambulance facilities they provide at racecourses throughout the United Kingdom. They have been commended for the dedication shown in dealing with casualties suffering from scratches and broken bones to paralysis - on occasions risking their own lives for the safety of others.

Worshipful Company of Coachmakers and Coach Harness Makers

149, Banstead Road, Ewell, Epson, Surrey KT17 3HL

Tel: 081 393 5394

Clerk: Major W H Wharfe RM

The World Equestrian Games

The first World Equestrian Games took place in Stockholm from July 24th to August 5th 1990. For the horse loving population of the world this provided a feast of equestrian entertainment. The disciplines covered in the Games were Dressage, Show Jumping, Three-Day Event, Endurance Riding, Vaulting and Carriage Driving.

The scale of the whole operation was tremendous and attracted both competitors and spectators from all over the world to what is known as the 'Venice of the North'. The teams for the different disciplines were housed throughout the city where there were independent stables and exercise areas for dressage, show jumping, three day eventing, driving and vaulting. Security at each stable compound was extremely strict.

It was an unfortunate event that only days before the Games were due to start the sport's seamier side was pushed into the limelight. The German Animal Protection Association accused West German show jumping star, Paul Schockemohle of cruelty for 'rapping' - raising a pole to hit the horse's legs as it is jumping in order to encourage it to jump higher and using devices that would cause pain in order to encourage obedience and better performance.

The sport's main German sponsors demanded a guarantee that rapping, de-nerving and doping cease at once or they would withdraw support. The FEI, under the presidency of the Princess Royal, Princess Anne, announced the setting up of an independent inquiry.

Endurance Riding

The British Endurance team won the only gold medal at the Games. The ride was completed in a total riding time, for the six riders and horses, of 35 hours 54 minutes and 31 seconds. Jane Donovan, on her horse Ibriz, won an individual silver medal. Jane was not included in the team as Ibriz had been injured after having been cast in his box and, although declared fit by the vets, was thought could become unsound if knocked.

All horses were required to carry a minimum weight of 75 kgs. Throughout the competition each horse had to pass through vetgates - the first being at 25 miles. Having passed the vet inspection the horses were held at the stop for 30 minutes before being allowed to continue. At any gate, whatever the allotted hold time, an advantage could be gained for horses and riders taking the least amount of time to present to the vets.

The British riders, who finished five hours ahead of the Belgian silver medalists, were a prime example of dedicated riders who had achieved fitness - both for themselves and their horses and a team effort at just the right time to achieve both success and worldwide acclaim.

Show Jumping

Britain acquitted herself very well in the show jumping event, winning both the team silver and the individual silver medals.

The course, built by Olaf Petersen, was impressive and also extremely photographic. The theme for the colourful and extremely imaginative set of fences featured scenes of the country. The course, although large was inviting, although horses of less calibre would have found it extremely difficult.

The arena was covered with fibresand, which, although requiring a great deal of preparation and care to work to peak condition, was impervious to extremes of weather. This consistency of 'going' took away that particular imponderable from the competition. Although the cost of this type of surface would be prohibitive for any but the super-wealthy because of the cost of maintenance, it would be hardly surprising if this surface were not adopted for other major equestrian events.

France dominated the show jumping at the World Equestrian Games winning the team gold, and both the individual gold and bronze medals.

Dressage

The British dressage team for Stockholm consisted of Jennie Lerriston-Clark on Dutch Gold, Diana Mason on Prince Consort, Auni Macdonald-Hall on Floriana and, the youngest member, Carl Hester on the 14 year old Rubelit von Unkenruf.

The German team, as had been expected, dominated the dressage event, taking both team and individual gold medals. Jennie Lorriston-Clarke and Dutch Gold obtained their highest marks ever in the Grand Prix. She obtained a score of 1323, 30 marks above her previous highest score achieved at the Seoul Olympics.

The British team have moved up in the world dressage table, finishing 5th out of 15.

For many the high spot of the dressage competition was the magical sight of Nicole Uphott on the superlative Rembrandt dance their way through the test.

Three-Day Event

The Three-day event at Stockholm proved to be a true test of the event horse, not just an event that was dominated by the dressage competition. The cross-country element was a severe test where there was little chance to settle the horse into a rhythm and innumerable changes in both direction and terrain. There were many fears that a course that demanding would cause an undue amount of injuries to the horses, although, in fact, out of the 84 horses entering this phase only one broke down. Out of these 84, 66 completed the course - the rest either not starting, retiring or being eliminated, 24 went clear and 3 of those were within the time. Going into the cross-country phase only 10 months separated the first 24 horses, with the USA in the lead as a team, followed by Great Britain, Germany, France and New Zealand - in that order.

The British team were lying second overall after the dressage. The cross-country was held over a difficult course in the severe heat of 35°C by midday. There were misfortunes with the first three members of the team to go, two having a stop and one a fall. The day, however, was saved by Lan Stark on Murphy himself. Lan and Murphy 'performed' a clear round that had the watchers alternating between holding their breath and cheering wildly. Murphy bounded around the course at tremendous speed with the exuberance for which he is noted taking, what appeared to be, wild chances but coming through - may be with the luck of the Irish. Lan and Murphy's heroic round left the British team lying in second place and Lan in Individual fourth. The show jumping

took place on the final day of this discipline amid great excitement with Lan Stark and Murphy clinching the team silver and individual silver. However, Lan's tremendous success and exuberant riding could in no way over-shadow the achievement of Blyth Tait and Messiah, individual gold medalist and members of the winning gold medal team.

Vaulting

For the first time Britain was able to produce a team for the World Vaulting Championship in Stockholm. Some six months prior to the month in which the Games were due to take place Britain did not have a team, indeed it could not be said that Britain has taken to this discipline as have many of the countries of Europe.

Vaulting in Britain has been done in a small way under the auspices of the British Vaulting Association. When one considers the limited number of competitors to choose from it is very creditable that a team was formed, especially when you consider that Germany has some 40,000 vaulters to choose from.

The British team should feel proud of their achievements and, although they finished last it was only by 0.057th of a mark. Not a bad effort for these British pioneers!

World Equestrian Games: Results

Endurance

Team

1. Great Britain
2. Belgium
3. Spain

Individual

1. Becky Hart on R O Grand Sultan US
2. Jane Donovan on Ibriz GB
3. June Petersen on Abbeline Lionel AUS

Show Jumping

Team

1. France	18.88 pts
2. West Germany	28.56 pts
3. Great Britain	29.91 pts

Individual

1. Eric Navet on Malessan Quito de Baussy Fra
2. John Whitaker on Henderson Milton GB
3. Hubert Bourdy on Morgat Fra

Dressage

Team

1. West Germany	4.389 pts
2. Soviet Union	4.124 pts
3. Switzerland	4.091 pts

Individual

1. Nicole Uphoff on Rembrandt FRG
2. Kyra Kyrklund on Matador FIN
3. Monica Theodorescu on Ganimedes FRG

Three Day Event
Team

1. New Zealand 205.9 pts
2. Great Britain 246.65 pts
3. West Germany 259.85 pts

Individual

1. Blyth Tait on Messiah NZ
2. Ian Stark on Murphy Himself GB
3. Bruce Davidson on Pirate Lion USA

Vaulting
Team

1. Switzerland2. West Germany
3. United States

Individual
Men

1. Michael Lehner FRG
2. Christopher Lensing FRG
3. Dietmar Otto FRG

Women

1. Silke Bernhard FRG
2. Silke Michelberger FRG
3. Ute Schonlan FRG

Carriage Driving

	Team	Individual	
1.	Holland	Ad Aaarts (HOL)	131.2 pts
2.	Sweden	Thomas Eriksson (SWE)	131.4 pts
3.	Hungary	Josef Bozsik (HUN)	131.8 pts

Medal Table

Country	G	S	B	Total
West Germany	4	4	4	12
Great Britain	1	4	1	6
France	2	0	1	3
United States	1	0	2	3
Holland	2	0	0	2
New Zealand	2	0	0	2
Switzerland	1	0	1	2
Sweden	0	2	0	2
Hungary	0	0	2	2
Belgium	0	1	0	1
Finland	0	1	0	1
Soviet Union	0	1	0	1
Australia	0	0	1	1
Spain	0	0	1	1

Olympic Games

Show Jumping

	Team	Rider	Horse
	Team	**Individual**	
		Rider	**Horse**
1900		Aime Haegeman(Bel)	BentonII
1912	Sweden	Jean Cariou (Fra)	Mignon
1920	Sweden	Tommaso Lequio (Ita)	Trebecco
1924	Sweden	Alphonse Gemuseus (Swi)	Lucette
1928	Spain	Frantisek Ventura (Cze)	Eliot
1932	No medals awarded	Takeichi Nishi (Jap)	Uranus
1936	Germany	Kurt Hasse (Ger)	Tora
1948	Mexico	Humberto Cortes (Mex)	Arete
1952	Britain	Pierre d'Oriola (Fra)	Ali Baba
1956	West Germany	Hans-Gunter Winkler (Ger)	Halla
1960	West Germany	Raimondo d'Inzeo (Ita)	Posillipo
1964	West Germany	Pierre d'Oriola (Fra)	Lutteur B
1968	Canada	William Steinkraus (US)	Snowbound
1972	West Germany	Graziano Mancinelli (Ita)	Ambassador
1976	France	Alwin Schockenmohle (FRG)	Warwick Rex
1980	USSR	Jan Kowalczyk (Pol)	Artemor
1984	United States	Joe Fargis (US)	Touch of Class
1988	West Germany	Pierra Durand (Fra)	Jappeloup

Dressage

Team

1912			
1920			
1924			
1928	Germany		
1932	France		
1936	Germany		
1948	France		
1952	Sweden		
1956	Sweden		
1960	Not held		
1964	West Germany		
1968	West Germany		
1972	USSR		
1976	West Germany		
1980	USSR		
1984	West Germany		
1988	West Germany		

Individual

Rider	Horse
Carl Bonde (Swe)	Emperor
Janne Lundblad (Swe)	Uno
Ernst Linder (Swe)	Piccolomini
Carl von Langen (Ger)	Draufganger
Xavier Lesage (Fra)	Taine
Heinz Pollay (Ger)	Kronos
Hans Moser (Swi)	Hummer
Henri St Cyr (Swe)	Master Rufus
Henri St Cyr (Swe)	Juli
Sergey Filatov (SSR)	Absent
Henri Chammartin (Swi)	Woermann
Ivan Kizimov (USSR)	Ichor
Liselott Linsenhoff (FRG)	Piaff
Christine Stuckelberger (Swi)	Granat
Elisabeth Theurer (Aut)	Mon Chérie
Reiner Klimke (FRG)	Ahlerich
Nicole Uphoff (FRG	Rembrandt

Three-Day Event

Team

1912	Sweden
1920	Sweden
1924	Holland
1928	Holland
1932	United States
1936	Germany
1948	United States
1952	Sweden
1956	Britain
1960	Australia
1964	Italy
1968	Britain
1972	Britain
1976	United States
1980	USSR
1984	United States
1988	West Germany

Individual

Rider	Horse
Axel Nordlander (Swe)	Lady Artist
Helmer Morner (Swe)	Germania
Adolph van der Voort van Zijp (Hol)	Silver Piece
Charles P de Mortagnes (Hol)	Marcroix
Charles P de Mortagnes (Hol)	Marcroix
Ludwig Stubbendorff (Ger)	Nurmi
Bernard Chevalier (Fra)	Aiglonne
Hans von Blixen-Finecke (Swe)	Jubal
Petrus Kastenman (Swe)	Iluster
Lawrence Morgan (US)	Salad Days
Mauro Checcoli (Ita)	Surbean
Jean-Jacques Guyon (Fra)	Pitou
Richard Maede (GB)	Laurieston
Edmund Coffin (US)	Bally-Cor
Frederico Roman (Ita	Rossinan
Mark Todd (NZ)	Charisma
Mark Todd (NZ)	Charisma

World Championships

Show Jumping

Individual | | Women | |
	Rider	Horse	Rider	Horse
1953	Francisco Guyoago (Spa)	Quorum		
1954	Hans- Günter Winkler (FRG)	Halla		
1955	Hans-Gunter Winkler (FRG)	Halla		
1956	Raimondo d'Inzeo (Ita)	Merano		
1960	Raimondo d'Inzeo (Ita)	Gowran Girl		
1966	Pierre d'Oriola (Fra)	Pomone	Marion Coakes (GB)	Stroller
1970	David Broome (GB)	Beethoven	Janou Lefebvre (Fra)	Rocket
1974	Hartwig Steenken (FRG)	Simona	Janou Tissot (Fra)	Rocket
1978	Gerd Wiltfang (FRG)	Roman		
1982	Norbert Koof (FRG)	Fire II		
1986	Gail Greenbough (Can)	Mr T		
1990	Eric Navet (Fra)	Malesan Quito de Baussy		

Team

1978	Britain
1982	France
1986	United States
1990	France

Three-Day Event

Individual

	Rider	Horse
1966	Carlos Moratorio (Arg)	Chalon
1970	Mary Gordon-Watson (GB)	Cornishman V
1974	Bruce Davidson (US)	Irish Cap
1978	Bruce Davidson (US)	Might Tango
1982	Lucinda Green (GB)	Regal Realm
1986	Virginia Leng (GB)	Priceless
1990	Blyth Tait (NZ)	Messiah

Dressage

Team

1966	West Germany
1970	USSR
1974	West Germany
1978	West Germany
1986	West Germany
1990	West Germany

Individual

Rider	Horse
Josef Neckermann (FRG)	Mariano
Yelena Petrouchkova (USSR)	Pepel
Reiner Klimke (FRG)	Mehmed
Christine Stuckelberger (Swi)	Granat
Anne Grethe Jensen (Den)	Marzog
Nicole Uphoff (FRG)	Rembrandt

Endurance

Team

1986	Great Britain
1988	United States
1990	Great Britain

Individual

Rider	Horse
Cassandra Schuler (US)	Skikos Omar
Becky Hart (US)	RO Grand Sultan
Becky Hart (US)	RO Grand Sultan

Vaulting

Team

1986	West Germany
1988	West Germany
1990	Switzerland

Men's Individual

1986	Dietmar Ott (FRG)
1988	Christopheer Pensing (FRG)
1990	Michael Lehner (FRG)

Women's Individual

Silke Bernhard (FRG)
Silke Bernhard (FRG)
Silke Bernhard (FRG)

Carriage Driving

Individual

		Team
1972	Auguste Dubey (Swi)	Great Britain
1974	Sandor Fulop (Hun)	Great Britain
1976	Imre Abonyi (Hun)	Hungary
1978	Gyorgy Bardos (Hun)	Hungary
1980	Gyorgy Bardos (Hun)	Great Britain
1982	Tjeerd Velstra (Hol)	Holland
1984	Laszlo Juhasz (Hun)	Hungary
1988	Jisbrand Chardon (Hol)	Holland
1990	Ad Aarts (Hol)	Holland

European Championships

Show Jumping

Team

1975	West Germany
1977	Holland
1979	Britain
1981	West Germany
1983	Switzerland
1985	Britain
1987	Britain
1989	Britain

Individual

	Rider	Horse	Women Rider	Horse
1957	Hans Gunter Winkler (FRG)	Sonnenglanz	Pat Smythe (GB)	Flanagan
1958	Fritz Tiedemann (FRG)	Meteor	Giulia Serventi (Ita)	Doly
1959	Piero d'Inzeso (Ita)	Uruguay	Ann Townsend (GB)	Bandit
1960	Susan Cohen (GB)	Clare Castle		
1961	David Broome (GB)	Sunsalve	Pat Smythe (GB)	Flanagan
1962	David Barker (GB)	Mister Softee	Pat Smythe (GB)	Flanagan
1963	Graziano Mancinelli (Ita)	Rockette	Pat Smythe (GB)	Flanagan
1965	Hermann Schridde (FRG)	Dozent		
1966	Nelson Pessoa (Bra)	Gran Geste	Janou Lefebvre (Fra)	Kenavo
1967	David Broome (GB)	Mister Softee	Kathy Kusner (US)	Untouchable
1968	Anneli Drummond-Hay (GF)	Merely-a-Monarch		
1969	David Broome (GB)	Mister Softee	Iris Kellett (Ire)	Morning Light
1971	Hartwig Steenken (FRG)	Simona	Ann Moore (GB)	Psalm
1973	Paddy McMahon (GB)	Penwood Forge Mill	Ann Moore (GB)	Psalm
1975	Alwin Schockenmohle (FRG)	Warwick		
1977	Johan Heins (Hol)	Seven Valleys		
1979	Gerhard Wiltfang (FRG)	Roman		
1981	Paul Schockenmohle (FRG)	Deister		
1983	Paul Schockenmohle (FRG)	Deister		
1985	Paul Schockenmohle (FRG)	Deister		
1987	Pierre Durand (Fra)	Jappeloup		
1989	John Whitaker (GH)	Next Milton		

Dressage

Team		Individual	
		Rider	**Horse**
1963	Britain	Henri Chammartin (Swi)	WSolfdietrich
1965	West Germany	Henri Chammartin (Swi)	Wolfdietrich
1967	West Germany	Reiner Klimke (FRG)	Dux
1969	West Germany	Liselott Linsenhoff (FRG)	Piaff
1971	West Germany	Liselott Linsenhoff (FRG)	Piaff
1973	West Germany	Reiner Klimke (FRG)	Mehmed
1975	West Germany	Christine Stuckelberger (Swi)	Granat
1977	West Germany	Christine Stuckelberger (Swi)	Granat
1979	West Germany	Elisabeth Theurer (Aut)	Mon Cherie
1981	West Germany	Uwe Schulten-Baumer (FRG)	Madras
1985	West Germany	Anne Grethe Jensen (Den)	Marzog
1985	West Germany	Reiner Klimke (FRG)	Ahlerich
1987	West Germany	Margit Otto-Crepin (Fra)	Corlandus
1989	West Germany	Nicole Uphoff (FRG)	Rembrandt

Three-Day Event

Team		Individual	
		Rider	**Horse**
1953	Britain	Lawrence Rook (GB)	Starlight
1954	Britain	Albert Hill (GB)	Crispin
1955	Britain	Frank Weldon (GB)	Kilbarry
1957	Britain	Sheila Willcox	High and Mighty
1959	West Germany	Hans Schwarzenbach (Swi)	Burn Trout
1962	USSR	James Templar (GB)	M'Lord Connolly
1965	USSR	Marian Babirecki (Pol)	Volt
1967	Britain	Eddie Boylan (Ire)	Durlas Eile
1969	Britain	Mary Gordon-Watson (GB)	Cornishman V
1971	Britain	HRH Princess Anne (GB)	Doublet
1973	West Germany	Aleksandr Yevdokimov (USSR)	Jeger
1975	USSR	Lucinda Prior-Palmer (GB)	Be Fair
1977	Britain	Lucinda Prior-Palmer (GB)	George
1979	Ireland	Nils Haagensen (Den)	Monaco
1981	Britain	Hansueli Schmutz (Swi)	Oran
1983	Sweden	Rachel Bayliss (GB)	Mystic Minstrel
1985	Britain	Virginia Holgate (GB)	Priceless
1987	Britain	VirginiaLeng (nee Holgate)(GB)	Night Cap
1989	Britain	Virginia Leng (GB)	MasterCraftsman

Major Show Jumping Competitions

British Derby
Hickstead

1969	Seamus Hayes (Ire)	Goodbye III
1962	Pat Smythe (GB)	Flanagan
1963	Nelson Pessoa (Bra)	Gran Geste
1964	Seamus Hayes (Ire)	Goodbye III
1965	Nelson Pessoa (Bra)	Gran Geste
1966	David Broome (GB)	Mister Softee
1967	Marion Coakes (GB)	Stroller
1968	Alison Westwood (GB)	The Maverick YII
1969	Anneli Drummond-Hay (GB)	Xantos
1970	Harvey Smith (GB)	Mattie Brown
1971	Harvey Smith (GB)	Mattie Brown
1972	Hendrick Snoek (FRG)	Shirokko
1973	Alison Dawes (Nee Westwood)(GB)	Mr Banbury
1974	Harvey Smith (GB)	Salvador
1975	Paul Darragh (Ire)	Pele
1976	Eddie Macken (Ire)	Boomerang
1977	Eddie Macken (Ire)	Boomerang
1978	Eddie Macken (Ire)	Boomerang
1979	Eddie Macken (Ire)	Boomerang
1980	Michael Whitaker (GB)	Owen Gregory
1981	Harvey Smith (GB)	Sanyo Video
1982	Paul Schockenmohle (FRG)	Deister
1983	John Whitaker (GB)	Ryan's Son
1984	John Ledingham (Ire)	Gabhram
1985	Paul Schockenmohle (FRG)	Lorenzo
1986	Paul Schockenmohle (FRG)	Next Deister
1987	Nick Skelton (GB)	Raffles
1988	Nick Skelton (GB)	Apollo
1989	Nick Skelton (GB)	Burmah Apollo
1990	Joe Turi (GB)	Vital

Volvo World Cup

1979	Hugo Simon (Aut)	Gladstone	1985	Conrad Homefeld (US)	Abdullah
1980	Conrad Homefeld (US)	Balbuco	1986	Leslie Burr-Lenehan (US)	McLain
1981	Mike Matz (US)	Jet Run	1987	Katherine Burdsall (US)	The Natural
1982	Melanie Smith (US)	Calypso	1988	Ian Miller (Can)	Big Ben
1983	Norman Dello Joio (US)	I Love You	1989	Ian Miller (Can)	Big Ben
1984	Mario Deslauriers (Can)	Aramis	1990	John Whitaker (GB)	Henderson Milton

King George V Gold Cup

1981	David Broome (GB)	Mr Ross
1982	Michael Whitaker (GB)	Disney Way
1983	Paul Schockenmohle (FRG)	Deister
1984	Nick skelton (GB)	St James
1985	Malcolm Pyrah (GB)	Towerlands Angelzark
1986	John Whitaker (GB)	Next Ryan's Son
1987	Malcolm Pyrah (GB)	Towerlands Angelzark
1988	Robert Smith (GB)	Brook Street Boysie
1989	Michael Whitaker (GB)	Next Didi
1990	John Whitaker (GB)	Henderson Milton

Queen Elizabeth II Cup

1981	Liz Edgar (GB	Everest Forever
1982	Liz Edgar (GB)	Everest Forever
1983	Jean Germany (GB)	Mandingo
1984	Veronique Whitaker (GB)	Next's Jingo
1985	Sue Pountain (GB)	Ned Kelly
1986	Liz Edgar (GB)	Everest Rapier
1987	Gillian Greenwood	Monsanta
1988	Janet Hunter (GB)	Everest Lisnamarrow
1989	Janet Hunter (GB)	Everest Lisnamarrow
1990	Emman-Jane Mac (GB)	Everest Oyster

Nations Cup

1981	West Germany
1982	West Germany
1983	Britain
1984	West Germany
1985	Great Britain
1986	Great Britain
1987	France
1988	France
1989	Great Britain

Three-Day Event: Badminton Horse Trials (1956 event at Windsor)

1949	John Shedden (GB)	Golden Willow
1950	Tony Collings (GB)	Remus
1951	Hans Schwarzenbach (Swi)	Vae Victus
1952	Mark Darley (Ire)	Emily Little
1953	Lawrence Rook (GB)	Starlight
1954	Margaret Hough (GB)	Bambi
1955	Frank Weldon (GB)	Kilbarry
1956	Frank Weldon (GB)	Kilbarry
1957	Sheila Willcox (GB)	High and Mighty
1958	Sheila Willcox (GB)	High and Mighty
1959	Sheila Waddington (nee Willcox)(GB)	Airs and Graces
1960	Bill Roycroft (Aus)	Our Solo
1961	Lawrence Morgan (Aus)	Salad Days
1962	Anneli Drummond-Hay (GB)	Merely-a-Monarch
1963	Susan Fleet (GB)	Gladiator
1964	James Templer (GB)	M'Lord Connolly
1965	Eddie Boylan (Ire)	Durlas Eile
1966	not held	
1967	Celia Ross-Taylor (GB)	Jonathan
1968	Jane Bullen (GB)	Our Nobby
1969	Richard Walker (GB	Pasha
1970	Richard Maede (GB)	The Poacher
1971	Mark Phillips (GB)	Great Ovation
1972	Mark Phillips (GB)	Great Ovation
1973	Lucinda Prior-Palmer (GB)	Be Fair
1974	Mark Phillips (GB)	Columbus
1974	cancelled after dressage	
1976	Lucinda Prior-Palmer (GB)	Wideawake
1977	Lucinda Prior-Palmer (GB)	George
1978	Jane Holderness-Roddam (nee Bullen)(GB)	Warrior
1979	Lucinda Prior-Palmer (GB)	Killaire
1980	Mark Todd (NZ)	Southern Comfort
1981	Mark Phillips (GB)	Lincoln
1982	Richard Maede (GB)	Speculator III
1983	Lucinda Green (nee Prior-Palmer)(GB)	Regal Realm
1984	Lucinda Green (GB)	Beagle Bay
1985	Virginia Holgate (GB)	Priceless
1986	Ian Stark (GB)	Sir Wattie
1987	cancelled	
1988	Ian Stark (GB)	Sir Wattie
1989	Virginia Leng (GB)	Master Craftsman
1990	Nicola McIrvine (GB)	Middle Road

Burghley Horse Trials

1961	Anneli Drummond-Hay (GB)	Merely-a-Monarch
1962	**European Champianship**	
1963	Harry Freeman-Jackson (Ire)	St Finbar
1964	Richard Maede (GB)	Barberry
1965	Jeremy Beale (GB)	Victoria Bridge
1966	**World Championship**	
1967	Lorna Sutherland (GB)	Popadom
1968	Sheila Willcox (GB)	Fair and Square
1969	Gillian Watson (GB)	Shaitan
1970	Judy Bradwell (GB)	Don Camillo
1971	**European Championship**	
1972	Janet Hodgson (GB)	Larkspur
1973	Mark Phillips (GB)	Maid Marion
1974	**World Championship**	
1975	Aly Pattinson (GB)	Carawich
1976	Jane Holderness-Roddam (GB)	Warrior
1977	Lucinda Prior-Palmer (GB)	George
1978	Lorna Clarke (nee Sutherland)(GB)	Greco
1979	Andrew Hoy (Aus)	Davy
1980	Richard Walker (GB)	John of Gaunt
1981	Lucinda Prior-Palmer (GB)	Beagle Bay
1982	Richard Walker (GB)	Ryan's Cross
1983	Virginia Holgate (GB)	Priceless
1984	Virginia Holgate (GB)	Night Cap
1985	**European Championship**	
1986	Virginia Leng (nee Holgate)(GB)	Murphy Himself
1987	Mark Todd (NZ)	Wilton Fair
1988	Jane Thelwall (GB)	Kings Jester
1989	**European Championship**	
1990	Mark Todd (NZ)	Face the Music

The World of Horsemanship: Useful References and Listings

Stud-breeding Services

Chiltern Connemara Stud
Combe Cottage, Presteigne, Powys, LD8 2LH
Tel: 0544 267026

Fieldguard Ltd
Grove Heath Farm, Ripley, Woking, Surrey, GU23 6ES
Tel: 0483 225224
Fax: 0483 222087

Kebroyd Stud
Delf Field Farm, Kebroyd Lane, Triangle, Halifax, W Yorks, HX3 6HT

Zara Stud & Training Centre
Highleigh Road, Sidlesham, Chichester, Sussex, PO20 7NR
Tel: 0243 641662

Stud Management Equipment

The Wyke Equestrian Services, Shifnal, Shropshire, TF11 9PP
Tel: 0952 462982
Fax: 0952 462981

Bloodstock Agents

Arabian Bloodstock Agency
Water Farm, Raydon, Ipswich Suffolk IP7 5LW
Tel: 0473 310407
Fax: 0473 311206

Beresford Bloodstock Services
Fairview Cottage, Wicks Green, Binfield, Berkshire RG12 5PF
Tel: 0344 860976

Curragh Bloodstock Agency Ltd
Crossways, 23 The Avenue, Newmarket, Suffolk
Tel: 0638 662620

Derek Lucie-Smith
12/13, Henrietta Street, London WC2E 8LH
Tel: 071 836 8833

Rondo Horse Insurance
29 High Street, Newhaven, East Sussex BN9 9PD
Tel: 0273 611555
Fax: 0273 611666

Veterinary Bloodstock Agcy Ltd
Burley Lodge, Hyde End Road, Shinfield, Nr Reading, Berkshire RG2 9EP
Tel: 0734 882553

Western Saddles and Wear

John Skeleton's Western Store
602 High Road, Benfleet, Essex SS7 5RW
Tel: 03745 2769

Newton Horse Ltd
Hotham Hall
Hotham
E Yorkshire YO4 3UN
Tel: 0430 423636

RPM Western Trading
The Avenue Riding Centre, Hanley Road
Malvern
Worcs
Tel: 0684 310783

Zara Stud & Training Centre
Highleigh Road
Sidlesham
Chichester
Sussex PO20 7NR
Tel: 0243 641662

Section 5: A Career with Horses

Chapter 31: Choosing a Career
with Horses   348
Chapter 32: The Fortune Centre 353

Careers with Horses

The world of horses offers a wide diversity of opportunities for those who wish to follow a career with horses.

The increase in the interest in equestrian sports has brought with it a demand for more people to work within the industry. Although many would prefer to be involved with horses at a competitive level in this sport it takes not only skill and ability but also extended training, financial backing and, perhaps most importantly - the opportunity. If the person is determined to work with horses it may be that they wish to work directly, or in an allied field such as saddlery, farmery or in the vetinary services.

Work that is directly with horses can be pretty much unrelenting since horses require attention seven days a week, 52 weeks a year. Anyone even considering full-time work must be physically fit, capable of withstanding even the most inclement weather and totally committed. Add to this the long hours and extremely modest financial remuneration and if the person is still determined to pursue a career in horses then they must be dedicated.

As the interest in the horse industry has increased so has the need for establishments to be run on a sound and efficient business footing. What establishments will be looking for, therefore, are employees who can complement their business and help with its administration not just muck out horses and fetch and carry. It would, therefore, be wise for any youngster considering entering the horse business to complete their education and consider taking one of the horsemastership courses at the growing number of colleges that provide these type of 'courses for horses'.

The British Horse Society is widely recognised as the authoritative body in the field of horse education. The British Horse Society Horse Knowledge and Care Examinations include both riding and horsemastership/stable management. These examinations are undertaken in four stages and will lead ultimately to the British Horse Society Stable Manager's Certificate.

The requirements at the different stages are:

Stage 1

Walk, trot and canter on a quiet horse in an enclosed space safely. Take care of the horse both before and after a ride. Perform simple stable duties under supervision.

Stage 2

Ride a quiet horse at walk, trot and canter outside and in an enclosed space. Walk and trot with stirrups. Jump a horse around a 2 ft high course of 6 - 8 jumps. Show improvement in knowledge of stable management under supervision. Be at a level to prepare a horse for a local show and perform reasonably in clear round jumping or Preliminary dressage test.

Stage 3

Ride a trained horse energetically forward in good form. Be able to assess the way a horse is going and discuss ways in which it could be improved. Ride and assess 2/3 horses on the flat. Jump two horses round show jumps/cross country course of 6 - 8 fences at a height of 3 ft. Show knowledge of horse's conformation, physiology and psychology. Have a sound working and technical knowledge of feeding shoeing, veterinary care, clipping, lungeing, grassland management, work/exercise.

Stage 4

Show that he/she is a competent rider on the flat - assess several horses on the flat up to and including work found in Elementary dressage tests. Ride a horse 'on the bit'. At show jumping/cross

country be able to assess and suggest ways of improving performance. Work a horse at the lunge. Take complete care of a competition horse in all aspects of stable management and horsemanship.

Stable Manager's Certificate

Show that he/she is knowledgeable and experienced in the management of stables in a variety of situations. Undertake all aspects of the business management of an enterprise, including book-keeping, accounting, insurance, staffing and general business management.

The above are basic qualifications in horse related training that can be used in conjunction with other more specific qualifications, e.g. teaching to give a qualification in that field.

Riding Instructor

BHA Assistant Instructor

Preliminary Teaching Test plus BHS Horse Knowledge and Care Certificate Stage 3. This qualifies the holder to give riding instruction at novice level and look after horses under supervision.

BHS Intermediate Instructor

Intermediate Teaching Certificate plus BHS Horse Knowledge and Care Certificate Stage 4 and either Pony Club 'A' test or Riding Club Grade 4 certificate.

This qualifies the holder to teach up to Elementary Dressage and Novice jumping and to hold a responsible position in a stable or riding business.

BHS Instructor

Hold the BHS Instructor's Certificate and the BHS Manager's Certificate. Includes riding up to Medium Dressage level, jumping to Novice Horse Trials and training horses and riders to this level. The BHSI is an experienced rider, trainer and manager and capable of taking charge of all aspects of a riding business.

Fellow of the BHS

Top professional qualification. Fellows have shown their competence in all aspects of riding, training and horsemastership.

Groom

There are various examinations for the person wanting to take up this particular career, some involve on the job training, some day release and some can be done full-time at college. The ABRS have an award tier system leading to the Assistant Groom's Certificate or the Groom's Diploma.

The duties of a groom include:

1. Grooming

2. Mucking out.

3. Watering and feeding.

4. Exercising.

5. Sick nursing.

6. Preparing for travelling (horses).

7. Track clearing.

8. General yard maintenance.

Farriery

The person wishing to take up farriery work must work as an apprentice with a qualified blacksmith prior to taking the RSS (Registered Shoeing Smith) examination. Apprentices are required to attend one of the Company of Worshipful Farriers' recognised training centres for training once a year. Apprentices are sometimes eligible for grants from the Company for books, tools, clothing etc.

Both physical strength and skill in the use of tools and iron are necessary to undertake this course of training. The apprentices will be given detailed instruction on the conformation of the horse and its action in order to perform this job with skill.

Stud Farm Assistant

The groom on a stud farm is expected to have the same basic knowledge and skills that any groom working on any yard would have. It is, therefore, necessary for the person wishing to work as a stud groom to have gained experience in general horse care before specialising.

The work of a more specialised nature includes:

a) Daily care of stallions - including mucking out, exercising, grooming and covering mares.

b) Care of the mares, both before, during and after foaling.

Training can be gained both on the job and at a course run by several colleges throughout the country. The National Pony Society award two qualifications for those employed full-time in stud work: The Stud Assistant's Certificate - for candidates 17 years and over; The Diploma in Pony Mastership and Breeding - for those 21 years and over.

Veterinary Profession

All vetinary surgeons must train first in general animal practice before going into a specialised field.

The vet will usually employ a veterinary assistant; these will have trained as a Registered Animal Nurse Assistant. Training for this can be gained at a training centre approved by the Royal College of Veterinary Surgeons. These centres are sometimes general veterinary practices, sometimes colleges of agriculture, sometimes RSPCA or Blue Cross Centres.

The period of training to become a RANA is two years. Details of the course are available from the Royal College of Veterinary Surgeons. Trainees pay a small fee to enroll, a further fee for the two examinations they sit and a further fee to be placed on the register of RANA's.

One of the perks for the mounted policeman is to represent the force at International event held in this country

The army representatives at the N.E.C. Birmingham.

Saddler

There are two ways of entering into the skilled craft of saddle making: Through the Cordwainers Technical College or through an apprenticeship to a master saddler.

The Cordwainers College is a specialised training college for those engaged in saddle, bridle and horse equipment production. The course is a full academic year and covers all the work - both theoretical and practical - that a rural saddler would be expected to do.

The apprenticeship to a master saddler will be longer than the college course, probably with day release for an appropriate course.

Grants may be available for further training from the Local Education Authority.

Mounted Officers in the Police and Army

Entry into the mounted divisions of both the police force and army are available to suitable officers who have successfully completed their basic training.

Further training is given to those candidates who are considered suitable.

Details of a career in the Police Force are available from your local police station, and for the army from the Army Careers Office.

The Fortune Centre of Riding Therapy

A look at some of the innovative work being carried on at this registered charitable organisation

The Fortune Centre is a registered charity located at Avon Tyrell, Bransgrove, near Christchurch, Dorset. It is a residential Further Education Centre for school leavers with special needs and a Training centre for able-bodied people who, through the training provided at the centre will be in a position to help those with difficulties to benefit. It is a separate Registered Charity from the Riding for the Disabled Association.

The centre, whose motto is 'Hold fast to Reality', is under the patronage of Her Grace the Duchess of Devonshire, with Mrs T D Holderness-Roddam as president and Mrs Jennifer Dixon-Clegg is the director. The Fortune Centre's aims are to:-

Extend the education of slow learning school leavers and those with emotional and behavioural difficulties;

Offer occupational training to young people who have experienced problems bridging the gap between school and the world of work, by a two year 'Further Education through Horsemastership' programme, fostering the development of life and social skills.

Introduce to young people the working concept of training alongside those less able than themselves by a one year foundation course culminating in the British Horse Society Assistant Instructor's Examination. This qualification is a pre-requisite for those wishing to train as Riding Therapists.

Through short courses for allied professionals, promote an increased understanding of the working practice of Riding Therapy.

By a residential in service course, train mature and/or graduate professionals as full-time Riding Therapists.

Provide for the long-term care of those whose disability prevents them entering employment, by supporting an 'Ostler' Home; demonstrating the value of horses in the lines of individuals to whom they offer an unprecedented opportunity for worthwhile occupation.

Offer a riding facility for groups of handicapped children from local schools on a once a week basis.

The students' needs vary - from difficulties with basic literacy and numeracy, to behaviour that makes living or working with others a problem. The two year course is designed to help the young people learn in a horse environment. The curriculum will cover:

Riding and lungeing.

Stable management (including all aspects of horse care)

Gymnastics and vaulting

Voltige

Sports (including swimming and team games)

Banking

Maintenance and Life Skills

Supervised recreation and social skills.

During the course students are given the opportunity to experience various potential work situations and consider future options. The students may not have had very much horse contact before they begin the course and may not be able to ride, but during the compulsory five day assessment course their motivations must appear genuine.

The long term objections of the course are to:-

1. Extend existing knowledge in basic literacy and numeracy,

2. Encourage an enquiring mind,

3. Develop a care for the need of others,

4. Improve self-esteem and foster self-control.

For those able-bodied youngsters embarking upon a course at the Fortune Centre they must meet the following criteria:

1. Be, at a minimum, 16 years old before 1st February in the year in which the course commences.

2. If under 18 years in the year in which the course is to commence applicants must hold a minimum of four GCSE's at Grade A,B or C - one of which must be English Language or Literature.

3. To have successfully attended a five day residential trial period in which they have shown ability to:-

Integrate with their own peer group and the handicapped group they will be learning to teach

Ride to a satisfactory standard to enable them to complete the course without undue stress and strain.

Present themselves in a reasonably efficient manner in an interview situation and express their commitment to their choice of training in a reasonable and convincing manner.

In addition to these extended courses the Centre also runs two day residential training courses. This course is available to anyone in an allied profession - teachers, nurses, social workers, occupational therapists etc.

and PDA workers, regardless of whether they have any experience with horses.

The aim of the course is to familiarise participants with the basic concept of horses as an educational and therapeutic medium. All participants will have the opportunity to take part in mounted instruction and voltige and also to observe a Riding Therapy session in all its aspects. In addition there will be discussion periods where the course members will have the opportunity to examine the concept of therapeutic riding.

In whatever direction your interests lie it would be well worth your while to investigate further the skills and facilities available at the Fortune Centre. If you have a desire to increase your knowledge about therapeutic riding you can be sure of a warm welcome - however, do ring up and make arrangements before visiting this very busy centre.

Tables of Suppliers

Boots	357
Breeches and Jodhpurs	359
Compound Feeds	362
Hats	366
Horse Trailors	367
Jackets	369
Rugs	372
Saddles	375

Boots

Company name	Brand name	Type	Material (upper)	Material (sole)	Colour	Sizes	Rec. Retail Price	Comments
Allen & Caswell Ltd Regent Works, Cornwall Road, Kettering, Northants NN16 8PR Tel: 0536 512804 Fax: 0536 411085	Regent Cotswold	Riding boot	Leather	Leather	Black	3x11		3 calf fittings Quality leather
	Regent Europa	Riding boot	Leather	Resin	Black	3x11		3 calf fittings Two lengths
	Regent junior	Riding Boot Europa	Leather	PVC	Black	3x8		2 calf fittings
	Regent junior steed	Jodhpur boot	Leather	PVC	Black Oxblood	5x2 3x8		Scuff free leather
	Regent steed	Jodhpur boot	Leather	Resin	Black Oxblood	3x8 ladies 6x12 men		Stitched sole. Scuff free leather
	Regent super steed	Jodhpur boot	Leather	Leather	Black Tan	3x8 ladies 6x11 men		Quality all leather boot
	Regent Newbury	Strap jodhpur	Leather	Leather	Black Tan	3x8 ladies 6x11 men		Quality all leather boot
	Regent Chepstow	Strap jodhpur	Leather	Resin	Black Oxblood Navy	3x8 ladies 6x11 men		Stitched sole. Scuff free leather
	Regent junior Chepstow	Strap jodhpur	Leather	PVC	Black Oxblood Navy	3x8		Scuff free leather

Boots (continued)

Company name	Brand name	Type	Material (upper)	Material (sole)	Colour	Sizes	Rec. Retail Price	Comments
Allen & Caswell Ltd (cont.)	Regent Paddock	Lack boot	Leather	Resin	Black Brown Navy	4x10		Stitched sole
	Regent junior Paddock	Lack boot	Leather	PVC	Black Brown Navy	3x8		Scuff free leather
	Regent Ascot	Riding boot	PVC	PVC	Black	13x11		Budget priced boot
J Barbour & Sons Ltd, Simonside South Shields Tyne & Wear NE34 9PD Tel: 091 455 4444 Fax: 091 454 2944	Barbour	Field & Country	Rubber	Rubber	Dk Green Navy Black			
		County Lady	Rubber	Rubber	Dk Green Navy Black			

Breeches and Jodhpurs

Company name	Brand name	Style	Type	Material	Size Range	Colour Range	Rec. Retail Price	Comments
Caldene Clothing Co Ltd Mytholmroyd Halifax HX7 5JQ Tel: 0422 883393 Fax: 0422 885925	Colt	Colt	Jods	Stretch	All, Ladies & girls	Beige, White, Navy, Black	N/A	100% Nylon
	Crusader		Jods	Stretch	As above	Asabove	N/A	Inner cotton surface
	Reflex		Jods Breeches	Multi-stretch	As above plus breeches for ladies	As above	N/A	
	County		Jods Breeches	Corduroy	As above plus br. for men	Beige, Navy, Grey, Black	N/A	
	Cavalier		Jods	Multi-stretch	As above	Beige, White, Navy, Black	N/a	
	Cavalry		Breeches	Hard wearing wool lining	Ladies & Men	Beige, White	N/A	Winter hunting/hacking
	Cattistock		Jods Breeches	Multi-stretch	Ladies	Beige, White, Navy, Black	N/A	
	Contact		Breeches	Stretch	Ladies	Beige, White, Buff	N/A	
	Piaffe		Breeches	Stretch, cotton lined	Ladies	As above	N/A	Eventing
	Cord Piaffe		Breeches	Stretch Corduroy	Ladies	Beige, Navy	N/A	Exercising

Breeches and Jodhpurs (continued)

Company name	Brand name	Style	Type	Material	Size Range	Colour Range	Rec. Retail Price	Comments
Gorringe Sportswear Ltd 2 Short Street West Midlands WS2 9EB Tel: 0922 28131 Fax: 0922 724336	Gorringe Dressage	Ladies & gents	Breeches	Nylon, lycra	Ladies 24/32 gents 30/40	black, grey beige, canary green, navy white		
	Gorringe 1500	Ladies & gents	Breeches & jodhpurs	Nylon, lycra, acrylic	Ladies 24/32 gents 30/40	black, grey white, beige navy, canary		
	Gorringe 400	Ladies & unisex	Breeches & jodhpurs	Nylon	Ladies 24/32 unisex 16/30	light grey, med grey, beige, white, navy, black, canary		
Lavenham Rug Co. List House Works Long Melford CO10 9LL Tel: 0787 79535 Fax: 0787 880096		Comfort	Jodhur & breech	Nylon 80% cotton lycra 3%	20" to 40"	beige, black, navy		
		Cavendish	Jodhpur & breech	Nylon 60% cotton, 37% lycra 3%	20" to 40"	beige, black, white		
		Snug	Jodhpur	Nylon 100%	20 to 28"	beige navy		
		Cotton	Breech	Cotton 94%	24" to 40"	beige, white		
		Corduroy	Jodhpur & breech	Cotton 48% modal 32% polyamid 17% elastane 3%	24" to 40"	beige, navy black, green, wine		

Breeches and Jodhpurs (continued)

Company name	Brand name	Style	Type	Material	Size Range	Colour Range	Rec. Retail Price	Comments
Saddlemaster Riding Wear Burnley Road Mytholmroyd Halifax HX7 5QJ Tel: 0422 883393 Fax: 0422 885925	Trekkers		Jods	Stretch	All girls & ladies	Fawn White Canary Black Brown, Navy	N/A	Britain's best-selling jodhpurs Great value for money
	Banbury		Jods & breeches	Stretch	Men	Fawn White Black, Blue	N/A	
	Beverley		As above	Stretch	Ladies & Men	As above	N/A	Self-seat for serious riders
	Event		Jods	Stretch	Girls & Ladies	As above	N/A	For year-round riding comfort
	Cattistock		Jods & Breeches	Stretch	Ladies	Beige White, Navy Black	N/A	

Compound Feeds

Company name	Brand name	Mix	Type	Main Ingredients	Supplements	Protein	Rec. Retail Price	Comments
Baileys Horse Feeds Four Elms Mills Bardfield Saling Braintree Essex CM7 5EJ Tel: 0371 850247 Fax: 0371 85169	Cooked cereal meal	No. 1	Non-heating meal	Cooked cereal meal		15%		Ideal for inclusion as part of concentrate ration
	Horse & pony mix	No. 2	Non-heating cubes	Cereal meal fibre, molasses	Vitamins & minerals	11.5%		A complete range of feeds, each suitable to be fed as the sole concentrate source.
	Stud cubes	No. 3	As above	As above plus soya	As above	15%	As above	
	Top line cubes	No. 4	As above	As above	As above	12%		As above
	Performance mix	No. 6	Coarse mix	Traditional grains, concentrate pellets	As above	12%		As above
	Stud Mix	No. 7	As above	As above	As above	16%		As above
	Meadow sweet	No. 8	Coarse mix	Micronised cereals, conc pellets, hay chaff	As above	10%		As above
	Horse & pony mix	No. 9	Coarse mix	Trad grains, conc pellets	As above	10.5%		As above
	Buckeye gro'n win		Pellets	Soya based	As above	32%		A nutrient-dense ration balancer

Compound Feeds (continued)

Company name	Brand name	Mix	Type	Main Ingredients	Supplements	Protein	Rec. Retail Price	Comments
Baileys Horse Feeds (cont.)	Buckeye foal starter		Pellets	Blend of milk products & full-fat soya	Vitamins & minerals	18%		A milk-based creep feed
British Horse Feeds (BHF) Ltd Victoria House 50 Albert Street Rugby CV21 2RH Tel: 0788 567475	Coarse horse	Mix		Cereals proteins		11%	Supplied to the trade, POA	
	Horse-pony		Nuts			10.5%		
	Natural country blend	Mix		Grass meal, micronised cereals molasses, minerals, vitamins		10%		
	Natural country nuts		Nuts			16%		
	Stud nuts		Nuts			16%		
	High energy nuts		Nuts			15%		
	Natural country cooked barley nugget	Nuts	Extruded barley linseed oil		10%			
Charnwood Milling Co Framlingham Nr Woodbridge Suffolk IP13 9PT Tel: 0728 723435 Fax: 0728 724359	CMC	Foal creep	Pellets	Cooked cereals, animal & vegetable proteins	Vitamins, minerals and trace elements	18%	POA	
	CMC	Yearling developer	Nuts	As above	As above	16%		

Compound Feeds (continued)

Company name	Brand name	Mix	Type	Main Ingredients	Supplements	Protein	Rec. Retail Price	Comments
Charnwood Milling Co. (cont.)	CMC	Stud	Cubes	Cooked cereals, animal and veg. proteins	As above	15%	POA	
	CMC	Racehorse	Nuts	As above	As above	15%		
	CMC	Hunter/ eventer	Nuts	As above	As above	14%		
	CMC	Horse & pony	Nuts	As above	As above	12%		
	CMC	Horse concentrate	Pellets	As above	As above	26%		
	CMC	Hi-Fi Horse	Nuts	As above	As above	14%		
	CMC	Pony	Nuts	As above	As above	12%		
	CMC	Coarse Horse 14		As above	As above	14.5%		
	CMC	Coarse Horse 11		As above	As above	12%		
	CMC	Calm Horse		As above	As above	11%		
	CMC	No oats coarse		As above	As above	13%		

Compound Feeds (continued)

Company name	Brand name	Mix	Type	Main Ingredients	Supplements	Protein	Rec. Retail Price	Comments
R & E Bamford Ltd Bretherton Preston Lancs PR5 7BD Tel: 0772 60067 Fax 0772 600340	Bamford's	Coarse Mix	General Purpose	Cereals	Added minerals & vitamins	12%	5/20	
	Bamford's	Nuts	General purpose	Cereals	Added minerals & vitamins	11%	4/50	

Hats

Company name	Brand name	Model	Type	BS No.	Size Range	Chinstrap/ Harness	Colours	Rec. Retail Price
S Patey (London) Ltd 1 Amelia Street Walworth Road London SE17 3PY Tel: 071 703 6528			Riding hats		All		Any	
			Riding bowlers		All		Any	
			Hunting toppers		All		Any	

Horse Trailers

Company name	Brand name	Model	Horses Carried	Length (int)	Height (int)	Width (int)	Ramps	Flooring	Outside shell	Axle units	Towing wt (unl)	Capacity	RRP
J and B Towing The Trailer Centre Cottismore Farm Kingsclere Tel: 0635 298928	Cottismore	Light horse	2	9'	7'2"	5'	1	hardwood	Aluminium	Indep. susp'n	2000kg	1200kg	£1995 +VAT
		Heavy horse	2	10'	7'2"	5'8"	1	hardwood	Aluminium	Indep. susp'n	2000kg	1340kg	£2050 +VAT
		Light front unload	2	10'	7'2"	5'	2	hardwood	Aluminium	Indep. susp'n	2000kg	1240kg	£1725 +VAT
		Front unload full size horse	2	10'6"	7'2"	5'8"	2	hardwood	Aluminium	Indep. susp'n	2000kg	1150kg	£1895 +VAT
		Front unload	3	12'6"	7'2"	5'8"	2	hardwood	Aluminium	Indep. susp'n	3000kg	2005kg	POA
Rice Trailers Ltd Portland Street Cosby Leicestershire LE9 5TG Tel: 0533 866666 Fax: 0533 7504398	Junior Foxhunter		2 x ponies	7'11"	6'7"	4'7"	Rear	Single wooden	Aluminium	Avonride	520kg	810kg	£1495
	Eventer 16.2hh		2 x	9'	7'	5'	Rear wooden	Single	Aluminium	Avonride	610kg	813kg	£1750
	Europa		2 x 16.2hh	10'	7'	5'4"	Front & rear	Single wooden	Aluminium	Avonride	737kg	1263kg	£2225
(* All Beaufort s have 7'6" headrm)	Beaufort single		1 x 17hh	10'4"	7' *	3'10"	Front & rear	Single rear	Aluminium	Avonride	610kg	700kg	£2150
(Single floor models have double avail.)	Showman Deluxe		2 x 16.2hh	3'11"	7' *	5'5"	Rear	Double wooden	Aluminium	Avonride	953kg	1547kg	£3495

Horse Trailers (continued)

Company name	Brand name	Model	Horses Carried	Length (int)	Height (int)	Width (int)	Ramps	Flooring	Outside shell	Axle units	Towing wt(unl)	Capacity	RRP
Rice Trailers Ltd (cont.)	Beaufort popular		2 x 16.2hh	10'4"	7'*	5'5"	Front & rear	Single wooden	Aluminium	Avonride	742kg	1308kg	£2895
	Beaufort double		2 x 16.2hh	10'4"	7'*	5'5"	Front & rear	Double wooden	Aluminium	Avonride	914kg	1286kg	£3495
	Beaufort 60		2 x 17.2hh+	12'2"	7'6"	6'	Front & rear	Double wooden	Aluminium	Avonride	1110kg	19990kg	£3995
	Beaufort Treble		3 (1x15hh 2x16hh)	12'2"	7'*	5'5"	Front & rear	Double wooden	Aluminium	Avonride	1011kg	1539kg	£4075
	Badminton Side unload		2 x 16.2hh	13'5" & rear	7'*	5'5"	Side	Rubberised	Aluminium	Avonride	1120kg	1380kg	£4950
Richardson Trailers Ltd Shipton-by-Benningbrough York YO6 1AB Tel: 0904 470282 Fax: 0904 470486 (Cheaper models also available)	0217	2	132"	84"	69.6"	Front Unload. Ramp Lifting Aid	Tongue & groove tanalised floor	Timber or Aluminum	Avonride Axle Unit	850kg	2-Horse 17 Hands	£850kg	£2,575

Jackets

Company name	Brand name	Style	Type	Size Range	Colour	RRP	Comments
Caldene Clothing Co Mytholmroyd Halifax HX7 5QJ Tel: 0422 883393 Fax: 0422 885925	Aachen Belvoir Richmond Olympic (men) Tailor's choice		Show	Girls, Ladies, Men	Tweeds, Black, Blue	N/A	
	Goodwood		Dressage	Ladies, Men	Black	N/A	
	Wessex Roxborough		Semi-hunt	As above	Black, Navy	N/A	
	Rockwood	Frock or Morning	Hunt	Men	Hunting Pink Beaufort Blue Beagling Green	N/A	
	Grosvenor		Hunt Tails	Men	Scarlet	N/A	Traditional Hunt Ball Tails
	Side Saddle			Ladies	Tweeds, Plains	N/A	Tailored
Bob Church & Co Ltd 16 Lorne Road Northampton NN1 3RN Tel: 0604 713674/27052 Fax: 0604 250051	Bob Church	De-Luxe wax riding coat tartan lined		28" to 44" chest	Navy, olive & burgundy		Approx £50
	Bob Church	Unisex Full length Australian style wax riding coat		Small, med, large, X-large	olive & brown		Approx £65

Jackets (continued)

Company name	Brand name	Style	Type	Size Range	Colour	RRP	Comments
Gorringe Sportswear 2 Short Street Walsall West Midlands WS2 9EB Tel: 0922 28131 Fax: 0922 724336	Gorringe	Show jacket polyester	ladies girls boys men	34/44 22/32 22/34 36/46	black, navy red green		
	Gorringe	Show jackets all wool SERGE	gents	ladies 34/44 36/44	black, navy		
	Gorringe	Tweed all wool hacking	ladies girls boys men	34/44 22/32 22/34 36/46	brown, blue grey		
The Lavenham Rug Company Ltd List House Works Long Melford Suffolk CO10 9LL Tel: 0787 79535 Fax: 0787 880096	Lavenham	Various in diamond quilt and duvet		24" to 50"	Various		Nylon, Poly cotton, Cotton, Tweed, Wax, Corduroy, Polyester.
Puffa of Suffolk Parka House Little Waldingfield Suffolk CO10 0S Tel: 0787 248474 Fax: 0787 248133	Puffa Childrens	Parka & Vest		24"/26"	bottle, navy olive, black watch, blue/white stripe, navy/red/white stripe, Housecheck Navy snaffle design,		
		Zip out sleeve reversible parka & vest		24"/26"	Navy, green, white stripe		

Jackets (continued)

Company name	Brand name	Style	Type	Size Range	Colour	RRP	Comments
Matlock Brown Ltd Bath Road Kettering NN16 8NH Tel: 0536 512435 Fax: 0536 513146	Rosette		Girls Boys Ladies men	24-32 30-36 34-42 38-46			
	Puffa	Parka &		32"/46"	Various		
	Puffa	Parka only		32"/46"	Jade, kingfisher navy, sky blue		
	Puffa	Zip-out		32" to 46"	Various		
	Puffa	Fleece reversible blouson emerald & grey/ grey		32" to 46"	navy &jade/navy mulberry/navy serge & navy/navy		
	Puffa	Quilted	Blouson	32" to 36"	Grey/jade/navy		
Saddlemaster Riding Wear Burnley Road Mytholmroyd Halifax HX7 5JQ Tel: 0422 883393 Fax: 0422 885925	Fenland Romsey Essen		Show	Girls Ladies Men	Tweeds Blacks Blues	N/A	A wide range of Tweed and plain show jackets
	Beaufort		Semi-Hunt	Ladies Men	Black Blue	N/A	Traditional High Quality Semi-Hunt Coats
	Fieldmaster		Anoraks W/Coats Quilts Blousons Showerproofs	All	Various Plains and prints	N/A	A wide range of casual country wear in quilts, super-showerproofs and fleeces

Rugs

Company name	Brand name	Type	Material	Colour	Roller available	Size	RRP	Comments
JP Rug Co Downs House Childrey Oxon OX12 9UF Tel: 0235 59400	JP	NZ NZ NZ Coolers Day rugs Day rugs	Flax Rip-stop Cordura Cotton Wool Melton					We manufacture all types of rugs to a high standard.
Lavenham Rug Co. List House Works Long Melford CO10 9LL Tel: 0787 79535 Fax: 0787 880096	Heata	Stable	Nylon/Cotton	Black bound grey		60" to 81"		12oz filling
	Super	Stable	Nylon/Cotton	Navy		60" to 81"		8 oz filling
	Cosy chevron	Stable	Nylon/Cotton	Navy/lt blue, Navy/red		48" to 81"		8oz filling
	Standard	Stable		Navy/red		48" to 81"		4 oz filling
	Standard Box	Stable		Navy/lt blue		48" to 81"		4 oz filling
	New Zealand	Turnout	Flax	Green		60" to 81"		21 oz
	Cordura	Turnout	Cordura	Navy/red		60" to 81"		
	Multi-sheet	General purpose	Polyester	Black with white, navy or red		60", 66", 72, 78		
	Wool	Travel	100% wool	Black watch stripe		60", 66", 72, 78		Washable

Rugs *(continued)*

Company name	Brand name	Type	Material	Colour	Roller available	Size	RRP	Comments
Newton Horse Ltd Hotham York YO4 3UN Tel: 0430 423636	Newton	Pocket numnahs	Equitex fleece	White		All sizes	From £29.96	Non-slip washable Hard wearing
	Newton	Standed	Equitex	White		All	From £29.66	Non-slip washable Hard wearing Available in dressage fitting.
	Newton	Stable	Equitex	Brown	Xed S.S.	All	From £49.99	A fabric that breathes but reflects body heat back to the horse
P.I. Associates	PolyPads	PolyPad				3 thicknesses	From £17	THE back protector for horses
		PolyPad plus one				3 thicknesses	From £17	THE back protector for horses
		Doubler				3 thicknesses	From £17	THE back protector for horses
		RollerPad				3 thicknesses	From £17	THE back protector for horses

Rugs (continued)

Company name	Brand name	Type	Material	Colour	Roller available	Size	RRP	Comments
Polywarm Products Ltd Cambusland Road Farme Cross Rutherglen Glasgow G73 1RS Tel: 041 647 2392 Fax: 041 613 1569 Telex: 779968	Polywarm	Stable	Outer siliconized 4oz nylon, lining 100% cotton	Navy with red bindings	X-over circingle included	5'6" increasing by 3" steps to 6'9"	£74 to £86	All rugs in the Polywarm range are extra deep

Saddles

Company name	Brand name	Models	Type	Size Range	RRP	Comments
G Fieldhouse Saddlery (Walsall) Ltd 18-19 Green Lane Walsall WS2 8HE Tel: 0922 38094 Fax: 0922 22921	GFS	International event	GP	16-18	£495	Adjustable version £100 extra
	Club	Synthetic saddle GP	GP	15-17	£199	Synthetic saddle made on laminated beechwood tree
	City	GP	GP	16-18	£425	
Sabre Leather Company Ltd 19-21 Sandwell St Walsall West Midlands WS1 3DR Tel: 0922 29925 Fax: 0922 723463	Dortmund	17"	GP		N/A	Ideal for the competition-minded
	Dortmund	17"	Dressage		N/A	
	Windsor	17"/18"	GP		N/A	Ideal riding-club saddle
	Working-hunter	16"/17"/18"	W/H		N/A	Showing & W/H classes
		All				Available in ebony or salamanca

Index of Directory Entries

4 K's Riding Centre 94

A

A D Mackenzie 288
A R G Cherry-Downes
Abbotts 124
Aberdeen Equestrian Training Centre 88
Aberdeen & Northern Marts Ltd 125
Abott (Chartered Surveyors) 124
Abotts 124
ACA Forage (Buckingham) Ltd 266
ACA Forage Ltd (Warnford) 266,292,296
Acorn Bridle Manufacturers 258
Acorn Rugs 172,276,282,292,294,302ff
Acre Cliffe Riding School 84
Acreliff Stables 275,278
Action South 74
Aerborn Equestian 164,166,274,282,283,286,302ff
Agriservices 124
Aldborough Hall Equestrian Centre Limited 40
Aldersbrook Riding School Limited 61
Alfred Cox (Surgical) Ltd 259,264,276,292,302ff
Alison Hammett (Equest Servces) 172
Allen & Caswell 162,164,168,176,281
Allendale Stables 53,107
Alton Riding School 34,101
Ambassador Saddlery Limited 271,288
Andell Equestrian Services Ltd 264,284,292
Andrew Oliver & Son Limited 126
Andrew Thomas 169,173
Anglesey Equitation Centre Limited 96
Anglo German Bloodstock Agency
Animal Bedding Company 257
Animal Portraiture 169,173
Animals Unlimited 173
Animart Ltd 266,268
Appin Equestrian Centre 90
Applefield Riding School 85
Appletree Stables 53
Apthorpes
Aquacrop 280
Arden Horsebox Company 275
Ardfern Riding Centre 128,90,119
Armathwaite Hall Equestrian Centre 33
Arniss Riding & Livery Stables 44
Arundel Riding Centre 82
Ashbrooke Riding Centre 98
Ashdown Forest Riding Centre 39,104
Ashfield Riding Centre 98
Ashley Green Riding Centre 26

Ashridge Equestrian Centre 50
Ashtree Riding School 38
Asthall Show Jumps 174290
ATG Horseboxes 275
Attadale Trekking Centre 89
Auster Lodge Riding Stables 60
Autosteer Controls Ltd 275
Avon Industrial Polymers 271
Avon Insurance PLC 170
Avon Livestock Centre 126
Ayrshire Equitation Centre 91,119

B

B & R Intl Horse Transport 280
B 1st Riding School of Equitation Centre 30
B F P Rosettes 172,174,285,290
B G S Plastics Ltd 174,261,262,272,290
B T Batsford Ltd 171
Bableigh Riding School 36
Backhurst, C P & Co 257
Backnoe End Equestrian Centre 25
Badminton Horse Feeds 260,265
Bahill Trailers 278
Bailey's Horse Feeds 260,266,284,311
Bairstow Eves 124
Baker Reeve & Co 170
Ballintean Riding Centre 89
Ballyknock Riding School 98
Balnakilly Riding Centre 92
Bambers Green Riding Centre 50
Barend Riding Centre 87
Barnby Training Centre 75
Barnes Green Riding School 73
Barnfield Riding School 77
Barnham Broom Hotel Golf & Country Club 110
Barrington Stables 70
Barrowby Riding Centre 65
Barton Stud & School of Equitation 79
Batchworth Heath Farm Stud 50
Bateson Trailers Ltd 278
Battle, Hayward Bower
Limited 265,276,280,292,308ff
Bay Horse Inn 68
Bayer (UK) Ltd 265,311
Bayford Stud Farm and Training Centre 71,112
Bearwood Riding Centre 26
Beauport Park Riding School 39
Beaver of Bolton Limited 164,165,166,168
Becconsall Farm Stables. 56,108
Beck Isle Ponies 65,110

Becks Lane Riding Centre 60
Bedford Horsebox Co Ltd 275
Bedgebury Park Riding Centre 53
Beech Equestrian Centre 85
Beech Tree Farm Riding Centre 56
Beechmount Equitation Centre. 56
Beechwood Riding School 77
Belle Vue Valley Equestrian Centre 36
Bellet Ltd 272,276,281,292,306ff
Belmont Riding Centre 61,109
Belmont Riding School & Livery 65
Belmoredean Stub & Livery Stables 82
Belper Riding Centre 34,102
Belstaff Int. Limited 164,166,168
Belton Riding Centre 63
Belvoir Horse Feeds 266
Bennington Artistic Iron Prods 262
Benridge Riding School 68
Berriewood Stud Farm 71,112
Berrisford Hill 169
Beta Fencing Limited 268
Better Tack Riding Centre 60
Bewerley School of Horsemanship 65
Bicton College of Agriculture 36
Biggar Auction Market Co Ltd 126
Bigland Hall Riding Centre 33
Birch Farm School of Equitation 50
Birchwood Riding Centre 34
Birmingham Equestrian Centre 34
Birmingham Land-Rover Services Ltd 296
Birrs Sportswear Ltd 163
Bishop Burton College of Agriculture 52
Bitchet Farm Riding School 53
Black Birches 71
Black Mountain Riding Holidays 96,121
Blackburn Auction Mart Co. Ltd 126
Blackdyke Farm & Riding School 33,101
Blackslade Riding and Trekking Centre 36
Bladbean Stud 107
Blaenau Farm 120
Bleach Yard Stables 52,107
Blenheim Riding Centre 70
Blewbury Riding & Training Centre Limited 70
Bloodstock & General Insurance 170
Bloomsgorse Trekking Centre 68
Blue Barn Riding Stables 108
Blue Well Riding Centre 53,94,120
Bob Church & Co. Limited 163,164,166,168
Bob Lillie Leisurewear 166
Bodysgallen Hall Farm 121
Bold Heath Equestrian Centre 30
Border Trails 112
Boreland Riding Centre 92
Botterills Ascot Bloodstck Sals 126
Bourne Vale Stables 81,116
Bowfield Riding Centre 91,119
Bowlers Riding School 63,110
Bowley & Coleman Trucks Ltd 292
Bowling Riding School 94
Bowmont Trekking Centre 117
Brackenhurst College 68
Bradbourne Riding & Training Centre Limited 53
Bradfield Riding Centre 26
Bramhill Riding School 52
Brampton Stables 127,67
Brandon Riding Academy 75
Brawlings Farm Livery Yard Limited 26,99
Braymont Riding School 80
Breckonborough Riding Holiday Centre 65,111
Brendon Riding School 39,104

Brentwood Riding Centre 40
Brian Lawrence & Co 163
Brian Lindsay 163,172,173
Brian Scrivener 288,295
Brickfields Equestrian Centre 53
Bridge House Riding School 82
Bridgedale 162
Brigg View Farm Stables 65
Brighouse Bay Outdoor Activity Cntre 87,117
Brimington Equestrian Centre 102
Brinsbury College 83
Bristol Horseboxes 275
British Bata Shoe Co Ltd 162
British Cod Liver Oils Limited 265,304ff
British Equestrian Centre 80,170,171
British Gates & Timber Ltd 256,269,270,292
British Horse Feeds Ltd 260,266,277
British Leathergoods Association 258,272,288
British Sugar Plc 267,268,277
Broadfield Stables 269
Broadlands Riding Centre 45
Brockholes Farm Riding Centre 73
Brocks Farm Equitation Livery & Training Ctre 45
Brook Farm Equestrian Centre 40
Brooklands Farm Riding School 58
Brookwick Ward & Co Ltd 259,264,272,276,307ff
Broomhall Riding School 30
Browns of WEM Ltd 292
Brownside Trekking Centre 111
Bryan Fradgley 288,290
Bryan Lawrence & Co 278,286
Brympton Riding School 85
Buckingham Harness 164,262,264
Buckinghams Property Cons 124
Buckminster Lodge Equestrian Centre 60
Budleigh Salterton Riding School 36
Burches Riding School 41
Burcott Riding School 72
Burley Villa School of Riding 45,105
Burstow Park Riding & Livery Centre 77,115
Burton McCall 162,164
Busby Equitation Centre Limited 91
Bushy Park Riding School Limited 77
Buxton Riding School 34

C

C & T Trailors 278
C M Stanford & Son 126
C P Backhurst & Co 268,277,302ff
C Vet Ltd 272
CAM Equestrian Joinery &
Equip 172,276,288,290,292
CAM Stables & Farmbldgs Ltd 172,269,292
Caeiago Trekking Centre 94
Cairnhouse Trekking Centre 91
Caldecote Riding School 80,115
Caldene Clothing Co Ltd 163,165,276,292
Calders & Grandidge Ltd 268,269
Caledonian Equestrian Centre 93,119
Calloose Riding Stables 31
Cambs Horse & Pony Agency 126
Cambs. College of Agriculture & Horticulture 28
Camel Hill Farm Stables 72
Camnant Centre 96
Canaan Farm Riding School 58
Canac Horse Products 283
Cane End Stables Limited 26,99
Canters End Riding School 39

Capton Equestrian Centre 36,102
Carbex-Munroe (Handles) 162,281,286,292,320ff
Carlton Forest Equestrian Centre 69
Carlton Grange Riding Centre 65
Carr Day & Martin Limited 265,276,281,305ff
Carrier House Riding School 52
Carrington Riding Centre 44,104
Carry on Stables 80
Carter Jonas 124
Castle Farm Livery Yard 47
Castle Hill Riding School 80
Castle Riding Centre & Argyll Trail Riding 91,119
Castle Sportswear Ltd 163,164
Casual Riding Manufacturing
Ltd 167,274,282,283,284
Caswell & Co Ltd 281
Cathay Equestrian Centre 88
Catherston Stud & Equestrian Centre 45
Catterick Army Saddle Club 66
Catworth Manufacturing Co. Ltd 167
Causeway Farm 34,101
Causeway House Stables 45
CB Horseboxes 275
Cefn Coch Pony Trekking Centre 121
Centaur School of Equitation 59
Chagford Riding Centre 36
Champerene Ltd 265,267,310
Champion & Wilton Limited 162,163,258,288
Champion Services Ltd 175
Chapman's Close Riding Establishment 67,111
Charles Owen & Co (Bow) Ltd 164,166,170,290
Charles Walker & Co Ltd 291
Charles Wilkinson Ins Brokers 170
Charnwood Milling Co Ltd 257,260,265,267,272
Chase Organics (GB) Ltd 265,311
Chaskit New Zealand Rugs 292,295
Chattis Hill Riding Centre 45,105
Chaucer Riding and Livery Stables 53
Chavic Park Farm 53
Cheffin Grain & Chalk Messrs 126
Chelsfield Riding School 53
Cherry & Cherry Limited 69
Chestnut Farm Riding School 52
Cheston Farm Equestrian Centre 36,102
Chevalier Ltd 163
Chiltern Connemara Stud 171
Chimney Mill Riding School 75
Chiverton Riding Centre 31
Chorleywood Equestrian Centre Limited 127,50
Chris Adams 258,271,284,288,291
Christy & Co Limited 166
Church, Bob & Co Ltd 164
Church Farm Stables 67
Churchgate Farm 41
Churchill Equestrian Est Agnts 124
City of Cardiff Riding School 97
Civil Service Riding Club 61,109
Claire's Riding School 38
Clare Lawson 258,261,262,271,274,282,288,291,294
Clevedon Riding Centre 24
Cleveland Riding Centre 31
Cloud Stables (School of Equitation) 26
Clyn-Du Riding Centre 94,120
CMS Trim 174,291
Cobham Manor Riding Centre 53,108
Coldwaltham House 83
Coleman Croft Saddlery 162,171,258,261,271,302ff
Coles Knapp & Kennedy 126
Colin Whittaker (Saddler) 258,288
College Farm Equestrian Centre 69,112

Colne Valley Riding Stables 41
Coltspring School of Riding Ltd. 50
Cone Rosettes 285
Connel Trekking Centre 119
Conquest Remedies 272
Constant Laboratories 272,276,309ff
Contessa Arabian and Riding Centre 50,106
Continental Car Centre 296
Coombe Park Equestrian
Centre 36,102,257,277,280
Coombe Wood Stables 54
Coopers Animal Health Ltd 310ff
Cophall Farm Stables 39
Copley Stables 97,122
Corby Rosettes 285
Corrow Trekking Centre 91,119
Coton Equitana 80
Cotswold Equitation Centre 70
Cottage Farm Stables 82
Cottage Ind. (Equestrian)
Ltd 258,261,271,277,288,292
Courtlands Riding Stables 50,107
Courtyard Equestrian 264
Cowley Riding School 73
Crabbet Park Equitation Centre 83,116
Craen Riding Centre 96,121
Craig Fawr Livery Stables 96
Crimdon Park Rig School 31
Cringleford Riding School 63
Crockett & Jones 162
Crockstead Equestrian Centre 39
Croford Coachbuilders Ltd 262
Croft House School Limited 38
Croft Riding Centre 30
Cromloch Riding Centre 96,121
Crook Brothers 280,296
Crooklands Riding Establishment 56
Cross Country (Equestrian) Ltd 176,286,288,291,292
Crossways Riding School 36
Crown Chemical Co. Limited 276,292,302ff
Culm Vale Riding Centre 36
Curland Equestrian Enterprises 72,113
Cwmfforest Riding Centre 96,122
Cwmyoy Pony Trekking Centre 121

D

D & J Watson 173,268,290,291,292
D I & J G Young 260,267
D Mears 269,292
D Thurgood 259
Dalchenna Riding Centre 91,119
Dale School of Equitation 74
Darby Rosettes 285
Dartmoor Pony Society 171
David Bedford 124
David Cemmick 169
David Marsh (Manchester) Ltd 165
David Wells Fencing 269
Davis Mead & Partners 269
Day Son & Hewitt Limited 265,311
De Beauvoir Farm Livery Yard 41
Dean Castle Country Park Riding Centre 91
Dean Hall Riding Stables 84
Deandane Riding Stables 44
Deanswood Equestrian Centre 50,107
Decoy Pond Riding & Livery Stables 45
Deepdene Riding School 54
Deepleigh Farm Riding Centre 72

Deepwater Equitation Centre — 88
Denefencing — 269
Denewear — 165,166,167
Dennis Coe Supplies — 269
Derby House Saddlery — 175
Derriboots — 162
Derwen Stud — 94
Derwentoak Riding Centre — 80
Devenish Pitt Riding Centre — 36
Devitt Midland Limited — 170
Devon River Riding Centre — 87
Diane Onions (Harness Maker) — 258,262,288
Dickinson Dary & Markham — 124
Ditchling Common Stud Riding School — 83
Dodson & Horrell Ltd — 260,265,267
Doe House Riding School — 73,113
Donalds McLellan
(Saddler) — 165,258,272,285,291,295
Doncaster Bloodstock Sales Ltd — 126
Doone Valley Riding Stables — 36
Dores Riding Centre — 89,118
Dorking Riding School — 77,115
Dormit Riding Surfaces — 256
Douglas Farm Riding School — 56,108
Down's-side Riding Centre — 97,122
Dressage of London — 164
Drift End Stables — 28
Drumbrae Riding Centre — 87
Drywell Farm Riding Centre — 36
Duchy College of Agriculture & Horticulture — 32,100
Dulwich Riding School — 61
Dunsford Land-Rovers (Bath) Ltd — 296
Durham Equestrian Skills Limited — 31

E

E F Birchall — 278
E J Wood & Associates — 170
E Ward & Sons — 278
E Williams & Co — 174,291
Eaglesfield Equestrian Centre — 54
Earnsdale Farm Riding School — 57,167
Earswood Riding Centre — 95
East Anglian Farm Rides — 41
East Hope Equestrian Centre — 98
East Lodge Farm Riding Establishment — 67
East Midlands Riding Ass for the Handicapped — 35
Eastern Equitation — 41
Eastminster School of Riding Limited — 41
Ebbisham Farm Livery Stables — 78
Ebborlands Farm & Riding Centre — 72,113
Eccleston Equestrian Centre — 57
Eclipse Jewellery — 173
Edergole Riding Centre — 98
Edinburgh & Lasswade Riding Centre — 90,118
Eldonian Brookes Limited — 286,288
Elizabethan Insurance Co. Ltd
Elliot Right Way Books — 171
Elvaston Castle Riding Centre — 35,101
Emsby Field Sportswear Limited — 165,166,175
Endon Riding School — 74,113
Engraved Signs — 173
Enterprise Biddenden — 275,278,280
Entertainment & Leisure — 170
Epic — 165
Epsom Veterinary Remedies Ltd — 302ff
Eqinis Polymer Ltd — 274,286
Equestrian Agencies Ltd — 265
Equestrian Book Society — 171

Equestrian Manufactng & Supply — 162,258,288
Equestrian Products International (UK) Ltd — 85
Equestricare — 265,267,311
Equi Study Centre — 61,68
Equi-Bed — 257
Equi-Study — 171,172
Equicushion Ltd — 264,272
Equifence — 269
Equiform Nutrition Ltd — 265,267,311
Equimix Feeds Ltd — 260,265,267,280,293,308
Equine & Livestock Ins. Co Ltd — 170,293
Equine Products UK
Limited — 260,261,265,267,272,303ff
Equinomic Products Limited — 272,283,286
Equiquip Ltd — 174,176,283,298
Equitred — 256
Equitus Ltd — 128,277,280
Equivite — 260,265,267,293,304ff
Equus Equestrian Centre — 78,115
Eston Equitation Centre — 100
Euroclip Ltd — 259
Exeter & District Riding School — 37

F

F B Davis Saddlery
Limited — 166,258,261,265,281,302ff
F J Alton & Partners Ltd — 265,267,311
F J Chandler (Saddler) Ltd — 288
F J Lucas — 270,293
Fagg, H J & Son — 162
Fancy Free Race & Event Wear — 165,175,286,294
Farm Forest Equestrian Centre — 48
Farmkey Limited — 269170
Farsyde Stud and Riding Stables — 66,111
Farthing Down Stables — 78
Faulks & Jaques — 175,267,271,290,293
Fawcett's Tarpaulins Ltd — 168
Feedmark Ltd — 265,267
Feeney & Johnson Ltd — 278
Fencing and Farm Services — 269
Fenix Enterprizes (Equestrian) — 263
Fenn's Equestrian Centre — 57
Ferniehurst Mill Lodge — 87,117
Field Bottom Riding Stables — 84
Field Farm Stables — 35
Field House Equestrian Centre — 74
Fieldguard Ltd — 268,269,284
Fiesta Rosettes — 285
Finmere Equestrian Centre — 27
Finningley School of Equitation — 73,113
Fir Tree Equestrian Centre — 45
Fisher Foundries Limited — 262,293
Fisons Animal Health — 276,306ff
Flanders Farm Riding Centre — 45,105
Fleckney School of Equitation — 59
Fleetwater Stud — 105
Flettner Ventilator Ltd — 275
Flexalan Products Limited — 281
Fly Laithe Stables — 84,116
Folkes Farm Riding & Livery Stables — 41
Ford Close Riding Centre — 31
Forecourt Signs Limited — 173
Forest Lodge Equestrian Centre — 38
Format Ltd — 271
Foto Focus — 173
Four Acres Equestrian Centre — 60
Four Oaks Livery & Training Stables — 82
Four Seasons(British Sugar PLC) — 260,267

Four Winds Equitation Centre 60
Fowlers Farm 45
Fox & Sons 124
Foxes Farm and Riding Centre 30
Foxhill Farm Equestrian Centre 67
Foxhound Riding School Limited 41
Frank Hill & Son 124,126170
Fred Sales (Jersey) Ltd 295
Fredericks Stables 293
Friar's Hill Riding Stables 66
Friendly Feeds 267
Frogwell Riding Centre 37
Fulwood Riding Centre 57

G

G C Smith (Coachworks) 275,278
G Fieldhouse Saddlery 258,285,288
G K Parson & Sons 269,270,293
G L C Williams 269,270,293
G M Daly 263,264
G R Bailey Limited 267
G T Palmer & Son Ltd 288
GA Property Services 124
Galgorm Parks Riding School 98
Gallon House 113
Gardner, H Cameron Ltd 259
Garry Gualach 118
Gartmore Riding School 74
Gatewood Stables 39
Gecko Leisure Products Ltd 166
General Accident Fire & Life 170
General Chip Co. Limited
George Hobbs Trailers 278,280
George Jeffries Gloves 165
George Parker & Sons Ltd 288
George S Forbes 170
GGH Equitation Centre 52
Gidden, W & H Ltd 259
Gillian's Riding School. 63
Glebe Equestrian Centre 41
Gleddoch Riding School 91
Gleneagles Riding Centre 45,105
Glenfarg Riding School 93
Glenrothes Riding Centre 88
Glentona Textiles (1977) Ltd 302ff
Glynhir Lodge Stables 95
Golden Castle Riding & Livery Stables 97
Golden Pheasant Riding Centre
Goldswell Ltd 266,276,281,293,303ff
Gooseham Barton Stables 32,100
Gordon Ford Carriages 263,275
Gorringe Sportswear Limited 164,165
Goulds Green Riding School 63
Grange Pony Trekking 95,121
Grange Riding Centre 90
Grangefield Children's Riding School 83
Granilastic Haltopex 271
Gransden Hall Riding School 25,99
Greenmeadow Designs 283
Green Meadow Riding Centre 96
Greenacres Riding Centre 67
Greenacres Riding School Limited 54
Greenham Saddlery Co Ltd 286
Greenmeadow Designs 290
Greenways Farm And Stables 78
Greggs Riding School 72
Grey Horse Riding Stables 101
Grove Riding Centre 88

Gunstone Hall Riding Centre 74

H

H & W Auto's (Ewell) Ltd 296
H Belfield & Sons Ltd 263
H S Jackson & Son (Fencing) Ltd 256,269
H S Jackson & Son Ltd (Bath) 256
H-M Veterinary Ltd 266,273,293,312
Hadham Mill Riding Centre 51
Hadleigh Equestn & Sportswr Ltd 167
Haford Equestrian Centre
Haggis Farm Stables 28
Hall Place Riding Stables 26
Hallingbury Hall Equestrian Centre 51
Hallow Mill Equestrian Centre 48
Halsall Riding & Livery Centre 57
Hampsley Hollow Riding Centre 85,117
Hampton & Sons 124
Hamsterly Riding School 31,100
Hanburies Riding Centre 48,106
Hargate Hill Riding School 35
Harlow Bros. Limited 293
Harris Meyer (E.P.) Limited 164,167,264
Harrods Estate Offices 124
Harrogate Equestrian Centre 66,111
Harrops Horseboxes Ltd 275
Harroway House 45,105
Harry Hall Limited 164,167
Hartlebury Stables Ltd. 48
Hartwell Riding Stables 27
Hastoe Hill Riding School 51
Havering Park Riding School and Club 41
Hawkins, G T Ltd 162
Hayacre Farm Ltd. 28
Hayfield Equestrian Centre 88
Hayfield Riding School (Aberdeen) Limited 117
Hayne Barn Riding School 54,108
Hayside Stables 69
Haywood Design 278
Hazeldean Riding Centre 87,117
Hazelden School of Equitation 91
Hazelwood Equestrian Centre 35
Headley Equestrian Centre 45
Headley Grove Riding & Livery Stables Ltd 78
Heart of Wales Riding School 97
Heathcote House 70,112
Heazle Riding Centre 37
Hebden Cord Co Limited 162,164,165,166
Heddington Wick Children's Riding School 85,117
Hedley Riding School 57
Heighstead Riding Centre 54
Hendre Eynon Stables 95,120
Henry Bowers 170,278
Henry Smith & Son 124
Herbert Johnson 166
Heron Bloodstock Services Ltd
Heron Stream Stud 41
High Beech Riding School 42,104
High Crundalls Stables 48
High Herts Farm Riding School 51
Higham Farm 39
Higham Ferrers Boot Co 162
Highbarn Horseboxes 275
Highfield Riding School 51
Highfield Stables Riding School 81
Highland Horseback 118
Highland Riding Centre 25,89,118
Highlight Hardware 268,293

Hill House Riding School 60
Hill View Riding Centre 72
Hillcrest Riding School Limited 64
Hillside Riding Centre 103
Hilltop Riding School 37
Hippomatic Ltd 174,276,288,309ff
Hobbs & Chambers 124
Hobbs Parker 124,126,170
Hobby Holidays 88,118
Hockwold Lodge Riding School 64,110
Hoechst UK Limited 310ff
Holdenby Riding School 67,111
Hole Farm 82
Hollins Farm Riding School 57,108
Holly Riding School 81,116
Holmescales Riding Centre 127,128,33,101
Home Farm Riding Stables 64
Honeybourne Stables Ltd. 48
Honeysuckle Farm Equestrian Centre 37
Hope Equestrian Centre 71
Hope Farm Riding School 30
Hopes Auction Co 126
Hopes Grove Farm 54
Hopperstore Bins 268
Horam Manor Riding Stables 40,104
Horse & Hound 171
Horse & Jockey Limited 171
Horse & Pony Magazine 171
Horse & Rider 171
Horse & Rider Insurance Service 170,263,275
Horse Advancement Co. Ltd 273,291,292,293,302ff
Horse Requisites Newmarket Ltd 162,176,256,266,308ff
Horsegear Limited 280,293
Horsemaster Coachbuilders Ltd 275
Horseshoe Farm Riding School 43
Horseshoes Riding School 54,108
Horwood Riding Centre 37
Houston Farm Riding School 90,118
Howarth Lodge Riding Centre 84
Humberts 124
Hunstrete Riding School 24
Hunters 124
Huntersfield Farm Riding Centre 78
Huntley School of Equitation 44
Hurdcott Livery Stables 86,175
Hurdcott Livery Stables & Saddlery 286
Hurst Vale Riding School 74
Husky of Tostock Limited 167,168
Husseys 125,126
Huxton Farm Riding Centre 37,103
Hwylfa Ddafydd Country Farm Holidays 94
Hydrodan (Corby) Limited 256,280
Hydrophane Laboratories Ltd 259,273,274,294,303ff

I

Ian McNeill Saddlery 288
Ideal Saddle Co. Limited 258,288
Ifor Williams Trailers Ltd 278
Ilex Riding Centre 54
Impala Sales and Marketing 174,281,282,286,289,293
Ingestre Riding and Livery Stables 75,114
Instant Signs 173,174,262,291
Integral Cabs 275,278
International Air Cargo Ser. 281
International Saddlery Ltd 289
Intervet Laboratories Ltd 266,312

IPC Video 175
Irene Wilson 165,167,175
Irish Draught Horse Society 171
Irrigation & Slurry Services 256,280,293,296
Isle of Arran Riding Holidays 91,119
Ivy Lane Riding School & Livery Stables. 60,109

J

J A Allen & Co 171
J & B Towing 278
J & C Gibbins 164,173,264,273,274
J Barbour & Sons Limited 162,167,168
J C Footwear 163
J C Gapp 263
J E Goodrick & Co Ltd 293
J Gordon Stirrat 275,278
J J Morris 126
J J Robinson & Son Ltd 290,293
J M H Harness Makers 263
J P Rug Co 172,283,287
J W E Banks & Sons Ltd 175,296
J W Wilkinson & Co Ltd 287
JAI 274,282
Jabez Cliff & Co. Limited 261,285,286,286,289,292
James Calder 168
James H Wood Printers Ltd 174,285,291
James Lock & Co Limited 166
James Walkers & Son Ltd 287,289,303
James Windsor of Mansfield Ltd 296
Jane Bertram Products 274,278,287
Jane Neville Gallery 170
Januarys 125
Jaytone Riding Wear 167,287
Jean Goodman Riding 287
Jefferd, S R (RRS) 265
Jeffries, George Gloves 165
Jennings Coachwork Ltd 275
Jofa UK 166
John & Judith Nead 170,172
John Goodwin (Int.) 277,289
John H James & Co 125
John James Hawley 272,281,282,283,287,289,295
John Palmer Ltd 276
John Partridge Sales Ltd 166,167,168
Joseph Clayton & Sons 282
Judith Cochran 174,265
Jump Off 295
JWE Banks & Sons Limited

K

K D Hampson 173
K G Products 172,259,310
K/L Pharmaceutical Ltd 308ff
Kampkit Limited 167
Kangol Equestrian 258,261,272,284,285,289
Kays 125
Keith Bates 254,263,289
Keith Luxford (Saddlery) Ltd 174,287,289,295
Kembroke Hall Riding School 75,114
Ken Johnson 270,293
Kentish Town City Farm 61
Kersey Stables 55
Kielder Adventure Centre 68
Killiemor Riding Centre 89,118
Killiworgie Mill Riding Centre 100
Kilmardinny Farm & Riding Establishment Ltd 91

Kiln Saddlery 175,276,295,312
Kimberley Riding & Livery Stables 80
Kimmerston Riding Centre 68
King & Chasemore 125
King Thomas Lloyd-Jones & Co 126
Kingfisher Ltd 167
Kingshill Riding School 55
Kingsthorpe Garage 296
Kingston Riding Centre 78
Kingswood Equestrian Club 82
Kingswood School of Riding 81
Kininmouth School of Horsemanship 90,118
Kivell & Sons 125,126
Kiwi Rug Co Limited
Knight & Co 285
Knight Bridge Riding, Training & 45,105
Knight Frank & Rutley 125
Knights End Riding Centre 28
Knowle Riding Centre 72,113
Kyre Combined Training Club 127,128,48

L

L & A Holiday & Riding Centre 97
L M Hickling 295
L W Faulkner & Son 163,285,290
La Corbiere Riding & Livery Stables 29
La Haie Fleurie Livery & Riding Centre 30
Lacock Riding Centre 86
Lacys Cottage Riding School 66
Lady Northmpton Boot Co Ltd The 163
Ladyland Stables 91,119
Lambourn Coachbuilders Ltd 275
Lanarkshire Riding Centre 92
Lanehouse Equitation Centre 38
Langbury Assoc Services Ltd 170
Langshot Equestrian Centre 78
Larkin the Saddlers 289
Lassell House Riding Centre & Livery Stables 57
Laurels Stables 75,114,277
Lavenham Rug Company Ltd 165,167,173,287
Lawrie & Symington Limited 126
LEP Bloodstock Inc (USA) 281
LEP Bloodstock Limited 280,281
Lea Bailey Riding School 48,106,48
Lea Bridge Riding School 61
Ledard Riding Centre 87
Lee Bennett 166
Leigh Equestrian Centre Ltd 38,103
Lely Iseki Tractors 291
Leonard Coombe 289
Lessans Riding Stables 98
Lettershuna Riding Centre 92
Levett Burchett 293
Levington Equestrian Centre 76,114
Lex Mead Cheltenham 296
Leyland & Birmingham
Rubber Co 163,262,273,274,286
Leyland Court Riding School 24
Lilleshall Riding & Livery Stables 71
Lillyputts Equestrian Centre 42
Limbuffs Limited 274
Limes Farm Equestrian Centre 55,108
Lineside Riding Stables 60
Linthwaite Textiles Ltd 287
Listers Clippers 259
Little Brook Equestrian 42
Little Montrose Riding Establishment 42
Little Paddocks 42,104

Littledean Trekking Centre 44,104
Livestock Fencing Ltd 269
Livestock Marts Ltd
Llanddona Riding School 96,121
Llangorse Riding Centre 97
Llanrhaedr Y M Pony Trekking Centre 112
Lloyds Bank PLC 175
Loch Ness Equi Centre 128,89
Lochore Meadows Riding Stables 88
Loddon Livestock Equipment
Ltd 262,269,270,293,310
Lodge & Thomas 126
Lodge Riding Stables 28
Logie Farm Riding Centre 89,118
Lomondside Stud & Equestrian Centre 92
London Thoroughbred Services Ltd
Long Distance Riding Centre 43,104
Longacres Riding School 62
Longfield Stables 58,109
Longham House 38
Longmead Riding School 42
Longton Riding Centre and Tack Shop 58
Longtown Outdoor Education Centre 106
Longwood Equestrian Centre 42
Loughton Manor Equestrian Centre 27,99
Lovanne Riding Centre 30
Lovatt & Rickets Limited
Loveston Mill Stables 120
Lower Bell Riding School 55
Lower Burston Riding School 37
Lower Downstow Stables 37,103
Lower Farm Riding and Livery Stables 78
Lowfold Farm Riding Centre 31
Lulworth Equestrian Centre 38
Lumsdaine Farm Equestrian Centre 87
Lydford House Riding Stables 37,103
Lynch Farm Riding Centre 28
Lynx Park 55,108

M

M J Ainge & Co. Ltd 163,167,282,303ff
M M B Farmkey 271
M S Racegear 173
Magnetopulse Ltd 311
Magnevet Therapies Ltd 311
Magnum Equestrian Centre & Tutorial Academy 40
Main Ring from Rumenco 261,266,267,312
Mallon Brother Transport Ltd 257
Malthouse Equestrian Centre 86,117
Manor Farm Equestrian Centre 68
Manor House Riding School 37,103
Manspence Developments 273
Manx Equestrian Centre 52,107
Marches Equestrian College 48
Mark Saddler Limited 165,284,287
Mark Westaway & Son 256,267,304ff
Markeaton Riding Centre and Stud 35,101
Markfield Equestrian Centre 59
Mars Oil Co. 274,276,282,305ff
Marsden School of Riding 59
Massarella School of Riding 73
Matlock Brown Ltd 167,174
Matthews Comfort & Co Ltd 170
Mawer Mason & Bell 125,126
Maxicrop International Ltd 266
Mayeston 95
McHardy's of Carlisle 164,167
McRostie of Glasgow 264,295,296

Meadows School of Riding — 59
Mechanical Services — 278
Medi Equus PLC — 266,304ff
Medway Riding Centre — 42
Meon Valley Equestrian Centre — 46,105
Merage Clothing Co (Ipswich) Ltd — 164,166,167
Merrie Stud Riding School — 46
Merry Pierce Thorpe — 125
Messenger May Baverstock — 125
Messrs Sawdye & Harris — 126
Messrs Taylor & Fletcher — 126
Methuen London Ltd — 172
Michael Stewart Fine Art Ltd — 170,173
Midgeland Indoor Riding School — 58
Midland Marts Limited — 126
Mike Doyle Marketing Ltd — 303ff
Mill Bridge Riding Centre Limited — 98
Mill Cottage Riding & Livery Stables — 28
Mill Farm Riding School — 60
Mill Green Riding School — 51
Millbrook Equitation Centre — 25
Millfields Riding Establishment — 76
Millfield School — 72
Millview Equestrian Centre — 73
Milton Lodge Hotel — 103
Miss E A Pickard — 28
Mistley Riding School — 42
Mitre Bridles — 259
Moat House Farm — 55,81
Mobberley Riding School — 30
Moddershall Riding School — 75
Moelfryn Riding Centre — 95
Mogridge Rosettes Ltd — 285
Monfort — 264
Monomet Ltd — 256
Montague Harris & Co — 126
Montpellier Riding Centre — 24
Moor End Stables — 42
Moor Farm Riding Stables — 95
Moor House Riding School — 66
Moorbridge Riding Stables — 35
Moorlands Trail Riding — 114
Moorside Equestrian Centre — 84,116
Mopley Farm Countryside Activity Centre — 46,105
Moss Farm Riding — 32
Mottingham Farm Riding Centre — 61
Moulton Riding School — 68
Mount Mascal Stables — 55
Moy Riding Centre — 98
Moyfield Riding School — 48,106
Mr & Mrs Wiegersma — 267
Mudchute Park & Farm Riding School — 61
Muir Landscape Services — 256
Multina Ridinch — 30
Murphy Chemicals Limited — 284
Murton House Riding School — 80
Myothyill Farm Riding Centre — 87

N

Naburn Grange Riding Centre — 66,111
Naldretts Farm — 83
Natural Animal Feeds Ltd — 256
Naval Riding Centre — 46,105
Nelson Park Riding Centre — 55
Nenthorn Stables — 86
New Farm — 28,99
New Forest Equestrian Centre — 46
New Forest Riding, Driving & Watersports — 46,105

New Forest Saddlers Limited — 289
New Hall School Riding Centre — 42
New Park Manor Equestrian Centre
and Hotel — 46,105
Newark Equestrian Centre — 69
Newcastle Riding Centre — 98,122
Newham Riding School & Association — 61
Newin Equestrian Centre — 64
Newmaster Ltd — 278
Newport Shredded Paper Products — 257
Newson Show Jumps — 174,259,262,291
Newton Hall Equitation Centre — 76,114
Newton Horse Ltd — 173,175,277,282,303ff
Nine Tor Riding Centre — 32,100
Norchard Farm Riding School — 95,120
Norfolk Rosettes — 285
Norris & Duvall — 126
North Farm Riding Establishment — 71
North Gellan Stables — 88,118
North Haye Riding Centre — 37,103
North Herts Equitation Centre — 51,107
North Humberside Riding Centre — 107
North Humberside Riding Centre — 52
North Wheddon Farm — 113
Northern Equitation Centre — 58,109
Northfield Farm Riding & Trekking Centre — 35,102
Northfield Riding Centre — 62,110
Northgate Riding Centre — 37
Northgate Riding School — 37,103
Northowram Childrens Riding School — 84,116
Norwich Union Insurance Group — 170
Nottingham Equestrian Centre — 128,69
Notts Equestrian Video Library — 175
Nursey & Son Ltd — 284
Nuway Manufacturing Co Ltd — 271

O

Oakfield Riding School — 70
Oakington Riding School — 29,100
Oakley Coachbuilders — 275
Oathill Farm Riding Centre — 55,108
Oatridge Agricultural College — 90
Offley Brook Riding School — 75
Old Hall Mill Riding School — 58
Old Mill Stables — 32,100
Old Park Stables — 78
Old Stowey Farm — 72,113
Oldencraig Equestrian Centre — 77,78
Ollard Westcombe & Co Ltd — 261,272,283,287
Orchard Cottage Riding Stables — 78
Orchard Farm — 109
Ordell Enterprises — 287,303ff
Osbaldeston Hall Farm Riding Centre — 58
Osborne Poultry Services Ltd — 256
Otterdene Riding Stables — 37
Outdoor Life — 164
Overland Pony Trek — 97,131
Owenmore Stables — 89
Oxford Riding School — 70
Oxhey Grange School of Riding — 52

P

P G Flower & Co — 170
P G L Young Adventure Limited — 71
P I Associates — 165,167,284,287
P J Godsmark — 269

Paglesham School of Equitation 43
Pakefield Riding School 76,114
Pantiau Farm Trekking Holidays 96,121
Par-le-Breos Trekking Centre 97
Paramount Horse Clothing Co 287
Park Farm School of Riding 63
Park Lane Riding & Livery Stables 43
Park Riding School & Livery Stables. 60,109
Park Stables 84
Park View Leicester Equestrian Centre 59
Parkhurst Horse Training Facilities 78
Parklands Riding School Limited 73
Parkway UK Ltd 257,262,280,285
Parkwood Feeds Ltd 261,267
Parry's Signs 173
Partridge Stables 78
Passmores Portable Bldgs Ltd 270,293
Patchetts Equestrian Centre 51,107
Patey, S (London) Ltd 166
Pattullo & Partners 126
Peacehaven Riding Centre 128,94,120
Pearce Horseboxes 275,278
Pearson Cole 125
Pebworth Vale Equestrian Centre 80,115
Peden Int. Transport Limited 280,281
Pelham Books 172
Pembrokeshire Riding Centre 95
Pencoed College 96
Pen-Llyn Stud & Trekking Centre 121
Pengelli Fach Riding School 96,121
Pennwood Saddlery 289
Penrith Farmers & Kidds plc 126
Pentac 261,289
Personalite Ltd 290
Peter Cliffe 293
Peter Vastl Saddler 259,262,264,272
Pevlings Farm Riding & Livery Stables 72,113
Pewsey Vale Riding Centre 86
Pfizer Limited 312
Pharmacia Ltd 302
Phillips, Sanders & Stubbs 125
Phoenix Stables 68,111
Pine Lodge Riding Centre 43
Pinewood (Toyota) 296
Pinnocks Wood Stables 26
Pittern Hill Stables Limited 81
Plas-y-Celyn Riding Centre 96
Plumpton Agricultural College 40
Polhill Riding Centre 55
Polpever Riding Stables 32
Polywarm Products Ltd 287
Ponsbourne Riding Centre 51,107
Pony 172
Pony Press 172
Pooh Corner Stables 83,116,172
Poplar Park Equestrian Centre 128,76,114
Popples Equestrian Centre 76,114
Porlock Vale Equitation Centre 72,113
Porth Hall Riding Centre 32
Portmans Farm 48
Pottersheath Riding Centre 51
Pound Cottage Childrens Riding School 39
Pound Farm 39,103
Prescott Equestrian Centre 71
Presfield Fabrics Limited 295
Priory School of Equitation 78,115
Proctors Woodflakes 257
Propack 256
Prudential Assurance Co Limited 170
Puffa Ltd 167,174

Purnell Books 172

Q

Quadrant Video 175
Quality Showjumps 174,291
Quarnhill School of Equitation 35,102
Queen Margaret's Riding School 66

R

R & E Bamford 261,267,277,312
R B Biddescombe Ltd 278
R E Tricker Ltd 162
R Ellis 269
R S Assemblies Ltd 257,293
R W Stephen Equestn Prods Ltd 174,291,293
Radiol Chemicals 274,305ff
Radnage House Riding School 27
Ragwood Riding Centre 43
Raikes Hall Riding School 84,116
Rainbow Horse Suppliers 168,287
Rainbow Rosettes 173,174,285,291
Range Rides 97
Raud & Malet 264
Rayne Riding Centre 43
RCR Sales 167
Rectory Road Riding School 64,110
Red House Farm Riding & Livery Stables 43
Red House Stables Carriage Mus 128,35,102
Red Rose Horseboxes 275
Rednal Products Ltd 294
Rednil Farm Equestrian Centre 61
Redport Equestrian 284,303ff
Redport Net Co Ltd 287
Reed Saddlery & Co Ltd 259,289
Reeves Hall 64
Regent of Huddersfield Limited 285
Remploy 257
Rendells 125
Rennies 126
RHM Pegasus Horse Feeds 267
Rhiwiau Riding Centre 96,121
Rice Trailers Limited 278,296
Richard Briggs Riding Stables 62
Richard Field Insurance Brokers 170
Richard Gill & Son Ltd 264
Richard Mayers 125
Richardson Trailers 280
Ride-Away 169,173,174,290
Ridgeway Rug Co 286,287
Riding 172
Riding Farm 55
Ridry Waterproof Clothing 165,168,265,277,278
Rillington Manor Riding School 66
Rimell Saddlers 289
Ring Croft Farm Riding School 27
Riverdale Riding Centre 52
Robin Hood Riding Centre 101
Robinson Healthcare 277,302ff
Robsons of Wolsingham 294
Rockingham House Farm Riding Centre 74
Rocklane Riding Centre 25
Rockmoor Stables 49
Roddimore Stud 294
Roehampton Gate Stables Ltd. 62
Ron Barry & Co 294
Rondo Horse Insurance 171,175

Rose Hall Farm Riding and Livery Stables 51
Rose-Acre Riding Stables 64
Rosebank Horse and Pony Centre 87
Rosebrook Farm Equestrian Centre 64
Rosehill Riding Centre 37
Rosemary Riding School 53
Ross Nye's Riding Establishment 62,109
Rowan Lodge School of Equitation 25
Rowanlea Riding School Limited 93
RPM Western Trading 162,165,259,272,289
Ruari Construction 270,294
Rugby Livestock Sales Ltd 127
Runton Hall Stud 64
Russell Baldwin & Bright 125,127
Russell Equitation Centre 46,105
Ruthin Riding Centre 94
Rycovet Ltd 294
Rycroft School of Equitation 46
Ryecroft Riding Centre 29

S

S Patey (London) Ltd 166,170
S Robb & Son 281,283,289,294
S W Halford & Son 264,289
Sabre Leather Co Ltd 259,274,289
Sachs Motor Services Ltd 296
Saddle Craft 289
Salcey Forest Timber Products 174,291
Salhouse Equestrian Centre 64
Sandon Saddlery Co 289,295,296
Sands Farm Equitation Centre 83
Sandwell Valley Riding Centre 82,116
Savills 125
Savills (Colchester) 125
Sawdust Marketing Co 257
Sawdye & Harris 126
Saxilby Riding Club 61,109
Schnieder Riding Boot Company 162
School Farm Training Centre 47
School of National Equitation 59,169,175,302ff
Scotrug Ltd 287
Scottish Equitation Centre 93,120
Scotts of Thrapston 294
Seechem Equestrian Centre 106
Selston Equestrian Centre 49,69
Senior & Godwin 125
Severn Valley Riding Centre 49
Shade Stables 29
Shana School of Riding 27
Shandon School of Equitation 92
Shanter Riding Centre 92
Shaw Mills Chrome Leather Co 284
Shay Lane Stables & Saddlery 84
Shieldbank Stud Riding Centre 88
Shilstone Rocks Stud & Trekking Centre 38,103
Shires Equestrian Products 274
Shreddabed 257
Shukburgh Riding Centre 68
Side Farm Trekking Centre 34,101
Signs Familiar 173
Silver Fox Showjumps 174,291
Silver Horseshoe Riding Centre 47
Silver Knowes Riding Centre 90,118
Silverdown Riding School & Equitation Centre 70
Silvretta Haflinger Stud & LDR Centre. 82
Sinclairs Trailers 275,280
Singleton Flint 257,285
Sky Farm Riding School 40

SMC Ltd 257
Smith, Kline Animal Health Ltd 175,266,303ff
Snainton Riding Centre 66,111
Snaresbrook Riding School Limited 62
Snowball Farm Riding and Livery
Yard Limited 27,99
Snowdonia Riding Stables 96,121
Snowflakes Wood Shavings Ltd 257
Somerset Zero Grass Ltd 256,280
South Essex Ins Brokers Ltd 170
South Leicestershire Riding Establishment 59
South Lincs Fencing 269
South Wales Equitation Centre 96
South Weylands Equestrian Centre 79
Southdown Riding School 40
Southern Equitation Livery Centre 79,115
Sparkford Sawmills (Bsgstke)Ltd 294
Sparkford Sawmills Ltd 269,270,294
Spillers Horse Feeds 261,267
Sporting Developments Int Ltd 167
Sportsline Plastics Ltd 174,262,291
Springfield Horseboxes 271,275
Springfield Stables Limited 49
Springfield Universal 280
St Clements Lodge Riding School 69
St Leonard's Equitation Centre 32,100
St Quentin's Stables 97
St. Stephen's College Riding School 55
Stags 125
Stainsby Grange Riding Centre 31
Stanbrook Riding Centre 64
Stangrave Hall Stables 79,115
Station House Farriery Supplies 265
Staughton Riding School 29
Steele Hill Riding Club 38
Stephenson & Son 127
Sterivet Supplements 176,266,277,284,294,304ff
Steve Russell Sales 261,277,294,306ff
Stewart, Michael Fine Art Ltd 169
Stiffkey Valley Stables 64
Stockbridge Riding School 47
Stocks Farm Equestrian Centre 39,103
Stoke-By-Clare Equestrian Centre 76
Stonar School 86
Stone Lodge Equestrian Centre 59,109
Stourton Hill Stables 82
Strathearn Stables 93
Stretton Riding Centre 59
Stromsholm 265
Strong Fabrications 268
Strumpshaw Riding Centre 64
Stubley Hollow Riding Centre 74,113
Stylo Manufacturing Int. Ltd 162,167,274
Sue Usher 29
Summerhouse Equitation Centre 43
Sunnydale Cottage 51,107
Sunrising Farm & Riding Centre 32,101
Supreme Stables 270,294
Surewood Products 174,259,270,291,294
Sustan Showjumps 174,259,262,291
Sutton Manor Farm Riding School 69
Suzanne's Riding School 63,110
Swallowfield Stables and Training Centre 25
Swiss Cottage Stables & Saddlery 65,110
Swordhill Equestrian Training Centre 58
Sylvandene Stud 79

T

T M International School of Horsemanship 32,101
Talat International Leather Co 168,259,261,264,272
Tall Trees Riding Centre 33,101,127,128,175
Tanarside Riding Centre 118
Tarden Farm Stables 30
Taunton Saddlery 289
Taunton Show Jumps 174,291
Taylor & Fletcher 126
Taylor's Riding Establishment 55
Tedman Harness 264
Thanet Show Jumps 174,291
The Avenue Riding Centre 49,106
The Avon Riding Centre for the Disabled Ltd 24
The Barn Book Supply 172
The Beacons Riding School & Holiday Centre 38
The Blindley Heath School of Equitation 79
The Bloodstock Breeders Review 172
The Boston Saddlery Co. 289
The Claife & Grizedale Riding Centre 34
The Clock Tower Riding School 79,175
The Coach House Stables 29
The Diamond Centre for Handicapped Riders 79
The Dyfed Riding Centre 95
The Equestrian Centre 94
The Fortune Centre 39
The Gatehouse Range 166,167,170
The Gleneagles Mark Phillips
Equestrian Ctre 93,120
The Golden Pheasant Riding Centre 94,120
The Grange Riding Club & Livery Yard 43
The Grove Riding Centre 89
The Haven Equestrian Centre 33
The Inett Farm & Equestrian Centre 71
The Ivory Equestrian Centre 51
The Kingston Riding Centre 79
The Limes Equestrian Centre 59
The Lion Royal Hotel & Pony Trekking Centre 97
The Malt House Stud Training Centre 70
The Marches Equestrian College 49,106
The Melfort Riding Centre 92
The Mendip Equestrian Centre 24
The Mill Feed Co Ltd 261,266,267
The Mounts Equitation Centre 49,106
The National Stallion Assocn 172
The Playmate Riding School 44
The Quantock Riding Centre 72,113
The Royal Engineers Saddle Club 56
The Spanish Bit Riding School and Livery 26
The Talland School of Equitation 44,104
The Wellington Carriage Co 264
The West Somerset Riding Centre 73
The Wharf 59,109
The Windmill Stables 29,99
The Wirral Riding Centre 31
The Worlebury Riding School 24
The Wyke Equestrian Centre 71,162,304ff
The Wyke Equestrian Services 257
The York Riding School 66,111
The Yorkshire Riding Centre Limited 67
Thimbleby & Shorland 127
Thomas Pettifer and Co. Ltd 266,267
Thomas Townend & Co Ltd 166
Thomdon Roffick & Laurie Ltd 127
Thorley Riding Centre 51
Thorndon Horse Boxes 275
Thornproof Riding Wear 168
Thoroughbred Horseboxes 276
Thoroughbred Saddlery Co 258,272,284,290,308

Thorpe Grange Equestrian Centre 61
Three Gates Equestrian Centre 81
Thurgood, D 259
Tildesley, W H Ltd 259
Tim Hawks 264,295,296
Tinsleys Riding School 25
Tiverton Timberware 294
Tollgate Livery Centre 76
Tollgate Riding Stables 56,108
Tomintoul Pony Trekking Centre 89,118
Tong Riding Centre Limited 71
Tony Riding Centre 71
Top Holidays 49
Torlundy Farm Riding Centre 89,118
Totteridge Riding School 62
Town and Country Prodns Ltd 176
Townley Cross Country Vehicles 296
Towy Valley Riding Centre 95,121
Tracey's Riding Centre 33
Tranby Equestrian Services 307
Tregaron Pony Trekking Association 95,121
Tregoyd and Cadarn Riding and
Trekking Centre 97
Trenance Riding Stables 33
Trenissick Riding Stables 33,101
Trent Park Equestrian Centre 62
Trevillet Parc Farm Riding Centre 101
Trew Well Hall 111
Trewalla Equestrian Centre 101
Trewysgoed Riding Centre 95,121
Trickers (London) 162
Triple Bar Riding Centre 79,115
Tuc Plastics Ltd 162
Tufnell & Partners 125
Tuka Limited 294
Tullochville Trekking Centre 93
Turf & Travel Sadd &
Harnss Ctr 259,264,283,287,290
Turner Griffiths Ltd 259,264,272,285,290
Turners Footwear & Country Clo. 162,165
Turville Valley Stud Riding 70,112
Twinstead Riding School 76,114
Ty 'N Lon Riding Centre 96,121

U

Umberslade Riding School 81
Unitex Limited 257,274
Uplands Equestrian Centre Ltd. 68
Urchinwood Manor Equitation Centre 24,99
Ushers Equestrian Services 257

V

V E Byrom (Mail Order) 173
Vale Bros ltd 162,277
Vale Lodge Stables 79
Vale of Belvoir Leathers 165
Valley Farm Equestrian Centre 70
Valley Farm Riding & Driving Centre 76,115
Vastl, Peter Saddler 259,262
Vet Health 176,261,266,277,304ff
Veterinary Field Station 90
Video Replay 176
Villa Farm Riding School 25
Village Farm Riding & Livery Stables 68,112
Vita Salford 169

W

W & H Gidden Ltd	162,169,287
W B Stubbs (Hawksworth) Ltd	290,294
W H Cowie Limited	274
W H Gidden Ltd	290
W H J Fagg & Son	256
W H Tildesley Ltd	274,277
W J Farvis & Sons Ltd	282
W R Outhwaite & Son	262
W S Hodgson & Co Limited	270,294
W S Johnson & Co	127
Wagg Foods Ltd	261,266,277,304ff
Walker Walton Hanson	127
Walkers Outdoor Leisure Ltd	162
Wallets Mart Ltd	127
Wallhead Gray & Coates	125
Walmer Riding Centre	56
Walsall Riding Saddle Co. Ltd	290
Ward Trailers of Easingwold	276
Warner Sheppard & Wade Ltd	127
Warrenwood Stables	52
Warwick School of Riding	80,115
Warwickshire College of Agriculture	81
Waterstock House Training Centre	70
Watson's Quality Products	174,262,291
Waverley Riding School	81
Waverton Riding Centre	31
Wearite Clothing Co	287
Weftmuir Riding Centre	90
Wellington Riding Limited	47,106
Wellow Park Stables & Saddlery	69,112
Wellow Trekking Centre	25
Wembury Bay Riding School	38,103
Wern Riding Centre (Crickhowell) Limited	97
Wessex Farm Machinery Sales Ltd	291
West Dorset Equestrian Centre	104
West End Farm	27
West Essex & Kernow Saddlery	175,290
West Runton Riding Stables	65,110
West Sussex College of Agriculture	83
West Wolves Riding Centre	83
Westcroft Stables	47
Westerham Riding Centre	56,108
Westertoun Farm Riding & Holiday Centre	87,117
Westfield Farm Riding Centre	70,112
Westlands Riding Centre	75,114
Westway Riding School	63,110
Westways Riding School	85,116
Westwood Riding Centre	75
Wethersfield Riding Stables	43
Wheal Buller Riding School	33
Whispers Equestrian Centre	31
White Cat Stables	25
White Hart Stables, Childrens Sch. of Riding	29
White Horse Stables	71,112
White Horse Trekking Centre	86
White's Place Riding Club	43
Whitemoor Stables	58
Whitewalls Farm Stables	93
Whittington Mill Riding Stables	80
Whitton Farmhouse Hotel	68

Whydown Riding School	40,104
Wickham Riding School & Stud	47
Wildbrook Arabian Stud & Riding Centre	86
Wildwoods Riding Centre	77,79,115
Willow Farm Horse Centre	56
Willow Farm Livery	47
Willow Farm Livery Stables & Riding School	257,266,267,304ff
Willow Farm Riding School	65
Willow Royd Stables	85,117
Willow Tree Riding Establishment	62
Wilton House Riding Centre	40
Wimbledon Village Stables	62
Windsor Stables	294
Windy Edge Stables	68
Winton Street Farm Stables	40
Witham Villa Riding School	59,109
Withington Hill Stables	294
Witney Horse Blanket Co	275,287
Wivenhoe Riding Centre Limited	79
Wm R Pangbourne	264,292
Wokingham Equestrian Centre	26
Woldingham Equestrian Centre	79
Wolviston Livery and Riding School	31,100
Wood Farm Riding School	75,114
Woodcraft Riding Centre	47
Woodfoot Riding School	92
Woodhurst Riding & Livery Stables	29,100
Woodland Riding Surfaces	257
Woodlands Riding School	97
Woodlands Riding Stables	33,101
Woodlands Stables	93
Woodlands Stables (International) Ltd.	77,115
Woodpecker Products Ltd	258,266,280
Woodredon Riding School	43
Woods Rosettes	285
Woodville Riding School	63
Woodward (UK)	294
Woodward, A & E	259
Woosham & Tyler	125
Wootton Riding School	26
Wrangler	165
Wrea Green Equitation Centre	58,109,128
Wright-Manley Auctioneers	127
Wrights Riding Academy	92,119
Wychwood Sportswear	168,169
Wynlass Beck Stables	34,101

Y

Yafforth Equestrian Centre	111
Yorkshire Riding Centre	67,111,127
Your Horse	172

Z

Zara Stud & Training Centre	83,116,128
Zenophon Publication	172

General Index

A

A Career with Horses	348
Allergy-Free Horse Hay	256
Allweather Riding Surfaces	256
And so to Ride	8
Anti-inflammatory Treatments	297
Antiseptics	297
Aqua Sprays	257
Associations	316

B

Bandages	297
Bedding	257
Best-dressed Horse: All Rugged Up	237
Better Safe than Sorry	140
Bits	203
Bits	258
Blood Tonics	298
Boots	274
Boots and Bandages	234
Breeches & Jodphurs	163
Breeding Supplements	304
Bridles	258

C

Cavaletti	259
Chaps	164
Choosing a Career with Horses	348
Clippers	259
Clipping	231
Clothing Manufacturers	162
Clothing Retailers	169
Coat Glosses and Dressings	299
Cod Liver Oils	299
Compound Feeds	260
Cough and Cold Treatments	300
Crib-biting Preventatives	300

D

Digestive Treatments	300
Disinfectants	261
Draw Reins	261
Dressage	127
Dressage Supplies	262
Drinking Troughs	262
Driving	127
Driving Vehicles and Accessories	262

E

Endurance	128
Equine Faults and Vices	241
Estate Agents Specialising in Country Properties	124
Eventing	128

F

Farriery Supplies	264
Feed Additives & Supplements	265
Feed Manufacturers	266
Feed Storage Bins	267
Feed Suppliers, General	268
Feeding your Horse or Pony	185
Fencing	268
Fencing	268
Fencing Contractors	269
Fencing Gates and Shelters	269
Fencing Suppliers	268
Floor Covering	271
Fly and Insect Repellants	306
Fortune Centre	353
Freeze Marking	271

G

Galleries	169
Girths	271
Grooming	226

H

Harness Manufacturers	272
Hat Covers	170
Hats	165
Healing Creams and Gels	306
Hoof-care Products	272
Hoof-care Products	276
Horse Boots	274
Horse Boxes	275
Horse Dealers	277
Horse Eye Protectors	277
Horse Feed Suppliers	277
Horse Holiday Homes	277
Horse Hoods	278
Horse Insurance	170
Horse Trailers & Accessories	278
Horse Transporters & Agents	280
Horse Treats	280
Horse Walkers	280
Horse-care Products	276
Hydroponic Grass Machines	280

I

Indoor School Maintenance Equipment	280
Insurance	170
International Forwarding Agents	281

J

Jackets	166

K

Keeping a Horse at Grass	210

L

Lead Ropes	281
Leather-care Products and Supplies	281
Leg Guards	282
Liniments	307
Linseed and Barley Boilers	282
Louse Powder	307
Lungeing Equipment	282

M

Magazines & Books	171
Mail Order Supplies	172
Making the Decision	130
Manufacturers and Suppliers of Horse-care Products	297
Measuring Sticks	282
Milk Replacers	308

N

Name Plates	173
National Bodies and Associations	316
No Foot No Horse	207
Numnahs	282
Nutritionists	284

P

Pasture Maintenance	284
Plaits, Bands, Threads and Needles	284
Polo	128
Portraits & Momentos	173
Poultices	308
Public Rights of Way	151

R

Reins	284
Riding Equipment, Clothing	162, 169
Riding Equipment, Tack	284
Riding Establishments	24
Riding Holidays	99
Riding Surfaces	285
Riding Wear	137
Rosettes and Trophies	285
Rubber Stops and Pads	286

Rugs & Blankets/Tail Guards	286

S

Saddle Stands and Racks	290
Saddle Manufacturers & Sole Agents	288
Saddles, Retailers	290
Safety Equipment	290
Safety on the Road: Medical Emergencies	144
Safety on the Road: Riding Out	148
Shampoos and Conditioners	308
Show Jumps/Sundries	290
Side-saddle	128
Side-Saddle Habits	174
Skin-care Products	309
Small Tractors	291
Some Human Faults and Problems	154
Spurs	175
Stable Equipment	291
Stabling your Horse	217
Stirrups and Leathers	291
Stud Breeding Services	346
Stud Management Equipment	346
Surcingles & Rollers	294

T

Tack Repairers	295
Tack Shops	175
Tacking Up	190
The Healthy Horse	179
The Healthy Horse: Useful References & Listings	254
The Responsible Rider	130
The Responsible Rider: Useful References & Listings	161
The World Equestrian Games	331
The World of Horsemanship	310
The Worlds of Riding	14
Ties & Stocks	175
Towing Vehicles and Accessories	296
Training	127
Transporting your Horse	247
Treatments and Tonics	309

V

Vaccines	310
Vaulting	128
Veterinary and Homeopathic Remedies	310
Veterinary Equipment	310
Videos	175
Vitamin/Mineral Supplement	311

W

Watering Devices	296
Waterproofs	168
Western Riding	128
Western Saddles and Wear	346
Where to Ride	8
Whips	176
Wormers	307
Wound Dressings	313

Notes

Notes

Notes

Notes